W9-BZG-413

The Iron of Melancholy

The Iron of Melancholy

Structures of Spiritual Conversion in America from the Puritan Conscience to Victorian Neurosis

John Owen King III

Wesleyan University Press
Middletown, Connecticut

ACKNOWLEDGMENTS:

Portions of *The Iron of Melancholy* appeared in somewhat different form in "Labors of the Estranged Personality: Josiah Royce on 'The Case of John Bunyan,'" *Proceedings of the American Philosophical Society* (February 5, 1976), and in "Demonic New World and Wilderness Land: The Making Strange of America," *Prospects; Annual Journal of American Cultural Studies*, vol. 7 (1983), and in "Of the Effectual Work of the Word: William James and Practice of Puritan Confession," *Texas Studies in Literature and Language*, vol. 25, no. 1 (Spring 1983).

The author gratefully acknowledges permissions to reprint:

Excerpts from THE INTERPRETATION OF DREAMS, by Sigmund Freud, Translated and edited by James Strachey. Published in the United States by Basic Books, Inc., Publishers, New York by arrangement with George Allen & Unwin Ltd. and The Hogarth Press, Ltd.

Extracts from letters of Sigmund Freud published by permission of Sigmund Freud Copyrights Ltd.

Excerpts from *The Origins of Psychoanalysis: Letters to Wilhelm Fliess, Drafts and Notes: 1887–1902*, by Sigmund Freud, Edited by Marie Bonaparte, Anna Freud, and Ernst Kris. Authorized translation by Eric Mosbacher and James Strachey. Copyright © 1954 by Basic Books, Inc., Publishers, New York.

Lines from "Howl" from *Howl and Other Poems*, by Allen Ginsberg, copyright © 1956, 1959 by Allen Ginsberg. Reprinted by permission of CITY LIGHTS BOOKS.

Lines from "The Snow Man," by Wallace Stevens, copyright 1923 and renewed 1951 by Wallace Stevens. Reprinted from THE COLLECTED POEMS OF WALLACE STEVENS, by permission of Alfred A. Knopf, Inc.

Extracts from letters of Josiah Royce from *The Letters of Josiah Royce*, edited by John Clendenning (1970) by permission of the University of Chicago Press.

Extracts from THE STANDARD EDITION OF THE COMPLETE PSYCHOLOGICAL WORKS OF SIGMUND FREUD, Translated and edited by James Strachey by permission of Sigmund Freud Copyrights Ltd., The Institute of Psycho-Analysis and The Hogarth Press, Ltd. (British publishers)

Quotations from *An Autobiographical Study* and *Civilization and Its Discontents* by Sigmund Freud by permission of W. W. Norton & Company, Inc. (American publishers)

Quotations from the writings of William James by permission of Alexander R. James, Literary Executor.

LIBRARY OF CONGRESS CATALOGING IN PUBLICATION DATA

King, John Owen.
The iron melancholy.

1. National characteristics, American. 2. United States—Intellectual life. 3. Conversion—History. 4. Psychology, Religious. 5. United States—Religious life and customs. I. Title.
E169.1.K533 1983 306'.0973 83-6490
ISBN 0-8195-5070-1

All inquiries and permissions requests should be addressed to the Publisher, Wesleyan University Press, 110 Mt. Vernon Street, Middletown, Connecticut 06457

Distributed by Harper & Row Publishers, Keystone Industrial Park, Scranton, Pennsylvania 18512

Manufactured in the United States of America

First Edition

I wish to extend my appreciation to Paul Conkin, whose gentle rigor long ago helped to shape a tenuous form.

And I wish to dedicate this book to my two children, Richard and Brian, and to the memory of the Marines I knew who died in I Corps, Vietnam.

Contents

ACKNOWLEDGMENTS xi

Introduction 1

1. Twice-Born and Sick Soul: The Awakening of New England's Conscience 13

The Den 17

The Melancholy Desert 19

The Temptations that the Melancholy Experience 22

Obsessional Temptation and the Movement of Puritan Conversion 29

The Pilgrim's Progress 36

The American Spiritual Relation 40

Self-Murder 49

The Self-History and Melancholy 54

The Transit of New England's Conscience: Jonathan Edwards 65

2. Conscience to Moral Psychology: The Elder Henry James 83

Inheritance 85

Vastation 90

Composition of the Crisis 100

The Nature of Swedenborg's Temptations 103

James's Confession of Temptations and Compulsion 105

The Conscience of Sin and the Conscience of Crime 110

Moral Works 113

James's Otherworldly Endeavor 118

The Moral Desertion of Henry James's Father 123

The Moral Wilderness of Henry James's Sons 129

Hawthorne 133

Bequest 138

3. Conscience to Neurosis: William James 141

Nature 144

Brazil and the Lost Garden 148
James's Fear of His Father's Ascetic 154
Panic Fear 159
The Context of the Crisis 164
Renouvier, Bain, and Obsessive Ideation 170
Work 175
Compulsion and Doubt 183
Radical Empiricism 194

4. Conversion through Ethical Salvation: Josiah Royce 198
Imitation 201
California and Royce's Childhood 207
James and Harvard 212
Breakdown 216
The Reconsideration of the Crisis 220
Modern Psychiatric Literature 222
Kant and the Constructive Imagination 231
Bunyan and the Mocking of the Tempter 234
Work as Self-Creation 237
The Contrite Consciousness 242
Modern Alienation 244
Death 251

5. Conversion through Psychoanalysis: James Jackson Putnam 254
Working Through 255
Putnam's Character 258
Family and Neurasthenia 261
The Memoir of James Jackson 264
Freud and the *Analerotik* 268
Moral Regeneration 274
Analysis 279
Putnam's Ethical Bias 284
Freud's Mechanics 286

6. American Apocalypse: Max Weber 289
Work and Person 291
Work and Text 293
Weber's Collapse 298
Weber's Obsessive Actions 302

The Worldly Ascetic Ethic 308
The End of the Worldly Ascetic Ideal 317
Work and Death 319

Conclusion 323

NOTES 337

INDEX 445

Acknowledgments

Historians have chosen fresh symbols with which to portray the American ideal, drawing from the nation's literature images of a virgin land, a pastoral ideal, an American Adam. Though this book attempts the reconstruction of another vision, it is indebted to these histories, which are finely wrought art. It is indebted as well to more recent works: in the manuscript's revision, to the writings of Sacvan Bercovitch and his idea of the jeremiad, to Edmund S. Morgan and his *Visible Saints,* and to Stanley E. Fish and his *Self-Consuming Artifacts: The Experience of Seventeenth-Century Literature*—indebtedness that the end notes fail to substantiate. The notes also fail to acknowledge, except in the most cursory way, the themes of Erik H. Erikson. His motifs run throughout this book, which, in one of its original conceptions, planned to locate Erikson's place in American thought. A much earlier version of this work, a dissertation, received uncommon care from my thesis committee: Paul K. Conkin, my advisor, Richard H. Sewell, and Daniel T. Rodgers. To the last I owe many discussions on the ethic of labor. David Hollinger offered words which I have used in the Introduction. Robert Berkhofer, whose ideas and approach to the study of history have greatly influenced my own thought and this work, offered care and advice. Genevieve Berkhofer offered a phrase, "conscience to neurosis"—words that were received as a moment of light and that became crucial conceptually in work toward a revision.

The Iron of Melancholy

Introduction

Study of the American character continues in some of the most exciting, and debated, of recent historical writings. The idea that a national character has existed no longer works in these histories as the idea did work little more than a decade ago—certainly not, given the historians' concern today with conflict as opposed to consensus, within the broadest view of pursuing America in terms of a holistic culture and personality. And yet many historians are using words analogous to "character" to portray the American past, words such as "self," "temperament," "*mentalité*," or simply "culture." These historians are arguing that though psychological styles have never enclosed the whole of the American people, such styles, including—most intriguingly—neurotic styles, can lead us to understand the behavior of one or another groups important in the nation's past. In addition, within the last twenty years a new discipline, psychohistory, has emerged and has received a certain amount of legitimacy within academic circles, and though the focus of this method rests upon the individual rather than the group, often psychohistorians consider their subjects as in some manner representative of a wider culture. Studies of the American character, then, which at first glance appear to have been abandoned during the last decade or so, continue to be written and to draw our interest. One thinks of such books as Sacvan Bercovitch's *The Puritan Origins of the American Self*, Philip Greven's *The Protestant Temperament*, and Christopher Lasch's *The Culture of Narcissism*. This concern with the anxiety of the American character is not surprising; as the present book argues, psychological analysis of the American character has been itself a part of American culture, or a part of an American textual culture, for the past three hundred years.

The present book addresses itself to earlier writings on the American character and particularly to the themes, present in these writings, of psychological anguish and spiritual birth. If the historian is still to be allowed to point to a controlling "myth" of America, then that myth is one of estrangement and bewilderment and the accompanying idea of the wilderness rather than that theme threaded so many of the classic studies of American culture, the myth of the garden. The wilderness, and all of the psychological implications that the word "wilderness" allows, has provided American writing, especially American autobiographical writing, with a distinctive character of trauma from the seventeenth century to the present. Whereas the garden rests as a pastoral retreat where no effort or will need be applied, where no work, in other words, need occur and therefore no change, the wilderness can confront the American as a demonic otherness. Literally, in Puritan writings, America was the place of Satan, where a great amount of work must be done just to carry the self through its time of alienation. The wilderness, most simply, is the place where spiritual conversion occurs. Thus whether conceived externally as wilderness and desert or internally as bewilderment and desertion, the landscape of America and its historically various forms of alienation—the land's frontiers, demons, and savages, as later its strange machines and machine-like labors—have been found by authors to be ideal places to make an attempt at personal transformation. This book looks at writings of spiritual conversion, stories of diseased souls wandering within the desert of Christ's temptations in hope of achieving through virtuous labor, through that which Max Weber termed a this-worldly ascetic ideal, what wholeness may be said to exist.

This book traces the origin of this struggle to the settlement of New England. No necessity existed in the seventeenth century to define an American character, but a necessity did arise to define rather precisely the character of the Puritan saint. To become admitted to the body of the church, and thereby to the full body of the community, the hopeful "visible saint" had to recount his character as a "case of conscience." He had to present a psychological history, that it be given, a requirement that remained unique in the Western world.

This "national" requirement that a Puritan saint confess the troubles of conscience, more than the presence of a disrupting frontier or the existence of a particularly guilt-inducing family or social structure, accounts for the idea of a distressed American character. While existing in American writing from the seventeenth century, the idea was to undergo change. Indeed, in a movement from what the Puritans termed "conscience" to what Victorians called "neurosis," the significance assigned to the traits of this personality altered radically. What was not to change was the necessity to articulate a particular consciousness of self. By the nineteenth century, of course, there was no requirement to make a confession of psychological ordeal, but the need to articulate for a community the intimate experience of the soul remained, and remained joined in many cases with the specific models of articulation provided by the Puritans.

Introduction

In moving from Puritan to Victorian confessions, this book changes its focus to authors who, rather than creating a spiritual autobiography at a given moment in time or within the limits of a single text, chose to confess mental malaise in various pieces of writing that extend across their lives. William James, who made such a choice, spoke in *The Varieties of Religious Experience* of a mark which he found stamped upon the earlier life of the New England saint and, as he confessed, upon himself. It is this phrase, "the iron of melancholy," that this book used to bring together the Puritan and Victorian discourse of confession.

By the time James used this phrase in 1901 and 1902, the meaning of the word "melancholy" was no longer precise. In the seventeenth century, however, the word had pointed to a specific state of conscience. Melancholy referred to symptoms that Victorian alienists (the nineteenth-century term for those we call psychiatrists) and neurologists considered neurotic, symptoms they variously termed morbid impulsions, insistent ideas, fixed ideas, and obsessions. No single name other than melancholy encompassed such symptoms until Freud combined them into a second major neurotic form (the first was *hysteria*, a word contributed by the Greeks) that he termed *Zwangsneurose* or obsessional neurosis. Then too, like the words "obsessional" and "compulsive" today, melancholy pointed not only to pathological symptoms but also to a set of character traits—most particularly, in the seventeenth century, to the character of those called "precisians," or Puritans, men and women who seemed to others to be possessed by excessive doubts, by extreme guilt and convictions of sin, and by particularly laborious attitudes and actions. We still associate this obsessional or compulsive behavior with a so-called Puritan or Protestant character.

Today, beginning with the work of Erich Fromm, who in 1932 first brought the writings of Freud and Weber together (specifically, Freud's essay on "Character and Anal Eroticism" and Weber's essay on "The Protestant Ethic and the Spirit of Capitalism"), and continuing on in many American studies, both the obsessional symptomatology and the compulsive character traits have coalesced into a state of mind that Weber first phrased a "Protestant ethic." This uniting of an "ethic," "character-type," and "neurosis" is less complex if we understand it as an effort that scholars have undertaken to define a moral psychology. Moral psychology allows the idea of an ethic, character, and psychopathology to interlock. Like Freud's individual typology of superego, ego, and id, each of these words forms a layer; together the layers constitute what we have come to understand as the personality of a culture.

Concepts of obsessional pathology have remained fluid and never, as one might think of hysteria, clearly defined. Only sometime within the first two decades of this century did psychiatrists, psychologists, and the medical and academic communities generally, following the lead of the psychoanalysts, come to see the psychoneurosis as the neurosis is seen today. Obsessional behavior is a type of behavior in which persons use highly ritualized and quite privately composed acts, whether mental or physical, to lessen doubts, anxieties, and the sense of insecurity they feel pressing down upon them.

Freud called the physical acts "obsessive actions." (They are generally referred to as "compulsions" or "compulsive behaviors" today.) These "petty ceremonials" appeared to Freud to caricature publicly sanctioned rituals of religious propitiation. Josiah Royce, the American philosopher, called these behaviors "self-invented exorcising devices," a phrase that like Freud's connotes the idea of a strangely practiced religion. The compulsive behavior that was the most familiar to Victorians and remains the most familiar to us is the handwashing ritual. Victorian alienists and neurologists referred to it as *mysophobia* or the fear of filth. As the word "mysophobia" indicates, all sorts of phobias could become entangled in questions of obsessional behavior (as phobias still are today), so that a question as to what obsessional behavior is can quickly erupt.

Freud accepted the common term "obsession" to designate the acts performed mentally. For at least three hundred years this word has opened itself to far more meanings and interpretations than the sometimes obversely used word "compulsion." Unlike a compulsive act, an obsessional idea fails to be so readily pointed out as having occurred "like that." Obsession can indicate a mental manipulation carried out analogously to a physical ritual—for example, when a person feels that he must think (or not think) a particular series of thoughts in a particular way or according to some complex ritual scheme. Or the word can indicate the "fixed ideas" or "insistent impulses" that a person cannot banish from his mind—sudden, terrifying thoughts that one might commit some unpardonable crime such as killing one's child or friend. Because this last designation of obsession begs the question of whether the person might carry out the thought—that is, whether he might give in to "temptation" or, from a rather common Victorian view, become a victim of "monomania" or "moral insanity"—this aspect of obsessional symptomatology became of great importance both to seventeenth-century Puritan divines and to nineteenth-century Victorian physicians.

Whether performed mentally or physically, for Freud, these obsessional behaviors involved the self-renunciation that any magical ceremony demands of its practitioner. Acts are to be performed or not performed according to the rules that some invisible otherness prescribes, and ideas are to be thought or not thought again as if, in Freud's words, some "ancient gods" were tugging at the mind of the patient. In all, speaking most generally, obsessional behavior is behavior in which a need to secure one's world may be expressed in these incessant works, in a seeming use of magic and superstition, or in behaviors that Freud likened to a primitive's use of totem and taboo. Obsessional behavior is behavior in which conscience may be expressed in paralyzing doubts, in seemingly silly forebodings and apprehensions, in methods of self-castigation, and in feelings of loathing and self-hate. And it is behavior in which anger may be expressed whenever the defenses of the compulsive acts and obsessional ideas are breached, anger reflected from the world and redirected towards the self as times of severe depression, times when one is unable to work and when one very much desires to gain a renewed sense of order.

Pointing, as the pathology does, to seemingly strange temptations and to privately composed rituals, it is not surprising that well before Freud's writings likening obsessional practices to religious behavior began to appear, obsessional pathologies became the concern of divines who also wrote as physicians of the soul. Much has been written about the English concern with melancholy that developed sometime in the late sixteenth century and runs through some of the most famous of seventeenth-century English literature, but little has been said about how this melancholy, specifically that which Robert Burton claimed to have first called "religious melancholy," was perceived in terms of its symptomatology, and almost nothing has been said concerning the obsessional symptoms that the English idea of melancholy included. It is difficult enough to speak of neurosis today when psychiatrists and psychoanalysts are speaking of neurotic behaviors as "mixed" and when they are redoing some of Freud's diagnoses; it is more difficult to work one's way into the seventeenth-century English world and try to fathom something as obviously complex and variously interpreted as melancholy. To understand the English and later American Puritan concern with melancholy, it is necessary to move past the idea that the Puritans were, or were at least thought of, as "melancholy" and to move toward just what, rather exactly, this melancholy was thought to entail.

As anyone familiar with the present understanding of this neurosis knows, obsessional behavior is intimately tied to questions of identifying self-fulfilling forms of work. As one may gather from a reading of Erik H. Erikson's study of Luther, and from the numerous studies of compulsive behavior that have been written under the influence of Erikson, the obsessional neurosis (which, from a fear of labeling, often goes unnamed in psychohistorical studies) vividly demonstrates the alienation of labor. The neurosis clarifies the "works" that Erikson argues so plagued Luther's life as to create Luther's valuation of worldly work or calling. This book looks at compulsive works, but it focuses more upon obsessional ideations—upon mental rather than physical absurdities. For seventeenth-century Puritan divines, religious melancholy demonstrated not only the futility of physically erasing a pressing sense of sin but also the hollowness of mentally manipulating fear. Given the Calvinist decrying of works, whether of a physical or mental nature, it is understandable that English and American Puritan authors should have seen the symptomatology of melancholy as a horror to be worked through on the way toward a knowing of one's true vocation. This time of trial and estranging temptation, an "other-worldly asceticism" to use another of Weber's concepts, could express a stage of false labor in a journey toward unalienated labor, work to be carried out productively within the world.

The history of the idea of the obsessional neurosis has yet to be written. Though the present work hardly accomplishes that, it does look at the changing use made of the symptoms of this mental pathology by authors who have attempted to carry themselves through a long and often laborious time of personal regeneration.

From the seventeenth century, Americans have confessed to behaviors that psychiatrists today label as obsessional or compulsive, giving rise to the argument that because of the Protestant or simply capitalist nature of America, the New World has induced a peculiar anxiety. Historians suspicious of the use of psychohistory push this argument aside. The brilliance of William James's pragmatism was to push aside the whole debate and to focus instead upon the making rather than the finding of truth. And questions of long debate do begin to dissolve if we ask not whether a historical person was neurotic, but why the evidence for neurosis appears. We could ask, for example, whether John Bunyan, who composed a psychological writing of his own life toward the end of the seventeenth century which includes such vivid accounts of obsessional thoughts and compulsive acts that his words appear in modern psychiatric textbooks, was neurotic. But the issue, as James told us long ago, is not whether Bunyan was neurotic, but why Bunyan chose to write about a particular psychopathology in the way that he did, thereby helping to create a formidable tradition of confessional narrative that has survived, most particularly, in America. The questions become why authors should have chosen to express a psychopathology, what use they made of it, and why literate cultures should choose to preserve the documents in which the evidence of psychopathology appears. These are the kinds of questions that historians can approach before they probe such documents for unconscious significance; before they probe them, that is, for evidence of other forces lying hidden beyond the texts. In the parlance of semiotics, one looks at writing without looking for anything in excess of the sign itself, anything that does not involve language.

This book proposes to recreate the discourse within which an argument of American psychopathology has worked. The tradition of confessional writing started by the Puritans is so distinctive that it can be called a discourse of its own: texts that participate in this tradition follow the same rules, invoke the same models, and testify to the same struggles. By tracing the origin of this confessional discourse to the settlement of New England and to the implantation there of a particular idea of spiritual conversion (a quite well delineated structure of conversion that comprises several steps), the present book is not attempting to find reflected in various texts the fact of pathology, but rather the expression of pathology. This writing out of pathology is not a "mere expression," or rhetoric as opposed to reality. Men and women in America could use the practice of confession to give meaning to their lives. They could use past texts to organize their experience—a thought common to structuralism. In the words of Mikhail Bakhtin, quoted by Marshall Sahlins: "It is not experience that organizes expression, but the other way around—*expression organizes experience*. Expression is what first gives experience its form and specificity of direction." As much as any other material substance, people use past texts to give meaning to their lives. This book analyzes the efforts of a series of individuals living at different times to find spiritual peace through the narration of their own psychological experience, narrations that build experience according to formulas established in the Puritan generation of John Bunyan. The book is not looking at commonly considered reasons for the presence of a pathology of American character, the material practices or the physical presences that are often said to have created character: the force of an environment like the American frontier, the use of certain child-rearing methods, the formation and change of particular social and economic structures. Rather, it looks for writings about an American character that are considered to be in themselves efficacious for giving shape to reality. Textual expressions, this book argues, are in themselves capable of creating a person's character.

Whether obsessional pathology is said to have been caused by particular patterns of child-rearing, certain family structures, or, most often, disquieting transformations in the American economy, the fact of anxiety commonly is assumed to have existed "out there"—as an object—because, simply, neurotic symptomatology is to be found described in certain historical texts. Rather than being given force to shape reality themselves, these texts are considered the reflections—the signs or symptomatic evidence—of something material going on outside of writing, something of a personal, social, or economic nature taking place outside of the act of writing down the pathology itself. Even though we are accustomed today to hearing ourselves described by cultural critics as in the grip of mental malaise, we may remain critical of the argument that Americans have suffered unique psychological estrangement. Still, we should acknowledge the power that writings on alienation have had in America—the power that a particular language structure can have for making sense out of our lives and therefore for actually "making" our lives.

Many studies have presented the importance of a Protestant character in America, particularly in reference to an American ethic of work, and many others, including most brilliantly the writings of Fromm, Erikson, and Norman O. Brown, have argued for the existence of a pathology of the Protestant ethic. Several recent histories have applied both psychohistorical and social historical techniques to American Puritans and to American Victorian intellectuals, asserting, whether directly or by implication, that a neurotically obsessional personality can be identified. Other cultural histories have looked past this "classical" neurosis, tied, as obsessional behavior is thought to have been, to an earlier capitalism and its work ethic. These more recent books have cited the formation of modern neuroses like narcissism which are thought to be akin to the "other-direction" that C. Wright Mills, David Riesman, and Herbert Marcuse first described thirty years ago as the temper of postindustrial society. All of these studies, whether on the obsessive-compulsive or the one-dimensional, narcissistic personality, remain characterological portraits; although they impute neurosis to the American, they rarely offer specific symptomatological evidence.

Evidence of obsessional mental pathology is to be found in the period of classical American economy, both in the spiritual autobiographies of Puritan saints and in the lives of such Victorian intellectuals as William James. This evidence begs to be looked at for the meaning that an expression of psychopathology possessed for the author who decided to reveal his life in writing, the meaning an author gives to suicidal thoughts, for example. The historian should seek this meaning before he makes an argument that the expression of such a thought reflects another material nature, whether the innateness of an author's character, the personality of his culture, or the forces of his economy. Questions of discourse precede arguments that writing acts like a mirror, presenting the virtual image of unseen but real forces elsewhere. (As James argued, a sign like writing is as tangible, and as efficacious in building reality, as that which it signifies.) We therefore reject the method of "culture and personality" that seeks an economic or social cause for a group's psychology. Nor do we pursue the history of the disembodied idea that certain authors have had about the existence of a particular psychology. Both these methods—the one which considers the personal and social causation of thought (the past expression of which is in writing) and the other which seeks the timeless idea—remain inadequate, if we wish to understand the force within a culture of discursive practices and the material production of writing.

Discursive formations, in the phrase of Michel Foucault, determine the presence of particular types of reading and writing, including the ways in which an author's life and character become merged with the particular texts he writes. The discursive reading Foucault requires refuses to ask the traditional questions of whether a historian should relate an author's personality to his texts, or how the historian should go about making such a relation. A discursive reading asks instead why such a relation within a particular historical formation has in fact been made. A method of discourse asks why a literate culture has chosen to produce certain writings that require close attachment with an author's name—that is, why a culture chooses to authorize certain texts.

A discursive method also seeks the ways in which people read their lives against past scripts. One thereby returns the word "character" to its literal meaning as a type face or scripture. Within the most traditional of understandings, meaning has adhered in the past to the idea that ideal lives are to be led according to, and in fulfillment of, scripture. ("And he began . . . , and interpreted unto them in all the Scriptures the things which were *written* of him.") This book, in presenting a series of lives set against a background of Puritan confession, asks how each of these lives reinterpreted and represented earlier writings of the self's trial and change.

Puritan confession first presented itself as an oral "relation" addressed to the body of a congregation. This confession then expanded into a variety of autobiographical and biographical lives, writings that also acted as movements of spiritual conversion. Within the earlier lives, whether oral or written, Puritan authors described symptoms of melancholy that they read as signs of salvation—the hellish or blasphemous temptation, for example, which when carefully observed reflected for the Puritan not the depravity but the grace of one so tempted. By the end of the nineteenth century the meaning attached to such obsessional ideation had precisely reversed: a horrid thought indicated that one might become morally insane. The Puritans' case of conscience had transformed itself into the Victorians' neurological "case."

The Puritans' understanding of melancholy as it related to spiritual conversion lasted through the writings of Jonathan Edwards. In the face of a turmoil of religious awakening, Edwards attempted to preserve the meaning that he had found in an experience of melancholy. By the end of the eighteenth century, a half-century after Edwards's death, the relationship of Puritan conversion to the humoral psychology of melancholy no longer worked. Against Edwards, the elder Henry James rewrote the psychology of his own "moral destruction" and rebirth, despising the terrors he thought Calvinism had wrought, and against the elder James, William James attempted to reformulate the idea of how it was that "religion and neurology" were intertwined. Josiah Royce, the younger colleague and close friend of James, sought to give a social expression to James's personal psychology, and James Jackson Putnam, a friend of James and a disciple of Royce, turned finally to Freud and psychoanalysis. Psychoanalysis, as Putnam thought, offered an analogue of Puritan conversion.

In their academic writings and in the writings that they composed of their lives, these men fashioned different interpretations of the process of Puritan conversion. To do so they reinterpreted the obsessive and compulsive psychopathology that they attributed to themselves, each asking through his own perspective what the symptoms of such a pathology now meant. Like the early American spiritual autobiographers, these intellectuals could discover a significance threading through their lives by writing of themselves within a specific structure of conversion. They could come to understand their turmoil by describing again the melancholy out of which a conversion journey—in the sense of both a travel and a travail—begins.

With the possible exception of Freud, no writer became more important in explicating an argument of American estrangement, and in defining the character of America, than Max Weber. His essay on the Protestant ethic works like a spiritual biography writ large for all of

America. Weber, having read James's lectures on *The Varieties of Religious Experience* and spoken to James during a visit to America in 1904, upon his return to Germany and following years of an incapacitating depression, wrote the last half of his essay—the portion that so many American scholars use to begin their own histories of America's despair. Weber provided the idea that a Protestant ethic had existed, most especially, he thought, within America. And as important, he furnished what is by now a well-known image of modern alienation, the image of an "iron cage." This image makes visible the mechanism that Weber believed the Protestant ethic had, by the end of the nineteenth century, twisted itself into—"mechanized petrification," a concept that has become timeless in that when Weber's image is used by historians, it can be relocated at a variety of points in time.

Invariably, Weber argued, a historically unique this-worldly or innerworldly ascetic ideal (the Protestant ethic) had created its own destruction. By the beginning of the seventeenth century, Weber believed, this ethic had begun to create an enormous outpouring of work and, unintentionally, wealth and material goods, fashioning an economy that brought the ascetic ideal to its end. Protestantism and most especially the radical sects of Protestantism had created, through the sanctification of work, a machine so furious that it tore itself apart. An ascetic religiosity that had demanded virtuous labor within the world, with the laborer to be in but not of the world, could only build such an enormous work (whether of goods, machines, or bureaucracies) in a way such as to remove the need for any further religiosity itself. The phrase "spirit of capitalism" refers to a certain German historicist idea of a cultural mentality. But the phrase, as when Weber spoke of "specialists without spirit," is also an ironic play of words.

Thereby Weber drew a pathology across America of economic and psychological "compulsion." He also drew America before the "iron cage of despair"—the cage in front of which, in Bunyan's *The Pilgrim's Progress*, Christian stands, facing there a temptation to commit the unpardonable sin of the man locked in the cage. In Bunyan's allegory, the scene of the iron cage begins rather than ends the story of Christian's conversion. (The scene is not unlike one that James related in the *Varieties*, describing the sudden fright he had felt that he might become like a man convulsed in epilepsy, a man he said he had actually seen in the cell of an insane asylum.) As a renewed expression of spiritual conversion, Weber's essay transposes this sight of God's desertion from the self to the whole of the American state. His essay returns America to the desert in which, as his Puritan had argued, life could begin. Another image, from the Psalms, also offers an understanding of why within an alienation of labor, conversion and pathology are intertwined:

> They wandered in the wilderness in a solitary way; they found no city to dwell in.
>
> . . .
>
> Such as sit in darkness and in the shadow of death, *being* bound in affliction and iron;
>
> Because they rebelled against the words of God, and contemned the counsel of the most High:
>
> Therefore he brought down their heart with labour; they fell down, and *there was* none to help.
>
> Then they cried unto the LORD in their trouble, *and* he saved them out of their distresses.
>
> . . .
>
> For he hath broken the gates of brass, and cut the bars of iron in sunder.

Such could be the experience for saints of a desert. And with the beginnings of America, the wilderness was found.

I

Twice-Born and Sick Soul

The Awakening of New England's Conscience

> Beloved, think it not strange concerning the fiery trial which is to try you, as though as some strange thing happened unto you.
>
> 1 Peter 4:12

The word "Puritan" appears to freeze the variousness of life in seventeenth-century New England, the flux of experience that one should imagine no word could contain. To define a Puritan "imagination" as a type, or to offer the presence of a "mind" or "temperament," singles out a particular character. An important definition of Puritanism, however, rests upon the necessity of definition—the necessity that different men and women felt in the seventeenth century to name themselves pilgrims. Though the textures of early American society permitted no singular Puritanism to hold as a center, there was a singular need to create a beginning and a sense of difference from others, a need that enfolded diverse doctrinal and experiential disputes. Before the English settlements in America, words had attached themselves to men and women who, whether speaking derogatorily or not, others held to be precisians—words that spoke of men and women who required such purity that they cast themselves into wildernesses and deserts. With the migration to America, these words received the material substance that a strange land offered. The separation continued in New England as men and women searched for the marks of experience that they believed defined the pilgrim or the "visible saint"; the separation continued as churches, in various degrees of rigor, established the requirements of experience for those they would allow to attend the Lord's Supper. Eventually, the land itself became marked and separated; a character, that is, came to define the "American."

The men and women who settled in New England had of course separated, though they could hardly dissolve or even conceive of dissolving their English traits and culture. The frontier now before them—a horrid wilderness, as it appears in their writings—remained incapable of changing anything of their character. The frontier that did demand a laying to waste of their old ways—the estrangement that, by the end of the seventeenth century, gave an irrevocable sense of beginnings to the American character—stood as an internal bewilderment. The Puritans' new world waited as an experience of spiritual conversion.

Puritan conversion began in an awakening. The eyes of a hopeful but still sleepy saint opened suddenly to a satanic sight lying before him, a sight that strikes the saint and creates his conviction of sin. While others have slept, content with the state of their souls, the saint, who is about to become a pilgrim, begins a trial of mental and physical anguish that may continue for years, perhaps continue for a lifetime. He has begun a battle with the devil's temptations. He sits for the moment frozen in terror, fearful that he has committed unpardonable sin, including the fear now that he is committing the unpardonable sin of despair. Held in this prison the devil has wrought, and fighting despair, he cries for the meaning of the horrors filling his mind, horrors that his neighbors can readily dismiss as a melancholy. He asks if he is damned, or simply mad, or whether, if he resists the thoughts obsessing his mind, he can work his way out of his prison. If he works, then perhaps he can travel from the fright of his sin to the promise of a coming salvation. If he accepts the travail a wilderness demands, then perhaps he can cross to a new kingdom.

Before the migration to New England, English Puritan divines had begun to define conversion not as a point in time but as this long journey (a narrative, in other words) that began in isolation and terror. Ministers proposed "steps" through which a person was to pass to achieve this most important of all separations. Though experience, spiritual conversion necessarily required interpretation and guides, conventions by which the saint could understand his trials and thereby make a sensible case out of his troubles of conscience. However human the authorship of these steps appeared, the divines marked out the boundaries and provided the skeletal forms for a story of conversion, providing a structure that each person's own experience then filled with substance. Conversion often entailed years of unfoldings; thus metaphors of journey, so deeply embedded in English culture, lent themselves to the understanding of this inward change. These internal migrations entailed "strangeness," a sense of one's alienation from God that began when the person suddenly sensed his own destruction and set about to understand why it had occurred. Given this terror or a conviction of sin, the person seeking salvation could easily enough look upon himself as entering into a wilderness. The satanic trials of this lonely desert would test his faith. The estrangement he experienced, however, others might simply call his melancholy.

The absolute necessity some English men and women felt for seeking the signs of an experience of conversion centers any understanding of Puritanism. This search, because it was often described in a written spiritual story and because it is, of course, the story of a war in one's soul (a psychomachia), inevitably brought to the Puritan the charge of melancholy. The charge focused the characterology of Puritanism in the seventeenth century, just as it continues to focus the understanding of the temperament of Puritanism today. Melancholy offered the definition that the Puritan had sought, by setting the Puritan's self aside. The charge appears, that is, not from the fact of a melancholy—certainly not in the first instance—but from a psychopathological discourse that English Puritanism itself helped to create in the late sixteenth and seventeenth centuries. Melancholy was a way of understanding otherwise chaotic mental experiences.

The Puritans' psychology appears in writings that range from bodies of divinity to barely literate spiritual relations, writings in which both ministers and ordinary men and women explained and then applied the occurrence of melancholy to their lives. The word "melancholy" defined the stricken in conscience and the outcast. The Puritan accepted the essence of the charge, providing, in the story of his conversion, the evidence of his alienation down to the finest of psychological peculiarities. Most particularly, the Puritan wrote of various temptations that beset his mind—of terrible thoughts of suicide, for example, the acting out of which he abhorred, but the significance of which he came to understand when a melancholy temptation spoke not of his damnation but of the play of Satan upon his mind. He could then read his life of temptation as an imitation of the temptations of Christ.

This understanding that melancholy, a corporeal fluid that along with blood, phlegm, and choler constituted man's humors, and spiritual re-creation did combine, lasted through the middle of the eighteenth century. Most prominently in America, the understanding lasted into the writings of Jonathan Edwards. The necessity to seek and properly interpret the signs of spiritual conversion created the need for Edwards, as it had for English and American divines before him, to lay out an anatomy of conscience. By defining as precisely as he could different types of temptations and the relationship that existed between certain temptations and acts, Edwards was asking how he could read salvation from the marks of a stricken conscience, just as a physician might read the signs of recovery, or of death, from the symptoms of a bodily ailment. A "semeiology," in other words—in a traditional understanding of that word as an art of reading symptoms—came to be applied to the study of spiritual conversion.

American Puritanism had differed from English Puritanism in two important respects, both of which Edwards confronted. First, most if not all the seventeenth-century churches in New England had required, for varying periods of time, that a person tell the story of his conversion. Second, a land was at hand that, like an interior of mind, one could call wilderness and desert. A land had opened out before the pilgrim upon which he could place the story of his spiritual re-creation, locating his psychology in time and space. Puritan authors, including the illiterate who spoke before their congregations, could externalize their experience, attributing their spiritual reform to the exigencies of a satanic new land. When seventeenth-century New England ministers like Cotton Mather applied spiritual conversion corporately, they applied it to the whole of the American body, locating the temptations Satan injected into the minds of the saints not only within the material humor of melancholy—the humor in which divines considered that Satan worked to tempt the children of God—but also within the corrupt landscape of America. They could make the whole of New England a devilish place.

Edwards, though he could still portray the desert of America as the desert of the temptations of Christ, began to take the source of melancholy away from the physical contours of the land. New England, obviously, had become industriously improved. He turned the location of the spiritual journey inward, and as he did so, he watched the corporate necessity for a spiritual story of conversion collapse. When Edwards demanded of his own congregation that they reinstate a relation of conversion, and when his Northampton, Massachusetts, parishioners refused, feeling that Edwards was demanding too much when he asked that they give voice to a state they felt they already knew, he became the outcast, sending himself out into a farther Massachusetts frontier. His own exile to Stockbridge expressed the dispersion of the story of alienation itself.

Edwards's writings on the religious affections, along with the story of estrangement he made out of his own life, provided the setting not for the American pastoral (which could be set in place amid the country's busy farms) but for the Victorians' internal, neurological journey. By the nineteenth century the Puritans' community of psychological revelation had fragmented into isolated spiritual texts. The Puritans' corporate case of conscience, like the wilderness, had turned into the Victorians' individual psychopathological case.

The Den & "In The Den"

From the sixteenth century on, various literatures have depicted America not as a garden—or as a garden only in a first naïve moment before the discoverer opens his eyes—but as a desert. America furnishes the landscape for the story of the pilgrim's progress. Like the prairie of Cooper, the woods of Thoreau, or the whale of Melville, America presents an untouched sheet of wilderness upon which to record the trials and spiritual conversion of a saint. In the idleness of an Old World—the City of Destruction of John Bunyan's allegory—the pilgrim awakens. He falls sick with melancholy, retires to his chamber, then travels from this world to that which is to come, moving alone across a bare common, heading toward a Celestial City that remains always in the future of his eye. The present nature of his travel, like the confusion besetting his mind, confronts him as a wilderness that speaks of his distance from God.

The present land is a terror. America will fulfill its promise, but only after America offers the temptations that Christian faces in *The Pilgrim's Progress*, the desert Christian must experience before he can turn his eyes to the Celestial City high above his nature. The temptations and trials of the Western world, fanciful and real, signify the American's passage: savages, torture, blood feasts, flesh, lust, greed, gold, filth, later the presence of monstrous machines. The pilgrim's re-creation begins where, two hundred years later, Frederick Jackson Turner argued that the American character did begin, not in the garden but at the "fall line" that marks the opening into the frontier.

The historian of early America places this allegory in time. He re-creates the European vision of America by beginning in a city of similar sadness, in the "sombre melancholy" of the fifteenth century, in Thomas Huizinga's words, that "weighs on people's souls."[1] He then takes his remnant from their prison and carries them through a narrative journey: his people begin east of Eden, in the Old World, and sail toward the west, for theirs too is the hopeful flight to a far world in the dream of redeeming their sin. Like the Celestial City of *The Pilgrim's Progress*, the New World garden waits, but it waits always within an ever receding future. The most quoted words of early New England history remain the words that John Winthrop spoke aboard the *Arbella* in 1630. Sailing toward America, Winthrop chose words that express a promised utopia, but a utopia that lies nowhere in the present: "for wee must Consider that wee shall be as a Citty vpon a Hill."[2]

There was no thought for Winthrop that the city could be attained without the saint's "preparation"—preparation that begins with attending to the Word and then, when one had dreamed only of pastoral innocence, suddenly feeling corrupt. The best of our histories tell how Americans have dreamed of progress and how the progress has failed. They speak of the seductive nature of America, the easy promise the garden makes that they turn to fancy and make, through history, the stuff of dreams. For it is not the garden, the pastoral, the virgin land that lies at the heart of the historian's America, but this revelation of the fall of the New World Adam, the discovery of sin that turns his work from chronicle to art and joins his history with the myth he describes—the myth, that is, of the American garden as a demonic land. These histories open the garden to horrid intrusions of iron and machines. They probe the American unconscious and there find a mechanistic pathology that feeds the desire to engineer a perfectly good order, the kind of order that covers up what it is that has been done. Like Freud's *Totem and Taboo*, American history weaves textures of chronology and myth, speaking of specific times when Americans have lost their innocence but also speaking of the timeless desire to build such enormous works across the space of the virgin land that the works turn and devour their creators. Like the Puritans' Word, history incites the conviction of sin. As the histories turn from chronicle to art, the American begins a transit across a "strange New World," and history begins the story of a nation's spiritual awakening.

In beginning *The Pilgrim's Progress*, John Bunyan imprinted such a setting of both wilderness and iron. His allegory opens in both the "wilderness of this world" through which the narrator of Christian's story walks, and the jail in which the author of the allegory actually lies in

1660. "I lighted on a certain place where was a den,* and lai place to sleep; and as I slept I dreamed a dream." The nar then, with his pilgrim's conviction of sin. But the spiritual Christian curiously mixed Bunyan's life into his own alleg thor notes that the den represents "*The Gaol*," and various the book entail further commentary, as in this asterisked n

In addition to such notes, many editions include a prelimi "The Life of John Bunyan," that further weaves together the and the universal. In biography and allegory, both the author grim create cages for their realization of sin: Bunyan lies in jai retires to his "chamber," struck, his wife laments, with mela bodily personification, melancholy etches the natural sin of tracing the sickness of their souls in the material of a humo apply a carnal physic to cure the men's convictions, whethe which society tries to imprison the word of God, or the de medicine that Christian's relations prescribe to mask his con of sin: "When we begin to be wise unto salvation, carnal fr nounce us mad unto destruction; and administer carnal me our sin-sick souls."[4]

Melancholy, a physical malady, foretells of spiritual awake from such prisons of sickness that both Bunyan and Chri emerge to begin their journeys of conversion. They will enter derness and into the temptations of Christ. What neither Bu his editors could ever actualize was the notion of the pilgrim's

The Melancholy Desert

In America, this metaphoric play of words—*ferus*, or "wild, *rum*, or "iron," and the *insanus* to which "wild" points[5]—c shape in the land. A textual expression, that is, could organiz ence. Though Bunyan realizes himself within his own alle landscape of *The Pilgrim's Progress* stays as timeless and spa Freud's landscape of the id.[6] Puritan histories of America cou the wilderness and implant the prisons, thereby providing s time for those who appeared to be living the pilgrim's text. Earl can historians could reveal the garden as a melancholy desert: b ing, satanic, beset with unimaginable crimes and, as trials in the

*Mr. Bunyan wrote this precious book in Bedford gaol. . . . The se Christ, when restrained by penal laws, from publishing the word of life pulpit, have become more abundantly useful by their writings.[3]

New World saints, inflamed with monstrous fictions that Satan presented only to the mind. Acts of crime erupted in New England, but thoughts of crime erupted as well, an ideation that seventeenth-century historians most simply termed melancholy.

William Bradford professed the acts in 1642 when he recounted the distempers of Plymouth: the "breaking out of sundrie notorious sins," "unclainnes," "incontinencie," "even sodomie and bugerie." There mingled with the saints a corruption, as Bradford wrote, of "natures," marvelous crimes considering how much his people had witnessed against wickedness. Bradford preferred to think such acts a matter of Satan's "spite," as well as the sociology of recording crime, the close keeping of accounts the magistrates required among the pilgrims of Plymouth. "I would rather thinke thus, then that Satane hath more power in these heathen lands, as som have thought, then in more Christian nations, espetially over Gods servants in them."[7]

By the century's end Cotton Mather, considering horrors worked in the minds of the servants themselves, willingly accepted the satanic presence Bradford had refused. He wrote of the very "PLOT of the Devil, against *New-England*, in every Branch of it," including himself. "The *New-Englanders* are a People of God settled in those, which were once the Devil's Territories; and it may easily be supposed that the *Devil* was exceedingly disturbed, when he perceived such a People here accomplishing the Promise of old made unto our Blessed Jesus. . . . I believe, that never were more *Satanical Devices* used for the Unsetling of any People under the Sun."[8] Mather termed the assault melancholy, a special disease in that it had attacked a people in Christ's hands.

Horrors existed in New England, but the bare possibilities of an estranged setting had become this writing of a wondrous evil. In imitation of the temptations of Christ, the children of God had "embraced a . . . squalid, horrid, *American* Desart" on the edge of civilization where the devil reigned. Mather's Christ lived as the Son of the wilderness, as the Christ that William Perkins, an important English Puritan minister, had analyzed with close psychological scrutiny. Christ, as the Cambridge divine had argued, prior to the errand of some of his students to America, had been tried by melancholy "euill suggestions." Perkins's Son had been cast in the place chosen by God for combat, not in Jerusalem but in a land low and base, void of pomp and glory.[9]

Mather wrote of America as such a waste in ritualized phrases without so much as a glance at the land. He had, instead, read Perkins's sermons, including Perkins's discussions of Christ's melancholy temptations. The people of New England had found themselves driven into

"temptation," assaulted in a land whose agony was prefigured in the assaults of Satan upon the Lord Jesus Christ. Mather speculated that Satan had perhaps driven himself from prosperous regions into New England because of his envy of the civilization God had wrought—more likely, because the Old World was living in sin and God had sent the devil for his own vexation into the desert of a purer people continually calling upon the name of the Savior. Whatever the reason, Satan lived in New England and had become aroused. The evidence Mather provided lies in a variety of psychopathic cases, cases of conscience that Mather studied with all the interest of an inquiring physician.[10]

America had become the visual analogue of the desert of Christ's temptations. For Mather, America lay before the pilgrim as a landscape of melancholy. The immediate fact of witchcraft had presented itself, though the satanic occurrences in Salem Village in 1692 represented for Mather but an instance of a long-besetting pathology. There existed not simply the visible fits and convulsions of young women but invisible "*Possessions* and *Obsessions*." In themselves, the obsessions appeared "very marvelous," something New Englanders had been experiencing since the founding of their land: *"things . . . then Darted into their minds. Darted!"* Now men and women had become tempted again, haunted even in church, and by the devil "that is the Author of all such Melancholy Suggestions," the "most Hellish *Blasphemies* often buzz'd by the *Temptations* of the Devil, into the minds of the best Men alive." Mather built his case for the conversion of New England upon this heaving "Mire and Mud," the "*Brimstone* even without Metaphor, . . . making an hellish and horrid stench in our Nostrils." There "are incredible Droves of Devils in our way," horrors such that Mather wrote of his own need to be *"fenced with Iron, and the Staff of a Spear."* The pathology remained communal: "The ill Humors or Vapours in the Bodies of such Good Men, do so harbour the Devil that they have this woeful motion every day thence made unto them; *You must kill your self! you must! you must!*"[11]

Mather was writing of witchcraft, recording, he said, his observations. Salem had presented an occasion, however, and Mather was choosing his phrases traditionally. He was drawing for his reader images that reflected not bare observations but writings such as Robert Burton's *Anatomy of Melancholy*, a copy of which he had in his library.[12] Mather's words reflected little of the anguish of the village in 1692, no more than they did the material fact of the New England frontier or the physical presence of savages and beasts. He was using this sight of Satan to envision a coming national salvation. Mather possessed the reason now for reminding his countrymen of their fears, of why, indeed, others would think them mad. For rather than fleeing from a melancholy world to a garden, the pilgrim had arrived in a psychopathic land. Here he was "accounted," as Thomas Hooker had written three decades before *The Pilgrim's Progress*, "a silly sot, and a mad man, in regard of the horror of heart." In the words of Thomas Shepard, another early New England minister, "We are here but strangers, and have *no abiding city* . . . ; and therefore let . . . Satan tempt, and cast his darts at us . . . ; let us be shut up in choaking prisons, . . . nay upon dung-hils."[13]

The Temptations that the Melancholy Experience

What, then, for a Puritan minister, was an experience of melancholy? There remained a maxim, Cotton Mather wrote, "*That a Wise Man will be Melancholy once a Day.* I suppose, they mean something more than, *Serious*, and, *Thoughtful*. . . . I must rather say, *My Son, Be thou in it all the Day long.* I am sure, a *Dying Man*, as thou art, has Reason to be so."[14]

From the time of the writing of the Greeks, melancholy had fashioned chambers into which men, as later in "monastic melancholy," could enter and there craft forms of unique understanding. Melancholy offered perhaps the beginnings of inspiration or frenzy.[15] Since the Middle Ages, theologians had portrayed melancholy not only as this chamber but also as a progression of stages or steps. Raymond Klibansky, Erwin Panofsky, and Fritz Saxl have brilliantly reconstructed this course moving from matter to spirit. One series, from Agrippa of Nettesheim, moves from *Imaginatio*, the mechanical and natural, through *Ratio*, the human and political, to *Mens*, the divine and prophetical. As these historians argue, Dürer's engraving, *Melencolia I*, with its depiction of structural and geometric precision, becomes the portrait of the first stage of one such possible series.

Also, when Dürer applied the four humors to the Apostles, he chose to portray Paul as melancholy.

> Dürer thought the best way of characterizing the tutelary genius of Protestantism was to represent him as a melancholic. . . . he not only emphasized the asceticism so characteristic of the historical Paul, but endowed him with a noble sublimity denied to the other temperaments.[16]

From the opening of the sixteenth century on, Protestantism and melancholy were somehow becoming intertwined.

The maxim Mather cited presented a pale reflection of the earlier, inspirational understanding of melancholy. More vividly, Mather drew words from English texts on melancholy that involved not only sadness but also a horror of heart and a striking consciousness of sin. Here a specific symptom exists; something that Mather considered a sensible impression, a type of thought that centered Mather's own understanding of the desertion that melancholy expressed.

> It is not without a Cause, that *Melancholy* has been called, *Balneum Diaboli* ["Bathing place of the Devil," in the editor's translation]. Some *Devil* is often very Busy with the poor *Melancholicks*; yea, there is often a Degree of *Diabolical Possession* in the *Melancholy*. King *Saul* is not the only Instance to be produced for it. The *Diabolical Impression* appears very Sensible, Either when *Thoughts* full of *Atheism* or *Blasphemy* are shott like *Fiery Darts* into their Minds, and so seriously infest them, that they are even *Weary of their Lives*; or, when their Minds are violently impelled and hurried on to Self-Murder.

For this trouble of mind, no physic the self could hope for existed that could cure the sickness, and "God forbid," as Mather played his words, "that you should make Light of the Matter." Only the profane would make this "but a *Mechanical Business* in our *Animal Spirits*."[17] Only God could bring light to the matter that a saint should so suffer an animal spirit's corruption.

The word "melancholy" appears as more than an offhand expression of sadness or ennui in the writings of seventeenth-century scholars. Writers such as Mather chose the word precisely, for "melancholy" possessed a history and a set of agreed-upon meanings. The significance of the word, however—that is, to what sort of person the word should be attached—depended upon chosen traditions. Melancholy had emerged as a popular expression on the eve of the Puritan settlement of America; the pathology and America would become intertwined, arising together not within an English imagination or as a cultural pathology of *mentalité*, but within important English texts.

Timothy Bright, an Anglican divine and a former physician, published the first book in English on the disease in 1586. Robert Burton, then an Oxford scholar, published the first edition of his *Anatomy of Melancholy* in 1621, a year after the separatists' settlement of Plymouth.[18] This timing became important, particularly because Burton was attributing melancholy to "a mad giddy company of Precisians," to "our . . . peculiar churches of Amsterdam." The Puritan settlement coincided with Burton's claim to have discovered a certain "species" of the pathology—"religious melancholy"—and he brought an enormous amount of learning to his pages to support his point. Like the Pilgrims he derided, Burton desired a beginning. He wrote that concerning religious melancholy he had "no pattern to follow," "no man to imitate." He in fact derived all his cases from books, and some of his most important discussions of religious melancholy he took from the writings of Puritan divines.

The "Schismaticks" or "Separatists" that Burton described stood before the Word terrorized. They were held in fear by "rigid preachers," and more important, by their own determination to settle the matter of their salvation. They had taken it upon themselves to determine the presence of visible saints, and that inquiry, Burton thought, had created a frenzy. The orthodoxy of Massachusetts, in fact, though never rigidly barring men and women from the sacraments, was about to make this examination of spiritual estates requisite for full church membership: "to define how many shall be saved," as Burton now said of separatists living in England and Amsterdam, "and who damned in a parish." Any such definition remained a mystery to Burton, as it had to Bright. Only a melancholic, Burton argued, would pursue such ineffable marks of salvation. Only one so filled with doubt would have to be so certain. Precisians doubted "of their Election, how they shall know it, by what signs. And so forth, saith Luther, with such nice points, torture themselves and crucify themselves, that they are almost mad."[19] The doubt the precisians carried with them, Burton said, drove their compulsive quest for certainty; within writings on Puritanism to this day, historians and even, perhaps, the popular imagination use this "compulsion and doubt" to portray an obsessional Puritan mentality.

Melancholy did offer a good representation of those who chose to speak about the depths of their experience. For nineteenth-century romantic poets, melancholy fell from a weeping cloud. For seventeenth-century physicians and divines, however, melancholy sat in the bowels or perhaps in the spleen. It was a humor possessed by all persons, of course, but sometimes its "excrementitious humiditie" rose, and when it did, the humidity excited terror. Melancholy appeared not a "distraction," or the possession of those, in Burton's words, who seemed "mad or desperate." It was not insanity or psychosis. Nor did melancholy appear as hysteria, a malady long described as something quite different.[20] Melancholy focused upon particular themes: solitude, dryness, wilderness, desert; slime, mud, foulness, slough; sorrow, fear, darkness, despair; doubt, weariness, exhaustion, strain—themes that expressed a certain ascetic attitude of turning away or facing the back of God.[21] The humor—"muddie," "earthie," "meere excrementall"—was a sediment or "grossest part of the blood," and when out of balance with the other humors, its vapors rose to shut "vp the hart as it were in a dungeon of obscurity." The "fogge of that slime" then created the mental torment: "feare, distrust, doubt, dispair." The vapors fashioned imaginations—rather than real visions—that the victim held before him: "monstrous fictions," "phantasticall apparitions," "counterfet goblins," "disguised shapes, which giue great terror." They were not the internal possessions of the truly mad, but external shapes that the victim held as alienations and not as a true part of his self. Closed first in this "dungion of melancholy," the self now began its trial by entering "into straunge natures."

The humor's corruption actually offered perfect representation of those about to settle New England: "These most seeke to auoyd the society of men, and betake them to wildernesses, and deserts." All these words are Bright's. Like Burton, Bright was an author of distinct antisectarian opinion who nevertheless offered the metaphors that a century later described the pilgrim's journey: sloughs of despond, valleys of darkness, castles of doubt, iron cages of despair.[22]

Burton repeated the metaphors. He most particularly discussed the fear that Bright had argued was the ground of melancholy sorrow. Burton's melancholic feared things that for Burton could never be: goblins, hobgoblins, devils, bugbears, ghosts, witches, black dogs, fiends, mormeluches. Whether "uncouth shapes" or "noisome smells," these things came to the melancholic not like the hallucinations or visions of the mad, but like fanciful frights. The melancholic gazed willfully upon "filthy excrements," when he might have turned to the "fair Garden" or to God. The melancholic also feared possibilities that he himself knew to be ridiculous: to walk alone, for he might meet a thief; to meet some man, for the man might seek his ruin; to "go over a bridge, . . . lie in a chamber where cross beams are, for fear he be tempted to hang, drown, or precipitate himself. If he be a silent auditory, as at a sermon, he is afraid he shall speak aloud unawares, some thing indecent, unfit to be said." This last fear especially spoke not of paranoia but obsession.

Burton's melancholic, in other words, was superstitious; he was not mad. He drew superstitious inferences from things both seen and read of: death, carcasses, executions, burnings, and unusual diseases such as an epileptic's convulsions. He feared, again, what he really knew was impossible: that he might be falsely accused of some crime and brought before the king, questioned, imprisoned, perhaps even hanged. He suspected in a shamefaced way that he stood responsible for any small crime, "thinks every man observes him, aims at him." His fears became trifles as "every small occasion" brought new troubles: "always afraid of something . . . which never peradventure was, never can be."[23]

Within Burton's text a character overlies the fear, the personality, in effect, of those haunted. Bright had distinguished his melancholics with traits of hesitation and a "ielousie of doubt." Their flurries of uncertainty "causeth them to be the more exact & curious in po[n]dering the very moments of things"; they created a "pitte" by questioning everything. Burton also wrote of incessant plans and hesitant action. If, however, "once . . . resolved," his melancholic became "obstinate, hard to be reconciled." He chased obscure speculations or puzzled himself with scriptures. For example, as applied to the sectarians: "Many are called, but few are chosen . . . strike them with horror, they doubt presently whether they be of this number of no. . . . How shall they be assured of their salvation, by what signs?"

Always fearful if "any small business or circumstance be omitted," this melancholic emerges in Burton's *Anatomy* as a laborious personality striking upon rocks of doubt and ready, if provoked, to strike others. It is a personality that modern psychiatry would readily label as obsessional or compulsive. For Burton it was an austere, intent, and distrustful personality ready to snarl and to take everything seriously, to interpret every occasion for the worse, but a personality above all fearing to leave anything out, to leave the world somehow open to doubt.[24]

Burton revolved the *Anatomy* itself in endless speculation. His book, as it ran through various editions, left nothing out as Burton added to his writing again and again, extending a compendium's already considerable length by piecing together in an endless stream whatever point he found. He led, he said, "a Monastick life in a College."[25] Burton interwove his own life and text, setting his character as an author upon his melancholy description, the two forming a palimpsest. His *Anatomy* presents a particular discourse in which the personality of the author and his work interplay.

With his welter of quotations, Burton feared that his writing had become a Babel. He spoke of his book as akin to "this chaos of Melancholy." A center did exist, however, in the obsessional fears that histories of the English idea of melancholy have ignored. The center locates itself in what Burton called "possessions, obsessions." He meant by these words the certain intensity of the melancholy mind: "still, still, still, thinking of it, macerating themselves. Though they do talk with you, and seem to be otherwise employed, and to your thinking very intent and busy, still that toy runs in their mind, . . . that cross."[26]

This last point should be stressed. Unlike the symptoms of hysteria or psychosis ("distraction"), the fears of the melancholic remained invisible. Rather than displayed, the symptoms stayed in the mind where the melancholic often (most often, one must assume) kept them hidden. As Burton observed, the possessions were not at all akin to the quite visible "possessions" of a person, say, struck by hysteric convulsions. Given this secrecy, the most obvious question becomes why certain persons chose to present their cases of melancholy publicly to the extent that an author like Burton could find and write of them.

The question that concerned seventeenth-century divines was the object that such a compelling thought signified. What spiritual condition, if any, did the melancholic obsession express? When such possessions came as "fiery dartes" to punish the wicked for sin, such fear was to be considered a normal one of the well-deserved wrath of God. In addressing his own book to a godly and proper friend "M.," however, Bright had written "of disguised scarres of the heart, without abilitie to worke the pretended annoyance." He meant by the phrase an external temptation coming from beyond M.'s nature, working in his mind but *not* carried out by M. This distinction between thought and act—a distinction that was lost to nineteenth-century psychiatry until Freud—was important in seventeenth-century writings about melancholy. If a temptation appeared "most straunge, and such as they [the children of God] abhorre . . . , & finde no parte of their nature to incline vnto them," then the temptation, no matter how compelling, expressed only the alien designs of Satan and not the potential criminality of the victim himself. "Of this kinde," Bright continued, "are certain blasphemies suggested of the Deuill, and laying of violent handes on them selues, or vpon others neither moued thereto by hate or malice." Bright meant by this a compelling thought so repugnant to the subject's conscience that he "vtterly abhorreth" it, here the thought of killing oneself or hurting another without any seeming reason.[27]

Burton too wrote of staid men and women bothered by strange fear. "It happens, willy-nilly, do what they may, they cannot be rid of it, against their wills they must think of it a thousand times over . . . ; if it be offensive especially, they cannot forget it." The thoughts were "rods to scourge ourselves, since we carry them in our bowels"—again, "compelled" thoughts of killing oneself or a friend or stranger, fixed ideas that came in prayer and meditation. Burton cited cases: a nun so troubled she thought herself mad; a man who feared to go into a church because of his thoughts, or go near the Rhine "for fear to make away himself"; persons thinking "such horrible and execrable conceits, not fit to be uttered," speech that simply was not to be spoken in this language "opposite to God."[28]

The problem was to answer the question Bright posed when he entitled a chapter of his *Treatise*, "Whether the conscience of sinne and the affliction thereof be melancholy or not." Ministers pondered the question for the next two centuries, for Bright had asked, in effect, whether any psychopathology existed at all—whether within the abhorrent thoughts there had simply appeared "that heauy hande of God [acting] vpon the afflicted conscience." The fascination with melancholy lay in this question, for though "natural," melancholy produced a conviction of sin unlike that of any other psychopathological form. Melancholy created a conscious sense of criminality that the victim could well consider quite deserved.[29] In that there was nothing of madness.

Melancholy remained a corporeal fluid, but Elizabethans held to a psychosomatic theory of disease that envisioned the body acting upon thought and thought in turn acting upon the humors,[30] so no question existed, as in Burton's mind, but that what the mind thought—or heard, as in the case of "Our indiscreet Pastors"—could cause the humor to rise, setting in motion a vicious cycle. From this view, body and mind interacted as thundering preachers provoked the humor—or as Satan did the same since, again, melancholy was "the Devil's bath." In the words of William Perkins, melancholy lay as "the *Deuils bait,* because the Deuill beeing well acquainted with the complexion and temperature of man, by Gods iust permission, conueyes himselfe into the humor, and worketh strange conceits."[31]

Melancholy was the dry and hot humor that, like a desert, Satan chose to gall the conscience, and, of course, Satan could only act through the agency of God. Thus the question of distinction could blur, for the fluid's eruption reflected God's work; a "neurosis," in other words, adhering to the physiological meaning of that term, held purpose. Being ministers themselves, neither Bright nor Burton could evade such a problem or, in the case of Bright, tell quite so clearly just what expressed "the particular difference betwixt melancholy, & the distressed conscience in the same person." Indeed, for Burton, "God's anger justly deserved" provoked melancholy, while for Bright, in the case of his conscience-ridden friend, it was a "fatherly frowning only for a time, to correct that which in you is to be reformed."[32]

Ultimately M.'s fear did emerge as a case only of gall and misplaced humor—a matter, as Bright said, of "accidents." But Bright could never ignore what he also wrote, that the melancholic more than any person suffered the conscience of sin. Even in the physic Bright chose to emphasize, the shedding of M.'s blood to purge the humor, he wove material and symbol together. Burton turned the *Anatomy* as well upon the conscience of sin, and thereby turned the tone of his whole discussion. He let go of his acidic wit by writing now of God often working by mysterious "contraries," of God wounding first before He healed. Burton too offered physic—purgatives, bleedings, sundry emetics, anything to void the humor—but never, he wrote, as the "sole" cure. There remained the case of Paul's "extremity" and his words on sufficiency of grace—"*My grace is sufficient for thee, for my power is made perfect through weakness*"—the case of innumerable saints imitating the Christ whom the devil had beset, saints to whom the angel had spoken as he had spoken to Peter—"the Angel . . . that opened the Iron-gates, loosed his bands, brought him out of prison, and delivered him from bodily thraldoms."

The *Anatomy* ends with Burton offering this vision: the breaking of the bars that the conscience of sin has wrought. If this release became the promise, then melancholy expressed a significant spiritual disease; certainly it came not as a mere accident.[33]

Obsessional Temptation and the Movement of Puritan Conversion

By what signs, Burton asked, did one know of one's election? Burton considered the question absurd. This was as impossible an act of signification for him as pointing out the objects that melancholics feared. Among the sectaries he chastised, however—William Perkins, for example, whom Burton used to pattern his discussion of religious melancholy—the question of knowing of one's election moved some to separate themselves in all but word from the Anglican Church and others to sail for Amsterdam. The problem became one of finding the marks that made the saints visible, of determining, however hesitantly, those whom God had elected for salvation before the beginning of the world, and thus of seeking particular signs.

The search for the distinguishing marks of the saints never appeared without doubt. The inquiry nevertheless led English Puritans to analyze conversion structurally. They outlined various steps of conversion, creating a process that Edmund S. Morgan has termed a "morphology of conversion." Although as Norman Pettit discusses, Puritan divines could never deny conversion as a singular moment because of the scriptural model of Paul, they came, Pettit continues, to view conversion as just such an unwinding narrative, a narrative whose complexity spoke against those who, like "antinomians," would have their conversion come suddenly. Spiritual conversion became the story of a journey up to, through, and then beyond the possible point of rebirth.[34]

Puritan divines used the Biblical order of salvation—election, vocation, justification, sanctifiction, and glorification—to categorize a spiritual trial that Darrett B. Rutman has aptly termed a "scale." English ministers, most important among them William Perkins and William Ames, imagined an experience that, while reflecting certain portions of the *ordo salutis*, specified and humanized the immediate "actions of God." For Perkins, "*workes of preparation*" led to justification, while "effects of grace" followed therefrom. Perkins offered ten steps in all, beginning with "the ministry of the Word." His and similar outlines of a way to salvation would provide the narrative structure for Puritan spiritual autobiographies. In brief, and using some of Perkins's phrasing, the steps run as follows: the provision of an outward means of salvation; the bringing into mind of a consideration of the Law; the knowing of one's own peculiar sins; a smiting of the heart with legal fear, or the fear of punishment and hell that any man or woman, saint or not, might have; the consideration in the mind of the promise of salvation; the kindling in the heart of some sparks of grace; a combat in the heart with doubts, despair, and distrust; a quieting of conscience and resting assurance; a stirring in the heart of evangelical sorrow; and lastly, the provision of the ability to obey God's commands.[35]

The first four steps, ending with legal fear—again, the selfish, quite understandable fear of anyone who pays attention to what he has done—involve a breaking and a crushing of the pride of the person's nature. They are the works, again, of preparation. The last six steps, with the penultimate step of evangelical sorrow or "a griefe for sinne, because it is sinne, & because God is offended"—not, that is, a grief for sin because the saint is afraid—follow as the effects of grace. The new faith is tested in the seventh step, where one comes to understand that in combat one relies upon faith and faith alone.

Ames spoke of eleven steps, the first seven of which, in showing the person his sin, begin with self-examination and end with the consideration of particular sins, most particularly with "the sight of some one sin" that is analogous to Perkins's legal fear. Following this sight—one is now considering the life of the saint—appears the setting for grace: hope, thirst, union with Christ through effectual vocation, and finally true repentance and a giving up.[36]

In New England, Thomas Hooker and Thomas Shepard most thoroughly described the structure. (Hooker first settled in Newtown, later to be Cambridge, then moved with his congregation to Hartford, Connecticut; Shepard remained in Cambridge.) In a simplicity absent from Hooker's works, Shepard joined the two orders, bringing into a single series the preparatory works of the English divines and the scriptural order of salvation. In his *Sound Believer*, published in 1645, Shepard outlined the first movement as a "fourfold act of Christ's power" to rescue from Satan the prisoner of sin. The acts unfold as conviction, compunction, and humiliation, followed then by faith, with a translation then to the benefits of grace: justification, reconciliation, adoption, sanctification, audience of all prayers, and finally glorification. Glorification, which unfolds out of time, is "immediate communion with God," a rare something few have barely known.[37]

The first portion of this scale, the works of preparation, speaks to its own destruction. As a legality that many men and women might pass through, these steps appear, as Perry Miller complained again and again in his great histories of Puritan thought, like a manufacturing of spiritual progress. As a preparatory structure, however, the pilgrim's awakening to sin and the legal fear he suffers define exactly what his faith is not. Faith is not the smiting of the heart "with a legall fear, whereby when man seeth his sinnes, he makes him to feare punishment and hell, and to despair of salvation, in regard of any thing in himself." These last words that Perkins used to describe preparation—most simply the terror that a person feels and the works by which he tries to erase the sight of his sin—define faith by creating faith's difference. These are the mechanics involved when the pilgrim moves from here to there, from his conviction of sin to his humiliation, but they are the mechanics that level a space the saint then fills with his faith. In the end, not his work but only the work of Christ prevails.

This preparation became the center of Puritan thought on salvation (an always controversial center because of a radical antinomianism on the "left" with its "hysteric" beliefs and a solemn Arminianism on the "right"). Preparation and the fear it entailed became the special case for America. The New World seemed pregnant with possibilities for awakening the saint to his terror and objectifying his sin. Also, a fresh land was spread out before the saint upon which he could apply his mechanics in an attempt to remove his sin. A journey that in England remained inward, spaceless, and scattered among isolated sects, could be enacted in place. In a wilderness a community could turn the divines' writings on spiritual progress from speculation to practice.[38] It appeared as if America loomed as a void (or a blank text) into which the saint could bring his trial of preparation.

English Puritan theologians posed the question as to whether melancholy, given the strange terrors of conscience it induced, offered a sign of salvation along this preparatory journey. By asking, the divines reformed the opinions of nonsectarians like Bright and Burton and turned the physics of melancholy upon its head. Perkins, in his *Cases of Conscience* of 1609, in which he designed his early and important structure of conversion, considered at length the immediate problem Bright had posed. He asked whether, in a possible case of conversion, any difference existed between "the trouble of Conscience and Melancholy?" He answered yes, but only after making some careful distinctions. The melancholy compulsions that Bright had considered a disease of unfortunate accidents, Perkins saw as works with more significance. Most particularly, he looked at the symptoms that Burton later referred to as "obsessions."

In presenting an anatomy of those suddenly troubled in conscience, Perkins spoke of a "distempered" conscience that included both a general despair and a lesser fear, the distinct fear that awakens the self to its sin. Perkins then linked such fear to an involved discussion of various types of temptations, some of which, he argued, could be cured not by the "physicke" of man (and certainly not the work of preparation) but only by the shedding of the blood of Christ.[39]

Perkins's *Cases* acts rathers like Burton's *Anatomy* in that it pushes a taxonomy of troubles to the point of minutiae. His types of temptations reflect his melancholic's own complexity of points. By analyzing closely a process of conversion and working finely into kinds of fears, Perkins created a therapeutic discourse—a concern that a person would experience fear coupled to advice as to how the fear should be treated. He put forth a set of rules for ministering to those in terror, rules that Burton read and included when he wrote, for example, of never leaving such patients alone. When Perkins approached melancholy, however, he argued that the body more often followed the mind, whereas physicians, he felt, were arguing too strongly that a horridly stricken conscience merely reflected a humor's eruption. Here, through the will of God and God alone, and for reasons that no man could ever render, since God simply acted as He would have it so, a state was effected worse than that which any physician had seen: "a burning ague, and it causeth the entrails to rise, . . . and consumes the flesh, more than any sicknesse can doe."[40]

No question existed, again, that the damned could be so stricken. Here the question involved the kind of fear, the type of temptation, and the manner in which a person reacted. Some fear came slowly as persons languished by degrees; other fear came by custom or through the nature of a soul; and there appeared fear, not like these others at all, that "astonished"—"the *foule Tentation*" with "strange" effects such as "blasphemous cogitations" suggested by the devil and troubling the "phantasie." These were Burton's obsessions; unclean thoughts "not fit to be vttered," "excecrable, as any can be conceiued," "forced into the minde by violence, so as the partie cannot auoid them; and they come into the minde againe and againe, yea a thousand times in a day."

Such thoughts, Perkins said, which the will struggled to oppose, offered comfort, for if the "damnable cogitations" actually adhered as a part of a man's own "selfe," then they would never have arrived with such "vehemencie and celeritie, but with leisure"; they would appear, that is, without the labor of conscience the melancholic suffered. The detested thoughts offered comfort because they came, as their estranged nature evidenced, from the devil himself against "the very light of nature," against God Himself and all natural-born reflections of His majesty. They came against the nature of the victim himself, appearing as his difference, defining his holy significance. These convictions offered comfort because this astonishing impurity of mind never troubled those of reprobate behavior, but parties "honest, ciuill, and such as profess the Gospell, at least in shew."

It remained a question of making a fine distinction—"This distinction of thoughts must be remembered"—of analyzing with precision the origin of a horrid image and then asking of the conscience what the image did in fact show. Perkins was asking whether an idea reflected behavior, whether it worked out. Perkins demanded an inquiry into whether a thought translated into action; here he answered that the victim abhorred his blasphemous ideas and—a distinction to be lost in nineteenth-century neurology—that the victim would in fact leave his compelling urge to act on his thought unconsummated.

These horrors, then, appeared not so directly to be reflections of sin as trials to be suffered in an imitation of Christ. The word Perkins chose, "tentation," expresses a trial, the testing of a work through an experiment. Tentation opposed the connotations that the word "temptation" held of allurement, of enticing and beguiling evil sweeping over and around a deceived soul. Tentation implied labor, undertaking a trial to test the worth of one's soul.[41]

For Perkins, melancholy offered the "occasion" rather than the "cause" for the pilgrim's awakening conviction of sin. As Perkins stripped away the conviction's fears that he considered normal, however, melancholy proper as a functional disease became for him a pathology that disturbed the imagination and left the conscience alone: "exceeding horrors, . . . and yet the Conscience for all this vntouched, and not troubled or disquieted." Perkins's melancholic acted like the person nineteenth-century alienists would call morally insane and twentieth-century psychiatrists a psychopath. The seeming irrationality Perkins was considering—a struggle of the self with its own imaginations—held its sanction, on the other hand, in the words he quoted of Paul, *"That he did not the good which he would doe, . . .* that *he did the euill which he would not."* These are the words of scripture ("For I delight in the law of God, in my inmost self, but I see in my members another law at war with the law of my mind and making me captive to the law of sin") that provided for a psychology of the irrational. Paul's words offered the Puritans not a case of abhorrent acts willingly undertaken ("it is no longer I that do it, but sin which dwells within me"), but a psychology of the conscience embattled with the fancy and of the mind pitted understandably against the will. They stand as central words in the Puritans' writing of a divided self and in the Puritans' attack on scholastic theories of a rational will and a reasoned imagination.[42] As such, the words focused the Puritan vision of salvation upon the sense of awakening as a psychomachy. A pattern of expression was set, a language with which a person could force his own abhorrent desires to make sense.

Perkins's anatomy of conscience continued in the work of his student, William Ames. As a minister equally important for expressing within English Puritan writing the idea of conversion as a progressing or narrative structure, Ames offered the seven steps leading to the possible reception of grace and the four following therefrom. He wrote his own *Conscience with the Power and Cases Thereof,* however, not to ring in dogma how a person won his salvation, but to offer what a minister like Ames thought of as a necessary verbal model—an "Effectual Work of the Word," to use a title by Thomas Hooker. The purpose of offering a verbal guide was therapeutic in that Perkins and Ames were analyzing the permutations of a conscience gripped by fear, making the distinctions between thought and act that Perkins demanded, and informing their listeners of how they, as ministers of the Word, interpreted seemingly strange behaviors. Perkins had offered advice, but ultimately an irony embraces the set of rules he provided, for the efficacy of his therapy becomes, in the end, naught. There is no mention of emetics, bleedings, and other voidings, and there is no indication that the pastoral therapeutics stand sufficient or even efficacious, except in the sense of seeing a patient through. The ministers wished to inform, to offer an understanding, and to demand finally that the listener make his own self-examination, while yet understanding his suffering against their particular texts. Comfort awaited because, concerning "manifold temptations," "we must not thinke it [the trial] strange, but rather count *it exceedingly great joy."*[43]

This careful consideration given to melancholy temptations elevated a minor point of present psychiatric observation, obsessional ideation, to importance.[44] The "sudden or vehement temptation," for example, was doctrinally to be written into the *Westminster Confession of Faith*.[45] For in the "foule temptations," as Ames wrote, a sign appeared, "a demonstration of a sanctifyed heart." "The reason is because the opposition which is apparent in this perturbation, is a signe that there is some thing in the soule contrary to the temptation, and a quietnesse doth betray some consent." The mark of prevailing temptation, again, was its commission. Here the temptation came "although there be no purpose to commit it," and it came, as Ames repeated Perkins's account, vehemently, in the manner of lightning; it appeared repugnant to nature, "reason itselfe," "our naturall inclination," arising not as inherent to the soul but through an invasion and seizing. Rhetorically, one rejected the blasphemous suggestion and detested its presence, but the saint who was not to leave this temptation unmarked. The idea expressed "the common condition of all the faithful, who this notwithstanding are in Christ beloved, and accepted of God." Rhetorically, one avoided melancholy as overmuch sorrow, as Richard Baxter, the English Puritan writer, entitled a sermon, yet the saint carefully described its occurrence. English Puritans like Arthur Hildersam argued that it was better thus to accept the charges of madness that others made against the children of God. John Preston, close to Hildersam and also important in delineating the saint's preparation, argued that the truly disordered conscience did not condemn enough. For Hildersam, the point stood to gaze upon death "and carefully to call to mind, the foulest, and grossest of all thy sinnes," creating one's death in the mind's eye. Melancholy served to demonstrate what no other psychopathological form could: that no person could resist or turn away the evil that God presented at the very edge of conversion. For John Flavel, as Norman Fiering has discussed concerning the writings of this seventeenth-century divine, the hellish suggestion argued against scholastic writings on the efficacy of the will.[46]

Baxter, one of the most influential of the Puritan divines, summarized these points by separating melancholy not from an inclusive monomania as Perkins had—that he simply assumed—but by drawing distinctions between those who consciously felt themselves alienated from God and their own natures and those (usually women, he thought) who appeared childish and impatient of temper, a form of hysteria he hardly considered. Melancholy appeared sadder, more serious, and though never a distraction or insanity, it almost always involved being "violently *haunted with blasphemous Injections*." Again, one distinguished melancholy from the temptations inherent in the life of a glutton, drunkard, fornicator, or gamester, and from the vanity of the proud and ambitious. Think carefully, Baxter said, and notice that "of all Men none love their Sin which they groan under so little as they," "and this is Matter of great Comfort to such Melancholy, Honest Souls, if they have but Understanding to receive it." Melancholy served as the devil's last effort to haunt those whom he could not allure. Obsessive temptations were tangible marks of salvation: the "comfortable Evidence [that] you carry about with you."[47] It is understandable why Puritan autobiographers should have chosen to express such temptations in the writing out of their spiritual journeys.

The Pilgrim's Progress

The charge of melancholy against the Puritans survived Robert Burton. The psychologism survived because Puritan authors provided the evidence for their own psychopathology, celebrating in their writings this sickness of soul. The cases of conscience of the Puritan divines remain obscure in themselves, but when Bunyan wrote the case of his own pilgrim's conscience, visualizing in one of the finest pieces of Puritan literature the technicalities of Perkins and Ames, he translated the divines' involved texts into popular literature. It is, of course, unnecessary to have read Bright, Burton, Perkins, and Ames to appreciate Bunyan, authors Bunyan probably received only through derivative texts. His own location remains an obscure setting within a larger textual field. A re-creation of the seventeenth-century understanding of melancholy, however, indicates that Bunyan employed significant psychopathological stereotypes. Rather than simply recording experience, he used past texts to create an understanding of himself. He composed the psychological history of his own life and then of his pilgrim Christian, using the language of the disease of melancholy. Bunyan reworked scenes from his own spiritual autobiography, *Grace Abounding to the Chief of Sinners*, first published in 1666, in writing *The Pilgrim's Progress*, published twelve years later. But given the obsessional pathology the Puritans employed and the use they made of its peculiar signs, Bunyan exposed no more of himself than that which appears in his writing. He chose to reveal his mental life as part of his own allegory and thereby to authorize, or to place his life against, the story of Christian's progress.

The revelation of the pilgrim's thoughts could appear scandalous, for Bunyan in his time had not only his celebrators but also his detractors for whom the chief of sinners was simply proving the absurdity of the quest.[48] This sense of scandal exists as a discursive tradition that runs to the present, for the suspicion one has of the use of psychology—for example, analyzing the excremental language the Puritans employed—remains a crucial part of the whole of a larger text. Puritan psychologism, or the use of psychological analysis to undercut one's motives, like psychologism today, immediately draws a reply, and thereby those who use psychologism and those who become appalled remain together in an ongoing dialogue.

Christian himself is marked as speaking ridiculous words and is then cast from society as melancholy. This is his wife's lament, that she had thought her husband of "foolish fancy," "over run with Melancholy Humours," "that some frenzy distemper had got into his head." Others put Christian to bed, administer physic, deride and eventually neglect the man who will leave their city behind. The charge repeats itself in Vanity-Fair when Christian and Faithful are judged "Bedlams and Mad," besmeared with dirt, and placed in a cage. The cage is reminiscent of the Iron Cage of Despair that Christian had earlier witnessed:

> Now, said *Christian*, let me go hence: Nay stay (said the *Interpreter*), till I have shewed thee a little more. . . . So he took him by the hand again, and led him into a very dark Room, where there sat a Man in an Iron Cage.
>
> Now the Man, to look on, seemed very sad: he sat with his eyes looking down to the ground, his hands folded together; and he sighed as if he would break his heart. Then said *Christian, What means this?*

Here Christian witnesses the fate of the commission of unpardonable sin: "threatenings, dreadful threatenings, fearful threatenings of certain Judgement and fiery Indignation."

The juxtaposition of the two scenes of the cage creates an ambiguity. Friends and relations call the pilgrim melancholy or even mad and thus hold him in suspicion, and the pilgrim becomes mad as charged, for he is actually sick in soul in Vanity-Fair as he had been in the City of Destruction. Christian, of course, is not the Man in an Iron Cage, for he has not committed the unpardonable sin of despising God by considering His blood an unholy thing. He is tempted to do so, however, as he stands before the Man, and in his victory over the temptation a sign of salvation materializes.[49]

Bunyan's allusions to melancholy in *The Pilgrim's Progress* occur in four important scenes that follow Christian's retirement to his chamber and his subsequent walk into the wilderness. The first scene appears as the Slough of Despond. It is Christian's conviction of sin, a descent into "scum and filth," a mire of "many fears, and doubts, and discouraging apprehensions." These he will work past by following barely visible

"Steps." Without their guide, his confusion could overwhelm him and drive him to lasting despair.

The second scene, in which Christian's fear becomes more specific, opens at Mount Sinai, the hill that Christian fears will fall on his head. He has been persuaded to go to the house of Mr. Legality for help, and now, like any useless but compelling ritual, legality becomes a pathology that paralyzes Christian, who is now frozen in his steps. This is an irrational fear, Bunyan makes clear, and one that parallels a fear that Bunyan wrote he had experienced. "I begin to think," Bunyan had recounted in his autobiography, "How, if one of the Bells [of his church, for which he had once been a ringer] should fall: then I chose to stand under a main Beam . . . : But then I should think again, Should the Bell fall with a swing, it might first hit the Wall, and then rebounding upon me, might kill me for all this Beam; this made me stand in the Steeple door. . . . but then it came into my head, how if the Steeple itself should fall, and this thought . . . continually so shake my mind, that I durst not stand . . . , but was forced to fly."[50]

For all its involved complexity, the fear remains irrational enough, and for Burton, as for his man fearing to lie beneath crossbeams, the fear remains without meaning. For Bunyan, the fear becomes of immediate symbolic importance. The seemingly silly fright allows a piece of psychopathology to merge with the morphology of conversion and thus to become a testament to the efficacy of terror under Mosaic Law. One knows of one's legal fear under the sight of the Law, or stands condemned, as in Bunyan's case, beneath the bells whose ringing Bunyan once loved.[51]

The third scene occurs in the Valley of the Shadow of Death—"*A Wilderness, a Land of Desarts,*" of hobgoblins and devils and fiery darts that only a Christian passes through. Here, in the wasteland that Bunyan believed Jeremiah had described, Christian faces his worst trial:

> Just when he was come over against the mouth of the burning Pit, one of the wicked ones got behind him, . . . and whisperingly suggested many grievous blasphemies to him, which he verily thought had proceeded from his own mind. This put *Christian* more to it than any thing that he met with before, even to think that he should now blaspheme him that he loved so much before; yet, could he have helped it, he would not have done it: but he had not the discretion neither to stop his ears, nor to know from whence those blasphemies came.

In a note, Bunyan explained in the manner of Perkins and Ames the origin of such thought from Satan. He also presumed the divines' understanding of the melancholy temptations when he spoke in his "brief relation" or autobiography, *Grace Abounding*, of the temptations that had seized him: "after which [darkness] whole floods of Blasphemies, both against God, Christ, and the Scriptures, was poured upon my spirit, to my great confusion and astonishment." "These suggestions (with many other which at this time I may not, nor dare not utter, neither by word nor pen)" became so continual as to leave "room for nothing else." They were words that he so feared he might speak that he clapped shut his mouth. They were thoughts that leaped into his mind, with his head in "some Muckhil-hole or other." They were thoughts against which he battled, lest "sometimes it would run in my thoughts not so little as a hundred times together." Bunyan fulfilled Perkins's words ("yea a thousand times in a day") without any sense that such a textual repetition made his story untrue. Bunyan was violently assaulted, for example, to sell out Christ: "Sell him, sell him, sell him; against which, I may say, for whole hours together I have been forced to stand as continually leaning and forcing my spirit against it, lest haply before I were aware, some wicked thought might arise in my heart that might consent thereto." Here Bunyan undertakes a compulsive act, or a physical piece of magic, to ward off his fear of selling Christ. He wrote, "This temptation did put me to such scares, lest I should at some times, I say, consent thereto, and be overcome therewith, that by the very force of my mind, in labouring to gain-say and resist this wickedness, my very body would be put into action, or motion, by way of pushing or thrusting with my hands, or elbows."

An attempt to perform a miracle is also attempted, as Karl Joachim Weintraub has pointed out. Like the compulsive act, the performance vies with a manner of Protestant rationalization—"Max Weber gave the beautiful term *Entzauberung der Welt* to this process"—rationalization that proves its worth only against Bunyan's crazy testing: "I must say to the puddles . . . , Be dry, and to the dry places, Be you the puddles."[52] The testing proves such magic false. The works, both mental and physical, create nothing but Bunyan's despair, throwing him back to a faith in Christ.

The fourth scene brings the pathology to conclusion. In Doubting-Castle, where Giant Despair attacks Christian and Hopeful, the pilgrims find themselves in another "nasty and stinking" dungeon. Here in darkness both men become tempted to take their own lives, "either with Knife, Halter or Poison." They escape from this, the last of their melancholy prisons, the Giant's hand becoming unaccountably paralyzed in one of his "fits," in what appears to be a hysterical seizure.[53]

The psychopathic journey ends, and the relation of spiritual conversion that has begun in a wilderness of temptation ends with the Celestial City in sight.

The American Spiritual Relation

As a form of popular literature the spiritual autobiography, like Bunyan's *Grace Abounding*, arose with the sectarians. The cases of conscience of Perkins, Ames, and other Puritan divines were placed in time by autobiographers by being given a particular author's character.[54] This literature, which promises to reveal the self nakedly, necessarily works with rhetorical devices as constructive as those of *The Pilgrim's Progress*. The self is exposed, but only as the autobiographer remembers, writes down, and thereby understands his life, making his self-history as textually complete as an allegory. Like oral traditions, conventions of writing become a force capable of fashioning a person's reality.

Throughout the seventeenth century Protestant sectarians produced ever increasing numbers of writings about themselves, initiating a type of confession that brought the private dialogue of penitent and priest into the open arena of publication. Usually they were not writing "autobiographies" in the modern sense. That late eighteenth-century term defines the boundaries of a single enclosed book, whereas Puritanism encouraged both speaking and writing down the self's journey in ways for which no single concept exists. Seventeenth-century spiritual confession moves through a continuum, embracing expressions from the recorded speech of the illiterate to allegorical biography such as *The Pilgrim's Progress*. Puritan confession includes various texts: the oral spiritual "relation" delivered before a congregation, the diary and journal, letters between family members and friends, as well as the autobiography itself, as for example *Grace Abounding*. At the heart of Puritan confession lay the oral spiritual relation, which was probably the first form in which Bunyan presented his autobiography, the one type of confession that uniquely shaped early American life.

Whatever form of literature he chooses, the Puritan autobiographer offers his soul's anguish as an exemplum or as an affliction for emulation. He offers a gift, particularly to his children, to whom the spiritual writing was often addressed. Beginning in the century in which Bunyan wrote the history of his "iron yoke" and then designed his dream of Christian's iron cage (by the nineteenth century the two books were often published together), it is a gift that forms a single extended text of historical personality woven in typical or allegorical character. It is a gift of literature in which Increase Mather, the American Puritan minister, rewrote his journal for his children, recounting for their edification his hypochondriacal vapors, meaning the melancholy that had once possessed his mind.[55] It is literature that reflects the Psalms:

I am counted with them that go down into the pit: I am as a man *that hath* no strength: . . .
. . . *I am* shut up, and I cannot come forth. Mine eye mourneth by reason of affliction: . . .
I *am* afflicted and ready to die from *my* mouth up: *while* I suffer thy terrors I am distracted.
Thy fierce wrath goeth over me; thy terrors have cut me off.

The psychomachia was not a Protestant invention. Its roots lay deep in the lives of the saints, most profoundly in the *Confessions* of Augustine. It remained for the Protestant to develop the self's examination in a peculiar way, however, with "an uncompromising analytical ferocity," as Sacvan Bercovitch writes, "that scandalized humanist and Catholic alike."[56] If one reads the words of trauma without a sense of the words required to express the excellency of Bunyan's broken heart, then the Puritans stand revealed as the selves they celebrated: broken, nervously strained, even suicidal. Historians may then argue that seventeenth-century Americans suffered from the composition of the self that the sectarians themselves conceived of: crises of identity, high rates of suicide, an abnormal number of nervous breakdowns. Their words are read as the immediate reflection of their strained hearts: "The struggle entailed a relentless psychic strain; and in New England, where the theocracy insisted upon it with unusual vigor—where anxiety about election was not only normal but mandatory—hysteria, breakdowns, and suicides were not uncommon." "In all, the theological developments of the 1640s and 1650s in New England bred 'uncertainty of outcome [which] could lead and often did to an inner tension and agony of soul disruptive in a new society.' Nervous breakdowns and suicides were not uncommon." "The conscience was . . . ferocious in its attacks." "For some evangelicals, the quest for nothingness occasionally verged upon actual suicide."[57]

With the exception of studies of witchcraft and hysteria, the historians' argument lacks specificity in terms of symptomatological expression. Words like "nervous breakdown" or "hysteria" are only loosely employed to connote the tensions assumed in early American society.[58]

In opening the self or going beneath a character, the historian forms oppositions of mind and emotion, thought and feeling—facings, that is, of exteriors and interiors.[59] A sheet of writing, in contrast, holds nothing within. To argue that one can look behind words into the emotional piety of New England, assumes that one can read through the texts into the heart of the writer.[60] This is to consider the writing that an author uses to make an understanding of his or her heart a verbal façade and not an efficacious presence.

For the psychologically informed historian looking at early American writing, an interior does seem to appear—because of the metaphors Puritans used—the excremental language, for example, that erupts in Puritan literature. This language molds the confessional world of which the historian himself becomes a part—the promise, for example, that Susanna Anthony, in an eighteenth-century spiritual confession, offers of opening her heart:

> O methinks I never knew the plague of my heart. It bursts out like a putrid sore, that never was truly healed. Lord, rip open the inmost sides, and let me be ashamed and confounded, because these things are yet such horrid remains of the abominable thing.[61]

Early American authors published their loathsome thoughts to such an extent that historians have presumed that psychic struggle became heightened when the Puritan became an American. The analysis of this self becomes an analysis of American culture, and thus a people become distinguished by their psychomachy. If the historian turns the "automachia"—for Bercovitch, the "auto-American-biography"—into the psychobiography, then the self's struggle becomes a microcosm of national psychic trouble.[62]

Bunyan reconstructed his life and the pathologies entailed most likely as a confession required by his church, a confessional requirement that remained local and peculiar to his Bedford congregation. In New England by the 1640s, orthodoxy stated that all churches were to require—uniquely so in the beginning, as Edmund S. Morgan has brilliantly shown—an expression of conversion for full membership in the church and thereby for full participation within the community. This requirement provided the whole of American Puritanism, for a moment of ideal time, perhaps five decades, with the stamp that Burton had derided. Precisians were attempting to determine by sign, through an expressed oral or written work, whether they were to join with the saints.[63] This spiritual "relation," as the small narrative was called, sights the beginnings of what has become an American national literature.[64]

New England churches variously interpreted and applied this requirement for something other than a ritual confession of faith, and they terminated the requirement at different points in time.[65] The oral narrative of confession nevertheless created a broad cultural literature in that all within the community were expected, if they were to join with the saints, to create at least once in their life a "writing" of their past history. They were to compose themselves against the "past written texts" (in a phrase of Sande Cohen) that the structure of Puritan conversion offered. Within the framework of the morphology of conversion that Morgan and others have described, men and women in early New England did not simply record an immediately sensible experience or, conversely, have a structure of words forced upon their lives; they instead used past writings to build experience out of the innate confusion of sensation. In a requirement that was uniquely "national" in scope, and with the spiritual relation eventually creating a written confessional literature that has marked American writing to the present, men and women extracted meaning out of the chaotic frontiers now before them.[66]

The relations that New England churches required in the seventeenth century reflect, in a compact form, the ministers' structure of conversion, most particularly that portion of the narrative leading from the Word, through the sight of sin, to faith. Scholars have variously described these relations, but perhaps the simplest formulation remains that of a sleepy person suddenly experiencing fear or terror, feeling convicted and humiliated by his sense of sin, entering then into a condition of malaise that often includes a melancholy temptation such as a Christ-like impulsion to suicide. The narrator then describes the formalisms or works by which he tries to remove his fear, proving thereby the inefficacy of any healing except through the blood of Christ. The testifier acknowledges his inability to undo his sin and thereby gives himself to Christ. He experiences, finally, further trials of temptation but suffers the temptation differently. Of course within these stories of conversion, to use a phrase of Jonathan Edwards, there appears "a vast variety" of God's work upon his saints.[67]

New England placed this narrative of the war of the saint's soul within the oral discourse delivered before the congregation, although the woman, perhaps excluded from public testimony, told her story in the privacy of the minister's chamber.[68] The discourse involved an "enquiring," as Increase Mather wrote, defending the tradition, "into the spiritual estate, of those who are admitted unto [the] Lords Supper." The relation was to express an "*experience of a work of grace*," a "practice," or most simply a "story." For Increase Mather, the story became a material practice in the sense of the efficacy the relation might effect: "Some have been converted by hearing others relate the story of their conversion—others have been comforted, and edifyed thereby."[69] Puritan ministers like Mather encouraged confession not because they considered a profession of conversion a substitute for an ineffable experience, but because they held the word of conversion to be a moment of experience itself. While certainly making use of a person's past, confession remained a present act. Speaking or writing of one's terror and transformation made one capable of realizing that experience before others. From the ministers' view there existed not two sorts of saints, one called "visible" (or professed) and another "real," not apparent saints and real saints who should ideally coincide. The idea of testimony was not to uncover a truth but to profess a truth already present. Without the always real presence of conversion made sensible through the spoken word, no conversion was real.

In defending the New England way a century later, Edwards also offered Mather's commonplace of the word's means. Edwards focused, however, not on the means but on the necessity of naming, arguing the nonexistence of the two sorts of saints. The scriptures, he wrote, never used the word "saints" in different ways—on the one hand for the visible, apparent, or professed, and on the other hand for the real—no more than there existed two names for gold. The application of a name could of course prove false. Naming remained, nevertheless, to account for a reality no one could sensibly question. Edwards thus asked for a testimony of conversion not to make visible a hidden truth, since the presence of saints was hardly that—not, that is, to get at the confessor's "*inward feelings themselves*" by turning his heart "*inside out*" and viewing it "immediately"—but to realize the truth already presented. Words of conversion never acted as a certainty, but they acted as the necessary moment of naming, drawing the confessor from his standing as a "spectator" to a "knowing as one *knows his own*."[70]

The spiritual relation Edwards wanted to revive had never functioned as a test. Rather, the relation served as anthropologists have conceived of the gift. An exchange occurred between the narrator and the audience who would receive the person's experience, the congregation being obligated, as it seems, to accept the presence of the testimony and to offer in return membership within the visible church. At least ministers like Increase Mather pleaded that they had no intention "to impose this or that mode, or to insist upon a relation of the time and manner of conversion." "I should think," Edwards wrote, "that such a person, solemnly making such a profession, had a right to be received as the object of a public charity, however he himself might scruple his own conversion." The "talk," for Edwards, "obliges, and as it were forces full charity."[71]

Beyond reworking the past by narrating an adequate history, the professor stood in the church presently to create a current experience, to offer a sound moment of the "special presence" of Christ. Congregations provided room for maneuver, for the relation would serve to bring the seal into the congregation, drawing the often disparate church body together. This community of interpretation remained the sectarians' ideal.[72]

Serving as a gift, the oral relation worked as a writing in the sense that, whether or not men and women in early America could read, they would hear the written word, the prepared sermon, for example, in which the minister would offer the understanding that lives were related to printed texts and to the interpretation of scripture. The effect of a past written text in the organization of a person's experience becomes plain when the relation is reorganized in the hands of authority, as in a relation recorded and then straightened out in writing by the Reverend John Fiske:

> 23 of 1st. [16] 45. Lord's day. . . . the congregation stayed and the wife of Brother William Fiske made a declaration of the work of grace to good satisfaction. . . . And being so voted by the church as meet for fellowship was received into the numbers.
>
> In her relation she held forth her first conviction from a sermon upon Col. 3:9 where a jesting lie was reproved and she was guilty. We heard of many other sins and of her miserable condition in case of sin, even of original sin. She was stayed somewhat by a place in scripture . . . , from Psalms 28. . . . She was taken off them again by Eccles. 11:9 [?] and going with her mother to a sermon she heard from Jer. 31. . . .
>
> Then she set upon prayer for it and had thereupon some stay from the power of God. Afterward from Ezek. 33:14–16 she found some comfortable hopes. . . . At length, in private, from Mat. 11:28 she saw Christ tendered to her. . . .[73]

By the middle of the seventeenth century, Max Weber has argued, Puritanism had created a new authority of self. Because of the radical removal of "magic" from the lives of the saints that a Calvinist theology of predestination required, Weber's Puritan found himself standing alone before God, without intermediaries like priests or rituals to guide his salvation. Weber's Puritan discovered "personality," a whole self that developed when all compelling authority (whether priestly or ceremonial) was taken away as a determinate of salvation. Only the saint, in other words, could authorize, or become the author of, his own salvation. Whether or not personality was actually discovered (as intractable a problem as pointing to the origins of capitalism), this personality did become expressed in the new autobiographies that Weber read—not a unique economic, but a unique spiritual display of bookkeeping.

The availability of printed models fed this discourse: the presence of the sermon, the Bible of course, and writings of both melancholy and the morphology of conversion. Rather than standing alone before God, the saint could use spiritual guides. He could find a book that would lead to his awakening. As one spiritual relator testified: "Reading Mister Hooker's book called The Soul's Preparation for Christ [one of the most important books on the morphology of conversion] it pleased God to let me see I was one needed preparation for him which as it moved me to consider seriously of my condition to resolve to pray and read Scriptures and attend to sermons that I might be able to give account to my parents and to mend my life which was the farthest thing I amed at[.]"[74] To give account, one read or heard writings that pulled together and wove a texture from experience.

Increasing Protestant literacy rates also fed the body of this confessional discourse, along with the sectarian requirement for a story of conversion. Though oral in form, the confession at times was recorded by the minister at the moment, presumbly, of its presentation or else the minister reconstructed the confession later from notes. Some relations were signed then or marked by the relator just as if they were a property will or civil testament.[75]

The demand emerged for an expression of utter wasting, moving the autobiographer past the point of merely mending his life. Thomas Shepard demanded an expression not of "noyse" or "violent and tumultuous complaint"—not, that is, of hysteria but an inrushing sorrow, a breaking sea, a becoming "sick" with "strange temptations, hellish blasphemies" such that forced the sight, stirred the "dunghill," and allowed the self to see that "all its righteousnesses is a menstrous cloth."

For Shepard, in his fourfold act of preparation, compunction and then humiliation follows this conviction of sin. Compunction is a compulsive attempt to work the sight of sin off. The purpose of both these stages of preparation is to humiliate the self into the realization that its "works" always prove false. For in attempting to undo his foulness—afraid as the suppliant is, standing before the writing of Mosaic Law—he undertakes an estranged labor until "the soule feeling it selfe to labor . . . , and to be still as miserable . . . , hereupon it is quite tyred out, and sits down weary, not only of its sin, but of its work." This, "the irritation of the law," or endeavors that Thomas Hooker referred to as "crazie holds" or a resting upon "thy owne crazie bottomes," expresses the self's attempts to undo its acts in a mechanistic or compulsive way. Such acts lead the saint through his preparation only to further "shame and confusion." In the end his self finally breaks. A willingness then follows in the fourth stage of faith, a contentment "to be a cipher, a stepping-stone, the very offall of the world."[76] And like the saint's works, even the narrative structure appears to collapse; the very work of the story itself, it seems, becomes stepped upon.

Whether speaking or writing out this story, the narrative of conversion contains forms learned through the models of written texts. Writing has cut into oral traditions of learning what a person is to make of his or her life. A training up has occurred as to how one should speak "for the record," and speak without any sense that, because of the presence of written forms, one's speaking has become false.

Psychohistorians must consider certain questions before arguing that something hidden is going on within such texts. These are questions of discourse. For example, why should a literate consensus choose to call one text (a diary, say) personal and another (a treatise) formal? Is the documentation "left" for the historian to read discursively determined in its preservation—in the passing, for example, of a diary through a family's hands? Is an expression of psychopathology inherent in a text the historian employs, and is it of historical interest why a writer should have chosen to put it there? Did early American authors —including the illiterate whose lives were shaped by writing —form a new psychological discourse by employing more commonly certain types of writing, most especially the spiritual relation New England congregations came to expect? These questions stand prior to historical probes for culture and personality. The question remains why certain texts got written, not how a writing in some manner reflects a deeper or hidden nature.

The preserved confession is written, of course, and even a transcription differs qualitatively from the oral word before its inscription. This is most obviously the case for illiterate New England authors for whom the minister recorded words. Psychohistorians will argue that they can spread out written documents across some measure of formality, judging the degree of intimacy between an author and his texts and thus gauging the amount of personal revelation a certain writing contains. It is as though, while treatises reflect mind, writings such as diaries, journals, and autobiographies reflect the heart, the spoken and even unspoken word that registers an emotive presence. It is as though writing only copies experience or acts as an index of *mentalité*. Writing becomes a witness, tracing, or copy mark of something more significant inside or below. Writing can even be held as merely copying rather than making sensible an experience presumably as complex as religious conversion, the conversion that is found in Puritan ministerial texts as the structure of stages or steps. The points of conversion, again, are listed in order, whether as the ten stages of Perkins or the eleven stages of Ames, and are sequentially numbered, yet the historian can still write: "The morphology of conversion thus described is in large part empirically based; this is the process as Puritan divines observed its occurrence among their people."[77] What the historian finds is not the immediate witness of spiritual conversion but the analytic power—lists, for example— that writing allows.[78]

For the authors of spiritual relations and autobiographies, the generative motive or determination of their histories is psychology rather than their state's polity, economy, or society. As if a metonymy, the body of the person giving his story expresses the sin of the entire state. "At this time the Lord set in with me to show me I was a son of God by outward covenant yet had corrupted my way *therefore* I thought it just with God to bring distraction on the whole country society congregation that belonged to me and I thought that was the cause of all the crosses they met with[.]"[79] The troubles of the person, while individualized, are projected upon the state, creating the idea of a national personality.

At the same time, autobiographers have authorized their self-histories to the extent that the historian may argue that their selves do stand discovered, or that the Puritans did achieve for the first time in history the personality that Weber believed their radical predestination forced. Discursive patterns of writing have shifted, however, in that autobiographies have been written and published in ever greater numbers.

Though as much typing exists within the new autobiographical literature as in the earlier lives of the saints, the spiritual relation is written to be read as if type were removed. Unlike the earlier hagiography, a distinct personality becomes immediately attached to the history, even if the spiritual relation reads as little more than the recitation of a standard confession of faith. Even when such recitations are recorded in the hand of the minister, they are marked or signed by the person speaking, and enough variation of wording is submitted to allow for a particular person's expression. Such written documents, though knowingly copied from former texts such as the *Westminster Confession of Faith*, the sectarians held as no less true or less personal a testament than a *Grace Abounding to the Chief of Sinners*. Writing per se, it seems, became a mark of singular truth.[80]

No sense of hypocrisy exists in speaking or in writing of oneself in the terms of former scripts. The seventeenth- or early eighteen-century author writes within the Biblical typology of understanding that one's life should in fact be in imitation or fulfillment of scripture. The presence of writing and the understanding that one is enjoined to employ scripture to make experience sensible is, in Christian culture, clear enough. Writing becomes a usable material in that it allows one to construct meaning out of the chaos of one's life. With the exclusions and inclusions made, one can make of one's life a "work." This is also to make one's life work, analogous to the oral culture of which Claude Lévi-Strauss writes: "The shaman provides the sick woman with a *language,* by means of which unexpressed, and otherwise inexpressible, psychic states can be immediately expressed."[81]

Seventeenth-century sectarian autobiographies express no naiveté—that is, no "inarticulateness" such as has been attributed to Bunyan's self-history, or childlike "candour and simplicity" as found in *Grace Abounding.*[82] In drawing the analogy between the use of written language and the use of oral discourse that Lévi-Strauss discusses, one sees language ordering confusion, making sense of experience, and providing material meaning:

> And it is the transition to this verbal expression—at the same time making it possible to undergo in an ordered and intelligible form a real experience that would otherwise be chaotic and inexpressible—which induces the release of the physiological process, that is, the reorganization, in a favorable direction, of the process to which the sick woman is subjected.[83]

The Puritan used the language of melancholy to provide such a form, expressing how it was to be sick and the signs that could be read if one were to heal. It is possible then to answer the question Edmund S. Morgan posed, "whether the pattern of Puritan spiritual experience was produced by the prescriptions of men like Perkins and [Arthur] Hildersam, or whether the prescription was itself based on experience."[84] It is not a question of choosing between words and experience, or between a language of conversion and conversion itself. Prescription is not opposed to experience; prescription is language with which to order and craft experience.

Self-Murder

The question of the truth contained in early American autobiographical writing perhaps nowhere better presents itself than in a Puritan author's expression of his temptation to suicide. If a Puritan author describes his thoughts of making an end to his life, then he was used the story of Saul, or the story of the jailer of Paul and Silas, and of course the account of the suicidal temptation of Christ, as models for his own story. For Increase Mather, a suicidal temptation such as that of the jailer signified the jailer's conversion, "proved the *Conversion* of the Gaoler. . . . We have herewithal a Relation of what proved the occasion of that strange *Conversion*."[85] The keeper of the prison becomes bound by his thought of killing himself, until Paul declares himself present, light is brought, and the transformation is wrought.

The Puritan author places his thoughts of doing away with himself as well, of course, next to the inscription of Christ.

> Then the devil taketh him up into the holy city, and setteth him on a pinnacle of the temple,
>
> And saith unto him, If thou be the Son of God, cast thyself down: for it is written . . .

When the author of a spiritual relation describes his temptation to suicide, he writes of himself in light of this scripture and marks himself as Christ is marked by temptation. The author is not making a lie out of his life, but neither is he reflecting an immediate suicidal pathology. Rather, he is making true his relation—both his relation to scripture, which he most certainly regards as true, and his relation to the congregation to which he is presenting the story of his conversion. He is marking the truth of his text by describing perhaps this specific temptation, organizing the understanding of his own self's history:

> The Lord showed me so much sin in me that I thought myself unworthy to breathe in his air or live upon his earth I thought it were better for me to die than to live upon his earth I thought better for me to make away with myself than to live here to dishonor God. . . . Temptations grew stronger but I thought I had more need of Christ Jesus to be my savior. Temptations grew so strong that I was even resolved to give up myself to evil *ways* and forsake the Lord but then the Lord came and visited me with this that I heard how that the Lord Jesus offers himself to those that can't save themselves or deliver themselves [.][86]

As in the life of Christ, Satan's asking for the attempt at self-murder is a sign of salvation. To make such an attempt, however, offers proof only according to Satan's wishes, for the act Satan requests is proof only of the fact of the existence of the devil. The attempt to do away with oneself works like any device so conceived to change one's life, in that it works not at all. To take one's life into one's own hands is to act as if one could, of one's own, do away with oneself, or efface one's pain, or rid oneself of one's sin. The thought of making an end to one's life, however, in striking the mind of the confessor, reflects the mark of Christ. The temptation to so act and then the refusal to do so reflects Christ's ability to see through the falsehood of any such sign. The temptation, then, becomes itself significant, in that it actually demonstrates the inefficacy of any such act to effect anything at all. The temptation proves its own absurdity, and the obsession proves the lengths to which Satan will go to draw the believer from Christ.

The distinction between thought and act that Perkins and Ames demanded needs still to be drawn, particularly if the historian reads a temptation to suicide as an actual expression of American cultural pathology. The distinction needs to be drawn between alien "suggestions" seen and so claimed as foreign to the self—as truly satanic in relation to the body of the believer—and therefore to be welcomed (and often expressed), and temptations felt as inherent in the self and thus an execrable part of one's own nature.[87]

When Puritan ministers warned of self-murder, their words did involve an irony, for an authority's admonition became the suggestion that one should in fact think about suicide. Increase Mather worked the irony by presenting a sermon on what he took to be a wave of suicides infesting New England in the 1680s. The self-murders existed as terrible acts and yet, Mather said, the temptation to so act worked in the minds of others as a sign of salvation, if the self-murders were suggested and not carried out. "The *Best of Saints* upon earth may be so"—tempted to kill themselves, that is—when "in the pangs of the *New-Birth*," both before conversion and after. For "when the *Devil* has no hope of prevailing, yet he will *Tempt* unto Crime. He will do it, only to vex and molest the faithful Servants of GOD!"[88] Such became the established guides, the forms the autobiographer could use to express the unthinkable.

New England ministers provided sermons of the horrid temptation, as to suicide. In building upon the work of Perkins and Ames, the ministers analyzed the pangs of conversion in terms of the blasphemous suggestion that Satan would inject—a notion considered as coming "irrationally" only if one thought such a temptation strange. In this form melancholy offered "a good servant." The hellish injection had attacked "some very godly men," "some of the choicest."[89]

The words of the ministers worked themselves into the lives of men and women from the college-educated to the barely literate. "The Relation of Mr. Collins," for example, which Michael Wigglesworth, New England's author of *The Day of Doom*, appended to his diary, is the relation of a Harvard graduate:

> My temptation increased so far as to provoke me to murder my self or some of my friends that so I might be soon brought to an end for this temptation did almost bodily distract me as inwardly distress me. I did not tell the president when he spoke to me the chief cause.

I was resolved to tell nobody but to fill my measure to my self. Afterward that I might let the president know I intended not to follow his counsel I sent to borrow an idle book out of the Library &c. I was kept under the lash of Satan's terrors that he might give me the more easily a false peace[.][90]

"John Dane's Narrative, 1682," reconstructed perhaps from a church relation, offers a less educated man's story, and an even finer example of this seventeenth-century naturalism:

. . . uppon a time walking, with my Gun on my shoulder charged, in the myle brok path, beyond Decon goodhewes, I had seauverall thouts cam flocking into my mynd, that I had beatter make away myself then to liue longer. I walkt discosing with sutch thouts . . . , with manie other satanecall thouts.[91]

Whether in oral discourse before a congregation or in a slight spiritual narrative such as Dane's, the self is patterned in its expression on past written texts the author may never have read, texts like Mather's sermon "On the Horrid Crime of Self-Murder." The editor of Mather's printed sermon, most likely his son Cotton, turned Increase into a figure of Paul. Like Paul to the jailer, here in the words of Cotton quoting from his father, Increase calls to his people not to kill themselves:

"*Tears gushed from my Eyes. And it seemed as if it were said unto me,* Preach on that subject. . . ." . . . The next Lords-Day, he Preached the Sermon . . . And Behold, soon after it, there came such to him, as informed him, That *at that very Time*, the Temptations to *Self-Murder* were impelling of them with an *Horrible Violence*; but GOD had blessed that Happy Sermon for their Deliverance! They afterwards joined to his Church.[92]

The "call to the tempted" voices a call for an alienated people's conversion. The New Englanders' thoughts of self-murder, far from marking the sins of their land, occasion the beginnings of this people's regeneration.

Cotton Mather used a similar occasion of a people's thoughts of suicide to declare, in sight of the devil at Salem, a cultural conversion. In his *Wonders of the Invisible World*, he wrote of "this woeful motion [made] every day . . . ; *You must kill your self! you must! you must!*" Jonathan Edwards, in his *Faithful Narrative of the Surprising Work of God*, wrote a half century later of these same horrors. Edwards was giving, however, not a history of witchery but an account of religious revival: "And many . . . had it urged upon 'em . . . 'Cut your own throat, now is good opportunity: *now, Now!*'"[93] The reader may then move from these formal writings of the work of conversion spread across a suicidal land, to the "spiritual Travels of Nathan Cole," composed during the Great Awakening and the tremblings of which Edwards wrote. He finds, in the historian's use of Cole's words, a similar phrasing—

words that allow Mather, Edwards, and present history to work within the same pattern of expression: "Nathan Cole, too, found himself tormented with suicidal impulses early in 1745. . . . Satan was always at his elbow, telling him to use his knife 'now, now,' but he kept resisting the impulse."[94]

The words cannot be read as mirroring Cole's state of mind, nor can they be read as fiction. Cole's words reflect earlier writings that offered him his own understanding. Throughout his narrative, Cole frequently mentions books he is reading or being given, and as the modern editor of his narrative notes, some of Cole's words reflect Bunyan's phrasing in *Grace Abounding to the Chief of Sinners*: ". . . then I was worried nine days by Satan with blasphemous thoughts, and I was Shut up and could not pray being fill'd with blasphemous thoughts, sometimes I would bite my teeth together to keep my mouth from speaking."[95]

Cole understood his impulse to suicide within the pattern of temptation the ministers had drawn; for him it made sense.

> Satan was my Enemy and was permitted to tempt me, and he told me I was not converted. . . .
>
> Well Satan comes upon me and says there is one way to know quick; destroy your self . . . ; for if you be converted you will certainly be saved; . . . I told him I will not on no account; but he follow'd me day after day . . . with this horrible temptation.

Cole seeks advice, and another tells him that "the bible don't tell of any Saint that was [so] tempted." Cole's own writing then becomes the reflection of a regressing series of scripts, and as so often happens in the spiritual narrative, a book of advice is placed in the doubting saint's hands:

> Well they put a book into my hand entitled Mr. Hookers doubting Christian drawn to Christ; . . . but I labour'd under great darkness some time; . . . Satan close to my elbow . . . [who] would say now, now, is a good time you may do it in a minute . . . ; my wife bad me leave my knife at home, which I did many a Day. [1746]

Now he is told in truth "that Satan tempted our blessed Lord to destroy his most Sacred body. . . . A ray of divine light broke into my Soul . . . and when I got home I took the bible to read."[96]

Concerning the trials of his wife, Cole too described "a drove of temptations and horrible thoughts" that had attacked her, "blasphemous temptations" that he fought to make her understand. He then undertook a struggle of scripture against scripture to work the meaning of her temptations out:

And as he [Satan] tempted by Scripture, I answered by Scripture, and he strove to make the Scriptures clash one against another, Satan all the while said they were her Sins, and strove to prove it by Scripture; but I proved by Scripture they were not hers.

An ordinary man, Cole could reason as closely as Perkins or Ames. He could ask in his own writing whether his wife had in fact delighted in her thoughts, and when she replied no, "I told her if her heart acted freely in them then it left a guilt upon her Conscience; but if her heart strove against them then they were not her Sins . . . ; and I told her it was no sin to be tempted, but it was sin to yield to the temptation."[97]

Aside from the question of what Cole and his wife did suffer, his advice, in present historical knowledge, surpasses the understanding of such insistent impulses provided by nineteenth-century psychiatry. A similar confession of obsessional thoughts such as the thought of murdering oneself or another would have led, in the Victorian era, to commitment in an asylum. Such thoughts, that is, would be read literally as an indication of "moral insanity." For Cole, the temptation suffered by himself and his wife becomes the mark not of their insanity but of their identification with Christ.

The Self-History and Melancholy

Beyond the public spiritual relations orally offered but in themselves reflective of past written texts, stand the Puritans' diaries and their lives or autobiographies. Coined at the end of the eighteenth century, the word "autobiography" signifies the author's self enclosed within the limits of a book. Various methods existed for composing a spiritual text, however, methods that expanded the limits of autobiography beyond even an author's own particular words. An editor could compile an author's "life and writing," for example, by publishing a series of letters along with portions of a diary, cementing the whole with his own interspersed comments to form a single book. As in the example of a minister's unpublished compilation, "A brief Account of the Life and Character of Mrs Sarah Pierpont, In Four Parts," such a text could form a progressive sequence that moves the subject from nature to spirit:

Her Natural & Civil Life
Her Moral & Religious Character
Her Domestich Character
Her Hidden Life[98]

The progress here from the natural to the spiritually hidden works gradually behind the façades of Sarah Pierpont's civil, moral, and domestic life, tearing at the outward presentments of her character, thereby allowing her self to see the life her moral works hide.

Sarah Pierpont had not just left pieces of writing behind; she had composed a public spiritual autobiography, at least in the sense that she probably knew that others did often collect such spiritual manuscripts. More simply, an author might translate a diary into an autobiography, having then a present of writing to offer directly to his children prior to his death. Whether a diary, journal, series of personal letters, or written spiritual history, these writings extended in real time the single moment in which the oral confession was given. They also presented movements of conversion, but now were worked out in the hand of a consciously literate elite. Early American authors thus widened the discourse of the psychological history. Eventually, that discourse became expansive enough to encircle historians within its radius.[99]

The recomposition of diary notes to make a spiritual autobiography, the turning of a diary of daily spiritual "fact" into a lasting remembrance and exemplum—the autobiography itself—warns that even under the author's own hand such self-explorations were discursively composed according to particular traditions. Most important, the reader should not confuse the first-person narrator of the autobiography with the person of the author. Such confusion remains inherent in this genre of literature, for the author, Increase Mather for example, does present his "life," his written spiritual history, as that which he lived. As Mather wrote to his children: "I have thought that the relation of what the Lord has done for your father . . . might be a meanes to cause you to give yourselves entirely to the Lord Jesus, and to endeavor to walk with God."[100] For Mather, again, his writing existed to pass his life on to his children and to create in them his character as he had written that character out.

The process of turning daily spiritual occurrences into a written memory demanded, then, a conscious distancing between the author and his works. Cotton Mather recognized this distancing when, in translating his own diary into an autobiography addressed to one of his sons, he kept the name of the subject of his autobiography, *Paterna*, hidden.[101] The spiritual compositions required this standing back of the author from his own narrator—the narrator whose life was to stand in imitation of Christ and for the imitation of the author's children. When the reader refuses to recognize this distancing—ignoring a practice demanded by the authors of such histories themselves—then confusion erupts and the charge is made that such authors intended to declare themselves to be the Christ they imitated. The separation of author and subject that the historical allegory demands upsets the "play-frame" for the modern critic of just whom the autobiographer is writing about. That considered as purported "truth" and that considered as the relation of type or "fiction" have become a mix that the contemporary historical critic sometimes attempts to separate.

If the critic attempts to make this separation, then the author of the spiritual history, most notably Thoreau in relation to *Walden*,[102] is accused of mistruths.[103] Thoreau is seen as posing and is charged with recounting things that the historian, in his knowledge, knows never occurred at Walden. Apologies may be offered for Thoreau's mistakes of fact,[104] or he may be accused of self-infatuation.[105] The author becomes a narcissist, whether as the chief of sinners or of egoists. As Sacvan Bercovitch recounts in relation to the Puritans, however, and as Bunyan wrote in relation to Christiana in his *Pilgrim's Progress*, the mirror (Thoreau actually took one to Walden) serves not for looking upon the self, the ego, or the individual, but for looking through the self, for gazing, that is, upon the image of Christ: "Nay my Daughter, said she [Christiana], it is no Shame, but a Virtue, to long for such a thing as that [a looking-glass]." "Now the Glass was one of a thousand. It would present a man, one way, with his own Feature exactly, and turn it but another way, and it would shew one the very Face and Similitude of the Prince of Pilgrims himself."[106] The glass for Thoreau becomes Walden pond, reflective yet infinite, and his own imitation of another gives meaning to his statement "that I can live on board nails. If they ["a certain class of unbelievers"] cannot understand that, they cannot understand much that I have to say."[107] There are enough allusions in *Walden* (showing the ignorant, for example, where to fish) to show that Thoreau could offer himself as Christ.

New England writers also used semeiology to provide otherwise illogical psychopathological symptoms with religious significance, making such incoherent symptoms like the marred self in the mirror into meaningful signs. They created, then, not only Christlike images but also portraits of the worst defilements of character. Here too, however, the pilgrim's glass, in this seeming realism of being melancholy, juxtaposes a "Feature exactly" with an immortality of what has come to be considered a typical Protestant character.

The wording of this character in terms of its melancholy appears peculiar today, pointing to something amiss in the lives of those who chose to record their sense of bodily filth. This seems most especially true when the record is found in the lives of some of the most benign of seventeenth-century ministers such as Edward Taylor. A poet, Taylor insisted on sensing, like Thoreau two centuries later, just what the natural self consisted of: "a Dish of Dumps: yea ponderous dross, / Black blood all clotted"; "A bag of botches, Lump of Loathsomeness"; "fumes of muck"; "Dunghill Damps"; "A Sty of Filth . . . / A Dunghill Pit, a Puddle of mere Slime." "Lord," the poet finished, "clear these Caves."[108]

Like Taylor, Anne Bradstreet could write in verse of cleansing a body of sin without conceiving that hers figured as a character abnormally described. Within her poetry, melancholy serves as an appropriate voice for the self's own nature, for the creation, indeed, of a Protestant character. Melancholy works as the "sink," "The Kitchen Drudge, the cleanser of the sinks / That casts out all man e're eats or drinks," its blackness hated by the other humors in the personifications that Bradstreet used, particularly derided by the blood or sanguine character. Melancholy casts its shadow as a necessary difference the other humors can hold then in "spight," rather as historians read such words today: the "charging me to be thy excrement." And yet melancholy is a humor that Bradstreet defends from this, "your slanderous," "loathsome imputation." Melancholy served to contrast its blackness with the desired light, to provide a necessary anatomical "passage," to exonerate "filth" and "nature," to provide in image an ascetic function of drawing from blackness the purity of a character that choler, phlegm, and blood deny. Bradstreet's melancholy portrays the virtues that Weber termed a worldly ascetic or Protestant ethic: "constancy," "patience," "Temperance," "Chastity," "prudence," "judgement." It is a character still both defiled and defended, but in any event analyzed as appropriate to New England. Bradstreet distinguished her character as best with but one "malady," not "Ague nor Plurisie, / Nor Cough, nor Quinsey, nor the burning Feaver," but "Chymeraes strange." They, she wrote, "are in my phantasy, / And things that never were, nor shall I see / I love not talk."[109]

The Puritan autobiographer gave witness to this character and its maladies by composing his melancholy psychology. He faced himself as "*The true Picture of Cotton Mather* . . . with *black* . . . Characters," as Mather himself recorded, resolving to look upon his writing without any horror.[110] The author composed himself not in hagiography but in analysis—a psychological history of one who stood witness before the empirical evidence of the demonic feature at hand. He was to observe, record, and introduce argument only when argument was needed. His record of words was to speak for itself.

While a young minister in England, for example, Thomas Hooker witnessed the melancholic's terrors in the years when Burton was drawing his cases from books. Observing a woman diagnosed as melancholy for whom physic had failed, Hooker provided a meaning for the woman's sickness in accordance with the ministerial understanding of melancholy. He provided a "new answering methode," an involved psychotherapeutic disputation, arguing against the woman, who simply thought herself damned.[111] Cotton Mather, who had early toyed with the idea of becoming a physician, demanded this same empirical experience. Nothing stood prescribed, though like Hooker, Mather employed a script for his own understanding. He could observe in his home, as a case of conscience, Mercy Short, a young woman afflicted by witches. He would record, as Mather thought it important to say, "not as an *Advocate*, but as an *Historian*."[112] He could only make sense of her case, however, by using a standard narrative of spiritual conversion, drawing the girl from her horrid temptations, through her struggles of resistance, toward her peace of salvation. At least to his own satisfaction, Mather felt he had given Mercy Short understanding.

In becoming one's own historian, one offered not an account as dramatic as Mather's but a story of seemingly inconsequential pains, small encounters contrasting with and yet reflecting the heroic battles of Bunyan's Christian with Apollyon and the other great monsters Christian finds in his way. The modern reader of Bunyan's autobiography feels closer to a true relation than when he reads Mather's relation of Mercy Short, hearing in Bunyan the relation of a man who has lived as but a tinker. Bunyan's own monsters remain small: petty doubts, absurd fears, a year-long search for certain words of scripture, and a temptation producing an unaccountable "motion, by way of pushing or thrusting with my hands or elbows." "These things," as Bunyan said, "may seem ridiculous to others, even as ridiculous as they were in themselves, but to me they were most tormenting cogitations." The detail becomes finely set and the realism appears strong, while a mold has still been provided into which the pilgrim can pour his agony and thereby make sensible his chaos and seeming confusion—the "anomie," as Perkins has said, of his sin.[113] Divines had offered words such that if one suffered, one could come to understand why and find some reason for the agony of mind.

In his own remembrance of his Christian experience, John Winthrop made this point—the force of the word to make sense out of experience. Winthrop emphasized his need to read and to listen so as to make his life meaningful. As a young man newly married, about eighteen years of age, Winthrop had come under "exercises of Conscience," recurrences of earlier struggles that now appeared stronger and yet still seemed ill-defined. The ill definition represents an important stage of his journey. Winthrop counseled others in their cases of conscience, cases he simply defined as vague troubles of mind, and then, growing in pride and in "employment and credit," he read Perkins. Now the agony Winthrop suffered appeared less chaotic, more focused: "I grew very melancholy and mine own thoughts wearied mee, and wasted my spirits."

Winthrop had suffered behaviors that he termed his bondage to the Law. Fashioning his understanding by writing only to himself, he remembered that he had put himself to "many a needlesse task," attempting compulsively to work out of his sin. If need be, he would forsake his occupation so that he might reside in some form of safe ascetic retreat. Finally, when about thirty years of age—the approximate age that will so often be mentioned in these texts—Winthrop broke down: God "laid mee lower in myne owne eyes then at any time before, and showed mee the emptiness of all my guifts, . . . so as I became as a weaned child."[114]

This is Augustine's age of conversion in the *Confessions*, the age that Puritan spiritual histories often recount as the point of crisis and turning. It is the age, of course, of the crucifixion of Christ. It is also the age of terror and transformation expressed by such nineteenth-century cases as the "vastation" of the elder Henry James and the "panic fear" of his son. William James referred to these mature conversions as "sporadic adult cases," and to these he wholly gave over his own discussion of religious conversion. The age also allows the moratorium to occur that Erik Erikson perceives as necessary for the conversions of his great men to work themselves out. The age reflects textual practices, however, rather than innate psychodynamic forces. The age provides an example, indeed, of the force a text holds, the ability of "expression" to organize "experience."[115] Until the Great Awakening, at least, this "middle age"—not adolescence —appears to have been the actual time for the organization of experience into a relation of conversion, and for a presentation then before the church.[116] Conversion, in this sense, works like a text, becoming an expression not of life cycles and Eriksonian stages of development—a natural history of conversion—but of past scriptural models.

Winthrop's own life is quite open to an interpretation of obsessional psychopathology. Winthrop wrote of striking himself compulsively upon empty works rather as Bunyan would push and shove his hands and elbows, but Winthrop used this behavior as his way to understand the inefficacy of his power—his inability to remove his sin. Free justification and the grace of Christ alone could "wash away all those spots," "fouler" than anything seen. Winthrop also organized the understanding of both his character and conversion by employing words of obsession like the "fearefull temptation" or "wind" of Satan he found disturbing his brain; he had felt "lumpishe," filled with obsessive thoughts "as I could not for my life gett my minde from them, but they interrupted my prayers, brake my sleep, abated the wonted relish of heavenly things." In character, Winthrop said he remained a man of excessive doubt, hesitant and yet overcareful. He provided an almost perfect representation of the behavior that modern psychology considers obsessional or compulsive: "My disposition is ever fittest upon the first apprehension of any thinge; if . . . I beginne once to beat my head about it, and meet with any rubbe or discouragement, I cannot for my life proceed to make any dispatche, etc; as in writings of lettres, etc, whilst I have some tymes been over carefull and studious for the forme, I have cleane lost both my matter and invention."[117]

Such becomes the composition of seemingly trivial behavior, if only to show how carefully one must consider one's faults, and how trivial, ultimately, this analysis of the self becomes. There emerges a further issue, to so open the self that others will call the precisian mad. For Winthrop suffered, he said, the pathology of those "called puritans, nice fooles, hipocrites, hair-brainde fellowes," "those which doe walke openly . . . despised, pointed at, hated of the world, made a byworde, reviled, slandered, rebuked," those who secluded themselves from wordly pleasures and thus became warned: "he will be over-runne with melancolie." His only "madnesse," Winthrop rejoined, was in ever having left the fellowship of Christ.[118]

Privately composed at a variety of times and seemingly as odd notes, Winthrop's spiritual history nevertheless remains archetypal and in this sense communal, initiating a form of self-history for America as a model of Christian conversion and melancholy intertwined.[119] The form may be traced through the more famous surviving diaries and autobiographies (preserved as received family texts), traced through this extended text as truly, in the present title of Thomas Shepard's journal and autobiography, a "God's Plot": Shepard's temptation to suicide; Michael Wigglesworth's "Melancholy scrupulosity"; Increase Mather's "melancholy Hypochondriacal vapors, and all splenetic infirmities"; Richard Mather's woven themes of time, work, and death composed in the biography by his son; and the "Power of Melancholy" so incessantly expressed by Cotton Mather, his compulsive habits and horrid temptations of every kind.

When Thomas Shepard of Cambridge came to write of his own case of conscience, he first remembered his mother's affliction verging at times on "distraction," then recorded his own, like Winthrop, locating his worst moment as a conviction of fear. He was about twenty, living in doubt, unable either to read or to hear the scriptures "without secret and hellish blasphemy"; he felt "strong temptations to run my head against walls and brain and kill myself." He spoke to no one, felt ashamed, and even following upon the mercy of Christ, his doubts and fears remained—the awareness that he had, as Shepard repeated again and again, of his distemper, impotency, nakedness, emptiness, of his self as "utterly wasted," "a clod of filthy earth," and of his thoughts as "cloudy, dark, black." Shepard only asked to have the Lord smite his affections by cutting off his dirty hands.[120]

The Reverend Michael Wigglesworth, who like Shepard recorded the spiritual relations of parishioners, recounted the same for himself: his filthy dreams and escaping pollutions [nocturnal emissions], his unnatural lusts, his vexations, weariness, confusion, shame, and the want of natural affection for his father. Wigglesworth observed that he actually felt "*secretly glad*" when he learned that his father had died. Such became the demand that Wigglesworth made for analysis, that concerning his father he "feared least there should be some root of bitterness that I were not willing to part with, unsearched out." He spoke too of petty crimes that beset his mind, "scruples of conscience" such as a small untruth told about a Mister Mildmay's sword, "so triviall a thing," "*a business so old* ," but a business he incessantly considered as he tried to justify himself, but a business about which he worried again at length as he attempted to work the point out. He indeed wrote of the untruth once again when he learned of his father's death.

Wigglesworth called his rigors his "Melancholy scrupulosity," oppression of mind he asked God to bear for him: worries about journeys not yet undertaken, thoughts about evils not yet met, atheistic irreverences seizing his mind, and a long, terribly involved consideration as to whether or not he should shut a neighbor's stable door beating to and fro on a sabbath evening. Given all this—the scrupulosity which even made his words appear as foolish as his foolish intent—Wigglesworth followed the advice, he said, of Perkins: "To fight against Melancholy and unbelieving thoughts not by debating with them (for so they are too hard for me) but by sleighting them and not attending to them."[121] He would give up, but only after he had carefully designed a narrative to reflect his scrupulous intent.

Wigglesworth recorded no single moment of collapse as Winthrop and Increase Mather did. The time came when Mather, at thirty-one, thought himself mad. "Now Satan set in with my melancholy to persuade me (though there was no ground for it) that this last [a mania] would be my condition." Mather was minister of the Second Church in Boston, a position he had assumed six years earlier, in 1664. Now, living fearfully in Boston, Mather first went to a mineral spring in Lynn to take the waters as a cure for his hypochondriacal vapors. He prayed and did receive some comfort, then left the waters, only to feel beset again with anxiety and harassing temptations.

Mather was portraying the inefficacy of the water's physic. But he was also joining within his awareness the sickness of his body with that of his soul, for by turning to physic he had also turned to prayer to ask for the healing of both. Only upon his return from Lynn could Mather become aware of the meaning that his bodily sickness portrayed. He now met a poor, godly woman who spoke of afflictions so close to his own that she appeared a messenger from God. In a moment of astonishment, he found that his ridiculous troubles made sense; through the voice of his adviser, Mather now understood that his "melancholy distempers" reflected the rest of his "body of sin." He had established that no cure of man could cleanse such sin, and also that his estrangement (and imaginary fears) could bring him closer to God by giving him this understanding. His fears now left, and he turned to work and the husbanding of time. He would control his "precious Time" by establishing some method. Inscribing his experience in words for further emulation by his children, Mather resolved to spend no more than seven hours in sleep, the rest in duties attending to his calling, including sixteen hours of work alone in his study.[122] He would move from physics to the faith attending his calling.

In the biography of his father Richard, Increase Mather wove these same themes of time, work, and death. The morning of his death, Richard Mather importuned friends watching over him to carry him into his study, lamenting that he had lost so much time, saying that he had a great many things yet to do.[123] Like his son (in his son's portrayal), Richard would attempt to manage the impossible: here, the hour of his death unto a new life.

This theme of time and ultimate loss, and of the hopelessness of the self ever working against its own decay, informs the meaning of the Puritans' ethic. Most vividly, the theme was displayed when Increase's son, Cotton, who became his father's colleague at the Second Church in 1685, came to compose his own diary and autobiography. In seventeenth-century New England no minister suffered so much or labored so hard, for Cotton Mather made it all so plain, setting his strict methods against a wilderness of anger and depression. He would engineer a perfect state that he knew he could never achieve.

Certainly no minister wrote so much; a bibliography of more than four hundred published items and numerous manuscripts, the sheer number of words of which remains unsurpassed in America.[124] Cotton Mather could take exceeding care, even in a diary never meant for publication. There, fourteen years after noting the thought for a book, Mather returned and, searching through the vast pile of his manuscripts for the entry, noted in the margin the book's completion. Mather's biographers have preserved this scrupulous act as a meaningful sign, noting its occurrence and thus begging the question of just what is meant by one of Mather's compulsive behaviors.[125] What Mather meant was that he would, if he could, work himself to death, understanding all along that nothing he could do would give him any life.

Cotton Mather feared idleness. Idleness had become his own special fault, at least in childhood, so like his father and grandfather before him, Mather worked with an ever increasing fever to the moment of his own death: "*In this year*, . . . I have written many Illustrations. I have sent more than a dozen Books to the Press. I have cultivated many Correspondences . . . , I wrote for *England*, above Thirty Letters. But, O my God, I lie down in Confusion before thee. Sloth, and Folly, have devoured an Incredible deal of my Time this year."[126]

Throughout his life, Mather sought what he most often called "Regular *Method*" or "proceeding *Methodically*." He would fill up "the little Parcels, Fragments, and Intervals of *Time*," and he would cultivate his mind, attending to that wildness ("*overgrown with Weeds*") like the American plotting out his garden. Rhetorically, Mather hoped to control himself completely—his evil thoughts, for example, that expressed a danger, in that such ideas might come true.[127] Thus Mather wrote of setting about to think expressly before his every act: before he studied, preached, or heard a sermon; before he made a visit, ate a meal, fell asleep, or set upon a recreation. He sought, "anatomically and particularly," to consider every part of his body, its function and use thereof, to think a certain way before dressing, undressing, or washing his hands. He wished to "improve the Time" during "Evacuations of Nature" by reflecting upon the horrors of his body's demands. He also undertook various "mortifying" and "macerating Exercises" to drive out "the Temptations of a filthy Divel." He used ascetic practices like fasting to punish his body to the point; and lamented (a lament common in spiritual histories) that he was damaging his health. Of all New England's early ministers, Mather most plainly used such methods to construct an emblem of compulsion. He would cut across chaos by attempting to structure his every move.[128] He would draw bars across his sight of dirt. Like the image that Bunyan used for Vanity-Fair—"they took them and beat them, and besmeared them with dirt, and then put them into the Cage, that they might be made a spectacle to all the men of the *Fair*," (an image that reverses the position of damnation by placing the real spectacle of mocking evil outside the cage)—the image that Mather built around himself is one of trading in asceticism to emphasize that he could only fail to hold such an economy together. His trading becomes a sport.

In his autobiography, Mather reported discovering his first fears of bodily sickness at about fourteen. He wrote that his fears were imaginary, though he carefully documented the physics with which he tried to cure himself. Like his father at the waters of Lynn, Mather was using his trial as an occasion for his conviction of sin. The sin of his soul was to be reflected in his bodily "Confusions." He was to see the first light coming from his "Condition of *Midnight*."

In his diary, Mather's melancholic sufferings extend to the end of his life. He incessantly mused upon this death, variously calculating and predicting his and other endings, offering in the meantime his continual refrain of the methods he would use to control his time and therefore the hour of his own death. He would work as if he alone could accomplish his end. He would "*Die Daily*" instead.[129]

Mather recorded the "Furious *Temptations*" that continually broke his good intentions apart. These were ideas that haunted, vexed, assaulted, and buffeted his mind, strange dejections, melancholy apprehensions, vapors rising from his spleen, impure ideas, foolish ideas, wretched ideas, fiery darts, temptations to atheism, blasphemy, suicide, and infidelity let loose by Satan, horrible, violent pollutions that surprised and astonished, forcing him again and again to lay with his mouth tasting the dust of his study's floor. Lesser worries erupted, no less ritualistically intoned; a certain superstitious inclination, as Mather considered it, to open the Bible and accept whatever word he found, or persistent worries rather like Wigglesworth's over small crimes such as borrowing books and finding them years later unreturned. Mather considered such particulars rather silly, but like Bunyan he considered his worries carefully. He could still, however, not quite admit of any more general fault.[130]

Mather did make an examination of what he described as his "Disposition to *Anger & Revenge*." If he had designed methods to circumscribe his death, the impossible point, then he would use his meticulous labors to control his attacks of sudden anger as well, for the anger, he feared, might end in another's death. He would "examine what lies at the Bottom of my Designs," probing his laborious methods, asking again and again when it was that his works would ever end his sin.[131]

Mather wrote the diary to himself. His words, while offering the genuine understanding that he had of his daily life, form a typical character: "Was ever man more tempted, than the miserable *Mather*! Should I tell, in how many Forms the Divel has assaulted me, . . . it would strike my Friends with Horrour." That "strange praecept" remained, however: *Count it all Joy, when you fall into diverse Temptations*."

Mather, in the writings that the minister made out of his life, has become a model of a compulsively sick American character: in his rage for control, in his frightening thoughts, in his harassing vexations, in his anger and stern moralism, in the methods with which he tried to cure himself, the strange ascetic practices that he made so readily apparent and that could only end in his terror. However privately intended, Mather's diary has become a public expression of the Puritan character. The mechanics Mather sought, like his father's physic, could only prove worthless.[132]

The Transit of New England's Conscience: Jonathan Edwards

A half century later the Reverend Benjamin Colman, of the Brattle Street Church, spoke again of New World saints' living in a "garden of his Agony." Colman republished in 1744, for the occasion now of the Great Awakening, a set of sermons that he had entitled *The Case of Satan's Fiery Darts in Blasphemous Suggestions and Hellish Annoyances*. The sermon summarized and brought to completion the seventeenth-century understanding of melancholy. In a rigid outline of points, Colman made melancholy so plain, and his own words so shrill, that he seemed to think his readers had forgotten the meaning the malaise was supposed to entail.

"It is *strange*," Colman wrote, "to observe the dreadful *Fears*" of those "alienated from GOD," those who found "all this odious Filth at the Bottom in me," "humble and gracious Persons, . . . annoy'd with *unaccountable irreverent, foolish, vile, filthy*, *base*, abominable Thoughts; They know not *what*, *how* or *why*! but they seem to *buzz* about 'em like *Swarms of Flies* . . . ; more especially when they would set themselves to *meditate* and *pray*." The "*Mire*," still, became "their Prison, . . . *Dirt and Sand* . . . us'd to *scour*" and wash "foul Hands." The assault, again, came in imitation of the Christ who had said to Satan, "*Get thee behind me*." Colman offered three points to consider: "1. That the most *upright* and dearest of the *Children* of GOD . . . may be sometimes [so] *annoy'd*. . . . 2. That these *hellish* Thoughts and *Injections* should be most *grievous* and *abhorred* to their holy Souls, and *rejected* with utmost Detestation. 3. That then they are not *their* Sin, nor will ever be imputed to them by the Holy GOD." The second point remained absolutely crucial: that "these hellish *Suggestions*, . . . be . . . abhorred to a Holy Soul, . . . *rejected* and cast out." These points still represented the map for an appropriate pathology of mind, one Colman simply called melancholy.[133]

In letters to Colman, extracts of which were later published, Jonathan Edwards provided the first descriptions of the Great Awakening, using these familiar terms of melancholy. Edwards had transferred Mather's rhetoric of a people suffering terrible impulsions from witchery to revival, writing now of the possibilities that Mather had implied of a people experiencing horrific temptations prior to the conversion of all the land now beset by Satan's hand: "'now is good opportunity: *now, NOW!*' So that they were obliged to fight with all their might to resist it, and yet no reason suggested to 'em why they should do it."[134]

Toward the end of the Great Awakening, however, with his hopes for national conversion diminished, Edwards turned inward and chose to publish some of the literary remains of the young missionary David Brainerd. Brainerd, traveling from one Indian settlement to another, suffered his temptations alone and outcast, while a sea erupted of an almost too popular awakening. Writing in 1743, for example, Brainerd was traveling through a "hideous and howling wilderness," mentioning, as he wrote to his brother, that "I live in the most lonely melancholy *desert*, about eighteen miles from Albany."[135]

The landscape had become almost too familiar, this "desert of hell" where "souls, who are in darkness, and, as it were, in a wilderness, have no cause to be discouraged." Cotton Mather had written of a satanic land "without Metaphor"; Jonathan Edwards spoke of his wilderness in the phrase "as it were." The phrasing still allowed Edwards to create a farther land, but it was a metaphysical land, and even there Edwards held tenuously—almost apologetically, and certainly with an ever greater amount of device —to the idea of salvation manifest in strange signs.

Some of the more feverish symptoms of the Great Awakening had tested the determination of salvation through the peculiar behavior of the saints, and because of the seeming hysteria, Edwards would need to defend, in a manner that Shepard and Cotton Mather had not, the idea of an awakening woven with moments of terror. Edwards thus returned the metaphor Mather had removed. He left the land itself for more benign transformations, for Emerson's ethereal scholars, for Thoreau's walks at Walden. Although the physical landscape of America would be industriously improved, the progress, as it seemed, actually made, the howling trek could reappear in wilds psychically removed.[136]

The sweetness of resting in Christ continued to follow the buffetings of Satan. "Often he raises needless and groundless scruples," Edwards preached, "and casts in doubts, and fills the mind with such fear as is tormenting . . . ; and he often raises mists and clouds . . . and sometimes wearies out the soul." But the words were softer than Mather's and the imagery was diffuse. Stronger imagery came in the economic metaphors that Edwards now used to portray the work of conversion. He spoke of any significant transformation not as quick or hysterical but as a "laborious, careful, self-denying business" without "relaxation" or "rest," a work of "*great expense.*" Here the labor that melancholy entailed could again serve its rhetorical function by describing the need for watch and employment, a need, simply, to be about one's business.

It was to make a statement of such "a melancholy habit"[137] that Edwards published Brainerd's diary. The revivals of the Awakening had unleashed a variety of moments that could well appear too cheaply wrought; sudden, hysterical fits that the Awakening's detractors could denounce—as they did, in an outpouring of derogatory scripts—as silly or obviously mad. Melancholy offered a pathology opposite to hysteria in that it remained tedious—expressive, that is, of the wearing labor Edwards demanded, suited not to fast or easy assurance but to the life of conversion Brainerd had experienced as he traveled across his howling land.

Brainerd spoke almost daily of his "vapoury disorders" or "melancholy" while living, he said, as a "hermit in the wilderness," "alienated from God." He mortified his body, heard the whisper of awful suggestions, and experienced an anguish that he described as "strange." His heart, he said, seemed like a cage of unclean birds, his thoughts appeared "wandering and distracting," his mind felt "overwhelmed with melancholy" and had been beset with all manner of "damping doubts and fears"—fears that drove the young minister to the verge of despair.[138]

However private his own account, Brainerd had stylized to the point of making barren the themes embedded in the Puritan self-history. His autobiography remains one of the last cast in purely spiritual tones, without the intrusion of any particular psychological explanation beyond what the metaphors of melancholy and the imagery of the Bible allowed. Franklin's *Autobiography*, Emerson's *Nature*, and Thoreau's *Walden* would approach such matters quite differently and more freshly, and without any obvious trauma. Brainerd simply offered himself in terms then familiar: he felt cold, dejected, gloomy, exhausted, terribly exhausted from his strenuous work; he lay weak from study, impotent and dry, depressed, brokenhearted, barren, confused, pressed and oppressed with his burden of work, hurrying about in wasted labor. He readily described his shame and his sense of bodily filth.[139]

Brainerd offered a case of conscience, to be sure, at least within the terms set by Perkins, Ames, and seventeenth-century Puritan psychomachy. Given those terms, Brainerd's phrases became acceptable to Edwards for the very nature of their stereotype: "I was much dejected, kept much alone, and sometimes envied the birds and beasts their happiness." "I was from my youth somewhat sober, and inclined to melancholy . . . but do not remember anything of conviction of sin." "About six at night, I lost my way in the wilderness, and wandered over rocks and mountains, down hideous steeps, through swamps, and most dreadful and dangerous places."[140] These terms safely characterized Brainerd, for they hardly made him a hysterical character.

Given the fears the Awakening had induced of men and women running mad, and the loss of sense in America of the meaning melancholy was supposed to draw, Edwards felt the need to defend his friend and thereby to re-establish the long journey of conversion that the melancholy expressed. Edwards himself had been at least partially responsible for disestablishing the interrelation of any kind of pathology and spiritual conversion by going so far in his own enthusiasm as to publish, in the early heat of the Awakening, two cases that his readers might take as extreme or at least as nonsensical: Abigail Hutchinson, a young woman who had traveled from horror to fainting enthusiasm in what appeared a matter of moments; and most particularly Phebe Bartlet, a four-year-old girl who had taken to her closet five or six times each day to pray, feeling quite assured that she stood damned to hell until in "smiling countenance, 'Mother,' she said, 'the kingdom of heaven is come to me!' "[141]

Edwards celebrated this child's terror and accepted her conversion. With regard to Brainerd he became more careful. Indeed Edwards, through Brainerd's diary, attempted to write again of the weariness the journey was supposed to create, noting in the young minister the "one thing," that he remained "so prone to *melancholy*." "Christian experience," Edwards said, for too many "is little else besides melancholy vapours disturbing the brain." Melancholy, however, presented a model of behavior, in that Brainerd himself appeared "*discerning* and *judicious*." His laboriousness removed him from the hysterical habit of mind of those who could certainly become silly: the "gay and sanguine" who, if religiously inclined, became prone to sudden enthusiasms and "whimsical conceits." A religious experience such as that, for Edwards, was indeed imaginary. Before the reader now, Edwards explained, stood a man "most worthy of imitation," a case of benefit for the "careful observer."[142] Edwards was asking desperately for a repetition of a familiar text.

Brainerd became rather an alter ego for Edwards in that Edwards found in the young man his own portrait deeply hued, at least in regard to the melancholy that Edwards had claimed for his own youth.[143] In his youth Edwards had hoped to trace a traditional form of conversion. He had begun his own diary at nineteen, in December of 1722, searching for the preparatory steps of the transformation he sought. The steps he remained unable to find "exactly." He attempted nevertheless to model his experience properly, to find his terror and conviction of sin, and was thus "about three o'clock, overwhelmed with melancholy"—the word intoned as though spoken in ritual. He felt "dull, dry and dead." Less formalized in building his character were his thoughts: he felt "all this time decaying," wasting away in "listlessness and sloth," and thus wrote of his need to stay "so careful to improve time"—"precious time"—"to do everything quick, and in as short a time as I possibly can." Like Cotton Mather, Edwards set out to keep an "account." He would "live in continual mortification, without ceasing, . . . even to weary myself thereby"; he would deny himself in eating, drinking, sleeping, never expecting ease, rest, or "vacation time." When things seemed "out of order," he would work; when violently beset with evil thoughts he could not rid his head of, he promised to perform sums in arithmetic. He would analyze his dreams, work out a complicated set of resolutions, encode them, and then bring one to mind at the proper occasion. He would work himself, as he thought he did, until he "broke"—do anything, in other words, to kill "the old man."[144] He would become a machine, even while observing that such a machine always broke.

Even within the confines of his Puritanism, Edwards distinguished himself as a man who "*lived by rule*." Even his biographer Samuel Hopkins, who first brought together and published Edwards's "Private Writings," thought this type of living a bit alien to his own late eighteenth-century generation. Rising by four or five in the morning, Edwards spent thirteen hours alone in his own study. Yet others thought of him as Edwards thought of himself, as weakly and delicate—"his animal spirits were low"—for which, Edwards said, he watched his diet exactly. He remained reserved—"stiff and unsociable," as others thought—while he kept guard over his tongue, being careful to stay slow and exact in his speech. Edwards "practiced," Hopkins related, "that conscientious exactness which was perspicuous in all his ways."[145] In that, he made his character appear strange.

Edwards's character was nevertheless proper, and properly described, being opened for analysis by Hopkins as if such a life were a text to be explicated and applied. The minister was defective certainly in "conversation,"[146] but not in the manner of the conversion he won. A child always weak before God, Edwards still had never found all the steps of his conversion, particularly the terror that he had sought in his youth when opening his diary at nineteen. Edwards then had finally to admit that if he should die, he would die fearfully, and for lack of having experienced anything much in the way of fear itself. He had failed to experience "conversion in those particular steps, wherein the people of New England, and anciently the Dissenters of Old England, used to experience it." The important word is "used," for Edwards implied even then that he had not lived necessarily out of step at all. He would search, he wrote, until he got to the bottom of the matter, but the matter itself had become historical in that New Englanders "used to be converted in those steps," not necessarily that he now should be. Indeed, when Edwards came twenty years later to reconstruct his conversion, he quite freely said that nothing in his experience could be called "by the name of terror." The only "kind of vision, or fix'd ideas" that he mentioned consisted "of being alone in the mountains, . . . sweetly conversing with Christ, and wrapt and swallowed up in God."[147]

When he came to write of the nature of conversion in others, this lack of discovery, this stepping out, as it were, from the accepted text of conversion, forced the issue, and the void drove Edwards to find alternatives. In place of "a certain order" of conversion, Edwards offered a pragmatic evaluation. He termed the evaluation "Practice." One needed not to copy earlier stories of conversion, of which Edwards had become quite suspicious, but to examine the fruits of an experience—to make an inquiry, in other words, into whether or not an experience was, other than laborious, working.[148]

At the height of the Awakening, Edwards had seen the fancy let loose, or at least seemingly so. In a competing structure of conversion men and women, as he only too well remembered, had not only failed to locate any discernible steps but were also refusing to search. They appeared to deny the very labor Edwards thought so important to the experience of conversion itself. Edwards had to make clear, in a manner that Shepard or Hooker had not, some simple points of inspection: it became "no sign one way or the other" if the affections appeared gracious or seemed "raised very high"; if they produced some "great effects on the body"; or they caused one to speak incessantly of religion; or came seemingly without one's contrivance; or brought into the mind certain texts of scripture; or unfolded, indeed, in a certain order. Clearly the point of Edwards's attack became the variety of experience Shepard had called noisy; a superficial impression of transformation that for Edwards expressed a phantom or delusion. Counterfeiting impressions worked within the phantasy (within the mind's power to build images) and created "inward whispers, and immediate suggestions of facts and events, pleasant voices, beautiful images"—an experience, in other words, such as the "raptures" of "raving enthusiasts." As a correspondent from Scotland had noted to Edwards: "There is this difference in this parish betwixt the awakening last year and now; that some of their bodies have been affected by their fears, in a convulsive or hysteric way."[149]

If hysteria clearly impressed no sign at all, what of melancholy, what, in Edwards's words, of Satan's own operations "in those dreadful and horrid suggestions, . . . vain and fruitless frights and terrors, which he is the author of"? And what became of those in whom no immediate hand of the devil seemed visible, those "of a weak and vapory habit of body, and the brain weak, and easily susceptive of impression"? "For we know that alterations in the body, do immediately excite no other sort of ideas in the mind, but external ideas, or ideas of the outward senses" (like those Satan wrought, working upon the phantasy through the animal spirits rather than upon the soul itself).

> And this seems to be the reason why persons that are under the disease of melancholy, are commonly so visibly and remarkably subject to the suggestions and temptations of Satan: that being a disease which peculiarly affects the animal spirits, and is attended with weakness of that part of the body which is the fountain of the animal spirits, even the brain, which is, as it were, the seat of the phantasy. . . . And thus Satan, when he casts in those horrid suggestions into the minds of melancholy persons, in which they have no hand themselves, he does it by exciting imaginary ideas [fixed ideas], either of some dreadful words or sentences, or other horrid outward ideas.[150]

What, in other words, of Edwards himself, at least insofar as he called himself vapid, weak, and melancholy?

The Awakening was, to Edwards's mind, attended much with melancholy, with "melancholy humor," as he said, evidently "mixed." An extraordinarily careful reading of Edwards's words is required, to find that he considered such melancholy within the framework of Perkins, Ames, and the American ministers such as Shepard whom he had assiduously read. Edwards appeared to attack the malaise as making wrought false terrors and needless fears, for melancholy created only a notion and not a true conviction of sin. He distinguished carefully between melancholy terror and spiritual conviction—the one a function of the body, constitution, and temper, and the other a function of the heart, soul, and conscience—but so, as Edwards noted, had Perkins; again, it became a question of distinctions. Edwards appeared to attack the melancholics themselves, writing that "One knows not how to deal with such persons, [for] they turn everything that is said to them the wrong way." The case in point for the Awakening—and the case would become famous—remained Edwards's uncle, Joseph Hawley, a man "overwhelmed with melancholy," as Edwards wrote, who did in fact slit his throat. "After this, multitudes in this [Northampton] and other towns seemed to have it strongly suggested to 'em, and pressed upon 'em, to do as this person had done. And many that seemed to be under no melancholy, some pious persons that had no special darkness, or doubts about the goodness of their state, nor were under any special trouble or concern of mind about anything spiritual or temporal, yet had it urged upon 'em, as if somebody had spoke to 'em, 'cut your own throat . . . *now, NOW!*'"[151]

The terror in itself certainly expressed no sign of conversion, one way or the other. Clearly, however, when Edwards noted that "pious persons" seemingly innocent, persons with no "special darkness, or doubts," suddenly fell and felt a strange temptation, the melancholy worked for their own damned good, or gracious good, if they so resisted. As Edwards had written earlier in his narrative of the Awakening: "But it has been very remarkable, that there has been far less of this mixture in this time of extraordinary blessing, than there was wont to be in persons under awakenings at other times." Edwards's reader could well take his words as a denial of the melancholy experience altogether, but his words expressed something other than a denial, for writing when he felt most optimistic about the light the Awakening had brought, Edwards was speaking of persons once so entangled. He spoke of men and women now about to set upon their "liberty," their apparently "unprofitable and hurtful" distresses gone, Satan seemingly restrained at the very last moment, "the latter end of this wonderful time, when God's Spirit [having only appeared] was about to withdraw." The whole of the text, corporately applied, had not changed in its broadest structure. The satanic blackness had to precede the now dawning light.

Edwards could be misread, so much did he attack as false—as no sign at all—the horrid impressions that melancholy wrought. Melancholy remained a fancy—it was physical, temporal, and humoral—and it created almost mad impressions when it erupted and worked on the weakened brain. It was a fluid to be expelled, just as its fancies were to be resisted; it appeared indeed satanic, and that remained the point, for Satan could never touch the soul or spirit of the true children of God.[152] However much Edwards worked his distinctions, distilling from terror an actual conviction of sin, he held to the idea that a corrupted bodily humor and spiritual conversion did properly combine. Melancholy still offered itself as an otherness that a saint need face.

Recounting the conversion of his wife Sarah, for example, and with the example of Hawley still fresh in his mind, Edwards offered Sarah as another "often subject to melancholy, and at times almost overborne with it." Sarah had passed through the same foul "sink," but her estrangement had ended when her melancholy was seen for its nature, for what indeed it was. Sarah Edwards prevailed now "without one hour's melancholy or darkness from that day to this; vapors have had great effects on the body, such as they used to have before, but the soul has always been out of their reach." Constancy came (her own "great exactness of life") as she applied herself to her secular calling or "worldly business" that she found "as good as prayers." She used work to replace travail, and she appeared more ascetic. She refused "affecting" and "dress," or to give herself to show. "Now if such things are . . . the fruits of a distempered brain, let my brain be evermore possessed." If her struggle appeared a "distraction," then Edwards wished that the world would become so seized. The pragmatics of Sarah Edwards's conversion stood tested in the profitability of the final work she wrought.[153]

The question became the working—what, if anything, the wilderness produced. Edwards refashioned conversion into a vertical list of twelve signs, replacing the divines' narrative series of steps, because the truth of conversion now manifested itself only in a final "action." What Perkins had called "anomie" and Edwards called "alienation" expressed the distance the self discovered between its hopes and its own actions. A "moral distance" existed when the self discovered itself caught in false labor. Edwards, then, thought it particularly important to test the self through action to find whether or not the self's labors—including the story that one made of one's conversion—remained profit-filled or estranged. "Assurance is not to be obtained so much by self-examination"—that had become too much of a show—"as by action." Judgment now relied not on a person explaining the "method" or telling "his story of the manner of his conversion"; instead, "his works will be brought forth, as evidence of what he is."

Edwards transferred the morphology of conversion, the sequel of steps that he had failed to find in his own life, into practice, shifting conversion from a narrative to a life as expressed in production. It still remained, however, a question of whether the labor undertaken was merely "external," like "the motion and action of the body, without including anything else"—labor, that is, without an "aim or intention," such as that of a clock or "the motions of the body in a convulsion." Such efforts expressed outward, inhuman actions merely compelled—the alienated labor, say, of Bunyan's pushing and shoving of his arms and elbows. For Edwards the distinction lay in the meaning that a distant treasure assumed only when a man evidenced his grace by leaving home, but never with the motions of his body alone as his consideration—never, that is, without his purpose in mind as to why his body moved.[154]

Melancholy offered itself as an exquisite metaphor of alienated labor, for as a difference from faith, the strange temptations and bodily works showed the falseness of the self's own action, and the works demonstrated the external nature of Satan. For the children of God, the wilderness remained this other, beyond the soul and inner nature. When defined, the surprising temptations and automatic works—the rituals undertaken without purpose in mind—made visible the necessary alienation of the self. As a metaphor of spiritual disease, melancholy allowed the fancy of compelling acts and obsessing thoughts to be seen: both the alienation inherent in senseless works—works as compulsive as a clock, as inhuman as a machine—and the alienation inherent in false terrors; terrors held without any truth to their natures, held as foreign to the self, held, that is, without any real convictions, without any real conscience of one's internal sin. The terrors were horrid yet strange, and for all the fear such terrors wrought, there always remained the sense that such fear was false. The terror became the "Legall feare" of which Perkins had spoken—a part, as he had said, of the mere works of preparation. This fear opposed the feeling that followed upon grace: again the "Evangelical sorrow, . . . a griefe for sinne, because it is sinne."

Edwards remained quite aware of this important distinction so thoroughly embedded in Puritan thought: "The famous Mr. Perkins distinguishes between those sorrows that come through convictions of conscience, and melancholic passions rising only from mere imaginations."[155] Clockwork mechanisms and foreign fears allowed the self to understand its estrangement; the works and methods allowed the self to know its difference, to realize its emptiness and shallow fears, and thus to actualize its internal and gracious definition. The setting of the self against savage others, and the objectification of the self's own sin in distant works and foreign thoughts, did not allow the self projection, or cleansing by placing its guilt upon the acts and ways of foreign others, such as (in Puritan captivity narratives) savages and agents of Satan—aliens then to be fought in a repression of one's own sin—at least not as an end.[156] Rather, the alienation allowed inner light and inner understanding. The objectification of evil allowed the self to see itself and thus to see the nature of the evil that one could never hold apart from the self. Works and sudden fears came to be seen for the estrangement they expressed—to be seen for what they were: fictitious means for achieving grace, imaginary ways for understanding sin. In this manner, then, Edwards preserved the meaning of a melancholy experience. He placed the self in an estranged environment (akin to the setting of a Puritan captivity narrative) of such a kind that the self might experience its saving alienation.

With the distance closed, the alienation ended, and a work undertaken with purpose in mind, that work itself could become a significant sign. In the cases of his wife Sarah and himself, Edwards used a metaphor of work for the conversion won, the practice to follow upon melancholic depression. Edwards became adamant on the point. Thomas Gillespie, for example, a correspondent in Scotland who had read Edwards on the trial of temptation, asked the following of the Northampton minister:

> What should one do who is incessantly harassed by Satan; can by no means keep him out of his mind; has used all means prescribed in Scripture and suggested by divines for resistance, known to him, in vain . . .? what would you advise such a person to do? what construction, think you, should he put on the sovereign conduct and dispensation of Heaven toward him? I have occasion to be conversant about this case practically demonstrated, of many years continuance, without interruption.

Did "all things," Gillespie concluded, "work for good"?[157]

In asking for a "construction," Gillespie was asking for a new interpretation of what had happened, perhaps to himself, perhaps to a friend. The case of conscience no longer held together for the Scottish evangelical, at least not according to its former structure.

Edwards replied and asked for distinctions: what kind, exactly, were the temptations—were they in fact melancholic and therefore horrid to the mind of the victim, or did the temptations merely express the person's natural lusts? If the former, then they worked for the good—if the temptations, that is, were resisted. But Gillespie was unsatisfied, if not confused. He replied in greater detail, as though he could not believe such horror worked for anyone's good:

> A person finds himself beset by evil angels (what if I remember right *Voetius* [Gisbertus Voetius, a seventeenth-century Dutch Reformed theologian] terms *obsessio*, and one in that situation *obsessus*); they incessantly break into his body and mind. . . . They do all they can, perpetually to seize, defile and discourage; he is conscious of the whole transaction . . . ; but all is in vain, no relief for him, relish of divine things wore off the mind, no comfort, it rendered callous by cruel constant buffetings, he cries, but the Lord hears not.

So rushed became Gillespie's words (of which this is but a small portion) that, as he pulled away from earlier divines' reasoned texts, he left their advice broken and scattered. He knew the constructions that had formerly applied, but his words, and the freedom that his style assumed, indicated that, for Gillespie at least, such interpretations now lay sundered. Gillespie and Edwards now appeared worlds apart, for Gillespie wanted advice, some sort of psychiatric information so that his patient could "recover." He was approaching the case without ever calling it a case of conscience. He wrote of the spirit as "broken," but in another, more secular sense of how that word might be used. "[M]edical, moral and religious means" had not worked; there appeared no comfort, and his patient's suffering remained in vain.[158]

Edwards gave his last reply: "I don't very well know what to say further." He mentioned his own insufficiency "as a counsellor in such like cases, . . . : If the Lord do not help, whence should we help?" He mentioned the therapeutics of Perkins and Baxter, then set about repairing his own idea of the pragmatic test of whether or not a conversion existed. Edwards offered only "One thing" that he thought of great importance: such a patient should bear his general and particular calling without diversion, "properly ordering, proportioning and timing all sorts of duties."[159] Edwards was advising not so much physic, though physic worked certainly as a part of the plan. He was attempting to gather back the idea of work as an application of the self in a significant calling.

Edwards examined psychic labors such as Gillespie had described and found the alienation he, unlike Gillespie, demanded. Here was the withdrawal of God and the hiding of His face until men became sensible of significant things: of their guilt, their misery, their need for God's help, their weakness that only mercy could cure. "He found him in a desert land, and in the waste howling wilderness; he led him about, he instructed him, he kept him as the apple of his eye." Whether the forty years for the children of Israel or the forty days for Christ, a time of trial revealed the land in which God worked, the incredible waste that brought forth fruit.

Puritan psychomachy required this breaking of the self's prisons: "And I will break the pride of your power; and I will make your heaven as iron, and your earth as brass: And your strength shall be spent in vain." Pride—"Because I knew that thou *art* obstinate, and / thy neck *is* an iron sinew, and thy brow brass"—terror next, then only the memory remains of the dry places passed. The deliverance then is to appear as the psalm says:

> I will go before thee, and make the crooked places straight: I will break in pieces the gates of brass, and cut in sunder the bars of iron:
>
> And I will give the treasures of darkness, and hidden riches of secret places, that thou mayest know that I, the LORD, which call *thee* by thy name, *am* the God of Israel.

The alienation remained to be passed through. The saint was to be sent, as Perkins had explained, into the place chosen by God for the temptation of his children, but then the saint would return. He would refuse to remain hidden in some strange monastic or hermetical land.[160]

Martin Luther had portrayed the monastic life as one of estranged labor—as Erikson brilliantly showed—dipping water by using a sieve, rolling a rock with the rock always returning, "wearing oneself out with an inexhaustible and a useless labor." Never, Luther insisted, was one rid of temptation, of "mental depression, blasphemy, unbelief, or despair." Never did the Law prove in itself enough to remove the despair: "For one law always produces ten more, until they grow into infinity," and one could "never find enough works to make his conscience peaceful. . . . Therefore his conscience can never become sure, but he must continually doubt and think this way: 'You have not sacrificed correctly; you have not prayed correctly; you have omitted something; you have committed this or that sin.'"[161]

It was upon reading Luther's *Commentary on the Epistle to the Galatians* (rather as Winthrop had read Perkins) that Bunyan said he found at last his "condition." The book appeared written from his own heart. He "doth most gravely . . . , in that book debate of the rise of these temptations, namely Blasphemy, Desperation, and the like, shewing that the law of *Moses*, as well as the Devil, Death, and Hell, hath a very great hand therein; the which at first was very strange to me." Other than the Bible, the commentary became Bunyan's favorite book, fit, he said, for the wounded conscience.[162] The book could make him understand.

Whenever the Law became a rigid structure—the absurdity of compelling actions and punctilious fears that Luther displayed—the Law, like Christian's fear of Mount Sinai, could fall on one's head. Luther had established in life and text a movement out from the Law's enclosing walls: a movement from the monastery to the daily world itself, from a life behind iron closure, or the prison in which Bunyan lay, to worldly ascetic labor. The movement created a new world economy, as Max Weber took the significance of that movement to be: "For when asceticism was carried out of monastic cells into everyday life, and began to dominate worldly morality, it did its part in building the tremendous cosmos of the modern economic order." The removal also created a mental form, one describing the self's immaterial conversion. A passage opened out from the ascetic or obsessional estrangement that Luther described as the monastic life into what Luther first termed "*Beruf*" or calling. This was to be a profession of faith signified not by works but by work.[163] It was Edwards's practice. Intermingled as life and text, a pattern of the self's alienation and return to the world had been set.

In England John Winthrop wrote in his *Experiencia*: "I . . . must not ayme at a condition retyred from the world and free from temptations, but to know that the life which is most exercised with tryalls and temptations is the sweetest, and will prove the safest." "I resolve," Winthrop wrote to himself, "to keepe a better watche, and to holde under the fleshe by temperate diet, and diligence in my callinge, for I founde that there was no peace in any other course." The fruit of "idleness . . . [is] shame and guiltinesse." Worldly work could prove security, though in Hooker's phrase it might also prove another crazy hold. Was peace so easily won as a fruit of the self's new labor? Or would these words of recreating the self through worldly endeavors prove themsleves a cliché?

In his *Magnalia Christi Americana*, Cotton Mather considered these questions. Mather opened the life of his dead brother Nathanael ("Nathaniel" in the nineteenth-century text) by presenting a psychological history, perhaps the first so composed in America. Mather was writing biography rather than spiritual confession, composing a case of conscience with a single personality placed in a historical frame, and all to demonstrate the efficacy of a young man's labors. His text, one of killing one's natural self in work, completed the writing on calling that Winthrop had begun. Working within his chosen structure—"HIS INDUSTRY," "HIS PIETY," "HIS DEATH"—Mather presented Nathanael as a personality appropriate to an unplotted land, "an instance of unusual *industry* and no common *piety*" such that Nathanael did indeed work himself to death by attempting to build mental structures across the face of a chaotic American nature. Mather would have his brother close a wilderness that, ultimately, only the labors of Christ would deliver.

Mather showed his brother's "bookish," "plodding" manner and demonstrated once again, in the enormity of the very American history that he was then compiling, the strength of his own endeavor. Mather demonstrated the ease Nathanael found in being "hard," the manner of his thinking more and again before allowing any sleep. He showed the work his brother had undertaken in constructing almanacs, various types of calculations, and a chronology—works, that is, upon time, history, and death. "His *chronology* was exact unto a wonder," as indeed was Nathanael's "*adversaria*" itself. Nathanael had left this last document behind in his closet, and Mather interspersed the diary's relation throughout his discussion, using his brother's melancholy to cut against the almanacs and the wondrous calculations performed by a young man facing the terrors of "this American wilderness."

The calculations made of building a safe retreat in the middle of the American wilderness ended when Thoreau presented the expenses and profits of Walden. The work failed to pay.

> Of all the things which ever troubled him, I know not whether any were more grievious than the "blasphemous injections" which, like *fiery* venemous darts, inflam'd sometimes his very soul within him.
>
> It may be some testimony of *sincerity*, when persons are not a little *afflicted* for, as well as assaulted with, "blasphemous imaginations" about God; which rise within us in contradiction to all that reverance of him which we know not how to lay aside.
>
> This person on his death-bed complained to me, that *Horrenda de Deo* . . . buzzing about his mind, had been one of the bitterest of all his trials; and I find his private papers [now, again, made quite public, as they could only be intended] making sad lamentations over the miseries of this annoyance. You shall read how he did encounter these *fiends*.

This melancholy of mind was, as Mather said, one of the "*signs*" that Nathanael became, as he thought himself, "*deodatus melancholicus*. This became his way of—*living*, shall I say, or of dying?" Mather could barely contain the irony as his text revolved upon itself. The calculations, like any such industry, were consumed in this, the "old man['s]" death.[164]

Thus Edwards offered the case of David Brainerd and, to Gillespie, he offered the case of himself. Edwards was also about to be "cast" again into a wilderness, whence he remained unsure. Because they would have nothing less than the open communion that Edwards's grandfather Solomon Stoddard, had given to them a half-century earlier, Edwards's congregation had refused to accept his desire that it should reinstate some sign, however minimal, of saving grace, some profession of conversion prior to receiving the sacraments. He had been asked by his parishioners to leave. In June of 1750, the Northampton congregation fired their minister. The necessity to make a written work out of one's conversion again tore itself apart in this irony that consumed Edwards.

What remained sure to Edwards, if not to Gillespie, in the last of the books that Edwards submitted for publication (the defense that Edwards made of the doctrine of original sin) was the suffering that the work of conversion must still involve: "Another exclamation against the doctrine is, that it tends to . . . promote *melancholy* and *gloominess* of mind. . . . and tis fit, it should." What remained sure, as Shepard had said, was the labor of conversion, "not wishing," "shedding a teare at a Sermon, or blubbering now and then in a corner. . . . But it is a tough work, a wonderful hard matter to bee saved." It was the work of those content to be called "Precisions, and fools, and crazie brains," those who would "know the worst of themselves," hear the words that others said led only to suicide or distraction. But "madnesse" for Shepard stood as arrogance, ignorance, impiety, idolatry, security, sleepiness. Sanity for Edwards opened the eyes to what stood plainly there. One then labored hard in the face of the sin—a matter of working, if only to show the madness of man's self and his natural works.[165] In Edwards's last exile one finds the results of ever making a demand for any final sign.

It became a matter of choice: between works and grace, works and faith, or, for Emerson, between "works and days." The choice followed only upon an experience of the alienation of labor, the distance set between the self and its desired object. "When God is about to turn the earth into a paradise," Edwards concluded, "he don't begin his work where there is some good growth already, but in a wilderness, where nothing grows, and nothing is to be seen but dry sand and barren rocks."[166] Edwards was speaking of why the millennium would dawn in America, the most barren and void of lands. Emerson, too, found his wilderness place by casting himself into "our nineteenth century [that] is the age of tools": into "the vast production and manifold application of iron" that Emerson said was "new." Here one beheld "lucifer matches," "the McCormick reaper," "sulphuric ether," all disrupting "the answering brain and nervous structure"—all the machinery, as Emerson phrased it, that was unmaking the man. "These tools have some questionable properties. They are reagents. Machinery is aggressive. The weaver becomes a web, the machinist a machine. If you do not use the tools, they use you. All tools are in one sense edge-tools, and dangerous." The occasion had changed, but the choice remained: "Works and days were offered us, and we took works."[167]

Emerson rephrased Edwards's idea of life beginning in crossings, that "human life is made up of such transits. There can be no greatness without abandonment." By abandonment, Emerson almost meant play, and he could well have changed his "works" to "work," so seemingly new appeared Emerson's idea that work itself was becoming alien. The pattern remained, however, the meeting of the self with alien beings, whether hobgoblins, devils, savages, robots, or machines, and whether the alienation itself lay within a howling land, or in the industrial corpse of a wasted land. The structure, in other words, is archetypal, the compelling nature of which Paul had spoken, the sense of being acted upon as if the self had become a machine. History would provide the emblems, the occasion for speaking of one's alienation, but history would not cause the alienation to be. Life was to remain, as Emerson said, speaking of Tantalus, "always in crisis," "the new man always . . . standing on the brink of chaos."[168]

Among those for whom records remain, a person can only have written out his life, or like Nathanael Mather, had it composed by another. Writing is never to be differentiated as to the degree of its composition, some being deemed spontaneous, automatic, closer to the person of the author, and some not. The words here of Emerson reflect not the making strange of the American character, not the fact of a psychopathology, but the making of a national spiritual text. The text extends to the rewriting of the current psychobiographer.

The psychohistorian serves American identity when he portrays early American history as a peculiar quest driven by struggle, a struggle peculiar for the very reason that its terms become psychic. Neither economy nor society, but a nation's particular psychology, propels history. Thus the psychohistory becomes ours as the psychomachia became the Puritans', in that an individual's anguish comes to reflect a culture's malaise. The Puritan author used his own history, his own psychoanalysis, for just that. And for the Puritan who found his wilderness land—his errand to be completed in a physical land—his person, as Bercovitch writes, not only became a self and that self thereby a type, but that type became American as well. For Bercovitch, in pulling the jeremiad that Perry Miller defined out of the latter seventeenth century, has offered the spiritual autobiography—the "auto-American-biography"—as a genre unique to America, peculiar in its weaving of fact and fancy and in the narrative's use of an estranged self as a social exemplum. The narrative of Puritan conversion offers the beginning of an American literature. It is the writing of "History as a Novel, The Novel as History." In an "unscheduled scatalogical solo," the "antistar" begins: "Excretion, in fact, was his preoccupation of the night."

Now we may leave *Time* in order to find out what happened.

IN THE DEN

Here in *Armies of the Night*, Norman Mailer begins his narrative on "the steps of the Pentagon."

The language of Puritan conversion offered the script of a new psychology—a language that could contain nineteenth-century American writers. As a structure of discourse, however, Victorian authors could only work against the Puritans' words. The language, that is, worked to its own end in a series of its own transformations.

Perceptions change as to what behaviors mean, what they signify, and words unfold as persons try to reset meanings. Phrases turn from the serious to the shallow and then often fade from view while others, differently seen, come to replace the original meanings. Imitation becomes significant, then, when the attempt at mimesis fails, as the attempt always does.

In remarking on the "textualizing of nature," Joseph Riddel writes: "The poem as 'document' throws together . . . old texts, mapping them, so as to 're-enact' their making." The rewriting is to occur, however, only "with a difference."[169] In a contextual approach—using multiple lives rather than the undifferentiated singularity or "uniqueness" of biography—meanings are generated across lives in relationships, substitutions, the presence always of a possible "other" word. Such is a prosopopoeia, drawing a life against another that is not visibly present. This is the synchronic structure of difference that for Ferdinand de Saussure creates the understanding of language (the distinction a sound achieves only when the mind places that sound against a silent but internally voiced image). There is also the difference history creates, the chronology or diachrony that comes in tracing a movement—here, the Puritans' writing of conversion. The inexactness of a copy constitutes history, for the inability to repeat *is* history. After the death of Edwards, an American scholar like the elder Henry James could turn violently upon such "Calvinism," holding its language in hate. Yet, at the same time, he could re-embrace the significance of the type of conversion Edwards had won.

2

Conscience to Moral Psychology

The Elder Henry James

> What is guilt? A stain upon the soul. And it is a point of vast interest, whether the soul may contract such stains . . . from deeds which may have been plotted and resolved upon, but which, physically, have never had existence. Must the fleshly hand, and visible frame of man, set its seal to the evil designs of the soul, in order to give them their entire validity against the sinner?
>
> Nathaniel Hawthorne,
> "Fancy's Showbox: A Morality" (1837)

When Jonathan Edwards left Northampton for the frontier village of Stockbridge, he left ostensibly because, once again, his congregation had refused to reinstate, in some small measure, the spiritual relation that New England churches had begun to require a century before. His grandfather, Solomon Stoddard, having ended the practice in Northampton, favored a more evangelical and homogeneous church admission that he termed his "harvests." The appeal of mass revival spread from the Connecticut Valley, and fed by a transatlantic religious awakening, the harvests eventually developed into the Great Awakening that, in Northampton, Edwards himself led.

Edwards watched as the repeating seas of revival broke churches into factions and engulfed the professions of conversion in hysteria. The oral relations of a melancholy struggle that had corporately bound the lives of the early saints in New England, and that had served as New England's first and most important social literature, vanished. Edwards's attempt, in the aftermath of the Awakening, to replant the personally crafted conversion failed, though he had attempted to get from his parishioners hardly more than an open confession of faith. His Northampton congregation refused even that, and left the minister to walk westward, alone, into another wilderness.

The conscience of the saint would no longer receive its public address. Swept aside by the stereotypical conversions of the revivals—and to Edwards's mind, by a new faith in the benign works of an "Arminianism" he abhorred—the act of voicing a story of sin was necessarily transformed. The corporate relations of a long journey of spiritual conversion would scatter now into separate and far more private lives.

Also, of course, by the end of the eighteenth century, the humoral psychology of melancholy no longer worked to explain the saint's peculiar temptations of sin. The New England saint, so to speak, would now have to move out of this new City of Destruction, left in the wake of the Great Awakening, and into a new moral wilderness. There he would have to face his temptations anew. He would have to re-explain why God implanted terrors into the minds of the most moral men alive. When he encountered strange assaults upon his conscience, he would have to struggle to redefine just why his good behavior was so easily broken.

This struggle for new definitions found its expression in the life and writings of the elder Henry James. Necessitated by a desire to leave altogether the past—the "Calvinist" or "Orthodox" grip that he believed had destroyed his life—James drove himself into a lonely and at times angry separation. In his isolation (an obscurity that remains to this day), he constructed a spiritual confession, but with such eccentric words that even the few contemporary readers of his books and essays found him hard to understand. He had become one of the first of the alienated artists in America, and in that respect his life reflects the changing practice of telling the story of one's strangeness.

James attributed his estrangement to Calvinism. In the course of his writing he struck out against its authority again and again, and with such vehemence that, within early Victorian America, no recorded life appears to contrast more sharply with the conscience of the Puritan saint. No recorded life, in other words, so clearly outlines the use the Puritans had found in confronting an outside terror. For James, the terror was Calvinist theology itself. The arduous conversion that Edwards had watched shatter, James would attempt to re-create, and he would do so by employing the grip Calvinist "morality." He would use its authority and its terrible works to destroy himself unto another life.

The elder James assiduously studied Edwards, and like Edwards desired to preserve the understanding that conversion had to be a self-destructive process. Like Edwards, James set himself against easy moments of religious revival and benign transformations portrayed, he felt, by friends such as Emerson. While Edwards could work brilliantly within readily accessible spiritual traditions, James could not. What theological interest remained in America centered not upon the moral destruction of the self and the inefficacy of works—the effacements James demanded—but upon a philosophy of calculating rewards. Additionally, the flowering of an American literature that transposed the spiritual autobiography into works such as *Walden* and *Nature* and some of the darker tales of Hawthorne, fashioned the conscience, as far as James was concerned, into a fiction. The psychology (and psychopathology) of religion that his son William founded in America did not yet exist, and thus James found himself alone, embedded in the need to give confession to his conscience while refusing, he thought, all Calvinist conceptions. More than any other early nineteenth-century American intellectual, the elder James placed the terror of his conscience in writing, but all the while he had to struggle to redefine, or as he thought to reject, previous understandings of what such terror meant. Even in his obscurity, then, James stands as a bridge from Edwards's writings on the religious affections to his son's discovery of a new psychology of religion.

Inheritance

The elder James received his education from Concord idealists. They were Unitarian sons, gently rebellious in tone, who spoke of a perfect transcending Divine, a miracle of light residing within the breast of every man. Writing on the periphery of the transcendentalist circle, James became the friend of Emerson and an acquaintance of Thoreau. In contrast to them, James had received his religious inheritance from Calvinism, and though strident in rebelling against its Presbyterian authority, he refused to write, as he accused Emerson of doing, by removing the shadows that framed man's inner light.

James left behind, after his death in 1882, the manuscript of a spiritual autobiography that was published, in the tradition of Puritan confession, two years later by his son William. James began by describing his own first awakening as it came not in the dawn but in an artificially illuminated night:

I will not attempt to state the year in which I was born [1811], because it is not a fact embraced in my own knowledge [and because, like the Puritan autobiographer, James distained his natural birth], but content myself with saying instead, that the earliest event of my biographic consciousness is that of my having been carried out into the streets one night, in the arms of my negro nurse, to witness a grand illumination in honor of the treaty of peace then just signed with Great Britain.

It was "as if the animus [mind] of the display had been, not to eclipse the darkness, but to make it visible."[1]

The transcendentalists, for James, had forgotten this display that, like the Puritans' fiery dart, made visible not a peace but a war that would awaken souls. "To 'experience religion,' or 'become converted,'" as James thought, "means now not what it once meant, to pass from the noon-tide radiance . . . into the grimmest midnight of spiritual impotence and self-distrust." Within his intellectual circle, James dwelled upon this darkness in words that bothered his transcendental friends, men such as Emerson and Bronson Alcott, for whom the miracle of life did eclipse the tragic.[2] James brought their transcendent ease to question, or at least what he, like his son William, thought of as the once-born healthy-mindedness of Emerson's program, just as Edwards had questioned some of the "hysterical" conversions that the Great Awakening had fashioned.

James was writing of the self's destruction, however, while searching for the terms to replace the Calvinism he thought quite insane. The problem with Calvinism, as James saw it, was the stress it gave to the moral. He insisted that the religion of his own father, William James of Albany, had grown mentally deranged in its effect. As both a theology and a parental cudgel, Calvinism was sending its sons into terror and then breaking their necks in its mill, and because of that, such wretched authority must be left behind. James wrote of himself as a man manufactured to behave properly; then he wrote that his good moral works had shattered in a night of true illumination. By insisting that such moral insanity existed, in other words, James preserved the whole point of the Puritans' religious experience. Like the Puritan saint, James refused to claim that his justification and spiritual birth could ever result from anything that conformed to law. Instead, he cried of the terrible conscience that Calvinism had given to him, then called for the death of everything "moral."

Moving past the Puritans and Edwards, James turned his thoughts on the insufficiency of the moral to a question not only of works but of work. Henry James had written in 1863—in phrases William James quoted twenty years later when he published his father's literary legacy, and then repeated anonymously in his Gifford Lectures in speakng of an ascetic's retreat from the world—that "life is no farce; that it is not genteel comedy even; that it flowers and fructifies on the contrary out of the profoundest tragic depths."[3] The elder James embedded his wilderness—the "unsubdued forest where the wolf howls and every obscene bird of night chatters"—in a passage on toil. Man needed to labor to "vindicate" himself before this sight, rather than to live in a garden or upon his "inheritance, or accumulated ancestral fat." James, actually, was living on exactly that.

From the perspective of at least two of his sons, William and Henry, James was living on nothing at all. To this passage, William appended another of his father's declarations, concerning the "dread omnipotent power of conscience" that "anon scourges me with the lash of its indignation, as the father scourges his refractory heir."[4] As William only too well implied, his father, by refusing the worth of modern occupations, refused the efficacy of ever working his conscience off. On that point, the father and son would battle.

As is apparent, the elder Henry James had become something of a "character." While New England writers like Hawthorne were transposing the darker side of Puritanism into fiction, James was fashioning himself into an exemplum. Like the Mathers, James placed his moral self, most particularly his own too industrious behavior, outside of time, yet rather than creating an acknowledged fiction, he became a type—the Henry James laboring with a conscience that he found a "living death." He contrasted himself with "persons of good hereditary temperament," by whom he primarily meant Emerson, and facing the strictures of conscience that he claimed for his father's orthodoxy, he set death against life: he "soon . . . [began] to suspect," he said, "that the demands of conscience are not so easily satisfied; soon discover[ed] in fact that it [conscience] is a ministration of death exclusively, and not of life."[5]

With this beast held in his mind, James entered into a long struggle. He accepted the transcendentalists' own ascetic quest, and when he did, he accepted its ascetic completely. He lived as Emerson would only preach. James would reach for the infinite by transcending his senses; he would deny his body and thereby eliminate the last of his material bonds. He would forego, as Emerson had written, the "penny-wisdom" of calculation, the categorizing and analyzing of the "understanding" as opposed to "reason." Emerson, in speaking of this higher reason, gave his own understanding of Kant, but his ideal transcendental stands closer to the words of Edwards:

> I have been before God; and have given myself, all that I am and have to God, so that I am not in any respect my own: . . . this understanding, this Will, these affections that are in me; neither have I any right to this body, or any of its members: no right to this tongue, these hands, nor feet. . . .[6]

James came to this faith when he understood the inability of ever working his conscience out.

Emerson's poet was to be rid of himself by denying not only the sensual but the customary, or historical, as well—the poet's inheritance and ancestral fat. When James translated that erasure into his foregoing of an immediate occupation, it seemed too literal a reading. Whatever was preached, the poet was still to be about his business within his particular calling, as Edwards had demanded. Or like the scholar that Emerson personified, if a man stepped from the pulpit (which Emerson himself had), he could become a scholar of affairs. Even Thoreau, his monastic rituals at Walden complete, left his retreat and returned to Concord.

James stayed in seclusion, working in his chamber without a visible vocation (though he worked there incessantly). The books that he wrote went unread, which only added to the image of his ineffectiveness and incurred the wrath of his sons. The elder James did achieve the otherworldly asceticism that he so desired (the purity of which his son William questioned), but only by living as he wrote that a man should not. He had tied himself to the wealth that his father's quite worldly business had bequeathed.

William James of Albany had died one of the wealthiest men in the state. An austere and frugal merchant and a manufacturer of salt, he had lived a pious life that exemplified an ideal Protestant type. He had never intended for any of his children to receive their inheritance unearned, and this applied particularly to his son Henry, who had turned from his authority and fled. Henry had lived for a while as a rebellious spendthrift and had acquired debts that he was unable to pay, debts that his father refused to buy off. To "discourage" just this "prodigality and vice and [to] furnish an incentive to economy and usefulness," the father had placed his estate in the care of trustees. Henry successfully contested his father's will, got his money, and lived at his ease, a "reprobate" bemoaning the guilt of his class.[7]

Wrapped in this irony, James spoke of the lash of his conscience. He spoke of a pain so great that he envisioned a millennium in which persons would no longer need to barter for money, or gather spiritual credit, or hold themselves to any such calculating God. When America's moral destruction came, no one need placate any longer any petty, authoritarian creature. He spoke of a coming apocalypse that would inflame the moral affairs of the Protestants—the successes, as they thought, of their busyness that were simply the hustlings of men grown spiritually sick.

The elder James's intellectual life spanned the decades from the 1830s to the 1880s. The years were filled with this personal turmoil, and they were marked by one particular crisis. It was the meaning of that crisis that James worked hard to define. James had studied Edwards, the "Jonathan Edwards redivivus" that he always regarded as a needed antidote for modern trends,[8] and he had even studied for a while at Princeton Theological Seminary—that following the death of his father. He had discarded Calvinism, however, as morbid, and now was caught trying to explain. He was clinging, his son William lamented, to theology in a post-theological age, constructing spiritual systems the meanings of which appeared fantastic but twenty years later.[9] Trained to the vocabulary of Edwards, the elder James could never have considered his troubles in terms that his son more easily phrased as the problem of "religion and neurology." He could never consider a psychology or a sociology of religion, for that discourse approached religious experiences as natural phenomena capable of being studied like rock strata or varieties of finches. James, too, would have had to strain to understand a reification like the "Protestant ethic," or to sense the connotations employed when one used the phrase that his son Henry perhaps was the first to use (in 1879): "the New England conscience."[10] He struggled, then, to speak about a particular religious experience (his own "vastation") without on the one hand transcribing the Puritan idea of conversion, or on the other, knowing the new psychology of his son.

As the elder James's disdain for the empirical took him in ever obscurer flights, and as his strange books came to reflect the character of their author, he provided his son William with a model of personal and intellectual endeavor that could only be faced and grappled with. He offered his life, that is, as Shepard and the Mathers had offered theirs. The whole of his writing, an imitation rather than a repetitive copy of past spiritual struggles, becomes an autobiography given in provision to his children and thus made available for them, in turn, to work against.

James had worked so hard to rid his mind of criminal thoughts fixed within his consciousness, that ultimately he refused to work at all. Moral labors were pretense and worldly endeavors were vain. William worked to bring his father's ascetic back into the world of daily endeavor by arguing that such a quest for purity spoke of vanity, if not of neurosis. The father, performing labors that he took to be ridiculous gestures undertaken for a God who demanded only his faith, had lived struggling with his conscience; he had manipulated his thoughts and circumscribed his acts, and all in an effort to placate God in some strange way that he sought to explain. His efforts had failed to pay, as they had to fail if James were to find the meaning of faith. James suffered his vastation not, he thought, as a religious conversion, but not quite as a mental collapse either.

The elder James thus fought to describe the psychology of his moral struggle. He sought to describe the compulsive works that had broken his worldly spirit, thereby quickening his coming union with God. Eventually James did attain the detachment he had always sought; he ended his natural or moral self by starving his body away. His pilgrimage ended in his death, and in the terrible ambivalence of his son. James killed his natural self, a last eradication and final vindication of the type of conscience he had come so to loathe.

Vastation

In the early 1840s, when his son William was two years of age, the elder James, then almost thirty-three, experienced panic. He also felt a sudden deep undercurrent of rage. Within a few seconds he became, he said, like an infant, his self-loathing having stripped him to a sense that now, somehow, he stood closer to God. This moment became his conversion. James, however, required a more secular word to describe his experience, a word that could get past the piety of his father and thereby transcend the language of orthodox religion.

James could not ignore his fright, but neither could he readily describe its meaning. He was sure that his sudden sense of degradation had resulted from "the entire strain of the Orthodox faith" that he had felt bearing down upon him since childhood. He likened the behaviors leading to his crisis to a strange asceticism that had malformed his youth, stripping him of his natural innocence. "It aroused a reflective self-consciousness in me," he said as he looked back at himself, "when I ought by natural right to have been wholly immersed in my senses, and known nothing but the innocent pleasures." James established his right to a childhood of innocence, then declared in astonishment, in a faithful narrative of the surprising work of an estranged God, the "concrete truth" of his experience. "I doubt whether any lad had ever just so thorough and pervading a belief in God's existence as an outside and contrarious force to humanity, as I had. The conviction of his . . . attributes was burnt into me as with a red-hot iron." The iron came like the Puritans' fiery dart to brand his "childish sinews." His natural right to happiness the Calvinist God had destroyed through the "subtle terror of his name."

As James's closest psychological biographer has pointed out, the stamp that this hot iron made not only worked as a metaphor (or name) but also as a physical reality, for James had actually burned his leg in childhood, in an accident at play, and it had been amputated.[11] Two decades later James replaced the foolish child playing with fire with a man struck by a psychological terror. "A lightning flash," like the fireworks that had illuminated the night sky of his first awakening, marked his conviction of sin. James held his conscience, however, and not the body of his sin, responsible for the pain he suffered.

In his own word, James suffered a "vastation." It is a military term meaning a laying to waste. The term also connotes a voiding (analogous to the purging of a humor), but James's vastation served not to drive the devil out but to evacuate his diseased conscience. The word suggested more, however, than the "breakdown" that James also said he had suffered. Culled from the writings of Emanuel Swedenborg, a mining engineer turned mystic, vastation expressed a purification, emptying the self of all its natural filth (or, as Edwards had demanded, releasing the self from its bodily ties). The word thus bridged the sacred and the profane, the Puritans' conversion and mental collapse. Vastation was simply a strange new word for the kind of event that James often referred to as a necessary conversion of waste. A descent was needed into the sinkholes of experience to find the ground for spiritual flight.[12] James had discarded his Calvinism and was carrying about the collected works of Swedenborg, who was now fashionable, and even, for the moment, palatable to Emerson's taste.

James suffered his collapse in the spring of 1844, while living with his family in Windsor, England. He had left for England the preceding fall, from New York, undertaking a commonplace genteel journey. It is not at all clear that James experienced only one such collapse or indeed that the word "collapse" properly connotes what occurred. The breakdown—"my moral death and burial"—served perfectly nevertheless as the turning point that James required to make sense out of his life when he came to reconstruct it thirty-five years later.[13] Shortly after a "comfortable dinner," he recalled, "in a lightning flash as it were—'fear came upon me, and trembling, which made all my bones to shake.'"

> To all appearance it was a perfectly insane and abject terror, without ostensible cause, and only to be accounted for, to my perplexed imagination, by some damned shape squatting invisible to me within the precincts of the room, and raying out from his fetid personality influences fatal to life.[14]

William James repeated this description when he recalled the moment of his own sudden terror that came approximately twenty-five years after his father's fright at Windsor. In his Gifford Lectures of 1901–02, *The Varieties of Religious Experience*, James inserted a small personal narrative no more than five hundred words long—a spiritual autobiography that sits among the many other psychological confessions that James had collected and quoted at length in his lectures. As one might expect, James disguised the identity of the narrator. He mentioned only that he had freely translated the original writing, which he said was in French, and that the author was his "correspondent." James placed the confession, an example of "the worst kind of melancholy," "panic fear," in his lecture on the sick soul. He spoke of "prospects," the title of Emerson's last chapter of *Nature*:

> Whilst in this state of philosophic pessimism and general depression of spirits about my prospects, I went one evening into a dressing room in the twilight to procure some article that was there; when suddenly there fell upon me without any warning, just as if it came out of the darkness, a horrible fear of my own existence. Simultaneously there arose in my mind . . . [an] image. . . .

This, which his father had understood as a conviction of sin, was James's presentment of something squatting, the likeness of a "cat" or "Peruvian mummy" that appeared in his mind as an encaged man with "greenish skin." The sudden terror for his own existence came as "the image of an epileptic patient whom I had seen in the asylum, a black-haired youth . . . entirely idiotic, who used to sit all day on one of the benches, or rather shelves against the wall." This squatting "shape," William feared, represented the possibility that chance might make of him.

To this sense of fetid personality that his father had described, William appended, in a footnote, a statement by John Bunyan:

> There was I struck into a very great trembling, insomuch that at some times I could, for days together, feel my very body, as well as my mind, to shake and totter under the sense of the dreadful judgment of God, that should fall on those that have sinned that most fearful and unpardonable sin. I felt also such clogging and heat at my stomach, by reason of this my terror.

Then, in the only other reference that James made to his case, he noted: "For another case of fear equally sudden, see HENRY JAMES: Society the Redeemed Form of Man, Boston, 1879, pp. 43ff."[15]

Thereby William brought together as a single text Bunyan's fear of having committed unpardonable sin, recounted in Bunyan's autobiography; his father's sight of the "damned shape" in the "precincts" of his room; and his own image of the asylum patient. The whole writing points directly to the scene that Christian faces, in *The Pilgrim's Progress*, of the Man in an Iron Cage:

> Chr. *What wast thou once?*
>
> *Man.* The *Man* said, I was once a fair and flourishing Professor, both in mine own Eyes, and also in the Eyes of others: I once was, as I thought, fair for the Cœlestial City, and had then even joy at the thoughts that I should get thither.
>
> Chr. *Well, but what art thou now?*
>
> *Man.* I am *now* a Man of *Despair*, and am shut up in *it*, as in *this* Iron Cage. I cannot get out; O *now* I cannot.
>
> Chr. *But how camest thou in this Condition?* . . .
>
> *Man.* I have Crucified him to my self afresh, I have despised his Person, I have despised his Righteousness, I have counted his Blood an unholy thing, I have done despite to the Spirit of Grace: Therefore I have shut my self out of all the Promises, and there now remains to me nothing but threatnings, dreadful threatnings, faithful threatnings, of certain Judgment and fiery indignation, which shall devour me as an Adversary.
>
> Chr. *For what did you bring your self into this Condition?*
>
> *Man.* For the Lusts, Pleasures, and Profits of this World; in the enjoyment of which, I did then promise my self much Delight: but now every one of those things also bite me, and gnaw me like a burning Worm.

The elder James and his son provided appropriate images for the vileness the father attributed to the self. This was "the death and hell latent in ourselves" that both men objectified in the alien figures that they held, invisibly, before their eyes. In their respective scenes, both of which occurred at twilight, they experienced their convictions of sin. Neither man, though they both quite consciously took words and images from past texts, felt that because they used other writings to inform their experiences, their relations of fear somehow made their experiences false.

In his *Principles of Psychology*, for example, William James discussed the necessity for verbal models. There he argued not for the reception but for the making of experience. He argued an idealist position, but unlike the idealist, he would present even the most nominal of mental categories as itself a felt experience. That conception allowed James to view the speaking and the writing of a thing as the creation of the thing itself. For James, experience is achieved through a process of articulation and naming. Words constitute experience and thereby become a fact, a sensible fact, of experience itself. James looked upon the act of writing, then, as he did other language practices. Words presented themselves to make sense of the world, drawing reality out of the innate confusion of sensation. Thus James held that, like any act of signification, words did other than reflect or translate experience; they made the stuff of experience, the matter, for example, of religious conversion. Additionally, James held that the act of re-creating a past event was just that—a new experience wholly self-contained and separate from the past event itself. Whether telling the story of an event, if only to oneself, or writing the event down, memory served to make an experience or to fashion sense out of the past.

Henry James and his son differed from Puritan autobiographers by turning from their presentments, which they sharply focused, to wondering whether they were actually insane. Without the structural assurance that the Puritans' understanding of melancholy offered, they could only wonder what they had suffered. Having to make an altered sense of their experiences, they thought of their frights as dramatic onslaughts, moments that had quickly and forever changed their lives. "After this the universe was changed for me altogether," the son wrote, and the father, believing his vastation complete, used the event to destroy his morally energetic life. In ten seconds, the father wrote, he had traveled from vigorous manhood to "helpless infancy," his personality being reduced to a "cinder."[16]

Like Bunyan, both the father and the son managed to preserve their intellectual faculties during their crises. The father held fast to his chair for an hour as he writhed in doubt, anxiety, and despair; the son remembered (in the common refrain of earlier spiritual texts) that he had been "very careful" not to disturb his mother with any revelation of his troubles. As Henry James, Sr., recalled, "I felt the greatest desire to run incontinently . . . and shout for help to my wife, . . . but by an immense effort I controlled these frenzied impulses." He vowed "not to budge from my chair till I had recovered my lost self-possession." Later, while recovering from a terror that the Puritan had called legal fear, the father claimed surprise. "At first, when I began to feel a half-hour's respite from acute mental anguish, the bottomless mystery of my disease completely fascinated me."[17] The experience, that is, was now to be rather marveled at and studied as disease.

A pattern of crisis remains. The need to speak to no other during such a struggle reflects Puritan (and Biblical) writings of psychomachy. Then too, like Increase Mather two centuries before, Henry James first attempted to cure his fright by immersing himself in "pastoral beauty." He entered a park, as Mather had bathed in the springs of Lynn, undertaking a retreat to "a famous water-cure, which did nothing towards curing my malady but enrich my memory with a few morbid specimens of English insularity." As "diet" and "regimen" the physic failed, but like Mather, James now met a woman; indeed he sought her out—"a lady of rare qualities of heart and mind" who informed James that he had experienced "what Swedenborg calls a vastation."

Now suddenly his ills made sense as James reconstructed the meaning of his terror. He worked within the convention of Puritan psychomachy, but he turned abroad, to Swedenborg, for his particular understanding. Now the ills of his body could reflect his troubles of mind, and the physic could become what it was supposed to be, a worthless "cure." James now told his readers that he learned that his sickness had worked as a step in a journey toward his regeneration: "that, without pretending to dogmatize, she had been struck with the philosophic interest of my narrative in this point of view, and had used the word *vastation* to characterize one of the stages of the regenerative process, as she had found it described by Swedenborg." James wrote as though no other precedent than Swedenborg existed: "I was glad to discover that any human being had so much even as proposed to shed the light of positive knowledge upon the soul's history, or bring into rational relief the alternate dark and bright."

James turned to books. He ran to London, and "from the huge mass of tomes placed by the bookseller on the counter before me, I selected two." He studied furiously, despite doctors' warnings that he had to rest because his collapse had resulted from an "overworked . . . brain." James could never accept the secular understanding of medical physicians, no more than Christian can accept a diagnosis of frenzy or distemper. Now growing "frantic," refusing any longer to stand "shivering on the brink, I would plunge into the stream, and ascertain, once for all, to what undiscovered sea its waters might bear me."[18]

James hardly made up this story. He had to make a renewed understanding of the process of spiritual conversion, and for that, he felt, only Swedenborg could offer him a guide. He remained, of course, not quite so naive either of whence he had come (out of the "wreck" that Calvinism had made of him) or of where he was going—of where, indeed, a reading of Swedenborg might eventually lead him. The surprise he expressed—the innocence of being struck as if by a lightning flash—stood as the condition of the saint without any explanation for trials that appeared so strange.

Emerson, for all of the seeming innocence that James scorned, had also demanded this moment for his American scholar. The scholar was to experience not the garden but the "extremities of nature," "the worth of the vulgar." He was to return from the pastoral to the rawness of seventeenth-century nature. In the most famous of his addresses, "The American Scholar," given in 1837, Emerson had provided enough of a portrait of Swedenborg's thought to allow James a hint of the meaning he sought. (Eventually, though, Emerson would consider Swedenborg's rhetoric too strange, an "importation," he later said, of "foreign" talk.) "There is one man of genius. . . . The most imaginative of men, yet writing with the precision of a mathematician. . . . Especially did his shade-loving muse hover over and interpret the lower parts of nature; he showed the mysterious bond that allies the moral evil to the foul material forms, and has given in epical parables a theory of insanity, of beasts, of unclean and fearful things."[19] For Emerson, Swedenborg had uncovered the mask: men appeared as dragons who thought themselves men; "when the light from heaven shone into their cabin, they complained of the darkness, and were compelled to shut the window that they might see."[20]

His own reading of Swedenborg now led the elder James away from "the Green Park" opposite his room in Windsor. Swedenborg led James through his writings as he had once taken visitors through a garden maze with a rare collection of American plants, past a brass cage housing a variety of birds and into a small and opened house and another "garden," that garden actually a mirror reflecting the preceding scene and reflecting, too, of course, the wanderer looking ahead into his own image. It was as though the mystic had built a maze to trap his visitor into looking at the possibilities of himself. Swedenborg then revealed for James what lay within "the pleasant scenery" of the park that James had left behind him.[21] Like an interpreter, he opened for James the interiors of space.

In the score of books that James read, Swedenborg had constructed a cage. Out of his visions the mystic had drawn intricate maps of heavens and hells and had plotted the orbits of spirits and beasts. For Emerson, as assuredly for William James, Swedenborg's universe stayed cold and still. His graphs froze beings into steps, levels, and particular degrees, all set like a crystal or a mesmerist's sleep. It was a world, for Emerson, without effort or will, devoid of persons and spontaneity. It was a lamination of atoms, Emerson complained, lying in order. "Every thought comes into each mind by influence from a society of spirits that surround it, and into these from a higher society, and so on. All his types mean the same few things. All his figures speak one speech."[22] The structure appeared an *idée fixe*.

Henry James could work through Swedenborg's maze and come to the reflection of his own convulsing obsessions: the kinds of works and the types of temptations that had broken him and had brought him to his vastation. Swedenborg's incredible hells—both so precisely drawn and so filled with excrementitious horrors—drew James before the sight of himself, or rather, before the fear of what James thought he had suddenly become: "He sat there," William was to say, "like a sort of sculptured . . . cat or . . . mummy. . . . *That shape am I*, I felt, potentially."[23] Through looking at Swedenborg's hells, the elder James could understand just where, exactly, the evil within his own mind lay. In the alienation of the (imagined) evil that Swedenborg portrayed, in the distance that Swedenborg demanded that the visionary set between himself and the horrible objects seen, sanity developed. The pilgrim, with this interpretation in hand, could then place the temptation out of sight and move his journey onward.

When James read Swedenborg, he read of how fabulous the distance became between the self and its obsessions, for they were out of space, Swedenborg wrote, and out of time. If one thought of one's self as a truly compelled thing, the consciousness dissolved if the self came to see that its compulsive designs were metaphorical and therefore false. James, who knew something of Swedenborg before his vastation, and who of course had read the mystic thoroughly before he wrote out the memory of his crisis, patterned his life on the movement of the engineer who had turned away from carefully machined analyses to embrace direct revelations. James used his vastation—and the sight that he had of the squatting shape in the precincts of his room—to realize his own mechanical undertakings. He used that shape to make concrete before his eyes just how frozen his own activity had been. As James wrote in *Society the Redeemed Form of Man*, published three years before his death:

> It struck me as very odd, soon after my breakdown, that I should feel no longing to resume the work which had been interrupted by it; and from that day to this—nearly thirty-five years—I have never once cast a retrospective glance, even of curiosity, at the immense piles of manuscripts which had ere-while so absorbed me. . . . My studious mental activity had served manifestly to base a mere "castle in the air," and the castle had vanished in a brief bitter moment of time, leaving not a wrack behind. I never felt again the most passing impulse, even, to look where it stood, having done with it forever. Truth indeed! . . . Truth must *reveal itself* if it would be known, and even then how imperfectly known at best! For truth is God, . . . and who shall pretend to comprehend that great and adorable perfection?

Analogous to compulsive acts were the obsessive thoughts that Swedenborg discussed as well—again, to show that the self must come to realize the alienation of its labors. To imagine that one's horrid thoughts came from within as the function of one's property or *proprium* was to think like a "beast," but to imagine that they came from without as an actual determinate of one's behavior—the sufferer strung, as it were, between lines of force—was rather the same thing. In either case the self, if it held to its estranged motives, became itself estranged. For "he too," Swedenborg wrote, in one of the books that Henry James first read after his vastation, "who, because he knows that wisdom and prudence are from God, still waits for influx . . . becomes like a sculpture . . . : that he who waits for influx, is like a sculpture, is manifest; for he must stand or sit motionless, with his hands hanging down, the eyes either shut or open without winking, not thinking and not being animate; what then of life has he?"[24]

The figure of paralysis centers the spiritual narratives of the elder James and his son. It is as if Christian's interpreter has placed them before this object of damnation. William actually toured an asylum, from which he took the memory of his epileptic patient. Like his father, he was to see objectified in a stony horror the living (or dying, as Cotton Mather had said) of one, in the son's words, "who used to sit all day on one of the . . . shelves against the wall, with his knees drawn up against his chin, and the coarse gray undershirt, which was his only garment, drawn over them enclosing his entire figure. He sat there like a sort of sculptured Egyptian cat . . . , moving nothing but his black eyes and looking absolutely non-human."[25] The figure is also one of waiting inaction.

Henry James's son then moved away from the sight of paralytic convulsion. The Swedenborg his father had read he wanted simply to scatter to the winds, and yet for all the mystic's whispering spirits and incredible systems of heavens and hells, all of which spoke of an obsession with intricacy and precision, Swedenborg demanded that the alien sit distant from the self, exactly where William wished. Swedenborg placed the evil within an exterior of thought rather than within interior being. He held up the petrification like a manufactured object to explain that man was not a manufactured thing. He projected a virtual image of alien thoughts and acts to explain that man was not a virtual thing. The meaning formed when he spoke of the necessity to distance such thought—the terrors and fears and small, petty worries, the false image of man as a played-upon thing, as indeed a machine.[26]

Swedenborg's own first recorded dream, dated for a night in March 1744 and kept by Swedenborg in a *Journal of Dreams*, was just that, "a mechanical nightmare," as one of his biographers has said. Swedenborg experienced the fright of his arms becoming bound, crossed in the wheels of an enormous machine that was lifting him up.[27] The assayer of mines and the metallurgical engineer now became a seer. He immersed himself in psychical research, recording his spirits' words through what the Victorians would call "automatic writing."[28] He found little irony, and perhaps there was none, in writing automatically to discover that he was free.

Swedenborg, then fifty-six, had dreamed of mechanics, and his dream had initiated a religious crisis. In the first week of April, in the midst of a vast anatomy book he had undertaken—a physiology, as it seems, of consciousness—he sat before the embers of his fire (he was abroad, and he would soon move to London). "And still," says a biographer, "there he was, sitting before the fire in Delft the next evening full of the 'temptation' of doubt again." He had recently taken Protestant communion and, still feeling depressed, had read the fifth chapter of Paul's Epistle to the Romans, which begins: "Therefore being justified by faith, we have peace with God through our Lord Jesus Christ." "But he 'looked at the fire,'" the biographer continues, "and said to himself that he might better doubt the evidence of his fallible sense and say there is no fire than to doubt God who is Truth Itself, 'and so I passed the hour or hour and a half, and laughed in my heart at the tempter.'" Swedenborg went to bed and in less than an hour began to shiver, "and about twelve or one or two o'clock I trembled violently from head to foot and there was a great sound as of many storms colliding, which shook me and threw me on my face." It was Eastertime. Swedenborg folded his hands in prayer, and the Christ who came held his hands.[29]

Suspended between a mechanics and faith, Swedenborg was searching, as he said, for a "faith without reasoning."[30] Henry James, in the spring of the year, having compiled his own vast manuscript that worked, he felt, as a mere theological machine, was now moving from "my merely rationalistic interest" to a "struggle . . . more intimate and living." His crisis marked the breaking of an obsessive attempt to control God: "a fact of experience, interesting in itself no doubt in a psychological point of view, but particularly interesting as marking the interval." "I remained sitting at the table after the family had dispersed, idly gazing at the embers in the grate, thinking of nothing, and feeling only the exhilaration incident to a good digestion, when suddenly—in a lightning flash . . ." Henry James, too, sat shivering in frenzy.[31]

I was dumb with silence, I held my peace, *even* from good; and my sorrow was stirred.

My heart was hot within me, while I was musing the fire burned: *then* spake I with my tongue,

The Iron of Melancholy

Lord, make me to know mine end, and the measure of my days, what it *is*; *that* I may know how frail I *am*.

Composition of the Crisis

For all the textual similarity between them, no reason exists to doubt the accounts of breakdown by either the father or the son. Although both men composed their records at some distance from the event, and both accounts stand encrusted (visibly encrusted, because of their distance and texture of time) with literary device—too much so to provide a clinical record of the events that actually occurred—the compositions of the father's vastation and of the son's panic fear were not offered as fictions. William James separated the act of signification (such as telling a story) from the object or the event the sign signified. He did so not to disparage the sign, or to question its significance, or to bore past the word to a more real or thinglike truth. He made the separation between sign and signified to demonstrate the experience that the sign itself produced. The tangibility of the sign, or the experiential nature of all acts of representation and reproduction (such as the father's narration of his crisis) underscored for James not only the selective process of consciousness that his psychology emphasizes, but also the constructive process of memory that James considered presently effective. The reproduction of an event—telling, for example, what has happened in one's life—requires selection (which past texts can guide) and even the creation of fictions, and thus the telling differs sensibly from the experience. As Increase Mather implied, and as Jonathan Edwards touched upon here and there in his writings, only a wording (or a profession) of an event like conversion makes that event sensible and therefore real.

This is not simply to say that literary narratives like that of Henry James and his son warn that an objective record is impossible. The lack of design that may appear to distinguish a clinical or a sanitized case history is obviously in itself an illusion. The figuration here, however, fails to cover up an underlying truth, for the composition of the crises forms the truth.[32] Whatever the self-conscious lack of "style," or the closeness in time between an event and its text, or the effort to work for that which actually occurred, one will always place a construction upon an experience to make that experience work. To strive for the Victorians' own conception of realism, or for the naturalism that others incorrectly thought that William's stream of thought (or consciousness) expressed—an expression whose flow they sought to achieve through automatic writing—is to think that by automatism one can liberate expression. Here, in obviously creative texts, only a "literariness" plainly reveals the sensible intent that such writing had for its authors.[33]

In the imagery that here couches, however barely for the father, the conviction of sin, both relations serve as model nineteenth-century descriptions of what a sudden nervous collapse should be. The two narratives reflect the writings of Bunyan and Swedenborg, and (by the time Henry and William James made their compositions) they reflect as well the *Autobiography* of John Stuart Mill. The son chose to ignore his father's mentor altogether, though he re-expressed Swedenborg's religious crisis, if only because he chose to note the similarity between his fear and his father's. The son, who would dedicate his *Pragmatism* to Mill, understood his panic fear, along with his carefully considered suspicion of its significance—"I have always thought that this experience of melancholia of mine had a religious bearing"—more according to Mill's account of a mental crisis.[34] Readers could debate Swedenborg's sanity (his texts, indeed, could appear as the writings of a psychotic) and argue whether the aging mystic had considered his visions real or had employed them only as metaphors and types.[35] Mill's work, on the other hand, appeared secular and detached—composed, in other words, by a man of analysis. When Mill described his own breakdown, he used analogy to keep his distinctions clear: "I was in . . . the state, I should think, in which converts to Methodism usually are, when smitten by their first 'conviction of sin.'" Like Swedenborg, Mill used "the dissolving influence of analysis" to cut away at his mechanics: he looked back upon himself as "a 'made' or manufactured man, having had a certain impress of opinion stamped on me which I could only reproduce." His mental crisis, a "melancholy winter," finally shattered his reproduction. The distance that Mill now set between himself and the impress of his father provided the turn toward his own self-creation.[36] Mill's crisis came without Swedenborg's visions, however, and he wrote carefully with both the marks of quotation around the conviction of sin and the "I should think"—marks of analysis that removed any immediacy of religious feeling and placed a world between Swedenborg's writing and his own.

The moments of crisis of the elder James and his son focused their lives more sharply than any such moment in Puritan spiritual autobiography. The crises distract the reader from the lengths of their suffering, from the periodic and extended depressions both men experienced following their convictions of fear. In the father's case, such depression lasted two years. The vastation or sudden devastation of the self that the father required to speak of conversion, worked not quite so suddenly to complete his moral destruction as he at first thought. His narrative draws itself closer to the processional model of Puritan conversion. In the autobiography of John Bunyan, to which William James directed his reader's attention, extended periods of depression and various moments of acute mental distress alternate with more rigidly proscriptive behavior. The defensive mechanisms—fixed ideas, for example, such as blasphemous thoughts, along with time-consuming ritual exercises—forestall collapse. They function as barriers between the self and realizations that depression periodically breaches. Henry James, when his works gave out, felt depression as a rage turned inward upon his self.[37]

Henry James later rested his entire philosophical endeavor upon the destruction of his fear-ridden life when, in book after book and essay upon essay, he called for an uncreation of the self. He called for the final moral death and burial of the personality that had so tormented his mind in the years preceding 1844. One may question whether the elder James successfully committed the "moral suicide, or inward death to self in all its forms" that he demanded—the expulsion of "that cadaverous . . . thing" lying within. Nevertheless, he devoted the remainder of his intellectual life to laying his strange behavior to rest.[38] He called for an end to the insanity of conscience that had driven him to extreme exercises of propitiation. He asked for an education of the self away from the natural, the moral, and the ritually religious—behavior that he said had circumscribed his youth.[39] He sought a learning by unlearning or a doing by undoing, a final release from the "downright charlantry" of moral pretension. He cried as Bunyan had cried: "Good Lord, break it open; Lord, break these gates of brass, and cut these bars of iron asunder."

The loathing of his shut heart, James said, or his pretentious conscientiousness, had filled his mind with hatred at Windsor. He finally felt such revulsion at working out his conscience that he could but envy the "spiritual innocence" of the beasts.[40] "And now," William James recorded from Bunyan's autobiography, "I was sorry that God had made me a man. The beasts, birds, fishes, etc., I blessed their condition, for they had not a sinful nature." The imagery is Biblical, and yet for William James these words appeared distant; having found this pastoral longing not only in Bunyan but also in the confessions of a Mr. Henry Alline, an eighteenth-century evangelical of Nova Scotia and the man "upon whose soul the iron of melancholy left a permanent imprint," William James could only wonder: "Envy of the placid beasts seems to be a very widespread affection in this kind of sadness." He called the sadness "religious melancholy," and he followed the case history of Henry Alline immediately with his own case.[41]

The Nature of Swedenborg's Temptations

Henry James had to construct an understanding of the kind of conscience that he believed his crisis had begun to break apart. He required a source from which he could form an idea of the purpose that his hell of thought had served. Swedenborg used certain obsessional thoughts (which generally he called temptations) to prepare his case, including the case that he made of himself, for spiritual awakening. "This opening and conjunction," Swedenborg had written in his *Apocalypse Explained*, first published posthumously in 1785, "is possible only through temptations, because in temptations man fights interiorly against the falsities and evils that are in the natural man. In a word, man is brought into the church and becomes a church through temptations. All this was represented by the wandering and leading about of the sons of Israel in the desert."[42] The years James spent prior to 1844 now became this desert.

Swedenborg wrote that this waste of thought created spiritual insight, in "that without temptations no one is regenerated, and that several temptations succeed one after another; the reason is, because regeneration is effected for an end, that the life of the old man may die." The "anxiety" of mind represented the moment, for Swedenborg, of Christ on the cross, the time of both greatest forsaking and closest conjunction with God.[43] Swedenborg offered this internal wilderness as the assaults of spirits, genii, and demons, torments that rendered the stricken person "first unquiet, then anxious," thereby allowing the self to actualize its "*proprium*" or property. This property the demons used as if a humor to gall the conscience. The realization of the demonic source of this thought offered a significance that foretold of regeneration: "I have heard the combat; I have perceived the influx; I have seen the spirits." "As soon as they perceive anything whatever of conscience, they form to themselves an affection out of the falsities and infirmities of man. . . . Besides which, they tenaciously keep the thought on one thing, and so fill it with fantasies, and then at the same time clandestinely involve lusts into the fantasies." "It is this combat which is perceived in man as temptation; but so obscurely that he scarcely knows but that it is merely an anxiety."[44]

With his reading in Jonathan Edwards, James perhaps had little need for Swedenborg's discussion of melancholy obsessions. James did require a system to replace the humoral psychology, however, and even Swedenborg's understanding of satanic temptations as the work of real spirits attacking the mind in a manner that Edwards would have considered absurd, offered a psychology of conscience James could grasp. In the first of the volumes he had purchased in London, he read not so much about genii as about the distinction that Swedenborg (like Edwards and Puritan divines) demanded the victim of temptations draw between temptations proper—spiritual temptations—and temptations of a merely disordered mind:

> Such disorders are melancholies, spurious and false consciences, fantasies of various kinds, griefs of mind [*animus*] from misfortunes, anxieties and anguishes of mind from defect of the body; which things are sometimes regarded as temptations, but are not; because genuine temptations have spiritual things for their objects, and in these the mind is sane; but those have natural things for their objects, and in these the mind is insane.[45]

Understanding the false consciousness of obsessional convictions of sin—the spurious conscience of the melancholy—allowed the alienated to create a genuine understanding of sin.

Swedenborg offered himself, and the foreign influx that had attacked his mind, to support his point—twice in one of the books that James first read. "To this I will add my daily experience: evil spirits have very often injected evils and falsities into my thoughts, which appeared with me *as if they* [emphasis added] were in me and from me, or that I myself thought them; but because I knew that they were evils and falsities, I sought who injected them; and they were detected and driven off, and were at a remarkable distance from me." ". . . this has been done a thousand times," Swedenborg wrote, that is, "to compel them to retreat," "and I have remained in this state now for many years, and still remain in it." The question Swedenborg asked was whether he acted like a man simply compelled to make some kind of movement. He asked whether, because of his influx, "I do not think and will anything of myself, and therefore that I am like some empty thing." He answered yes, in that he neither thought from himself nor willed from himself, and he answered no, in that he had never lived like some empty, mechanical thing. He possessed internal thought and therefore thought himself free—free to perceive the evil that flowed into his exterior thought, free thus to accept or to reject it, in this paradox of compulsion. "Now because man does not wish to know that he is led by others to think, but wishes to think from himself, and also believes this, it follows that he is in fault [for the evil he does], nor can reject it from himself, as long as he loves to think what he thinks: *but if he does not love it* [emphasis added], he releases himself from connection with them [the spirits of hell]; this is done when he knows that it is evil, and therefore wills to shun it and desist from it; then also he is taken by the Lord from the society which is in that evil."[46] The mental detestation the victim had of the foreign invasion that racked his mind signified the victim's conversion, exactly as such detestation had signified conversion in Puritan writings of the seventeenth century.

Thinking of the self as unbound and not determined—however false such an idea of freedom was, the very idea of self or of "*proprium*"—Swedenborg demanded to allow his sufferer a sense of personal choice, commitment, and direction. A determined act of self, that is, did appear, one for which God could indeed level blame if the choice made was evil.[47] Like Edwards, Swedenborg could thus argue against the freedom of the will and yet maintain in all consistency that man's acts were not "compelled"—neither by miracles nor signs, neither by visions nor discourses with the dead, neither by threats nor punishments. Man received his reformation, as Swedenborg wrote, not in a state of fear, misfortune, disease of the body, or disorder of the mind—not out of legal fear, in other words, or externalities that strike against us all. Like the frozen shapes that stand before Swedenborg, James, and James's son, such thoughts—that one had, for example, without choice committed unpardonable sin—remained so distant and alien from the interior of one's sorrow of mind that they could be, through an act of choice, cast off. "Now because the internal and the external of the mind are so distinct, the internal can also fight with the external, and by combat compel it to a consent: combat exists, when man thinks evils to be sins and therefore wishes to desist from them; for when he desists, the door is opened; . . . the . . . evil . . . cast out."[48] This external temptation personified the regenerate soul rather than, for Swedenborg, the truly sick or melancholy mind.

James's Confession of Temptations and Compulsion

By introducing Swedenborg, James obscured his own discussion of spiritual regeneration. Swedenborg had offered one of the most thorough discussions of obsessive ideation since the Puritans. If the elder James were to break out of the seventeenth-century concept of melancholy, then the European mystic's writings at least allowed for a seemingly newer understanding. Within his own often abstract discussion of the conscience of sin, James did weave in his own confessions of temptation, making concrete the types of thought and the compelling acts he loathed—not the acts of man but the criminal thoughts of James, trained up to the kind of selfhood he wished to expel. The Protestant conscience appeared as an "insane career" to James, as he searched for whatever word he could find to attack as morbid the guilt his mechanical self possessed. "I soon found my conscience . . . acquiring so infernal an edge, that I could no longer indulge myself in the most momentary deviation from an absurd and pedantic literal rectitude . . . without tumbling into an inward frenzy of alarm." James had turned to destroy the precisian's conscience. His moral quest had become an "insane pride" and his obsessive fear of doing wrong a "'morbid' natural temperament." His need for "personal purity" had led only to "self-distrust and self-deprecation," all of which led to his conversion.[49]

James placed the fullest account of his youthful moral endeavors in the disguised spiritual autobiography published by his son. Just as Cotton Mather related portions of his brother's secret diary, and as Samuel Hopkins gathered together and published Edwards's "private writings," so William James as his own first book published his father's manuscripts, including the pseudonymous autobiography. In his introduction William also quoted extensively from the father's account of his vastation, thereby drawing together in a single text a good portion of his father's internal life. In his autobiography, the elder James attributed his conscience's morbidity to his early indoctrination into the utter vileness of man within the sight of a powerful and all-perfect God. This estrangement had compelled acts of "insane superstition" and a desperate attempt at propitiation. As a youth, James recalled, he had found within himself a natural boyish sensibility—an ardor, often sexual in tone, that he thought his Calvinism and his family's bond had quite unduly proscribed. At the expense of his innocence a harsh God had forced out his moral consciousness, so that he soon found himself "in an attitude of incessant exaction—in fact, of the most unhandsome mendicancy and higgling—towards my creative source."[50]

The Calvinist God and the merchant father merged in this memory as James recounted his childhood efforts to purchase salvation: the "indebtedness" he felt and his need "to *transact* with God." Whatever his pleasure or youthful excess, he was plunged "incessantly into perturbations." To get out, he tried mental maneuvers. The metaphors he used to describe his compulsive efforts spoke to his father's kind of economy. He tried to haggle with God. He entered into "flatly commercial" transactions. He assumed a "bargaining or huckstering attitude" and became God's slave. "This insane terror pervaded my consciousness more or less. It turned every hour . . . ; made me loath at night to lose myself in sleep, lest his dread hand should clip my thread of life without time for a parting sob of penitence."[51] He meant to cut apart Calvinism, but his satire preserved the meaning that legal fear, along with the accompanying attempt to buy out of sin, played within the Puritan spiritual autobiography.

James also likened his becoming "studiously, even superstitiously pure in thought and act," to "an ascetic regimen." His theology and family, having placed him at odds with his nature, blinded him to the way of life that opposed the ascetic: the "spontaneous" or the actively faithful. The merchant father thus became the symbol of all that the son revolted against. James's commercial Calvinism projected this father as an external authority, an other against which James could push and thereby define an internal place for his faith.

James failed to elaborate the account of his schemes of credit and debit, but he did explore the behavior that had produced the need for self-punishment. First, overt acts of misdemeanor and even crime had existed—an ungenerous word toward his sister, for example, or the exposing of himself (as Bunyan had) to physical dangers that left his parents in dread. He had even transacted criminally with his father, stealing small sums of silver left enticingly available to the child, who needed to pay a confectioner. Yet James remained quite clear, in his autobiography as elsewhere, that "not any literal thing I did, so much as the temper of mind with which it was done, had power to humble me before God."[52]

James's conscience arose, in other words, from no "overt iniquity." Indeed, there seemed to exist an inverse relation between the goodness of his acts and the vileness of his conscience. James thus set about to understand why those purest in act should feel the greatest of guilt, while criminals should feel little or no remorse. James's own propitiation had only added, he said, to his anguish; the better he had acted toward God, the further he had found himself removed from His grace. He became momentarily confused, unsure whether he had in fact committed acts that justly alienated his Creator: "understand me here, I beg. I have not the least idea of representing myself as ever having been especially obnoxious to the rebuke of conscience. On the contrary, I am willing to admit that I have been tolerably blameless in all the literal righteousness of the law."[53] That was the point: literal righteousness accounted for nothing at all.

James often wrote, without elaboration, that he had felt tempted to commit various crimes: "inasmuch as I perceived in myself great moral infirmity, that is, a ready proclivity under temptation to lying, theft, adultery and murder, my religious life had always been of intense anguish." Again, in an essay on Emerson, James asked how his innocent friend could ever in fact have known evil without having borne such horrid impulsions:

> I am satisfied that he never in his life had felt a temptation *to bear false-witness* against his neighbor, *to steal, to commit adultery,* or *to murder*; how then should he have ever experienced what is technically called a conviction of sin? . . . One gets a conviction of the evil that attaches to the natural selfhood in man in no other way . . . —as I can myself attest. . . . For I myself had known all these temptations—in forms of course more or less modified—by the time I was fourteen or fifteen years old; so that by the time I had got to be twenty-five or thirty . . . I was saturated with a sense of spiritual evil—no man ever more so possibly.

His vastation had supposedly relieved James of these self-condemning thoughts. He denied neither their continuing iniquity nor their irony, however. The irony, again, was the inverse relation between the consciousness of sin and the committed crime: "irresistibly prone . . . thus tempted like as we are, yet without sin—being thus touched with a feeling of our infirmities, and yet rigidly self-debarred from the actual disorder." Emerson, by failing to acknowledge not the act of evil but the impulsion to crime, had washed out the conviction of sin.[54]

Still, James was expressing Christian themes of moral depravity. He was re-expressing Swedenborg's thought on external temptations, though his own phrases remained stereotypically Biblical. In three slight essays, all somewhat removed from his theological endeavors, he returned to these themes and now did speak (first in "A Very Long Letter") with a greater specificity of a pathology he had found in his "mental history." He wrote here of "the morbid susceptibility of my conscience," which had "secured my general inoffensiveness, while it left me a prey to the most poignant sorrows for mistakes and accidents so trivial that I am ashamed to mention them."[55] However ridiculous such thoughts and now also actual behaviors might seem, James, like Bunyan, would bring the history of his morbidity to light.

In a small essay on "Spiritual Rappings," James considered the notion of the returning dead. Whatever his obsession with Swedenborg, James allowed that no ghost, if such exist, would return for the good of its recipient. "They . . . get hold of a criminal remembrance on the part of the subject, and keep urging it home upon him until they drive him almost frantic with remorse." James said that his own weak-willed self had once writhed under such a "despotic grip," a "foreign influx" too strong for his prayer and, most particularly, for his undefined "ritual observance," but not quite so strong as to crush his life. This was not a matter of derangement. These articles inflamed the "ascetic ambition" and left the will "a dismal wreck . . . on the sands of superstition." "I am not speaking of impossibilities. We have all heard of tender and devout persons, who having through some foolish asceticism . . . come under the influence of this attenuated despotism, have at last got back to their own firesides, so spent with suffering, so lacerated to the very core."[56]

Again, as James attacked a popular spiritualistic movement that would encourage a spirit's invitation, the language reads like a drama. This is not the case in his discussion of habit and intemperance. Here James allowed an admission that only a later generation, had they paid attention, would have considered a confession of neurotic behavior. He published the essay in 1846, after his conversion to Swedenborg, but because the essay lacks the imagery of demons and ghosts, his statement appears to speak more to the everyday life of compulsive behavior that he said he led. However ridiculous, as Bunyan had written, such petty activities might seem, their confession becomes significant when it appears within a text. James was speaking of alcoholism as a malformed system of habit in need of "medication" rather than "malediction." He placed his confession in a formal writing, almost as an aside, and therefore begged the question of his intention:

> There is no mystery about drunkenness. *Like all habits, its strength lies in a diseased will.* I have been in the habit of saying "good morning" to my mother when we meet at breakfast. If I set myself seriously to forego this salutation of a morning, I find the task superior to my powers. All my spiritual forces appear on the point of deserting me, and my thoughts become a complete chaos. This experience upon so trivial an occasion, arises from the feebleness of my will or practical faculty. The bent of my nature is towards affection and thought rather than action. I love the fireside rather than the forum. I can give extatic [*sic*] hours to worship or meditation, but moments spent in original deeds, such as putting a button upon my coat or cleansing my garden-walk of weeds, weigh very heavily upon my shoulders. Habit, therefore, is my tyrant. What I have been accustomed to do I do easily, nor can I forego the doing of it without extreme pain. My will, or practical faculty, being so small, I can scarcely do anything else but what I have been accustomed to do all my life.

James continued by mentioning his lack of ambition in the presence of women, then spoke generally of his passivity and life of reflection that, he believed, had opened his mind to temptations.[57] What James expressed here was a slight, almost inconsequential compulsion to act which, if the words were left undone, produced an excessive amount of anxiety. A "complete chaos" of mind erupted unless, each day, James repeated the ritual morning salutation to his mother.

Blasphemous thoughts, criminal thoughts, and ritual excesses of devotion could intrude themselves to such an unwarranted degree that

James devoted a good portion of his intellectual life to explaining their purpose. Ultimately, he defended their infernal edge as Edwards had, for the pathologies worked as a sign of contrast. The ascetic devotions provide a necessary preface of material death prior to spiritual birth. Whether James wrote his lines intentionally against a work like Bunyan's autobiography, or whether he was actually unaware of their significance in terms of Puritan psychomachy, this slight moment of autobiography functions within a larger textual history of confession.

The Conscience of Sin and the Conscience of Crime

The habits to which James confessed worked as a wondrous symbol of James's natural attachment to automatism. The "diabolic infestations" worked to break his habits apart, smearing his moral behavior with dirt. James was to live in what he termed the basement of personality. Abhorring not his sin so much as that "iron domination" of his church, an authority of false but painful "hereditary shackles" that had forced his cruel thoughts, James's self-illumination came when he managed intellectually to work himself out of this belief in his crime. He concluded, as the Puritan had concluded, that his particular fears expressed not his criminality in the sight of God but his goodness, or rather his immediate preparation for goodness.

Before his massive depression of 1844, James had attempted to buy God's approbation by working "studiously." The more he tightened his conscience, however, allowing not that "momentary deviation" from "literal rectitude," "the fouler grew its fetid breath. A conviction of inward defilement so sheer took possession of me, that death seemed better than life." This conviction had troubled him in his youth, and also in the years up to his depression. He spoke of a cross word toward his child (William) or a petulance toward his cook, petty angers that would send him into frenzied fear lest he should have provoked God's wrath.[58] He worked out of this worry by concluding that only a "subjective" personality had produced the fear: both the small crimes and the compulsions that the anxiety then created. This was a momentary and unreal personality, unexpressive of James's real relation with God (or the personhood that James would have for himself). God had merely imposed this phenomenal self upon James to ratify his moral sense, thereby preparing James, as God was preparing the whole of humankind, for his ultimate return to His pure and creative self. God allowed the pride of selfhood as a curse to force persons to solicit, morally but ineffectually, His countenance. They had to perform a "legal and accredited righteousness" that soon turned into what James called "a perpetual discipline of cleansing and oblation"—a "ritual and figurative drapery of sacrifice and lustration," as if one could on one's own wash away the bloodguilt. The frustration of attaining such purity, James concluded, made the pretension plain, as the rituals became but a painful attempt to buy God's grace. By seemingly demanding such ultimately useless rituals, God was showing the futility of ever appropriating His grace.[59]

James demanded this "morality" as a preparatory step—strange propitious acts that, in the end, served only to unmask all such undertakings. The conscience of sin lifted man out of "the mud of animality," creating his soul. Conscience acted to prepare man for the death of the self brought by the self's own ridiculous distortions. Out of His infinite love, God was wooing man from his selfhood by making him hate it, unsuspectedly wooing him from his own self-created death.

James, in other words, had used the Puritans' distinction between legal fear and evangelical sorrow to write the preparatory history of a last vision. This was the time when nothing the self did or felt worked to effect anything at all. Even the fears the self felt for deeds actually done counted for nothing. Is, then, James asked, "the conviction of sin which I feel a real conviction," truly expressing "my individual rottenness, . . . my personal alienation," "reflecting the truth of things as far as it goes?" Did man feel a righteous guilt created by a hateful and wrathfully paternal God? If God had only used the conviction of fear as a sham to magnify His power, then an omnipotent God was trading in deceptions and was unworthy of man's consideration. No, James concluded, for man would realize that his actual sin, for which he would feel sorrow, had begun in a primal deed actually performed, but lost within his past. As one began to investigate "the mental judgment" of this deed, it soon became apparent that its reality "becomes altogether spiritual. In other words, it is a matter of daily observation that a genuine conscience of sin . . . is out of all ratio to the amount of evil actually [or consciously] done, much more actually doing." The necessity to distinguish legal fear from true sorrow remained. One needed to make a distinction between the conviction of sin as "real . . . or . . . mere[ly] dramatic" by understanding that true sin, for which no act of removal existed, distinguished itself from a show of sin that was in fact a drapery of ritual. Concerning this "religious drama," as James said in other regards, the necessity now existed for "dropping metaphor and speaking truth."[60]

Those who had felt the "evil thought" remained the least prone to "evil-doing." Those who had so carefully watched their "secret thoughts" and who had so "laboriously" sought their righteousness, found their rottenness now all the further exposed. At this point James made the distinction that Perkins, Ames, and then Edwards had made, the distinction that nineteenth-century alienists, neurologists, and psychologists, including his son William, would fail to make again for almost another half century. Swedenborg had made the distinction between a compulsion to act horridly and an actual acting out of the horror itself. "Let us make up our minds then at the outset," James wrote, "that a very great distinction obtains between the conscience of criminality and the conscience of sin, between the mere doing of evil and the feeling oneself to be evil. To do evil is one thing, the lowest thing a man can do; to feel oneself a sinner is a totally opposite thing, is indeed the height of a man's spiritual achievement, for this world at all events." Those who had become closest to God and to their own spiritual birth, James concluded, lived in the greatest mental alienation.

In his wish to explain his own conventional deportment along with his temptations to crime, James had arrived at certain therapeutic conclusions. By distinguishing acts of crime from thoughts of crime, he made "Evil-doing" and "sin" "as distinct as earth and heaven." The saint—not, as alienists were concluding, the morally insane—remained "more than all others averse to evil doing, and [yet] feels the soil of an evil thought . . . more poignantly than others do the grossest contact of literal defilement."[61]

By virtue of the Adamic experience, all men lived as evildoers, but to think and then feel abhorrence for what you thought belonged to the spiritual mind, the mind "disengaged from sense." So disengaged, indeed, was this mind for James, that he felt it could never bear to speak or write out its abhorrence. As opposed to the Protestant revival and the Catholic confessional, this confession of sin remained a wholly private affair. The contrite conscience felt itself so humilated in the presence of its very outward righteousness that it humbled itself into the dust and could not "possibly endure to publish itself." By publishing his own confession as the tradition of Puritan psychomachy demanded, James did catch himself within a contradiction, though his point is well taken. Bunyan's autobiography, for example, remains frustratingly vague as to just what, exactly, its author thought that seemed so horrible. The biographical celebration of an obsessional mental disquiet, by its own nature hidden even by modern psychiatric patients who remain embarrassed about such thoughts, demands a reason for its publication, which James did have. He had no reason, however, to become specific.

In writings that were going unread, James said he doubted if anyone even spoke of such thoughts to another: the "glimpse of the uncleanness enclosed in one's ritual righteousness" that "baffles utterly our ordinarily florid dramatic capabilities." He was declaring against any dramatic writing out of sin that could, in itself, act only as another ritual, this time a ritual of confession. An expression of sin could never exist, except in the sense that such an expression erased all man's conventions. One had to break through utterly to "one's unlikeness," through "the ineffable smallness, filthiness . . . wrapped up in [the] conventional virtue."[62] James would use his own writings to cut against convention by attempting to create an estrangement similar to God's estrangement from him. He would alienate himself, a human author of words, from his reader who, James felt, could only discover his own sorrow for sin.

James psychologized Calvinism to preserve the Puritans' terror of conversion. The sense that he had of his life as a progressing mental history allowed James to use the "extreme mental suffering induced in me by that theology" to preserve the psychology of that theology itself. As Emerson had mentioned, a "way of thinking" still existed, a perennial opposition to the "superstitious times" that "made protestants and ascetic monks [words that Emerson left historically ungrounded], preachers of Faith against preachers of Works." However much James conceived of Calvinism as a sickness and considered its morality a physic, he used the terms of his new psychology to reformulate the central tenet of his father's faith: *sola fides*. His demand for self-scrutiny and harsh self-examination was to lead to an awareness of the magical acts of morality itself, and his denigration of rituals as works was to speak of a quest for a complete personality that came only with the end of *proprium* or self. "It would be tedious to report the gradual dawn of the truth upon my understanding. Reading one day the Epistle to the Romans, my attention became arrested by the words, read before a thousand times without notice—*Faith cometh by hearing*. I said to myself, Faith then means belief of the truth, and not any magical operation in the bosom."[63]

Moral Works

An uncertain man, James had attempted to exact from God a surety he never found in life. He would do things—think proper thoughts, act certain ways—in an attempt to order an environment he found materially chaotic and decayed. His quest for a transcending absolute exaggerated the type of philosophical endeavor his son William would come to deny, for in expressing the transcendentalism and later the Spencerianism of his generation, he caricatured this Victorian quest for universal law. A year before his massive break at Windsor, for example, James asked Joseph Henry for a book to unify "*all* the sciences," making "all *one* at bottom," and Henry replied that no such book existed.[64] A year or so before his collapse, he wrote to Emerson, pleading for the help that he thought surely the sage could, but for some reason was refusing to, supply: "I am led . . . to seek the *laws* . . . —to get hold of some central *facts* which may make all other facts properly circumferential, and *orderly* so—and you continually dishearten me by your apparent indifference to such law and central facts. . . . Do you not feel the necessity of reaching after these laws all the while,—some inner fact which shall link together mighty masses of now conflicting facts." He could not say what he ached to say, James continued to Emerson. He was thirty-one and yet ignorant, but he remained patient in his meditations and weariless in his pursuits. "What shall I do? Shall I get me a little nook in the country and communicate . . . a fit word, once a year?"[65] His quest for certainty was dashed, and James soon suffered his nervous collapse.

William of Albany had afforded James the leisure to pursue whatever vocation the son desired.[66] Though James considered work exceedingly important, his choice of an occupation and the manner in which he pursued that choice drove him ever further from worldly affairs. Having abandoned his theological studies at Princeton, a debt paid to his father,[67] James had hoped to lecture and yet, though never shy, had experienced such a horror of writing and such depression whenever he tried to give his thoughts to others that he called this, his first "outgoing," a failure. He withdrew, and as he wrote to Emerson, he would need to look about for some other flight.[68] He vowed to make all his work a "sabbatical," to produce only by "impulsion" in order to keep himself "sane."[69] Unable to work as he romanticized, he labored incessantly. Just before he collapsed at Windsor, he piled up page after page of manuscript for the book that he later thought not so much a pursuit of truth as a ridiculous effort to prove he could in fact pursue some truth.[70] The book became an emblem of the studious laws James was revolting against; it became a text of ritually inscribed words that he used his vastation to rend. As he said, he never returned to the manuscripts after his collapse; indeed, the manuscripts probably never existed.[71] In any event, he was released from a legality. Now he searched for a spontaneous creation.

This was finally to make "allowance," James said, "to the weakness of my nerves." Now he would bring his work "to such orderly close"—

in this instance some letters—"as my infirmities will permit." His appeal to Emerson, his thrashing around, and the ever mounting bulk of his manuscripts had ended in paralysis. He was now compelled to write about it. Speaking of Windsor, James remembered that "most jealous scrutiny" of God's eye, "until my will, as you have seen—thoroughly fagged out as it were with the formal, heartless, endless task of conciliating a stony-hearted Deity—actually collapsed." The law was not to be broken; it was to be extinguished. He was frozen, unable to move: "No idiot was ever more incompetent . . . than I, at that trying period, felt myself to be. It cost me, in fact, as much effort to go out for a walk, or to sleep in a strange bed, as it would an ordinary man to plan a campaign or write an epic poem."[72] Having labored before a spying Creator, patching together frantically his words and acts, he sat, as William would say, entirely idiotic. Now he could write of a new beginning of spontaneous being. He would write of the free productivity of the true "artist," the saint that he held as working above the law.

So great did the elder Henry James feel his own humility before God to be that all ritual, the petty acts of the moral self, seemed void before a God who, after all, infinitely loved him. His criminality, his blasphemous thoughts, became but a part of his natural selfhood. His transactions, his youthful asceticism, were the useless acts of a contrite heart that, all the while, was returning to God. His debits and credits expressed the tradings of an ascetic. James thus attacked traditional forms of asceticism vigorously. "Reduce the appetites . . . , imprison them as you do a tiger, . . . and of course you insure them the tiger's force and ferocity. Thus the unhappy and unhandsome monk, who from some spiritual insanity, some morbid ambition . . . finds his whole life turned into a sordid conflict."[73]

James pointed his discussion of asceticism in the direction that Max Weber would take when Weber argued that Protestantism had created a historically unique ascetic capitalism.[74] The distinctive act of Protestantism was that it had carried ascetic discipline into the world, creating a "commixture," James argued, "of the secular with the 'religious.'" That, he continued, "is precisely what differences the Protestant evolution of religion from the Catholic." Catholicism retained its asceticism for monks; "Protestantism . . . proceed[s] to make it fruitful by marrying it to the secular life." James then looked with horror at the fruits this marriage produced. The "cheerful hum of industry"—this new worldly ascetic—had spilled out wastes "flatulent and sour."[75]

Swedenborg had demanded labor. Even in the mystic's heaven, there awaited some "office" or "function."[76] James demanded a probe, however, into Protestantism's "depths." He would look at even Swedenborg's heaven as he had looked at a nun's "mechanical dress." He found a new type of alienation.[77] He found that Protestant labor had become as compulsive as a nun's rituals. He called instead for "free productivity," envisioning a demoralization of labor itself. He called for a work that would bring "the object of all my action . . . *within the* conditions of my own nature." This work expressed the wholeness of personhood in which the subject and the object of its application became one. No longer looking at its object as a contradictory other, the self took its labor into itself. Having experienced its alienation, the self rested now above the law. Its new work became higher than any "LAW or fixity."[78]

The self defined itself now not in images fixed outside the mind but in the manifestations it experienced when it viewed itself in its action. "Our true individuality is our faculty of action, our power to do. By so much as I am able to do or produce, am I myself. A man *is* that which he *does*, neither more nor less. What I do, that I am." James offered a pragmatic valuation, one that he had derived from Swedenborg:

> Your image in the looking-glass is not the living expression of yourself, but only its lifeless effigy addressed to an outward eye, the eye of sense. It is not a reflection of your real *life*, but only of your phenomenal *existence*. . . . Your conscious or real self stands expressed only in your action, in your work, in what you freely effect. It is only your unreal and apparent self which reveals itself in the fleeting image impressed upon the glass.[79]

Not what you saw of your self but what you did with your self determined who you were. Ideally, work provided a process of self-creation. Modern work like moralism had become "fetichism, or superstitious worship," however, and its mechanical laceration was turning the self, as it had turned James, into hideous ashes. Work fashioned "a mere magical product." Work had become "the power of gratuitous or ostentatious productivity; the power to produce something out of nothing, consequently without labor-pains: thus a something which has no inward ground of being."[80] Work ended in "a gross mockery," creating nothing more than that which Bunyan had created when he tried to make the puddles dry.

Free productivity or spontaneity, on the other hand, held itself within as an internal of the self. It created personhood by releasing the self from compulsive, magical, or moral bonds. Before such release, an "impulsion," like one of Swedenborg's contrary spirits, grabbed the person and awakend him to his "diseased or abnormal life, [with] his action being perverted and inhuman." The divine life ended the alienation. Divinity appeared as a "new economy," "one which *interiorates* object to subject."[81]

James discussed the spontaneity of this new creation by drawing a distinction between the "artisan" and the "artist." James's artisan was bound to work by necessity; his artist discovered that he was free to choose and to work without material or dutiful constraint. The artist signified James's divine who interiorized the "property" or the object of his application. "Faculty" or a capacity for action defined spirit, for spirit lay in what something—a horse, say—did, in what its purpose expressed. But opposed to faculty, "personality" fulfilled the desire for self-derived activity—"the power of originating one's own action" without regard or even sympathy for the demands of someone else. If any external demand existed, then compulsion defined the action. And all worldly activity, James concluded, remained so constrained. "Man's natural activity degrades or obscures his personality. It is not spontaneous—nor does it originate in his internal self, but in a mere necessity of his nature." Ultimately, then, that "capacity of use" that defined a creature's spirit, remained alienated; the self and the object, the person and the property, were split one from the other.[82] The estrangement, which of course stood as an absolutely necessary step in the self's realization, allowed James at least to perceive of a time when society would break its bonds. An apocalypse of moral destruction, analogous to his own vastation, would then occur.

The age for James was hardly free or very divine. Caught in its fetishes and in a "grovelling mercantile commerce between God and the soul," society was trading things back and forth. It was making nothing but its own alienation: "man's object external to him instead of internal." Like Emerson, however, James used these mechanics as a metaphor. Rather than looking for any immediate social reforms, he was seeking the signs of a coming moral destruction. He did write vaguely of Fourierism,[83] but Fourierism, written as it was, like Swedenborg's visions, in the precise designs of a mathematician, provided a modern mechanical device just as morally encrusted as any other. Only an irony can explain James's infatuation with Fourier's social system.

James was focusing, in other words, on psychology rather than economy or polity to explain his state's estrangement. Modern labor was easily described as "mere toil," "servile and imitative." Modern labor, however, expressed James's own state of "compulsory work" or "ritual labor."[84] Ritual labor defined an insanity, in that in insanity the will became fixed: "a fixed will, a will pertinaciously anchored upon any thing or event, to the intolerance of any other thing or event, is the definition of insanity." The mind of the age had fixed itself, in its "mechanical process," such that James, prior to apocalypse, could declare the whole of the Protestant ethic compulsively sick.[85]

James had driven the distinction of faith and works to the question of work itself, to a point that Edwards could hardly have imagined. He even drove past the transcendentalists and their own preoccupations with the alienation of modern labor, even past Thoreau, who, though he was speaking the most cogently of work and its alienation, was still celebrating the organic labors of armies and sailors. James had, in fact, defined his own artist as ethereal to the point of meeting the worst of Emerson's fears. Emerson had unleashed his American Scholar, but when Emerson came to write of the sequestered transcendentalist, and of young artists' "solitary and fastidious manners not only withdraw[ing] them from the conversation, but from the labors of the world," his caustic lines ate away at the very poet he had come to celebrate.[86] James, again, had only taken Emerson at his word. If everyday work defined the understanding of the naturalist's cabinet and the merchant's mind, if it was mere classification and calculation—"manure" and "*scoriae*," as Emerson had said—then such natural work must end. Nature, as Emerson would remind his readers, promised something else: in "our fine Latin word, with its delicate future tense,—*natura, about to be born*, or what German philosophy denotes as a *becoming*."[87]

James's Otherworldly Endeavor

A measure of paradox surrounded Henry James's life. He celebrated the plain, the poor, and the unadorned, yet he lived off the inheritance of the type of man he said America should not honor—the rich financier and the bank cashier—all, he readily admitted, to his own discredit. He valued the holiday and the sabbatical, the occasional lecture and the impulsive letter, but he labored incessantly, driven, whether by a Fourier or a Swedenborg, to publish works which none of his friends claimed to understand.

Those who only pretended to work, James wrote, should never be fed. Emerson had written the same. Then James thwarted, famously, the vocational aspirations of his own sons. It was as if their work would (or indeed should) promise to become the waste that the moral life expressed. "Well do I remember," his son Henry wrote, ". . . how I was troubled all along just by this particular crookedness of our being so extremely religious without having, as it were, anything in the least classified . . . to show for it; so that the measure of other-worldliness pervading our premises was rather a waste. . . . Religion was a matter, by this imagination, to be worked off much more than to be worked in."[88] There was to be nothing "classified" in their religion, nothing with which to make a "show."

Having collapsed ostensibly from overwork, the father had plunged himself once again into labors as devoid of interest to his friends as the earlier Biblical exegeses. This time, despite warnings from his doctors, he moved into the immense complexities of Swedenborg. Swedenborg offered a writing that James could compose his life against, but his style of work remained, to his death, unaltered. Once again he entered into abstruse and demanding labors, becoming, as a friend remarked, a sect unto himself, repetitiously publishing, at his own expense, book after book of a very idiosyncratically interpreted philosophy.[89] He wrote, as William Dean Howells remarked, *The Secret of Swedenborg* and kept it.[90] "Probably few authors," his son William wrote, "have so devoted their entire lives to the monotonous elaboration of one single bundle of truths."[91] William presented his father's *idée fixe,* however, this other world of his obsession, to provide the monotony that he could, in his turn, work against.

"We took his 'writing' infinitely for granted," Henry James, Jr., wrote, "—we had always so taken it, and the sense of him, each long morning, at his study table either with bent considering brow or with a half-spent and checked intensity, . . . a musing lift of perhaps troubled and baffled eyes. . . . He applied himself there with a regularity and a piety as . . . if he had been working under pressure for his bread and ours."[92] "The rupture with my grandfather's tradition and attitude was complete; we were never in a single case, I think, for two generations, guilty of a stroke of business."[93] Within this composition drawn by his son, the elder James is working with the ascetic piety and regularity of his own Calvinist father. His labors are to stay otherworldly, however, most particularly in William's eyes: "My occupations are all indoors, so that I am generally at home."[94]

Henry James, Jr., wrote that as boys both he and William felt embarrassed by their father's lack of an occupation. The father had set his life so much against "the American ideal in that matter, then so rigid, [that we] felt it tasteless and even humiliating that the head of our little family was *not* in business."[95] To work without an office "of a rigorous sort was to *be* exposed . . . ; since it was a world so simply constituted [that is, of works] that whatever wasn't business, or exactly an office or a 'store,' . . . was just simply pleasure."[96] It was hardly that. When the boys asked their father what they should tell their friends he did, Henry James replied, again famously: "Say I'm a philosopher, say I'm a seeker . . . an author of books if you like; or, best of all, just say I'm a Student."[97]

It should be remembered that the son created this image of vacuousness for his own purpose. The father's exposure was the exposure of the American artist without a space, a context, or a culture to work within—the artist, like Henry James's Hawthorne, whom the younger James discovered buried within his chamber, writing through time and in a blankness that demanded a unique faith. Few would even remember the elder James, but for those who did, these patterns created by the son, in his own autobiographies, formed the most lasting impressions. They are the archetypal patterns of a saint working to deny all his past history. With exposure came dread. With exposure, as Henry Adams prefaced his own *Education*, the manikin forms of the self were removed. Exposure dissolved the self in a wasteland, and it made little difference whether that waste appeared opened or closed—whether it was spread across the vastness of the American landscape or constricted to a point devolving in upon the self—as long as the self remained, momentarily, without any business.

Like a prophet beyond the city's gates, James wished to expel in a breath what he wanted to say: "Oh, that I might thunder it out . . . the *whole* of it, and never speak a word again!" This smoldered as the fire in his breast, as William James expressed his father's fury. "This is why he despised every formulation he made as soon as it was uttered," William remembered, "and set himself to the Sisyphus-labor of producing a new one that should be less irrelevant."[98] Henry James wanted some central and controlling fact, some embracing structure, but he wrote instead in "anticipatory flights,"[99] his words evolving into a private language that William tried desperately but failed to understand. "You live in such mental isolation," he wrote his father, "that I cannot help feeling bitterly at the thought that you must see even in your own children strangers." The son thought the problem lay in his father's uncertain use of words—words that through "long brooding" had acquired a substance unapparent to another.[100]

The father became "a genius certainly,—a religious genius" and, for William, eventually a saint. The "discordance," however, which marked the relationship between the elder James and his oldest son turned quickly to a separation that, as William said, "makes it so hard for me to make him feel how warmly I respond." William then repeated his father's own rebellion against William of Albany, but he reversed the terms, demanding that his father place his faith in something concrete.

The adolescent son only too quickly had pointed out that his father's philosophical apparatus, for all the study he made of it, lacked any precision.[101]

Henry James placed the life he wanted so desperately to destroy in both his philosophy and biography. Like the Puritan autobiographer, he universalized "insane worry and superstition" such that his fear became the common condition of all preceding spiritual birth.[102] James often traveled from the personal to the absolute within a matter of paragraphs. The center of his universe alternated quickly between an intense egoism and an equally intense universalism—an acute consciousness of himself that vied with a desire to submerge himself in the whole experience of mankind. Ultimately, he would extinguish his self, he believed, within a universal socialism that would shortly arrive.

William called "self-conceit and self-reproach, pride and penitence" his father's "malady," and wrote that his father's philosophy had set itself to cure the division.[103] Within James's philosophy this division erupts at moments of creation when persons both receive "community with all other things" and at the same time stand "alienated from the creator"—receiving, that is, not only their community but also their "conscience of selfhood or freedom sensibly distinct." For James, the doubleness sets the moral conscience to work. Standing apart from God, wishing to become as God, man attempts to "placate" his Creator, but as his propitiation becomes futile and ever more insane, he drives himself further into "wilderness states . . . of frantic self-isolation." Hope turns to despair and love twists to hate as sons come to denounce the God whom once they had loved so closely. For this state, James called upon the Puritans' vocabulary, not his beloved Swedenborg: "I experience, in fact, what is properly called 'a conscience of sin'; that is to say, I undergo such a sickening. . . . Indeed, so lively a conviction besets me, . . . that I feel a distrust and distaste of his once lovely name, hardly stopping short now of . . . hatred."[104]

Creation or, more to the point, conversion remained for James an unfinished event, a process or constant need for re-creation that would only cease with the lifting of society as a whole from the base material to a spiritual plane. Until this millennium, no beginning existed; there remained instead a process of alienation and return: an estrangement from God the Father creating the sense of self and individual distinction, and the accompanying conscience of sin, the acute loneliness that drove sons into contrition and their hope for return. That had defined his relationship to his father, and James wished the rebellion and reunification to define the relationship between himself and his own sons.

To illustrate his thesis, James drew the most obvious analogy, the separation of the child from the parent—a divorce necessary, to his mind, for the child's growth. The early and habitual reverence of the child for the parent would become "chronic imbecility" unless the child grew "to be wise, not from his father but from himself." This was "the rise," James continued, "of a . . . Protestantism in the soul; a needful insurrection against all purely external or arbitrary authority." A new power over nature, a scientific pride and philosophic achievement—that which Weber termed rationalization—depended upon just such a "Protestant" effacement of patriarchal, traditional, or arbitrary authority. As the "awe" of the race toward God, like the child toward his parents, changed to this skepticism and "scientific consciousness," innocence turned not only to pride but to "vulgar self-assertion" and "blatant independence." The self developed and discovered itself, but a "sickening conviction" erupted as well as the new self viewed its now complete estrangement from its all-loving Creator.[105]

This "mental condition" commonly marked the fall, though James was loath to view the separation as such. The fall acted as a prelude fathers and sons were re-enacting before their lasting embrace. The fall acted to provide the shame that alone could drive the assertive self back to its creative source. God had not capriciously created man and then abandoned him to writhe. He manifested Himself not as "a holiday God" but as "a working God" who had toilsomely made that which was not Himself. God had alienated man from Himself to allow a return, to make men so "ashamed," to so sense their own "worthlessness," to so know their "own natural obdurancy" that they would yearn for a return. Man would then travel "from distant creatureship into intimate sonship."[106] James would expect this estrangement to occur in the lives of his own children. He would write out his theology of alienation and return as though planning the course he wanted his children's lives to take.

The hell of the alienated self, as James loved to quote from Swedenborg, was "the vilest excrement," "the most vile and filthy excrement," "a realm of ever active outward waste." Protestant rationalism and its rigid scientific grids held within itself this other: "ghastly dwarfs" haunted by "underhand and sneaking ghostly interference ["by stenches so infernal as to put us to our wit's end for a remedy"] permitted through the crevices and rat-holes of our still most disorderly natural . . . existence." The "mental sewerage" was creeping through chinks of consciousness, becoming the stuff that men had to make "utterly unconscious" before their return, in purity, to God.[107]

Confusion reigns. . . . And the entire scope of what we call *history* is to reduce this chaos to order, to lift up this sobbing and prostrate universe . . . , to train this mute and melancholy and boundless nature into . . . personality or character.

Man worked toward rational science as nature formed structures, for consciousness began in minerals and in the separation of such types as iron and sulphur, gold and lead. Then growth and motion began as the mineral moved to the spiritual.[108] Like Swedenborg, in all these quests for formulas James moved toward the point of his own separation. He then broke himself by engineering the abstruse formulations. He mined Biblical texts and constructed systems, just as Bunyan had got stuck in chapter and verse, and Cotton Mather had tried to work out methods. The designs, of course, proved false.

And the father's schemes did become distant and arcane, set as they were in a rigid natural theology of which Emerson was among the last to speak: "God never jests with us, and will not compromise the end of nature. . . . It is a natural consequence of this structure, that . . . we resist with indignation any hint that nature is more short-lived or mutable than spirit." "Nature's dice"—until the advent of Darwin—were "always loaded." There was no chance to break into nature's scheme. The "iron bars" that man paved did allow Emerson to prepare for the collapse of this structure, however. The scene could quickly change, "for nature is not always tricked in holiday attire, but the same scene[,] . . . the frolic of the nymphs[,] is overspread with melancholy today. . . . To a man laboring under calamity, the heat of his own fire hath sadness in it."[109]

To a young William James, writing now in the world of Darwin, the father's theology offered only confusion: "You posit first a phenomenal Nature," William wrote to his father, "in which the *alienation* is produced . . . , and from this effected alienation a *real* movement of return follows. But how *can* the real movement have its rise in the phenomenal? . . . I cannot understand what you mean."[110] It would be left for the son to offer a natural history of the estrangement God wrought.

The Moral Desertion of Henry James's Father

It might be expected that the elder James's own father, the pious and eventually quite wealthy Calvinist, had unduly constrained his children. Indeed, Henry James wished to give the reader of his autobiography just that impression. James made it clear, in a statement that William would repeat in regard to his own family, that he never felt "so happy at home as away from it." He made it clear as well that he expected, and of course applauded, the "outward demoralization of the parental bond," a bond his father had impressed during his own boyhood.[111] The tyranny of the Calvinist parent, in other words, provided the figure of James's subjection to the Law, the Law under whose sight his terror had come, and the Law out of whose sight his civil disobedience could arise, opening his insight into a higher Law that demanded not his obedience but his faith.

Do as he might, however, Henry James could find little of the "tyrannous" in his father. He remembered that his father had appeared "weakly, nay painfully, sensitive to his children's claims upon his sympathy," and James used this sensitivity to argue for the parental detachment that he favored in relations with his own children: "and I myself, when I became a father in turn, felt that I could freely sacrifice . . . to save my children from unhappiness. . . . What sensible parent now thinks it is a good thing to repress the natural instincts of childhood?" The natural instincts must be allowed their play, for the instincts worked as the "educational forces" driving the self's destruction. The demoralization of the parental bond, the allowance of this free play, acted in behalf of making the child pay. There was enough "pregnant evidence" to show that authority was being transferred to the maternal, exalting men "out of the mire and slime of their frivolous and obscene private personality." Natural forces, in other words, created their own reaction; the child's instincts would turn and devour themselves. For all the guise of the "authoritative," the father, William of Albany, had managed just that. He had allowed enough freedom for his son to be left alone, suspended, as Henry James thought he had been suspended, in "contented isolation."[112]

James scattered comments throughout his autobiography that make his father out as distant and arbitrary but not authoritarian. When young, James remembered, he had little contact with his father except at family prayers and meals. His father often stayed away from home, but even when at home the elder William James seldom inquired of his son's interests or asked about his occupations or expressed concerns about his friends or standing in school. "He was certainly a very easy parent," James wrote, "and I might have been left to regard him perhaps as a rather indifferent one, if it had not been for a severe illness which befell me from a gun-shot wound." Suddenly William James of Albany turned and provided his son with an affection the mother thought imprudent. James had to suffer a terrible wound, however, to receive his father's love; he had to experience the eventual loss of his leg to know the sympathy his father in fact possessed.[113]

It appeared as though the father had abrogated his responsibility toward his child and left Henry James, as James thought, in direct communion only with God: "The parent, or whoso occupies the parent's place, should be the only authorized medium of the Divine communion with the child; and if the parent repugn this function, he is by so much disqualified as parent." James's uncertainty had placed him in that attitude of needing to huckster with God. Doubt as to where exactly he stood had driven James to try to bargain his way out.

The mother, the essence of "maternity itself"—"a good wife and mother, nothing else"—somehow in all of this remained both demanding and depressing. She had given herself to her child, as though she could never forget the gift of a child that she had received. Perhaps she could never let her child forget just what it was that he had received. She formed, in any event, not a personage but an essence for James—"maternity itself in form": "I remember . . . that I have frequently seen her during my protracted illness, . . . come to my bedside fast asleep with her candle in hand, and go through the forms of covering my shoulders, adjusting my pillows, and so forth, just as carefully as if she were awake."[114]

Beyond this autonomic image, James remembered that his mother had seemed "someway ashamed, as well as I could gather," so that she "would so willingly have remained mere lowly grass." She was willing, that is, to be crushed. Her children knew that she felt ashamed of her "distinguished relations," the "tacit quarrel" she maintained "with the fortunes of her life"—feelings of being tied to an inheritance that her son would repeat. Henry James would also attack his mother's good fortunes—his inheritance from a "great capitalist merely"—and for his own sons would condemn anything smacking of a "thrifty scheme," anything "paying." He would repeat his mother's feelings by idealizing lesser classes, all a part, as his son William said, of Henry James's own "*abasing* mood."[115]

James was in doubt whether his upbringing had been free or restrained. He appeared uncertain too whether his parents had been loving or indifferent. To say that he had experienced the authoritarian served his intellectual purpose, for then the Calvinist God and the Calvinist father could combine in the consciousness of the child to produce an unholy fear of sin, marking out the estrangement James required between the son and God the father. Henry James attacked not the authoritarian but the arbitrary God, however, the God who *could* strike or condemn him, who commanded all good and yet could, if He so chose, punish him under the most arbitrary of circumstance. He could never, Henry James wrote, worship a God who remained personal, finite, and sensuous, a God who would love him and yet could, if He so chose, crush him to death. Thus, "so long as I conceive Him in any manner *capable* of inflicting death . . . I cannot truly worship Him." Indeed Satan, not God, represented "the principle of arbitrary authority in human affairs whether secular or ecclesiastical." "I would renounce my own father as cheerfully as I would eat my daily bread, did I conceive him capable of a petty malignity like this."[116]

James did renounce his father, or at least ran rebelliously from home. He renounced the type of traditional or patriarchal authority that could act quite as it pleased. He renounced the irrational authority (in Weber's terms) that for James created the despair of persons who simply never could know whether their God held them within His grace. Man possessed a female nature as well, however, and for James the female, with the loss of patriarchal authority, was ascending to end the despair. Through the gradual demoralization of the family bond, accompanied by the sexual education of the child, the abolition of laws of divorce, and the decreasing bondage of wife to husband and of child to parent—through the arrival, indeed, of a universal family and parent—children and men would at last be freed from the faults of parental frailty. For the immediate parent, James claimed only a mediative role. The "putative mother" was "only a *quasi* mother," hiding the child momentarily while aggrandizing "its material bulk sufficiently to bring it under the care of the common mother, to be dandled thenceforth on her impartial knees, and nurtured to manhood upon the milk of her imperial breasts." And so for the father, "the child's immediate parents turn[ing] out abjectly mediate ones after all." James envisioned, most simply, a "more efficient" parent who would end the cause of the child's doubt.[117]

If a child experiences a distant and arbitrary environment, a family of whose love or even hate he feels unsure, then doubt and a compulsion to know will beset his mind. He may never know whether his family has offered love or disregard, or whether his environment has secured or divorced him. This portrait, used to fashion the etiology of a compulsive or obsessional personality, is a psychological analogue of a common reading of Calvinist theology. The person will live in a state of not knowing (whether of love or salvation), and thus might try to know by attempting to control the uncertainty. He will surely feel guilt as well as doubt, since being unable to attribute his misery to the simple malignancy of another, he will look for the cause of his hurt within himself. The authorities in his life offer both good and bad, both love and hate, all perhaps at the most incongruous of times. Parents may give much and then ask the child never to forget just how much he has in fact been given. They may offer love and then tell the child never to forget just how great the love has been—just how much it has cost that it might be given.[118]

The world appears far from a garden; it appears a wilderness. In the tangle of doubts created, a material fact of child psychology works like a Puritan spiritual convention. James imagined a paternal world stripped of humanity, a world of loathsome material holding humankind back, a world "we . . . cry aloud to be delivered." "Can any thing be presented to your imagination so ghastly and abhorrent as the conception of this fair universe given over to the dominion of [such] animal life, turned into a hot-bed of gigantic reptiles, and a nursery of nameless and obscene monsters, whose empire should know no law or limit but that of their own hideous might?" He wrote the words in 1855, four years before the advent of Darwin, and they became the words of terror that William would try to explain. The elder James offered this tangled bank and broken shore to his children, feeling, as he had, that he had seen this snake in sensuous form. His re-birth, like that of his children's, had to begin in this nursery of nameless monsters.[119]

One may only mark, then, rather than account for the uncertainty and rage James expressed. Not only did he compose a careful account of his fright, but later others composed their memory of him. They described the sympathy and the rebuke that he expressed, both toward himself and toward others. When "you took him to task for violating the feelings of others . . . ," William James quoted from a friend of his father, "he would score you black and blue . . . and all the while he made you feel that . . . his divine rage was with *himself*." If James were uncertain as to the attitude of the world he confronted,[120] that made him, as Ralph Barton Perry concluded, "in all his human relations at one time romantically tender, at another almost boisterously bellicose, and often both at the same time." No question existed as to "the tenderness and generosity" of James's character, and no question existed either as to the bite of his tongue.[121] He could offer cruel remarks to the best of his friends, as when, in a conversation with Bronson Alcott, he broke in: "My dear sir, you have not found your *maternity* yet. You are an egg half hatched. The shells are yet sticking about your head." Perry apologized for such by saying, in effect, that James never really meant it, that his abusiveness remained "impersonal" or "*merely* personal, for he continued to smile lovingly upon the universal humanity."[122] By remaining in the universal, however, James could strike and not *really* hit. If what remained personal failed to be of any account, then he could hurt and not mean harm; he could strike and still remain safe within the impersonality of all humankind, affording in that way gentle but only distant expression.

James called forth the coming community of man, the common universality of love and democracy wherein all would share together in the fruits of their civilization. Beside this prophet stood the vandal—the critic who, in the basest of his terms, would "convert *myself* . . . into an army of Goths and Huns," as he wrote to Emerson, "to overrun and destroy our existing sanctities." His "argumentative style" bothered Emerson—grains of gunpowder, as Emerson thought, instead of garden seeds sown in a book "full of nobleness." The distance of James's style, as well, bothered Emerson—"every technical *For* and *Suppose* and *Therefore*" that erected barriers between James and his readers.[123] This distance secured James, while the qualifications that he used to surround his doubt covered up his uncertainty.

Like his own father, for whom sympathies had remained emotionally taxing, James found relief by so universalizing his love for his children that his own sympathy no longer seemed intimate and therefore dangerous. "Your long sickness," he wrote to his son Henry, "and Alice's, and now Willy's, have been an immense discipline for me, in gradually teaching me to universalize my sympathies."

> It was dreadful to see those you love so tenderly exposed to so much wearing suffering. . . . But when I gained a truer perception of the case, and saw that it was a zeal chiefly on behalf of my own children that animated my rebellion, and that I should perhaps scarcely suffer at all, if other people's children alone were in question, . . . I grew ashamed of myself, and consented to ask for the amelioration of their lot only as a part of the common lot. This is what we want, . . . the reconciliation of the individual and the universal in humanity.[124]

This detachment and hesitancy to offer immediate love reflect, perhaps, an earlier time when the child could very well die.[125] James had set about to become a modern parent, however, claiming authoritarianism only for the generation of his father. "At that period it was very nearly altogether authoritative and even tyrannous with respect to the child; while in our own day it is fast growing to be one of the utmost relaxation, indulgence, and even servility." He was obviously ambivalent.[126]

Whether he was right, the moral faculties that the parent might expect the child to possess had changed in perception. One need only think of Edwards's thoughts, and the composition that he made, of the religious experience of Phebe Bartlett. The elder James wanted to raise his own children quite differently. He wanted to preserve, for as long as possible, their inborn innocence, their being as opposed to their doing.

Their doing was the work or the narrow pursuit that would crush their life, he said. Vowing that his children would never experience the forced morality and authority that he felt had marred his own upbringing, James set about, as he made it appear, to lengthen for his sons and daughter that "period of infantile innocence and ignorance." The words "innocence" and "ignorance" he carefully conjoined. He promised never to force a choice or cut short some possibility, however remote. "What was marked in our father's prime uneasiness," Henry Jr. wrote, "in presence of any particular form of success we might . . . propose to invoke was that it . . . dispensed with any suggestion of an alternative. What we were to do instead was just *be* something, something finer in short than being *that*, whatever it was, might consist of."[127] One must hold these words and the freedom they intone in suspicion, however. The words suspend, in their innocence, the terror that will come, thereby running the father's experience into the experience of the sons. The elder James would provide his children with sufficient freedom that they would rebel and thereby ruin their seeming innocence.

The Moral Wilderness of Henry James's Sons

Appearing to have rested upon his conception of "being," and having set about to check the vocational aspirations of his sons,[128] the elder James could only dream of that more efficient family, the incredibly defined common mother of impartial knees and imperial breasts who would replace the "abjectly mediate . . . , even ludicrously incapable" parents of his day.[129] But if he could not depersonalize the family institution, he could crack his own parental bond by prolonging the uncommitted childhood—"all those immunities and exemptions that had been, in protracted childhood, positively embarrassing to us," as Henry wrote. When the younger Henry James composed this memory, he informed his reader clearly enough that his father's efforts had failed. One suspects the father had fully expected as much.

Calvinism had served James well as an image of faith running amuck in business concerns. "Calvinist Orthodoxy" had demanded "tribute" while rendering his account "insolvent," damning his own child self to hell "on account of this natural insolvency." James gave the image of his childhood as a brokerage house without faith, a petty capitalist empire of bargains struck that God left broken. "I was born in the bosom of orthodoxy," and only Swedenborg had quieted his anxieties by teaching that religion was not an economy and that bargains were not to be made.[130] Calvinist authority (as it remains today) was a good figuration for explaining James's malaise. Such malignant paternity simply made no sense. James would be different; he would become a modern parent with "new ideas."[131]

James's allowance to his sons came, however, with its own particular cost. It came with the words that his son Henry continually used to describe *his* youth, a time, he said, of "disconnectedness," of "detachment." His father, he remembered, wrote before a window separated only by a pane of glass, but separated nevertheless, seeing out clearly, in the son's irony, into the reflection of the human condition.[132] And the father paid: he paid for the printing of his books, for his ideas—"Your father's *ideas*, you know—!"—and for his lack of the commonly defined success. The sacrifice he made "of such calculations" would entice and bother Henry Jr., whose own books would pay quite well. Henry Jr. wrote of "what I have commonly called our common disconnectedness positively projected and proclaimed a void; disconnected from business we could only be connected with the negation of it, which had as yet no affirmative, no figurative side." Business figured its own negation, the whole aura of being "methodically vague" that the novelist would consider and then project as the problem of American artists. Henry Jr.'s American artists removed themselves from time and took themselves from place. They were out of context—the right geography, in other words, for the Puritan saint. They devolved inward upon themselves, closing themselves in monastic rooms to write for years in pain, a problem Henry Jr. first approached, when a young man himself, in his study of the agony of Hawthorne.[133] Here he spoke of his father's amusement of "our pewless state, . . . as to where we should say we 'went,' in our world. . . . How as detached unaccompanied infants we enjoyed such impunity of range and confidence . . . is beyond comprehension save by the light of primal innocence, the absence of complications." "I read back into the whole connection indeed the chill, or at least the indifference, of a foreseen and foredoomed detachment."[134] That was the point, for the sons were to know that, in the absence of complications, the innocence would end in a chill.

He and William had lived as "nothing less than hotel children," Henry James said, their father having moved them from box to box to keep them free. The father's discipline is best described, it would seem, as passive aggression. "He was something very different withal from a parent of weak mercies; weakness was never so positive and plausible, nor could the attitude of sparing you be more . . . on occasion . . . comically aggressive." The elder James had given his exemptions to his children, but only with the utmost in parental watchfulness and interfering restraint.

Above all, for the younger James, a paradox evolved. He and William were to live to the point of their own growing confusion by re-experiencing the lack of parental consistency that the elder James had suffered:

> The literal played in our education as small a part as it perhaps ever played in any, and we wholesomely breathed inconsistency and ate and drank contradictions. The presence of paradox was so bright among us . . . that we fairly grew used to allow, from an early time, for the so many and odd declarations we heard launched, to the extent of happily "discounting" them.

The discounting too assumed some cost, for his father "only cared for virtue that was more or less ashamed of itself," and from that a crisis broke. The younger James suffered "that rather dreary time" when he found himself in a void, looking for "the object, the place, the person, the unreduced impression . . . [that] should give out to me something of a situation; living as I did in confused and confusing situations and thus hooking them on, however awkwardly, to almost any at all living surface I chanced to meet."[135] His father's abstraction had forced the younger James to find a concrete situation that he could pin himself on.

The children's freedom necessitated the creation of the very uncertainty that the elder James despised in his own Calvinist God. The modernity of James's family hardly existed, if by "modern" the father meant that the child's conscience should remain free—which the father did not. His own familial figuration ended not unlike the Calvinist pattern: uncertainty acted to expel the children from a garden of hardly innocent pleasure; to send them forth from the "insipid," the "impracticable," the "babyhood" of play; to move them from "childishness" into "progress" and "action," into the necessity of "history." They were to progress toward God rather than things, for history, or an uncovering of ties long past, remained the only calm that could ever rock one's "storms" to sleep.[136] The innocence ended in guise and so did its making, and that James would train his sons to see. They would find for themselves that in the protraction of their boyhood games, not peace but fire awaited, not innocence but reaction and death. "Accordingly, God endows him with conscience . . . (in scriptural phrase, *sends him forth from Eden*), and devolves upon this flaming vicegerent the task of humbling his conceit, and bringing him at last into the obedience of the truth." These words, for the father, formed the secret of Swedenborg, the fiery passage, the absolute necessity for "a long preliminary wrestle or tussle on the part of the individual or self-conscious man with himself":

> . . . a long, toilsome, most bitter, and vexatious conflict on his part with his own puny, crooked, insincere and ineffectual ways: before he can attain to that steadfast peace in God, which shall eventually leave him profoundly disinterested, indifferent, and actively inert in his own behalf.[137]

The younger Henry James, who so cemented the image that he and William were only to have experienced an extended youth—that their father had, in fact, left them infinitely free—furthered this first step of conversion by writing that his father had said what he said. The son then proceeded to uncover for himself the terror his own supposed innocence held. The Puritan structure, in other words, held: the claim to youth and the writhing skin; the sighting of the garden and the smell of death; boyhood games ending, as the father said, in fiery conscience, as though God sent fire as a heartfelt dart. When the elder James had lost his leg, he had been playing in a boyhood game, an experiment, with flammable ballons. The novelist son now wrote of his own bodily hell. He was chasing to put out a fire as his father had, and he too was caught: "a body rent with a thousand wounds" (like the rest of the nation, James was fighting a civil war), caught "in the presence of a crisis—the smoke of Charlestown Bay still so acrid in the air." "Jammed into the acute angle between two high fences, where the rhythmic play of my arms, in tune with that of several other pairs, but at a dire disadvantage of position, induced a rural, a rusty, a quasi-extemporised old engine to work and a saving stream to flow, I had done myself, in face of a shabby configuration, a horrid even if an obscure hurt."[138]

The image expresses a pouring of a stream of consciousness—fire and water, death and salvation—that provided twenty minutes of terror for the younger Henry James. James was working, quite ineffectually, like a machine. Leon Edel has pointed to the words in this obscure description to counter surmises that the hurt James experienced was actually castration: "it so made of these marked disparities," the younger James said, "a single vast visitation."[139] Henry Jr. had hurt his back, an infirmity, as William had earlier said of his own physical pain, that offered more than medical significance. In the James family, the body was tied to spiritual re-creation.

In a preceding volume of autobiography, the younger Henry James had described a similar fear. This time he recorded a nightmare, a sleep within a sleep. He fought for words to describe an immense hallucination of a struggle "lock and bar" against the presence of a "visitant."

"The lucidity, not to say the sublimity, of the crisis had consisted of the great thought that I, in my appalled state, was probably still more appalling than the awful agent, creature or presence, whatever he was."[140] This, again, is the damned shape of the father. Presumably this visitant also represented for the younger James his conscience of sin.

Like the father's memory of paternal tyranny, the son's memory of inconsistency, or the disconnectedness and the paradox that Henry James claimed for his and William's youth, did not cause their fear so much as give them a reason for saying why it should have come. Their doubts provide a reason for making them design. Doubt could drive the artist, as it drove the Puritan saint, to search for the figure that lay in the carpet, indeed to write of finding such an embedded form, just as the Puritan had spoken of conversion as a hidden design.[141] The chaos one remembers in one's youth provides one with a way out of chaos. A memory of chaos, like a memory of tyranny, expresses a means of control, for any memory placed upon experience orders experience. For both Henry and William James, the conscious artists of the family, the fear that came in the form of mechanical figures trapped in cells and moving convulsively, reflected the fear of their father. The father did not cause their frights; the father's figuration contained and structured their terror as they reconstructed his writing to make their own experiences make sense. Their obsessions, like their father's fixed structure, were to prove the need for their own eventual destructions.

Hawthorne

For the next half century, alienists posed the question. Though a man found his thoughts abhorrent and perceived his temptations to crime as silly or vividly repugnant, would he act his ideas out? The question was whether thoughts truly reflected nature, whether the mind reflected, in fact, the degeneracy of soul. Alienists and neurologists were to answer that an ideation like that of which the elder James spoke, represented not a fancy but a real psychopathic "moral insanity." Only James could have appreciated the irony of the phrase.

James wrote on the question prior to these neurological investigations. He worked with the intellectual equipment available to him: the theology and moral philosophy of sin, propitiation, guilt, and accountability that a new psychiatry was coming to replace. He worked as Nathaniel Hawthorne had worked, asking, as Hawthorne had asked, whether sinful thoughts, devoid of any factual substantiality, were to be held to a person's account. Was a person so haunted to be judged—and should he judge himself—on the basis of thoughts grounded in no specific act? Did there exist—in another variant of the question, and as Hawthorne seemed at times to imply—a compelling necessity to act the thoughts out, a weaving of influences beyond one's control which turned the projected consequences entailed by such terrible thoughts "into an iron tissue of necessity"?[142]

James knew Hawthorne—an "everlasting granite." To "one who didn't know him [he possessed the look] of a rogue who suddenly finds himself in a company of detectives." Hawthorne remained a center for James in a world "breaking up." The "death" of the world meant the resurrection of life, "that necessary rule," as James put it, "of inversion." "Let us then accept . . . destruction that chooses to come: because what is disorder and wrath and contention on the surface is sure to be the deepest peace at the centre, working its way to a surface that shall *never* be disorderly."[143] Hawthorne's writing, he had hoped, would hold.

Like Swedenborg, or William of Albany who had traded in salt, Hawthorne too had labored as an assessor of coal and salt. He had worked in the mines of ships in the custom house of Boston measuring the worth of contents. "A worse man than Hawthorne would have measured coal quite as well," the younger Henry James quite easily pointed out, "and of all the dismal tasks to which an unremunerated imagination has ever had to accommodate itself, I remember none more sordid than the business depicted." The life of the American artist began in such sordid occupations, while the artist's imagination went unpaid, and the younger James had no qualms in writing these lines while his father was still alive. The elder James, of course, would have quite agreed. Both Hawthorne and his early critic, the younger James, had worked this depiction out carefully: the assessing of coal, the measuring of salt, the blackened conscience of the customs house. James quoted from Hawthorne of "the doom laid upon me of murdering so many of the brightest hours of the day at the Custom-house that makes such havoc with my wit." "And when I quit this earthly career where I am now buried, nothing will cling to me that ought to be left behind. Men will not perceive, I trust, . . . that I have been a Custom-house officer."

They would, of course. Hawthorne was undertaking a passage. Through James's depiction, he had hermetically sealed the American artist in a chamber; now he was removing the self from its solitude to look back upon the national history this self exemplified: "this unblest Custom-house." It was knowing that which nature never taught, the mechanical endeavor that created naught. Because "the animal, or the machine rather, is not in nature," the saint in transition made his own bars. "It is good for me, on many accounts," the younger Henry James continued to quote, "that my life has had this passage in it." The feeling for Hawthorne was that of "the iron of my chain." It was his learning to work "with such materials," things, he wrote, "worth knowing."[144]

Hawthorne broke open the conviction of sin that his measuring had only briefly contained by breaking his measures down. In 1837 he provided a slight sketch—"it is a record merely of sinful thought, which never was embodied in an act"—entitled "Fancy's Showbox," in which he approached the same problem of signification that the elder James was to consider. Should "guilty thoughts—of which guilty deeds are no more than shadows"—draw down upon a subject the full weight of their approbation? He bound the tale on either side with a psychological inquiry. This is the story of a man beset by images of crime "so doubtful . . . , so faint and pale," as to make their viewer, a Mr. Smith, uncertain of his own criminality. The subject emerges from his innocence to become haunted and penitential, tearfully uncertain whether he has committed certain acts: they range from the murderous to the petty, from the vengeful killing of a close friend to the commencement of a lawsuit against three orphans ("blurred . . . he began to see . . . as stripping the clothes from the backs of the three half-starved children"). The images of these acts stay "cloudy," "devilish," "dull, semi-transparent," with the eye waiting "to fix them." Mr. Smith has sat deep in the luxury of his chair, his meal presumably just finished, a glass of Madeira in his hand, his children "gone forth about their worldly business," his solitude quiet, unfeared, until suddenly Fancy, Memory, and Conscience appear, as they were to appear for James, the glare of the light now muffled, his riches obscured. Mr. Smith becomes quite suddenly tortured ("Though not a death-blow, the torture was extreme"), fixing his sight "in a dusty mirror."[145] His, as T. S. Eliot would have it, becomes a wilderness of mirrors.

Hawthorne ended the tale by discussing prospective thoughts rather than memories. He argued the "cause" of Mr. Smith against his own conscience. Such a man "weaves his plot of crime, but [he] seldom or never feels a perfect certainty that it will be executed." He plots in dreaminess, his thoughts diffused, this mark "an indelible blood-stain." Here the imagination and actuality almost meet between reality and dramatic fancy. "Be it considered," Hawthorne continued, "also, that men often over-estimate their capacity for evil," for as they take their steps towards crime, "impelled . . . as in working out a mathematical problem, yet [they are] . . . powerless with compunction, at the final moment." Truth adheres, then, only at "the very moment of execution.

Let us hope, therefore, that all the dreadful consequences of sin will not be incurred, unless the act have set its seal upon the thought." This lack of a seal becomes a sign of something other than damnation, but the sign of uncommitment remains "slight fancy-work" if a man should disown his conviction entirely.[146]

The significance of this obsessional ideation had become less accessible, but the demand for a sickness and for a probing and recovery of buried thoughts remained. To take the poet out of his chamber of fathomless worries and endless self-reflections, as Emerson had demanded, remained problematical for Hawthorne, fraught with the possibilities of failure. Hawthorne's vision of such artistic alienation is in his *Blithedale Romance*—so well conveyed, indeed, that his readers considered the book itself a failure.[147] The narrator, Coverdale, seems distant and mechanical, fashioning characters that themselves appear hollow and manikinlike, form and content merging in a story the flat language of which estranges Coverdale from telling his own tale.

Hawthorne had spent a few months at Brook Farm, working, as he said, its gold mine,[148] and he used the occasion to move his narrator Coverdale from a bachelor's quarters of genteel musings and claret to Blithedale's promise of unalienated toil. This was to be the life of James's artist, mating the work of the head and the hand in a "Paradisiacal system" not unlike the Fourierist system that James projected for his nation's millennium. ("Speaking of the Phalanx," James was to write to a Swedenborgian friend, "I met . . . a young gentleman . . . and he said . . . , 'Mr. James, pray tell me did you ever visit Cambridge when Mr. Emerson, Mr. Hawthorne and others were trying their socialistic experiment there?' 'O,' replied I, 'I perceive you have been reading Hawthorne's new book, the *Blithedale Romançe*, rather inattentively.'" "'. . . and now, Mr. James, allow me to ask whether it is your impression that a great deal of *concubinage* was indulged in there?' *Did* you ever! I of course willingly protested against such an insinuation, on your account and Ripley's, but the *Herald* and *Express* have so bedevilled the idea of socialism in the minds of our spoon-fed people, that it conveys no thought to them but that of license.") Coverdale arrives, meets his utopian companion Zenobia, and promptly strips her naked in his mind. His Eve is becoming his New World garden. That evening, Coverdale falls sick.[149]

In "Coverdale's Sick-Chamber," shivering, the room "fireless," the narrator sets up his passions in distant crimes. He wonders, as an immediate question, simply whether Zenobia has ever been a wife. This wonder of her sexual past, asking just how innocent his new Eve is, becomes Coverdale's conviction of sin. The moment is set in a humoral corruption, but the language is strange, and for Hawthorne's reader the words may well have appeared inconsequential:

> There was not, and I distinctly repeat it, the slightest foundation in my knowledge for any surmise of the kind. But there is a species of intuition—either a spiritual lie, or the subtle recognition of a fact—which comes to us in a reduced state of the corporeal system. The soul gets the better of the body, after wasting illness, or when a vegetable diet may have mingled too much ether in the blood. Vapors then rise up to the brain, and take shapes that often image falsehood, but sometimes truth.

That night, Coverdale says, "proved a feverish one," his having caught a "tremendous cold," "a fit subject for a hospital." "During the greater part of it, I was in that vilest of states when a fixed idea remains in the mind, like the nail in Sisera's brain, while innumberable other ideas go and come, and flutter to-and-fro, combining constant transition with intolerable sameness."[150]

Coverdale calls his obsession mesmerism: satanic forces and magnetic feelings are ascribed to the tricks of others. The moment he allows to pass, and he returns to his garden and pose of innocence, and puts space between himself and his thoughts of sin. As narrator, he moves his actors stiffly across their pastoral stage, standing back as a passionless, untouchable, uncommitted artist peering through the lush greenery at his scenes, hiding in the vines of a tree, looking down upon his companions with the cold calculation of a transcendent, transparent eye.

It is left for Hawthorne, the artist further hidden, to reveal the nature of Coverdale's dream, and to reveal it consciously. As a portrayal of the transcendental quest, it is a biting commentary that ends with the plunging of a pole through Zenobia's dead breast, an orgiastic scene of three men probing and stabbing for her corpse drowned in a lake. Coverdale sits in the boat, looking into the blackness of the water, watching the search of the wasteland take place: "by and by, with a nervous and jerky movement, he began to plunge it into the blackness . . . , setting his teeth, and making precisely such thrusts, methought, as if he were stabbing at a deadly enemy." When the pole strikes, Coverdale momentarily senses what has been wrought, "for it was as if the iron hook had smote my breast." The men recover the body, and finally, for Coverdale, nothing is seen: "'See!' said Foster. 'That's the place where the iron struck her. It looks cruelly, but she never felt it!'" "'In God's name, Silas Foster,' cried I, with bitter indignation, 'let that dead woman alone!'"

Coverdale had anticipated this scene in his night of feverish, half-waking dreams. The "moral sand-waste of the world" that the oasis of Blithedale stood to repair overruns the garden in a midnight of terror.[151]

Bequest

Henry James, too, thought the innocents of the natural-born world the vilest of murderers. Though he understood his own mental anguish as but a last step before his spiritual return to God, his conscience of sin but a prelude or a crude seed of redemption, he paid his penitence. Like Hawthorne, James had arrived at certain psychological conclusions. The conception that men could think criminal thoughts and not commit them, that they could feel an impulsion toward acts and not perform them, allowed neither Hawthorne nor James to remove the bloodguilt from their hands.

True being arrived through "moral suicide," and Henry James thus ended his world. The final paradox of his character lay in his believing that God had rooted his particular contrition in his brain rather than in his spirit, that his moral hell remained but a part of a pathological self James called his phenomenal self. To release the spirit, persons had to render as naught the finite, the natural, the male, the material, the base, the sensuous, the mechanical—all the elements of man "*self*-alienated" from God. For nature was not "an ontological but only a psychological phenomenon." James asked his reader not to regard nature "as being, but only and at best as a seeming to be," "an appearance or semblance of being still uninstructed."[152] James's intelligence demanded that the natural and the bodily be of no account, that the self so painfully presented to his mind be sloughed off. He demanded that the world and its work be left to the devil, that the devil be given his due while men aspired to the holy and the unworldly, to something ultimately fragile and pale. Though he attacked traditional forms of asceticism as but some secret delight famishing desire, James killed his bodily self—slowly and, if his son Henry is to be believed, cheerfully, by starving himself to death. "He had no visible malady—strange as it may seem. The 'softening of the brain' was simply a gradual refusal of food, because he *wished* to die. There was no dementia except a sort of exaltation of his belief that he had entered into 'the spiritual life.' Nothing could persuade him to eat, and yet he never suffered, or gave the least sign of suffering, from inanition. All this will seem strange and incredible to you." Born into that darkness and its falseness of light, James had now looked through his pain: "He lay facing the windows, which he would never have darkened—never pained by the light."

Replying to this letter from his brother, William James wrote: "I must now make amends for my rather hard non-receptivity of his doctrines as he urged them so absolutely during his life. . . . Father's cry was the single one that religion is real. The thing is so to 'voice' it that other ears shall hear,—no easy task, but a worthy one, which in some shape I shall attempt."[153]

The "selfless detachment" of the father from his world could in retrospect be praised or damned. Though he accounted his father a religious genius, William James could only wonder, as Ralph Barton Perry noted, at those "left high and dry and abandoned by the tide as most men often are, only to be rescued from conscious annihilation by willingly forgetting their plight and taking no interest in it further, but looking out and sympathizing with the distant game, or with the tides as they flow. The obstructive ego says, unless I win (more or less) I won't play."

So William worked with the end of his father's life, killing again this old man who had lived, really, only the Calvinist demand, and who had extinguished himself. In his turn Henry James had damned those who were turning a deaf ear to being by simply doing—the gospel of the Carlyles: "He was used to harp so successfully on one string,—the importance of men doing, . . . and he no longer saw any difference between doing well and doing ill."[154] "The truth is," the father had earlier said, "we are moral and rational only because we have not yet intellectually realized our nature or spiritual creation, but stupidly insist on the contrary upon identifying it with our vulgar and pragmatical selves."[155]

The elder James had, he thought, broken the iron domination of the law, the sight of Mount Sinai that was about to fall. He had left Albany, his city of destruction, behind. He had written of the vanity of his father's cage—the telegrapher's cage of one of his son's stories—leaving the repetitive ritual and ugly business to walk alone. He was, he felt, besmeared with dirt; he felt, he knew, the whispers of monsters. He had composed his life like a pilgrim's chronicle, as if his life were that text. Henry James hated moralism, as his son William concluded, that thin plaster of "well-being" hiding the sores of being, small vanities covering cries and pains, efforts and wills prescribed for those who could only recognize their failings. William demanded in his turn some "practical fruits"—some material sign, some "wild" or "heroic" confrontation rather than what he took as his father's futile, world-forsaking quest for perfection. By opposing his father to America's gilt-edged perdition, "the general scramble and pant with the money-making street," he valued his father's saintliness, but whether that saintliness was to become a "moral equivalent of war," and thus a way to work off sanely such aggression, or a type of asceticism with which to work off what the son called an "obsession," discipline was to carry itself into the market and conduct itself productively.[156]

William James demanded the empirical, the workings out within the world that his father refused. The son would emerge from his own panic and fear and begin teaching the clear facts of physiology as an instructor at Harvard, while the father was still writing of Swedenborg and reading the mystic's revelations. William James would turn to vocation, to a small piece of reality, as he said, and attempt to reformulate his father's quest. As the elder James had attempted to break out of William of Albany's vain city, the son would attempt to break away from the waste that he took his father's other-world of purity to be. From a city of destruction, through a strange hermetic wilderness, a turn could be made back toward the world. A sequence of conversion could continue.

3

Conscience to Neurosis

William James

Everywhere the haunting
  Doubts
  Arrangements (Myself with hymn-books)
  numbers-combination
  Search for what is lost
  Metaphysics
  Moral intensity
  Belief in mission
    William James speaking of a psychopathic temperament, in notes for his unpublished "Lowell Lectures on Psycho-Pathology" (c. 1896)

Our own life breaks down, and we fall into the attitude of the prodigal son. . . . We want a universe where we can just give up, fall on our father's neck, and be absorbed into the absolute life as a drop of water melts into the river or the sea.

William James, "Pragmatism and Religion" (1907)

The elder Henry James had had to struggle to find modern expressions with which to describe his temptations and conscience of sin. He wrote out his confessions in published letters, books of divinity, and an anonymous autobiography. He worked with theology, punctuating his abstract texts with direct revelations from his life, while the most creative of early nineteenth-century American writing had left such theological pursuits behind and turned to the tale, the moral novel, and the essay to craft confessions of sin. James's obscurity, however, allowed him to live far more out of place than the estranged transcendentalists of whom Emerson wrote—in an actual alienation, as his children thought, of the otherworldly saint. One of his sons, William James was determined to draw the estrangement of his father out. William would take his father's struggle and place it back in the world.

New academic demands for professionalism and a German model of scholarship sharply divided William James's generation of American scholars from the world of Emerson and the transcendentalists, and of course from the world of James's father. For at least a portion of their lives, these men worked in universities, and even scholars as self-conscious of their Calvinist heritage as Josiah Royce, Henry Adams, James Jackson Putnam, and James himself did not conceive of their writing as theological or even as "religious," though in Royce, America had produced its greatest theologian since Edwards. This new generation thought of itself as working within established or emerging academic disciplines: philosophy, history, psychology, and in the case of Putnam, neurology. The men of these disciplines considered themselves, in our words, secular intellectuals.

Nevertheless, as Bruce Kuklick has shown, academics like William James felt a necessity to address wide audiences, and when they spoke to such popular concerns as the efficacy of religious belief, the technical mastery they possessed allowed them to speak with the authority of the scholar-ministers of early America. Victorian ministers themselves lacked the education in medicine or epistemology that Cotton Mather and Edwards had applied to questions of spiritual conversion. An academic like James, on the other hand, could assume the mantle of the publicly attached "intellectual," the kind of scholar who until the mid-eighteenth century could only work in America as a pastor.

At the same time the role James inherited, situating him somewhere between preacher and professor, encouraged him to present before the public not only his scholarly writings but also the writings he composed of his own life. Like the ministers of early America, and like his father, he allowed his most private struggles to become public documents. He gave voice to his life and the mentral struggles that his life entailed because, while a professional scholar, his self was still to serve as a moral exemplum.

Like his father, who often composed his writing in the form of letters addressed to a friend, James suffused his lectures and essays with a very personal confession. His confessional tone permeates even his most abstract writing. He interpositioned himself in his texts even when he refused the pronoun "I." Like his father, or like Hawthorne in his tales, he invites his reader to wonder and to make an inquiry—to make a psychological case out of James, in other words, much as James made such a case out of the lives of others. Consequently, William James has invited more psychological interpretation than any other American scholar.

James's confessional text—a "radical act of public confession" that he lamented as missing from his Victorian world—is embodied in no single spiritual autobiography, but rather is distributed through his collected correspondence, published diary entries, and personal asides within his publications. His autobiography obviously remains far more complex than a single written memory, but in its construction it can be conceived as a whole text, as indeed his son Henry James III, the first editor of his letters, and Ralph Barton Perry, his student and first biographer (*The Thought and Character of William James*), so considered it. This practice of gathering disparate autobiographical fragments and publishing them as a coherent story extends at least as far back as Samuel Hopkins's publication of the *Life and Character* of Jonathan Edwards.

The demand for professionalism that William James found himself immersed in not only enabled him to find a job in the new and rapidly expanding university setting; it also demanded that he compose his confessions differently from those of the elder James. He was not a "writer," so he could not create a spiritual autobiography like *Nature* or *Walden*. But as an academic scholar he could write about "natural religion." He could display the "neurology" of religious conversion for a Victorian audience he admonished for refusing to acknowledge the possibilities of spiritual terror; but as an academic psychologist writing his Gifford Lectures on natural religion (*The Varieties of Religious Experience*) from a bequest that, in the words of Lord Gifford, wished religion "considered just as astronomy or chemistry is," James chose not to assert that he had experienced religious insight. (All that he would say of his case in the *Varieties* was that "I have always thought that this experience of melancholia of mine had a religious bearing.") To claim that he was witness to an immediate action of God appeared nonsensical to

James. Given the new psychology, however, James could still use older confessional practices to make his struggle effective.

William's scientific training provided a vocabulary with which he could specify and make far more accessible his father's idea of spiritual conversion; his training included study of the psychoneurotic, which for the father was only medical materialism. One had to begin with the neurotic, the son insisted, if one wished to make accessible to the modern mind the spiritual insights that William fully believed his father had achieved.

The elder James, of course, possessed nothing of this nineteenth-century resort to the idea of neurosis. He certainly discovered nothing neurotic (only something moral or "insane") illuminating his own particular case. The case of conscience that he had struggled to express, his son could readily place within the purview of neurological science. William employed new expressions like "neurasthenia" and "psychasthenia" to speak of the religious conscience. He spoke in terms of morbid impulsions and obsessional ideations, and when he did, he reversed the seventeenth-century understanding of such thought. In forgetting the distinctions that Puritan divines had made between insistent temptations and real inclinations to crime, the new psychology failed (from the later perspective of Freud) to advance psychiatric thought. That in itself was significant, for by equating obsessional ideation with "moral insanity," or at least by equating horrid thoughts with an actual possibility of crime, William James could place himself in a position just as fearful and potentially damning as his father's position at Windsor. He could really believe that he might fail to hold himself in check, that he might, indeed, commit an unpardonable crime. He could then ask, if his grip failed, whether he possessed the faith not to seek what Thomas Hooker had called "crazie holds."

James demanded of alienists and neurologists that they realize the possible spiritual significance of the kinds of thought they explored. He would use an example like his father's vastation to found a psychology of religion, but he would do so in the hope of renewing the case of conscience. The most exposed of all such cases in Victorian America, again, is that which James made out of his own life.

Nature

William James was not, as he once described his father, a monotonous man. His own biographers have celebrated him as an impulsive and contradictory figure: the pacifist who wrote of war, the empiricist who engaged in psychical research, the scientist who disliked the laboratory bench and the classification of plants and fish, the experimental or "brass-instrument" psychologist who, having introduced the psychological laboratory to America, seldom experimented.[1] James drew a difference between science and faith, whether that meant adding a sermon on habit after he had drawn the diagram of a nerve, or preaching the power of positive thinking after he had explained the physiological determinism of the will. He offered himself as the exemplum of a divided self, the scholar searching, as he entitled a lecture, for the reality of the unseen, but searching where he began the chapters of his *Psychology*: in "the functions of the brain." Like his father, William placed himself between a theory of man as an automaton—*l'homme machine*—and a belief in the efficacy of the determined will, the will toward belief or the right to believe that he made so famous, and this in the face of the schooling he had had in British psychological mechanics. He wrote in spite of his father, but he wrote in accord with the empirics of his time, explaining his father's psychomachy in terms of neurology.

For late Victorian Americans, however, it was not the elder James but William who was re-enacting the history of "Poor patient Bunyan."[2] He was living out for himself the sickness involved, but the horror of the pilgrim's progress now hung mute upon a museum wall. It was displayed, by a young James, for new interpretations:

> I have been pretty busy this week. I have a filial feeling towards Wyman already [Jeffries Wyman, then his instructor at Harvard]. I work in a vast museum, at a table all alone, surrounded by skeletons of mastodons, crocodiles, and the like, with the walls hung about with monsters and horrors enough to freeze the blood. But I have no fear, as most of them are tightly bottled up.[3]

James was writing from Harvard to his sister Alice, asking about his family and mentioning everyone—everyone, that is, except his father.

Whatever the whimsy that William used to freeze his father's terror into these dead specimens, William held to history. One awoke and left ignorant parents behind: for the elder James, that had meant leaving Albany and its merchants; for the younger James, it meant leaving Swedenborg and his *Apocalypse Explained*. William juxtaposed the mystic's revelations with the natural history that hung on the museum's walls. He sat waiting, thinking a little of "medical business" and perhaps of becoming an alienist. In the meantime he would "go it blind," as they say, and watch for that bottle to open.

William was re-enacting in the modern setting of the Lawrence Scientific School the Puritans' drama. "I want you to become familiar with the notion that I *may* stick to science, however, and drain away at your property [his father's *proprium*] for a few years more."[4] He would use his father's money to make something different of himself.

If his father seemed archaic, to be read only by George Santayana by the end of the century,[5] then James appeared the modern man undergoing a modern crisis of faith.[6] He was to move himself through a series of occupations as if passing through the steps of a conversion. His occupations would run from the physiological to the immaterial: portrait artist, chemist, biologist and naturalist, medical student, anatomy instructor, psychologist, and by century's end, philosopher—this last the one vocation that William James had, from the outset, rejected.

When he came to pragmatism, however, James came to work. He came to Edwards's practice and to the awakenings that seventeenth-century ministers had presented as experiments to be enacted in place. Like Walden, truth was expressed; it was not expression. Belief was not an "origin, but the *way in which it* works." "By their fruits ye shall know them, not by their roots." These were the biblical words that Charles Sanders Peirce most favored for his pragmatism. "The *roots* of a man's virtue are inaccessible to us. No appearances whatever are infallible proofs of grace. Our practice is the only sure evidence, even to ourselves."[7]

James considered the truth of a matter like spiritual conversion a production, and he considered a narration of that conversion as itself a real experience, the experience that an artist used his memory to fashion. As for so many writers of American fiction, the artist had to accomplish his journey before he could begin to write,[8] but for James, only an act of articulation made such a journey visible.[9]

Radical Protestantism had created a new literary realism. The plain style of its confession included trivial incidents: absurd fears, petty worries, ridiculous scruples. The earlier lives of the saints appear to have denied that such things had any significance.[10] James scoured these earlier autobiographies anyway to find the "impulsions" he was looking for. He compiled a new vocabulary for what became no less than a natural history of the "neurotic": "Imperfect memories, silly jingles, inhibitive timidities," "*automatism*, sensory or motor," "morbid compunction," "fixed ideas and obsessions." It was a "*farther* side," James said, or an "ultra-marginal life." It was a neurological frontier. James placed his neurotic into this "empty waste"—"diseased, inferior, and excrementitious stuff." He then gave his neurotic a chance to work his barrenness out.[11]

James was opening the self at the extremities of nature.[12] He was arguing that "a thing's significance" appeared in "its exaggerations and perversions" in the bewilderment that the Americans, from their first crossing, had demanded. "Insane conditions have this advantage," James wrote, "that they isolate special factors of the mental life, and enable us to inspect them unmasked."[13] James always held that he was working against some conventional wisdom, a formalism that his empiricism would shatter. Here it was an academy that saw the mad as simply mad and not as the potential shape of the self as I.[14] James's unmasking, of course, reflected a Puritan trope. He could use the neurotic to strip away unwanted factors. He could hold the self in a bell jar to reveal its desiccation. The "crisis" of a "genuine saint"—David Brainerd, for example—began in a hermetical land of "contrivances and projects." The crisis began when the vanity of salvationist machinery was exposed at the edge of nature, in the automatism of a "melancholy state." James provided what he considered the best example of exploring the mind at nature's extremes, of why, indeed, his disbelieving audience should consider neurology before they spoke of religion: "Morbid impulses and imperative conceptions, 'fixed ideas,' so called, have thrown a flood of light on the psychology of the normal will; and obsessions and delusions have performed the same service for that of the normal faculty of belief."[15] One could never understand the will to believe as an act undertaken in a "blinding mist" without a study of obsession, or of the "phenomenon of automatism, be it motor impulses, or obsessive idea." This ideational "explosion" erupted, it seemed, from the subliminal or subconscious thought, and the eruption appeared to James intimately involved with the decisions of the saints. "We stand on a mountain pass in the midst of whirling snow. . . . If we take the wrong road we shall be dashed to pieces." This was the choice that Bunyan had given to his pilgrim.[16]

James, then, began the story of his conversion. When considering his confessional narrative, a reader must not only redefine the word "autobiography" to include temporally separate writings but also understand James's narrative within his definition of "conversion." James acknowledged sudden conversions but, like Edwards, held such onrushes in suspicion. He wrote instead that if a person's "conscious fields have a hard rind of a margin that resists incursions from beyond it, his conversion must be gradual if it occur, and must resemble any simple growth into new habits." The reader of James's lifelong confession finds himself drawn into Luther's and Calvin's idea of conversion, the spiritual preparation that in seventeenth-century New England Hooker and Thomas Shepard portrayed as a steplike journey, transformation punctuated by singular crisis while crossing still a person's entire life.[17]

Brazil and the Lost Garden

James undertook his own pilgrimage, then, beginning with a trek in 1865 out from behind the museum's walls and into the Amazon jungle. He had studied chemistry and comparative anatomy at Harvard. Now he became for the naturalist Louis Agassiz, "such a vast practical engine as he is," a collector of fish. "No words, but only savage inarticulate cries, can express the gorgeous loveliness of the walk I have been taking. Houp lala! The bewildering profusion and confusion of the vegetation, the inexhaustible variety . . . are *literally* such as you have never dreamt of." He stood, it seemed, in a park: "this placid Arcadia" or "Garden." Like his father, he was standing in an innocence of childhood prepared to make his fall.[18]

Agassiz, too, demanded that his students peer beyond their texts into nature. James could easily accept this antinomianism and hold it against the bookish life of his father. "O the vile Sea!" he had written in sailing to Brazil, "the damned Deep! No one has the right to write about the 'nature of evil' . . . who has not been at sea. The awful slough of despond into which you are there plunged furnishes too profound an experience not to be a fruitful one."[19] A decade earlier, the elder James had written *The Nature of Evil* from his study behind his glass. These lines from the son to his parents, tinged with parody and the slight bite of William's tongue, hardly concealed the challenge. If James were to reenact the pilgrim's progress, he would actually go into nature. He would find himself "sitting on a rock by the side of a winding mule-path. The mule-path is made over an 'erratic drift' which much delighteth Agassiz, but makes it truly erratic to the traveler. On my left, up the hill, there rises the . . . impenetrable forest; on my right the hill plunges down into a carpet of vegetation." "How often, my dear old Harry, would I have given everything to have you by my side to enjoy the magnificent landscape of this region! As for the rest I don't enjoy it so much."[20]

At twenty-three, the younger James had begun working his way through his profession. He could only write to his parents for the moment, however, about his indigestion: "I hope this letter has not a sombre tone. If it has it is owing to my digestive derangement."[21] Then he wrote to his brother Henry and mentioned that he wished that he might "hear Father's [lecture] on 'Faith and Science.'"

His garden was slowly turning to sickness. He now wrote to his father of his failing eyes and smallpox infection (later considered to have been varioloid). He wrote of himself as "an object of infection, . . . perfectly cynical as to my appearance" before "the good people of the hotel."[22] He wrote to his family of the "sensitiveness" of his eyes and of "the dismal potato existence I have been leading for the last three months. . . . Still in these ashes"—now his garden of ashes—"glow their wonted fires." "The fact was that my blindness made me feel very blue and desponding for some time. I only . . . thanked heaven that I kept on here, and put the thing through instead of going prematurely home."[23]

At the age of twenty-three, James was working hard to make something of himself, but found himself alone, sick, and mechanically collecting and packing biological specimens, his expedition having ended, he claimed, in failure. It was then that he finally wrote to his family that he had lost the use of his eyes.

In his diary, Jonathan Edwards had described his useless efforts to manage naturally his sin, attempts at self-improvement that ended always in "decay." "O, how weak, how infirm, how unable to do any thing am I!" Edwards's words, written at the age of twenty, contain sentiments similar to those James was now voicing. He felt caught, James said, and "owing to my eye," in the romance of an expedition that he now thought an "expensive mistake as regards what I anticipated." "You must know, dear father, what I mean, tho' I can't must[er] strength of brain enough now to express myself with precision. The grit and energy of some men are called forth by the resistance of the world. But as for myself, I seem to have no spirit whatever." His existence appeared "so monotonous," crossing this bare common of the Americas where nothing could befall him, and where everything would.[24]

> I am glad to the brink of fear [in the best known lines Emerson had written]. In the woods, too, a man casts off years, as the snake his slough, and at what period soever of life is always a child. In the woods is perpetual youth. . . . In the woods, we return to reason [to the spirit above the understanding, the calculation and collection] and faith. There I feel that nothing can befall me in life,—no disgrace, no calamity (leaving me my eyes), which nature cannot repair. Standing on the bare ground,—my head bathed by the blithe air and uplifted into infinite space,—all mean egoism vanishes. . . . I am nothing; I see all. . . .

Constructed in letters home, the Brazilian experience has achieved the proportions of myth in James's life: his failure to make a proper account, to make do in this, his strenuous life of taxonomy and collection.[25] James created his image of failure as Cotton Mather had created his, his own losing account to more practical, businesslike men. "I am convinced now" (lines that James's biographers often repeat) "for good, that I am cut out for a speculative rather than an active life. . . . I became convinced some time ago and reconciled to the notion, that I was one of the very lightest featherweights. Now why not be reconciled with my deficiencies?" Why not accept, indeed, that James had become the chief of failures? "By accepting them"—the "great many of my imperfections" that Professor Agassiz had pointed out, the fact that "he said I was 'totally uneducated,'"—then "actions cease to be at cross-purposes . . . and you are so much nearer to peace of mind."[26]

In the face of too literal a reading of James's words—that he had actually failed in his search for the "active life," as if that phrase, so reified, explains itself—one must remember that he recorded the Brazilian experience in "diary-like" letters to his family. Brazil expressed an "ideal type" that he would later explain: "As regards the narratives of conversion, . . . *no man's* account can be accepted as literally true. . . . Everyone aims at reproducing an ideal type which he thinks most significant and edifying. But . . . I think these inaccuracies of detail of no great moment; for ideals all are *pointed to* by experience."[27]

Experience, however, was not simply doing something; it was making a record (if only in one's mind) of what one thought had happened. Thus whether in letters to his father from Brazil in which he wrote of his convulsive labors, or in the later composition he made of a young man atrophied by the mind's seizures, James wrote not to recover his past but to move in new directions. He would take himself out of such prisons by remembering an event that has still "no connection with the first event except that it happens to resemble it." He would use what he termed this "revival" of memory that stands wholly self-contained, giving his narrations of fear a distinct truth that works separately from the moments of fear themselves. A testimony of any past experience becomes this tangible sign, reproductive, certainly, but also productive in that the necessary substitution functions as a new experience, creating its own consequences. Even speaking a fiction, of course, could create a truth, as James's theory of the emotions argued along with his "Will to Believe." James defended the necessity of signs not simply to make an experience visible—through a translation into words, for example—but also to make the actual stuff of experience, even the stuff of mystical experience that seemingly "defies expression." For this reason, James made true the "fallibility of testimony" itself: "We quote what we should have said or done. . . . But ere long the fiction expels the reality from memory and reigns in its stead alone."[28] When he came to write *The Varieties of Religious Experience*, James appeared little concerned with the literary devices of the autobiographies he studied, though he hardly appeared unaware of them. If the fiction works, the fiction works truly.

In the spiritual diary he was composing in his letters home, James was offering (like the Puritan) a gift of confession to his family. He was forming his experience into the failure demanded. He was looking at the Amazon's "mere vegetation" so as to see the state that he might become. He faced the vegetation as he would later face the asylum patient—to see his own estrangement. With this sight, he could then begin to work his fears out. "Men's activities," he now wrote, "are occupied two ways: in grappling with [such] external circumstances, and in striving to set things at one in their own topsy-turvey mind."[29]

This shutting down of the landscape, with which Emerson had concluded the first chapter of his *Nature*, represents the conventional ending for beginning the trek. One moves then through *Nature*'s "discipline" toward "spirit." Thoreau, for example, provided this ending for *Walden*, a conclusion that also appears to speak of a garden's failure:

> The sulphur-like pollen of the pitch-pine soon covered the pond and the stones and rotten wood along the shore, so that you could have collected a barrelful. . . .
>
> Thus was my first year's life in the woods completed; and the second year was similar to it. I finally left Walden September 6th, 1847.[30]

The American artist, and James was pre-eminently that, analyzes mind as Thoreau constructs his cabin, and begins his narrative of conversion as Ishmael arrays the lengths and breadths of the whale, in all the minutiae of detail that seem so objectively there. The artist grapples with this external circumstance and strives to set things right, laying out his warped boards to straighten in the sun. He then manufactures a safe ascetic retreat, a hut, ship, or raft, or for James, a carefully diagrammed physiological text of psychology, the measurements of which break the artist down. The I becomes transparent. ". . . such is the character of that morrow which mere lapse of time," measured by a clock, "can never make to dawn. The light which puts out our eyes is darkness to us. . . . The sun is but a morning star."[31]

The breaking seas of American fiction offer insight; for James's "genius," it is the farther land of the neurotic, in the psychopathic phenomenon he called "borderland insanity." This frontier provides the alien external the father had studied in his Swedenborg. Its measures provide the "very ancient slough" of which Thoreau had written—"*aes alienum*, another's brass; always promising to pay, promising to pay, tomorrow, and dying to-day." The estranged objects the self manufactures allow the self to know its works: they are industrious wastes; the artisan is a tool of tools in Thoreau's own phrase. "I went to the woods," Thoreau had written, "to front only the essential facts of life," and his readers expect his failure. The elder James, reading of his son's attempt to pack up the Americas' nature, expected a similar end for William's expedition. Like Thoreau, James had hardly set out to become an apprentice naturalist. "We must learn to reawaken and keep ourselves awake," Thoreau had lectured, "not by mechanical aids, but by an infinite expectation of the dawn." "We are made to exaggerate the importance of the work we do; and yet how much is not done by us! or, what if we had been taken sick? How vigilant we are! determined not to live by faith." It was to consider "for a moment" that Thoreau had taken himself to the "primitive and frontier." He was to learn of "the gross necessaries" of methods, "to look over the old day-books of the merchants" and read of "the grossest groceries" that their books "stored." The "improvements of ages"—the new alien labors Thoreau confronted—"have but little influence on the essential laws of man's existence: as our skeletons, probably, are not to be distinguished from those of our ancestors."[32]

The external force of the desert meant for the younger James wandering first in a garden to shatter himself. He could claim his initial "mistake" and then acknowledge his "strangeness." "I thoroughly *hate* collecting, . . . this elementary existence." "My whole work will be mechanical, finding objects and packing them [in barrels], and working so hard at that and in traveling that no time at all will be found for studying their structure. . . . Can I afford this?" This last comment concerned only in part the expenses involved, the rather large amount of money that Agassiz, like the father's Calvinist God, was now demanding—double or triple the amount he had first requested. The mental costs also increased: "I can't afford the excursion mentally (though this is not exactly the adjective to use)."[33] The adjective remains appropriate, however, as do the mechanics, along with William's feeling that he had to pay. He paid, and yet he had "no spirit": "our packing-work, its volume, its dirtyness, and its misery is wonderful. Twenty-nine full barrels of specimens from here, and hardly one tight barrel among them. . . . But when a good barrel presents itself, then the calm joy almost makes amends for the past." "If there is anything I hate, it is collecting. I don't think it is suited to my genius at all; but for that very reason this little exercise in it I am having here is the better for me. I am getting to be very practical, orderly, and businesslike."

The attempt to enclose nature could not end here, however. For years, James would try this economy again. No matter the failure he initially acknowledged in beginning his steps in Brazil, he would try other ways of managing his life. As for Brazil, "on the whole it was a most original month, . . . its strangeness I shall remember to my dying day." On the whole, it "was so much waste."[34]

The jungle collection offered the first of James's passages. He was plying into the matter of his nature, his natural history as opposed to Emerson's *natura*. He was re-enacting the morphology of conversion as a choice, now, that he had to make of profession. The problem of vocation that the American scholar faced, once the scholar had stepped from the pulpit, renewed the bewilderment of the pilgrim's quest.[35] James would work his way from the Brazilian fall through his panic or legal fear. Then he would attempt to set an ascetic life to work against his sight of horror; he would try, as Thoreau had tried, to build a safe place in the midst of his mental wilderness. The whole of his vocation would unfold like the stages of a conversion: an artist, happy and naive; a naturalist and medical student held in classification and physic; a psychologist bound up in the details of a long and meticulous writing; and in the end a philosopher working toward a mysticism and a final letting go. The last chapter of James's conversion spoke of hard work not as a means of salvation but as an expressed sign.

James's varieties of vocational experience contributed to an image of impulsiveness, however, not ascetic restraint. He appeared an "explosive self" flowing as freely in his character as he ranged and wandered in the subjects of his thought.[36] James did wander, carried by his father's immaculate quest, but always with insecurity and regret. He feared the sundering of "habit" that his father had envisioned. William disparaged any impetuous life as shallow, like the small depth nerves cut in their channels when they were not exercised enough by habit's passing. The father had dreamed of a spontaneous being, but the son demanded, for his time, a methodical self. His first passage in Brazil complete, he was now ready to open the sick chamber and return to life. "Knowledge about life is one thing; effective occupation of a place in life, with its dynamic currents passing through your being [for Emerson, "the currents of the Universal Being"], is another."[37] Whatever the effect the new history had wrought, the natural science of Agassiz and Darwin, or the observed as opposed to the transcendent, James placed his words close to Emerson's *Nature* and close to this older demand that the poet know but then leave his chamber behind. James asked that nature be seen from beyond his father's study—ultimately, however, and still, he asked this only to the end of transcending the eye, the I that, as for his father, had to become transparent.

James's Fear of His Father's Ascetic

William James reserved considerable time in his Gifford Lectures for a discussion of asceticism. It was a topic, he said, that his audience would find repugnant in their relaxed and optimistic age. Asceticism nevertheless "stood for nothing less than for the essence of the twice-born philosophy"; it stood, that is, as the only way to work a spiritual crisis out.

Portraits of the sick soul provide the most intriguing of James's case histories, a few of which appear but gruesome studies in self-immolation and insanity—"monstrously ascetic" forms that could only have served to horrify or titillate his audience. James refused such a purpose, although he did argue that religious experience could begin only with a study of the neurotic. "It is the work that is done, and the quality in the worker by which it [is] . . . done" that expresses the theme of his lectures, for only in the final product of a purportedly pathological mind could one determine whether that mind remained stuck in the pathological. The "industrial arts" offered the same truth: "Opinions here are invariably tested by logic and by experiment, no matter what their author's neurological type. It should be no otherwise with religious opinions."[38]

For those of healthy mind whose souls required but a single birth, asceticism seemed unnatural, but for those whom the iron of melancholy had stamped, asceticism provided a way out; its discipline arranged a method for "systematizing fear." In the end, James's interest lay with neither the insane nor the monstrously ascetic, but with those whom he argued had managed to purchase their safety, men such as Bunyan and Tolstoy. Saintly strenuousness or "austerity and singlemindedness" rather than self-immolation interested James, and he turned to such cases for examples.[39]

Though well read in the increasingly specialized literature of mental pathology, James used psychiatric terms loosely. He portrayed his divided selves romantically and sometimes, it appeared, overdramatically, particularly in his Gifford Lectures, in which he placed his literary skills above his medical training. When James said that asceticism expressed the essence of the twice-born philosophy, that it existed for persons who knew life as "neither farce nor genteel comedy," his listeners had to ask whom the twice-born were that James had in mind.[40] At least one was his father, whom James was quoting without acknowledgment.[41] However indirectly, the son pointed to the experience of the elder Henry James. He directed his listeners back to his "lectures on melancholy" for a reminder, he said, of persons who had felt panic and experienced the insubstantiality of life. There, within his discussion of the sick soul, James joined the three examples of the "worst kind of melancholy"—"that which takes the form of panic fear." The account of his own panic and depression—experienced in the early 1870s, perhaps in the winter of 1869–70,[42] and disguised in the *Varieties* as that of the "correspondent"—provides the main text. To this slight relation James appended the two footnotes earlier discussed: that of his father, which he referenced without comment; and that of John Bunyan, which he quoted at length. It was Bunyan's experience that James asked his reader to compare to his own.

It is also Christian's experience that James was making his own. Bunyan had translated his own temptation to unpardonable sin into the despair Christian sees as the Man in an Iron Cage, thereby providing James with an allusion for his correspondent. Like Christian, James's correspondent is viewing a man held in the room of an asylum. James's correspondent, in other words, is the figure of Christian.

It was Bunyan himself who provided an "exquisite" example, James said, of the divided self: "In the haunting and insistent ideas, in the irrational impulses, the morbid scruples, dreads, and inhibitions which beset the psychopathic temperament when it is thoroughly pronounced." Elsewhere in the *Varieties*, however, James joined this struggle with temptation or "obsession" to the need that some had for an otherworldly asceticism. "In psychopathic persons," he wrote, "mortifications may be entered on irrationally, by a sort of obsession or fixed idea which comes as a challenge and must be worked off, because only thus does the subject get his interior consciousness feeling right again."[43] Here he was speaking not of Bunyan but of his father.

James never precisely defined his understanding of the term "obsession." His meaning ran from a petty but unbanishable annoyance in the mind, to a blasphemous possession like Bunyan's temptation to sell Christ, to a seemingly irresistible impulse toward crime, and finally to a more popular, less anguished meaning of the word as an all-encompassing possession of mind toward some object or idea. He expressed the last meaning when he said that he had found Freud "a man obsessed with fixed ideas."[44]

Nevertheless, James repeatedly spoke of obsession as something that a person had to "work off." James expressed this idea as early as 1895 in an essay on "Degeneration and Genius" when he argued that genius, religious or otherwise, connoted "doggedness" and "staying power" rather than nervous debility. James repeated the theme in the Gifford Lectures when he spoke of religious geniuses who had "known no measure, been liable to obsessions and fixed ideas," but who like Bunyan had managed to put their lives "to active use." "As all effective initiators of change must live to some degree upon this psychopathic level of . . . impulse to action so obsessive that it must be worked off, I will say nothing more about so common a phenomenon."[45]

The phenomenon, however, had become not quite so simple. To become possessed and then to work the possession off expressed an idea easy to comprehend. In fact, it was too easy, for to conceive of an obsession as so closely tied to an act allowed a few persons to believe that they remained as "obsessed" as the "monomaniac" of the asylum and the novel. Such persons could use their criminal thoughts as sufficient reason for staying out of touch, uncommitted to some other person, perhaps, out of fear of doing that other person harm. They could use their obsessions, in other words, as laborious defenses. By the 1890s a few alienists had begun to distinguish what the elder James had simply demanded, that those who felt a seemingly irresistible impulse to act—often to the harm of someone they loved—would never actually commit the deed. Alienists, most particularly after Freud's writings began to appear, distinguished at times between those who found their criminal thoughts abhorrent and those who simply committed a crime.

James refused the argument and probably never considered it important. The distinction ran against the strain of his own psychology of the will and, as he thought, against his own experience. He equated the "inhibited" person with the potentially "explosive" person, or the compulsive with the impulsive. He wrote that if a thought possessed a person—a temptation to murder, perhaps, or to suicide—then unless some counter idea created through a sheer act of will overrode the original possession, the thought would quickly materialize. James considered the "irresistible impulse" irresistible unless an intervening idea painfully and always willfully brought to consciousness prevented the act from occurring. That conception allowed James to portray the obsessed as persons desperately needing to act. His religious genius, like his "psychopathic man," was "liable to fixed ideas and obsessions. His conceptions tend to pass immediately into belief and action; and when he gets a new idea, he has no rest till he proclaims it, or in some way 'works it off.'"[46]

Ascetic practices provided disciplined work to control such fear. Whether a "conviction of sin" or what James's father had called a "conscience of sin," religious melancholy expressed the grip of these "diversified temptations." In a passage from the *Varieties* following his description of Bunyan's "blasphemous obsessions," and in words that his father might have written, James portrayed the feeling of vileness and moral remorse and compunction that melancholy brought. Standing in "false relation" to God, with a conviction splitting the real from the ideal self, the patient sought a period of "order-making," a time in which he could relieve himself from doing what he hated to do and from not doing what he desired to do. James quoted from Paul.[47] But though he allowed his father's language, James would not allow the fact of an obsession to become immaterial. He required a real possibility of evil against which to test himself. Having taken his ideal religious genius from a chamber into nature, James placed his sick soul in Emerson's need for a grinding debt—discipline that Emerson expressed in a middle chapter of *Nature*. James made his saint undertake a moral act that his father, in his seclusion, had refused.

Though Henry James, Sr., appears but once in the *Varieties* and then only in a slight footnote, one can readily understand the Gifford Lectures as a dialogue between William and his father. To an extent, as Ralph Barton Perry noted, the lectures represented an exercise in "filial piety" for James, for immediately after his father's death in 1882, James had written to his wife, asking her not to "leave me till I understand a little more of the value and meaning of religion in Father's sense. . . . My friends leave it out altogether. I as his son (if for no other reason) must help it to its rights in their eyes."[48] Within two years, in the introduction to his father's literary remains, James began to investigate the psychological function of religion. There he included his father in "that band of saints and mystics, . . . [who had] prevent[ed] religion from becoming a fossil conventionalism."[49] Henry James had found in the Divine not arid theology but experience, the first of the varieties of religious experience that his son explored. It was the father's passive retreat that the son refused.

More than a note of ambivalence toward his father runs through this early introduction. At first James carefully separated his father out from a "common run of mystics" who had kept some tinge of voluptuousness in their lives, but then he remarked that his father's deconstruction of the self perhaps remained less complete than his father had thought, that his conversion from despair to salvation, in fact, was quite unsatisfactory. His father, he wrote, had appeared strange when in his "depressed mood," he murmured "the psalms of David to himself by the hour, apparently without a feeling of personal application." Though "drastic and unsentimental," his father had "lost himself . . . like a river in the sea," his "unity" expressing not a heroic meeting with evil so much as a relaxed sensuality—a desire at least for containment rather than will.[50]

As early as 1890, in his *Principles of Psychology*, James spoke of the self-love that an ascetic's life might contain. "If it be the 'other-worldly' self which he seeks, and if he seeks it ascetically,—even though he would rather see all mankind damned eternally than lose his individual soul,—'saintliness' will probably be the name by which his selfishness will be called." William James buried this remark in a footnote, but in his lectures on saintliness in the *Varieties*, he furthered the distinction at length. Otherworldly asceticism "occupied itself with pathetic futilities, or terminated in the mere egotism of the individual, increasing his own perfection." The heroic ascetic engaged the world through action. James proposed "some outlet" for encased futility by offering a new ascetic ideal, one that came when the "old monkish poverty-worship" he called "the strenuous life" transformed "the ascetic . . . impulse . . . [into the] objectively useful."[51] Otherwise, within a habitual, stereotypic world, only a "moral consistency," "monotony," "minuteness of uniformity," or "mental rest" existed. "Purity," James continued, ". . . is *not* the one thing needful; and it is better that a life should contract many a dirt-mark, than forfeit usefulness in its efforts to remain unspotted."[52] The father appeared to his son as too obsessively concerned with washing his hands of the natural to know that his life was sense-filled.

James had ended the introduction to his father's literary remains with a similar distinction and a faintness of praise. "To suggest personal will and effort to one 'all sicklied o'er' with the sense of weakness, of helpless failure, and of fear, is to suggest the most horrible of things to him. What he craves is to be consoled in his very impotence, to feel that the Powers of the Universe recognize and secure him, all passive and failing as he is."[53]

The father had failed, as he had to fail for his son, closed in the arid room of a perfect and, however ironically, a morally encrusted sick chamber. The trope allowed James, as the son, to complete the text by drawing himself out of such estrangement. This view of his father allowed James to fuse his father's life into the script of his own biography, thereby to form their lives into a single text in a single process of conversion. The son could hold the father's obsessive purity of perfection as a necessary, and necessarily futile, moment out of which he could emerge. His father's world-forsaking and quite sick desire for self-perfection had served its point.

Panic Fear

William James repeated the mental crisis of his father at approximately his father's age at the time of the father's vastation: the son was in his late twenties, the father just past thirty. William James's son, Henry III, the editor of William's letters and the person who revealed the identity of the anonymous French correspondent, would join William's narration of panic fear to a notebook entry William had made thirty years earlier: "dated April 30, 1870, [it is one] in which James's resolution and self-confidence appear to be reasserting themselves. This entry must be quoted too."[54] William's son would time his father's crisis by drawing together an unpublished manuscript and an anonymous publication, and by joining the presentment from the asylum to the diary entry of 1870 would also reflect a family tradition, in that he traced the event—"I think that yesterday was a crisis in my life"—to April, to spring, the season when the elder James and Swedenborg had also suffered. William's son smoothed out the complexities of his father's mental condition—in other words, fears and depressions that seem to have flowed throughout William's life—and provided contextual relationships with which to read the crisis. Henry James III would give his father's crisis a place and a time; he provided a "story." In a similar manner, William James had recovered the experience of his own father, unread in forgotten books and an unpublished autobiography.

In each of these scenes—William James to himself, then anonymously to his public, and then through the editing by his son to history—a text of conversion gradually worked itself out, as if James's writing reflected the natural evolution of his crisis and growth. It appears as if that text had existed all the while, uncovered simply through the light of history as in the archaeology of an artifact. James's conversion experience, however, remains this ever-evolving writing as it unfolds from his own, his family's, and his biographers' hands.

Although the "date of this experience cannot and need not be fixed exactly," Henry James III wrote, he in effect fixed the time of the sudden presentment of the crouching and petrified young man, the small study his father had made of the possibilities of human vileness and insanity.

The crisis occurred, as it had for William's father, in the midst of an extended period of doubts and depression. All through a time of "crass indolence" in Germany and then after his return home to Cambridge in November 1868, William James had been pulling and tugging at himself, attempting to set himself right. His breakdown did not come as his often feared meeting with insanity; rather, the panic allowed him to peer at his alienation: into the "pit of insecurity beneath the surface of life." He clung to scriptural texts, remembering passages such as "Come unto me, all ye that labor and are heavy-laden." Then for months after this panic ceased, he feared to go out into the night or to stay alone during the day.[55]

William James clung to scripture and thought his crisis had religious significance, but his fright failed to repeat his father's vastation. He later described fear like his own as agoraphobia, a wholly secular term which for James represented "the statue-like, crouching immobility of some melancholics" that, like an "instinct," crawled back out of man's animal past. It was "the accidental resurrection through disease," he wrote, of a once useful attitude. Meaning a fear of open spaces—literally, a fear of the marketplace—agoraphobia had emerged as one of the new phobic terms coined after 1870. Alienists used the word in a wide context to denote the fear of leaving any secure place such as one's home.[56] However insecure James now felt, he took pride in refusing to reveal his panic, preferring to reveal one face to his parents and another to himself. This portrayal of secretiveness remained characteristic, for in Germany James had admitted to his father that he had "purposely hitherto written fallacious accounts of my state home, to produce a pleasant impression on you all." Of course the confession tore down whatever façade James had managed to erect. Furthermore, James did communicate his insecurity to his parents and friends, though usually through indirect but incessant complaints of nervous fatigue and bodily ills. Thirty years after his panic, he thought that he had left his mother undisturbed, yet she knew at the time of her son's debility. "The trouble with him," Mrs. James wrote in 1874, "is that he *must express* every fluctuation of feeling, and especially every unfavorable symptom, without reference to the effect upon those about him. . . . Whenever he speaks of himself he says he is no better. This I cannot believe to be the true state of the case, but his temperament is a morbidly hopeless one."[57] The mother was writing as though she were Christiana, expressing disbelief that her son's troubles reflected anything significant.

James did suffer stoically from physical distress.[58] He never tired of revealing his body's ills, the "insomnia, digestive disorders, eye-troubles, weakness of the back" that his son Henry readily spoke of, because discursively the revelation of such ills was appropriate. James also used his ills as a reason to approach his world hesitantly; his body was a defense behind which he could continually plan and marshal his forces. Most often, James tied his body to his work. He argued that his eyes, for example, permitted only light reading and no writing, or that his back—his "dorsal infirmity"—disallowed work at a laboratory bench. If he had begun an experiment with baking powder (while a student at Harvard's Lawrence Scientific School in 1862), then ill health required him to forego the experiment because he could not eat bread; perhaps, it seemed, his body would force him to withdraw from Harvard as he feared it might. Throughout his career, James argued in the wake of considerable work that his ill-being permitted but little doing. In almost every letter he either introduced himself as presently infirm or mentioned in one way or another that he felt belabored, overworked, pressed, lazy, tense, or depressed. He called himself neurasthenic and then—when that term became dated—psychasthenic.[59] He repeated, as it seemed, the psalms of David.

There is no soundness in my flesh because of thine anger; neither *is there any rest* [or health] in my bones because of my sin. . . .

My wounds stink *and* are corrupt because of my foolishness. . . .

For my loins are filled with a loathsome *disease*: and *there is* no soundness in my flesh. . . .

My heart panteth, my strength faileth me: as for the light of mine eyes, it also is gone from me.

James also spoke of his detachment, his inability to experience religion, and his emotional coldness. This last was the sense that he possessed of his incompleteness: "I am a victim of neurasthenia and of the sense of hollowness and unreality that goes with it. . . . At present I am philosophizing as little as possible, in order to do it the better next year, if I can do it at all." James always managed to write letters about his sickness, though he claimed his "morbid pride" and "habit of secrecy" prevented him from doing so. He wrote of his "tedious egotism" and his "sickness and solitude," yet thought any hope for recovery "idiotic." James was not so much fighting a neurosis as his biographers have easily argued (because of the very evidence James chose to express); rather, he was living in a fight, running his life as if his body expressed a struggle reflecting the division of his soul. The fight in itself permitted certain luxuries—excuses for worrying and for secluding himself from family and friends. The psychomachy allowed James to brood, ponder, hesitate, and consider—to worry about his lack of pluck and then feel ashamed of his worry, "ashamed of those pusillanimities and self-contempts which are the bane of my temperament and against which I have to carry on my lifelong struggle. Enough!"[60] It never was, and although James kept apologizing for his complaints, he kept introducing them for others to hear and read of. In this sense, James calculated his behavior—never hypocritically, but with enough cold presentation to make one understand just how defensive and careful he was. When his friend Thomas Ward questioned his agitation, for example, James replied two years before his crisis that he was less quiet than Ward supposed; he was like a man "consuming his own smoke." When Ward greeted him "as the man of calm and clockwork feelings," James protested: "I was on the continual verge of suicide."[61]

James put himself into debilitating baths, hydrotherapies the benefit of which he doubted and a purge that he always complained weakened and unnerved him. He underwent galvanizing or mild electrical therapies and subjected himself to blisters and counterirritations—pains administered to battle bodily ones. He promised to take up a lifting cure and then allowed doctors to isolate and force him into rest, "though the listlessness that goes with all nerve-rest makes itself felt." One might surmise that physicians did these things to James, but James enthusiastically proposed such treatments himself, as for example a painful series of lymph injections to combat insomnia and nervous fatigue. He proposed the physic even after his alliance with the mind and faith cure movement in America.

The reader of seventeenth-century spiritual texts—Shepard's autobiography, for example, or Cotton Mather's *Paterna*—finds similar complaints of physical infirmity and notations of experiments with useless medicines. "Tormenting Pains in my *Teeth* and *Jawes*" for Mather physically signified the sin of his "Evil Speeches." His own physic spoke to the inefficacy of all but the physician Christ.

> And Studying *Physick* at this time, I was unhappily led away with *Fancies*, that I was myself Troubled, with almost every *Distemper* that I read of, in my studies: which Caused me sometimes, not only *Needlessly*, but also *Hurtfully* to use *Medicines* upon myself, that I might Cure my *Imaginary* Maladies. . . . Until once Crying . . . , and Casting my *Burdens* on ye Care of the Lord Jesus Christ, I sensibly felt an unaccountable *Cloud* and *Load* go off my Spirit.[62]

Besides the discomfort, James's preoccupations with his eyes and "that delightful disease in my back" permitted him "the life of a hermit." His back pains allowed him to claim almost complete infirmity and thence to make decisions that he could later revoke: "Of course, medicine is busted—much to my sorrow, for I was beginning to get much attached to it. The future is very uncertain." Or again: "My back will prevent my studying physiology this winter at Leipsig, which I rather hoped to do." It was as if James counted on his future in medicine being foreclosed:

It is only three months since I have taken up medical reading . . . and owing to the slowness . . . , I have not covered much ground. Of course I can never hope to practise; but I shall . . . work for medical periodicals or something of that kind—though I hate writing as I do the foul fiend. But I don't want to break off connexion with biological science. I can't be a teacher of physiology, pathology, or anatomy; for I can't do laboratory work, much less microscopical or anatomical. I may get better, but hardly before it will be too late for me to begin school again.[63]

At least twice—during the late 1860s and early 1870s, and then again in the late 1890s while preparing *The Varieties of Religious Experience*—James found himself in bed, lonely, weak, and depressed. During this latter period he worked quite hard, though he found his labors excruciating and slow. The ills permitted pains while the pains allowed James continually to castigate himself for his infirmities and moan his inability to study. The ills allowed him to hibernate and then to deride his seclusion, to lie indolent and then rebuke his laziness, to become contemptuous of himself and then to feel ashamed of this contempt.

The pain also allowed James to speak with his father. The infirmities tied the generations together and placed the men within a comprehensible structure. In Brazil, recovering from fever and acutely ashamed, his hopes for some active and romantic life seemingly dashed, he longed, he said, to see his father and explain, to tell him of his lack of grit and "mental pride and shame."[64] Henry James had centered his family around his eldest son, considering William dear for his morality and conciliatory demeanor.[65] The elder James had checked his children's moves to preserve their innocence, demanding their affection and their free allegiance while moving his children from one school and country to another, his sons remembering only how much they wanted more order and stability. His children were to remain pure and uncommitted, free of the authority that had ruined his own youth. But the elder James had generated as much insecurity, it seemed, as his own father—that pit of insecurity into which William looked during his crisis. Like his father, William chose to express this doubt as a problem in finding a vocation.[66]

The father's contradictory attitude could create guilt within a child who was spoken to as if he were precious and yet was carefully watched and therefore not trusted. William James felt close to his father, he said, only when he lived safely away. The father thought William perfectly generous, but even away from home the son could only think of his own snubs and harsh words, and remember his disrespect and impurity in behavior. In Germany, before his collapse, William could lightly refer to himself as "your despised child" and then undertake an extended criticism of his father's philosophy. "But I cannot help it and cannot feel responsible for it." William did, of course, acting out the necessary rebellion, for he also wrote during these same months of his seclusion, half-starvation, and thoughts of suicide; he attempted, in other words, to tell his father how pained he felt and how much he needed some care. His description, presented coldly and with an unnerving amount of the matter of fact, allowed for a bare literary and intellectualized account of his despair. He had lied about his condition, William reported to his father. He had sent home happy letters while actually confined in a small room—within a prison, it seemed—speaking to no others and feeling depressed. He had been thinking too often of "the pistol, the dagger and the bowel." Still, he might find some way to work himself out of this, his "repose." He apologized for the added expense of his sickness and then brought the personal part of his letter to a close: "So much for biz."[67]

The Context of the Crisis

Having joined his body to his work, James used his ills like a humor to propel himself from one occupation to another: if his eyes were bad, he could not be a painter; if his stomach was weak, he could not be a doctor; if his back was sore, he could not be a laboratory psychologist. James hoped to define himself, however ill-defined his special calling seemed (as he claimed, though given his genteel class, he soon cemented his profession as a scholar and academic). He would solve the problem of "method" rather than search for his father's "being"; he would take "hold of the reality of things—whatever that may be—in some measure." He believed his own salvation depended now upon finding a line of work—knowing "one thing as thoroughly as it can be known, no matter how insignificant."[68]

James had gone to Brazil and returned. Later in the 1860s in Germany, in and out of bed, alternately musing and depressed, he set up rigorous schedules of study and then called himself a mere wreck. He fingered bookcovers, looking, he said, for some "definite aim." "The patience of these Germans in their calling is something that is hardly known at all with us." James often felt that he had somehow taken a wrong turn, but in Germany that sense became acute. As he had in Brazil, he claimed his need for economy. "If six years ago I could have felt the same satisfied belief in the worthiness of . . . monotonous, scientific labor day after day (without reference to its results) and . . . had some inkling of the importance and nature of education (*i.e.*, getting orderly habits of thought . . .), I might be now on a path to accomplishing something some day, even if my health had turned out no better than it is."[69]

James wanted the "thoroughness and exactness" of the Germans' scientific work. He wrote back to Thomas Ward, praising him for a decision to take up bookkeeping as a discipline in getting down to "methodical habits." It was not so much the type of work they accepted, he wrote, but whether they could labor respectably and keep "a clean bosom" that stayed the aim. The "mere exercise" of work—"the work as a mere occupation ought to be the primary interest with us"—allowed men such as themselves to find their reality, though their wide sympathies and class "mobility" would make such work hard to accept. They could only choose and hope, and disallow fret.[70]

Labor, in other words, offered a means for achieving an alienation. James and Ward could use their activity to place evil beyond themselves—"be independent of our moods," "look on them as external, for they come to us unbidden, and feel if possible neither elated nor depressed, but keep our eyes upon our work." Later, again to Ward, James concluded that they should enter a brotherhood, however anonymously. "I know . . . this seems a cold activity for our affections, a stone instead of bread."[71]

James returned to Cambridge in this mixed state of volition and depression. He desired to assert a reality to achieve an objectification, but he still worried about his energies. He would need to draw his assertion narrowly and pay his own way; he would make "finally and irrevocably 'the choice of a profession.'"

From then until his death, James worried about just what work he did. He worried about what others thought his work was that defined his personality, for he feared that without a work in hand, he would become nothing: "There are few men who would not feel personally annihilated if a life-long construction of their hands or brains . . . were suddenly swept away. The miser feels similarly towards his gold, . . . a sense of the shrinkage of our personality, a partial conversion of ourselves to nothingness, which is a psychological phenomenon by itself."[72] He could not yet accept the nothingness.

James's "problem of vocation" became the best-known intellectual confusion of its kind in the nineteenth century. It came to appear a prototype of a twentieth-century crisis of identity.[73] James had translated the morphology of conversion into an agony of profession. He had begun to pull himself out of his depression through work—"by holding my own"—constricting his life through will.[74] He admitted that he might be fooling himself. He wrote that he might be "cultivating the moral . . . only as a means & more or less humbugging myself,"[75] but he dropped this attitude. He had to attempt the moral effort his father had decried.

Three months later, on April 30, 1870, James recorded the thought that his son Henry later accepted as his father's decision to end his melancholy depression. In his diary, James described the new disciplines that he hoped to draw upon:

> I think that yesterday was a crisis in my life. I finished the first part of Renouvier's second "Essais" and see no reason why his definition of Free Will—"the sustaining of a thought *because I choose to* when I might have other thoughts"—need be the definition of an illusion. . . . For the remainder of the year, I will abstain from the mere speculation and contemplative *Grüblei* [grubbing among subtleties (editor's translation)] in which my nature takes most delight, and voluntarily cultivate the feeling of moral freedom, by reading books favorable to it, as well as by acting. After the first of January, my callow skin being somewhat fledged, I may perhaps return to metaphysical study. . . . For the present then remember: care little for speculation; much for the *form* of my action; recollect that only when habits of order are formed can we advance to really interesting fields of action—and consequently accumulate grain on grain of willful choice like a very miser; never forgetting how one link dropped undoes an indefinite number. *Principiis obsta*—Today has furnished the exceptionally passionate initiative which Bain posits as needful for the acquisition of habits. I will see to the sequel.[76]

This portion of one of James's diaries, here condensed, is as often recounted as the Brazilian experience and the sight from the asylum to portray James's mental struggle. The three relations, if only because so often placed together, form one text. The entry of April, to be sure, stands as a symptomatic expression of what James then felt, but the entry is not free in the sense of being unrelated to other writings that James knew and even to words that he would only later come to write. The entry becomes no less formal because of the title "diary" or because it appears more private (until published by his son), and thus somehow closer to James's heart than a "literary" account. James carefully constructed the paragraph; it is not an automatic pouring from his unconsciousness. Like the letters from Brazil and the case from the Gifford Lectures, it stands fully developed. In telling his case, if only to himself,

James shaped an understanding of his suffering based upon his knowledge of other writings and his reading of his father's crisis. Like the letters and the case, the entry must be understood within this context, before one can probe its words for unarticulated meanings. Rather than a reflection of William James's nature—his psychopathological condition—the entry is another reflection of how James came to view himself.

The writing of April asserts a rebirth. At least the writing marks a period of further growth as James continues a journey through the bare common of Emerson's *Nature* he had begun in Brazil and in his meeting there with the efficacy of collection, a meeting that had resulted in the loss of the use of his eyes. Here he will again attempt to pack up his depression, like the miser, by using habit. What he has discovered here, however, but had not in Brazil, is a way to look upon his fears as an estrangement. He can now pack them away. Whether to the knowledge of his son Henry or not, James coupled the experience of panic, recounted in *Varieties* over thirty years later, to this entry of 1870, joining their meanings if only because James spoke here of leaving behind "my callow skin." He meant most immediately that he was becoming, as he said, or at least as he hoped, "somewhat fledged." He would strike out on his own by looking to "the *form* of my action." He would use activity, in other words, to oppose the passive reception or mere "speculation" that he later used to characterize the young man of immature, callow, or "greenish skin" waiting in the asylum. James, fearing he was sitting like the man in the asylum in mere speculation, could turn away. He would not, like that man, mentally contrive some picture, some fancy or image that his eye invented—a delusion in the broadest sense of the word—because such an image held no relation to an object. Two years earlier, in 1868, James had expressed a similar conviction:

> Tonight while listening to Miss Haven's magic playing, . . . my feelings came to a sort of crisis. The intuition of something here in a measure absolute gave me . . . an unspeakable disgust for the dead drifting of my own life for some time past. . . . It ought to have a practical effect on my own will—a horror of waste life since life can be *such*—and Oh God! an end to the idle, idiotic sinking into *Vorstellungen* disporportionate to the object. Every good experience ought to be interpreted in practice.[77]

The idiocy—again the young man from the asylum—expresses the sinking into ideas held without some visible object at hand. The idiocy is expressed in a word that Krafft-Ebing introduced in 1867: "*Zwangsvorstellung*."[78] It becomes the figure in the asylum in the sense that an idiot stays a separate person whose private words are unattached to things. "Callow" also means bare, as in the barrenness of youth.

The Brazilian experience and its voluptuous greens could only fail, at least in James's early letters of conversion. James would at first quit the strenuous life, foregoing the active for the introspective. He had defined the active as collection; the passive he defined as blind. With the April entry of five years later, James presumably recovered by turning himself once again to the "powers of action" or the pragmatic. He opposed the pragmatic to the "metaphysical," and he opposed the "manly" and "daring" to the "suicide" he now said had formerly seemed the only way out.[79] In this construction, the entry of April becomes the Jamesian myth, for James emerges as the heroic self asserting a healthy willingness to act. He becomes the Arminian as opposed to the predestinarian, the man of free will as opposed to an Edwards caught in the flow of Calvinist waves. James asserts a progressive self in the face of a morbid, brooding past and in the face, of course, of his father. Works, efforts, wills, "the self-governing *resistance* of the ego to the world," appear now to break James away from the sickness of the melancholy self he would later define. If the passive meant speculation, then James refused not blind faith but the works the mind continually, and falsely, creates. He called to himself not to become the strenuous but the unspeculative, unobsessive, man. Once again, in the words of Edwards, the act of professing conversion was to draw the confessor from his role as a "spectator" to a "knowing as one *knows his own*."

The "classic" James, because of the diary entry of April, adheres to deeds as Benjamin Franklin struck out against the bothers of a man like Cotton Mather. James wrote to his brother in December of 1870, however, in words that hold to Mather's past: "It seems to me that all a man has to depend on in this world, is, in the last resort, mere brute power of resistance. I can't bring myself, as so many men seem able to, to blink the evil out of sight, and gloss it over. . . . It must be accepted and hated, and resisted while there's breath in our bodies." As a re-enactment of the theme of the Brazilian experience, the April entry repeats the Puritan figure: "Not in maxims, not in *Anschauungen* ["regardings, or contemplative views," in the words of his son], but in accumulated *acts* of thought lies salvation." Expressed signs, that is, rather than ritually repeated dogma, or a true passivity of merely regarding the mind's own view, confirm salvation.[80]

The "contemplative *Grüblei*" that James said had stricken his life became words that for him meant a particular sickness of self. It is a psychopathology James later defined in his *Principles of Psychology*.[81] The words form the essence, or rather the exaggeration, of what he meant by doubt. Doubt is incessantly performed mental busywork—

mental works, that is, that in their opposition to belief define a meaning for faith:

The true opposites of belief, psychologically considered, *are doubt and inquiry, not disbelief*. . . . Both sorts of emotion may be pathologically exalted. . . . The pathological state opposed to this solidarity and deepening [of belief] has been called the questioning mania (*Grübelsucht* by the Germans). It is sometimes found as a substantive affection, paroxysmal or chronic, and consists in the inability to rest in any conception, and the need of having it confirmed and explained. "Why do I stand here where I stand?" "Why is a glass a glass, a chair a chair?" . . . etc., etc.

James appended a note to these remarks, citing from the case of a man who involved himself with thoughts more paralyzing than abstractions such as these. As James quoted, the man, whose case he found in T. S. Clouston's *Clinical Lectures on Mental Disease*, published in 1883, possessed an "imperative" to think that formed his ideas into magical serial chains: "thought about in a peculiar fashion [or order], . . . often when I am utterly wearied and would be at peace." "This goes on to the hindrance of all natural action." For example:

[If] told the staircase was on fire and I had only a minute to escape, and the thought arose—"Have they sent for fire-engines? Is it probable that the man who has the key is on hand: Is the man a careful sort of person? Will the key be hanging on a peg? Am I thinking rightly? Perhaps they don't lock the depot"—my foot would be lifted to go down; I should be conscious to excitement that I was losing my chance; but I should be unable to stir until all these absurdities were entertained and disposed of.

The case is like a small parable of whether or not one would be saved.

"And in the most ordinary circumstances," said the man, "it is all the same," as on a walk in the cold, proceeding only by jerks: "Once I got arrested, my feet in a muddy pool. One foot was lifted to go, knowing that it was not good to be standing in water." The water becomes a slough or perhaps the temptations against which Bunyan moves his arms and elbows: "but there I was fast, the cause of detention being the discussing with myself the reasons why I should not stand in that pool."[82]

Three years later, in March of 1873, Henry James, Sr., noted his son's improvement: "'then so hypochondriacal,'" he quoted from William, "(he used that word, though perhaps in substantive form)." And in the words of a foil, the father had written, "Why do you not resolutely close your mouth and forbear this insane and hypochondriacal course,"—forbear, that is, "a conscience of sin"?

The elder James mentioned that his son, as William also noted in the

April entry, attributed his newfound sanity to a reading, among others, of Charles Renouvier, most particularly the French philosopher's vindication in the face of nineteenth-century medical materialism of the freedom of the will. But the father most noted his son's "splendid confession": "his having given up the notion that all mental disorder [is] required to have a physical basis. This had become perfectly untrue to him. He saw that the mind did act irrespectively of material coercion." Increase Mather had used his trip to Lynn to discover just this point. In Germany, William too had sought out medicinal baths, like the hydrotherapy that his father had tried in England. As Henry James said, "unerring signs" now appeared that his son was gaining health (William most immediately had set to work teaching physiology at Harvard, his father watching his every step: "Willy is going on with his teaching. The eleven o'clock bell has just tolled, and he is on the platform expounding the mysteries of physiology"). The elder James, who had given his own struggle with harassing thoughts over to the work of his spirit's Creator, hoped that his son would now discard "men of mere science" and find a less coercive construction of the mind's alienation.[83] William, of course, could never turn from physics to the "universal" his father now mentioned, but embraced instead his reading in the pathology of brain.[84] Nevertheless, he could work against the materialism by demanding that the neurologists hear what his father had said. Toward this end, he used the new mental sciences to come to an understanding of just how coercive obsessional thoughts were.

Renouvier, Bain, and Obsessive Ideation

William James later erected an important part of his psychology upon the work of Renouvier. He used him both to shape his own theory of "ideo-motor activity"[85] and to offer his explanation of the will's power to induce difficult acts. The theory of ideomotor activity proposed that any idea momentarily dominating the mind proceeded almost immediately into action—"fatally and infallibly"—unless some obstructing notion worked in opposition.[86] Renouvier was not alone in holding the theory, nor did James have to draw upon the philosopher to support his contention.[87] James did derive his theory of volition as the forced introduction of an idea from Renouvier's second essay, however, and it was upon a reading of that work that James published, in 1888, an early essay of his own on "What the Will Effects."

James considered volition not an act but an idea to act. Following from the contention that ideas acted themselves out, volition could by itself proceed to a deed through "ideational coercion" in a type of forced "effort" that James opposed to the instinctive, blind, or impulsive behavior of the primitive, the mob, or the insane. The sustaining of a thought through choice, in other words, opposed the impulses of the untutored: the mental confusion of a drunkard, for example, whose nerves had unlocked and whose ideas had become a jumble, or the emotional confusion of a believer whose thoughts (and passions and explosions) held little or no reality for their substance. Whether the delusions of the insane or the stonings by a mob, a false reality or "mental vertigo" existed—the "belief of a thing for no other reason than that we conceive it with passion." The self created an image and then made that image real through continual mental excitation, the whole—a terror, for example—being brought about by some often inconsequential object, some small seed of reality that had grown out of proportion.[88]

James's belief in this explosive potential of ideation dominates his psychology of the will. Once the mind holds fast to an idea and "the empire of passion" reigns, then if a person wishes to turn away, perhaps from "a coquette's door," he has to force another idea into his mind, another "fixed idea." James spoke of "the forcible holding fast to an incongenial idea" to prevent the other idea from materializing. "The work of moral effort then . . . is neither more nor less than the work of attending to a difficult idea." To pull one's self morally out from under thoughts of "some particularly dirty" act, one needed to scour one's mind.[89]

In a portion of Renouvier's second essay—the essay that James cited in the diary entry of 1870—a similar discussion emerges. Describing vertigo or "*vertige mental*," Renouvier explained the false and sometimes absurd realities built by the imagination. He presented a state in which the mind plays upon itself, producing at worst hallucinations or at best vague feelings of suffering. The imagination constructs feelings that things are being done to oneself, that a disease, perhaps, has infected one's body. Such ideas appear familiar, Renouvier wrote, under the name of hypochondria. Though Renouvier mentioned that some persons still superstitiously thought of the condition as possession or demonic control, he presented it as an imagination feeding upon itself. The mind first imagined a possible act, then focused upon that act until the imagining led "*à l'obsession, au vertige*," and finally to committing the act itself. However bizarre, a thought demands an explanation, and thus the mind focuses on a thought, and the thought repeats itself and fixes itself more and more firmly, until the idea eventually becomes a reality. What has begun as an imagination becomes an obsession, and the obsession results in the commission of the bizarre. The false becomes the factual, and the imagined, the real. The *"la monomanie des idées"* began in this manner, too, Renouvier wrote, with constant thinking of the ridiculous, the criminal, or the absurd. At first a negation holds such thoughts in check, but eventually the germ of a possibility tends toward an act as the thought repeats itself and solidifies. The movement, for Renouvier, was inevitable *unless* the will controlled the play and offered mental negations. The will had to dampen the idea before the obsession established its grip—before *"l'empire d'une émotion"* possessed its subject.

In concluding—and this is the point James surely focused upon—Renouvier said that he did not dispute that such *"aliénation"* arose from bodily disorders. For this particular alienation, however, he argued that the mind could afflict the body as much as the body the mind. Nothing proved, he concluded, that a moral education would fail to suppress such obsessions and monomanias.[90] In 1870 James could read that he did not have to sit compelled, waiting for a horror to happen. Like Christian, he could realize that to be tempted to unpardonable sin was not necessarily to be forced to act such a horror out.

Twenty years after his panic, James still used Renouvier's essay to account for self-explosions. Here, in the spring of 1870, James wrote of his need to sustain "a thought *because I chose to* when I might have other thoughts," and that gave him hope. He would care little for what he later described as the mere form of thought, the unnatural philosophical brooding that for him bred "hypochondria." He wanted instead "some stable reality," and in 1870 he also wanted some habits, to "accumulate grain on grain of willful choice like a very miser."[91]

Next to Renouvier in the diary entry of 1870 stands Alexander Bain, the other psychologist to whom James turned for an explanation of his own despair. Bain was an English utilitarian and a standard text psychologist.[92] One of his books, *The Emotions and the Will*, supplied James with a chapter on "The Moral Habits." James never accepted the determinism of Bain's psychology, the argument that persons acted for pleasure and the avoidance of pain. Quite obviously, for James, many persons sought pain which, whatever one might argue, in nowise appeared pleasurable. He did accept, however, Bain's admonitions for accruing habits as one might gather moral credits, all of which James's father had denounced as tyrannous. William would in fact refashion Bain's chapter into the most popular chapter of his own *Psychology*. No more than here can James be read as the stereotypical moral Victorian, yet in the *Psychology* James also went to considerable lengths to point out "a terrible stumbling-block to the candid Professor Bain."[93]

Though his terminology changed through his book's editions, Bain admitted that a problem existed within the purity of his mechanistic psychology. The problem was the type of thought that Bain finally came to call the "fixed idea." It appeared, for the utilitarian, an oddity that some persons felt an impulsion to act from a fixation they abhorred rather than liked, that they experienced a need to act out of not pleasure but pain. The fixed idea thwarted the will, overturning the rational calculation that a normal mind would make. The "undue or morbid persistency of certain ideas in the mind" opposed the "proper course of volition." "A certain object has, by some means or other, gained possession of us; we are all unable to dismiss it: whence, by persisting in the view and excluding other things, it may at last find its way into execution, through that power whereby every conceived act has a certain tendency to realize itself." In his companion book, *The Senses and the Intellect*, Bain again wrote of those times when, in opposition to a will that urged a person toward pleasure, an idea occurred that, unlike other ideas, not only opposed the will but conquered it: "times, when an idea possesses the mind so forcibly as to act itself out in opposition to the will, and therefore in opposition to those interests that the will should side with—the deliverance from pain and the furtherance of pleasure."[94]

James based his critique of Bain's utilitarian mechanics precisely upon this exception of the calculus. "All diseased impulses and pathological fixed ideas are instances to the contrary," James wrote, for he could only reaffirm what was again obvious: the evil that all the natural-born selves were capable of seeking. There was no necessity to speak of grand evil when a small bit of pain demonstrated the same necessity:

> It is the very badness of the act that gives it then its vertiginous fascination. . . . But we need not go to minds diseased for examples. . . . Every one who has a wound or hurt anywhere, a sore tooth, e.g., will ever and anon press it just to bring out the pain. If we are near a new sort of stink, we must sniff it again just to verify once more how bad it is. This very day I have been repeating over and over to myself a verbal jingle whose mawkish silliness was the secret of its haunting power. I loathed yet could not banish it.

When James concluded this analysis of "morbid impulsion," he noted once again that a person's action sprang from possession rather than from pleasure. The fatal dominance of that which appeared "interesting," "morbidly fascinating," or "tediously haunting" impelled an act. "This is what we have seen in instinct, in emotion, in common ideomotor action, in hypnotic suggestion, in morbid impulsion . . . —the impelling idea is simply the one which possesses the attention."[95]

In attacking Bain, James attacked a scholastic, now utilitarian, doctrine of the rational will.[96] James, however, later rephrased one of Bain's admonitions in his diary and then again in his *Psychology*, when he spoke of the need for an ascetic that could, as much as possible, rationalize one's living. Thus, "above all," one was "never to lose a battle. Every gain on the wrong side undoes the effect of several conquests on the right." In accepting Bain's demand to habitualize conduct, James also accepted a pattern of child development that, as opposed the writings of his father, required an "education in submission." Habit and the repetition that habit required strengthened concentration, keeping the child's mind fixed, undisturbed by "sensual solicitations," by various objects that attracted his sight and touch and that could unduly detain him. "We have," Bain wrote, "to be put under training to resist those various solicitations, and to keep the mind as steadily fixed upon the work in hand as if they did not happen." Through what Bain described as "a judicious starving regimen," both child and adult could dampen emotion to give more energy to intellect and volition. Emotion, intellect, and will—the three capacites of human conduct—rested within a closed and economical system, the balance of one determining the reserves available for another. Within this popular Victorian image of the body as a bank, a person needed to lessen sensual desires to allow intellect greater play. Habit dampened emotion, particularly emotions that prompted the will to "detain" an exceedingly painful thought and thus to act contrary to its proclivities.[97] Habit prepared the organism to fulfill its proper mechanism or its already declared utilitarian law, a circularity of argument that Bain's texts could not erase.

The particular impasse that habit faced, Bain referred to again as the fixed idea. In 1859 he referred to this as fascinations, infatuations, monomanias, or "irresistible impulse[s]," all of which words upset the calculus of his ethics. Like the vastation that had broken the elder James's production of a rational theology, the "passion of fear," for Bain, was "an instance in point. . . . The usual course of volition is manifestly here perverted and paralyzed by some foreign influence"—anxiety, dread, panic, and consequent depression, all of which followed upon an experience with evil. William later described this type of terror when he recounted his own panic and crisis. He had read in Bain, however, that such fear related to no particular reality. This was the "excitement, the depression, the Fixed Idea" that exaggerated an "ideal evil"; the "utter loss of control, the breaking down of discipline, the ruinous persistence of a fixed idea" that led the subject, like a superstition, "farther and farther from the regular action of the will. The evils dreaded are unreal, and therefore unmeasured and indefinable." From his perspective, the elder James would have argued that one could measure legal fear; only true sin existed elsewhere. For Bain, however, habit or "measure"—not immediate change, but rather the painfully slow accumulation of concentrated efforts—could lead one from such fixed terrors. Through "a work of no little time and effort," a person could withdraw from these alien solicitations.[98]

Like Swedenborg, Bain externalized and made this ideation false, in the sense that it need not be acted upon. Thus, in this respect, Bain could serve William James as Swedenborg had served James's father. This estrangement of mental evil did not make evil false, but it did say that a horrid act did not have to follow. The Puritan conception of satanic melancholy had served the same function. Unlike James's father and like Renouvier, Bain did say that a criminal act could quite readily follow if some method was not used to suppress the fear.

Work

William James attempted to banish the figure of the epileptically convulsed young man that he feared for a moment was himself. If he would not become that, then he would focus his attention and estrange his moods to become, in a sense, a passionless man. James understood the emotion that he called the luxury of woe—the inclination to stay within the stony insensibility of melancholy depression. However painful, depression allowed one to revolve about oneself; to get out, James advised his daughter, "we must . . . set ourselves to some hard work, make ourselves sweat."[99]

James came to view a possible religious crisis like his as other than "imitative." His student, Edwin Starbuck, had advanced that point, James thought, when he typified conversion as an adolescent "statistical inquiry [James's words]." James opposed Starbuck's social psychology with the cases of his *Varieties*.[100] His examples appeared to him "more first-hand and original" because they existed not as adolescent but as "sporadic adult cases." They read as "forms of experience," James thought, on the whole self-consciously Protestant. James maintained this singularity to show the work conversion involved, the coming out of the new self not in predetermined and repetitive moves, or with the self stamped out as if by a behavioral template, but in choice and voiced profession. No matter how much James spoke of the will involved—the efforts and small habits and matters of choice—he never spoke as the Arminian. "It is needless to remind you," he said, speaking of conversion to his Edinburgh audience more than a decade after he had published his massive work on psychology, "once more of the admirable congruity of Protestant theology with the structure of the mind as shown in such experiences." "In the extreme of melancholy the self that consciously *is* can do absolutely nothing. It is completely bankrupt and without resource, and no works it can accomplish will avail."

Thoreau, offering himself as a common laborer rather as James, and working as far from the nature of the elder James as did the son in his own empiricist ways, argued the same, with the same use of psychology: "What I have heard of Bramins sitting exposed to four fires and looking in the face of the sun; . . . or dwelling, chained for life, at the foot of a tree; or measuring with their bodies, like caterpillars, the breath of vast empires"—these labors "of conscious penance" remained as useless as the twelve of Hercules and "trifling in comparison with those labors which my neighbors have undertaken: for they were only twelve, and had an end; but I could never see that these men slew or captured any monster or finished any labor. They have no friend Iolaus to burn with a hot iron the root of the hydra's head, but as soon as one head is crushed, two spring up."

Thoreau, as he proudly proclaimed, had also moved through various occupations, displaying in *Walden* his exercises in yoga, for example, in which he measured his body as he surveyed the pond. "As Protestants are not all sick souls," said James, "of course reliance on what Luther exults in calling the dung of one's merits, the filthy puddle of one's own righteousness, has come to the front again in their religion" (his neighbors' gilded age).[101] The slough of despond stays there in a writing like *Walden* or James's autobiography to show just how stuck the mind can get and how inefficacious one's moves become when faced with such excrement.

During these years of crisis and depression, James began teaching physiology at Harvard. The discipline came as a God-sent blessing, he said, and a responsible diversion for his ills. "You will like an account of my own condition. My eyes serve from three to four hours daily. . . . My other symptoms are gradually modifying themselves. . . . Perhaps the whole thing will soon smooth itself out." He made the choice of teaching physiology, which was the job he could get, as opposed to philosophy, but he also made the choice in a continuing motif of avoiding doubt-filled speculation. In "the anatomical instruction" he reversed the movement that his father had discovered in Swedenborg. He never changed the expressed goal of his father, however, which remained blind faith. At this particular step in William James's life, it was the metaphysician and not the anatomist who wallowed in doubt, acting much like his father's Biblical exegete. The metaphysician called "in question the grounds of his faith of the day before." The biologist's responsibilities, on the other hand, "form a fixed basis from which to aspire . . . ; and a basis, too, upon which he can passively float, and tide himself over times of weakness and depression, trusting all the while blindly. . . . A 'philosopher' has publicly renounced the privilege of trusting *blindly*, which every simple man owns as a right—and my sight is not always clear enough for such constant duty." "To make the *form* of all possible thought the prevailing matter of one's thought," again, "breeds hypochondria."[102] James had lost his sight over the matter of packing specimens, and now he would lose it again, metaphorically, the sight as I, over the problem of forever asking impossible questions.

James wished "to be settled and concentrated, to cultivate a patch of ground." He would utilize his energies carefully, for his nervous fatigue still required that he economize his strength so as not to waste his "small available store." "Last year was a year of hard work, and . . . I was in a state of bad neurasthenic fatigue, but I got through outwardly all right."[103] James sprinkled his letters with comments such as these, reminding correspondents just how fragile he felt and just how cautious he had to be. His neurasthenia served as a reason for not unleashing himself (perhaps killing himself) through impulses his weakened will might fail to contain. He of course did overdo, once to the point of damaging his heart. He even liked to experiment with drugs and intoxicants, with nitrous oxide and peyote, for example, simply to sniff and see what some substance might do. After each experiment in the loss of self-control, however, James rebelled and found the experience in itself revolting. He still interested himself in these experiences, examining dizziness, seasickness, alcoholism, anesthesia, hypnotism, hysteria, and mysticism—the degradation and the exaltation of minds detached from sense. The self-extinction states—the trances and illusions, dreams and visions—fascinated him. He found himself particularly drawn to those states in which he thought a person existed without emotion—the complete corporeal anesthesia approached by some hysterics and those few unfortunates born without bodily sense. James never partook of these experiences himself except through brief tastes of drugs and perhaps one mystical revelation while camping in the woods of the Adirondacks. He examined them, nevertheless, and feared the most impulsive of them, or at least drew such states to their wild unnatural extreme. He thought of dypsomania, for example, as a force that could drive a man to cut off his hand and ask for rum to cleanse the stump, and then, having plotted for his drink, gulp the bloody mixture.[104]

Nowhere did James more vividly display this image than in "The Explosive Will," an important portion of his chapter on the will in the *Psychology*. But what James described as impulsive thought—the "monomania" and the "irresistable impulse" that he believed led to such abhorrent acts—expressed behavior in which persons thought that they might commit some crime and therefore held themselves in strenuous check. James admitted to some confusion on this point: it remained difficult, he wrote, to tell whether one should term such a will explosive or obstructed. He dropped the consideration, however, and proceeded to discuss compulsion as impulsion.[105] The confusion (from the point of view of present-day psychiatry) became important, because upon it James rested his belief in the necessity of restraining the "weak" or "exhausted" mind—the neurasthenic mind, in other words, that he so often complained of himself.

James's *Psychology* appeared at the time when some alienists were beginning to question whether a person's fear that he might act necessarily meant that he would. Should a man who thought that he might slay a friend commit himself to an asylum, or did the fear work merely as an expression, and if it did, what significance did the expression have? James, however, noted references to literature in the *Psychology* that he had read in the midst of his own crisis in the 1870s: Bain's psychologies, Henry Maudsley's works on mental disease, Forbes Winslow's *Obscure Diseases of the Brain and Mind*—books written in the 1850s, 1860s, and early 1870s.[106] Writing when they did, these authors drew little or no distinction—as Puritan divines carefully had—among the homicidal maniac, the impulsive psychopath, and the person whose crimes resided solely in his mind. Instead, they viewed the obsessional mind as a broken and whirling Newtonian machine, a conception that allowed James's sister Alice, for example, to conceive of herself as a woman who could easily fly apart, wasted in the impulsion that her mind displayed:

> Owing to some physical weakness, excess of nervous susceptibility, the moral power *pauses* . . . and refuses to maintain muscular sanity. . . . I used to sit immovable reading in the library with waves of violent inclination suddenly invading my muscles taking some one of their myriad forms such as throwing myself out of the window, or knocking off the head of the benignant pater as he sat with his silver locks [his locks, as it were, of iron], writing at his table. . . . Conceive of never being without the sense that if you let yourself go for a moment your mechanism will fall into pie and that at some given moment and you must abandon it all, let the dykes break and the flood sweep in, acknowledging yourself abjectly impotent before the immutable laws.[107]

The "fight" of Alice James for her "moral . . . stock in trade" resembles the battle of her brother. Alice, however, bedridden for most of her life, placed herself in the category of permanent hysteric that disallowed much of a working out—anything, that is, other than "my life-long occupation of 'improving.'"[108]

James was fascinated by cases that turned thought into motor activity. Such examples of "automatism" revealed Renouvier's alliance of "*l'obsession*" and "*la monomanie.*" The alienists that James read realized that some persons struggled, heroically they thought, against images of the murderous and obscene, but alienists perceived the struggle from the sufferer's view. If such thoughts no longer reflected a degeneracy of soul, the impulses unleashed expressed a depression of brain. They arose, most simply, from a patient's nervous exhaustion. Though they did not speak of a tempter working through a humoral bath, these alienists nonetheless reinforced a conviction of sin in a manner that seventeenth-century divines never had, for the potential of actual crime, stored in the obsessional thought like the energy of an electric cathexis, pulsed with a sickening sense of the real.[109]

Isaac Ray, for example, in a *Treatise on the Medical Jurisprudence of Insanity* important for strains of pragmatist thought,[110] collected a variety of such cases from English and European literature. They are cases of indiscriminately mixed obsessive ideation and insanity that Ray termed "partial moral insanity." The cases illustrated his treatise's progressive theme that a criminal did not always act out of a rational, objectively determined will. Concerning "the last and most important form of moral mania that will be noticed," he wrote:

> [It] consists in a morbid activity of the propensity to destroy; where the individual, without provocation or any other rational motive, apparently in the full possession of his reason, and oftentimes, in spite of his most strenuous efforts to the contrary, imbrues his hands in the blood of others; oftener, than otherwise, of the partner of his bosom, of the children of his affection.

The book appeared progressive in that it expressed a controversial theme concerning the responsibility for crime in the case of the insane. Nevertheless, Ray confused his inquiry through the taxonomy he chose, for his cases of actual *monomanie-homicide* are in themselves rather few. The majority of his examples concern thoughts of crime that the person never carries out.

> A young lady who had been placed in a *maison de santé*, experienced homicidal desires, for which she could assign no motive. She was rational on every subject,

and whenever she felt the approach of this dreadful propensity, she shed tears, entreated to have the strait-waistcoat put on and to be carefully guarded, till the paroxysm, which sometimes lasted several days, had passed.

That, in its entirety, stood as the case—juxtaposed in Ray's text to that of a man who "abused" a woman, struck another with a hatchet, split open the skulls of a lad and a young man, scattering the latter's brains on the road before he hacked at the body.[111]

Of the typical cases that Ray provided of momentary images of crime, one is of interest in relation to James. James perhaps had this case in mind, among others, when he composed his memory of the asylum patient. The history concerns a peasant "who never enjoyed very good health, twenty-seven years old, and unmarried, [who] had been subject from his ninth year to frequent epileptic fits."

> Two years ago, his disease changed its character without any apparent cause, and ever since, this man, instead of a fit of epilepsy, has been attacked with an irresistible inclination to commit murder. He felt the approach of the fit many hours, and sometimes a whole day, before its invasion, and from the commencement of this presentment, he begged to be secured and chained that he might not commit some dreadful deed. "When the fit comes on," says he, "I feel under a necessity to kill, even if it were a child." His parents, whom he tenderly loved, would be the first victims of this murderous propensity. . . . During the fit, he preserves his consciousness, and knows perfectly well that in committing a murder, he is guilty of an atrocious crime. . . . When it is over, he cries out, "Now unbind me. Alas! I have cruelly suffered, but I rejoice that I have killed nobody."

In nearly all such cases, Ray concluded, "the criminal act," or rather the thought, followed from some disturbance of health "originating in the head, digestive system, or uterus, or by an irritable, gloomy, dejected or melancholy state."[112]

The new psychology still allowed the guilt-ridden, if they so chose, to convict themselves for their images of sin. James, who used Renouvier and Bain to walk past this feared correspondence between himself and crime, presented the most dramatic of such cases to show just how horrid the scene was that one had to pass by. He attributed the irresistible impulse to nervous exhaustion, as was common, but even when he observed "impulsive insanity" among the strong and inhibited, he could but applaud the self-control involved in refusing this "gnawing, craving urgency to act. Works on insanity," he continued, "are full of examples of these morbid insistent ideas, in obstinately struggling against which the unfortunate victim's soul often sweats with agony, ere at long last it gets swept away."[113]

James provided case histories of obsessional struggles that caricature the labors described in the Puritans' spiritual autobiographies. Here the conscience-stricken withdraw behind elaborate defenses to protect others from their murderous intent. In one account an unfortunate soul thinks he might kill his mother and so cries for restraint, gladly accepting commitment to an asylum. "Take a solid rope, bind me like a wolf in the barn," he first remarks upon imagining his crime. Then, on the eve of his commitment, he writes to the asylum's director: "Sir I am about to become an inmate of your house. I shall behave there as if I were in the regiment. . . . Never let me out." James introduced another as a case in the monomania of love, one for which "all of us are subject, however otherwise sane." "Contemptible in my own eyes," James quoted from the autobiography of Vittorio Alfieri, "I fell into such a state of melancholy as would, if long continued, inevitably have led to insanity or death." Once again a man has devised an "insuperable barrier"—"Isolated in this manner in my own house"—determined never to break out lest his lust should explode and destroy a lady he knows. James believed that Alfieri had, at least, learned one thing good: [the need for] "gradually detaching me from love, and of awakening my reason. . . . I no longer found it necesary to cause myself to be tied with cords to a chair."[114]

These examples of melancholy prisons remain extraordinary. They represent the natural extremes that James thought so telling. James cited less dramatic fears, however, to illustrate his explosive self:

> Often the insistent idea is of a trivial sort, but it may wear the patient's life out. His hands feel dirty, they must be washed. He *knows* they are not dirty; yet to get rid of the teasing idea he washes them. The idea, however, returns in a moment, and the unfortunate victim, who is not in the least deluded *intellectually*, will end by spending the whole day at the wash-stand. Or his clothes are not "rightly" put on; and to banish the thought he takes them off and puts them on again, till his toilet consumes two or three hours of time. Most people have the potentiality of this disease. To few has it not happened to conceive, after getting into bed, that they may have forgotten to lock the front door, or to turn out the entry gas. And few of us have not on some occasion got up to repeat the performance, less because they believed in the reality of its omission than because only so could they banish the worrying doubt and get to sleep.[115]

When James included examples of compulsive handwashing and annoying acts of checking and rechecking the details of everyday behavior, the inhibition displayed could only outweigh any potential for explosion. Nevertheless, because such cases expressed a struggle, he celebrated the will whenever the will interjected another idea to conquer some dramatic or trivial obsession. He wrote of "a rarer and more ideal impulse . . . called upon to neutralize others of a more instinctive and habitual kind; it does so whenever strongly explosive tendencies are checked, or strongly obstructed conditions overcome. The . . . child of the sunshine, . . . does not need much of it in his life. The hero and the neurotic subject, on the other hand, do."[116] No matter how "icy" the new thought might seem or how difficult forcing the attention might be, James's neurotic had to submit his self to "this cold-water bath" to clear out his impulsive thoughts. "To sustain a representation, to think, is, in short, the only moral act, for the impulsive and the obstructed, for sane and lunatics alike."[117] The elder James could have only wondered at the moral the new psychology had wrought.

Within all souls, the son admonished the "average church-going civilizee," and assuredly within the neurotic hero who had become for James the Puritan saint, lay an instinct to fight, an unsuspected "aboriginal capacity for murderous excitement which lies sleeping." These "deeper currents of human nature" lay like a wilderness in the American mind. If one offered the "slightest diminution of external pressure," one unleashed murder. One unleashed "the carnivore within," which he, like his father, had seen. Thus rather than allow the emotions to remain the romantics' vision of sublime flight, James tied the emotions to the body. He struck hard at those who would leave feeling as an ambiguous, unfathomable, God- or devil-inspired state of the mind. In James's most famous formulation (other than his stream of thought), the emotions result from bodily movements. Fear is an act of running, or terror an act of turning. Behind this "James-Lange" theory, brilliant in its conception, lies a calculation that, to become happy, a person can move his mouth into the shape of a smile. We "must assiduously, and in the first instance coldbloodedly, go through the outward motions of those contrary dispositions we prefer to cultivate. The reward of persistency will infallibly come."[118] By tying moods and emotions to physical functions, James could bring depression, fear, and even rage within reach. He could locate "in my body" all emotions except the most ephemeral.[119] James could become a clock. He could practice method as Cotton Mather had.

James's theory of instincts also expresses this quest for control. From innumerable possibilities, James selected instincts that represent defensive characteristics: pugnacity, resentment, secretiveness, jealousy, cleanliness, acquisitiveness, holding [hoarding], modesty, shame, and above all "constructiveness." For some of these instincts, James sought an "impulsive root." Fear, against which he pitted construction, turned into agoraphobia, the statuelike immobility that had resulted from "ancestral conditions, even infra-human ones." Acquisitiveness and holding twisted into an insane instinct for collecting, preserving pins and bits of thread without regard for their use. Shyness became fright and modesty became shame, and both secretiveness and cleanliness devolved into the servile terror of the child or the adult faced with a despot. That cleanliness expressed an instinct proved itself through the "insane symptom called 'mysophobia,' or dread of foulness, which leads the patient to wash his hands a hundred times a day."[120]

Whether one wishes to call James's portrait of instinctual behavior "compulsive" or simply "Victorian," it did offer a sociability that conflicts with these self-holding drives. James's divided self lives in a push and pull, however, reaching out and then withdrawing, even from love. For love a counterpart exists: "the *anti-sexual instinct*, the instinct of personal isolation. It . . . [is] the actual repulsiveness to us of the idea of intimate contact with most of the persons we meet."[121]

The irony of James's explosive self remains apparent: inhibition tightens existence into a lock, under the assumption that little inhibition exists. The "neurotic," like the Victorian hero, works his way from inherited sin or "the sensual propensity" that threatens him with delusion. "He speaks of conquering and overcoming his impulses and temptations." "It is deliberately driving a thorn into one's flesh"—"an excursion into a lonesome moral wilderness."[122] James almost begged his reader to ask whether the wilderness would not eventually turn the moral out.

Compulsion and Doubt

James's psychology revealed a certain irresolution. Little question existed that the *Psychology*, published in 1890—a massive, disheveled, and ultimately brilliant compilation of twelve years' labor that James had planned to accomplish in two—offered the moral act as the inhibited act. As James reiterated nine years later in his *Talks to Teachers on Psychology*, the highest type of character filled itself with scruples and acted along lines of resistance. The mind needed to act as a muscle acted, pulling and checking. The mind, however, had to work without paralysis.

In these same talks, then, James warned of the melancholic danger of overinhibition when fearful minds became cramped with indecision. He considered the possible self-delusion that he had spoken of three decades earlier. He looked at the New England conscience when it became locked in "repressive forms of self-consciousness, . . . condemned to express itself through a jungle of scruples and checks."[123]

In some of the essays James composed during and after the turn of the century, this same irresolution appears, particularly in his lectures on the "gospel of relaxation" and "the energies of men." A question erupts that appears again in the *Varieties*, where James spoke of an ascetic's moral efforts (or sanctification) and then of a mystic's letting go. The question is whether James hoped to tighten or relax, whether he spoke for moral exertion or repose—whether, in other words, he spoke of faith, if by faith one means a letting go.

James delivered his lecture on "The Gospel of Relaxation" to numerous women's colleges at the end of the nineteenth century, first at the Boston Normal School of Gymnastics. The lecture became popular, as James expected, for by calling for relaxation, he addressed a problem confronting many besides himself in the white-collar or new middle class of America.[124] The "intense, convulsive worker" who flailed about and accomplished little had become, by 1899, an American stereotype. "A saint in ecstasy is as motionless and irresponsive and one-idea'd as [such] a melancholic." The tightness and the scurrying about in a pretense of labor resembled a compulsion, and the monotony had become a national structure:

> We, here in America, through following a succession of pattern-setters whom it is now impossible to trace . . . have at last settled down collectively into . . . our own characteristic national type,—a type with the production of which . . . the climate and conditions have had practically nothing at all to do.

Though James never mentioned the word, Puritanism presumably had produced this national character. As in the seventeenth-century meaning of the word "efficiency," which was about to become a key word for reformers looking to renew the worth of American labor, James was arguing for grace. To say that men and women were collapsing from overwork, as many practitioners were arguing at the end of the century, represented an "immense mistake." Not work but unholy labor had created the problem, the morbidity of a New England people caught up in the fear of doing the trivial with the utmost precision—a form of melancholic depression, as James said, that fixed the mind. Men and women felt "threatened," "guilty," "doomed," "annihilated," "lost," exactly as Mather and Edwards had said. James cited not the Puritan figure of this wasted hell through which persons had to pass (which, in fact, had become the tradition to blame), but a certain "Viennese neurologist." Freud had discovered the *Binnenleben*, a secret prison house of wrath, an "unuttered inner atmosphere" out of which crept the self-loathing that James's father turned into the seed of his spiritual being. James was denouncing this prison as a laborious hell.[125]

James was voicing themes that had begun with the first English histories of America. Shakespeare's Caliban fashions a tempest that forces the self to order nature and work either like an automaton or like Prospero, an engineer.[126] One lives or dies, Emerson had said of his own industrial world, in "amputation from the trunk, . . . so many walking monsters,—a good finger, a neck, a stomach, an elbow, but never a man." "I do not know but it must be confessed that . . . melancholy cleaves to the English mind as to the Aeolian harp. But I maintain that all melancholy belongs to the exterior of man; I claim"—as Swedenborg had claimed—"to be a part of the All. All exterior life"—this division of one's labor—"declares interior life. . . . The constant warfare in each heart is betwixt Reason and Commodity." The elder James presented the alienation like Emerson—here, in Emerson's words, the need for the scholar to fight against being "wasted by nothings." "The manufacture goes forward at all hours," but only for a time: "The new deed is yet a part of life,—remains for a time immersed in our unconscious life."[127]

William James offered another expression of a convulsive America in which the alien would work itself out. Literally, alienation would burn itself out. "I am sure that your flesh creeps at this apocalyptic vision": "Wars will cease, machines will do all our heavy work. . . . Nay, I have heard a fanciful friend make a still further advance in this 'new-man' direction"—the eating of half-digested, "pepsinated" food prepared from a variety of atmospheric elements. ". . . what need shall we have of teeth, or stomachs even? They may go," while in their place would stand "the gigantic domes of our crania, arching over spectacled eyes." The deformation compares with Emerson's vision of a monstrous, utilitarian life.

James grounded the automatism in the coming of new industry; most generally, in his essay on "relaxation," he placed the automatic in the psychological principle of imitation: "*Become the imitable thing*"—here he spoke of the studies of his Harvard colleague Josiah Royce—"and you may then discharge your minds of all responsibility for the imitation." Imitation remained the one "law which we Americans most grievously neglect. Stated technically, the law is this: that *strong feeling about one's self tends to arrest the free association of one's objective ideas and motor processes*. We get the extreme example of this in the mental disease called melancholia." A melancholic patient's moves stay compulsive, his automatism offering precisely the figure that James sought, to spell the doom of American civilization. Automatism predicated birth: the breaking off, as Emerson had said, of "your association with your personality."[128] Mechanics offered the continuing drama for the nation's death and life. In James as in Emerson, it reads like a sudden awakening to sin. America is always the most mechanical of lands. America offers convulsion, the dark side of its Protestant character fixed in the moment prior to that which the convulsion will bring forth, when the terrible machine breaks into a spiritual clearing. "Perhaps the time is already come when it ought to be," Emerson spoke, "and will be, something else; when the sluggard intellect of this continent will look from under iron lids and fill the postponed expectation of the world with something better than the exertions of mechanical skill." "*Unclamp*, in a word," said James, "your intellectual and practical machinery, and let it run free"—"LET YOUR MACHINERY RUN FREE."[129]

There is some irony in watching James send himself abroad for the nerve rest he thought unnecessary for others, and in reading of the water cures and mineral baths he tried. James also wrote of habits that forced him to write, rewrite, and write again every sentence which, as he said, he forged, only to tear up his sheets and start again. Like his father, James never could alter these patterns, no more than his father could achieve that impulsive letter he often dreamed of penning. William spoke of forging "every sentence in the teeth of irreducible and stubborn facts. It is like walking through the densest brush-wood." "As for 'detail,' . . . it is the ever-mounting sea which is certain to engulf one, soul and body. You have a genius to cope with it.—But again, enough!"[130]

In 1908, as earlier, William James could write of "the strict routine of my hours. . . . I write on my Oxford job till one, then lunch, then nap, then to my . . . doctor at four daily. . . . To bed as soon after 8 as possible—all my odd reading done between 3 and 5 a.m., an hour not favorable for letter writing." "The fact is," he wrote two weeks later, "I've been trying to compose the accursed lectures in a state of abominable brain-fatigue—a race between myself and time."[131]

James ended his essay on relaxation with a small discussion and a long quotation from a seventeenth-century Carmelite friar. He moved his essay from Americans centering their work about themselves to a Brother Lawrence who found his mind troubled with thoughts of his soul's damnation. The monk ends his doubts by accepting whatever tasks God and his superiors assign.[132] This was the desire James expressed repeatedly in letters from his later years, at least in that he wished to simplify his life. Still, his horror of unfinished work stayed as he languished in a condition he thought endemic in his family and "morbid" in himself. He would still try "to construct the world" in a "fever." "But I verily believe that it is only work that makes one sick in that way that has any chance of breaking old shells and getting a step ahead. It is a sort of madness however when it is on you."[133] "I am *vastly* better in nervous tone than I was a year ago," he wrote again as he wrote so often, here a month after discussing his inward fever; "my work is simplified down to the exact thing I want to do, and I ought to be happy."[134]

James spoke repeatedly of an economy that concerned both his bank account and his nervous center. He could warn Henri Bergson to "economize all your energies for your own creative work," or ask Theodore Flournoy to preserve "your precious nerve strength," or express concern over his own small "store." It was to alleviate his and others' plaguing nervous prostration that he recommended the galvanization of the spine and the lymph injections. "The skin and the arteries softened almost immediately, and the nervous prostration . . . began immediately to improve greatly."[135] James liked honest businessmen, neat rows of houses, and the punctual meeting of one's engagements. He liked the American industry he found lacking in Brazil, and liked writing of "that fine economical instinct which distinguishes me." James was anxious in business matters, his son Henry reported, or at least he was unable to involve himself without "unprofitable worry."

James drew his economic values from another period, it seemed, or at least thought his values skewed to a "strange thinness and femininity hovering over all America," the "moral flabbiness," "bitch goddess of success," and "squalid cash interpretation" of the world that his brother Henry and he deplored. James closely watched his diet and drink, dressed neatly without adornment, and liked simplified spelling: "I'm sure that simple spelling will make a page look better, just as a crowd looks better if everyone's clothes fit." He was sure too that total abstinence from every stimulant remained necessary to keep himself living at a rapid pace. He wished forever to settle "upon a solid and orderly basis of general frugality. Keen cold weather, bare ground, and a clear sky."[136]

Like Cotton Mather facing a young Benjamin Franklin and the new civilization that Mather, too, thought he had seen, James frowned.[137] One could, however, misunderstand his values as they seemed intended. James himself felt that his essay on the energies of men had been misunderstood; how he did not say, though he perhaps worried that some should think he had called for the moral as a militant life. The essay itself originated as a 1906 presidential address before the American Philosophical Association and eventually evolved into a widely distributed article in *The American Magazine*.[138] The essay's fame rested, in part, on its originality, for in the face of an immense amount of literature in

America on nervous fatigue, brain fag, and general mental debility, James proposed that untapped reserves of energy lay buried within the subliminal self. Seemingly so wearied himself, James had become—mistakenly, he feared—America's spokesman for the strenuous life. The "Energies of Men," however, again uses compelling behavior to distinguish the sickness of the American temper. Now, having studied the malaise from another view, James argued more clearly that within compulsion lay the strength for America's redemption.

Neurasthenia, by definition, expressed fatigue. The word has remained little more defined than that in historical considerations of what Victorian alienists and popular writers synonymously called "American nervousness." In the opinion of George Beard, the American neurologist who popularized the term after the Civil War, neurasthenia had erupted in the nation as a result of the sociological exigencies of America's new industry, the nation's new rush and new concern with time. James spoke of an analogous sickness when he spoke of the convulsive American.[139] Beard brought forth a variety of neurasthenic symptoms, complications that ranged from the falling hair to biting one's fingernails. Nevertheless, because of Beard's work and despite this symptomatic confusion, neurologists commonly diagnosed neurasthenia for those persons manifesting obsessive, absurdly paralyzing fears. Alienists and neurologists also observed that some neurasthenics expended great energy performing absurd labors. This anomaly—that the nervously fatigued should work so hard—caused neurologists at the Massachusetts General Hospital under the direction of James Jackson Putnam, James's colleague and friend, to suspect that overwork did not cause, but rather resulted from, certain mental ailments. Nevertheless, until Freud proclaimed work a protection from, rather than a cause of, neurosis—and really not even then—physicians refused to drop overwork as an important component in the etiology of nervous disease.[140]

James's essay on the energies of men appeared at the time when questions of work and neurosis were emerging. James knew Putnam well. He had met the neurologist while they were medical students at Harvard, and he vacationed with Putnam at the Keene Valley camp they maintained in the Adirondacks. James had also sat in on the presentation of at least one of Putnam's papers on neurasthenia—a paper in which Putnam, as was common, included many of the obsessional manifestations of neurasthenia within his discussion.[141] James used his readings in the work of Pierre Janet, however, to argue for the energetic potential within nervously sick persons. Until the arrival of Freud in

America, the French alienist and psychologist dominated theories of mental disease, much as Weir Mitchell and his rest cure dominated American therapies. In particular, James used a 1906 essay by Janet that had appeared in the first volume of *The Journal of Abnormal Psychology*, an essay entitled "On the Pathogenesis of Some Impulsions."[142]

Prior to Freud, Janet's classification of mental diseases other than the insanities was influential in America, particularly the syndrome he called psychasthenia. Like neurasthenia, psychasthenia excluded hysteria and included both obsessive and compulsive activity, along with phobic fears. As he had with hysteria, Janet used two important devices to build a theory of psychasthenia: the amount of mental tension a person possessed, and the *idée fixe* which took dominion whenever mental tension, for whatever reason, relaxed. When tension lessened, an obsession or a fixed impulse could assume a grave disproportion, sweeping a mind no longer able to resist. For the hysteric, Janet assumed the fixed idea stayed buried and unconscious, causing disturbances without conscious awareness or knowing participation. An unaccountable paralysis or anesthesia, for example, expressed the fixed idea, or an amnesia or fugue—behaviors that seemed to occur quite beyond the consciousness of the person concerned. The psychasthenic, on the other hand, consciously held the obsession in his mind—an impulsion to act, perhaps, no matter how absurd.

Janet remained quite aware that persons often failed (as he thought) to commit the act. In this particular essay, however, he considered acts that did occur: "the patient may deceive himself, may let himself go farther than he wishes." Janet spoke about "the obsessed and impulsive" who performed sometimes silly, sometimes dangerous acts simply to excite themselves and alleviate their otherwise depressed states of mind. The cases included a man who drank too much, a woman who ate too much, another who at times walked incessantly, and a group of persons who inflicted suffering upon themselves: one who tore out her hair bits at a time, another who inflicted small burns on her hands and feet. For all these patients, only a few of whom later psychiatry would consider obsessive, there appeared an irresistible need to act—first a desire, then an act, then a measure of relief or satisfaction. Remorse, and a good but useless resolution not to act so again, concluded the cycle.

Janet also found a sense of unreality and of incompleteness—two words he thought important for defining the psychasthenics' feelings. To relieve their incompleteness, neurotic ascetics tortured themselves. As one of Janet's patients remarked: "I feel that I make an effort when I hold my hands on the stove, when I pour boiling water on my feet; it is a violent act, and it awakens me. . . . The means I use seem foolish, and I know that I abuse them; but what can you expect? . . . Why do you speak of my desire for mortification?" For these particular patients, Janet reinforced the necessity of a regimen that James had earlier read of in the work of Renouvier and Bain. Psychasthenics might channel their activities, ending their depressions through more useful occupations.[143]

In this particular essay Janet had unduly complicated some issues of impulse and act. Fitting as it did James's earlier references to the explosive self, however, the essay provided a model of obsessional behavior that closely approximated James's own. Within these "most bizarre obsessions and agitations," James found a store of energy periodically erupting in "freak-activity."[144] He proposed to tap the energy through the same procedure that Janet had observed in some of his patients: asceticism. He offered the example of the yoga discipline of a friend, a Polish intellectual named Wincenty Lutoslawski. Lutoslawski had undertaken a fasting regimen. He reduced his meals to two and then to one a day. He began breathing rituals and prayers. "Then concentration of thought on different parts of the body, and on the processes going on within them. Exclusions of all emotions, dry logical reading, . . . and working out logical problems." He broke under the stress, then he resumed his preparation. "However base and vile a sinner I had been, perhaps my sins were about to be forgiven, and Yoga was only an exterior opportunity, an object for concentration of will."[145]

In a letter to Lutoslawski, James mentioned having tried the breathing exercises himself, though they "go terribly against the grain with me, are extremely disagreeable." The "obstinate strength of will" was not working. "When could I hope for such will-power?" With the press of his work, James said he found but little "*ascetic* energy" left. "I shall try fasting and again try breathing—discovering perhaps some individual rhythm that is more tolerable."[146]

James eventually discarded yoga. By 1908 he was on to "my Roberts-Hawley lymph compound injections" for his own neurasthenia and psychasthenia; the medicine was "still working beautifully on *me*." As for Lutoslawski, he "came and went, and seems now very well lodged in California. . . . Egotism & silliness are all! He got no Yoga pupils here."[147]

Asceticism—the heroism in small, unnecessary points that James had spoken of in 1890—still remained a way past psychasthenia, but not if it led the penitent back to prison.[148] James spoke most beautifully of asceticism in his Gifford Lectures on "saintliness" and "the value of saintliness," lectures in which James brought the ascetic ideal out of imprisonment into the world. Odd impulsions and obsessions erupted from beneath, driving neurotics into themselves or, if they chose, into a selfless life. The process worked when conversion utterly annihilated the self, bringing the initial sense of foulness followed by the understanding that nothing the person merited, did, or hoped to perform could remove the sin. James had directed his talks toward the fruits of this experience when the obsessive desire "to break something, no matter whose or what," crushed the ascetic and offered his self-surrender. The ambiguity of asceticism arose at this point, for the breaking might, as James said, "become so passionate as to turn into self-immolation. It may then so overrule the ordinary inhibitions of the flesh that the saint finds positive pleasure in sacrifice." Here, as with yoga, asceticism became a mathematical function.[149]

> The practical course of action for us, as religious men, would therefore, it seems to me, not be simply to turn our backs upon the ascetic impulse, as most of us to-day turn them, but rather to discover some outlet for it of which the fruits in the way of privation and hardship might be objectively useful. The older monastic asceticism occupied itself with pathetic futilities, or terminated in the mere egotism of the individual, increasing his own perfection. But is it not possible for us to discard most of these older forms of mortification, and yet find saner channels for the heroism which inspired them?[150]

In these lectures James said that "taking refuge in monasteries was as much an idol of the tribe in the middle-ages, as bearing a hand in the world's work is today." James was speaking clearly enough to his father. "We must," he said, "test it by its economical relations." He could hope in that way to cut out his father's otherworldly structure. "There are no successes to be guaranteed and no set orders."[151]

Like Max Weber, who cited these lectures in his *Protestant Ethic and the Spirit of Capitalism*, James provided a metaphor of stepping from a monastic cell into a work ascetically but productively pursued. For both scholars, asceticism expressed a timeless ideal serving the mental health of its practitioners, but in its Protestant form, for Weber, or in its pragmatic form, for James, asceticism served best. As in the pragmatic economy that James measured, however, asceticism could turn and accomplish its own closure. It could fail in the end to pay, or to redeem anyone from fear.

The *Varieties of Religious Experience* hardly offered what its title invoked: the sense of James as a pluralistic wanderer studying species of natural religion. He carefully structured the order of his talks, moving his lectures—singly and in sets as personifications—through the morphology of conversion of the Puritan divines. If the first and last of the lectures are removed—the "Circumscription," "Conclusions," and "Postscript," along with the philosophical beginnings and ends—the steps appear.

James could never describe the morphology of conversion in the manner of Shepard and Edwards but, using the terms of modern psychology, he could re-enact their structure. In this sense the book lies in the tradition of Shepard's *Sound Believer* and Edwards's *Religious Affections*, providing for the third century of New England literature another great work of personal conversion. The word "varieties" encourages a reading of James solely in terms of modernism (though for Darwin, variety did express morphology, growth, and transformation, change actuated by chance and then suitably tested by the environment). In words that James quoted in another regard from the English Unitarian theologian James Martineau, however, only variety, or dissociation—not, that is, the utilitarian's association—allowed an original unity of consciousness to form. One "confused fact" presented itself, only to achieve its meaning as "unsuspected varieties" revealed themselves. In the sense of Shepard and Edwards, variety spoke to the manifold operations of God upon the spirit—in Edwards's words, "perhaps as manifold as the subjects of the operation; but yet in many things there is a *great analogy* in all."[152]

Edwards had broken Shepard's serial of conversion into a list of twelve signs. James returned to the narrative structure in his *Varieties*, using his lectures to tell the story of conversion that, in its simplest formulation, Edwards had never denied. The *Varieties* works as a composite biography, a course of lectures in which James, by piecing together bits of autobiography from a broad range of history, moves an ideal "religious genius" through a transformation, refashioning the landscape of the pilgrim's journey in the terms of the new psychology. The *Varieties*, a book of spiritual biography, reads like a synecdoche of James's entire life. James takes his allegorical figure from carnal security—"the religion of healthy mindedness" (liberal, ameliorative, and quick to be shattered)—through panic fear and crisis, to ultimate glimpses of glorification.

Broken into two ten-lecture series separated in their delivery by a year, the Gifford Lectures mark the two acts of spiritual trial that William Perkins and William Ames had described. Moving from "the sick soul" and its conviction of sin through "the divided self and the process of its unification" (unification that James also termed "vocation"), the first series ends with "conversion," a word that James once defined as "justification." The first series circumscribes Perkins's works of preparation. The second series begins with "saintliness" and "the value of saintliness"—or "sanctification," as James said—and ends substantively with "mysticism," Shepard's glorification and immediate communion with God. In the good works displayed and the peace achieved, the second series offers the effects of grace.[153] James used the *Varieties* not to write a psychology of the world's religions but to reconsider a quite specific structure of spiritual transformation.

The first of James's varieties of saintliness is world-forsaking and perfectionist in its pursuit of estranged labors. His second is world-accepting, with work replacing works. "Mysticism"—"and I can speak of . . . [it] only at second hand"—represents the final letting go, the willingness, through the door of asceticism, to open the self to the personality of its final end.

Mysticism neither exalts nor intoxicates, but offers an "anaesthetic revelation." In words of Tennyson to Benjamin Paul Blood that James reported, "the loss of personality (if so it were) [seems] . . . no extinction, but the only true life." And in the words (also reported by James) of a "subject, a gifted woman, . . . taking ether for a surgical operation":

> He went on and I came to. In that moment the whole of my life passed before me, including each little meaningless piece of distress, and I *understood* them. *This* was the piece of work it had all been contributing to do. I did not see God's purpose, I only saw his intentness and his entire relentlessness towards his means. He thought no more of me than a man thinks of hurting a cork when he is opening wine.[154]

The woman's words appear close to the father's experience: "a slight operation under insufficient ether, in a bed pushed up against a window," with the pain reflected back and then made transparent. "The eternal necessity of suffering" showed "the passivity of genius, how it is essentially instrumental and defenseless, moved, not moving, it must do what it does;—the impossibility of discovery without its price;—finally, the excess of what the suffering 'seer' or genius pays over what his generation gains." The price is exacted that God might show the supplicant his faith:

> (He seems like one who sweats his life to earn enough to save a district from famine, and just as he staggers back, dying and satisfied, bringing a lac of rupees to buy grain with, God lifts the lac away, dropping *one* rupee, and says, "That you may give them. That you have earned for them. The rest is for ME.")[155]

All of this, "communicated to me in manuscript by a friend in England," had come to James's correspondent in the revelation of "an ether dream."

Radical Empiricism

James had pulled out of his own worst depression by setting to work. He had predicated his sanity upon his ability so to sustain a thought that no other idea could intrude. Morbid ideas work to fill the mind with such pain that they can prevent even more painful ideas from intruding. Obsessions, so-called, place barriers between the self and others, family and friends, for example, that morbid thought so often includes. The impulsive insanity that James had read of included the fear of killing not a stranger but a loved one or friend. A fear of criminality, blasphemy, doing harm, or even a trivial fear of no apparent consequence, provides a logical reason for remaining rigid, emotionally tense, and detached. In his diary on December 21, 1869, William wrote that "Nature & life have unfitted me for any affectionate relations with other individuals—it is well to know the limits of one's individual faculties, in order not to accept intellectual[ly] the verdict of one's personal feeling & experience as the measure of objective fact—but to brood over them with feeling is 'morbid.'" On January 1, 1870, he resolved to read, among other books, a book by Henry Maudsley—not the book he cited in his *Psychology* but Maudsley's *Physiology and Pathology of the Mind*, an American edition of which was published the following year.[156] Among "Varieties of Insanity," Maudsley included a partial "ideational" form:

> C.K., aet. 36, married, had always been of an extremely religious character and of exemplary behavior. After he had been married for about a year, his present illness began with general depression of feeling and with the involuntary appearance in his mind of blasphemous ideas in spite of all his efforts to avoid them; . . . his gloom increased, and at last he concluded that "he had done it,"—namely, committed the unpardonable sin.

Such depression, Maudsley continued, allowed for "an automatic and spasmodic activity of certain ideational cells," manifesting itself in the irrepressible ideas. The patient himself was "very hypochondriacal, and fearful that he should die soon." Reasonable, intelligent, alive, as Maudsley said, to "all business relations," the patient lapsed into melancholy whenever his attention remained undiverted from his suffering. "He lived, as it were, two separate lives—as a sound, reasonable being, and as a morbid automatic being."[157]

If the defense of such ideation fails, then a person may feel enveloped by chaos. Depression ensues, the periods of intense control now broken with feelings of loss, fatigue, weakness of will. Control is swept aside by melancholic languor, and order is replaced by the sense of a mess. The person, then, seeks a new order. For James, the choice became one either of reverting to an order he called automatic and neurotic or of turning to an incompleted production. Philosophically, he proposed to choose between a universe as given—an iron block cold like the melancholy self he described, conceptually tight, mentally complete, and logical to the point of utter absurdity, rational to the point of a "mad absolute"—or a universe in the making. This was a creative world never finished in its construction. James offered a choice between positions on the one hand that he variously defined as intellectual, monist, absolute, rational, all of which were static and shut, hypochondriacal, as he had said early on, and positions on the other hand that held the rationalist's "disdain": "the particular, the personal, and the unwholesome"—a universe unfinished, open to experience, and radical enough in its empiricism to allow that death was not death but possibly rebirth.

> There are resources in us that naturalism with its literal and legal virtues never recks of, possibilities that take our breath away, of another kind of happiness and power, based on giving up our own will and letting something higher work for us, and these seem to show a world wider than either physics or philistine ethics can imagine. Here is a world in which all is well, in *spite* of certain forms of death, indeed *because* of certain forms of death—death of hope, death of strength, death of responsibility, of fear and worry, competency and desert, death of everything that paganism, naturalism, and legalism pin their faith on and tie their trust to.

The words appear no different from Edwards's as James pitted himself against anything that reeked of structure: intellectualization, conceptualization, verbalization, mechanization, anything of logical elegance, style, or legality that bred "foreignness" or so-called "rationality" itself. "Intellectualism," he wrote in one of his last lectures, "denies . . . that finite things can act on one another, for all things, once translated into concepts, remain shut up to themselves. To act on anything means to get into it somehow; but that would mean to get out of one's self and be one's other," a clear state of alienation "which is self-contradictory, etc."

> What really *exists* is not things made but things in the making. Once made, they are dead, and an infinite number of alternative conceptual decompositions can be used in defining them. But put yourself *in the making* by a stroke of intuitive sympathy with the thing and, the whole range of possible decompositions coming at once into your possession, you are no longer troubled with the question

which of them is the more absolutely true. Reality *falls* in passing into conceptual analysis; it *mounts* in living its own undivided life—it buds and burgeons, changes and creates.[158]

James's greatest works, his *Psychology* and *Varieties of Religious Experience,* reflect the productions of his own self-defined melancholy mind. They are flowerings that were preceded by horrid depressions (the *Varieties* itself was written in bed in James's neurasthenic chamber). He readily expressed all this: not so much why he lay depressed or what that expressed, angry as he remained with himself for days on end, but why he thought it important to write of this preparatory sadness at all. He had to speak of it, to his daughter Margaret, for example, using himself once again as an exemplum for his children to read of:

Now, my dear little girl, you have come to an age when the inward life develops. . . . Among other things there will be waves of terrible sadness, which sometimes last for days; and dissatisfaction with one's self, and irritation at others, and anger at circumstances and stoney insensibility, etc., etc., which taken together form a melancholy. Now, painful as it is, this is sent to us for an enlightenment.

He was writing from Bad-Nauheim, convalescing, the "baths . . . threatening to disagree with me again, so I may stop them soon."[159] He was writing in May of 1900; his Gifford Lectures were about to begin.

James believed that this form of expression—autobiographies like the letter to his daughter and the cases used in his lectures—was relatively new. He also believed that the expression used, in which the self becomes a moral waste, was also new. James spoke of this in his Hibbert Lectures at Oxford in the year before his death. He faced there, as he took it, monistic steel, an elegance of logic propounded by younger idealists, against which he was placing a variety of strange psychical experiences. He offered empiricism to such rationalist friends as his colleague Josiah Royce, a maker, for James, of the mad absolute.

By this I don't mean immortality, or the death of the body. I mean the deathlike termination of certain mental processes within the individual's experience, processes that run to failure, and in some individuals, at least, eventuate in despair. Just as romantic love seems a comparatively recent literary invention, so these experiences of life that supervenes upon despair seem to have played no great part in official theology till Luther's time. . . .

Luther was the first moralist who broke with any effectiveness through the crust of all this naturalistic self-sufficiency, thinking (and possibly he was right) that Saint Paul had done it already. Religious experience of the lutheran type brings all our naturalistic standards to bankruptcy. You are strong only by being weak, it shows.[160]

For that, James said, as he finished his lectures, he had "brought in [G. T.] Fechner and [Henri] Bergson, and described descriptive psychology and religious experiences, and have ventured even to hint at psychical research and other wild beasts of the philosophic deserts."

It was in sight of this wilderness that James had hoped to "make my *nick* . . . in the raw stuff the race has got to shape, and so assert my reality."[161] Royce, one of his closest friends, was also writing of work as self-creation, but Royce had found his own immediate vocation early in life. James feared that a vastation into obscure speculation like that which his father had experienced was devouring his friend Royce as well. He feared losing himself too in such a philosophic sea, brooding about questions for which no answers existed. James asked that this devil be forestalled by carrying one's labors into a world itself in the making, a world never to be closed or made by the eye so terribly complete.

4

Conversion through Ethical Salvation

Josiah Royce

> Strain, endurance, sacrifice, toil—the dear pangs of labor at the moments when perhaps defeat and grief most seem ready to crush our powers, and when only the very vehemence of labor itself saves us from utter despair.
>
> For most of us the higher life is to be gained only through weary labor, if at all.
>
> Josiah Royce, *The Philosophy of Loyalty* (1908) and "The Decay of Earnestness" (1888)

In America following the Civil War, a few vestiges of a formal Calvinism survived. Certainly for a young man educated at Berkeley, where Josiah Royce received his undergraduate education, or at Harvard, where Royce taught, it was simply not expected that one believe in predestined damnation. One could, however, if one needed to make sense out of a burden of conscience, re-enact a pilgrim's progress. Of the American intellectuals writing in these years, Royce expressed this need most thoroughly. A Harvard professor who represented the best thinking of that college's great age of philosophy, Royce appeared to his colleagues to be living like a latter-day Bunyan. Educated after Berkeley in Leipzig and

Göttingen, then the recipient of a doctorate from Johns Hopkins in 1878, Royce had well under way, at the age of twenty-three, a difficult journey through the intricacies of Kant and the German idealists.[1] The trek, technical and abstruse, was to remain a deeply moral and religious experience for Royce.

Royce used German idealism to write a salvationist history both for himself and the estrangements he suffered, and for America and its alienation. Early American authors like Cotton Mather and Jonathan Edwards could employ the Biblical typology of the wilderness—the desert of temptations of the Israelites and Christ—to explain the significance they found in the evils facing America: times for them when God had loosed Satan's hand to tempt a people at the very edge of national salvation. Victorian authors could employ the typology only by using newer forms of estrangement. Early national America in its progress provided examples of alienation as mechanistic and satanic as the Puritans' alienation: the factories, kilns, and stones of Wall Street that had replaced the witch, the savage, and the body of a suicide. In authors like Hawthorne and Melville, these metaphors had become just as real and efficacious for making sense of spiritual desertion as Edwards's American "desert"—industrial landscapes that lead a people not into economic struggle but spiritual insight. They are landscapes, in other words, that create revelation rather than revolution.

Royce also engaged America in an ethical struggle with the "tempter." The struggle he portrayed, however, is not with satanic mills but even newer forms of estrangement: impersonal structures like corporations and bureaucracies that create machines large enough to drive a people into amoral work and eventually into despair. It was Royce, influenced by German idealism, who first used the words "alienation" and "estrangement" in America in their modern or social meaning. The words served him perfectly to speak of spiritual desertion, and provided him with a new way to write a Calvinist text of salvation.

Before Royce considered the question of national alienation, he focused his writings on the estrangement of the person. Like James, the case that he opened most immediately was the estrangement he found in himself. Royce, like James and James's father, used his philosophy to form an understanding of himself. When a literate culture expects writers to make their lives a part of their texts, which was the case not only for Victorian fiction but also for Victorian philosophy, then it is appropriate to make a "personal" reading of texts, even texts in a field as formal as philosophy. Royce wrote an ethical and religious philosophy so abstract at times that it made James impatient (James attributed the impersonality to his friend's personality). What is of interest is how and why that reflection should be there—the cultural context, in other words, or the textual culture that permitted Royce to write of himself by using his philosophy as a confession of sin.

By the nineteenth century the spiritual relation that had held particular significance in mid-seventeenth-century New England, possessing the power to place its author within the visible church, had scattered into the privacy of letters, diaries, journals, and personal asides within otherwise impersonal texts. Nevertheless, these Victorian testaments, even one as hidden as the panic fear of William James, held as much public intent as the earlier spiritual confessions. An editor could gather the dispersed confessional pieces together and have them published as a single text. One could collect and publicly place such confessions in an archive or in print. Preparing even as Thoreau had a "pine box" to hold his journals—a box measured by Thoreau to the last inch to fit his most personal observations[2]—a New England writer could expect eventually that some type of library shelf would contain his life. He could also expect that others would construct his life further by writing memoirs and publishing selected letters.

Texts do emerge, then, that appear to reflect the most private things an author has suffered. Within practices of discourse, however, received texts exist that an author can work both with and against to give his self psychological meaning. An author can write out tracings of past self-revelations, but if he remains creative and desires to give himself distinction, he never makes a perfect copy. The process of imitation, as Royce never tired of reminding his readers, works like a process of "mocking." The self learns to distinguish itself by attempting, but failing, to copy. The son, for example, becomes himself by *not* becoming his father.

Royce of course was right, for late Victorian lives could hardly copy a Calvinist text of salvation such as the one Royce most closely studied, Bunyan's *Grace Abounding to the Chief of Sinners*. Still, for the intellectual composing his life in the years following the Civil War, the necessity remained to express the last phrase in this chapter's epigraph from Royce, the "if at all" that collapses the worth of even the most excruciating labor. The necessity remained to express the careful construction of Thoreau's cabin, also measured to the last inch, and then to watch as the cabin is left behind and eventually sold, finally abandoned and lost beside some decaying railroad tracks. Royce, whose own conversion extended over years, left a similar text of wearying labor behind.

In the prelude of a diary written in 1879, for example, he held the irony of this self-consumption within a single line: the "denial of activity; it is death." "The individual moments of our lives," he wrote, "must be full of action, the fuller the better: but they must also be, for the very same reason, full of unrest. No content of the moment, however great, must lead us to wish to remain stationary. This content in the present moment . . . is death."[3] In refusing to remain stationary, Royce would refuse to have his life simply impressed.

Royce was beginning his diary as Cotton Mather had begun his, with a promise to practice method, and as Edwards had begun his, with a promise to watch his time. These earlier beginnings had ended as they would for Royce, in the scholar accepting the death denied. By composing his life not in a single spiritual text but in letters, in a small, anonymous confession, and in the ethical philosophy that he publicly preached, Royce allowed his readers to see this composition of the self as it works toward its own destruction. He could show then the one work of atonement that for him remained of any significance.

Imitation

The composition that Royce made of himself is that of a man "beset," "driven," "overtasked," a composition similar to that which James made in his own letters. Like James, Royce found his mind harassed by "temporary vexations" of one sort or another.[4] Like James's father, Royce also spoke of his need for seclusion like that provided by the sea, isolation that he once called "my place of safety." There he toiled. As James Harry Cotton has recounted, Royce's son Stephen remembered that once, when he was a young boy, he and his father were out sailing when a sudden storm appeared. While the son steered for harbor, the father sat in the bow, pondering theorems in symbolic logic, his son warning whenever a wave threatened to drench his father's papers.[5] The story tells of the barriers Royce could erect between himself and others. He could approach those closest to him with uncanny detachment. When his son Christopher fell mentally ill, for example, Royce began referring to his son as "the patient,"—someone he had to provide for against "pauperism, which I of course regard with peculiar horror." "Should the patient soon recover enough to begin anew a fight with the world," Royce continued in a letter to James, thanking his colleague for a gift of money, "his guardian could use the sum to help start afresh. Should recovery be followed (vain hope!) by any chance worldly success, then the patient could himself return the sum to you or to your heirs."[6] Like the elder James, Royce wrote as if his love for his children came at too great a cost.

In the image of one of his students, Royce had constructed a "cabin" for himself. He died with this same effacement. Only recently, through the publication of his surviving letters, has the life of one of the most eminent American philosophers begun to emerge. A few nights before his death in 1916, Royce entered his study to burn many of his personal papers.[7] Still, he revealed his life—though never so openly as James—particularly in the letters that others preserved. Here Royce presented himself, again like James, as physically and morally exhausted. Most significant, however, Royce also left behind an unpublished lecture that he had given in 1893, containing one small personal revelation, a confession that appears like a piece of clinical evidence.

This confession is slight and achieves significance only when read within the context of the Puritan confession of such a small mental detail. Royce was illustrating imitative behavior as a learned response, using the work, among others, of Bain. He spoke first of a mockingbird copying sounds, then of a child performing a prohibited act because a parent had vividly described it and intrigued the child with the very thing forbidden. Finally, in a "personal confession," he continued with an example of "imitation" from his own experience. In a German library, he remembered, authorities had discovered patrons lighting matches in dark alcoves to read book titles and had posted a sign prohibiting the practice, threatening punishment for anyone discovered. Royce said that he had never thought of lighting matches in the library, and yet—in the words of a secondary account of Royce's remark, buried in a footnote without seeming significance—"he begged the authorities to remove the sign, for within a week he'd have a compulsion to light matches in every dark corner."[8]

Royce was narrating a fear of performing a criminal act. The ideation that Royce confessed, James had called an explosive self. A similar though certainly more serious example of such obsessional fear is that of a mother who, beset by an idea that she will stab her child to death, removes all knives from her kitchen. As Royce said, he had never thought of lighting matches to read book titles, though he remained unclear whether he believed he would have actually committed the crime. But he did beg the authorities to remove the precipitant of his fear, so as to quiet his apprehension.[9] The posted words held a magical and indeed compelling power for him. It was as though he wanted the sign erased.

In the spring of 1893, Royce termed his insistent fear one of imitation. Imitation offered a psychological concept, to be sure, but the word indicated no abnormality, no more than that of a mockingbird distorting a sound. Royce was then writing essays on psychology, however, and even went so far as to attempt some experiments using the brass instruments of James. As in his studies of imitation, Royce was designing these experiments to show the significance of the self in its relation to others. He was arguing that only imitative behavior allows the self to distinguish itself, for when the self attempts to copy another, it inevitably fails, and thus the self comes to know of its own self-distinctions. Through the caricatures or imperfect tracings that the self makes of another's acts, it comes to know of its internal possessions. This other that the self tries to copy, or feels attracted to, serves in the same way as the demonic other of a Puritan captivity narrative where the saint, in conversion, stands before a savage and feels at first compelled to act like the satanic object that will sooner or later tell the saint just what his own self is not.[10] Ultimately, Royce argued, harmony results from such a distortion, for the self's rationality (or indeed the Hegelian absolute) requires that the self first experience what it is not. In an estranged effort, the self comes to know itself only by trying to become its other. Because the imitation fails, and turns into a mocking, one learns of one's difference by failing to grasp something that stands beyond the self. A child, for example, plays with its fists, and a young man looks to the example of his father.

Royce moved through experimental and pathological psychology, looking for the manner in which a subject made such tracings. Whether making studies of a person tapping a brass key, attempting to copy a previously heard rhythm—Royce's own experiment—or reading of neurasthenia, impulsive insanity, and hysteria—states in which the self appeared to mock itself—Royce looked for examples of the self facing an estrangement, an other that was saying what the self was not.[11] The humoral psychology, of course, no longer sufficed to explain the feeling of a body pitted against itself, but there did remain the assumption that one could and indeed should substantiate "the problem of Job" with the latest writings in nervous physiology. Royce held that the irrational was there as a measurable other. Like the absolute, the sanctity of personhood became evident only when the body was held in physical tensions and in mental divisions. Royce, outcast as an intellectualist by colleagues and students and forever pitted against James, nevertheless dabbled as a metaphysician with these tapping keys and revolving drums to employ muscles and nerves, "merely physiological fact," to prove the necessity of evil. In his finest essay, for example, he wrote of Job in just these terms: that for "every rational life" there existed "this crossing." Will and reflex, or conscience and impulse, battle continually against one another, only together forming a whole person.[12]

> Now it is easy to say that such states of inner tension, where our conscious lives are full of a warfare of the self with itself, are contradictory or absurd states. But it is easy to say this only when you dwell on the words and fail to observe the facts of experience. As a fact, not only our lowest but our highest states of activity are the ones which are fullest of this crossing, conflict, and complex interrelation of loves and hates, of attractions and repugnances. As a merely physiological fact, we begin no muscular act without at the same time initiating acts which involve the innervation of opposing sets of muscles, and these opposing sets of muscles hinder each other's freedom. . . . We do nothing simple, and we will no complex act without willing what involves a certain measure of opposition between the impulses or partial acts which go to make up the whole act.[13]

From this, "I admit, philosophically speaking, trivial" point of human physiology—as trivial as the bodily moves and pushes that Bunyan had written of—Royce could pass to the dialectics of Hegel: "There is nothing . . . there till you win it, nothing consciously known or possessed till you prove it by conflict with its opposite, till you develop its inner contradictions"—and from thence to the biography of the world spirit. As Edwards could pass from the basest of humors to the plight of man in the state of temptation, as Thoreau could pass from the hoeing, the knowing of beans, to the selling of his base product for the purity of rice, and Melville from the measures of the whale to the absolute—so Royce could move, a few paragraphs later in his essay on Job, to the resolution of spirit from errors, conflicts, and physical "repugnances." This was the moment of thwarting the most elemental of impulses, "the moment of victory over the tempter." As Royce had written earlier: "Such triumph alone does the supreme spirit know, who is tempted in all points like as we are, yet without sin. Holiness, you see, exists by virtue of its opposite. Holiness is a consciousness of sin with a consciousness of the victory over sin. Only the tempted are holy, and they only when they win against temptation."[14] The struggle had evolved from conscience to consciousness as a modern word replaced a less acceptable one, but the words are like Edwards's own words and Royce's struggle was like Edwards's own struggle to make Gillespie, his correspondent over the meaning of horrid temptations, understand.

> Here we are with the world in our hands, beset already with temptation and with all the pangs of our finitude. For us holiness means, not the abolition of worldliness, not innocence, not turning away from the world, but the victory that overcometh the world, the struggle, the courage, the vigor, the endurance,

> the hot fight with sin, the facing of the demon, the power to have him there in us and to hold him by the throat, the living and ghastly presence of the enemy, and the triumphant wrestling with him and keeping him forever a panting, furious, immortal thrall and bondman. That is all the holiness we can hope for.[15]

Royce thereby discarded portions of Hegel and all the evolutionary optimism Royce ascribed to his generation, for the person could hold but through history never subdue the alienation or the tempter. The struggle stood as ancient—as universal—a text as Job's struggle with God. Royce was "heir," George Santayana observed, "to the Calvinist tradition," preaching "the most terrible truths about one's depravity," thereby appalling Santayana and bothering James. They both sensed that Royce was resigned and was now apologizing for every conceivable horror, and suspected that Royce truly felt, as he had prefaced his diary, that before nature and God he stood "but as a worm."[16]

Royce had received a heritage that his father's family liked to remember as having included militant seventeenth-century Baptists.[17] Royce, however, preferred to recall how stubborn he became in his rebellion against his church and against the rigors of his family's Sunday observances,[18] as stubborn as the elder James had been against his family's religion. And like Henry James, Royce thought of himself as returning to explain how doubt and incessant error proved the existence of an all-knowing Being. The elder James had died in his obscurity with only Santayana, for whatever the reason, reading his works. To Santayana, Royce now had become another prophet for troubled Victorian Protestants, those who still wished their unsuspecting ill fortunes justified. "In his age and country all was change, preparation, hurry, material achievement"[19]; Santayana claimed this mercantile mentality as Cotton Mather had claimed it his. Royce had taken the occasion to stand against America's progress, working to seek Santayana's own ascetic island of certainty amid America's doubt.[20]

Royce achieved his fame at the age of thirty for his validation of the absolute through the existence of error. In a masterful exercise in logic, he sought to reaffirm what the elder James had expressed in a flurry of Swedenborgian mysticism: that only impurity presaged perfectly pure being.[21] He is less acknowledged for his thesis of modern man's alienation and for his ideas of work as self-creation, a theme he fashioned for his "century of nerves" from his reading of Hegel's "self-estranged spirit." It was the same idea of the power of work to define the self that had influenced Marx.[22] Royce had begun to compose his trauma, that he was holding a ghastly presence by the throat and must thereby set to work. He proposed in his diary that only this discontent prevented one from sinking "into nothing"—into "*Das Ewig-Weibliche*," the everlasting feminine. "Life is action. Passivity, the negative aspect, must at every moment be set up and conquered[.] Every moment we must enter into contract with the devil; every moment use his services for our own development." "The goal of activity once found," Royce wrote six years later, just before a severe nervous collapse, "the problem will be solved, and the devil's wager lost."[23]

Royce was hardly turning to a foreign ideology, no matter what suspicions his colleagues held of the Storm and Stress of German literature, of this "autobiography of the spirit," as Royce described the work of Hegel. He was no more turning than Henry James when James discovered Swedenborg, no more than his friend James Jackson Putnam when Putnam discovered Freud. The estrangement—the making strange that was so important to a Puritan vision of a demonic New World and wilderness land—Royce alone, of the Americans, captured from the modern idealists' quest for identity. The Germans provided Royce with a meaning for alienation by predicating unity only in the self's initial division or in the distance first to be held between subject and object, self and other. For the so-called young or Hegelian Marx, it became the distance between man and his manner of working. It is the barren that is capable of bearing fruit, the working out in dialectics of the seed of destruction held within, the "on-coming fatal future," in the words of Royce, providing his own illustration of Hegel, "that constitutes the deepest pang of loneliness, of defeat, of shame." It is the contrite conscience of which Hegel spoke, the alienated laborer—unknown to Royce—of Marx. "I exist for nobody; and erelong," Royce wrote, again of Hegel, "perhaps to my surprise, generally to my horror, I discover that I *am* nobody. The one thing means the other. In the dungeon of my isolated self-consciousness I rot away unheeded and terror-stricken. Idiocy is before me." It was the idiocy that had sat before James in the asylum's cell.[24] And it is the idiocy that first frightens the self before it tells the self what the self can become. The self can become different.

In Royce's later writing it became the devastation (and therefore the hope) of America as the most alien of lands, strangled now in an economy of corporate loneliness. It became a question for Royce of interpreting the necessity of evil. For "it is not those innocent of evil," Royce wrote, "who are fullest of the life of God, but those who in their own case have experienced the triumph over evil. It is not those naturally ignorant of fear, or those who, like Siegfried have never shivered, who possess the genuine experience of courage; but the brave are those who have fears, but control their fears. Such know the genuine virtues of the hero," or the saint.[25] A higher life grew from an evil impulse, but the pain survived so that struggle and conversion could continue.

California and Royce's Childhood

Though Royce had warned others away from his life, he thought of his personality as intimately tied to his philosophy. In a last, brief autobiographical sketch provided just before his death, he portrayed his childhood in words that he considered significant. "I was a born nonconformist," he remembered. "I was not a very active boy. I had no physical skill or agility. I was timid and ineffective, . . . more or less given to petty mischief." He was like Bunyan. With red hair, freckles, and a "countrified" appearance, he feared his schoolmates thought him "quaint" and "disagreeably striking." Because he stood apart, lacking the confidence, for example, to play boyhood games, his playmates had introduced him to the "majesty of community." They had provided him with a particularly joyless lesson in "the Pauline doctrine of original sin." Through his estrangement, the boy who possessed "so much of the spirit that opposes the community" first learned that difference did create a definition. He learned the irony that only opposition saved outcasts such as himself.[26]

Royce was raised in a family that was not rigid in its prescription but rather arbitrary in its authority, as arbitrary as the lack of "interpretation" he feared when two parties confronted each other without a third party (an interpreter) to mediate between them. The push and pull to which Royce attributed self-division and uncertainty expressed itself in a family in which ethics appeared split. A strong mother watched her son's every move, while a passive or at least absent father left his son behind.

Although information about Royce's childhood is scanty, his family may readily be seen as having instilled the doubt that, everyone agreed, drove Royce's life. This is the "outrageous vacillation" that Royce denigrated in others, and the doubt that Santayana remembered as having tormented the philosopher's life.[27] Royce's parents appear to have been strict, yet aloof and divided. If so, then Royce was caught in a "dual orientation," in the phrase of Andras Angyal, unsure, one may surmise, whether his family acted lovingly or cruelly. He never discussed his father in his surviving letters in any significant terms, except for a few offhand remarks about the father's "permanent ill-health" and his eventual death in 1888.[28] Josiah Royce, Sr., seemed himself a study in contradictions, for while zealous in his Protestantism (he was once a member of the Disciples of Christ) and given to memorizing the Bible, he lived as an idler. In John Clendenning's words, he was a "hopelessly quixotic" man who could converse for hours on end as he restlessly pursued some undefined purpose. Often away from home, he stood as an absence to his only son. He moved his family as often as he changed jobs; he was, at one time or another, a farmer, storekeeper, traveling salesman, mailman, and, as known by San Franciscans, an odd peddler of produce and fruit.[29] His son reacted to this mismanagement, the bewildering vocations that the frontiers of America could produce: "I wish that just for this moment it were given to me to summon every man to a calling that should remain his calling for life."[30]

The mother, Sarah Royce, encased her son's early years. Though Royce celebrated his mother and his three older sisters for becoming his first philosophy teachers, Sarah Royce appears, in another's words, a "solicitous mother" who overprotected her son by providing Royce with such an "imaginative world" that he became "disqualified" from participating on any physical frontier, although she seemed rather daring herself.[31] Throughout a memoir of the family's westward travel and early years in California that Royce had asked his mother to write in the 1880s, Sarah Royce preached self-sacrifice, yet at the same time flaunted her ability to do things well, whether ride a horse or kill a tarantula. She too seldom mentioned her husband in her autobiography. Only a refusal to rest had protected Sarah's husband and her firstborn child in their crossing of the Carson desert in 1849 on their way to the California goldfields. Her loyalty had protected her family in the moral wilderness of California as well. She opposed herself to her husband as "the patient endurance that is faithful to sacred ties, even when suffering from coldness and neglect." She set the temptations of ease and "the fatal gift of beauty" against her own strength. Royce would do the same after he had left his barren childhood state.

Royce never rejected the strength that his mother taught.[32] He never forgot to mention his own "passive resistance," however, for in the midst of other false gardens, he could use his rebellion, or his conviction of sin, to express his need to find a more lasting "community." If Sarah Royce did overindulge and solicit her son while preaching a sacrifice that verged on martyrdom, and while expressing a hardly concealed terrible rage, then she placed her son in a "double-bind" that could only have caused him shame and, of course, confusion.

In constructing this history, one must ask why this image remains so composed. The elder Henry James had written of fathers as rigid, certain, and tyrannical, and of the women he knew as lowly grass, for such figures made sense for an author who was turning against Calvinism and the authority that Calvinism presupposed. Henry James had declared that such authority would vanish in apocalypse, and it appeared that it had. The family Royce remembered, solely his mother and sisters—his father, again, he placed quite out of sight—resembles the memory of the younger Henry James. The younger James mentioned the uncanny sense of no one being there, however much his father had followed his every move. The loss of the fathers, in other words, presents a figure of malaise as sensible as the tyranny the elder James imagined. The loss of male authority accounts for the uncertainty that late Victorian intellectuals in America felt, or at least incessantly expressed—the uncertainty of a disrupted culture, ending in the entropy, or in the lack of information, that Henry Adams plotted out to the point of his nation's collapse. The fathers become reclusive or wandering men; in either event, the image appears the same: the fathers seem uncertain of their place; the children search for new vocations; and stronger, more assertive, indeed domineering mothers come to fill their husbands' void, caring for the ineffectual men. Images of authority's impotency run through William's and Henry's accounts of their youth, for such worked as a meaningful text. If the Calvinist God had turned his back, the Victorian father simply left. If he stayed and educated a prodigious son in a traditional way, then he remained an anachronism, like the father of John Stuart Mill's *Autobiography*, the best known of the contemporary fathers who stayed, to the point almost of destroying a son.

The Royces thus appear like the family of William James, moving across America as the elder James moved his family through the cities of Europe, for theirs is another expression of the search for a security never to be found. For Royce's mother, quite literally, the wandering became a pilgrim's journey. For Royce, the wandering reflected the necessity for an alienation and return. Royce could embrace an ethic of labor all the more harshly because his family, or rather his father, appeared lost as to the meaning of the ethic itself. Royce, again, could complete a text of salvation by working against his father. He could struggle to work out the meaning of his father's estrangement.

Such, however, remains an interpretation. The interpretation (or Charles Peirce's "interpretant") mediates between an "object," the cause of Royce's suffering, and a "sign," Royce's story, that is taken to be that object's effect. The sign in this case remains the repeated display that Royce made of his weakness and of the need that he expressed for work. The question is how to interpret Royce's words. For as Peirce argued for Royce, this trinity of object, sign, and interpretant becomes a whole or a further sign that requires another interpretant. The whole analysis thus spins off into ever further, recursive texts.

As an example of this problem of interpretation, Royce composed his own portrait of a mother and son in a novel that he wrote in the 1880s about California's early years, *The Feud of Oakfield Creek*. If the reader approaches the novel, the plot of which centers upon a land feud, as reflecting the conflicts in Royce's early years, then the novel has received an interpretation. This interpretation then becomes a sign of what Royce actually meant to say, and what Royce is said to have meant becomes the sign of what Royce actually lived. Here the various writings of fiction, autobiography, and biography require ever further interpretations. One assumes that the various texts somehow work down, eventually capturing the object or the origin of Royce's own admitted guilt. For Peirce, however, the end of interpretation, other than a God that he seldom acknowledged, is not an origin, but a working definition, a communally agreed upon, pragmatic definition of truth.[33] It is a convention that people agree makes sense. For Royce the end of interpretation, other than the absolute of which he always admitted, likewise results in a working definition, a communally sensible making of sense. For both men, truth evolves not from an origin but out of a habit or convention, through "habituation," as Douglas Greenlee has remarked of Peirce.[34] No nature, then, directly creates a sign, or in this case a writing, that reflects back upon itself. Instead, a sign remains paradigmatically interpreted by a body of persons in "convention," as Greenlee has also remarked. As for Royce's novel, interpretation makes sense only when the interpretation takes place in a context, or in a habit or convention, that Royce himself could use to make truth.

In the character of Margaret Eldon, Royce presented in his novel his own figure of a strong, spirited woman who dominates her household, an athletic horsewoman who is widely read, yet a brooding woman who fears spontaneity. Her morality and business sense stand without question, and her feelings appear "hard and cold," a lack of sympathy for which Royce tried to apologize. A part of this coldness consists of a carefully, almost neurotically ordered life, that of a "country lady who announces her fixed arrangements. 'I've set that for such a day,' was one of Margaret's commonest expressions. She delighted to predetermine her simple life down to all the smallest details, and it was in vain that you sought to suggest any unnecessary change in the predicted order of her doings"—suggest, that is, any "accidents." "'I suppose I seem to brood a good deal. I do it whenever I'm much alone for a while.'"[35]

Within this order, little room exists for a child. Others think of Margaret as "a very cold mother," though Royce tried to write of her as "plainly trying" to satisfy her son's demands. She keeps her child clean and his hands unmuddy, but in her obsessive care she expresses guilt for the anxiety that her child's mere presence creates. The boy thus becomes "lonesome," "somewhat ill-tempered," and suffers from inconsistency, "a little from a too frequent change of nurses, and from a constant change of the plans for his welfare." He reacts to this tangle of doubt and overprotection by fearing to show his own affection in the morning hour that his mother allots to his attention.

> With his mother, therefore, he was restless, hiding much of his delight in her presence beneath a certain anxious care to keep her attention fixed upon him, and to be sure that she should not leave him. . . . When she complained that he had got his feet wet . . . , he made her sit down on a rock, and then nestled close beside her, and patted her arm and her cheek very nervously with his little muddy hands. She smiled, but forbade any more such caresses, and begged the nurse to take him at once to wash his hands. At this he cried and showed temper, while she frowned, looked unhappy, and wandered off to the front lawn.

The boy, who has offered his mother a gift of moss, becomes frantic and finally enraged, and Margaret pulls further away, thinking

> that if her boy had no love for her, and could take no joy of her efforts to please him, it must be hardly worth while to spend even so much time with him.
>
> Then she grew anxious about his health, and began to question the nurse. He was pale; had he slept well? She wondered if that room was the best for him, after all,—the room that they had last fixed upon for the nursery. They were always changing nurseries in this house. . . . Margaret, who was very conservative in all her other habits, could find no rest as to this matter.[36]

If uncaring appears disguised, then a child cannot blame another for his pain. If even brutality is hidden beneath a "constant thin veneer of convention and sweetness and light," Harry Stack Sullivan observed, then a child has only himself to blame for the trouble his existence creates. He can only feel guilt because the anger he feels seemingly has no cause, and he will know only confusion because a parent tells him he has no reason for having the hurt that he feels. His anger becomes frightful because it seems so unaccountable. It is this unaccountability, the nature of his rage and the sense of his evil, that he must above all else control.

Within Royce's depiction of the mother and son, a clear issue emerges as to the quality of Margaret's love. Having begun his novel by describing their estrangement, Royce ended with a passage that affirms their love while it also affirms their bondage. Having lost everything in the family land struggle and feud, Margaret turns to her son as her only cause for living. The son in turn embraces her, but now only as a distant absolute. She becomes Royce's ideal, his "cause" or "beloved community," here "the source of all good, the ideal of ideals, the playfellow, the teacher, the friend." Resolution is achieved, but the son can conclude that only "some day" would this being teach the boy to understand her heart.[37]

One might wish never to touch another, for close relations punish at the same time that they provide and care for one. Margaret's son, nestled in his mother's lap, is told to run and wash his muddy hands. Thus only in an absolute, as Royce would affirm throughout his philosophy, can any lasting communion form—communion that comes not in face-to-face relations but through the mediation that his idealism demanded. For the present, Royce could only accept his uncertainty and repeat his parent's compulsion. He could, however, write again from a received text to make his troubles meaningful.

James and Harvard

Royce portrayed Harvard's "pragmatists" also as persons who had pushed him aside, so that he stood alone as their seemingly ineffectual enemy. "The 'Pragmatists' wag their heads and mock when I pass by."[38] After the arrival of James's pragmatism, and toward the end of his own career, Royce portrayed himself once again as the outsider. Like his childhood companions, others were enjoying popular activities while pushing Royce out of the play. He pointed to James to explain this estrangement, but like the figure he made of Margaret, Royce also portrayed James as the one man who had "found me" and "accepted me with all my imperfections." James became a close friend and benefactor, the one person who had been able to take Royce from the "madness" and the "wilderness" he had found in California.[39]

Immersed in an abstract philosophy, Royce seemed to float in vacuous irrelevancy. He taught and lectured to those who he thought would rather have listened to James. James, for all of his complaint of weakness, was considered by his students a physically awesome professor who, most agreed, met and probably surpassed his own criteria for "tough-mindedness." Among colleagues and students who seemed enthralled by tough thoughts, strenuous habits, and active lives, Royce acquired a reputation as "the tender-foot Bostonian," a physically and to many a philosophically effete little man. James was the "realist" and pragmatist, Royce the idealist and representative of what Santayana disparagingly called "the genteel tradition," a style said to be as timid and ineffectual as this cumbersome professor who, "feeling his own physical impotence in a world of struggle, asked to have the victory written in the stars in order to contemplate and relieve it in imagination." This remained one impression Royce encountered throughout his career, an image that must have stung all the more since it was Royce who had been raised on a California frontier, while James—"the philosophical 'Rocky Mountain tough'"—had been nurtured by urbane Bostonians.[40]

This "Roycean myth," as it has come to be called, pitted the two philosophers against each other, creating the struggle of a father and son.[41]

> I lead a parasitic life upon you, for my highest flight at ambitious ideality is to become your conqueror, and go down into history as such, you and I rolled in one another's arms and silent (or rather loquacious still) in one last death-grapple of an embrace. How then, O my dear Royce, can I forget you, or be contented out of your close neighborhood?[42]

James would then accuse his colleague of counseling a "moral holiday" by using the absolute as a sublime retreat for those who wished to retire. Stung, Royce attempted to explain:

> And it is true that some of these have said: "The saints . . . do enter into this rest. And for them there is indeed nothing left to do." To such, of course, the moralists may reply: "You enlightened ones seem to think yourselves entitled to a 'moral holiday.' We strenuous souls reject your idleness as unworthy of a man. Your religion is barren aestheticism, . . . an ascetic and unworldly contemplation. . . ." In these lectures, as I ask you to note, I have never defined salvation in such terms. Salvation includes triumph and peace, but peace only in and through the power of the spirit and the life of strenuous activity.[43]

James would also declare a "protestant reformation" for philosophy, scolding Royce's idealism. He attacked the absolute as he had his father's Swedenborg, calling it "incantation" and "unlawful magic." Royce's absolute favored "formula" rather than "work"—"the view that truth in our ideas means their power to 'work,'"—meaning that James's pragmatic philosophy never sought Royce's perfectly machined truth. James's pragmatist sought God instead "in the very dirt of private fact." Royce replied, arguing that signification did remain a process of infinite measures, as Peirce had shown, for signs required other signs for their own interpretation. Meaning, in other words, was never self-contained. In rejecting Royce's pure absolute that did create a lasting interpretation, James used words similar to words Royce had already chosen: "We receive . . . the block of marble, but we carve the statue ourselves." "Must *all* be saved? Is *no* price to be paid in the work of salvation?" Were men willing to forego an immediate solution and work ceaselessly upon an "unfinished" edition of the world, or were they to collapse into a single text, "the infinite folio," the "*edition de luxe*, eternally complete . . ."?[44] James knew his friend's answer—the answer of Thoreau at the end of *Walden*, where Thoreau speaks of the artist's always unfinished staff. James's father now being dead, Royce became the man who could entice him to look for immediate perfection. Royce always replied by saying that it was left only for God to complete the works of man.

The struggle marked the men's difference. Within this mimesis or the "mocking" that Royce imagined imitation involved, Royce and James embraced, reinvigorating technical philosophy by struggling, in James's image, as they played against each other. Only when James found within his colleague's philosophy the monism that he believed had destroyed his father did he caricature idealism, turning upon Royce as he grappled with the question of his own father's estrangement. The quest for structure, James feared, as though he sought none at all, compelled one to decay into "a mass of morbid melancholy."[45] James made Royce into a sickly and tender patient, the kind of patient that he had made of his father. The elder James, the son, and the younger colleague were held thus in interpretation.

In his approach to authority—an attitude that Royce had described upon his departure for Harvard in 1882 as his mixed feelings of "trembling" and "impudence"[46]—there existed a self-discord that psychologists only later called "ambivalence." Royce may well have spoken correctly in 1897 when he said the common psychology held that, while love and hate could intertwine about an object, the two feelings excluded each other at any one moment. Until Eugene Bleuler proposed the concept of ambivalence and Freud discussed it as a clinical fact, common sense proposed that one loved this and hated that, but never at any given moment both loved and hated the same object. Royce objected, thinking perhaps of Paul's epistle to the Romans ("For that which I do I allow [know] not: for what I would, that do I not; but what I hate, that do I . . . . For I delight in the law of God after the inward man: But I see another law in my members, warring against the law of my mind, and bringing me into captivity"). Royce noted how a person could "consciously have an impulse to do something, and at that very moment a conscious disposition to hinder or to thwart as an evil that very impulse." One pulled away from objects one desired, and one possessed objects one abhorred. In this way a man could "love his own hates" and "hate his own loves," opposing his will to assure his "dissatisfaction."[47] Royce used this psychology to destroy the utilitarians' mechanics of simply choosing between this or that.

Here also, as in the push and pull of muscles and bone, unity emerged out of tension, for here was the ability to tense and to make the self work. One of the most common memories of Royce is his work. Friends cited his manner of lecturing, for example, and as expected, they contrasted Royce with James. A former student remembered James as "varied, broken, at times struggling for expression," but Royce standing before classes "composed" and "immovable." His lectures were "continuous, even, unfailing." The memory of Royce's mechanism agrees with Santayana's, who recalled Royce as a water tap, lecturing for up to three hours without stopping, "according to demand or opportunity." "The voice, too, was merciless and harsh. You felt the overworked, standardized, academic engine, creaking and thumping on."[48] Royce had become, in this caricature, "a sort of automat restaurant," a place to stop for information. While Santayana would characterize Royce as effete, friends imagined him a "monster of pure intelligence" who "knew everything" and touched upon every subject. His mind was thought "a card-indexed cyclopaedia," and his life was considered an existence for "nothing . . . but philosophy." Like the elder James, Royce seemed to flail out at his own sense of impotency. He appeared pugnacious with students, a "terror" in the 1890s—"sleepless," "ready for all comers," "the John L. Sullivan of philosophy." In company with others, he was thought "untouchable." On one occasion John Jay Chapman remembered his teacher entering a room for tea and a discussion of philosophy. Royce never removed his coat or his muffler or sat down, but "took his stand" next to a chair and spoke for an hour.[49] Others protested the compulsion, as they did Royce's disengagement. This is why once, in the third person, Royce had written that "faithful disciples had certainly never understood him."[50]

Alone, belabored, at times belligerent, Royce was suffering in bondage as an exiled prophet. He railed at those who failed to meet his exacting demands. "I speak plainly," he wrote in reply to Francis Abbot, initiating an unfortunate affair. Abbot had taught one of Royce's courses, while Royce was suffering from mental collapse, and based on his lectures, Abbot published two years later, in 1890, *The Way Out of Agnosticism*. Royce acknowledged Abbot's humanity, but, in a devastating review of Abbot's book, continued to write, for "in judging of the actual work of philosophical writers," he concluded, "we must lay friendly esteem aside in so far as it is necessary to do so for the cause of the 'greater friend.' In brief, . . . we must show no mercy,—as we ask none."[51] Printed on the page of a single book review, these words came literally to destroy Abbot even as they lashed back upon Royce and expressed his travail. In other writing and in other words, and for his "greater friend," Royce constructed his beloved community, a community of Peircean interpretation, a triadic community of "signs."

Those who knew Royce thus recorded his tendency to spin webs of intellect and then accuse his students of not understanding, to counsel love and then appear terrifying, to favor company and then refuse to associate. Royce composed his own life as one of a wanderer who seemed to seek out the circumstance that would allow him to describe his travail. To James, for example, he wrote: "I suppose that I have seemed hopelessly unfaithful, but the fact is that the second half year's work, on my return, proved very exacting, giving me, towards the end, . . . a sense of being driven, a discomfort . . . that left me, at the close, morally tired,—mildly aboulic, so to speak." James easily agreed and complimented Royce's self-image: "We are both to blame for not writing. . . . You have the excuse of over-industry in other directions, I that of over-idleness in every direction." James ended a note to Royce with the comment: "I'm afraid you've over-worked."[52]

Breakdown

Royce had used activity to assuage his loneliness in California,[53] and upon his arrival in Cambridge, he continued in intense occupation. In 1888, at the approximate age when the elder James suffered his vastation and William his panic fear, Royce brought his activity to a climax: he became, he confessed, "broken down with too much work."[54] At the age of thirty-three, Royce underwent an experience that he later described in letters to James, letters the whole of which compose an autobiographical text. He wrote "indeed [of] a long period of depression—not exactly the sort of discontent that was to be feared, i.e. not exactly a *longing* for anything good or evil, but simply the dullness that Tolstoi describes in his Confession or the 'grief without pang, voiceless and drear,' that Coleridge so well portrays. It was a diabolically interesting nervous state." Understandably, he used past writings to make his experience meaningful for James. Royce described not a period of psychosis but a depression that had left his intellectual faculties intact. His breakdown had not brought delusions but rather "an absolute negation of all active predicates of the emotional sort." Royce wrote that he felt nothing except "a certain (not exactly 'fearful') looking-for of judgement, and fiery indignation," the Biblical words Bunyan had used. He appeared to be looking for some vague punishment to absolve imprecise feelings of guilt.[55] He was searching, too, for a meaning that he could attach to an experience that, unlike James, he never said had a religious bearing.

In her own "Pilgrimage Diary," rewritten as the memoir that her son requested, Sarah Royce had recorded the "sloughs" and "Wilderness" of her own desert experience, using the journey she had undertaken across the Carson desert in the gold rush year of 1849 as the analogue of a spiritual crisis. Again, like so many in the seventeenth century, she turned a diary into an autobiography and then presented the work as a gift to her child. She spoke of "gloomy forebodings" that had rushed into her mind and oppressed her for hours, and then of the strength she had gathered when she refused to turn back. Alone, exhausted, her firstborn child fainting of thirst, Sarah Royce had become Hagar, the mother of Ishmael, and had spoken to God. Amid a smoldering fire of sagebrush and burning sands, her conversion occurred. For her it was a deeply mystical experience of knowing of God's presence rather than simply believing in His existence.[56]

Thirty-nine years later Royce was writing of his own despond. He cited his favorite Buddhist homily: "I feel 'like a fire that returns not to the place once burnt over.' . . . New lands and new worlds call for me now, so . . . I *can't* go back"—meaning that he refused to return to his depression. The son was reaching as well for Sarah's "new land," his own "new life" that he hoped to create out of his despair. He would recreate his mother's westward journey by traveling now from Cambridge to Australia. For the moment he had simply broken down, and he refused to conceive of his crisis in terms of any allegory. "The break-down is nervous of course and needs nothing, I am assured, but a long sea voyage all alone, to make me myself again."[57] Sarah Royce had understood her trauma as the title of her diary foretold: hers was a pilgrimage during which the wheels of the prairie schooner had become stuck in "mean, vexing" mudholes and in sloughs hidden unsuspectedly beneath the appearance of firm grass. She had crossed a desert in which she had been tried, forsaken, and then given to God. Josiah Royce approached the image in his own "looking-for of judgement," but his depression had stemmed from "carelessness" and leaning too much on "superhuman aid." His case was one of "pathology," "abnormal nerves," and a case, he said, "no longer in order."[58]

For his cure, the mere physic, Royce temporarily left Harvard—"my consequent desertion of my post"—and yet aboard ship, writing to James from the mid-Pacific, he said that he found his wits growing "more constructive." The voyage itself was becoming "a very highly educating experience," not indeed a leave from school at all. He was going to try to work again. "I am holding myself back from any hard work, but by the time I get back I think that I shall be ready for an outburst of literary toil." Within these letters, Royce reminded James, even in the depth of his illness his wits had all along "been working"; he had read mechanics and mathematics,[59] and without any hint of the irony, he wrote back to James that he had "largely straightened out the big metaphysical tangle about continuity, freedom, and the world-formula, which, as you know, I had aboard with me when I started." Of his breakdown and depression: "*That* experience is done for and over forever."[60] Such physic could never last, nor the senseless formulas.

In the winter of 1888 Royce had peered for a moment into a ruin. His own "over-work" and "overtasked nerves" had caused the break, but his activity was still to hold his confusion at bay. He appeared healthy, he wrote, and thought "nobody meeting me on the street would call me ill, but the little devil in the brain is there all the same, and this kind goeth out but by travelings and hard fare." "When the Devil by Afflicting of us," Cotton Mather had written, "drives us to our Prayers, he is *The Fool making a Whip for his own Back*. Our Lord said of the Devil in Matt. 17.21. *This Kind goes not out, but by Prayer and Fasting.*"[61] The journey Royce undertook to Australia became the fare or the difficult passing through, a ritualized search for a hopefully still primitive frontier where Royce could renew his strength for a return to civilization. James's transit to Brazil had expressed the same theme of going to nature's extremes and then turning back to this world, as do the crossings of so many American literary figures who dissolve themselves in a myriad of frontiers. An unnamed friend had paid for the voyage and for the support of Royce's family while he remained away, alone among sailors and outlanders. His city of destruction appeared behind him.[62]

Before his collapse, Royce had stood enmeshed in abstruse speculations. He had attempted to touch ground with his novel of California as well as with a history of California's Anglo pioneers. His work on these past frontiers only furthered his worries, for once again he found himself entangled in problems he thought he could never resolve. He was violating his own often repeated maxim by living as an eccentric lost in a swirl of meticulous regards. He eventually broke, as he thought, under the strain, under the type of work that had led to the vastation of the elder James.[63]

Royce's own too private concerns involved the two books that he had labored upon, most particularly the history of California in which, in an untoward number of pages, he pursued the legend of John C. Frémont—"a household name"—bitingly, almost mercilessly, convicting the man for having wrenched the peace of California's order. And in the novel, admittedly of "portentous length," Royce again confronted themes of deceit in his native state.[64]

The California history did not become the book that Royce had promised, "an amusement for idle hours," for it absorbed Royce as he pored over documents and sources, hoping that when he finished, his reviewers might "express something of my respect for thoroughness." Royce was never satisfied with it and when he did finish, he apologized to a friend for not writing; there had been, he said, "the fearful sloth wherewith my California work has been distinguishing itself. I have been ashamed to confess my inefficiency." Royce momentarily thought the book itself a product of sloth, for he had failed to use some misplaced Frémont letters to try his case further. Through the "basest negligence," he had not taken the time to search for the letters and, "like a lazy novice that I am," he had proceeded without them.[65]

Both writings had kept Royce frightfully busy. His anger was obviously intense, and probably hideous to him, and when the defense of writing the books crumbled, Royce found himself preoccupied with a vague but besetting guilt. He refused to look further within himself to discover just what had gone wrong, believing as he did that to inspect oneself too closely simply furthered the depth of an already spitefully "personal aim." The collapse had resulted from carelessness; he had lost control. Vowing never to collapse again, Royce would inspect himself only from an anatomical distance by saying that he found his breakdown—what he now called his "mishap"—"peculiarly edifying, instructive, and even fascinating to one who loves to study his own mental states." About to leave for Australia, Royce considered himself but a case study awaiting cure, a piece of mental anatomy available for examination.[66] The case of conscience, however, had to express more.

Suffering his break and recovery less than a year after publishing his novel and two years after the history of California, Royce found himself "no longer tired," and he knew no reason why he should not return from Australia "a very much cured man." "I am," he wrote back, "anxious for work again."[67] Upon his return to Cambridge, he again set about to lecture, his nose "in the neighborhood of the grindstone, if not flat against it," waiting "until the task of grinding is done. And so," Royce ended a letter to a friend, "for still another season I dare not try to come to you."[68]

The Reconsideration of the Crisis

Royce's crisis could emerge all the more clearly in an America that wished to alleviate the burden that Calvinist forebears, presumably, had placed upon the child: a theologically liberal and Progressive America whose gospels of relaxation and "new thought" appeared in consonance with the times, where the Puritan's struggle for conversion had emerged as but an unfortunate episode of the mind breaking down. At the end of the century, when neurasthenia had become the most popularly discussed of all medical syndromes,[69] Royce could never explain his crisis as a step in a process of conversion. In the winter of 1888, like so many Americans jostled by machines and working with incessant speed, he felt he was simply suffering from nervous fatigue.

Royce had begun reading "modern psychiatrical literature," however, including a by then classic essay by Edward Cowles on the obsessional trauma of a "Miss M." Royce studied Cowles's work closely. The essay had appeared during the winter of Royce's collapse and now, by 1893, Royce was reading the essay in preparation for his own study of the "pathological character" of John Bunyan. Royce had turned from his California histories and the struggle he had had with his family's past to examine his symptoms in whatever clinical histories he could find. He remained discontented: such literature, he felt, was merely groping for a definition of the type of character to which insistent thoughts and acts adhered. Each day alienists and neurologists were inventing some "new mental disorder," bandying about "endless '*manias*' and '*phobias*.'" They were also unduly characterizing such sufferers as "degenerate," turning their insistent impulses into neurasthenic "stigmata" when something else—something with "a deeper ethical meaning"—was going on.[70]

Royce had come to reconsider the meaning of the crisis that was now weighing heavily on his mind: the depression from which he had emerged, aboard ship, "entirely cured," but after which he had learned, upon his return from Australia, of family illness and the death of his father. Help from "a good son . . . wouldn't . . . [have been] a bad thing. So once more I have cause to feel that when we play with our strength, we hurt more people than one." Royce could never let his trauma pass now without searching for a meaning beyond the mere neurasthenic collapse.[71] He found an understanding for his crisis first in the travail, the harsh work, and eventual self-creation, as he thought, of Immanuel Kant, and then, most significantly, in the spiritual struggle of Bunyan. From Bunyan, Royce recovered a "struggling with the 'Tempter,' with the Demon in personal presence," a mocking by the devil that allowed Bunyan to distinguish the presence of his faith. Royce, of course, could never accept Bunyan's account of the struggle: "We now have the power to recognize, much more exactly than Bunyan could do, the nervous nature of his enemy." Royce set himself to the problem of describing Bunyan's mental alienation "in more modern forms," without dismissing, as he felt other alienists had, the ethical significance of the struggle that sufferers such as Bunyan had won. Bunyan "gave us," Royce said, "an instance of a concrete solution of the problem of evil whose philosophical significance is not made less by the fact that Bunyan's theology is no longer acceptable in Bunyan's form." Bunyan had faced his strangeness, a "dramatic crisis, . . . a long period [in words that Royce had used to write of his crisis] in a condition of secondary melancholic depression." Royce could insist on offering a "psychological analysis" of the "still too much neglected" personal experience of the author, for the strangeness or the mocking of the self by the devil in a place of temptation implied the presence of grace. The occurrence of melancholy was still the occurrence of possible spiritual insight.[72]

Royce could now use past writings such as Bunyan's autobiography to provide significance for his own crisis. He could transform his mishap and carelessness into a more meaningful text: a renewed version of the sectarian struggle understood in terms different from those his mother had used, and yet understood in terms not quite so different after all. Royce transformed Bunyan's psychomachia into a clinical psychobiography, the first such psychological history written in America. Royce wrote without the religious refrains of Cotton Mather describing his brother Nathanael's troubles, but he wrote with the same signification. Bunyan's psychomachy provided Royce with what he later called a community of memory, a history and a cultural context with which to understand the meaning of the present.[73] In this case, the community of memory provided significance for Royce's own depression, along with his travail and the "morbidly insistent mental processes" that, at first glance, he had called imitation.[74] Royce could find in Bunyan, and to a lesser extent in Kant, a discourse into which he could place himself so as to make his crisis meaningful.

Royce had to pursue his case of conscience, given the terms imposed by the new discipline of neurology. His colleague at Harvard, James Jackson Putnam, had become one of the first American physicians to designate his calling by that name. Writing in the early 1890s, Royce was nevertheless working with a barren literature. James had yet to provide his *Varieties of Religious Experience*, and the *Psychology*, published in 1890, said little of psychopathology. Putnam, as yet, could not discover Freud. The neurological literature available on neurosis remained disparate and void of unifying themes. To explain, it presented the seemingly self-evident observations that physicians expected medical histories to use. When an author did employ psychology intertextually to interpret character—Jonathan Edwards's for example—he could use terms of pathology all too ridiculously: "That poignant gloom and distress over purely fictitious sins is the evidence of delusional monomania. A boy to-day with such symptoms would be put under the care of a skillful neurologist." Edwards, for the Reverend Joseph H. Crooker, writing in 1890, had lived as a "theological monomaniac"; he was simply "mechanical," "and not one of his sentences contains a theory that the modern mind cares to preserve as a precious possession."[75]

The Puritan psychomachia had shifted, but a writing like Crooker's one simply ignored. Other contemporary cases existed, and just as one needs to set Perkins's and Ames's cases of conscience within English writings of melancholy, so one needs to place Royce's study of Bunyan within the strata of late Victorian neurology.

Modern Psychiatric Literature

If New Englanders no longer heard their ministers speak so violently of an angry God as they had heard Edwards speak little more than a century before, and if for some of the affluent, Puritanism had evolved into a graceful Unitarianism—the benign faith, for example, that James Jackson Putnam celebrated, when he attended to formal theology at all—then what remained of the "New England conscience" could appear in itself ridiculous. Indeed, Victorian authors had invented the New England conscience, the "soil and climate" of a strange region the remains of which Crooker lamented. A man like Crooker could never understand the ideational struggle Bunyan had suffered as foretelling of spiritual salvation, or read Bunyan's terrible account of the fiery trial exactly as Bunyan had portrayed it, as the selected trial of the visible saint. Outside of Puritan psychomachy, writers in England and America had considered the melancholy described by Bright and Burton abnormal from the beginning, and thus examples of obsessional behaviors are scarce; the behavior is invisible and there appeared no reason to speak of it. In Boswell's biography of Samuel Johnson one does find various compulsive behaviors and obsessive fears recounted, but the observations stand aside as interesting relations unlinked to any particular religious experience. These are small abnormalities adding color and depth to Johnson's personality, but little else.[76] For the Puritans, of course, the case had been different.

By the end of the nineteenth century, accounts of insistent behavior—though still few—emerged in America with a renewed significance. Expectedly, New Englanders wrote many of the accounts, for obsessive behavior now appeared to reflect, like a distorting mirror, the moralism of the remains of the Puritanical mind. Alienists sought alternatives for the "insistent" or "imperative" partial insanity (or neurosis): rest for women, occupation for men, discipline for boys. American alienists and neurologists began to give the malaise greater attention, though accounts of hysteria, with hysteria's quite visible signs, still took up the most pages in the journals of mental disease. Gradually, though, for at least a few American neurologists, obsessive behaviors—which had as yet received no single embracing name or designation—came to represent, as if a metonomy, the mutilation of Puritanism within Victorian society.

In the latter half of the nineteenth century, American neurologists often called neurotic behavior a habit. Neurosis formed a bad habit, to be sure, a form of mental estrangement that physicians, in their capacity as alienists, attempted to treat. Today the word "style" has replaced habit, but this conception of neurosis as an integrated structure remains.[77] A neurologist would search for the cause of mental pathology within the pathways of the body, among the nerve channels where a neurosis by definition occurred. He would look for reasons why a nervous system had failed, and if unable to locate a lesion or a visible tumor or scar, then often ascribed the behavior to fatigue. Excessive strains, he assumed, the wear and tear of body and brain, dampened the nerves much as anemia weakened the blood. Mental tension lessened, allowing the normal checks and inhibitions to subside, thereby permitting abnormal habits to form and solidify. A particular thought, for example, could assail the mind whenever a weakened nervous system failed to offer a defense. For such "neurasthenic" patients, ridiculous fears or foolish ideas of no more than passing interest normally could become implanted and fixed. With the nerve paths opened and flowing like a sluiceway without dams, intermittent activities such as washing one's hands could become habitual and set, repeated again and again as if by an insensible fool.

The causes ascribed to such behavior were changing. Emphasis was shifting from the brain to the mind, from a strictly neurological etiology to causation somewhat less somatically imbued. The conception of neurosis as a malformed structure continued, however, for within distended behavioral patterns, the neurotic appeared to take social values and rip them apart, putting together otherwise appropriate behaviors and making a caricature of Victorian living.

Until well into the twentieth century, alienists labeled aspects of behavior now called "obsessive" or "compulsive" with a variety of names. Sometimes alienists joined various symptoms into a single syndrome; more often they analyzed such behavioral signs only in parts—the "content," in other words, rather than the relationships between parts that Royce wanted. Compared at least to the quite apparent effects of hysteria—the amnesias, the partial paralyses, the fugues, the "fits"—the malaise remained invisible, possessed by a person embarrassed and secretive about his troubles. As a mental and bodily disorder, hysteria had a name, a history, and a sense of what its symptoms entailed dating from the medicine of the Greeks.[78] The syndrome Freud eventually called *Zwangsneurose* or obsessional neurosis had never received any such naming other than "melancholy." In the nineteenth century either a single symptom or an ill-defined word represented the neurosis as a whole, and thus a confusing array of names began appearing, particularly after 1870: mysophobia or the fear of filth, metaphysical insanity, introspective insanity, doubting insanity, impulsive insanity, imperative insanity, fear of touching, neurasthenia, psychasthenia. Little mention remained of melancholy; the word appeared to have extinguished itself.

This is not to say that a single neurosis existed that confused alienists and neurologists failed to find. Debate existed—as it does today—as to what forms of neurotic behavior belonged together, what constituted, for example, a hysterical, paranoid, impulsive, or compulsive style of pathology. Classifications changed and questions remained: for example, whether the phobic reactions that Freud called anxiety hysteria properly belonged to the obsessional neurosis or formed a separate syndrome.[79] Perceptions were also changing, and no observer looking back can label someone something as though words and things stand together naturally (or universally) related, or reduce a person's behavior as if it should fit a naturally given taxonomy. To set the kind of universal definitions that William James warned against—"iron block" constructions that fail to account for how words act and, indeed, make reality—and then to place such definitions within timeless frames, is to accede to the notion that psychological models are somehow laws, and that when once discovered they can be turned around to reveal the past. Words become wrenched from their historical culture, and neuroses or complexes become universal themes rather than variations of ongoing constructive motifs.

Indeed, how an alienist described neurosis in the nineteenth century—what types of behavior, in other words, an alienist had come to expect—could determine how a patient responded. From 1870 through the turn of the century, for example, alienists asked, as William Perkins had, whether a person who incessantly thought he would kill someone might in fact commit his feared act. Now, even though the sufferer abhorred his insistent idea or considered his thought foolish, many American alienists believed, along with James, that an act expressive of the thought could readily occur. The distinctions Perkins had demanded among various types of temptations were reduced to a single impulsive "act." Since this reduction could only add to the doubts and the guilt of someone involved with abhorrent thoughts, a question remains whether this belief enabled the neurotic symptom to work properly. Believing one might commit the act is, of course, the point. Believing in the real potential of one's criminal thoughts allowed some men and women to castigate themselves, to punish and seclude themselves in a room or an asylum in order, they thought, to protect those they loved. They could believe they remained truly "obsessed," in a more horrid manner than any Puritan had considered. Their thoughts reflected not an alien or satanic device impinging upon their minds, but an internal potential of how they might readily act. The neurosis was a part of their self. For insistent disease the Puritan reading, speaking as it did of salvation, was of course far more comforting.[80]

As perceptions of the obsessional neurosis changed through the latter decades of the nineteenth century, alienists did gradually distinguish its most acute forms from insanity or from the "monomania" of ideas that seemed to grip the psychopathic killer and the obsessional alike. Gradually, too, alienists began bringing together symptoms under a single heading, drawing out the relationships that Royce wanted between one or more confusing behaviors. Nevertheless, not until the work of Janet and then Freud became familiar, did a second major neurotic style become identified.[81]

The choice of the word "obsessive" remains significant. The connotations of the word still appear derogatory: that someone, obsessed with sex or money or fame, has fixed his mind upon a desire and thus set himself to accomplishing his aim. As with the word "compulsive," "obsessive" connotes a sense of surety proper only to maniacs and fools. The sufferer's expressed concern reflects doubt rather than fixation—self-alienation, in other words, rather than self-assurance. The "alienated" in the nineteenth century were the mentally sick, both those who appeared overtly insane and seemed alien to others, and those who appeared "partially insane" or neurotic and seemed alien to themselves. Neurotics possessed "split" personalities, "dissociated" thoughts, "estranged" selves. And while alienists might discover a hidden personality, a subliminal self, or an unconscious wish, such patients could discover the alienation for themselves, consciously knowing how heterogeneous, foreign, or incomplete their own thoughts and actions seemed.

As alienists began describing obsessional symptoms, it became apparent that many such symptoms caricatured religious expressions. Some mental pathologies appeared as simple degeneracies, the decayed remains of enfeebled, immoral, or unregenerate selves, men and women who were thought to possess bad heredities or poor educations, or to have suffered from unfortunate accidents. For some of the sick, however, "degeneracy" or "immorality" seemed quite improper words. Often alienists described these men and women as intelligent persons from proper families, having a good education and conservative regards, persons who sat before the alienist with their consciences tightly drawn. In a word, and in a pejorative meaning of the term, they appeared ascetic. They isolated and punished themselves. They preoccupied themselves by holding to painful thoughts and by performing careful acts. They feared to touch this or do that. Some washed their hands by the hour as if attempting to wash guilt from their souls. Others brooded, incessantly questioning why they had sinned, how they could atone, or whether they might commit some unpardonable act. Faced with general anxiety or perhaps a specific painful thought, some patients said that they had to think out a certain complex chain of ideas to replace their dread. One particular image had to follow another without omission or mistake. If their thoughts slipped or if their attention failed, then they had to repeat the serial, sometimes running through the ideas again and again until they had completed the chain in a particular way. Others had to perform some physical ritual or ceremony seemingly as if to atone. Perhaps they methodically straightened up a room by first positioning a chair, then a lamp, then a pillow, again without the allowance of omission or mistake. If they touched the pillow improperly, then they had to start again by first restraightening the chair, working their way through the complex act until it, like the ideational series, appeared properly completed. They found no reason for such mental and physical exercises—as Bunyan had, in the pushing and shoving of his arms—only insignificance. These small self-tortures but momentarily released such neurotic penitents from whatever they feared.

This need to order could drive a person into a well-arranged chamber. In 1883, for example, a physician observed an American schoolteacher in her room, her hair shorn and her hands wrinkled from frequent washings. "She was equally particular about the arrangement of things in her room," the alienist wrote. "When the doctor came in, he had to sit in a particular chair placed in a particular position, and he was not allowed to step on particular parts of the carpet. The presence of a fly in the room, alighting here and there, annoyed her to the last pitch. It seemed to her to be 'mixing things up.'"[82]

Because of the reticence of such patients, and despite the use that George Borrow, the English Victorian autobiographer, made of the ascetic symbolism provided by the obsessional malaise,[83] few good descriptions of these behaviors exist in nineteenth-century American medical journals. Often the sufferers lived well enough with their secret occupations. Even if they became incapacitated and turned to another for help, they might still conceal many of their actions. Whereas hysteria became popularly displayed in the late Victorian era (hysterics, indeed, often found themselves dramatically placed upon the medical stage), this malaise produced only embarrassment and shame. When portrayed, the obsession emerged now as the abnormality of Protestants who thought of the harsher aspects of their religion as having destroyed their lives. Through only barren confessions, such patients offered their conscience of sin as a "Protestant ethic" or a "New England conscience" stripped to the pathos of pure pathology.

In the "Confessions of a Psychasthenic," for example, a slight medical autobiography, an anonymous American used his Protestant upbringing to explain why he had fallen into what he considered insanity. Writing only that his father had thought of him as an excessively pious young man, the author divorced his blasphemous thoughts and strained conscientiousness from any expected Calvinist behavior. He had received warnings as a young boy against taking various paths to hell. He remembered as well that when he was either five or six years of age, the daughter of a neighbor had "seduced" him. This memory of an incident he left undefined focused his guilt. Later, after reading the story of Francisco Spira, he became troubled over having committed some unpardonable sin, "although," he said, "I did not really know in what it consisted." Anguished, the man wrote that he felt compelled to shut his mouth tight out of fear that he might speak some horrible thing. None of this, however, seemed to make any sense.[84]

What becomes meaningful in this confession is the lack of meaning the anonymous author found in his condition. He thought of his "insane compulsion" as simply a trivial pathology. He thought inexplicable what the Puritan autobiographer had considered meaning-filled and indeed Biblical in its sensibleness: thoughts of defilement, for example, or an impulsion to throw oneself from a window. The anonymous author's rigidity and carelessness were simply that. The fear that a dictionary might fall and break open, or his drinking excessive amounts of water—both subject to any number of possible interpretations—held nothing for him in the form of symbolic content. The only analogy he allowed was that out of fear of some sexual excess he did become "ascetical," "at times even like a monk. Thus I tried to sleep on a bare floor." Here again, however, one finds nothing that points to anything significant, as one does, of course, within Puritan autobiographies. A lack of "literariness" fails to account for this insignificance, for the man's education certainly stands above that of many earlier autobiographers. He simply lacked a context in which to make his troubles meaningful. Engaging small worries, incessant questions, trivial doubts—wondering, for example, what would have happened if he had not decided to read this or do that—the man arranged his life into a meaningless cloister. He offered description, but gave no explanation for his travail other than his having become insane.[85]

In 1888 Edward Cowles, a Boston physician, had published a fuller account of obsessional behavior. This is the case history of Miss M. that Royce read. She was an asylum patient, twenty-eight years old, of a "good family in heredity and otherwise." Cowles, an established Bostonian, was an acute observer of partial insanity, a sometimes obtuse and overly meticulous writer whose study of Miss M., entitled "Insistent and Fixed Ideas," explored obsessional behavior more thoroughly than any case available in an American medical journal. By implication, Cowles used the case of Miss M. to probe the damage that he thought his own New England Protestantism had wrought.

The importance of Cowles's study rests in part on his allowing his patient, an intelligent woman, to speak for herself, while at the same time distinguishing the behavior that he observed from the insanity that she, like the anonymous autobiographer, thought she had fallen into. He made uncommon distinctions between men and women who feared they might harm some other person and men and women who might actually do so, or between persons who contemplated suicide and those who might actually kill themselves. He also distinguished an "obsession" from a "delusion," or a "fixed idea" from a "monomania," by arguing that for patients like Miss M., intelligence and judgment stayed intact while thoughts and behavior otherwise appeared to run riot.

For at least the last fifteen years of her life, Miss M. had alternated between periods of depression and discipline. In the latter phase, facing fears that she might harm someone or come to harm herself, she made up and then secretly repeated counteractions, both of an ideational and behavioral kind. She became caught, Cowles thought, "in a complicated system of methodizing all her acts." When she walked, dressed, and undressed, she felt "obliged" to act according to a rigid scheme, fearing that otherwise some disaster would occur. She performed such rituals only when unobserved, and spoke of the worries that had provoked her compulsions only to her mother, and then only when she became fatigued and eventually physically ill.

Cowles's patient also revealed that she sometimes methodically arranged her thoughts to control her most pressing fear, one that involved a distant relative she had met at school. This was a young girl of her own age, "C.," whom Miss M. said she admired and even loved. Jealous of the attention her friend received, Miss M. began to think of possible harm that "C." might receive; she wondered, in fact, whether she might herself do violence to "C." She thus undertook "vows" and performed repetitious acts to ward off the idea, using such mental and physical "operations" as atonements, feeling that otherwise she would be to blame for whatever happened to "C." "To reinforce this process, . . . vowing became swearing, and then came the necessity of the most fearful and blasphemous imprecations upon herself, to compel herself to do or not to do certain acts, then or thereafter, upon pain of inflicting injury upon her friend, and all of its dreadful consequences upon herself."

Agonized with thoughts of her friend's suffering, Cowles's patient now began to think of suffering herself. Eventually any mention of death drove her to make patterns of ideas, much as she had repeated particular acts. She began allaying her fears of hurting her friend by substituting another person in her mind for "C." Then she elaborated the process by requiring that the mental substitute have a different age, sometimes a different sex, as well as different name initials, color of eyes, place of residence, and so on. Next she began preparing three or four alternatives for whatever an occasion seemed to demand. Then she felt she had to think of the entire set in a certain way, until the relief she received waned and she had to imagine a new set of substitutes.

Then she reformed the entire structure again as her magical operations proceeded.[86]

Until the age of twenty-five, Miss M. had managed her world tolerably. Then, for reasons inexplicable, she became more and more depressed and gradually withdrew from others, until neither she nor her family could ignore her troubles. Having concealed her anguish, Miss M. now began thinking of herself as truly insane. Before, she had maintained an intellectual awareness of her obsessional behaviors by regarding her obsessions as an estrangement (rather like the Puritan's reflection), as the product of some self-accusatory "Satanic double of her own mind, that tyrannized over her conscience and thought with a world of intricate formulae." Now the devil became herself, as she internalized the fears and made them a part of herself. She left school and began a listless, aimless life, holding on to friends for a while, but gradually abandoning them to prevent painful associations from occurring in her mind. It appeared as though any friend or object could, through a complicated scheme of interrelationships and differences, produce ideas of violence. Thus she began avoiding certain foods and kept from going certain places. She stripped her room bare, removed all colors, and took away pictures and ornaments. Once fond of colors, she now felt forbidden to wear particular shades. "Certain days were tabooed for shopping, because they were anniversaries of painful events in her morbid calendar; and certain shops could not be entered. When the new dress was obtained, very likely it would not be worn because of some newly imagined danger of potential harm to her friend." Worried, her relatives sent Miss M. to a doctor and then to the country. For a year following that she often secluded herself in her room, becoming more irritable and despondent. She stopped going to church and gave up her remaining friends and all social activities. She could not sleep. She thought at times that she would kill anyone young, old, or weak whom she happened to meet. Once she actually drew a razor across "C."'s throat and said she had made a joke, but then experienced waves of anguish and self-reproach. She thought perhaps that she had become a murderess and after a year of such worry, secretly drew a razor again across another's throat, canceling out, she thought, her former act. Then for ten months she refused to leave home, and for a year she never left her barren room.[87]

The punishment Miss M. inflicted gradually became worse as her life evolved into this strange monasticism. Cowles never labeled this life; he simply presented his history without readily discernible interpretations. Miss M. was eventually committed, probably to the McLean asylum that Cowles managed on the outskirts of Boston. There she dressed plainly and spoke of her conscience that compelled her to do everything contrary to her wishes. "She had to make herself disagreeable and hateful to the people she liked best and respected the most, just because they were sources of comfort to her." She considered such persons the "creditors of my conscience." Once Miss M. thought of substituting physical pain for her mental torment, and with a small pistol shot herself quite carefully in the shoulder and hip. "She was perfectly calm about it and explained that she tried to wound the joints, which she thought would cause permanently painful and crippling injuries. She protested that she had carefully avoided endangering her life; for she had virtually pledged herself not to do that."[88]

Miss M. continued her ascetic occupations, and Cowles, though he of course realized the seriousness of the case, continued to distinguish Miss M. from the insane. At the base of her need to damage herself lay a neurasthenic condition, a depleted soil from which insistent ideas had grown and formed according to the laws of association and habit. There also remained, Cowles thought, a mental soil of "rare conscientiousness," a plasticity of mind so warped that traditional questions of sin had become horribly twisted.[89]

As a neurologist, Cowles had committed himself to an understanding that bodily fatigue and nervous exhaustion underlay Miss M.'s behavior. Like other American neurologists, he therefore faced an irony. A weakened nervous system had dampened the body's resistance, allowing abnormal thoughts to assail and eventually possess the self. Miss M. had thoroughly controlled herself, however, working as she had throughout her odyssey to place a barrier between her self and others by mechanically performing her secret litanies even when, for example, she had to speak to another. She made her malaise into a cloister, and the asylum itself into a world of control. Unlike Bunyan's Christian, she had no thought that any interpreter could point to a meaning in such a cell. Nor did Cowles, a medical professional, have any thought that in such acts lay a sign—that is, an ethical significance.

Kant and the Constructive Imagination

Royce had probably read Cowles's study by the time he completed *The Spirit of Modern Philosophy*, published in 1892. Using the life of Kant and Kant's philosophy of the constructive imagination, the book presents a theme that Royce would touch upon throughout his later writing, that of work, and of the objectification that work allows as a process of self-creation. Cowles had established certain neurological themes: the weakening of nerves that, like a humoral corruption, could provide a soil for the compulsive work of the tempter, and the medical physic that could prove a worthless cure. What the tempter furnished was a mocking image of the self's travail that could allow the self to see its alienation, and then to see how it might use that alienation to fashion a world of its own. In his examination of the life of Kant, and then of Bunyan, Royce asked whether insistent activity could provide any lasting purpose. Both men, for Royce, had confronted obsessional behavior. Neither had eradicated the neurosis, but both had used the fixed activity inherent in the neurosis to work their way from demonic chambers.

Ultimately Royce promised an undivided selfhood and an eternal godhead weaving a perfect and final interpretation. As firmly as he believed in this lasting sign, however, Royce set the "brute facts" of psychology against the moral order of idealist philosophy, most particularly the fact of a tempter. The satanic trial of melancholy had become an uncanny experience demonstrating that self-possession remained the most "evanescent thing," that the self of finite man was "the most delicate, unstable, and intricate of all the phenomena studied by psychology." A headache, an annoyance, a passing mood could upset or even derange the self, and a foreign idea could possess the mind even when a person recognized the idea as other than his own. A person found it not uncommon to "play" with his self, to address his self as another, "and upon occasion observe myself . . . as if I were a wholly alien personality." ("She says," Cowles had written of Miss M., "she has lived two lives.") Though "possession" of such a difference marked a deranged mind, a mind some still superstitiously believed invaded by an evil spirit, healthy personalities provided similar examples when they felt their selves wavering or new and unreal. Given this fragility of self, this seeming existence of "a strange self," Royce asked: "Am I not a mere child of circumstance, . . . a chaos of bodily products?" Where did one find his abiding personality, the unity and fixity the absolute promised?[90]

For Royce, alienation expressed a struggle to create a work with which to order and make sensible the otherness that appeared to the self as this strangeness. For Kant, that work became his writing, his *Critique of Pure Reason* that emerged after years of travail. For Bunyan, that work became his decision for vocation, the ministering that Bunyan undertook to justify his confrontation with Satan. Both men, according to Royce's understanding, had transformed years of alienated activity into a penultimate and productive work by turning an estranged asceticism into a this-worldly ideal.

Personality and ideas remained thus inextricably bound together for Royce, so that he often used biographical portraits to explain and judge the worth of a person's writing. His discussion of modern idealism began with a portrayal of Kant as the philosopher who had set about to destroy the clockwork mechanism of an eighteenth-century philosophy of reason. Kant is to order his own life in the face of unknown, unknowable things—the "things in themselves" that he will place beyond the understanding of the mind. Raised in a pietist family, a "spare, small, insignificant-appearing man," "almost fleshless," Kant has first approached a pathological edge. Before he can build his constructive imagination to order that which is to be known, he has incessantly stumbled about by pursuing his every thought, jotting down on innumerable scraps of paper, on invitations, envelopes, discarded letters, every fact and idea that he happened to come upon: Latin verse, bits of metaphysics, heights of water in capillary tubes, notations of paid lecture fees, geometrical computations, all of which degenerate into "illegible marks." They are the unreadable signs of a discordant mind that refuses to waste a fact or lose a thought or let an idea slip by. Kant forgets past notes, rushes on to new, and creates nothing.[91]

Royce described Kant's "odd fashions of work" as those of Kant's "student" or young instructorship years. They were to Royce's mind habits like those he chastised himself for in the diary he had kept as a young instructor at Berkeley. "Spent the evening on my new beginning under changed title 'The Work of Thought.' When shall I come to the end of these everlasting beginnings? This one strikes me well. But so, alas, did they all." Following this entry, Royce noted that once again "my plans have shifted," and these plans shifted in their turn until, with ever new and more elaborate outlines following one upon the other, Royce's "numberless" sketches and bits of essay had emerged as nothing.[92] They are the resolutions and methodism that textually precede the giving up.

In the face of such "chaotic activity," Royce offered the *Critique* as a map of "sanity." Daily Kant has walked his own "regular path," precisely, at the same time every afternoon, rigidly controlling his steps, a famous emblem that Royce derived from Heine of the philosopher working like "the great cathedral clock." As a guide to man's constructive capacity to shape and form a world of his own, the organized world that has eluded Kant for over a quarter of a century, the *Critique* reflects the drawing of an author who has gathered his "mass of flightly seemings," a person who "*continually collects* himself, . . . binds this to that," and who through an ability to link facts, achieves a rational knowing of himself. At this particular step of Royce's own career, the essence of sanity works to make the connections and to discover the relations that mere sense can never provide. "In the world of sense there are facts, but there are not links. You see things happen; you can't see why they must happen." Thus the philosophy of neither Descartes nor Locke—neither a compelling reality of dogmatic, innate ideas nor a mere impression by sense upon a blank mind—can form a world, but only the creative acts of the mind itself, the "constructive imagination" of man himself. To know an ordered world is to know an ordered self, a self that is making sense, unconsciously creating a world that appears other than the self's own—a world, nevertheless, that becomes the self's own. Although a person creates objects from an environment of sense, he does not create chaotically or incoherently; he does not create, in other words, objects that make no sense or that stay alien to his self. If I am sane, Royce wrote, then the phenomena that I order and bind together will come to "know me, that is, recognize the authority of my thought-forms, or categories." A world of alien others, like an insanity of mind, stands as a world predicate to this making of sense; it stands like a wilderness set against the self, so that the self comes to know itself when it comes to know that it creates this other. The self creates itself against impressions that make no sense, and thereby the self creates its sanity. A world of clocks and mechanical endeavors appears, with the self thinking that an other acts upon it, to the point of the self coming to know that it is acting itself by creating its time and fashioning its space. One creates, that is, when one has thought that one stood merely created.[93]

Bunyan and the Mocking of the Tempter

A year after Royce published his text on the spirit of modern philosophy, he began focusing explicitly on obsessional mental illness. In his study of Kant, of course, Royce had offered no particular diagnosis of the philosopher's travail, but now, with Bunyan, Royce began speaking clinically. With readings in psychiatry and his philosophic idealism, Royce was eventually to join the neurosis to Hegel's theory of alienation, coming to believe that the malaise represented more than a medical curiosity—that it stood as an archetype of the human condition, in that it belonged to the ethos of whole societies. Royce juxtaposed "self-alienation" with self-possession, the first term as yet rarely used in English. When he found the malaise peculiar to a Hegelian stage of social consciousness, to a society's as well as a person's winning of possession, he juxtaposed "estrangement" with community.[94] In all, Royce was marking a path from isolation, through the insufferably active and painful search for an unattainable bliss, to the discovery of a new life as a working, social being. Only then would Royce come to destroy the lineal progress of this self and social conversion.

Royce first introduced Bunyan, in correspondence, to attack utilitarian or "hedonistic psychology." As early as July of 1890, a month prior to the publication of James's *Psychology*, Royce explained in the manner of James that Bunyan's case and that of a "friend of mine, a professional man who has studied with me," failed to support the utilitarianism of persons pursuing pleasure and avoiding pain. In a case of "morbid impulse," for example, the fear of having misaddressed a letter tormented a man; he felt compelled to tear the letter open and check the address, to seal it and then to reopen it again, his better judgment notwithstanding. Though the impulse to reopen and recheck the letter annoyed and indeed pained the man, when the compulsion came, he obeyed. "Where then is the pleasure in it?" Royce asked. Clearly in this example, as James was arguing, an act of will led consciously to pain: "the morbid patient gloats with horror and tormenting fascination over his 'fixed ideas' or 'insistent impulses,' which he regards with loathing, and yet hugs to his consciousness with a sort of gloomy frenzy."[95] In the case of his friend, no delusions existed that might indicate insanity. The man possessed an above-average intelligence. His morbid impulses remained nevertheless "insistent, agonizing,—his daily burden. They are impulses to doubt himself, to draw back from life, to wonder whether he isn't lost, helpless, a wretch, to wonder whether others don't think wrongly of him or misjudge him, etc., etc., *ad. inf.* They affect his will deeply. Their results are agonizing. They themselves are *never* pleasure-giving. Have you looked into facts of this sort?"[96]

In his essay on "The Case of John Bunyan," Royce followed Bunyan through the course of his insistent illness. Royce described the tormenting thoughts, the notions of bartering Christ, the fear that church bells would fall and strike, together with the annoying yet, for Royce, "senseless motor acts" that Bunyan had repeated in an attempt to quiet his apprehension. Royce contrasted Bunyan's petty acts with the large questions of good and evil that had aroused Bunyan's fears. The compulsions were ridiculously small behaviors that for Royce held no theological meaning, whereas for Bunyan they had.[97]

Royce nevertheless recovered the Puritans' sense of this psychomachy by drawing out a structure of spiritual conversion from a welter of clinical terms: "the essential psychological equivalence of several of the various sorts of *manias* and *phobias* which some authors, imagining that the content rather than the relations of the impulses concerned is important, have so needlessly chosen to distinguish." Royce most particularly recovered the signification of the automatism that had resided in Bunyan's life, the "loathsome triviality of the motor impulse itself, in its pettiness"; the "imperative motor speech-function"; the "loathsome motor irritations"; the "associative processes . . . all the more marked, automatic"—in all, "the automatic processes" and "automatic evolutions" that had driven Bunyan to become a machine. In an eventual "nervous crisis," Bunyan had simply broken down, his compulsive efforts to win salvation sundered by "secondary melancholic depression expressed . . . occasionally in praecordial anxiety," or the terror that Bunyan felt splitting his breast. In the alienation of his horrid works, Bunyan had come to know himself by knowing the tempter as this other, "mocking self." "The doubts and other motor inconveniences were of course still in the background . . . , but it is interesting to note how, whenever they appear, they are now simply overshadowed and devitalized by the fixed presence of the ruling melancholic ideas. The tempter is thus at length known as a relatively foreign and mocking other self, whose power over Bunyan's will grows less even while his triumph is supposed to be final."

> Bunyan, so the tempter suggests in his old metaphysical way and with the old doubting subtlety—Bunyan had better not pray anymore, since God must be weary of the whole business; or if he must pray, let it be to some other person of the Trinity instead of to the directly insulted Mediator [the Mediator, that is, whom Bunyan would "sell," "assent to the 'selling' of. The proposed transaction involved, as a matter of course, no actual conceived exchange whatever"]. Could not a new plan of salvation be devised by special arrangement, the Father this time kindly acting as mediator with the otherwise implacable Son, to meet Bunyan's exceptional case? . . . Bunyan knows by the very contrast that these suggested words of the tempter are *not* his own. This is the mere fooling of the exultant devil. It is meaningless. . . . A better device than this for the "segmentation" of insistent questionings could not have been imagined by any physician learned in the cure of souls. The victorious tempter had unwittingly dug his own grave. He could never again get possession of this man's central self.[98]

Bunyan, in other words, learned through the very absurdity of the devil's request (that there in effect be no mediation and therefore nothing of Christ) that the temptation to commit unpardonable sin was not a temptation that adhered to his own self. The mocking evil built up such a caricature of evil that Bunyan could see this other, or this difference, as coming to define his grace. Bunyan thus gave in to the demon's "automatic play," and Royce thereby rested his case for the necessity of alienation to make this difference. The play or the mocking of the self as if by another served the point that this estrangement had served through two hundred years of mental biography. Bunyan never sold out the Mediator (the mediation that later for Royce became the interpretant between an object and Peirce's sign); he sold out the satanically false words that his mind had heard in contrast. The external world existed, so that one could find the truth of internal words. In Bunyan's mechanism, the interpretation was told, for the automatism, the devices the devil's suggestions fashioned, became such a mockery as to promote Bunyan's faith. There existed no "better device" than this insistent mocking labor for showing up the transactions of the self, the buying and selling, the contracts and arrangements, or the bargaining in which the self finally became "lost." "One is lost; only eternal mercy can save." "And 'now,' [Bunyan] says, in narrating this last experience, 'did my chains fall off my Legs indeed.' Such is the healing virtue of true resignation."

The importance for studying Bunyan's apparently trivial mental case was to read of his resignation. This was "not to cheapen our sense of the dignity of genius, but to heighten our reverence for the strength that could contend, . . . that could conquer the nervous 'Apollyon' on his own chosen battle-ground." The importance of looking to Bunyan's spiritual autobiography was to read of the creation of a "genius," or a saint, in the face of a peculiar psychopathology that had fashioned its own destruction.[99]

Work as Self-Creation

First in Kant—the "good father"—then in Fichte and Schelling, and finally in Hegel, Royce hunted in writings of philosophical idealism for that which could win for the self the stubborn world of the other. He found his answer in unalienated work. He was to find that such a work, in the hands of man, never existed.

Bunyan's tempter created an automatism so absurd that through this demon's difference it told Bunyan how he was not to fashion his belief. How he was to fashion his belief in spite of these works, was by fashioning his self through what Royce referred to as Bunyan's "extraordinary and persistent power of work." Like James, who turned away from an image of convulsed labor to winning his world through vocation, Royce moved his ideal self from estrangement to self-possession. Royce wrote of the need first to assert a foreign world, an object world the self regarded as alien, and then through activity to come to know that world, to regard it as one's own, as the product of one's self, and ultimately *as* one's self. "I have a foreign world as the theatre of my activity; I exist only to conquer and win that apparently foreign world to myself; I must come to possess it; I must prove that it is mine. In the process of thus asserting a foreign world, and then actively identifying it as not foreign and external, but as our own, our life itself consists." By continually asserting an object in either fact or reflection and then claiming that object for one's self, as the expression of one's self, a person came to know his identity and eventually to possess himself as he possessed the alien matter. One worked to build from nature a small piece of experience, for as man acted, so he thought, and so he thought of himself. How a person acted upon his world, what he struck from the material of the world, determined how he saw his world, and how he saw his world determined how he saw himself.[100]

The struggle in making this other world brought knowing to the self, for in possessing this other, the self possessed itself. "In knowing nature we are but learning to know ourselves," and thus self-possession and ultimately the question of a person's "sanity" remained inextricably bound up with how he created his world, with whether he came to find his environment rational or crazed. To know "The Absolute" meant simply to know the self, to understand that this vague expression for which idealists were so often derided stood for nothing more mystical than "self" and "self-possession," for "identity," for "precisely that which the self . . . has been trying to be."[101]

If asked who he was, any man could reply by stating his name, or his home, or his birthplace, or his country, "but the answer to the question, 'Who are you?' really begins in earnest when a man mentions his calling, and so actually sets out upon the definition of his purposes and of the way in which these purposes get expressed in life." From his earliest philosophical explorations, Royce counseled work as the one course toward self-definition. In middle age he gathered an ideal from Fichte which stated: "My life, my existence, is in work. I toil for self-consciousness, and without toil no consciousness."

> But this process, thinks Fichte, is essentially an endless one. The more of a self I am, the more of a world outside me I need, to develop and to express my energies. A busy man needs, and therefore posits, a world full of the objects of his business. Without this asserted world of objects, he, as busy man, would cease to exist; he would, so to speak, retire from business; he and his busy world would stagnate together. This, then, is Fichte's central thought: Your outer world, your not-self, is just as large as your own spiritual activity makes it.[102]

Such too was Hegel's lecture on the master and the slave, where the toiling servant again realizes himself through labor. It is the slave,

Royce recalled, who attains "genuine selfhood. For self-consciousness is practical, is active, and depends upon getting control of experience. The slave . . . works over, reconstructs the things of experience. Therefore by his work he, after all, is conquering the world of experience, is making it the world of the self, is becoming the self." Without labor, self-creation ceased. "If I merely saw my world as already my own completed work, I should have nothing to do. But I am essentially a doer. With the completion of all deeds, both I and my world would vanish together." Royce committed a major portion of his philosophy toward reconstructing the argument of the German idealists, piecing together threads, working ceaselessly himself as if his own sanity depended on suffering and toil. "For . . . the only way in which self-consciousness can attain its goal is through such a conquest over self-alienation, through a becoming finite, through suffering as a finite being, through encountering estrangement, accident, the unreasonable, the defective, and through winning thereby a self-possession that belongs only to the life that first seeks in order to find."[103]

For the Puritans, the argument had been that the end of man's alienation, and thus his spiritual conversion, was in itself endless. No one moment of conquest, no sudden conversion, no washing of sin eradicated evil and left persons in a state of passive grace. The end of alienation represented "a ceaseless determination," "a continual conquest over self-estrangements that are meanwhile inevitable, but never final." The conquest never ceased and it never ceased to be painful. "For the triumph of the wise is no easy thing," Royce preached. "Their lives are not light, but sorrowful. Yet they rejoice in their sorrow, not, to be sure, because it is mere experience, but because, for them, it becomes part of a strenuous whole of life. They wander and find their home even in wandering. They long, and attain through their very love of longing. Peace they find in triumphant warfare. Contentment they have most of all in endurance. Sovereignty they win in endless service. The eternal world contains Gethsemane."[104]

Yet such was the detachment of Royce's idealism that he could celebrate the labors of a lighthouse keeper as long as his work was pursued for a community which waited, ultimately, only within the future. "The devotee as an individual may always remain in his cloister, but the *Weltgeist* transmigrating awakens in new individual form . . . , as a man who has found his task and to whom the world is in the larger sense his business."[105]

Works, of course, or the performance of carefully regulated repentant deeds, had always focused the Protestant's grappling with the question of faith. The question was what constituted an act of sincerity and what did not. In a century Royce was celebrating for its "rediscovery of the inner life," he could attack the problem psychologically.[106] He could employ observations from the neurological clinic, declaring for his young Bunyan what a later—and much more influential—post-Freudian study of Martin Luther would do. The acts that the elder Henry James had called superstitions emerged now as compulsive rituals, the senseless "motor" performances that could plague a man's being as they made a farce of his faith. Throughout the tradition of the Protestant spiritual confession, from the seventeenth-century psychomachia to the psychobiography of a Royce or a William James and thence to the "psychohistory" of a later generation, writers could turn their subjects from travail to "identity."[107] Though the terms would change, the point would not: a person was still to win for himself, through the hell of lacerating mental and physical acts, a faith declaring all such acts profane. Often the conversion was to arrive with a reading of Paul and an understanding of Paul's preaching against works. Work, on the other hand, becomes acceptable not as the cause but as the sign of grace, whether for Royce's century of nerves and spiritual sorrows or for Erik Erikson's age of anxiety and hedonistic cant.

Forms of activity must still be differentiated, however, as Marx wrote when he set himself against Hegel's valuation of the slave. The question is the kind of activity that remains in alienation. Max Weber distinguished between the tortuous productions of a person in a cell, his "other-worldly" ascetic, and work performed within the world. Erikson writes of a movement from preoccupation to occupation for his Luther, from "works" to "work," or, for his Gandhi, from "vow" to "vocation." Hannah Arendt draws her distinctions: *facere* or *fabricari, ouvrer* and *werken*, words that turn away from an estranged infinitive of labor: *laborare, travailler, arbeiten.*[108]

The question for Royce was whether America was offering the work to provide the identity, or whether America had progressed to the point of its own convulsing, almost wondrously in the sense that America could be seen collapsing in a mechanics of its own design. In the last of his work Royce became one of the first intellectuals to declare America neurotically sick—in a clinical sense, void of the satanic imagery of Cotton Mather. Royce described America as estranged, appearing strange, or lost to the meaning of its work. Like Mather, he presented the alienation as the last of the signs before the coming of his beloved community of faith.

Royce composed his beloved community of mediation by holding

Charles Peirce's language of signification not as a metaphor but as a faithful transcription of the reality of reconciliation. The triadic logic that fascinated Peirce, the interpretation that the sign of an object requires for the sign to possess meaning, held for Royce the promise of ending conflict, whether such interpretation worked in the form, actually, of a vast insurance company buffering the conflict of nations or, more lastingly, in the form of a more ineffable interpretant resolving inner peace. But it was in the last of his writing that Royce collapsed Peirce's triadic language of object, sign, and interpretant into a last sign of mediation. This became the one moment of atonement for Royce that erased whatever other logic the mind had so conceived. Royce spoke only then of lasting mercy.

> Once in a while I have a dream of your house. . . . I wander in my dream about Baltimore, live there maybe for some time, and fear to go near you lest you should have forgotten me. Then I go, clamber into the house by the front window or walk in without knocking, feel frightened and confused, cannot explain my self, am afraid to see anybody, hear you all perhaps in another room and cannot enter, or meet you and have nothing to say. . . . I wake up highly amused, and resolve to write forthwith.

Royce was twenty-six when he dreamed of emptiness and awoke amused. His amusement hardly masks the estrangement he felt and wanted desperately to express, in spite of the elliptical metaphor Royce chose or his quick discarding of the whole matter. He was writing to George Buchanan Coale, a prominent insurance executive and Baltimore civic father who had taken the young philosopher under his care five years earlier. Nine years later, in 1885, Royce dedicated his first book to Coale. Now, as he thanked Coale and his wife for their help and uncommon goodness, Royce matter-of-factly described his shame. He had not, he confessed, written enough, and now that he was writing to the Coales, he chose to recount a dream in which he expected no one to notice his presence for some well-deserved but still unaccountable reason. He hoped the Coales would not think him ungrateful; he was not, he explained—he was simply the same "unspeakably raw little boy" they had once befriended. Royce thanked the Coales: "you did what you could for me."[109]

In correspondence, Royce often felt guilty about the belatedness of his letters, but his apologies, like his dream, were to hint of a greater, less specific need for atonement. In his novel, *The Feud of Oakfield Creek*, Royce expressed this same sense of unaccountable guilt, and the desperate attempt of a prodigal son to return. William Harold is a young

California intellectual who, like Royce, dreams of an estranged visit to an old and familiar home. For a mysterious yet compelling reason, Harold is prevented in his dream from returning home until, persisting in his efforts, he is brought before a crime. Outside the house, Harold's dead wife points silently to a field of freshly dug graves covering a nearby hillside. Harold, by attempting to return, knows he has "somehow" killed all of those now buried.[110]

The Contrite Consciousness

Through his career of philosophy, Royce was to construct various objectifications of evil against which to set the self to work. As a process of self-creation, work was to allow the self to objectify its definition by fashioning its own image, to look upon itself by looking upon the matter that it had fashioned with its own hands. When the self refused to labor, then, like Harold, the self had committed itself to estrangement. Like Bunyan for a time, Harold is a "great dreamer," and like Bunyan, Harold holds to thoughts he will only keep secret. He broods too often. He believes superstitiously in omens. He plans a trip (the visit of his dream) with "childlike precision" for weeks on end, then daily remains undecided whether to go. Pursuing a life Royce so much feared for himself, Harold is without any "fixed calling." He is absorbed with too many inconsequential affairs and irrelevant pursuits. Deeply religious, he has no religion save a "sacred sorrow," the worship he makes in memory of his dead wife. Within his own sect Harold contemplates his world from afar, surrounded by black arts, odd pets, and antiques, smoking all day, as Royce himself smoked, remaining unexercised just as Royce—the author of an essay on physical training—remained sickly, clumsy, and overweight.[111]

Following his study of Bunyan, Royce had begun attributing the obsessional malaise—"rebelliously insistent" habits, "e.g., the habit of counting or of examining gas-jets, locks, etc., to see whether they have been safely adjusted, or of asking useless questions about some sort of topics"—more and more to abstracted personalities: the philosopher, the ascetic, "our English stock," and in his last major work, "modern man."[112] As a preface to his discussion of the alienation of modern man, Royce considered another analogue for neurotic behavior like Harold's, this time an entire social stage that becomes a penultimate chapter in modern man's realization of his sin.[113] From Hegel's *Phänomenologie des Geistes*, a portion of which Royce first translated into English in 1908,[114] Royce took the "Unhappy Consciousness," or what he translated as "The Contrite Consciousness," and drew a likeness between it and James's sick soul.[115]

For Hegel, "who knows not the modern psychological vocabulary," the experience is one of neurotic self-alienation: "shut up in his cell with his sorrows," Hegel's ascetic "seems wholly self-estranged and foreign to himself." The unhappy soul has in fact learned Hegel's lesson of the slave, but he is still alienated in the work he has sought to serve his lord: "*Quantus labor ne sit cassus*, and so at length perhaps, through self-discipline, self-abnegation, endless self-chastisement, the imperfect self does come to some consciousness of a new and sanctified and redeemed nature."[116]

Within Hegel's portrait, Royce saw a state of perfect watchfulness and self-control finally emerging.

> But hereupon, for the unhappy consciousness the enemy appears, as Hegel says, in his worst form. The former self-abnegation changes into spiritual pride. The sanctified person becomes the home of vanity, and needs a constantly renewed casting down into the depths of humility. . . . It becomes intensely overcareful as to every detail of its fortunes and of its functions. Its existence is one of painful conscientiousness, of fruitless dreariness.

The unhappy consciousness needs a work, an "intense and absorbing work, but not the labor of conquering these fantastic spiritual foes."[117]

Like Marx and Weber, who viewed compulsive activity as the supreme symbol of the modern human condition, Royce presented the ascetic slave as one who has sacrificed himself and driven himself for a foreign master. Unlike Marx and Weber, Royce placed the estranged compulsion within the ascetic's mind. In Royce's free translation of Hegel's words, the contrite consciousness "abandons, in a measure, whatever it has earned by its labor" by undertaking instead some "mysterious task" for a foreign will. Because "its own reality appears to it as an obvious nothingness, the result is that its actual work seems to it a doing of naught, and its satisfaction is but a sense of its misery. Work and satisfaction thus lose all universal content and meaning." Knowing the "worthlessness" of its own petty acts, the unhappy consciousness sits like James's epileptic patient—"only a brooding, . . . miserable personality, limited solely to himself and his little deeds." Sinking back into itself, this divided self is "explicitly aware of its own doubleness," aware of "its own uncleanness." "[C]onsciousness is a doer of works, and knows itself as such," but the contrite consciousness performs its activity for a might it regards as strange to its own nature. The contrite consciousness "works," but it works "as a thing remote from itself."[118] Otherworldly, it has yet to bring itself into the world wherein Royce thought it would find its fulfillment, the "bliss of an activity which rejoices in its tasks," a field for Royce of unalienated labor.[119]

Most obviously the question becomes, what is to be made of the self when the thing the self makes is estranged. What is to be made of the self when its greatest work becomes an image of its crime? How defensible, in other words, is any work that is used against an ineradicable sin of man?

Within the whole of a text—one that links Royce's discussion of the unhappy consciousness (his "Baltimore Lectures" on modern idealism of 1906), the translation of Hegel he published two years later, and finally the lectures on the "Problem of Christianity" that Royce was to deliver seven years later—a movement appears. There is first the cutting of the self into these pieces of estranged labor, and then the attempt to cleanse the self by building for the monastic slave a this-worldly labor—to provide for the penitent a calling, a "loyalty," or what Royce most generally termed a "cause." In the end, Royce would describe the need for the self to give itself to a "lost cause." As Royce prefaced his last lectures on the problem of Christianity, on the first page of the resulting book, there will at last be a religion "free from superstition." Only one work is to remain.[120]

Modern Alienation

Royce had returned to a theme of James's father by turning from William James's singular cases of conscience to a social history of pathology. He spoke now of mental pathology as a developmental interrelationship. This social construction of psychopathology had appeared in Royce's writing as early as 1894.[121] Royce now so universalized alien experience that he used a singular abstraction, a neurosis that he left unnamed, to renew the meaning of original sin breaking the works of the industrial world.[122] The tempting denial of mediation that Royce had approached in the case of Bunyan, along with the discovery that Bunyan had made of his self acting like an "automaton," Royce by the end of his career transposed as a national problem. He spoke now of a society of automation, one, indeed, that he himself remained wont to design by speaking out for the need for such enormous mechanisms as world insurance corporations.

However much Royce seemed at times to place his boyhood memories of Grass Valley, California, into the American East by denouncing city and machine, Royce never became the local communitarian that so many of his interpreters, including himself, declared him to be.[123] He spoke not for traditionalism but for rationalism. For California, he celebrated not the pan-mining of gold, a singular and distraught labor, but the arrival of a complex of sluiceways and corporate machines that had created a saving division of labor. He spoke of the "severely impersonal relationships and language of official life"—in Weber's terms, the moment when the self is sacrificed for its role, or for Royce, the moment when an "official function" erases personality by eliminating individual quests.[124] In essays on "war and insurance," he drew up a monetary contract for guaranteeing the peace among belligerent states.[125] Royce's "beloved community" was to re-create not Edenic America or his past, or even bring about the mediation triadic logic demanded for corporate states. Like great communities that mocked themselves when they used machines to save themselves, Royce's industrial designs mocked his own quest for insurance—"the plan—the saving plan"—that he had given to estranged quests like Harold's.[126] His lasting community forms only when all such causes are lost and when nothing of insurance is left.

Alienation, in other words, ever evolves out of its own attempted elimination. In matters of even the greatest design (for world insurance, Royce had turned to the newly formed Harvard Business School for his financial calculations), Royce could only discover that his modern man became ever more estranged, as distraught in his new corporation as James's pan-miner of gold. Royce designed and then collapsed a progressive future by industriously turning here and there, working himself to such points of exhaustion that he left the modern self to the only mediation that ever mattered, the last work —"Christ's work"—which became the one interpretant that made sense. Whether an insurance company or a civic father, authority could turn and consume itself. Royce could then leave himself with nothing left to say.

In the books written in the final decade of his life before his death in 1916, Royce considered the alienation of the contrite consciousness inherent in an industrial America. Again using Hegel, he spoke of the "self-estranged social mind" of a split society whose collective consciousness has become "estranged from itself" or, with another translation of Hegel's term, alienated.[127] Royce attributed the malaise to the peculiarities of what he called "higher civilization," an imperialistic stage of society in which the individual stands removed from the vast and ever more impersonal institutions surrounding him.[128] Confronting a society he but dimly understands, Royce's confused American ponders a destroyed patriarchal family, a remote but irrepressible government, the large and still growing corporations for which he feels but little attachment, and all the other organizations of mere "mechanical bondage" that seem so "estranged and arbitrary." ". . . our nation," Royce wrote, "has entered these days into the realm of the 'self-estranged spirit'"—self-estranged because the individual both covets and fears the society that provides him safety and material comfort, but which also arches so huge and unintelligible that it only furthers his alienation from the machine in which he moves. A stranger in his land, Royce's American becomes easily distracted, or escapes into the security of impersonal authority, or stands confused before too numerous objects of attention. Even if he escapes his freedom and welcomes his submission, he finds that any governmental or corporate form that he chooses becomes but a "fact" rather than an object of lasting devotion. With increasingly familiar phrases, Royce sketched a nation of persons upset by being "a mere spoke in the wheel," persons who felt the "unsettlement," the "restlessness," and the "chaos of conflicting passions" in their morally confused and complicated society.[129]

Several American analysts were describing such traumas by the turn of the century, though Royce was the first to apply the Hegelian concept of alienation to his own society. More significantly, Royce went beyond description to offer a complex explanation for the increasing alienation he found not in the vast complexes of modern bureaucracies and machine labors, but in the psychological development of the individual. For Royce, man's alienation from society was intertwined with man's alienation from himself: the "self-estranged social mind," in other words, was but a reflection of the individual's "own self-alienation."[130] Joined as they were, Royce searched for an end of alienation within the awareness rather than the institutions of men. What was required was a new perspective: "the problem of educating the self-estranged spirit of our nation to know itself better."[131]

Royce's discussion of the destruction of an organic community by a mechanical society—"the dreary complexity of mechanical labor"—appears commonplace. Less common is the rising sense of self-alienation Royce found in the modern mind—an estrangement brought for him not by impinging technologies and the division of labors alone but, again, by the increasing consciousness of guilt a person finds within himself as he confronts high civilization. The original sin of modern society is that it has expended community, but just as important for Royce is the original sin of man, a "moral burden" that increasingly weighs on the conscience as one attempts to reconcile a new awareness of self with the ever vaster forces confronted. With a measure of tragic irony, Royce portrayed a socially conscious society that breeds an increasingly acute sense of self, a new value of individualism that eventually vies with the state's own collectivism. The angered self vies with the great community that Royce had designed. In what amounts to a theorem, Royce stated that as the "corporate capacity" or "collectivism" of a society increases, so too does each person's estimate of himself and of his own particular worth. Individualism and collectivism, in other words, intensify and reinforce each other as high civilization advances. Royce extracted this theorem from his theory of imitation and the development of self-consciousness, which states that a person's awareness of self grows in proportion to his awareness of society, that self-awareness only develops, again, as the person becomes increasingly aware of the differences around him—conscious of those others who offer the conflicts and provide the comparisons so necessary to define a self. Thus as a child grows he develops a self-conscious will, and as a society grows and intensifies difference, workers develop an increasingly distinct sense of their own particular expression. They become "deliberate, cultivated, and therefore dangerously alert."[132]

Within this theorem, a variant of the mocking of which Royce had written long ago, Royce found a despair he clearly thought more profound than any external conflict between capital and labor. Against modern society, men revolt; they choose, however, to "revolt inwardly" rather than to oppose authority overtly. Within a dialectic, the corporate will produces not only its own external and most obvious enemies, but also "spiritual enemies" who turn inward upon themselves, becoming the enemies of their souls as they collapse in front of their endeavors. The alienation of modern man becomes as much an affair of guilt, in other words, as it does a conflict between warring industrial parties. Corporate society trains its own enemies through an education of "personal wants," but mechanism also gives persons a more cultivated conscience—a "socially trained conscience" that heightens despair. The "inner rebellion" of modern man breeds a conscientious regard and a secret hate for an authority persons both covet and despise. Submissive, trained well in morals, and given to respect the authoritative will, modern man nevertheless finds that his own self-will is becoming "fastidious, and abiding love for a community difficult." Modern man remains, then, as "lost" and as "dead" as Paul had decreed, his inheritance as "tainted" and his guilt as "hopeless" as any Puritan forebear believed. If persons remain normally intelligent and "orderly" in their habits, then they will not set out in "a merely stupid attempt to destroy all social authority." A "sensitive self-will, which feels the importance of the social forces," will not become "childishly vicious" and simply attack all authority, but will actually favor that authority's development. Thus the "individualism of such a man wars with his own collectivism"; thus "in its rebellion against authority, when such rebellion arises, it is a consciously divided self-will." "I am the divided self. The more I struggle to escape through my moral cultivation, the more I discern my divided state. Oh, wretched man that I am!"[133] Like the ascetic slave, modern man must understand the inviolate nature of his sin.

For Royce, the "moral" now appears as a curse upon man, hidden behind man's seemingly correct conduct. "[W]e are all naturally under the curse," Royce wrote; we are plagued, no matter how good our deeds. The curse comes as a disease brought by civilization and bred by individual conscience. A training of the child has occurred, as in the training that Royce remembered having learned from his childhood companions. A well-behaved child and good works are produced, while an inner rebelliousness remains. A man obeys, but he does "not obey with the inner man."[134]

More than a causal connection existed between Royce's memory of his childhood and his analysis of this alienation. He presented the slight remembrance of his life and these lectures close in time, his autobiography and his discussion of automatism, his self-history and his social history, thereby conjoined as a particular type. Modern man's sense of self had to grow from early childhood encounters that were fraught with the inevitable rivalries, the uncertainties, the quest for order, and finally the angry compulsion that erupted in rebellions unknown to distant tribal communities or to the small cultures that embraced the person in consistency, forcing his natural and unthinking submission. Within the surety of such culture, no bewildering occurred, until a moral curse eventually drove the primitive from his garden.

Like Freud, Royce was collapsing anthropology and psychology into a single moment of primordial crime. He was conflating historical place and personal time by equating the childlike devotion of a primitive for his tribe with "mother-love," an untainted devotion "from which cultivation inevitably alienates us, by awakening our self-will," and by awakening man's guilt. Just where in history the crime had occurred Royce no more than Freud could say, other than to speak of the crime by turning from chronological to mythical time. When Royce asked whether the family could return to primitive affection, he answered that, for "the wayward youth," "herewith his father's house ceases to be, for him, any longer lovable."[135]

With both a "fastidious" and "rebellious" will, no child could return to the house of his father. Tempted to perfection, to become ambitious, men became self-divided gods fascinated by their own transgression. Estranged from mothering love and fastidiously rebelling against authority, "sin means alienation from the Kingdom and from the Father; and hence, in the end, means destruction." "This, if you choose, is the root and core of man's original sin,—namely, the very form of his detached individual. This is the bondage of his flesh; . . . this is his alienation from true life; . . . a stranger in his father's house."[136]

From a later perspective, sin lies embedded in that unknowing rebellion of the son against the father, an Oedipal rebellion, Royce had earlier noted, that Hegel found in the unconsciousness of small commonwealths where family loyalty had pitted itself against the state.[137] Royce had no need to imply any such specific origin here for the guilt of Hegel's imperial society, for he was re-expressing the psychology of Paul: the secrecy involved in having committed the unpardonable act that left man without a community and without a home: "Sundered from them, he . . . wanders in waste places, and, when he returns, finds the lonely house of his individual life empty, swept, and garnished."[138] As in the dream Royce had recorded more than thirty years earlier, lonely men returned home to find the house of their childhood empty.

Herein lay "the problem of the traitor." For this "act of treason," fixed and "irrevocable," persons, if they really knew themselves, could never forgive themselves. Given this "sense of sin," this "hell of the irrevocable," Royce asked how the person could achieve his grace or even possibly face himself knowing or sensing that he had committed the crime. Most particularly, Royce asked how the person could face his guilt without succumbing to that "dangerous brooding" now considered appropriate only for an atavistic, Puritan mind.[139]

The answer remained the same as the Puritan's. No traitor could ever "undo" his deed, for "all seeming, all worldly repute, all outward conformity to rules," all of the moral so cultivated, "avail nothing in the eyes of the Master, unless the interior life of the doer of good works is such as fully meets the requirements of love." There existed, in other words, no "elaborate code" with which to remove the sin.

> If any new deed can assign to just that one traitorous deed of mine any essentially novel and reconciling meaning,—that new deed will in any case certainly *not* be mine. I can do good deeds in the future, but I cannot revoke my individual past deed. If ever it comes to appear as anything but what I myself then and there made it, that change will be due to no deed of mine. Nothing that I myself can do will ever really reconcile me to my own deed, so far as it was that treason.

Royce countered what he considered easy humanist prescriptions for sin—whether "good deeds" or petty acts—by stating, "If I ever say, 'I have undone that deed,' I shall be both a fool and a liar."[140] There waited, that is, no act of canceling out like Miss M. drawing a razor across another's throat to cancel her sin of "killing" her friend. Royce remained uninvolved with any specific mental pathology, and yet pathology and theology had become so homologous that he could only imply that no ritual behavior—no elaborate code—could undo the original act. If any man held to such an act, then that act was alienated, not of his own expression, not of his own possession.

Within this realization of the inability to perform an atoning deed lay the lesson for Royce in the parable of the prodigal son. Those brethren who had sinned "against their father" could receive a new, reunited family through the community symbolized by the father's rejoicing. Through the "labors" and "atoning work" of a Joseph, good could come from evil as the "old man" was ever made over into a new: "Atoning deeds, deeds that, through sacrifices, win against the lost causes of the moral world, not by undoing the irrevocable, nor by making the old bitterness of defeat as if it never had been, but by creating new good out of ancient ill." Crimes filled childhoods and fathers waited for their rebellious sons to return, but until that homecoming, an absolute that awaited in the future, men were estranged from their "moral hearth and fireside." For the traitor, good works remained that could open "the tomb of the dead and treacherous past," works that could never eradicate the sins of history, but that could create goodness from hate and take life out of death and triumph out of treason. Suffering servants could assuage their grief or "use their grief as the very source of the new arts and inventions and labors whereby they have become such valuable servants of their community."[141] Guilt, the very compulsion Royce so feared, could create from its own mechanics a newfound art, a whole new way of envisioning vocation.

Royce had proposed to give a modern, psychological meaning to Paul's writing. Using "the now favorite word, the subconsciousness," he stated that he was searching for the "subconscious" ideal of the Christian Church, looking for Christian undertones beneath surface phases of modern man's estrangement. On the one hand there awaited something so ineffable and yet so redeeming as the life of Christ—"Christ's work"—a perfectly objective fact of salvation. On the other hand, there remained a call for an active expression of Christ's service in the face of each man's irrevocable sin. Religionists admonished men to flee to their "cloisters" if they wished to grapple with sin. "If thus you flee, they say, you may find what the saints of old found in their deserts."[142] The contrite could emerge, their grief becoming the engine of their own self-construction; their sin, however, only their faith could erase.

In this, his last writing, Royce offered the devastation and therefore the hope he found in America's "alienation."[143] If Royce's modern man was neither deranged nor alienated from his Creator, but held to the "old faith," then he was estranged by the very force of a rationality whose security he both coveted and hated. The demonic of Cotton Mather's New England had become for Royce an apocalypse, "this law of constantly accelerated change." "Physical science and the industrial arts are altering the very foundations of our culture"; "alteration is now taking place at a rate for which no previous age of human history furnishes any parallel." Without any "right" to predict the future, Royce envisioned the rapid "mental" change and the "bewildering alterations." The morbidity of the "Puritan spirit" had waned, but the American remained as strange to himself as those Paul had declaimed about, confronting the compulsive evil that Bunyan had experienced and that worked now as a national neurosis, a compelling fastidiousness, a rage for order, and yet a rebellious anger and thus a shame stemming not from the tempter but from the ambivalence inherent in social discord and family strife. An original sin did remain, the sin of the man who had attacked whatever symbolized the security he loved: his family, for example, or the "Father."[144]

Like Luther centuries before, like Hooker, Shepard, the Mathers, and Edwards, Royce was returning to Paul and the psychology of the irrational he found therein. He found not only torn acts but also health, for in the burning of the self like in the melting of iron, the self could never return to its original shape. Royce thus continued his earliest themes by rejecting ritual and self-mechanics to embrace vocation, or what he now termed the "cause."[145] As a vocation that never removed the conviction of sin, a cause allowed modern man entry into a beloved community of faith, but only as the cause became lost. The cause became a *Walden* for Royce, carving from chaos a small abode or machine that becomes a reflection—or for Royce, an objectification—of the self's alienation, to the point of knowing the machine and then leaving the machine behind.

Death

Royce had become well aware of Freud by the time he presented these lectures, *The Problem of Christianity,* at Oxford in the winter of 1913. His friend at Harvard, James Jackson Putnam, had been reading extensively in psychoanalysis for the past three years, and Putnam, an avid follower of Royce, certainly communicated his findings. If Royce in a sense became James's creation, then Putnam became Royce's, being locked in with his mentor (though Putnam, a contemporary of James, was almost a decade older) just as James acknowledged being in an "embrace" with Royce. Of the three, of course, Putnam possessed the far lesser intellect. He worked as a pastoral mind ministering in his capacity as physician to those who heard the teachings of his two Harvard friends. He attended to Royce in the months of late spring and early summer of 1916 as Royce approached death, months in which Royce walked (in John Clendenning's phrase) distractedly about. Royce's own cause, it seemed, was falling around him. As Horace Kallen remembered: "His steps seemed hesitant and unnaturally short, all his movements suggested an uncertainty, a reluctance to make them. When I greeted him, his round blue eyes looked staring, and without recognition. It was a moment or two after I had spoken my name that he remembered who I was. And then he said in a voice somehow thinner, and more dissonant than I remembered: 'You are on the side of humanity, aren't you?'"[146] Royce had fixed his mind on the war, "wholly inhibited," as he said, "by the war, and by its chaos of sorrows and of crimes,—a chaos from which, as I well know, . . . my dear Oxford friends suffer in a vastly more manifold and intimate way than is possible to me." Against the spirit of community of which he had spoken, Royce had unleashed his own terrible anger—words, as he said, of "hate," though "it is not hate, but longing and sorrow for stricken humanity, which is with me."[147] Royce died in the fall of the year, his beloved community sundered, his students accounting the whole as irony, preachings of peace as opposed to the anger in his life. Toward another understanding of such self-division—of such anger, that is, held within—Putnam was now writing of Freud.

Evil and error, as Kallen related, remained the matters of Royce's entire career.[148] He made an absolute demand that one perceive the alien or the ever contrasting sin that flowed through the community's history, holding the community responsible. Like Edwards, Royce found himself cast out. Like Edwards, who left for Stockbridge, and there wrote *The Great Christian Doctrine of Original Sin Defended*, he spoke to the city beyond its gates of matters that appeared misplaced again—of original sin, for which the community would not let its prophet stand too near. Alienation, as that word became acceptable coin—a popular way to say nothing at all—lost its meaning yet it retained it all, for Royce became the figure of vacuousness, of dryness, the automaton busy to the point of killing himself and dying like Edwards into life. Royce became an emblem in the memory that was made of him as a mechanical figure. Royce, looking for the Absolute, the One, appeared, by the middle of the twentieth century, as he had to appear: the authoritarian character.

From all his words, out of the vastness of his writings—moral philosophy, history, biography, fiction, symbolic logic, psychology, empirical probes, and rationalist proofs—one phrase, "loyalty to loyalty," stuck, and drew from Royce's critics either a musing smile or a suspicious fear. Having cast himself in a wilderness land, placing himself as Cotton Mather had against the state, unleashing hate, he imploded to the point of self-collapse. Eyeing the waste, Royce remains the American figure, his compulsion still the wondrous symbol.

5

Conversion through Psychoanalysis

James Jackson Putnam

> The times and seasons at which divine mercy is sought must be specifically indicated; the patient must submit to physical toil, to the trials and sacrifices of a pilgrimage, before he can become worthy of this divine mercy.
>
> Sigmund Freud, "Physical (or Mental) Treatment" (1905)

The intellectual background of Sigmund Freud owes nothing to the tradition of Puritan conversion. It owes much to European philosophy, nineteenth-century neurology, and Judaism, though in retrospect, and especially considering the avid reception of psychoanalysis in America, scholars have likened the arduous work of Freud's method to the Puritans' idea of spiritual conversion. Freud did speak of his psychoanalytic method as a long pilgrimage, and when his task of bringing the self out of neurosis is placed within the framework of Protestant psychomachy, his ideas can be read, either now or by a contemporary intellectual working within the tradition, as offering a renewed vision of spiritual salvation. James Jackson Putnam, the colleague at Harvard of James and Royce, made just this reading of Freud.

It was following Freud's visit to America in 1909 that Putnam turned his attention to Freud. It is fair to say that he converted himself to

Freud. Putnam suddenly left his work in neurology and stopped his use of mind cures and various suggestive psychotherapies, all of which Freud was disparaging as cheaply wrought physic, and became America's first practicing psychoanalyst.

Putnam's conversion, made after he had turned sixty, amazed Freud. Given Putnam's New England heritage, Freud could only think of the physician as the last man who should accept psychoanalysis. His history, of course, had made Putnam the first. By 1909 Putnam had already achieved eminence within the Boston medical community, but he was not ready to retire. Instead he had turned his attention to a less material approach to the problem of evil, studying Royce, whom he considered his mentor in philosophy. Putnam himself had experienced little psychological struggle. He had not suffered, or at least he had not given any expression to vastation like that of the elder James, or a panic fear like William James's, or a breakdown like that of Royce. After 1909, in long letters to Freud, Putnam did begin to open himself up, using Freud as a guide to explore neurotic symptoms in his everyday life. Perhaps the fact that, like Jonathan Edwards, he had never found terror within his own experience demanded from him this deeper exploration. Psychoanalysis concerned itself with an original sin so frightful that the staunch morality of a man like Putnam could be read as a mask for that sin. Freud thereby could renew the meaning of the Puritan claim that the worst sin was hidden in the most ordinary occupations of man and woman, especially when those occupations appeared to work so well. In this sense Putnam would complete the thought of Royce, for though far less accomplished intellectually than his teacher, he could struggle to find with Royce that an original sin did lie in the unconsciousness of the most beloved of human communities.

Working Through

A Victorian invention, the "New England conscience" speaks to sin lurking like a regional atavism within an otherwise progressive age. It speaks to the same concern as the "Protestant ethic" that Max Weber created for the late Victorian mind. Weber, who had met and been influenced by William James,[1] offered the Protestant ethic as a pacific ideal, rather as James had envisioned corps of young persons working off their natural aggression, or as Royce would speak of a beloved, mediated community as another moral equivalent for the "man of war."[2] Weber designed his this-worldly ascetic ideal as an ethic that was to serve the mental peace of its creator, but under dissection—most obviously at the point of psychoanalysis—Weber's ethic could be revealed as containing latent sadism and thus serve other than peaceful interpretations.

Freud also met James and by then, in the fall of 1909, had re-created the Protestant's ethic, or at least he had stripped away the Protestant's methodical, punctilious moralism to reveal what an outward display of good behavior hid. Freud created an obstinate, angry, acquisitive character, in effect a stern capitalist entrepreneur, a person whose posture of rectitude covered his sadistic urges and rage. Freud turned up the underside of the Protestant conscience to reveal its desire for bodily filth. This compulsive or anal-retentive sadistic character was the most scandalous of all the character types that Freud envisioned. In all this, which Putnam quickly read of, there was also a method of analysis that could take the person through this revelation of his sin and thereby renew the meaning of Puritan conversion, a method that Freud called "working through."

Putnam's Unitarian faith seemed to have precluded any traumatic conversion, but his turn to Freud at sixty-three became an event as meaningful in his life as the elder James's vastation and James's discovery of Swedenborg. He read now of an intense and laborious process of transformation that rejected quick or seemingly miraculous aids.[3] Freud asked for a vast amount of work from his patients, work that the patient had to conduct outside the neurological asylum and the pastoral retreat. Since neurotic symptoms substituted for denied pleasures, Freud proposed, as a fundamental rule of psychoanalysis, that a person carry himself through the process in a sort of this-worldly asceticism, outside any personally or institutionally constructed cell but still "under privation—in a *state of abstinence*." Laboring within "patienthood" himself, the analyst was not to permit a therapy for himself or for his other that could become a pleasurable chamber within which both he and the neurotic might reside.[4]

In his American lectures of 1909, given at Clark University in Worcester, Freud spoke of the need to touch such sore spots of the mind, and he promised, through the work of his therapy, to release a great amount of energy that neurotic repression consumed.[5] In speaking to the American press, Freud attacked as thin plasters the mind and faith cures then sweeping the nation, therapies that William James embraced for a time and therapies that Putnam, eyeing them like a physic, could now set himself against as too easy a way out. Psychoanalysis, Freud countered, "makes difficult demands": the "instrument of the soul is not so easy to play and my technique is very painstaking and tedious."[6] Conversion came slowly and only with cost. Psychoanalysis demanded money, the payment of which Freud thought essential for any therapy to work. His patients had to pay to extricate themselves from Adamic gardens, out from under the substituted pleasure of their neuroses. "This working-through of the resistances may in practice turn out to be an arduous task for the subject of the analyst. Nevertheless it is part of the work which effects the greatest changes in the patient and which distinguishes analytic treatment from any kind of treatment by suggestion."[7]

With Freud's arrival, Putnam began to question. He looked to his dreams as he began to search for the cause of the suppressed anger that Freud told him lay buried within his immaculate character. He also sought to reconstruct his "history," by which he meant his childhood, a history that he held responsible for much of the "mischievous" he now discovered in his life, including his inability as a beginning psychoanalyst to write frankly of childhood sexuality.[8] By that history, Putnam also meant his New England legacy, however, one typically described as "a distinguished heritage on both sides," "the very best [of] New England traditions."[9] Putnam had become particularly engaged with this inheritance prior to his meeting with Freud. Four years earlier, in 1905, he had published a massive *Memoir of Dr. James Jackson*, an account of the ancestry of his mother.[10] The history that Putnam never alluded to in his writing, and the history that no memorial of Putnam has ever mentioned, is the ancestry of his father. As the most landed and influential family in Salem, the grandchildren of John, the first Putnam in America, had lent powerful backing to those who accused others of being witches. One of the elder John's great-granddaughters, Ann, had acted as a witch's victim.[11] Unlike Hawthorne, Putnam himself protested no peculiar guilt for the judgments of his paternal forebears. He had decided to record, however, in a series of neurological writings that act like a medical history, a plague of obsession that he found besetting the mind of nineteenth-century New England. It was this personal history that Putnam could now refashion and cast in Freud's light as if reopening a hidden text.

Before his turn to Freud, Putnam had examined a "New England character" in terms of an obsessive pathology. More than any American, he had clinically examined the New England conscience that Henry James, Jr., was perhaps the first to name, using the terms of George Beard's neurasthenia. Now, with his turn to Freud, he could use the concept of Freud's *Zwangsneurose* or obsessional neurosis. He could re-express a demand long embedded in his American culture that an outward moral look covered an inner hate, that a mask was in place that the analyst had to lift. He chose to cast himself into a desert to make his discoveries, having at the age of sixty-three, as he felt, left the comfort of friends and a genteel profession to undertake a search within the writings of Freud. There he found, in the waste of neurosis, the possibility of a new life.

Putnam considered Royce perhaps his closest friend, but while Putnam was older—a contemporary of James—he was now, so he thought, to push Royce's psychology of religion further. Royce had early on warned "romantics" against digging too deep within their bowels lest their experience become, as Royce said, a bad dream. By the end of his career, Royce did speak of the unconscious, but the Oedipal guilt he recovered remained a metaphor for man's alienation from God. Having accepted Freud, Putnam could no longer speak in metaphor, for the anger he found expressed the trauma of an actual physiological experience. The Oedipal struggle, in other words, was real.

Putnam's Character

In the memory of A. Lawrence Lowell, James Jackson Putnam had lived like a "saint."[12] The grandchild of James Jackson, one of New England's most esteemed physicians, Putnam had begun his career as an "electrician" at Massachusetts General Hospital. There he founded a Department of Neurology where, in 1872, he located himself in a new electrical apparatus room, a small and confining alcove where colleagues pictured him as sitting under an arch, toying with a battery, receiving cases no other doctor understood. The following year the hospital board voted to change Putnam's title from "electrician" to "physician to out patients with diseases of the nervous system," a position that Putnam held under one name or another until his retirement in 1912.[13] Like his grandfather, Putnam also taught at Harvard, where he became the first Professor of Diseases of the Nervous System in 1893, retiring in 1912 as Professor Emeritus.[14]

The youngest of four children, Putnam came from a reserved and, in his daughter's opinion, unaffectionate family. Friends remembered his father, an obstetrician, as a grave, unassuming man who had sat honorably but silently in the shadow of his father-in-law and "revered master." Like Royce, who had pushed his own father out of sight, Putnam devoted but a half page to his father in the family memoir he wrote, though there he echoed these remarks by speaking of Charles Putnam's happy marriage to Elizabeth Cabot Jackson and of his humane, unselfish life of "few words and simple tastes."[15] Putnam's older brother Charles had studied pediatrics, but it was Putnam who received from

Miss Anna Lowell, a relative, the key and seal of James Jackson. He also received her admonition: "to keep his love, and holy, spotless example ever before you, so that you may live to be truly worthy of the name you bear."[16]

As Putnam inherited this legacy, his parents, or at least his mother, watched the youngest child closely. Unlike Miss Lowell, Putnam's mother could offer confusing advice: "Pray don't over-walk this hot weather, but do all to make yourself all right for good honest study next year." Again, she wrote to her son that "some good society must not be entirely neglected, yet you are surely right in guarding carefully *any wasted* time."[17] Her family called Elizabeth Putnam nervous, but in these subtly contradictory admonitions there emerge the words of a woman in doubt, advice to "do all" but "don't over-walk," to become "good society" but not "waste time." They work as double binds, and if such admonitions were placed upon Putnam as a young child, then they could have instilled the sense of insecurity that Putnam would finally confess when he sought to understand such trauma in analysis with Freud.[18]

Whether from his mother's confusing admonitions or simply, and contextually, from his Puritan inheritance and Victorian culture, Putnam lived (in Austin Warren's figure) with a rage for order. Like Royce, he sought to perfect himself, most particularly through an ethic of labor. As an adolescent, he tried to emulate men like William Ellery Channing, the revered Unitarian minister, who had expressed, as he thought, the devotion of St. Francis. This "marvelous fanaticism" furnished Putnam's only slightly more secular, now scientific ideal of giving his life to some well-defined, controllable endeavor, to the study of a "fly's wing or some other microscopic subject."[19]

Putnam's daughter remembered her father as a "tremendous worker" and a "poor sleeper," a "gentle, overconscientious" man who accomplished most of his reading and his writing of some one hundred articles—more, even, than James Jackson had published—between the hours of three and seven or eight in the morning. After his morning labor he ran along the Charles River, commuting between his lectures and practice, and saw two or three patients during each of his evening meals. Even by Victorian standards, Putnam excelled. In his daughter's words, he remained "thoroughly purposeful in his every undertaking, whether personal or professional. Even while gardening or sailing on summer weekends with his family . . . he was constantly thinking about problems philosophical."[20] Not uncommonly, Putnam would awaken at midnight "with the beginnings of 40 things going through my mind, . . . part by the general tendency to think over my paper forever and ever."[21]

Putnam read continuously and wrote "assiduously and even laboriously," producing a painstaking but never self-satisfying output of work that veered between minute decription and a vague, rather inexpressive speculation often ending in the commonplace. As a teacher, Putnam apparently failed because of his extreme care. The failure arose, a colleague wrote, "from a certain lack of clarity of expression and an overconscientious attempt to impart to elementary students the profundity of his own knowledge. The result was a failure at times to differentiate essentials from the more unimportant details."[22] Freud considered this representation the mark of an obsessional character.

In his appearance as well, Putnam bore the marks of an ascetically controlled character. He was a spare, tall, rather frail-looking man who dressed simply and immaculately. In one photograph taken during his later years, he appears with a neat, white, close-cropped beard, wire-rimmed glasses, and a dark suit that accentuates the length and rigidity of his body. He is sitting firmly on the edge of a short-backed cane chair, composing at his desk.[23]

Putnam, a gentle, "almost childlike" man, was always a mediating person who in Royce's ideal shunned controversy, hoping for nothing so much as to rid his world of conflict and his mind of unreflecting passion.[24] Though sensitive to criticism lightly given, he lived as a deferential, thoroughly honorable man, remembered for his vigorous walks, rather poor conversation, and a self-effacement sometimes verging on unwarranted extremes. He was called a dreamer and was thought to be inclined to philosophy, but though he followed Royce and called himself an idealist, his metaphysics never approached any degree of rigor. He was a religious man, though of no particular doctrine beyond the most simple of Unitarian faiths, so that in the years before his death, and after his conversion to Freud, he could readily believe that he had "had no religion at all, properly speaking," except for a youthful, now suspect celebration of natural law.[25] He was, above all, a sympathetic man who burdened his mind with the cares of others, identifying so readily with the poor and the sick that he eventually advocated, albeit privately, what he called socialism. In his sixties he said he believed now in communal forms of sacrifice, and thus would refuse to let "personal comfort and prejudice stand in the way." He wrote his daughter after midnight one night that he felt "inclined to go in for socialist movements" and that he had also decided to abstain from wine.[26]

As his character became reconstructed, Putnam was seen as allowing impersonal burdens to weigh as personal guilt. "His attitude toward the First World War was characteristic," a colleague remembered; "it was constantly in his mind, to the detriment of sleep and of personal pleasure; he seemed to feel toward it a certain personal responsibility—that somehow he was in a measure to blame."[27]

In all, Putnam gave himself to his profession. Only at thirty-eight did he marry Marian Cabot, a family friend eleven years younger whom he had known for years. "Boston was a small place . . . while family clans were large," and Putnam married properly. Together with his wife and children, he shared his Boston home with his oldest sister, a favorite grandchild of James Jackson to whom he would dedicate his long family memoir.[28]

Family and Neurasthenia

When approaching sixty, Putnam undertook a common task for the most literate son of a prominent New England family. In November of 1905 he presented the memoir of his namesake, Dr. James Jackson, "one of the best types of the practicing physician that New England has as yet produced."[29] Putnam acknowledged the risk of idealization, barely hinting that he had discovered flaws in his grandfather's character, but he still believed that the good in men measured their worth. Even that which physicians disparagingly called disease represented but feverish symptoms of a body and perhaps a soul laboring not in decay but in a trial of reformation.

Rather than a diary, journal, or autobiography, Putnam had chosen a set of selves, a family genealogy, to offer an exemplum for the edification of others. It was obviously with a measure of reverence for the details of his genealogy that he had gathered together and published a host of hitherto scattered memories. Two years after he published the memoir, Putnam, in a forum less public than the Boston community that received his book, spoke of another, parallel history, a recently completed "Study in Heredity" in which he had inquired into the problem of inheritance and mental disease. The published account of Putnam's paper remains brief. It simply mentions "the study of a large family . . . well known to the writer, many of them personally." The discussion following the paper discloses that Putnam had spoken of his own family, undoubtedly the forebears of his mother whom he had so extensively researched in the years preceding his talk. In his censored abstract, Putnam offered a summary of the case to the American Neurological Association:

The husband and wife, with whom the history begins, were persons of active minds, but showing symptoms in the former case of neurasthenia, in the latter of hysteria. One object of the inquiry was to ascertain to what extent these disorders had been inherited and whether they gave place in subsequent generations, to more serious affections of the nervous system. Apparently the former of these inquiries could be answered in the affirmative, at least so far as the neurasthenia was concerned, the latter in the negative.[30]

The two histories together form planes of a single text. Above lies one of the most productive of New England families; below, a neurasthenic heritage—not a degenerative disease, but an otherness against which the Jacksons had worked their sickness out. Prior to Putnam's meeting with Freud, the neurasthenic (or obsessional) disorder was something that one simply did work out. What such a sickness was for Putnam is evident in the many articles that he wrote on the subject prior to 1909.

Putnam's assistant at the Massachusetts General Hospital referred to neurasthenia as an indecisive and overly sensitive "New England conscience." It was an "exaggerated ego." For Putnam neurasthenia, along with its complications, involved fears of contamination and filth, anxieties about becoming insane, unceasing doubts and indecisions, and a sense of shame. These symptoms, along with imperative or obsessional ideas and the embracing apprehension of nervous fatigue, could and usually did pass physically through generations.[31] Such "signs" appeared and reappeared, coursing through a family's history "like a bit of paper on a stream . . . perhaps to be dissolved, or possibly to reappear again a good deal later." Such inheritance, however, rarely portended "degeneration," as William James had also argued, for neither physical inheritance nor even the increasing strains of industrialization led to diseased families or decayed communities (a popular thought at the turn of the century), as long as relationships remained large and inviting to new members. With greater or lesser force, neurasthenia had erupted down through the decades of a family's history, as indeed in a contextual sense it had throughout writings about New England. Putnam refused, however, to discourage further marriage or to counsel eugenics that might eliminate, as he thought, a sickness that could actually provide a great measure of production. The eruptions remained periodic, and even with the knowledge that inheritance brought mental disease, "we ought not to throw over the chance of gain." With genius came excitability and a certain "danger," but a danger one accepted as a "sacrifice" for the sake of bearing "our great leader."[32]

No bedridden—perhaps feigning—New England invalids, Putnam's neurasthenics possessed the ability to make themselves over. They had vague feelings of "isolation and dread"; held undue suspicions and at moments felt self-distrust and losses of identity; suffered morbid fears and obsessions; and carried out foolish, repetitive acts.[33] Still, if "fastidious, or over-conscientious," they remained "hard and good workers," though often incomplete and inefficient workers. They tired easily, and therefore they had to economize by shunning stimulants and excessive sex, protecting their limited strength. They could profit, in other words, by emphasizing the ascetic inclination of their particular character. They could become "over-systematic and business-like."[34] They might readily profit if they could turn their minds from intruding thoughts and their bodies from foolish acts and undertake other forms of labor.

Putnam emphasized these therapeutics of labor to overcome popular conceptions of the neurasthenic as a nervously exhausted invalid. He subtly played upon the common image of the neurasthenic as a saintly but "worn worker." A "simple life" and absorption in tasks devoid of the stress and undue competition embedded in much modern American living offered a way to health.[35] Fatigued in body or not, the neurasthenic should work, but within rules and at carefully prescribed times, avoiding anything "irregular" that might activate his inherited disease. He was to avoid the fear of routine that his lack of strength and confidence was apt to induce.[36] He was to become, as it were, a machine.

Like Cotton Mather's method and Jonathan Edwards's play with time, this Jamesian turning of "morbid energies into channels of active work" was to place the neurasthenic upon a new, even religious plane. The new labor was to effect the kind of life that religious conversion sometimes achieved, perhaps a desire for plainer dress, but more important, the beginning that the new dress symbolized, "personal identity" and a capacity for "being a different person; for different he must be."[37] The neurasthenic could profit from new surroundings, seclusion, or even removal from home, but above all he needed simple, repetitive labors—the recitation of a foreign tongue, for example, to scour his mind harassed with unclean thoughts, or some artistic expression to redirect "the cogwheels of his habitual and false logic." "The brain is a machine for grinding out work, and if it can be made to do this effectively, . . . the patient is sure to be the gainer."[38] Neurasthenics needed to work out their counting manias and their senseless repetition of words. As for their sexual relations, "it should be recognized that sexual intercourse is not the main object of marriage. On the other hand, an unnatural struggle for extreme abstinence is not good for the neurasthenic patient."[39] The whole seemed a vague cliché, so simple, it appeared, and innocuous, had the idea of conversion become.

Putnam had continued his grandfather's research in subjects such as exercise and neuralgia, where James Jackson had pioneered.[40] Most important, as his grandfather had, Putnam took issue with the precepts of the "Brunonian system," which attributed disease to "debility" or the lack of some bodily substance or force.[41] The theory, for example, had led to George Beard's attributing neurasthenia to a lack of nervous force,[42] and had led to rest cures and forced feedings as the prescribed therapies for those thought anemic, fatless, and nervously ill. Like his grandfather, Putnam looked to words such as "vital" and "activity" instead,[43] for like James, he was searching for the hidden energies of men. He was demanding that his nervous patients become some sort of new and productive machine. Only then would Putnam's turning to Freud make sense.

Putnam was asking that the neurasthenic accept the travails of Bunyan, whose mental pathology Putnam had studied in the essay by Royce,[44] although Putnam said nothing about any conviction of sin or about evil other than that the neurasthenic had inherited a physically determined disease. No cure awaited, but the possibility of a new life did, a life of good order, careful devotion, and economized strength, the life of a Protestant ethic that Putnam found and lovingly described in the heritage of his mother. Again, one can easily become suspicious as to how simple the ethic appears.

The Memoir of James Jackson

As an overside to his private inquiry into heritage, Putnam's memoir reads like a celebration of ancestors. In four hundred and fifty pages of text and commentary including a mass of letters and testaments—the longest such work he had ever undertaken—Putnam offered no comments on hysteric or neurasthenic strains. When he included comments on mental aberration, they came in letters from his forebears rather than from Putnam himself, and these concerned the nervousness of the women rather than the men, most particularly the wife of Dr. James Jackson, a nervousness Putnam would if anything have called hysteric.[45] He mentioned no neurasthenic heritage in the father, brothers, and son of Dr. James Jackson. With a characteristic regard for the achievements and organizational abilities of his family, Putnam chose to stress the theme he reported clinically in 1907, two years later: if sacrifices of mental debility did occur, then they occurred for the sake of community gains, accomplishments in law, politics, manufacturing, and medicine that made the Jacksons a family of moderate wealth and some intellectual achievement. Neurasthenia had occurred, though its discussion would remain ostensibly private, for the malaise embraced men with a "moral sense" lacking in enfeebled, grossly selfish hysterics fond of exaggeration and display.[46] Neurasthenia, again, was a model pathology in the display of the moral it wrought.

Putnam began his memoir with an estimation of his great-grandfather, Jonathan Jackson, and the inheritance that he provided for his sons. This inheritance included a certain "ceremoniousness," a requirement that his children upon entering the breakfast room each morning recite, "Duty to father and mother and love to brothers and sisters"—a habit, as it seemed, or a ritual. The inheritance also included a meticulous regard for fairness, a love of law and order, and a "scrupulous integrity and fidelity in matters of business"—an interrelation of economy and religion that marked Jonathan Jackson as it marked his children, sons whom their father admonished. He admonished his son Henry, for example, when Henry was about to ship out to sea: "Remember it is by strict frugality as well as by industry and perseverence that property is to be acquired and accumulated by those who begin with little or nothing—it is only by the most exact economy you give it a chance like the snowball to increase in size."[47]

What Max Weber meant by describing the Protestant ethic as a this-worldly asceticism received no better display than Putnam's chronicle of the energy and selfless devotion of Jonathan Jackson's descendents. One of these descendents, Patrick Tracy Jackson, became a developer and manager of the mills at Waltham and Lowell. Of all the Jackson brothers, Patrick gave himself most to enterprise, but enterprise bound with obligations that often diminished his gains. He refused, for example, to speculate in stocks, to make, that is, what he considered unearned money, at least as Dr. Jackson recalled.[48]

This conscience fell with its greatest weight upon James Jackson himself. With his own love for ceremony, Dr. Jackson liked to recall his boyhood days in school, days of recitation and of blackboard mottos such as "*Labor omnia vincit*," days not of play but times when his life stood in "perfect silence." In the memory of a friend, his face shone like a benediction, while for another, he "walked in our midst, our perpetual monitor." A dutiful yet gentle physician, demanding from himself "a scrupulous degree of exactness," Jackson advised his only son also "to be methodical" and told matronly invalids to walk instead of rest. He gave "hard" prescriptions like cold baths, harsh rubbings, simple food, and good exercise, and above all, for men, no suspensions from work, no foregoing of one's "mission . . . to do business and make money, so that . . . you may do a great deal of good."[49]

Putnam judged the character of James Jackson much as his grandfather might have wished. Putnam established an ideal text, venerating the man not only for his medical acuity and scientific accuracy but also for his "patriarchal authority," an authority Putnam feared young doctors with better instruments and skills than their elders might disregard. As a founder of the Massachusetts General Hospital and one of the first lecturers at the Harvard Medical School, as well as a practitioner with more published articles than any in the new medical journals of New England, James Jackson cast an impressive profile for his grandson. Putnam reached his majority before his grandfather died at ninety, and thus he knew him well in these later years when, relieved of a part of his practice, Jackson made "each morning, a round of visits to . . . his children. . . . As he started before eight o'clock, the neighbors came to regard him as a thermometer, so many different coats had he . . . according to the weather, and he was so punctual that the clock could have been set by his ring at the door."[50]

In all this portrait no sign appears of the neurasthenia Putnam described two years later as embedded somewhere in the males of his ancestry. A hint came from James Jackson himself, however, when he wrote in a letter to Miss Anna C. Lowell (here preserved by Putnam) of his "stomach" and dyspepsia and the "clouds" that arose to his mind. Here his life appears not quite as methodically attuned as his walks to his grandchildren:

> It is hard to fight with the demon in his moment of power. I believe the best one can do is to fix in the mind a conviction that the black and motely crew of despondent thoughts are of fleshly origin, and not, as they would pretend, from a spirtual source. And second to engage the mind as much as possible in some occupation.[51]

Whether Jackson was describing the pain of his thought rather than the ache of his stomach, and whether he was describing himself or simply prescribing to Miss Lowell, his life did approach, in this play he made of body and mind, a pathological edge. Putnam, among the most eminent of American neurologists, assuredly at least believed that it had, and whether through conscious intention or not, Putnam began offering documents that undercut the ideal he had established of his grandfather's life. A distant and almost forgotten melancholy began to reappear in his memoir. As Jackson wrote to William Ellery Channing, his friend and the brother of his former assistant at the Massachusetts General Hospital, he feared only that he could "never be good enough—but it is a holy fear."[52] It was a fear that drove the physician to strange behaviors, for like Channing, James Jackson disciplined himself unsparingly. As Putnam wrote:

> As a college student, and though he was fond of pleasures, he denied himself for a time even a sufficiency of food, and lived on prison fare. . . . Throughout his professional life he bound himself by certain rules of conduct, and saved himself thus from needless wasting of his slender store of strength. . . . He carried two watches, and did not, for that, leave his conscience at home.[53]

Putnam continued with example after example of his grandfather's punctuality and orderliness, moral behavior that Freud, to whom Putnam later sent a copy of his *Memoir*, conceived as a reaction formation or a defense against unconscious urges quite the opposite of the tidy and clean. For Putnam, writing in 1905, four years prior to his meeting with Freud, such "habits" appeared only "hampering." Putnam was not yet ready to acknowledge any abnormality, though he continued to record the extremes of his grandfather's behavior:

> It was his habit to decide beforehand, so far as possible, how many minutes—usually twenty or thirty, as the case might be—were to be allotted for each visit; . . . the limits set . . . but rarely overpassed.
>
> It was also his prudent custom never to hand over a prescription to his patient at the first moment of writing it, but to lay it aside while finishing the examination, to be scrutinized a second time, lest a mistake should have been made.
>
> These orderly tendencies and fixed personal habits grew upon him with advancing years. His hat and coat hung always on a certain peg, and were not to be removed without cause. . . . With some men such habits are hampering, but Dr. Jackson's conservative and tranquil spirit found in them a natural expression.[54]

His grandfather's regard for time and regularity, for checking and rechecking his every act, served his work. The practice of medicine required care, and the conventions of a prudential society fused easily with Jackson's character. Nevertheless, in the eyes of a neurologist, the proper could slide into the pathological. Jackson's ethic of order distends itself ever so slightly in Putnam's memoir until a caricature of a well-ordered person evolves, an extremity of a proper Victorian world. Putnam regarded his grandfather's actions as but a natural expression, and yet he continued with another example of Jackson's behavior that seems, even by Victorian standards, less than natural. Reciting another's remarks, Putnam presented an excellent example of how mental pathology related to social expectations. Within a single recitation, an ethic of time and regularity slowly slips into a form of neurotic behavior. Quite unobtrusively, the normal "goddess of orderliness" becomes the abnormal as Putnam portrays how close a New England conscience stood to behavior that, from another frame of reference, represents a pathology of a Victorian ideal:

> He breakfasted at seven, and always took his place at the table at that hour whether the meal was served or not. He never would use a silver fork, but always a three-pronged steel fork. He lunched at twelve, dined at five, and went to bed at half-past nine. Before retiring he always took a foot-bath. The tub had to be carried to his dressing-room at 8:30 and placed on a certain flower on the carpet. He had two pitchers brought, and these were placed on certain flowers on either side of the footbath. Both basin and pitchers had patterns of large flowers upon them, and they had to be arranged so that the flowers would seem to grow away from him. He never excused any one for being late. He lived by rule, but was very good and kind, although exacting.[55]

Still, Putnam found no abnormality, and certainly Jackson's due regard for caution and time, however hesitant yet demanding, or his desires for steel instead of silver, expressed good Boston if not Puritan traits. Putnam could not look for any symbolic representations or ask why his grandfather had to watch his minutes or look only at flowers as they grew up from his feet. He even appeared unconcerned with the recitation of his grandfather's need to have water basins arranged in particular ways on particular spots of his carpet. "These are small matters," he wrote, "but with men of consistent characters such habits are like floating chips, that serve well to mark the setting of the stream," to mark as it were the progress. "Through and through, Dr. Jackson . . . believed in the saving force of habit," thereby preserving days of "usefulness" before his inevitable decay.[56] The fears, the doubts, the compelling ideas, and the senseless rituals of neurasthenia floated through generations like bits of paper on a stream, but Jackson's habits had marked his course; in Putnam's opinion, these works had preserved his grandfather's sanity. With this text displayed, and placing his own life as he so clearly did against James Jackson's history, Putnam could now uncover the moral. He could fulfill the Puritan scripture by bringing down his grandfather's law. He could question, in other words, the meaning of his grandfather's rule.

Freud and the *Analerotik*

Four years after he had his memoir published, Putnam, as established and conserving as his grandfather, embraced Freud. To the detriment of his medical practice and the embarrassment, even "tragic bitterness," of his wife, he became, as noted earlier, the first practicing psychoanalyst in America.[57] Unlike most if not all of Freud's converts in America, Putnam came from a traditional medical discipline. He was a neurologist and as such a founder and past president of an American professional association unalterably opposed to Freud's teachings. He was also considerably older than most psychoanalysts, ten years older than Freud himself, and possessed of a reputation that quite naturally endeared him to those in a new and as yet unestablished cause.

"That old man is a magnificent acquisition," Freud wrote to Karl Abraham. To Carl Jung, Freud wrote that "the old man has indeed worked his way brilliantly into the field, he understands almost everything."[58] Jung agreed: "An amazing man, a natural aristocrat." "It is really amazing how a man of his age has been able to work his way into the material."[59] There remained a bit of hesitation as to how far Putnam would be willing to go ("Today I received a letter from Putnam bearing witness . . . and good intentions; of course with puritanical reservations about the sublimation"), but Freud wished to hold on to Putnam and the few other American converts at all costs. Putnam turned out to be worth the trouble of Freud's trip to Clark University, where Putnam heard Freud lecture: "Putnam seems to be *truly ours* . . . My prophecy come true! Our trip to America seems to have done some good, which compensates me for leaving a part of my health there." Putnam, until his death in 1918, continued to be, in Carl Jung's words, "a real brick."[60]

Six years after the publication of the *Memoir* and two years after his first meeting with Freud, Putnam sent a copy of his book to Vienna. "I shall read it with much interest," Freud replied. Putnam's family history would serve as an "example [to] disprove the idle gossip of those scientists who believe in the inevitable degeneration of civilized man," a falling away from "one's ancestors."[61]

In 1911, when he sent his memoir to Freud, Putnam understood the teachings of psychoanalysis. In the months following his conversion he had read and reread every published work by Freud and many by Freud's circle as well.[62] He had reviewed a few of Freud's articles prior to 1909 (James had given the first American book review), one of which he had thrown down in disgust, carefully but firmly rejecting psychoanalysis along with its dredgings of sometimes "revolting" memories.[63] At Worcester, when Freud lectured in 1909, and during a following three-day visit with Freud at his camp in the Adirondacks, Putnam changed his views. From then until his death nine years later he deferred rather reverently to Freud. He wrote three years later from the same camp where he and Freud had talked together that "your visit of three years ago was a more significant event to me than you can easily imagine, for it helped me to change radically the whole course of my life and thought." Whether radically changed or not, Putnam no doubt felt as he wrote that his study and share of work for the psychoanalytic movement, "small though it has been, has meant more intense and more engrossing labor than I have ever spent on any previous task—a labor often involving much readjustment, sometimes far from pleasant."[64]

Putnam wanted to learn, and he promised in his opening letters to Vienna that he would lose no time in reading the body of Freud's and Jung's work. He began immediately, initiating correspondence with Freud, Ernest Jones, Sandor Ferenczi, and Jung, inquiring, tentatively proposing, probing for answers to numerous questions and expressing a few carefully guarded hesitations.[65]

The questions began in his first letter to Freud. After enclosing some photographs of the Adirondacks retreat and expressing his sense of new faith, Putnam asked:

> One [question] is, just what you mean by the 'Geld [Money]-complex' as brought out by the Psychoanalyse. I have carefully noted what you say on that point in the paper on *Analerotik*, which I have just read with much interest, but wish that I knew more fully to what you refer. I dwell on this because your reference to it shows me that in my own 'Analysen' I have not as yet learned to go deep enough to find all that can be found. In spite of this . . . I think you have thrown new and important light on the great subject of character-formation.[66]

Putnam had written of character formation just prior to his meeting with Freud. It was a subject that had increasingly fascinated him as he abandoned his particular neurological studies for broader psychotherapeutic concerns.[67] Here Putnam began his inquiry into Freud's writings by asking about the most inflaming of Freud's early essays—a terse twenty-five-hundred-word exploration written six months before the American lectures. Freud's essays remain the most thorough of the few examinations that he made of character types. He had considered the infantile sexual origins of a type of character that he took as a complex of related personality traits.[68] "By the term 'money complex,'" Freud replied to Putnam, "we mean the individual's attitude towards money: the intrinsic value he attributes to it; his tendency to attach to it a variety of unconscious complexes. The attitude towards money should be especially revealing in the United States, where anal eroticism has undergone quite interesting transformations."[69]

With a fondness for the play of opposites,[70] Freud sought the sexual origin of ethical and, at least by implication, economic formations in contrasting unconscious pleasures, here the pleasure a person had found in excretory functions. In what is by now one of the most familiar of Freud's formulations, persons react to their pleasure, and against those who have trained them to deny their pleasure, by asserting moral positions, by looking for substitutes like money and by hiding their rage. Generally they appear the opposite of or different from what their desires urge—different, at least, until Freud's characterization became so familiar that one could readily "see" in the strict moral attitudes and in the "withholding" what the tightness and the morality meant. Thus embedded within the most considerate of persons were defiance and scorn, rage, and even desire for revenge. Putnam quickly began to perceive himself in Freud's terms: "I remember that Dr. Freud pointed out to me in the very first of our few conferences in Zurich, that I was a murderer! Think of that." To a depressed patient, as Nathan G. Hale has related, Putnam quietly confessed that he, too, in Hale's words, knew that he "sometimes felt like killing someone."[71]

Repugnant to many, Freud's article on character and anal eroticism did fashion a double-edged sword, for in plumbing to the depths of men's sensibilities, the sketch raised an issue of sublimation (a subject Freud seldom discussed in the prewar years[72]) that Putnam could hold on to. Whether the product of reaction formations, counterforces, or sublimations (Freud used all three phrases with fine distinctions), this most fully developed of his characters could, if stripped of avarice, rage, revenge, and shame—and stripped too of the neurotic compulsions and doubts to which Freud drew an obvious connection five years later[73]—become a person better at least than the one who perverted anal eroticism, or the one who remained encumbered by manifestly neurotic obsessional symptoms. Putnam could use Freud's obsessional neurosis as a step in a dialectic of working out good.

In an essay entitled "The Disposition to Obsessional Neurosis," written five years after he wrote his character study, Freud finally tied his character type to the obsessional neurosis. Why Freud waited remains unclear, for he had more than implied the connection in a case study completed shortly before the essay on anal eroticism.[74] In any event, when Freud had focused on the obsessional neurosis, he emphasized themes of ascetic self-renunciation that are not to be found in his discussion of anality. In 1907, a year before the essay on anal eroticism, Freud had published a paper entitled "Obsessive Acts and Religious Practices," in which he drew a careful analogy between ordinary religious ceremonies and ritualistically performed neurotic activities (the "obsessive acts" or compulsions) that some of his patients described. Any Victorian essay describing these neurotic activities remains rare. A person who performed such acts, as Freud noted, concealed them and seldom if ever spoke about them, out of embarrassment, certainly, or out of ignorance if he had so worked them into his life that they seemed normal and inconsequential. The ceremonies remained secret affairs conducted out of sight and usually, Freud wrote, during but a part of the day.[75]

A thought that one might commit a crime or maim a loved one could force a person to seek help. Not uncommonly, then, one finds many discussions of imperative ideas, fixed ideas, obsessions, impulsive insanity, or "monomania" in nineteenth-century psychiatric and neurological literature, particularly since alienists often conjoined these mental ailments with the insane, sinful premonitions of impulsive killers and criminals. Yet with the exception of compulsive handwashing or mysophobia—often an incapacitating form of the obsessional neurosis—alienists seldom discussed compulsions or, in Freud's term, "obsessive actions." In fact, such actions might seem almost normal within the context of a well-ordered society. Distinctions between a life led regularly and a life led compulsively could blur and engender debate. This appears, for example, in Putnam's reiteration of his grandfather's behavior. Freud, though he had no doubt as to what was neurotic, approached this problem when he opened his 1907 essay on obsessive acts and religion:

> The performance of a ceremonial can be described by replacing it, as it were, by a series of unwritten laws. For instance, to take the case of the bed ceremonial: the chair must stand in a particular place beside the bed; the clothes must lie upon it folded in a particular order; the blanket must be tucked in at the bottom and the sheet smoothed out; the pillows must be arranged in such and such a manner, and the subject's own body must lie in a precisely defined position. Only after all this may he go to sleep. Thus in slight cases the ceremonial seems to be no more than an exaggeration of an orderly procedure that is customary and justifiable; but the special conscientiousness with which it is carried out and the anxiety which follows upon its neglect stamp the ceremonial as a "sacred act". Any interruption of it is for the most part badly tolerated, and the presence of other people during its performance is almost always ruled out.[76]

Within this paragraph Freud drew a careful line between neurosis and habitual living, implying that seemingly inconsequential neatness could be torn from the framework of Victorian society and labeled neurotic. As he drew this boundary where habit and compulsion met, Freud also drew a controversial analogy between such ceremonials, as he thought of them, and religion. It was with the sense of a sacred demand or prohibition that the patients he observed performed such acts—the little things they had to do, such as record the numbers of every bank note they spent, and the petty things they could not do, such as sit in a particular chair. These unwritten laws, taboos, or superstitions appeared as invocations—things a neurotic did to insure himself, but from what, Freud often could never tell except within a broad origin of sexual reaction and Oedipal anxiety. When questioned, Freud's patients did not know why they performed such activities except to say that they experienced a great deal of anxiety if they tried not to perform them or made a mistake, omitted a part, or changed them slightly. Freud likened this mystery again to religion, where usually only a priest or a magician knows the signification involved in particular ceremonies. Like the beneficiaries of a sacred taboo, these neurotics performed their rites with dreadful precision. Unlike communal religions, however, such rites stood without the sanction of others, "a travesty, half comic and half tragic, of a private religion."[77]

An "unconscious sense" of guilt appeared to have driven some patients to renounce things or forbid themselves this or that—something as foolish as always leaving the best portion of a piece of meat untouched at dinner. Within such renunciations the sense of guilt seems overt, and Freud's analogy to religious practices, especially to ascetic practices, appears clearly drawn.[78] Freud drew no analogy between such rituals and asceticism, however, nor did he draw any relationship between these preoccupying acts and other, more productive forms of labor. Work itself could possess nothing of the neurotic for Freud because of the working-through of the psychoanalytic therapy itself: the arduous, detailed sweeping of the mind that could become an intellectualized game with its own obscure symbols—a ceremonial, in other words, that some of Freud's obsessional patients could engage in as enthusiastically as they did other complex, personally distancing endeavors. Freud discussed this problem of psychoanalysis becoming a private religion, but he failed to resolve the irony.[79]

Putnam found himself drawn to psychoanalysis at least in part because of Freud's opposition to alienists who were withdrawing their patients, most often women, from family and friends by placing them in rooms, forbidding them even to feed themselves for up to six months or a year. Such patients received strict schedules, times outlined for forced feedings with bland foods and milk, and other times for rubbings or electrical massage. These were chambers in which a professional nurse ideally made all decisions,[80] an otherworldly ascetic that Freud was working against by arguing that his patients should work their neurosis out as much within the "real world" as possible. The "element of 'overwork,'" Freud wrote in 1898, "which physicians are so fond of producing to their patients as the cause of their neurosis, is too often unduly misused." "Intellectual work is rather a protection against falling ill . . . ; it is precisely the most unremitting intellectual workers who remain exempt."[81] Labor could resolve affairs of the mind, though the question remained whether psychoanalysis could itself form an interminable therapeutic chamber. The question Freud became concerned with was whether a patient might remain in analysis just because it was a safe game.

Moral Regeneration

In Freud's writing, Putnam found a conviction of sin and an excremental analogy that turned sin into physical fact. He could easily accept the insight that the most moral of persons were deluding themselves by thinking themselves clean. But he admonished Freud for stopping there. Actually he undercut his acceptance by demanding something else, that the patient accept "sacrifices," "effort," "*will*." He confirmed Freud's analysis of obsessional behavior by demanding not only insight but "moral" improvement as well. "Now I do not ask that we should simply say, 'Be moral.' I have a wider plan than this."[82]

Putnam's wider plan slipped into something about "the Hegelian and Froebelian philosophy, and the psychology (and philosophy) of Harris and Bergson and Judd, etc." Putnam appeared to be missing for the moment whatever deep chains Freud found linking avarice and money with duty and morality. He was looking instead for "the community and social aspects" of Freud's investigation into anality, and of course he was thinking of Royce. He congratulated Freud on his new insights, but while Freud was poking at the American's affinity for money, Putnam was asking what he was to do with an intelligent, morbidly self-conscious woman whose work bored her and whose life offered few ideals.[83] Freud's essay had not broached the question of work or even extended to his character an inclination for labor.[84] Money lent itself more readily than work to sexual interpretation (and Freud never involved himself with a Protestant question of "works"). "By the way," he wrote Putnam, "the inter-relations between the money complex and anal eroticism only recently have been established. With us, people are just as dishonest and as repressed in their attitude towards money as they are towards sexual matters."[85]

Putnam replied by speaking only of "moral regeneration," using words Freud considered vacuous. To preach simply, "'Be moral and philosophical,' . . . is too cheap and has been said too often without being of any help." Too many patients of "inferior endowments" remained incapable of achieving any sublimation: "it is therefore more humane to establish this principle: 'Be as moral as you honestly can be and do not strive for an ethical perfection for which you are not destined.'"[86]

Freud, the empiricist of which Putnam had once dreamed, drew his metaphors from hydrology and the study of electrical fields.[87] Any other metaphor, any sense of sickness as presaging light, he relinquished. Psychoanalysis became more pervasive in America than in any nation, however, for Putnam's sense of what the moral struggle of conversion entailed hardly stood, as Freud thought, as a wondrous anomaly to it.

Quite understandably, Putnam had turned to psychoanalysis precisely for the "ethical perfection" Freud slighted. He envisioned a therapeutic process working toward a purity of self quite beyond any of Freud's expectations, a cleansing of the soul for the therapist certainly, if not for the patient himself. Analysts, Freud admonished, remained far from "perfect human beings." But Putnam continued, beginning his own self-analysis by persistently voicing disappointment when others' expectations failed to match his own. In the longest, most intellectually involved of his preserved and now published letters, a letter that he chose to write on Christmas Day, Putnam said that he wished "to make perfectly understood: 1. I *desire* to practice this branch of medicine (Ψa). in accordance with the very best principles, and if I fail to do so it will be because I cannot rise to my own standards, on account of resistances which I realize to exist but find hard to master." He assured Freud that "I am trying more conscientiously than ever before, and with better results, to work out my 'infantile fixations'. . . ."[88]

Putnam strongly affirmed the need for an analyst, whether through individual effort or the intercession of another, to undergo psychoanalysis himself, an early requirement of the movement. "Not a day passes that I do not feel the need of this with regard to myself. But on the other hand a great many psychoanalysts have been analyzed, and yet they are far from being perfect human beings from any point of view." If one asked, Putnam continued, why analysts failed to achieve their "best sublimation," then the answer must lie in the failure of either themselves or their intermediaries to know of the goal toward which they were striving, something again of "an ethical sort" such as Royce's ideal of loyalty. A "patient *capable of such work*" could, "by a strictly logical process of introspection," achieve this end.[89]

Putnam set about to examine himself. He would give his repression a chance "to work itself out" by allowing his buried emotions to make some sense, "an opportunity," as he said, "to . . . work themselves off by making themselves articulate."[90] He began this articulation by re-examining his past through reporting his dreams, looking out for the undersides of his character he now knew to exist. "The dream-interpretation goes better," he wrote to Freud, "and I think I have had a 'baby-diapers' dream of comfortably lying in excretions (warm water and mud, turning into a bed). . . . I have also recognized *Uebertragung* [transference] towards yourself, and a 'revenge' in which I took you through a church (my philosophic ideas) and then made you (indignantly) confess that you had symptoms of depression (as I, *formerly*, and slightly of later) which ψ an. could not remove." Since little remained for Freud to interpret of the obsessional events that Putnam had dreamed, Freud simply replied with an expression of delight that such an analytic effort had not left "a bad aftertaste. Self analysis is a never ending process that must be continued indefinitely."[91]

Putnam did continue. To Ernest Jones he described the same as well as another dream. The mud-bath dream Jones thought "doubtless an excretion phantasy in the main"; a bicycle dream involving earth, defiles, and stones he thought "certainly a homosexual dream with analerotic aspects; it portends a conflict between male and female tendencies." Jones explained again "the well-known relation between money and faeces," and he thought since the mud bath occurred in the richly appointed home of Morton Prince, Putnam was undoubtedly envious of the American neurologist's leisure and wealth.[92] If perhaps surprised at this last interpretation, Putnam doubtless knew the others before his report. He knew that by the terms of his analysis he would find beneath his orderly character evidence of filth and revenge, desires for particular erotic pleasures, and a need to bring down authoritarian friends. He said that he knew most of his complexes by name, but still they troubled him and held him in their grip. Now a psychoanalyst, he had to reach some "millenium of perfection" before he could truly begin his profession.[93]

Exactly what bothered Putnam he never made clear. He did spend six hours in analysis with Freud during his trip to the Weimar Congress in late September of 1911, an experience that apparently encouraged him to undertake his ongoing *Selbst-analyse*. The meeting also prompted Putnam to write to Freud about his personal concerns rather as William James had written from Brazil. To the disappointment of his correspondent, however, Putnam said he cared to write about such matters only once. The night before he left Weimar, Putnam explained, he had dreamed about descending a hill in a cart—a dogcart, he thought; suddenly he had found himself leaving the road, perhaps the safe road, taking a shortcut instead. As the new grassy route became steeper and more difficult to manage, he found that his goal—point "E," for Putnam diagramed the entire geography of his progress out—seemed marshy and filled with bumps and holes. He tried to stop his horse, but to no avail, finding himself instead pulling with great effort but accomplishing nothing.

Putnam's interpretation followed: the horse represented his sexual drives that he wished so desperately to control; leaving the safe road expressed his desire for independence; while the bog symbolized a dependence on both his brother and wife. In all, he thought the dream told of "dependence," "'protest,' and sometimes irritation—really, at myself," a hesitant and rather couched interpretation he thought possibly related to attitudes toward his parents or perhaps toward feelings of homosexuality and heterosexuality. "The holes containing water may have sexual meaning, as I seemed to be going into them, yet dreading the fact."[94] The whole, it seemed, represented a renewed and terribly jumbled version of a pilgrim's difficult progress.

For all the complications, diagrams, and endless qualifications—all the logic that Putnam thought he could readily use—Putnam arrived nowhere (and everywhere, of course). He spent considerable effort to accomplish little except to express his finely drawn doubts and ambivalent feelings. If he protested anything, he thought, he protested himself. If he dreaded anything, he dreaded his sexual drives. Putnam continued his letter to Freud with a less intellectualized description of his fears, speaking of his rather infrequent sexual relations with his wife, of his actual dread of intercourse, partly because he thought it perhaps improper for a man of his age, mostly because of the exhaustion, depression, and sleepiness that would follow for days. The act itself, however, provided a "great relief from a very unpleasant state of tension and anxiety." Putnam then drew back to say that though he believed sex his one uncontrollable drive—something he could never "satisfactorily drive or restrain"—he never meant to imply he was "in any sense, a 'pervert'. . . ."[95]

Putnam then related a youthful fantasy he apparently thought beyond reach, a longing to sit comfortably by a fire with a wife and, more important, with children, reading aloud, playing, caressing, and attending to one another in a darkened room—a common portrait of "domestic happiness, I suppose,—perhaps idealized somewhat from personal memories, but possibly referring to a close feeling for my mother and father."

He then ended his letter with a jumble of self-attributed traits and personal concerns: early childhood experiences of "affection, readiness to be caressed, narcissism, 'protest,' autoeroticism, homosexuality, heterosexuality," along with a sense of sexual and social inferiority that had led to his desire for self-recognition. As compensations, he listed his need to purchase things and to win influential friends, to have "little successes" such as looking into a shop window without intending to buy, "as I am 'sparsam' [frugal], even in essentials." With a feeling of living "not at harmony with myself," Putnam confessed to duplicity for his occasional "extravagant" living. "I owe you an apology for writing at such length, but you can help me very much by even a few words, and I *must* get myself *free* and able to use my powers."[96]

"You certainly describe yourself as a very bad character," Freud replied. The dream Putnam had interpreted correctly, except to say that perhaps the safe road represented the older, presumably easier therapies, while the new and steep road represented the psychoanalysis "of which you seem to be very much afraid. You are much too frightened by your fantasies," Freud continued. "On the whole I see that you are suffering from too early and too strongly repressed sadism expressed in over-goodness and self-torture."[97]

Thus after six hours of analysis, Putnam ended his own mostly private examination. He had rigorously reported a few dreams and had looked as he knew he should for the undergirding of his character. What he discovered he could never clearly explain, at least not without the qualifications and hesitations that left Freud a bit wary. For all the detail Putnam displayed, he had really "described the underlying motives so hastily and piled up everything disagreeble" in such a way that Freud could offer little more than the obvious. Putnam reported his mud-bath dream again and wrote of his desire for solitude and frugality, and admitted suspicions of a desire for revenge toward authority. He then sent a copy of his *Memoir* to Vienna and left his self-analysis behind, turning his thoughts once again toward his hopes for sublimation. If anything, his memory of James Jackson still expressed more fully than his fantasies the life Putnam thought accessible and certainly therapeutic, even if he knew that Freud could easily interpret the book differently. Since Freud never mentioned the book again in correspondence, he probably never read it. In that sense, Freud threw away Putnam's moralism.

"Pain, disappointment, the necessity of sacrificing cherished hopes; the necessity of ceaseless struggles with the sense of weakness, of exhaustion, of isolation; the necessity of living in almost perpetual companionship with some parasite or demon or phantom of the fancy, hardly less hard to bear for being recognized as fictitious . . . ; trials such as these may mar, but often make a fine character."[98] Putnam maintained these words as though copying them from Royce. If Putnam had allowed himself the fantasy of a caressing home, children "playing about and receiving the usual caresses and attentions," then he managed something different. He believed now in infant sexuality, but from that he drew the lesson to dampen undue excitement, as though such excitement might destroy the moral he sought. In these last years of his life, then, Putnam would not allow his daughters to sit upon his lap.[99] In the preservation of this fact, no repression exists; it is the most open of personal texts.

Analysis

In retrospect, psychoanalysis appears an onrushing wave. In September of 1909 Pierre Janet held the Bostonians' attention, however; it was he who spoke to appreciative audiences in universities and at expositions and claimed the respect of men such as James, Prince, Hugo Munsterberg, and Putnam himself. While Freud was being mistaken for Freund,[100] many of Janet's essays were being quickly translated into English. Quite appropriately, Janet dedicated his Harvard lectures to Putnam, for Putnam had invited Janet to speak.[101] Psychoanalysts called their movement a cause, and those surrounding Freud stood close to the beleaguered cause they proudly remembered in later years. It is easy to exaggerate their tribulations, as Freud himself became apt to do, but it is also understandable why Putnam appeared so valuable—"not only the first American to interest himself in psycho-analysis," in Freud's memory, "but soon . . . its most decided supporter and its most influential representative in America." When Freud remembered Putnam, he thanked him not for his intellectual contributions but for his "established reputation," the "lofty ethical standards and moral rectitude" that allowed Putnam more than any American to "protect" psychoanalysis from its enemies.[102]

Rather than suggest, explain, hypnotize, or command, Freud gave to the individual the burden of achieving his own insight, as well as the duty of accepting responsibility for his acts. And rather than accept confession, Freud asked for more, arguing that his patients must labor hourly and for years to wean knowledge from the most stubborn recesses of mind. Some regarded psychoanalysis as a Catholic confession, but for Putnam the therapy became a "long and patient searching" that began "where the confessional leaves off."[103]

The somatics of neurasthenia had become for Putnam a mere humor now, as the occasion emerged to move from body to mind. To know the self, "to see things as they are," required a "radical" therapy: "'Suggestion,' 'isolation,' improvement of the bodily nutrition, persuasion, explanation, all of which have their valued place, leave many of the great springs of emotions and of motive untouched." Putnam thought he had learned a lesson in pagan mythology. Buried within the unconscious lay impulses that rest cures and therapeutic suggestions left intact, rejected experiences that erupted as depressions or sometimes as rituals undertaken to relieve the self from dread. There existed "the impulses to adopt ceremonies and observances which are practically analogous to pagan ceremonies of propitiation and expiation," acts of both ignorant races and neurotic men. Freud's therapy never provided all the self required for "spiritual progress," but psychoanalysis prepared a "way" and opened "a long path." Too often alienists simply "veneered" mental disease with optimistic slogans and friendly advice, shutting the patient off from "obvious darkness" while shunting him toward some "imagined light." Too often Americans blamed their malaises on anxious times, forgetting that worry rather than overwork contributed to their plight. If the patient was willing to make his life as transparent as glass, and if the physician stood like Faust before the enormity of his task, then an understanding of the self might begin. The patient might relieve himself of the need to defile his thoughts and entangle his life with superstitious tasks. He might "adjust himself to some workable conception of community life."[104]

Until his meeting with Freud, Putnam had used rest cures, forced feedings, hypnotism, and suggestion. He had toyed with the veneers of new thought, mind cures, and such lay psychotherapeutics as the religious balms brought by the Emmanuael Movement.[105] He wrote extensively on hydrotherapeutics,[106] cautiously approved the surgical removal of ovaries—surprisingly advocating the procedure more than Weir Mitchell, the father of the rest cure—and for the obviously unbalanced and "excessively lascivious," proposed castration. As he explained in 1891, "we should not permit ourselves to be too much controlled by sentimental considerations in dealing with the question of 'unsexing' the patient."[107] When the work cures of his cousin, Richard Cabot, arrived, however, Putnam favored those, and when he spoke of Weir Mitchell, he emphasized not rest but the strict schedules, regimens, and rigid prescriptions that regulated the patient's environment to the minutest degree. He always opposed control to the supposed benefits of repose.[108]

Before his encounter with psychoanalysis, Putnam had emphasized that cures seldom indicated causes. If a therapy broke apart a malignant pattern, then the reason for the pattern still remained undisclosed, and the physician might have applied other physics just as well. Putnam always kept his neurological training close at hand, never relinquishing his professional demands to fads or well-meaning ministers. He found little contradiction in studying heredity and searching for lesions while offering support to social and mental therapeutics. He moved continually from somatic to mental explanations of nervous disease, but moved glacially, always reminding his reader, whether early in his career or late, that thoughts and flesh were inseparably joined, acting reciprocally as body and soul reflected each other. He could still speak of "inherited tendencies" after his acceptance of Freud, even as Freud could never disavow the importance of some unknown toxin or physiological function for what Freud called the real or actual neuroses.[109]

The predisposition and preparation of which Putnam spoke worked together. Whether by inheritance, strain, or accidental shock, men and women could break like crystals along planes of least resistance. Given the lesion of an accident, particular men and women appeared to break more readily than others, and with a sense of the social causation of mental disease, Putnam thought he found nervous disease following lines of economic and occupational class. Hysteria, particularly the conversion hysteria or paralysis that followed accidents, seemed to occur more often among the lower class. Neurasthenia, for Putnam, remained a disease for the less prepared of the cultivated class.[110] The thought that "social status" could condition the forms and severity of nervous disease placed Putnam in a vulnerable position among his colleagues, particularly many stricter somaticists who threw other statistics and different interpretations toward him at will. Nevertheless, with the underpinnings of Royce, Putnam composed some of his most beautiful essays on the developing social consciousness of the child and the adult that could bring an acute sense of self-consciousness, doubt, and isolation. The aridity of an ever more isolating environment, a new mechanical garden, could readily strip a person of the very preparation he required to leave his childhood, "to leave the Garden of Eden for . . . conscious development."[111] What Putnam wished was "real work."[112]

Though a consistent physician, Putnam was realigning his interests as he approached his meeting with Freud. He had focused his early research quite naturally on hysteria, the readily seen and easily described affliction with acute, often traumatic physical symptoms. Sometimes appearing suddenly following a railway accident or another obvious shock, hysteria claimed the attention of neurologists like Putnam in part because of suits of accident litigation, questions of workmen's compensation, and an apparently increasing number of invalid women, all of which in the 1880s were opening areas of controversy into which Putnam and other neurologists could readily step.[113] With his interest drawn to the mental rather than physical manifestations of the neuroses he studied, however, Putnam was moving his attention to neurasthenia, the disease that he, like most alienists, thought less serious, less well defined, and certainly less dramatic than the vivid complications of hysteria. Neurasthenia allowed Putnam to examine the mental disorders of males and his own social class, the obsessive symptoms that appeared "among the best and keenest people in every community."[114]

Because these patients might well conceal their rituals and imperative ideas out of embarrassment, physicians imbued with the somaticism of American neurology concentrated on what they thought of as the physical symptoms—the languor and fatigue, for example, or the facial tics (and even rituals) that were thought of as varieties of chorea. Like other neurologists, Putnam wrestled with problems George Beard had presented as to just what symptoms defined neurasthenia, but he looked to mental symptoms—the phobias, counting manias, handwashings, and obsessions—and most important, he studied the less obvious, less readily described feelings of isolation and self-alienation. He began asking whether the fatigue and nervous exhaustion that Beard had used to summarize his syndrome remained as physiologically induced as American neurologists were claiming. Putnam never discarded neurasthenia,[115] nor did Freud, who even in his last writings maintained that neurasthenia existed as the functional disease that Beard had claimed it was.

As Freud was doing, Putnam began stripping neurasthenia of certain manifestations, reordering the remainder into a new complex with fatigue assuming considerably less importance. With the advent of Janet's psychasthenia, Putnam could more readily discuss obsessions, compulsions, and *sentiments d'incomplétude* without the expected litany of bodily incapacities, nerve fatigue, and physical strain. At a time when American neurologists looked first to overwork in the etiology of ambiguously caused nervous diseases, it was important when Putnam asked whether overwork did indeed function as "the real cause of . . . collapse."[116] Putnam now spoke of the "supposed demon of overwork," and he began to think of the mind fatiguing the body, creating the "depressions, obsessions, and morbid fears" that seemed "to strangle one's very breath."[117]

Putnam received support, of course, as he moved his considerations from the strains of the body to the compressions of mind. With James's essay on the energies of men and with Royce's earlier discussions of Bunyan and the anomalies of self-consciousness, Putnam had at his disposal a social portrait of potentially energetic men foundering in a morass. It had been Royce who, more than any neurologist or alienist in the Boston psychotherapeutic community, had emphasized the social rather than the somatic side of mental disorder, and Putnam's turn from neurasthenia to psychasthenia came upon the heels of Royce's essays. After the mid-1890s Putnam wrote exclusively of psychasthenia, just as after his reading of Freud he wrote only of phobic and compulsive disorders. His concern with hysteria and neurasthenia dropped completely from sight in the years preceding 1909. Putnam was now writing the social portrait of alienated Victorians who could not account for their conscience of sin.

Shortly before his meeting with Freud, Putnam asked once again whether family inheritance caused mental disease and seemingly agreed that it did. But then he quietly replaced inheritance with "forgotten experiences of the past." He spoke of "the skeleton in the closet, the tug of an evil spirit residing in the mysterious depths of our subconscious life, the misunderstood twists and tendencies derived from unfortunate experiences in childhood." Without preparing his reader, Putnam had suddenly changed "family" and "racial" into childhood, and he had changed an unworkable into a workable history. He refused to accept Freud at this point, but in the spring of 1909 asked, "Are we prepared to pay the price, in labor," for a life that refused to stay in "narrow cells."[118]

Though Putnam rejected psychoanalysis, he wrote appreciatively of the new cathartic method of Josef Breuer and Freud. Yet at this point he considered psychoanalysis but another way to substitute, sidetrack, or suggest, and when he spoke of Freud, he spoke of "a confession of principles, not of details." He did begin to write more of sin—the "power that thrusts an obnoxious act or thought into the current of our lives," for if no original sin existed, there did exist an "original limitation." One needed, like Christian,[119] to journey alone, for though physicians and alienists could suggest and intercede, they could not assume the patient's responsibility.[120]

Freud confirmed this inerrancy of sin for Putnam. The emblem of sin—the "estrangement, compulsions, obsessions" that most people suffered "in some measure"—reflected but a wish for a return to youth, to the "fantasy-weaving days of childhood" that in fact were "an intolerable prison-house." Childhood was a time of passion, assertion, egoism, and craving, a time one had to leave behind[121] for the Roycean world of disinterested labor where men and women were joined together through the lines and functions of their tasks, drawn together through forms, rules, and the triadic fact of mediation.[122] Royce's world existed as a realm of reason that negated "the sensuously emotional, illogical, time-neglecting cravings" of childhood.[123]

Ideally a person passed from the sensuous gardens of his youth, "work[ing] his way along, . . . [like] Christian passing through the Valley of the Shadow of Death, in the presence of only dimly appreciated dangers." Ideally a person renounced the sensual ego for the spiritual self. Even if the adult thought his passage eminently satisfactory and considered his life one of propriety, he thought wrongly, for he was "indulging himself, without knowing it, in the aroma of pleasures and excitements . . . banished to the 'unconscious.'"[124] As Putnam argued again and again, Freud had simply furthered the responsibility for sin. Freud demanded an awareness "not only for the visible, but also for the hidden sin" that the self-deception and disguise of neurosis hid, and that the "moral education" of psychoanalysis could open for rational analysis.[125]

Putnam provided this plain and ironic argument for those who wished to avoid the "dirt" of psychoanalysis. To shun this history meant seeking "enjoyment" rather than "doing work," and it meant refusing the obligation of a Western philosophy that demanded "the facing out of temptation."[126] Perversion existed as an obvious sin, undisguised and readily available for analysis. Neurosis worked as a worse sin. It was a "confidence game."[127]

Putnam's Ethical Bias

Freud thought Putnam's desire for a sublimation a rather decorative centerpiece, something to admire, perhaps, but not touch. And Putnam did leave it to others to look for sexual symbolism. He searched instead for Royce's triadic community in the number three occurring in dreams, or for hunger for knowledge in the theft of a book. He asked that psychoanalysts "be continually on the watch for the constructive element of the neuroses," refusing to believe that an "obsessive patient," for example, expressed "a simply destructive tendency." While Freud broke religion down to a primordial killing of the father and the compulsive rituals of expiation that followed—rituals that worked logically or ideally to cover the crime up—Putnam searched his obsessional patients for their duty, works, and goodness. He argued that ceremonials indeed served superstitious ends, but carried "the germs of something better" as well.[128]

More intrigued by character studies than Freud, and more willing to generalize than his fellow American clinicians, Putnam also rewrote Edward Cowles's essay on Miss M. by providing, as the "Sketch for a Study of New England Character," the case of a matronly Bostonian woman suffering obsessions and compulsive acts. The lives of this woman and Miss M. hold together in a progressive narrative, for having offered Freud's obsessional neurosis as a cultural malaise, the neurotic outcropping of a strict Protestant society, Putnam now proposed that his patient, in "a species of new birth," had found identity in social occupation. "It should be added . . . that this result, while it would have been impossible without psychoanalytic aid, has been greatly furthered by congenial work and an increase of social intercourse of a good sort." Putnam turned Miss M.'s neurasthenia into a psychoneurosis, displayed his patient's Oedipal struggles, then brought the woman from Cowles's asylum back to the world. She became his assistant, drawn into Putnam's own world of intense labor and social obligation. Exactly what she did, Putnam failed to say,[129] and his therapies could remain mundane. In the Out-Patient Department of the Massachusetts General Hospital, he supported small centers of labor—a pottery-making enterprise for women, a cement shop for men, groups producing articles together which they could then sell to others.[130] Given this value for their labors, Putnam's patients were to value themselves.

In the prewar years, Freud had shunned the word "sublimation" and was occupying himself solely with the ill effects of self-repression.[131] To an extent, Putnam had allowed his own patients to dig around in their past to uncover the infantile source of their grief, but his own interests lay ahead in the causes that he brought to his understanding of Freud. Freud wryly judged Putnam a sublimated man. "His closer personal acquaintances," Freud recalled after Putnam's death, "could not escape the conclusion that he was one of those happily compensated people of the obsessional type for whom what is noble is second nature." In this one sentence, Freud tore Putnam—his own wanted moral creation—apart. In "a reaction against a predisposition to obsessional neurosis," Freud wrote, Putnam's "ethical bias predominated."[132]

Anyone the least familiar with Freud's writing knew that a strong "ethical bias" is thought to cover impulses of sadism, although when Freud had lectured to the Americans in 1909, he had allowed a more willful text by explaining that the "energetic and successful man" was the "one who succeeds by his efforts in turning his wishful phantasies into reality." For the "estranged" intellectual, this might mean turning fantasies into artistic productions, but if neurotic rebellion remained strong or if the artistic gift was lacking, then persons regressed and entered the safety of cells. "To-day," Freud said in Worcester, "neurosis takes the place of the monasteries which used to be the refuge of all whom life had disappointed or who felt too weak to face it."[133] Freud placed his fullest statement on such asceticism in a historical essay he wrote in the early 1920s.[134]

A better way existed, Freud wrote in 1930, in terms reminiscent of Putnam: "that of becoming a member of the human community, and . . . going over in the attack against nature and subjecting her to the human will. Then," Freud concluded, "one is working for the good of all." By the time Freud wrote these lines, he had reconsidered Putnam's call for sublimation, asking his readers to appreciate structures he had formerly disparaged. Like cleanliness, Freud wrote, order "applies only to the works of man. But whereas cleanliness is not to be expected in nature, order, on the contrary, has been imitated from her. . . . Order is a kind of compulsion to repeat which, when regulation has been laid down once and for all, decides when, where, and how a thing shall be done, so that in every similar circumstance one is spared hesitation and indecision. The benefits of order," Freud continued, "are incontestable. It enables men to use time and space to the best advantage, while conserving their psychical forces."[135]

Before his death in 1918 at age 72, Putnam wrote often of the benefits obsessive patients could derive from their symptoms.[136] The ethic of work inherent in obsessional disorders provided values of order, and appropriately in the years in which clinical case histories of obsessionalism began appearing, Max Weber constructed a this-worldly asceticism, the ethic of which he, like Freud, presented as a therapeutic text. The calling for Weber became what he said only worldly ascetic labor created: an "idea of personality," a "unified personality."[137] Whether for Marx, Weber, or Freud, however, and even for Putnam in his simpler discussions of mechanics, this work could never hold. Work could no more hold its value or its lack of estrangement than the moral that remained so visibly shallow in the secondary figure of Putnam.

Freud's Mechanics

The drama re-enacted itself. Weber, who would declare any such work as Putnam might find dead, was to destroy the Protestant ethic. He had worked to break himself down as Freud had recorded in a "travel dream." "The scene is changed so often in dreams, and without the slightest objection." Freud was moving into another "compartment" within a dream that itself was of a moving train. The scenes were presumably flashing while the scenes, too, remained the same in their expression of the timeless id. "In the dream itself, accordingly," Freud continued, writing in the 1890s when Weber was suffering his breakdown, "I was declaring myself to be one of these cases of '*automatisme ambulatoire.*'" He had become, that is, like a machine:

> It was a hot night and the atmosphere in the completely closed compartment soon became suffocating. My experiences of travelling have taught me that conduct of this ruthless and overbearing kind is a characteristic of people who are travelling on a free or half-price ticket. When the ticket-collector came and I showed him the ticket I had bought at such expense, there fell from the lady's mouth, in haughty and almost menacing tones, the words: 'My husband has a free pass.' . . . the man uttered not a word but sat there motionless. I attempted to sleep.

There, in his iron compartment, Freud said he took revenge.[138]

Alexander Grinstein, who offers this dream, writes that Freud then "relates a case history as an association to his dream"—that of a "thirty-one year old patient with an obsessional neurosis." "He was unable to go out into the street," in Freud's words, "because he was tortured by the fear that he would kill everyone he met. . . . The analysis (which, incidently, led to his recovery) showed that the basis of this distressing obsession was an impulse to murder his somewhat over-severe father."[139]

The obsession itself reflects a primary scene or a primary "history," in that the dream sets the self against another or the ego against the id. It is a conscious scene of estrangement: "Hostile impulses against parents [a wish that they should die] are also an integral constituent of neuroses. They come to light consciously as obsessional ideas." With the alienation readily seen, logic is used and moralism works as a defense. In Freud's words, writing again of the neuroses of defense:

> The conscious ego regards the obsession as something alien to itself: it withholds belief from it, by the help, it seems, of the antithetic idea of conscientiousness, formed long ago. But at this stage [a conviction, as it were, of sin] it may at times happen that the ego is overwhelmed by the obsession—for instance, if the ego is affected by an episodic melancholia. Apart from this, the stage of illness is occupied by the defensive struggle of the ego against the obsession; and this may itself produce new symptoms—those of the *secondary defense*. The obsessional idea, like any other, is attacked by logic, though its compulsive force is unshakable. The secondary symptoms are an intensification of conscientiousness, and a compulsion to examine things and to hoard them. Other secondary symptoms arise if the compulsion is transferred to motor impulses against the obsession—for instance, to brooding, drinking (*dipsomania*), protective ceremonials, *folie du doute*.[140]

The use of compulsive logic becomes clear enough. The question for Freud remained that of an "architecture"—the architecture, say, of hysteria: "scenes . . . arranged in the order of increasing resistance: the more slightly repressed ones come to light first, but only incompletely. . . . The path taken by [analytic] work first goes down in loops to the scenes or to their neighborhood; then from a symptom a little deeper down, and then again from a symptom deeper still. Since most of the scenes converge on the few symptoms, our path makes repeated loops through the background thoughts of the same symptoms." This analytic method becomes the reflection of the neurotic's own "construction of symptoms," here, for example, in plotting out the functioning energy of a system that Freud became apt to diagram, figuring as he was the mechanics: "The repression of impulses seems to produce," for example, "not *variety* but perhaps depression—melancholia. In this way the melancholias are related to obsessional neurosis." The constructions, then, are revealed for what they are only with the word that Freud wrote next to one of his drawings of axes and arrows that depict the depths of repression: "—Work."[141]

Freud was writing at the end of the century, in 1896 and 1897, and he was writing, as he said to Wilhelm Fliess, in "preparation": "I still do not know what has been happening in me. Something from the deepest depths of my own neurosis has ranged itself against any advance. . . . For my writing-paralysis [continues] . . . Has nothing of the kind happened to you? For the last few days it has seemed to me that an emergence from this obscurity is in preparation. . . . The hot weather and overwork." "My mild hysteria (very much aggravated by work, however) has been resolved one piece further: but the rest is still at a standstill." "Things are fermenting in me, but I have finished nothing. . . . I am tormented with grave doubts about my theory of the neuroses. I am very sluggish in my mind and have not succeeded in calming the agitation in my head and feelings." Freud was readily displaying his own mechanics along with his working-through: "But I think it must be done, and is a necessary intermediate stage"—the paralysis, that is, of his "psychical strength," with the "chief patient" himself.[142]

6

American Apocalypse

Max Weber

If my own activity does not belong to me, if it is an alien compulsive activity, to whom does it belong? To a being other than myself. Who is this being? The gods?

Karl Marx, from the "economic-philosophic manuscripts" of 1844, in the translation of Norman O. Brown

The religious root of modern economic humanity is dead; today the concept of the calling is a *caput mortuum* in the world.

Max Weber, *General Economic History* (1919–20)

Puritanism gave expression to a struggle of soul so widespread within the writings of even ordinary men and women that by the end of the nineteenth century, historians—focusing like Royce on the development of cultural consciousness—could argue that the seventeenth century had given birth to the self. In Max Weber's argument, Puritanism had created the idea of personality. Radical Protestantism had pulled the self from webs of custom and had broken the bonds of ritual and ceremony, Weber argued, thereby placing the self alone, like Bunyan's Christian, to pursue its course as an individual. To live without even a semblance of works, to stand alone before God in a state of predestination, to forego the intercession of others such as patriarchs and priests, demanded, for Weber, a wholeness of person that other Protestant churches never conceived of requiring. The aloneness also demanded an incredible amount of work. Weber's portrait stands necessarily as an ideal, and his Puritan as an ideal type, but in itself his argument re-created the idea that Puritanism had given birth to a new character—and in capitalism to a new economy. With Freud, Weber created the understanding that a particular type of modern personality had come into being, a personality that defined—most particularly, Weber thought—the ethic of America.

Weber, at the close of *The Protestant Ethic*, then brought this new personality to its end. The worldly ascetic ethic that he had set upon its course found itself, at the end of its progress, strangled in a cage of its own ironic making. Weber left a nation to wonder at its works:

> The Puritan wanted to work in a calling; we are forced to do so. For when asceticism was carried out of monastic cells into everyday life, and began to dominate worldly morality, it did its part in building the tremendous cosmos of the modern economic order. This order is now bound to the technical and economic conditions of machine production which to-day determine the lives of all the individuals who are born into this mechanism, not only those directly concerned with economic acquisition, with irresistible force. Perhaps it will so determine them until the last ton of fossilized coal is burnt. In Baxter's view the care for external goods should only lie on the shoulders of the "saint like a light cloak, which can be thrown aside at any moment." But fate decreed that the cloak should become an iron cage.

It was Weber who, more than any modern scholar, composed a nation convulsing in its own mechanism. A new nation, having given up all works as a help in its salvation, had created a work before which it finally stood estranged.

Puritanism had in fact given unique expression to the self's individuality when churches enjoined men and women to articulate their lives. Discursively, a revolution had occurred when sectarian groups of English men and women, loosely gathered under the term of Puritan, had separated in various degrees from the Anglican Church and, as sects, now sought a definition for those who had chosen to covenant together. As opposed to the sects of radical Protestantism, it was birth and family, when coupled with certain ceremonial observances and a ritual adherence to creeds, that had defined membership within a church, whether Anglican or Catholic. Puritanism had set itself against this automatism of time and geographic location as fully as it had opposed other apparent "works." Puritanism had placed these spiritual locations within the self, giving to each person the necessity of defining, through a process of articulation, his or her own time and place of membership within the body of Christ. Puritanism had thus required a voluntary search undertaken across an internal space, the profession of an individual experience of conversion that alone, in the words spoken, defined the fellowship of Christ.

No term defined this character that the Puritan had given expression to until, for the opening of the twentieth century, Weber offered his phrase of "the Protestant ethic." American Victorian intellectuals such as James, Royce, and Putnam, writing within a practice of Puritan confession, and searching for meanings to renew the idea of spiritual conversion, offered perspectives that ranged from neurology to psychoanalysis to speak of their own and their nation's personality. Weber brought this discursive practice to completion by speaking now of an ethic. Writing within a developing European sociology, he turned to a question of religious consciousness and culture. By the end of the 1920s, when his writing began to appear in America, particularly within the guiding hands of Talcott Parsons of Harvard, the son of a Congregational minister, his work came to define the American character. When joined with the writings of Freud, Weber's work also came to define the type of mechanistic psychopathology that such a character was said to possess. By enwrapping a cultural psychology around a people, Weber gave time and space to the internal of Protestant psychomachy. Most particularly, Weber placed an ascetic ethic upon America and then drew the irony of the ethic out. He brought America through the course of a conversion, to its end in a new alienation. The psychological struggle that English Puritans had, upon their first migration, placed upon the New England landscape, giving place to their own psychomachy, Weber gave to the whole of the nation's history.

Work and Person

Max Weber's biography and scholarship have become woven together in such a way that his life and writing form—as in the context of modernity from the seventeenth century on they only can form—a single plain of text. His character as an author, in other words, is to give meaning or provide significance for his work. His writing stands not as an anonymous text akin to a medieval narrative, or as a text that Michel Foucault views as without authorial intent,[1] but as scholarship with a self—Weber's own Protestant character—as referent. Revealed as nervously exhausted or neurotic in the Victorians' forming word, Weber himself has become an expression of the Protestant ethic. The "rosy blush" of his Enlightenment, his sanguine figure of history, is seen as consumed in the coals of his own particular production, burned in the humor, as it were, of his melancholy. "Weber," then, has become a plain of discourse of self and script working together, himself a piece of Protestant psychopathology. His writing has become expansive enough to include the "fable" of the author, the modern writer, in Roland Barthes's words, who "inscribes himself in his text as one of his characters."[2]

One portion of this writing, recorded by Weber's wife Marianne, exemplifies the destruction that Weber gave to the Protestant ethic: "I am bone-tired. . . . I accomplish almost *nothing* aside from my lectures; one to two hours a day, then it doesn't go anymore." Weber was writing from Munich in the summer of 1919, explaining to a friend that he felt exhausted and lay under a terrible strain. "'Work,'" he wrote, "is coming along very modestly—one to two hours a day. I am astonishingly worn out, my head is in bad shape. But it will work out. . . . I am preparing [a new edition of] the 'Protestant Ethic' for publication, then I shall take up the 'Economic Ethic.' After that the Sociology." The new edition did come out and other work as well, including two lectures that Weber had presented on the sanctity of vocation. If he rested, however, and felt "tolerably well," remaining to walk in a forest at six o'clock in the morning, bathing in a sunlight "so wonderful" and "calm," then his lingering stood as an "escapade" that came only with cost—"the cost of tremendous laziness; the 'Spirit of Capitalism' is hardly making any progress in addition to the lectures!"[3]

The following spring Weber again expressed his "nervous exhaustion." Now he "had to pay," his wife Marianne explained, "for his extraordinary intensity." Some mention was given of a cardiac spasm—"The machine," as Weber told visitors, "wouldn't work anymore"; lying on his sofa "unable to work," he occupied himself with the meaning of death.[4] In these months preceding his death, in other words, Weber is to be seen as completing the dismantling of his own machinelike works.

Marianne Weber's biography (the source of much that scholars repeat of Weber's personality)—the words of Weber chosen, the intermingling of private letters, scholarship, and past remembered phrases spoken only to Marianne and now printed as dialogue—testify to a confessional discourse. These memories, even contemporary letters so often considered directly reflective of an author's personality, work together with the formal texts that Weber wrote to reveal the character or the cultural spirit of Protestantism. The great amount of psychoanalytically informed scholarship given to uncovering the Protestant character—modern scholarship that began in 1932 when Erich Fromm joined *The Protestant Ethic* with Freud's essay on "Character and Anal Eroticism"[5]—reveals that the pathology of a Protestant or "Puritan ethic" remains significant enough to become rewritten and extended.

A discursive field that had opened in the seventeenth century with the Puritans' disclosure of their own melancholy, has broadened, becoming a whole field of writings on Protestant cultural psychopathology. The presence is this text, however, from which persons can make sense; it is not hidden forces that persons reveal themselves in their writings or a culture that expresses itself in its books, as though writing lies above nature, simply absorbing and marking lower or material forces. This type of cultural discourse, including the fact that an author's life does become interwoven with his own printed words, completes itself in relation to other texts and within a textual region, a "geo-graphy"; the discourse remains universal.[6] It remains to be used, however, by persons who have chosen to write about themselves.

It is inappropriate, then, to speak of a new critical approach to writing, including some versions of structuralism, when writing is used to fashion meaning from lives. Clearly, Christian culture—most especially, one might think, Puritanism, in the sense of the broad publication that Puritanism demanded of the Word—has read lives as it has considered lives composed. ("These *are* the words . . . which were written in the law . . . , and *in* the prophets, and *in* the psalms, concerning me.")

Work and Text

In employing discourse as an interpretant drawing together oppositions such as personal author and formal text, Michel Foucault seeks the embodied text in a function that as a practice relates author and writing, inserting the one into the other.

> It is not possible to reexamine . . . the privileges of the subject? Clearly, in undertaking an internal and architectonic analysis of a work (whether it be a literary text, a philosophical system, or a scientific work) and in delimiting psychological and biographical references, suspicions arise concerning the absolute nature and creative role of the subject. But the subject should not be entirely abandoned. It should be reconsidered, not to restore the theme of an originating subject, but to seize its functions, its intervention in discourse, and its system of dependencies.

Literary critical theory has thus posed the issue to historians as to what constitutes an "author," a "work," and a "text." Turning the question into a matter for the history of ideas, Foucault writes: "The coming into being of the notion of 'author' constitutes the privileged moment of *individualization* in the history of ideas." "Certainly it would be worth examining how the author became individualized in a culture like ours, what status he has been given." Foucault speaks of a "reversal" that "occurred in the seventeenth or eighteenth century. Scientific discourses began to be received for themselves. . . . The author-function faded away. . . . By the same token, literary discourses came to be accepted only when endowed with the author-function." Reconstructing Foucault's essay, three points may be said to follow. First, that "it is not enough to declare that we should do without the writer (the author) and study the work in itself." Second, that the "work" remains a "problematic"—what is to be made, for example, of pieces of writing "left behind" or of disjointed markings that a critic collects and claims constitute a significant text? Third, that the authority newly given to literary texts newly creates a critical function, most typically that of psychologism:

> Nevertheless, these aspects of an individual which we designate as making him an author are only a projection, in more or less psychologizing terms, of the operations that we force texts to undergo, the connections that we make, the traits that we establish as pertinent, the continuities that we recognize, or the exclusions that we practice. All these operations vary according to periods and types of discourse.[7]

The psychoanalytic interpretation of a text, say, is itself a historical location—not a way that may be universally used to get at a particular text, but a part of the modern text that the analyst reads.

In the arguments of Foucault, pathological revelation emerges within historically delimitable fields, and thus one works not to recover a universal unconsciousness but to understand how traditions of writing and intellectual assemblages of thought make things like an unconsciousness appear sensible. One does not return, therefore, from a reflective reading like the cultural recovery of texts, the American approach of myth and symbol, to the older, more rarefied history of ideas, for such a return would erase whatever discursive practice is present, here one of spiritual confession that holds a work and person together. The practice of writing autobiography is to be broadly defined, then, to include a writing like Marianne Weber's biography of her husband and even bits of private letters. This makes for a "field of the text"[8] in which an author can work. In the pathology that Weber expressed of the Protestant ethic, and which he formed as a cultural character, he was not reflecting but making his nature; he was reworking writings of psychopathology inherent in a practice of religious confession. He was forming a composition of himself that reflects a certain "pre-text"[9] and the sense he could produce from that. He was composing his ethic much as the Puritan divines he read had done, placing his melancholy both in his books and in the writing that he was making of his life.

The composition that Marianne Weber offered in her biography continues: Weber's depression momentarily lifted, and writing to Marianne in April of 1920, Weber said that once again he was becoming what she had always feared, "this constantly 'working' grumpy *Ehemann* [husband]. Otherwise everything is going well. . . . Except work. . . . That'll come, too. It has to!"[10] By June, however, Weber became mildly delirious. He was occupied now with "fantasies" or with ideas that he had finally begun working as he thought he should. He remembered an earlier collapse in the last months of 1897, his moment of severest depression when, as Marianne earlier wrote, "he was overloaded with work, [and] an evil thing from the unconscious underground of life stretched out its claws toward him. One evening, after the examination of a student at which he had, as always, worn himself out, he was overcome by total exhaustion, with a feverish head and a strong feeling of tension." It was during that depression that Weber had also lain on the sofa he was resting upon now, examining the same patterns of the paper on the wall, "'but at that time,'" he said, "'I was able to think and I struggled with the good Lord.' . . . Did he feel remorse or have any feelings of guilt? He thought it over and said first hesitantly and then definitely: No." This time the final diagnosis was pneumonia, and Weber died quietly that spring.[11]

Within Marianne Weber's reconstruction of her husband's death, Weber dies from more than a lung infection. Marianne offers the sense that Weber quite literally labored to death, suffering his final collapse for the same reason that the "breakdown" of twenty-two years earlier was said to have occurred, from a nervous exhaustion deriving from a scholar's vast labors.[12] Weber becomes caught within the "irresistible force" that he had described within the most famous of his passages, in the end of his jeremiad, *The Protestant Ethic*, as determining "the lives of all . . . born into this mechanism." "To-day the spirit of religious asceticism—whether finally, who knows?—has escaped from the cage. But victorious capitalism, since it rests on mechanical foundations, needs its support no longer. The rosy blush of its laughing heir, the Enlightenment, seems also to be irretrievably fading, and the idea of duty in one's calling prowls about in our lives like the ghost of dead religious beliefs." His rational ascetic had built such an incredible machine that it had estranged its own motives. The irony for Marianne Weber was now "this complete halting," as she wrote of her husband, "of the precious machine."[13]

Marianne Weber's published biography mirrors Weber's completion: lines on pages are graphically set and justified in print to describe the mechanics that had failed to justify. Marianne stands as interpreter to Weber as the interpreter stands to Christian in *The Pilgrim's Progress*: "stay (said the *Interpreter,*) till I have shewed thee a little more, and after that, thou shalt go on thy way. So he took him by the hand again, and led him into a very dark room, where there sat a Man in an Iron Cage." Marianne offers Biblical meaning for this sight of the cage—the spiritual promise entailed in acknowledging one's bondage and affliction: "For he hath broken the gates of brass, and cut the bars of iron in sunder."

Marianne's narrative reflects neither a collapse of *fin de siècle* society nor, in the image of Ferdinand Töennies that Weber himself closely followed, an objective historical alienation, or a transition from *Gemeinschaft* to *Gesellschaft*. Her narrative expresses something other than what Weber had sought along with his generation of European scholars, the consciousness of society that H. Stuart Hughes has discussed so well[14]: a *Weltanschauung,* a *Geist,* a collective consciousness or unconsciousness that, as a cultural personality, is thought of as either reflecting or informing productive modes and nature. What is evidenced is material, but it is itself a way of writing. What is expressed is discourse, the text of such psychologism itself.

The structure of conversion entails an irony: first, establishing a process of salvation as a path charted to heaven, and then, tearing the process apart. The steps of conversion become, in Stanley E. Fish's phrase, "self-consuming artifacts."[15] The consumption reflects the Calvinist demand that the self and its works be displayed before the works become the waste they are. As Fish culls from a close reading of *The Pilgrim's Progress* (leaving aside the whole of Bunyan's own self-recorded obsessional life), no progress occurs in the sense that no relation exists for Christian between the geographic distance he covers and linear time. There is no way of saying just where Christian is, no more than there are actual historical locations in Weber's ironic text of Protestantism. In that text, Weber moves his ascetic as he moved himself: first from an obsessively constructed monastery to the world, and then to the ascetic's ending in a "compulsion" of high capitalism. Weber folds his text back upon itself, in other words, back to beginnings in other cells of despair. What has begun in a cage ends there, for in the end, progress is erased in order to create a timeless space for faith.

With Weber, a writing of Puritan conversion has broadened to become a whole cultural narrative. The narrative weaves culture with self to the extent of composing Weber's life just as he had worked to compose himself, writing of himself within the language that Puritanism offered, the measures of conversion against which Weber could "de-scribe" himself, or write from, thereby making his life "work." His writing becomes a testament: the "storie of those things, whereof we are fully persuaded." "And he began . . . , and interpreted unto them in all the Scriptures the things which were *written* of him."

This formation of personality argues the use of a typology, for the composing and the reading of a life is accomplished in relation to past texts. A person fulfills "pre-scriptions" when he discovers his self in writing. Through the words of interpreters, Weber provides a most important example of using writing in just this manner:

> During the course of his studies in ancient Judaism, in 1916 and 1917, he was profoundly moved by the analogies he saw between the situation of the ancient Hebrew peoples and modern Germany. It was not only the public and historical situation he saw as parallel; in the personality of many prophets and in their irregular and compulsive psychic states, particularly of Jeremiah, Weber saw features he felt resembled his own. When he read passages of this manuscript to his wife, she was touched in immediately seeing that this reading was an indirect analysis of himself.

What Weber described from Jeremiah were "compulsive acts," "compulsion," and the possibility "of a specific 'personality type'" involving "emotional depressions and *idées fixes*," the last, again, a psychiatric phrase for obsessions. What he valued from Jeremiah concerned "a strong devaluation of all ritual," a reaction against "massive ritualism," above all a "magic" analogous here to a "machine." What he celebrated of the Yahwe prophets stood "superior" to magic and ritual law: the "'call,'" the "*berith*-conception," "this workaday ethic."

> Perhaps it was only in this fashion that Weber, who since childhood was incapable of directly revealing himself, could communicate his own self-image. Thus, what was most personal to him is accessible and at the same time hidden by the objectifications of his work.[16]

Here in texts reflecting themselves—Weber's manuscript, Marianne Weber's biography, a commentary on the biography by Hans Gerth and C. Wright Mills, and then returning to read Weber's *Ancient Judaism*—sense is made of Weber; and Weber, through the prophetic writings, could make sense of himself. The revelation remains "direct," for rather than hiding himself, Weber was making an understanding of himself, here in past scripts. His "work and person" become related not in an interior boring to explain the production of an author's pen but, again, in an exterior delimitation.

Weber's Collapse

Weber completed *The Protestant Ethic* after he had made a visit to America in 1904. In America, he wrote, one could observe certain matters "in their most massive and original shape." He completed the essay after a tour through Oklahoma and then through Chicago, this last an industrial wilderness ("the whole tremendous . . . like a man whose skin has been peeled off and whose intestines are seen at work"). And he completed the essay after he had spoken with William James and read James's *Varieties of Religious Experience.*[17]

In those lectures, again, James had moved his religious genius through a process of conversion. He had taken his saint from once-born innocence through panic fear and crisis, a conviction of sin or melancholy, and then offered a step of worldly ascetic discipline, the building of a personal and social economy of saintliness. James had then ended by crossing work out. Having inserted himself into his own narrative ("William's melancholy about the universe is due to bad digestion [the disbelievers will say]—probably his liver is torpid"), and having described himself as coming out of the "wilderness," by which he meant America, and into the "dreamland" of Edinburgh, James spoke in "Conclusions" of a "kind of aimless weather, doing and undoing, achieving no proper history, and leaving no result." Nature, he finished, "appears to cancel herself," crossing herself out.[18]

Weber re-created this spiritual movement. Among the first writings Weber published following six years of incapacitating depression, his essay on the Protestant ethic was meant to end his own sighting of terror. The essay, which demands the saint's removal from self-imposed seclusion, was begun after Weber's own massive collapse of 1897.

After his father's death in the summer of 1897, Weber had become severely depressed. In Freudian terms, he had begun a long struggle with work inhibition. Unable to teach or to write, he had left his university, gone in and out of asylums, and had attempted long vacations. With the little energy that he said remained, he began to study religious values of rationality. In an early passage of his *Protestant Ethic* he wrote of a Pietist's "mental concentration," "strict economy," "cool self-control"—attitudes that his depression had seemingly dashed.[19]

During his collapse, Weber pulled within himself. His hands shook, his back ached, his nerves jangled at small noises, his sleep suffered. He spoke of exhaustion, broken nerves, and an inability to speak.[20] "The inability to speak is purely physical, the nerves break down, and when I look at my lecture notes I simply can't make sense of them." "All mental functions and a part of the physical ones fail him," his wife wrote. "If he nonetheless forces them to work, chaos threatens him, a feeling as though he could fall into the vortex of an overexcitement that would throw his mind into darkness."[21] His doctor prescribed hydrotherapy.[22]

Others variously debated the reason for Weber's depression, seeking the natural causes for what was taken as a physical collapse. As Mary James had thought of her son William during his crisis, and as Christiana thinks of her husband prior to Christian's leaving the City of Destruction behind, so Weber's mother considered him quite simply a hypochondriac.[23] Weber and the doctors he consulted attributed the illness to overwork, the alienists' then favored way of making sense of such breakdowns. In 1892 Weber himself had spoken of working too much: "an overestimation of my capacity to work." But now, five years later, with the death of his father having presumably shattered his world, Weber still labored to manage the smallest details of his life. He failed and, in the words of Marianne, interpreted an acute irritability over some minor points of vacation planning "as a sign of nervous exhaustion. . . . On the return trip the strained organism reacts with an illness. Weber becomes feverish and feels threatened." With a "strong feeling of tension," Weber collapsed at the age of thirty-one.[24] He was one of James's "sporadic adult cases."

This is the age of crisis that Erik Erikson's great men suffer—an experience, it is supposed, that should normally erupt in adolescence. Here the legal fear and conviction of sin of the Puritans is translated into the melancholic crisis of the Victorian intellectual. Weber, given an extended leave of absence from his university, remained nearly incapacitated for almost seven years, until 1904.[25]

It becomes a matter of further interpretation if one moves past the physical explanation of Weber's collapse to seek not structural configurations but genetic causations.[26] One may move, in other words, from the organic (overwork) to the Oedipal. One may place the Oedipal struggle either within the context of Weber's family or, more ambitiously, within the field of a whole European generational battle.[27] Coincidentally and almost wondrously in Freud's own terms, Weber's father had died shortly after a bitter quarrel with his son, a quarrel involving Weber's mother.[28] Weber's own illness followed. Strains do appear to have existed within the Weber household, for the piety and the quiet religiosity of Weber's mother more than once clashed with his father's genteel yet autocratic living.[29] Weber himself spoke of matters that had "completely alienated" him from his father,[30] and spoke too of the guilt that he attributed to a seemingly fatal decision, one that involved a vacation the mother was to spend with her son, that he had finally made to defend his mother before his father's demands.[31]

Contradictions marked the Weber household as well, where, in a post-Freudian interpretation, one may read parental behavior as confusing Weber as much as creating his anger. If the piety of the mother did clash with the anger and moodiness of the father, then the confrontation could only have contributed to Weber's doubts, doubts that come with the inability of any child to take sides easily while parents collide. Within the evidence of parental conflict, Weber found a contradiction in his father's behavior. His father, he wrote, "was always sanguine," and yet his "mood was often subject to sudden change from little external cause." Such whimsical moods could again create doubt and only be feared—here, the capriciousness that left a "painful impression" on the mother that the son had to consider.[32]

The ability to face out uncertainty, which remains at the heart of Weber's celebration of Puritanism, is the ability to engage the image of one's world as a jungle, the tangle created for the child, Andras Angyl argues, by conflicting and seemingly chaotic parental moods and decisions. For Angyl, such an image lies in the eye of a fearful, compulsive person, one who in terror would try to order nature completely.[33] It is an ascetic effort such as Weber tried, one that in American literature (in *Walden*, for example) eventually suffers its own collapse.

In the years of his breakdown Weber, in his reflection, was indolently living off the resources of his family and university. In his own term he had suffered an "emotional depression," one that he believed, or that his doctors informed him, only time and rest could cure. Weber hoped to regain a discipline through another physic by working his way out from the erratic moods that he said his father and now he himself experienced. "We may tolerate no fantastical surrender to unclear and mystical moods in our souls," Weber later wrote. "For when feeling rises high, you must fetter it, to be able to steer with sobriety." After the worst period of his depression, Weber began to study asceticism as a form "opposite" to "a positively hysterical character." He looked to an ethic of "strict and temperate discipline"—"the systematic life of holiness of the Puritan." He spoke now of those engaged "in the ascetic struggle for certainty."[34]

If overwork is irresponsive to other than a somatic interpretation of a breakdown and appears, especially for the psychoanalytically informed historian, too naive a cause for Weber's melancholic depression, work may nevertheless become as significant as Oedipal drives by becoming itself a full sign. If one abandons the search for the cause of psychopathology and studies instead the formation of a discursive plain of description, then meaning becomes attached to objects rather than revealed by them. Meaning is not simply found, but becomes a historically variable social production. Rather than searching Weber's unconsciousness, one watches as he manipulates his own work, which includes his own writing, within conventions to make a meaningful account of himself. Foucault, in speaking of "commentary"—a process of interpretation that says that something else (a remainder) has yet to be deciphered, that something still lies hidden behind the text—writes: "Is it not possible to make a structural analysis of discourses that would evade the fate of commentary [that of an infinite regression of interpretations, especially a regression of psychological interpretations] by supposing no remainder, nothing in excess of what has been said, but only the fact of its historical appearance." Foucault seeks neither a disembodied history of ideas nor a psychologically revealed reading of history—neither a timeless form nor an as yet unrevealed text, neither a universal aesthetic nor an author's hidden intention—to center a history of thought, but the arrangements that persons make between words and things. The question is how persons make an interpretation that draws together the object and the sign, the signified and the signifier. Foucault watches as interpreters point to what is behind the lines of texts, saying, as if to Christian, what for all time is meant. He watches, then, for the transformations of this interpretation as the relation made between things spoken and things said to have been thought changes:

> What counts in the things said by men is not so much what they may have thought or the extent to which these things represent their thoughts, as that which systematizes them from the outset, thus making them thereafter accessible to new discourses and open to the task of transforming them.[35]

Following his depression, Weber used familiar schedules to carve a certain economy out of his bewilderment. He set the significance of his labor against the "chaos" and the "vortex" that his illness had expressed. He structured his life carefully after his visit to America. He worked only six hours a day, while at the same time he refused the emotional entanglements of public lectures and social occasions and minimized his relationships with family and friends. Though he complained of slowness, as James incessantly did, following his depression Weber produced a great volume of his most important writing.[36] The depression, in other words, expressed the end of a cycle through which Weber had moved: an intense grasp for assurance which, when the grasp failed, could bring the sense of impending disaster.

Weber's personal mechanics are to be found within an extended text—a writing that moves from his own reported words to those words as explicated within secondary texts. "If I don't work until one o'clock [in the morning] I can't be a professor," Weber told his wife in 1894. When he was a student in 1884–85, Marianne Weber wrote: "he continues the rigid work discipline, regulates his life by the clock, divides the daily routine into exact sections for the various subjects, saves in his way." Weber described the function his work was to serve during the decade preceding his depression:

> When I had finally come to an inner harmony [through marriage] after years of a nasty sort of agony, I feared a deep depression. It has not occurred, to my mind, because, through continual work I did not let my nervous system and brain come to rest. Quite apart from the natural need for work, therefore, I am most unwilling to allow a really marked pause in my work; . . . I can't risk allowing the present composure . . . to be transformed into relaxation.

Weber routinized himself, to such an extent that he has become the exemplum of his own ascetic character type. He then probed for the meaning of the magic that he thought his routine contained. He considered, that is, the mechanics of himself, the signification of his own working.[37]

Weber's Obsessive Actions

Weber's habits of labor, along with the descriptions that he gave of himself and those provided by others—accounts of his conscience and forceful temperament—resemble the type of character that Freud was calling compulsive. These stand as the architectonics of a particular self-formation, however—behavior that signaled for Freud a character type, and for Weber an ethic. Neither considered the formation irrational; indeed, Weber viewed the repression required to hold such an ethic in place as a sign of productive activity. For Freud, the significance remained the same, at least as regarded the work that his character type performed. Freud found a crossing stratum running beneath the character, however, the faults of which could erupt and break into the overlying character, cutting his type into a neurosis: an obsessive-compulsive malaise. For the ill-productive labors that distinguish the neurosis, or again the behavior that Freud referred to as "obsessive actions," such as meticulously performed ceremonies, Freud sought unconscious significance. He sought to read the obsessive action by looking for reflective evidence of the unconscious wish that the action represented, symbolized, stood for, or replaced. The ideational manipulations that also distinguished the neurosis—thoughts the neurotic himself gave little significance to, except that he possessed them often in fear—also appeared to Freud to hold hidden meaning: to represent, in fact, an actual reverse of the moralistic character that the obsessive enjoyed. Freud could view the obsessions along with the compulsive acts as distorted signs or refractions of the unconscious desire that the neurotic, like a primitive, actually implied. Freud linked the neurotic and the primitive, for whether in the form of compulsions and obsessions or of totem and taboo, the same chains of significance were repressed: the attempt, through such works, to control a deed of primordial violence.

For Freud, repression never expressed the willful endeavor that it did for Weber. Weber is often held apart from Freud, as indeed he held himself, speaking as he did for what he thought of as the efficacy rather than sickness of repression. Weber nevertheless adhered to a similar discursive architecture. He also presented an underlying irrationality—his "other-worldly" ascetic—a psychological formation that gives significance to the reversal of meaning that his worldly ascetic enjoys. Weber defined his Puritan, and his own Protestant temperament, by this other-worldly difference, "psychological peculiarities" that run parallel to his this-worldly ethic. Behind the Protestant and his capitalist material production sits this peculiar psychological cell, its door slammed tight. Within the writing he made of himself, however, these irrationalities were opened, and Weber is revealed in the pathology these otherworldly eruptions entail.

Weber's depressions were unproductive enough, "irrational" within the terms he set for that word. Such depressions for Weber were akin to a mystic's or a hysteric's emotive elations and collapse, or to a Catholic's cycle of sin and expiation. Then, too, the question remained of the irrationality behind his ascetic's life, the pathology of "magic," that is, that his Protestant ascetic so adamantly opposed.

Weber was called neurotic, and his depressions are proof enough of that. As his own writing unfolds, however, it becomes apparent that

Weber considered more than depression and more than the loosely defined "hysteric" moods that he so feared as undercutting his life. The symptoms other than depression that bothered Weber in a clinical sense have remained unknown,[38] though evidence is present—or rather presented—in an extended public text. Weber was using his work to defend himself from depression and perhaps from sex (his closest psychological observer has argued that Weber left his marriage to Marianne unconsummated).[39] Although Marianne Weber destroyed a document in which her husband described his symptoms for a psychiatrist,[40] she did record that Weber likened his troubles to those of Jeremiah. In his study of ancient Judaism, again, Weber found in Jeremiah a mental pathology that he thought resembled his own.[41]

It is more correct to say that Weber produced from his reading in Jeremiah a mental pathology that gave significance to his suffering. Otherwise ill-defined behavior could be focused by becoming historically significant. Jeremiah offered Weber a text that he could read his life into, as the words impressed and made sense to him. One is tempted to say that in piecing together certain works—Marianne's own *Max Weber* and portions of Weber's *Ancient Judaism*—one has uncovered a hitherto concealed symptom in Weber. This of course has not occurred; rather one has, in the very assembling of texts—in a reading of *Ancient Judaism* now in the light of Marianne's biography—read a discursive field. One has redefined what is to be meant by a text, extending the definition from an enclosed book temporally defined by a publishing date (a date hard enough to define in relation to Weber's own rewritings and complex publishing history) to a set of books, one of Weber's self and the other of Weber's scholarship. A new temporal definition now encloses a wider field. This new text, by intermingling self and theology in a confession of a small piece of mental pathology, forms a spiritual autobiography.

For Freud, obsessions and compulsions buried their significance in the unconsciousness, becoming themselves but distorted reflections of the violence such magical acts replaced. For Freud, such acts (like taboos) guarded the consumed father, and defended sons through the sons' use of incredibly precise ritual detail. For Weber, such rituals pointed consciously to ethical questions of law and faith. Rituals of otherwise confusing significance pointed consciously to questions as to whether the self had enwrapped itself in irrationalities, or whether it could emerge from such magic into disinterested vocations, into callings bonded to faith. As Weber wrote in "The Social Psychology of the World Religions":

> Things have been quite different where the religiously qualified . . . have combined into an ascetic sect, striving to mould life in this world according to the will of God. To be sure, two things were necessary before this could happen in a genuine way. First, the supreme and sacred value must not be of a contemplative nature. Second, such a religion must, so far as possible, have given up the purely magical or sacramental character of the *means* of grace [magical asceticism]. For these means always devalue action in this world . . . and they link the decision about salvation to the success of processes which are *not* of a rational everyday nature. . . . The religious virtuoso can be placed in the world as the instrument of a God and cut off from all magical means of salvation. At the same time, it is imperative for the virtuoso that he "prove" himself before God, as being called *solely* through the ethical quality of his conduct in this world. This actually means that he "prove" himself to himself as well.

Not "merely ceremonious, ritualist, and conventional particulars," not "senseless brooding and events and long[ing] for the dreamless sleep," but a rational affirmation of the world through work confirms salvation—"methodical and rationalized routine-activities of workaday life in the service of the Lord. Rationally raised into a vocation, everyday conduct becomes the locus for proving one's state of grace."

In his portrayal of the "Psychological Peculiarities of the Prophets," Weber described Jeremiah as a prophet combatting magic, visions, and "dream interpretations," a clear enough reference to Weber's opinion of Freud. Jeremiah lived as a speaker rather than as a passive or emotional seer, a prophet who felt compelled to speak:

> One meets with compulsive acts, above all, with compulsive speech. Jeremiah felt split into a dual ego. He implored his God to absolve him from speaking. Though he did not wish to, he had to say what he felt to be inspired words not coming from himself. Indeed his speech was experienced by him as horrible fate. . . . Unless he spoke he suffered terrible pains, burning heat seized him and he could not stand up under the heavy pressure without relieving himself by speaking. Jeremiah did not consider a man to be a prophet unless he knew this state and spoke from compulsion rather than "from his own heart."[42]

Weber called some of Jeremiah's acts compulsions as well: the wearing of an iron yoke, the smashing of a jug, the burying of a belt, the later digging up the belt's putrid remains—"strange activities thought to be significant as omens." Weber refused interpretation, however; indeed, he refused the "act of interpretation *per se*," the "obscure and ambiguous" signs that pointed only to the prophet as type, to *his* mission as an interpreter. The significance of the prophet lay not in the meaning but in the possession of his signs, in his calling which used unfathomable signs to erase magical significance. There existed in the prophet's images of iron—iron pans, iron yokes, iron horns—and the eating of filth, motifs of hardness and decay. Images also formed of bonds and destructions: the wearing of yokes, the smashing of vessels, the decay of belts, the inflicting of bodily wounds—prophetic demands for tearing apart constructions or for tasting decay, for being, as it seemed, within a cage besmeared with dirt, caught in the machinations of a design that barely contained the filth behind.[43]

Whatever one means by "compulsion" or the obverse word "obsession," it becomes clear that Weber considered the prophet as necessarily driven—indeed, as vocationally defined—by these alien drives, himself forced to act like any running machine. Marx gave such alienation to the end of the capitalist consciousness. Weber gave the compulsion to the mouth of anyone crying from such a hell, here from Israel's own "bureaucratic machine." This is not to be considered evidence of a malaise that Weber suffered: "This is not the place," he wrote, "to classify and interpret, as far as that is possible, the various physiological, and possibly pathological states of the prophets. Attempts made thus far . . . are not convincing. It affords, furthermore, no decisive interest for us." But the compulsion becomes a meaningful text in that for Weber it could make sense by uniting his symptoms with those of the prophet with whom he so identified. In the midst of his own estrangement, Weber stood like Jeremiah, this "prophet of doom," "ridiculed, threatened, spit upon"—an image that Weber at times gave to himself and that his Puritan, standing in the midst of a great American desert, had also given to himself.[44]

Weber continued his analysis. He declared that for a prophet such as Jeremiah there had never existed the wish to lose control or to reside in mystic vision or, for that matter, to dream dreams or hear mysterious voices. Rather, as for Weber's Puritan, a drive had started toward "clarity and assurance." This quest for assurance and the rigidity involved came at the expense of, or held beneath it, behavior that, unlike the vague compulsive acts mentioned above, better delineates in Weber's reading a mental disorder. Like the sociologist just prior to his long depression—when Marianne recorded that every small thing seemed in need of control, and Weber grasped to order the smallest particulars of his world—so the prophet had fretted over the minutiae of life: "The typical prophet apparently found himself in a constant state of tension and of oppressive brooding in which even the most banal things of everyday life could become frightening puzzles, since they might somehow be significant."[45]

Significance becomes attached haphazardly as words and things normally scattered now link themselves in incredible chains of signs. Portents, meanings, omens, all could be located, in Weber's frame of reference, beyond the limits of a normal grammar, within a swirl of colliding sounds and interpretations. Moving now, however, in the sections of his text from "psycho-patholo(gy)" to "prophetic ethic," Weber stressed a way out of endless interpretation. The prophet now refuses to use "magical compulsion" to relieve his confusion, meaningless rituals that for Weber had come in the face of meaningless signs. Weber's prophet turns instead to an early form of occupation that for Weber faithfully replaces the magic: a productive work, calling, or vocation that effaces both magic and depression. For the prophet, the calling—not immaterial ritual—combats sin and, most important, frightening obsessions, compelled ideas that like the acts can pain while they still preoccupy and absurdly cement a mind: "Jeremiah's tender soul suffered grievously from emotional depressions and *idées fixes*," Weber finally concluded, "but he disciplined himself by force of his calling to a desperate heroism."[46]

Earlier Weber had written of his own work as a defense against depression. Now, in addition, he was writing of work as defending against an *idée fixe*, one of the less ambiguous phrases in turn-of-the-century psychiatry. It was one of the most common terms for an obsession—the hurtful, criminal, or blasphemous expression that one cannot banish from the mind. Weber had identified himself with an ancient text, if not with his Puritans' conceiving of their own melancholy, then with the malaise of the prophet for whom the Puritans so often spoke. He was reconstructing Jeremiah, and constructing himself, in modern terms within the oldest of prophetic psychomythologies.

Weber's reading, then, is to declare a psychopathology for any religionist who tries to make signs that are not common sense. Weber made Jeremiah's words unreadable, quite the opposite of Freud's approach to such ritual in *Totem and Taboo*. If words and things, meanings and materials, or sounds and conceptions—even such obvious signs as an iron yoke and putrid remains—fail to hold together through the interpretation of symbolism (what a sign represents), then the interpreter's production of meaning can itself become significant, rather than the interpreter's use of a particular sign. Meanings that become attached to banal everyday accidents, significance that is given to absurd intruding thoughts, worked for Weber as the psychological peculiarities of Old Testament prophets compelled by the Law. The prophet acts only through magical forces playing upon him from without. Weber, of course, attached significance to all this. The unreadable text he made a readable sign. He wrote of the inefficacy of such law itself, the unproductive labors that had been required for the law's interpretation. He wrote of the entangling alliances that persons make between words and things, immaterial productions that enchain persons in ritual circles of magic and superstition. Such expressions, repeated to the self while fixed in the mind, make for senseless acts performed again and again as if holding the self in check. Weber's reading of this text as a pathology, and his making a sign of that, allowed him to create a difference for Jeremiah. The reading allowed Weber to hold work or the calling against irrational compulsion, since the rationality of work, as a vocation, had erased such immaterial production. The psychopathology Weber spoke of—this particular piece of mental pathology of the *idée fixe* and the compulsive act that otherwise hold little significance—assumed incredible proportions by defining that which the prophet, as later Weber's Puritan, had worked against: the ritual law that precedes the giving up to faith, the prophetic Law of the Old Testament that had to be closed before the opening could be made into callings undertaken only in faith. For a moment in time in the protostruggle of Jeremiah, then in the opening light of the Reformation, rationality held no magic. Work remained unpossessed of the demonology that a later capitalism would, ironically, re-embrace, the commodity fetish and estranged labor that Marx, for example, portrayed.

The Worldly Ascetic Ethic

Erik Erikson has written of this movement in the life of his great men, extending Weber's text: a movement, again, from "works" to "work" or from "vow" to "vocation." When Erikson writes of man's reliance on magic—meaning, in particular, a neurotic's reliance on superstition—to control his world, he stresses the damage which occurs to one's sense of wholeness and identity:

> The dangers to man's identity posed by a confused realism allied with a popular demonology are obvious. The influences from the other world are brought down to us as negotiable matter; man is able to learn to master them by magical thinking and action. But momentary victories of magic over an oppressive superreality do not, in the long run, either develop man's moral sense or fortify a sense of the reality of his identity on this globe.

When Weber wrote of man's use of ritual to atone for sin, he stressed the same point, arguing that the periodic relief of fear which superstition allows opposes the formation of a "total personality pattern":

The vouchsafing of grace always entails the subjective release of the person in need of salvation; it consequently facilitates his capacity to bear guilt and . . . largely spares him the necessity of developing an individual planned pattern of life based on ethical foundations. The sinner knows that he may always receive absolution by engaging in some occasional religious practice or by performing some religious rite. It is particularly important that sins remain discrete actions against which other discrete deeds may be set up as compensations or penances. Hence, value is attached to concrete individual acts rather than to the total personality pattern which has been produced by asceticism.

Weber returned to Germany from America in 1904 and completed his greatest essay, *The Protestant Ethic and the Spirit of Capitalism*. "Stimulation and activity of the brain without mental strain is the only means of healing," he remarked upon the end of his American travel. He thought his health now good and felt he could, in 1904, complete things that he had formerly thought impossible.[47]

Weber composed the *"innerweltliche Askese,"*[48] the life of monastic virtue to be led beyond one's own self-imposed chamber, by describing an asceticism requiring that one construct some sort of "disenchanted" view. This was to be Weber's scientific ethic in which "no mysterious incalculable forces come into play, but rather . . . [one in which] one can in principle, master all things by calculation. This means the world is disenchanted"—freed, that is, from magical interpretations. As Weber would use this science to free inquiry, so he felt that his inner-worldly ascetic had freed himself from "spirits," "magical means," "mysterious powers," creating the world view to which, Weber wrote, early radical Protestantism had given completion.

That great historic process in the development of religions, the elimination of magic from the world which had begun with the old Hebrew prophets and, in conjunction with Hellenistic scientific thought, had repudiated all magical means to salvation as superstition and sin, came here to its logical conclusion. The genuine Puritan even rejected all signs of religious ceremony at the grave and buried his nearest and dearest without song or ritual in order that no superstition, no trust in the effects of magical and sacramental forces on salvation, should creep in.

Weber desired to study empirically this new rationality in man, an attempt, as he thought, to hold the demonic by the throat.[49]

Weber gave his most eloquent expression of this consciousness in the years 1904 and 1905, when he published *Die protestantische Ethik und der 'Geist' des Kapitalismus*. The essay was an opening expression for a new discipline that Weber called a *"Religionssoziologie."* The term was his own.[50] Beyond looking at a single religious form in terms of its social and economic behavior (and indeed, though Weber denied it, looking at

Protestantism in terms of its "neurology and psychology" as well[51]), Weber's essay provided the image of the "*protestantische Ethik*" itself, for that phrase was neither current in the vocabulary nor, as yet, was it reified. In a moment of clarity, as Marianne remembered, Weber conflated history and crystalized themes, drawing together already abstracted types (Pietism, Puritanism, asceticism, sect) until, for the opening of this century, his ideal type was made.[52] The sociologist had formed his ethic by offering a whole economy as *Geist*, arguing the existence of a historically unique spirit of labor and restraint. The Protestant ethic, Weber imagined, existed as a singular quest for "rational" behavior.

Rationality was not a new expression. When sorted out and conceptually seized, however, rationality, as Foucault writes, calls for an other. Rationality requires a reversal of image (as in a camera obscura) or a farther nature or frontier. Like Henry Adams's pile of coal hidden behind the dynamo, rationality demands a difference.[53] If placed in time and given origin (the Reformation), then, whether as a new mechanics, a Protestant ethic, a Cartesian graph, or simply a "machine," rationality requires a parallel, foreign history that offers the other side to the taxonomic sheet and its grid. The irrational too therefore begins, rising with the eruption of the self, both faults of which Weber plotted to the seventeenth century and measured with the new autobiographies upon which he relied. One should not view it as a matter of mere interest, then, that economic rationality received its most thorough sifting by a scholar psychologically revealed.

Weber constructed his essay on the Protestant ethic by equating "capitalism" with "worldly asceticism," choosing the latter term to emphasize the restraint and renunciation that any enormous enterprise requires. The first term, capitalism, remained in one sense merely a device, a convenient expression for the production that such an ascetic discipline had created. Capitalism arose, Weber wrote in the most powerful of his images (other than that of the iron cage itself), when asceticism emerged from its cell, when the Reformation carried the order of the monastery—the first institution that Weber believed man had run according to the dictates of time, efficiency, and ritual perfection—to the marketplace.

> Christian asceticism, at first fleeing from the world into solitude, had already ruled the world which it had renounced from the monastery and through the Church. . . . Now it strode into the market-place of life, slammed the door of the monastery behind it, and undertook to penetrate just that daily routine of life with

its methodicalness, to fashion it into a life in the world, but neither of nor for this world.[54]

This image commands Weber's essay and draws an irony for his reader: this removal from the chamber (as Emerson had demanded in his *Nature*) and the slamming of the chamber's door behind, then the entry into a strange arena—most pre-eminently, for Weber, America—which awaits to become a new cage.

Weber's finest psychological interpreter, Arthur Mitzman, has argued that *The Protestant Ethic* begins "those years when [Weber's] theoretical defense of the ascetic code began to crumble." Mitzman equates Weber's worldly ascetic with the authoritarianism of Weber's father, the iron cage that becomes, in literal translation, the "housing hard as steel." It is the house, that is, of the father.[55] This reading, however, demands that the critic equate two of the three types of capitalism of which Weber wrote—the ascetic Protestant and the high—and ignore Weber's description of the Puritan saint as, most particularly, "anti-authoritarian."[56] The equation—simply saying that Weber was writing about "capitalism"—remains analogous to the reading that Erich Fromm made in 1932 when, in an influential essay, Fromm equated the whole of the "Protestant ethic" with the acquisitive character of Freud's anal compulsive character type. Fromm made the link despite Weber's opening remarks that "the impulse to acquisition, pursuit of gain, of money, of the greatest possible amount of money, has in itself nothing to do with capitalism"—that is, with Weber's idea of an ascetic capitalism. Weber's Puritan was not given to "hoarding."[57] Both readings, however, are not simply misreadings; as modern psychological readings, they have informed a good deal of popular discourse on the Protestant ethic—important (and, one should think, almost inevitable) discourse, in that these additions take the Protestant or "Puritan ethic" back to earlier psychological charges, back to Robert Burton's *Anatomy of Melancholy*, for example,[58] and to the Puritans' own charges against themselves as the slandered and sick of the world.

In terms of a specific expression of obsessional psychopathology—whether of melancholy in the seventeenth-century understanding or of "*Zwangsneurose*" in Freud's formulation—the Puritan spiritual autobiography had opened the self to expressions of a ritually encumbered conscience, the *Grace Abounding to the Chief of Sinners* that Weber knew to be the pre-eminent example. The "meere excrementall" of the melancholy humor had interworked themes of psychopathology and theology by using obsessional ideation as a sign of the irrational satanic temptation waiting at the edge of spiritual conversion,[59] the temptation Satan used to create false impressions of the conscience of sin which, along with the ritual acts, expressed a merely legal fear and a legal way of getting out of sin. Obsession, again a rare point of psychopathology,[60] had become a way to distinguish such fear from a conscience of sin as sin, or to know of that which was not true sorrow. The attempt ritually to rid the self of its fear defined the kind of estranged works the self undertook prior to accepting the sacrifice of Christ.

Weber drew this writing to completion not by disparaging his Protestant ascetic but by unfolding its irony. His worldly ascetic saint, having rid himself of magic and having combatted doubt as but another form of temptation (one works simply for the work there is to do), begins to create wealth, making goods quite against his own intentions. As Weber quoted from John Wesley:

> "For religion must necessarily produce both industry and frugality, and these cannot but produce riches. But as riches increase, so will pride, anger, and love of the world in all its branches. How then is it possible that Methodism, that is, a religion of the heart, though it flourishes now as a green bay tree, should continue in this state? For the Methodists in every place grow diligent and frugal; consequently they increase in goods. Hence they proportionately increase in pride, in anger, in the desire of the flesh, the desire of the eyes, and the pride of life. So, although the form of religion remains, the spirit is swiftly vanishing away. Is there no way to prevent this—this continual decay. . . ."[61]

Weber's saint creates the machines and thereby the materials of his own destruction, so that in the end he finds himself lost as to the meaning of the ethic that had brought about his labor. The alienation comes as a new temptation: unintended vanity in which, as in Vanity-Fair, there sits a new cage.

The Protestant Ethic, then, becomes expressive not of Weber's turn against his own "work asceticism" of which Marianne wrote,[62] but of a narrative movement of conversion. Weber is to be seen as leaving a certain irrational work behind—his crisis and depression, certainly, and perhaps particular obsessional manipulations. He is to emerge from this enclosed chamber, psychopathologically wrought, to write of the Puritans' calling not as a means but as an expression of their faith. From "the ascetic death-in-life of the cloister," he brings his Puritan out of ill-productive works akin to the works (and ill work) of his own crisis and depression.[63] He brings his Puritan from an asceticism that can strive for such control that men are, in effect, incapacitated—an estrangement against which, in text, both Weber and his Puritan work.

As Weber wrote, such an estrangement is a "magical asceticism" that demands a host of encumbering devices. It requires the otherworldly production of things like fastings, chastisements, mortifications, taboos, petty rituals, precise ceremonies, prayers, chants, sanctioned thoughts—behaviors all of which disallow the production of rational material labor.[64] In an assumption that grounds the whole of Weber's argument as to why the Protestant chose to work ascetically, the guilt of all men must in one way or another be relieved. Guilt must somehow be read or understood. At times Weber looked almost nostalgically to Catholicism and its periodic use of oral confessions and priests (whom he considered magicians) to relieve guilt. He considered Catholicism as organically relieving such pressure by mating the person to the natural rhythms of his environment, matching sin and repentance to the movements of the seasons, making for a cyclical as opposed to a linear (or Puritan) text of salvation. A pragmatic question evolved, however, as to the "productivity" of such cyclical labor. And a psychological question emerged as to the "personality" of the magical worker himself.

Magic, ritual law, and taboo appeared to Weber as a "fear-ridden punctiliousness," "a mental alienation," a "slave-liked dread." Weber wrote of relieving guilt through a "methodical compulsion of the gods," and in words close to Freud's study of compulsion in his anthropology of totem and taboo, he wrote of the ceremonies of eating a sacred totem. Such practices created the "incredible irrationality of . . . painfully onerous norms," practices, for example, of those in "a fraternal community" who were attempting to placate a god. "Within this complex," Weber concluded, "there is little differentiation between important and unimportant requirements; any infraction of the ethic constitutes sin." Freud deemed such a complex neurotic; Weber considered such labors estranged. Marianne attributed obsessionally careful behavior to her husband, at least as regarded the banalities of Weber's incessant planning prior to his collapse—again, not symptomatic evidence, but a sign of that which Weber had set himself to work against by composing his writing on rationality. It "is perfectly obvious," Weber reiterated, "that economic rationalization would never have arisen originally where taboo had achieved such massive power."[65]

Whenever Weber explained the rise of "rational" work processes, he emphasized this importance of being relieved from magic, however ironic such an emphasis for "high capitalism" and its fetishes would appear. Weber used the idea in a variety of forms. In part, the release from magic allowed for economically rational decisions—such mundane choices as the location of a factory without reference to the place of spirits and demons.[66] More significantly, however, Weber stressed the author and the authority to be given to work, for when he contrasted the Puritan's productivity with what he saw as the Confucian's mere ceremony, he again emphasized the encumbrance that any magic style entailed. Caught in a "magical coercion of spirits and deities"—in a "vestigal ritualism" that Weber's Puritan considered "impudent blasphemy"—buried in observances and in obscure issues of law, the Confucian lives without an "inward core" or an "autonomous value position." He lacks "a 'unified personality,' a striving which we associate with the idea of personality. Life remained a series of occurrences. It did not become a whole placed methodically under a transcendent goal."[67] Weber opposed such piecemeal "ritual" to the "rational-ethical." He opposed this "merely apparent" of magic to the "real." The key becomes the release from "works": for those bound "hand and foot," rational ascetic prophecies could effect freedom by releasing the self from magic.[68]

In *The Protestant Ethic*, Weber wrote that this "radical release of magic from the world allowed no other psychological course than the practice of worldly asceticism." The decomposition of magic that the Reformation emphasized removed the types of devices other psychological formations could use to relieve stress. Without priestly intermediaries, for example, or confessions and penances, the Protestant faced his God and his sin directly. He had turned magic, that is, into a transparent sign, providing magic with no significance at all. With the Catholic cycle of sin and expiation removed, the Protestant had no other recourse but to live a linear working life unrelieved of pressure.[69] Though Weber denied that psychology or psychiatry could unravel the Protestant ethic, he nevertheless argued that it was the "psychological sanction" or the "psychological effect" of Calvinism that distinguished the ethic.[70] The doctrine of predestination disallowed works, but work, the hopeful proof of salvation—more properly, the sign—became a labor of grace. Logically, fatalism should have become the only outcome of predestination, but "on account of the idea of proof the psychological result was precisely the opposite." All men required some assurance of salvation, and some way to work out their guilt, and thus one's work represented not the means of grace but the signification, "the technical means, not of purchasing salvation, but of getting rid of the fear of damnation."[71] Work became a whole endeavor singularly written—authored, for the first time in history, by a unified "personality."

Again, the Puritans' signification of grace is expressed not in isolated contents, discrete signs, or "single good works"—not in a work bound like an enclosed book—but in a whole faith running through to infinity. The Calvinist had found himself forced to forego the "planless and unsystematic character" of those who could magically undo whatever transgression they thought they had committed. Thus they had replaced this doing and undoing, or the periodic acts of thought and behavior of undoing violence that Freud placed at the center of his obsessional neurosis, with the constancy of the calling. The Puritans had allowed the self its own writing.[72] The book of God stood absolutely prescribed: its word was made transparent, therefore the book could never be opened to anxious, intermediate, and peculiar interpretations.[73]

If one held grace to be other than plainly read, then one did leave the world open to doubt that only magic could periodically unravel. The ascetic labor Calvinism induced, as Weber wrote after his depression, eradicated doubt along with the magical sign: "it is held to be an absolute duty to consider oneself chosen, and to combat all doubts as temptations of the devil, since lack of self-confidence is the result of insufficient faith, and hence of imperfect grace." Never, for Weber, had the Puritans simply worked their way out, bargaining around unfathomable questions, no more than they had remained in states of abject doubt, anguishing over themselves as psychological peculiarities. The combatting of "temptations" nevertheless demanded that the temptations become fixed or conceptually defined as signs of the "irrational impulses" that the self was working against. The impulses needed to be expressed as the alienation, or the satanically induced other, that the self was holding itself against. Weber argued that asceticism first defined this estrangement by holding the body apart from its Creator. Monastic asceticism combatted depression along with the confusion that Weber's own exhaustion had itself only magnified. But only worldly asceticism provided self-identity, the sense of constancy and worth that Weber himself struggled to attain.[74]

It becomes, then, not merely a psychologism to move between Weber and his texts; such a reading is almost demanded. It is demanded discursively, for even if one seeks an impersonal text, psychologism presents itself from the seventeenth century on as a universal text, giving to narrative literature, for example, an author, while opening up the author psychologically within the newly popular autobiographical literature. Fascinated with types, Weber viewed his sociologies as studying such shifting patterns of consciousness. He was honing his analysis here to this point of the self, his concern being, as he said, with the historical formation of the "psychological sense" of personality that he believed his Puritan had, for the first time in history, achieved.

The achievement came as the Puritan removed himself from singular acts of contrition. Weber pitted the new personality against such "compensations," for personality came only with the ethical wholeness provided by Luther's *Beruf* or calling. William James argued the same, though never by so precisely locating the movement in history. James pitted the "automatic or semi-automatic composition" of the Hebrew prophets ("We have distinct professions of being under the direction of a foreign power, and serving as its mouthpiece") against "the teachings of the Buddha, of Jesus, of Saint Paul . . . of Luther, of Wesley." "And it always comes," James had quoted in the *Varieties* from another source, speaking in the main of Jeremiah, "in the form of an overpowering force from without, against which he struggles, but in vain"—"some strong and irresistible impulse," that is, "coming down upon the prophet, determining his attitude to the events of his time." The attitude strikes at the time when the Law appears about to fall, crushing the old toward creating the new. Topologically it becomes the space experienced for passing from Law to faith; typologically it becomes the juxtapositions that one makes of the Testaments.[75]

Weber struck out against his own manner of working only when he held that his work had become like a magic or "talisman." One may read Weber, however, as using much of his work as a form of ritual. He undertook incredibly precise studies to organize his world—perhaps to control the unpredictability of his emotions, perhaps to defend against the fact of his father's "killing," or perhaps to combat doubts instilled in childhood as to whether his world was sanguine or punishing. Weber fled not in the first and most readable instance from the sex of marriage or from an Oedipal reaction, but from the self-doubt any emotional entanglement could bring, doubt that work as a carefully performed ceremony could end. When minutely performed, labor could clear one's mind as one might clean a room. Weber worked carefully. He paused, rearranged, digressed, added clauses, reservations, balance, refusing to write freely as if he might let some unpredictable emotion show. Until the defense broke and depression ensued, scientific labors allowed Weber to mechanize his life, which Weber well knew and which he took as a sign.[76]

Clearly, to the end of his life Weber strove to return to the thoroughness of what he called the "malignant growth" of his footnotes.[77] The form of his labor expressed a prolonged quest to grasp and control every facet of his learning. The attempt, of course, gave Weber his genius, but his circumspection could further confusion, for in the multiplicity of sides, a chaos of reflections could blind a reader. Those who have translated Weber's German testify that his writing expresses a need for such mastery that at times his words evolve into a private, almost magical or totemic language, as if Weber were attempting to preserve his knowing through codes of secrecy.[78] He never apologized for this; he simply said that he wished his reader to labor as hard as he, to bring them, as it seemed, through his own travail.[79]

Doubt could also encourage the resolution of the world into predictable patterns, the figurations that Weber applied to history. These are the "ideal types" or structures that could make every block and being of the world fit for Weber and perform as they were supposed to perform. Weber opposed such structures to one such type: patriarchalism's "free arbitrariness."[80] It was asceticism that functioned to order patriarchialism along with other dangerously chaotic expressions. More than any religious form, asceticism strove to "devalue" the world. It banished "the peculiar irrationality of the sexual act," for example, along with the capriciousness of patriarchs, the demonology of magicians and artists, or anyone who worked with uncontrollable powers or emotions. Protestant asceticism, and the scientific devaluation that Weber proposed Protestantism had created along with capitalism, was, again, antiauthoritarian. It opposed monarch and priest, and it opposed the closed texts of a dogma's chambers, the study of life through circular, ratiocinative signs.[81] In all, ascetic prophecies demanded the release from the affections that ended in entanglements: "The sib has had to fear devaluation by the prophecy. Those who cannot be hostile to members of the household, to father and mother, cannot be disciples."[82] The text, of course, is the New Testament.

The End of the Worldly Ascetic Ideal

For a moment in history, grace was attained. Now, in the larger text that Weber gave to his Protestant ethic, the new work and its rationalism is to end itself in a terror, or more mundanely, in "sport." Ascetic renunciation ends in the mechanization and the fetishism of high capitalism. Adumbrations of Weber's theme appeared in 1904 in letters he wrote to his mother. He gave expression to an America transposing itself from an ascetic community of various sects into a Chicago. Weber's ascetic, in other words, fails to contain the forces within itself—in Oklahoma, for example, the "stench" and "smoke" and "numerous clanging railways," and in the fact of "lawyers" that Weber wrote about in quotes.[83] The "boiling heat of modern capitalistic culture" was transforming America, changing the physiognomy of the nation.[84] Weber stood as a prophet viewing the sins of a newly foreign nation. His European tongue was an appropriate emblem.

When Weber looked to America, he celebrated only remains—the vitality of the Oklahoma town he visited, for example, that was about to decay. "It is a shame," he had written his mother, but "within one year everything will appear here as in Oklahoma City, i.e., as in every other city in America. WITH FURIOUS SPEED EVERYTHING THAT COULD HAMPER CAPITALISTIC CIVILIZATION IS SMASHED."[85] America's high capitalism had thoroughly rationalized itself. It was introducing systems of standardized bookkeeping, aptitude testing, and a factory discipline that Weber saw as symbolizing the nation's compulsion for scientific management.[86]

Upon his return to Germany, in completion of his essay, in the final, most famous paragraphs, Weber spoke of the iron closing on the West, particularly on the United States. "The Puritan wanted to work in a calling; we are forced to do so"—forced as if by some external power. Of course the exigencies of the machine itself existed, along with the cloak of external goods that fell now as "an iron cage [*ein stahlhartes Gehause*]." An "economic compulsion" had replaced ascetic labor.[87] Like Marx, Weber destroyed the work of capitalist production through an irony, finding in high capitalism the same magic estrangement of otherworldly ascetic enclosure. Unlike Marx, Weber wrote now in timeless frames. He turned his text, as Freud was turning *Totem and Taboo*, from a chronicle of history to literature, ending outside of history in myth. He was fastening rebeginnings.

It was as though Weber were drawing for his reader timeless psychological conclusions, offering again Bunyan's portrayal of the iron cage of despair in the midst of the "Profits" of Vanity-Fair:

> Chr. *For what did you bring yourself into this condition?*
> *Man.* For the Lusts, Pleasures, and Profits of this World; in the enjoyment of which, I did promise my self much delight: but now even every one of those things also bite me, and gnaw me like a burning worm.[88]

The Puritan had rejected Vanity Fair, so Weber argued,[89] but in a modern economy the lusts, temptations, and fears reappeared. In an ambiguous statement, Weber appeared to join the entrapment to a new psychology—a secular Pauline psychology expressing the end of the inner calling and the beginning of the external compulsion of work in a high economy. As predestination could slip into mere fatalism, Weber wrote, so "there is a non-religious counterpart . . . , one based on a mundane determinism":

It is that distinctive type of guilt and, so to speak, godless feeling of sin which characterizes modern man. . . . It is not that he is guilty of having done any particular act, but that by virtue of his unalterable idiosyncracy he "is" as he is, so that he is compelled to perform the act in spite of himself, as it were—this is the secret anguish that modern man bears.[90]

In an economy without sanctions for work, persons felt inexplicable sin. They felt "inhuman," compelled to act in spite of themselves as if coerced by another. Weber worked the irony of his history by twisting his ethic into a spiritually barren renunciation of the self to specialized, totemic labor, "mechanized petrification."[91] Compulsion, the neurotic possession of but a few, still symbolized an appropriate nature. With the performance of penances seemingly to atone, and a fear of one's eternal damnation, no other neurosis so openly displayed the guilt that presumably underlay other neurotic structures as well. In compulsion the guilt becomes consciously felt, and the form of a strange act can retain its significance. Weber conceived his ascetic ideal out of such agony—too far removed, it seemed, to work any longer as a step in a morphology of national conversion. Ahead nothing awaited except a desiccated bureaucracy, the "Specialists without spirit" coveting the graph.[92]

As Weber witnessed the travail, he did offer the promise—the faith that could begin in such wastes. ". . . they burn soft coal. When the hot, dry wind from the deserts of the southwest blows through the streets, and especially when the dark yellow sun sets, the city looks fantastic. [He was speaking of Chicago and its "endless filth."] In broad daylight one can see only three blocks ahead—everything is haze and smoke, the whole lake is covered by a huge pall of smoke." "It is an endless human desert." "All hell had broken loose." "On the billboards there was a poster proclaiming CHRIST IN CHICAGO," Marianne remembered. "Was this brazen mockery? No, this eternal spirit dwells there, too." From all this, Marianne concluded, Weber had returned, "conscious [now] of the reserves of energy that had slowly accumulated."[93] For Weber, his genius expressed enough of a testament to the efficacy of such a hell. Weber thus brought America to its end, choked in its new world. In such deserts life began, in the forty years of national exile, or in the forty days of the temptations of Christ.

Work and Death

In a suspicion too of the completeness of any work at hand, Roland Barthes distinguishes a "work" from a "text." Barthes holds the text as an infinity, almost as an analogue of faith. "In other words, *the text is experienced only in an activity, a production.* It follows that the Text cannot stop, at the end of a library shelf, for example; the constitutive movement of the Text is a traversal . . . : it can cut across a work, several works." A text, then can cut across works—this crossing, for Barthes, being the only completion.[94]

As Barthes's translator quotes in other regards, post-structuralism becomes a matter of deconstructing "Law."[95] A critical despair of sterility appears, of order and ritual structures ("It is as if," Weber wrote, ". . . we were deliberately to become men who need 'order' and nothing but order, who become nervous . . . if for one moment this order wavers").[96] A "Protestant ethic" woven in script and in the figure of an author's life demonstrates Barthes's aim, to make of the work, that is, an "imaginary tail."[97]

Edward Said locates this violence within the earliest of structural expressions, works that for him remain totemic rituals for "cutting down" nature to size, carving out in desperation too much rationality in an intensity of structuralist industry. For Said, such writing becomes an "economy of means that renders every detail," closed orders the anxiety of which can be opened only in a dispersion of signs, in a realization of the buried irony, in a "beginning," then, again.[98]

This expresses Weber's text, and Freud's in *Totem and Taboo*.[99] For the post-structural critic, critical method becomes this text, as critic and subject reflect themselves; for Joseph Riddel, writing of the themes of beginnings in American literature, it is a language that "must build a machine to bridge the abyss its questioning repeatedly opens up, a machine that turns out to be the sign itself of the abyss."[100]

Like Freud, Weber had constructed a mechanics of personality interplaying (or for Freud, masking) the depths of a specific psychopathology. The personality represents the most rigidly structured of the Freudian character types and of David Shapiro's "neurotic styles."[101] Like Said's early structuralist, the neurotic structure possesses its own violent potential, one for cutting at the bars of its mechanical repression. Unlike Freud, Weber offered the personality as a historically unique formation. It is fairly argued that Weber recovered his Protestant ethic from American manuscripts, the archives of which he searched, as well of course from Luther and to a lesser extent from Calvin. In its renewing frontiers enclosed now by mechanism, and in the land provided—blank as it had appeared, and waiting for Puritan inscription—America presented the space for the development of Weber's iron cage. Now, as Weber wrote, his own work was breaking down.

Mechanism fails to work, having first been built before a demonic sight. The end appears when the technologically contrived plays the work out. For Barthes, this becomes the nature of a text, "its motto the words of the man possessed by devils," or "legion," "play," something never compulsively enclosed.[102] The text expresses Thoreau's "deep cut on the railroad" composed as a winter sand and mechanics exploding in an arrival of spring, and of a garden left in decay, the miles, as Thoreau said, of his garden's rows. The text expresses the labor of William James, who for all his will wrote in the end of letting go, of the mind that would "strike work" again in a crossing out.[103] This becomes the narrative movement of psychomachy that Weber recomposed. As Barthes entitles his own essay, the movement becomes one "from work to text."

Within an American literature that holds itself within spiritual narrative forms, such structures, as Leo Marx writes, work as tight buildings that authors leave in depression, factory ships that end in their own destruction, rafts that explode in the middle of their pilgrims' passage, banks of sand that erupt in an explosion from the bowels of the earth in spring. Weber's cage reflects the decomposition Henry Adams made of his own dynamo displayed at a Paris exposition. Within Bunyan's narrative, the waste is displayed when Christian is smeared with dirt and placed within his own cage before he can leave Vanity Fair behind. The narrative begins in the sealing of the self in methodical devices, in the ritual bathings of a Thoreau, in strange ascetic manipulations, in the whole neurotic primitivism that Freud gave to totem and taboo. There follows a worldly ascetic and then an opening to nature, a cutting out there of economical forms, the linear structure enfolding back with the arrival then of terror. In a moment of realization of what the self has committed, the structure turns, and in uncovering the trope of its irony, falls apart. Life begins now in the perfectly random dispersion of Adams's entropic void.

For the American audience who would receive his writing, Weber's importance lay in re-creating this theme of the nation's spiritual journey. America had become an archetypal reference, Weber thought, for all of what he wanted his ethic to say. In the years in which Freud was writing to America, uncovering an "especially revealing" money complex that obsessed the nation, filthy lucre of coin and dirt, Weber was also writing of what Freud called the "transformations" of American values, of turnings or tropes, of which the most significant is irony.

By creating a desert of ritualization, Weber offered a timeless cycle of death and birth. Works vanish at the point of faith, and ritualization is self-destructive, the machine being defined by its waste and insanity, paradigmatic oppositions of metal and dirt, effort and collapse, with America to become this narrative of wilderness turning to iron. "Wilderness" and "iron," as Hayden White points out, possess the same root.[104] The soil of America becomes this site of bewildering rationalizations, the land of the highest capitalism where the demonics of the machine are most visibly displayed. This penetration of nature, this machine in the garden (in Professor Marx's apt phrase), this cutting for Weber of organic forms with the edge tools that Emerson had described, with the calculation or "understanding" that Emerson had then denied, calls for an interpreter. The interpreter points to the lines of iron that have carved a graph from nature, and then to the terror crawling out from behind those lines. He points, as Bunyan or William James did, to the meaning of such "steps" or "progress," to the terror waiting when one makes such a satanic machine. As Marianne Weber to her husband or as Max Weber to himself, the interpreter points to the fear waiting when one attempts one's own conversion, making the self a progressive machine by writing the lines of the way to God as if the text were not already prescription, that is, preordained. The absolute Calvinist demand of the Protestant sects that Weber studied—beyond the capitalism created or the work performed or the contracts drawn—drew his interest, centered his essay, and in his own declaration of the mechanist's grip, brought him within the demonic of Puritan conversion. The debate enjoined, the "Weber thesis" and the question how a scholar could ever have celebrated—as Weber clearly did—the horror of the compulsion his worldly ascetic came to display, resolve before the understanding that Weber was rewriting the most radical of Puritan texts. He looked to the signs of the terrors of America, claiming that birth—for Emerson, "reason"—came at the end of the understanding (*Verstehen*) within sight of the cage. In alienation came the waters of separation, and the creation then of saints.

Conclusion

> Case 2.—Admirably brought up, but as a child nervous and sensitive. . . . Later on, severe headaches, and easy fatigue on moderate mental exertion, both of neurasthenic type, put an end to the projected professional life. Increase of neurasthenic symptoms and obsessions temporarily brought to a close the substituted commercial life which had been well begun.
>
> Depression; Obsession, the sudden assumption of the strangest attitudes; grimaces; morbid doubts. Calculations were vainly done over and over again for fear of making mistakes, rendering him worse than useless in business; repetitions and verifications of everything; dread of a simple and easy journey; paroxysmal morbid dread and insistent ideas as to the most simple undertakings; the writing of the shortest letter only accomplished after many attempts and repetitions, and even then not to his satisfaction.

Wilhelm Reich was to liken compulsive persons to "living machines."[1] This image turned a neurotic's behavior into the corporal symbol for mechanized societies, a grim counterpart to C. Wright Mills's "cheerful robot." Erich Fromm's "authoritarian personality," Carl Jung's "introvert," Harry Stack Sullivan's "obsessional"—each appears the appropriate product of an intense, calculating nation. The compulsive character fits well a society that demands precision; as in the case history cited above, such a person desires a life of bookkeeping, a "substituted commercial life" in which to bury his trauma in counting.[2] The enormous file room of Mills's America seems to provide what Jung said the introvert desperately seeks: "A lonely island where only what is permitted to move moves."[3]

America's Protestant heritage is said to have instilled an appreciation for conscientiousness, making the case cited above, though it came from England, all the more ironic. In this small portrait of mental illness from the late nineteenth century, prudence has destroyed all other considerations. Here a work ethic has turned on itself: a young man is paralyzed, his labor twisted into meaningless travail.

The American ascetic, in Thoreau's words, is "to truly worship stocks and stones." It is to eliminate, for the politician a century removed from the thought of Thoreau, "waste in industry." It is to forge a terrible steel: Henry Adams's dynamo, Weber's high capitalism. It is to weld from twelve rods and special nails a weapon. The maker then asks, like Ahab: "have I been but forging my own branding-iron, then?"

> Oh, Pip! thy wretched laugh, thy idle but unresting eye; all thy strange mummeries not unmeaningly blended with the black tragedy of the melancholy ship, and mocked it![4]

Cotton Mather ringed himself in iron: "But the man *that* shall touch them must be / fenced with iron and the staff of a spear; and / they shall be utterly burned with fire in the *same* / place." James Agee, three centuries later, measures a bed of iron in the midst of America's Great Depression: "For only Og king of Bashan remained of the / remnant of giants; behold, his bedstead was a bed- / stead of iron. . . . nine cubits *was* the length thereof, and / four cubits the breadth of it, after the cubit of a / man." Ahab too holds his steel, and he too is torn asunder: "The harpoon was darted; . . . the line ran through the groove;—ran foul." With the "ironical coincidings" with which Melville's book is made, "lances, and harpoons, mechanically retained," Ahab too is caught in the line of his own fashioning. "Now small fowls flew screaming . . . then all collapsed."[5]

"Are We Automata?" William James had asked, and the answer it seemed was obviously no. As David W. Marcell has shown, James asked for the building of a world, an extrication from "the primordial chaos of sensations." This is to be accomplished by the "slowly cumulative strokes of choice, . . . extricated out of this, like sculptors, by simply rejecting certain portions of the given stuff."[6] James's words are exciting in the creations they promise the self, carving from nothing a small camp like Walden, a clearing, and not the least a clearing of mind.

James's words come from the first of the two volumes of the *Psychology*. In the second, in the last sentence of the final chapter, James closed as Melville had, shutting his landscape down:

> Even in the clearest parts of Psychology our insight is insignificant enough. And the more sincerely one seeks to trace the actual course of *psychogenesis*, the steps by which as a race we may have come by the peculiar mental attributes which we possess, the more clearly one perceives "the slowly gathering twilight close in utter night."[7]

Steps and sincerity—and James offered both, his struggle in itself heartfelt enough—hardly matter.

William James—in the writings he offered and in the life he composed so as together to form his completed text—provides, in one phrase, this "sense of an ending."[8] By holding to history and working with the words of Thomas Shepard or Jonathan Edwards, tracings of which his reader could not fail to find in his own life, he brought his history to a close. In his meeting with Freud, the year before his death, he offered Freud the future. He harbored, of course, his suspicions.

James marks "beginnings" in another word as well. He wrote of the "I" as the real "me" physiologically determined and bodily placed as if the I were in Cartesian space, and then wrote of the I transparent, of the I diffused in relative space without that space holding to a particular center. He measured, and carefully, the steps of his conversion, then like Edwards listed the signs, twelve in all, of the religious affections (as Thoreau measured the breadth of his fields, or Melville the lengths of the whale), and declared the measures infinite. Like his father, James measured his labors and his bodily processes across time, thereby pushing himself through his preparation, then came to the end of never finishing his history. He held open the working God that his father had demanded. He held the process of the self's completion to be infinite—like an instantaneous point of conversion where diachrony (or history) and synchrony (or myth) cross. Conversion becomes the point where the Cartesian axes collide. He held to the absolute demand that no point of origin could ever be found, fixed in the survey of any ground so as to preclude a re-creation.

The moral tried by James could only in the end extinguish itself. The weekly charts of Franklin, made to plot his virtue; the lost steps of Edwards, sought to make his history; the ascetic methods of Mather, undertaken to make of himself a Christ; indeed the whole of this morality of American Puritan theology set now in the secular state of James—the lists and lines and points of resolution—could only erase themselves and consume their own makers.[9] The moral for James could only fail and become of no account, of no more account than the bookkeeping Thoreau tried when listing his own expenses. These are the efforts and the wills measured so precisely with the brass instruments of the new psychology. This is the point of their making: the iron is to be forged, and it is forged to be broken.

Ahab's monster—the whale upon which he projects his unfathomable quest—is of the mechanics of the image from the book of Daniel. Both Ahab and the whale are pieces taken from a mixture of parts, for the machined monster, as in the turnings that Daniel reveals of the king's dream, is also the captain's body, which he thinks of as an automaton, put together from contrasting materials such that he becomes terrible in the division his body displays. Ahab's "monomania" is at one with "his bodily dismemberment."[10] "Nebuchadnezzar dreamed dreams, wherewith his spirit was troubled." And when the magicians, astrologers, and sorcerers fail and "the interpretation" is unrevealed, Daniel appears and opens the image for the king: "and the form thereof *was* terrible." "His legs of iron, his feet part of iron and part of clay."

> And the fourth kingdom shall be strong as iron: forasmuch as iron breaketh in pieces and subdueth all *things*: and as iron that breaketh all these, shall it break in pieces and bruise. . . .
>
> And in the days of these kings shall the God of heaven set up a kingdom, which shall never be destroyed: and the kingdom shall not be left to other people, *but* it shall break in pieces and consume all these kingdoms, and it shall stand for ever.[11]

The self is held in division while its dream is revealed of iron and clay, its house "made a dunghill." The self is to know the limits of its measurements, the iron that breaks and is so broken, "broken to pieces . . . and became like the chaff of the summer threshing-floors; and the wind carried them away, that no place was found for them." Contrasting elements are for a moment to be held together as a machine: "all varieties were welded into oneness, and were all directed to that fatal goal which Ahab their one lord and keel did point to." It is a construction that can only be broken to declare another time of creation, and another kind of lord.[12]

The problem is to find not the historical aspects of a literature but the literary aspects of a history: not to deny materialism but to view the chains that literary forms create, not only for fictional characters but for nonfictional lives. It is to know what Ahab declares, that the act itself must play itself out whether in his own fictional re-creation or in the factual presentation of other lives, in the autobiographical accounts to be drawn from letters, diaries, small confessions, assembled like the psychoanalytic "taking" of a history or, as Erik Erikson has said, the "making" of a history. This documentary shows the constructions and re-creations of the iron that binds, and it shows the destructions and re-creations of the iron that breaks. Perhaps, in the interpretation of other prophets of dream, "the iron, the clay, the brass, the silver, and the gold" will finally be shown to be shattered and scattered like chaff in the summer wind as things to be forever sundered.[13]

When an entire culture becomes expressive of neurosis, re-creating the Puritans' satanic vision of America, then work turns to graceless occupation. The historian seeking to diagnose America's malaise finds a strange, mechanical thing: the "Protestant surrender to calling and to capitalism." Work is now the tempter, "a mode of surrender to the Devil and to death."[14] Norman O. Brown can thus write of Protestant history as but a movement toward death. The chapters of his own work *"plunge into a strange world and a strange language—a world of sick men," "the world we all of us actually live in."*[15] The titles in themselves are Puritan enough: "The Disease Called Man," "Neurosis and History," "Death, Time, and Eternity," "The Excremental Vision," "Filthy Lucre," "The Resurrection of the Body." Their ordering is precise. Again, it was not too far from what Cotton Mather had claimed, particularly when Mather eyed the new America of the Franklins or saw the words of John Wise: that verity was not to be found in the "transient," as Wise said, meaning in Mather himself, but in the worker who knew "the Nature and Qualities of an Edge-Tool which he hath wrought."[16] Wise's words held all the irony they needed when they reached the hands of Emerson. Given Brown's vision of a playful society, of psychic systems now boundless and open, the analytic historian can offer in a meticulous work of considerable labor, well manufactured in Wise's own terms, the history of the compulsion that is to precede the light.

Brown's book is literally to burn itself "out." His intelligence is to prove no end in itself, for such a display of carefully wrought history is to remain, simply, a display. For Brown, this is his own setting of Wallace Stevens's "Domination of Black" against "The Snow Man"—"And, nothing himself, beholds / Nothing that is not there and the nothing that is"—the setting of the analyst against his own "analysis." In finding the "cure," Brown removes all the work which *Life Against Death* so readily displays.[17] Liberation for Brown is neither eros nor a narcissistic inward turning, an "other-direction" in the then popular phrase of the 1950s, no more than it was for Thoreau. Liberation is the self revolting against "personality." Work has become a mask and masking is magic—"The mask is magic." Work is one's "*demon*" or alien other, as well as all the other words that Brown applied in his following book, *Love's Body*, to explain his meaning: "*persona*," "stage," "theater," "theatrical creation," "psychodrama," "dream-stuff," "thing," "fetish," "commodity," "mechanization," "compulsion," "masquerade," "carnival," "Larva," "ghost," "grub," "law," "ritual," "legal fictions," "personification," "reification," "conscience," "super-ego." These are all cases, in other words, "of demoniacal possession."

"Modern (Western) legalistic rationalism does not get away from magic: on the contrary, it makes the magical effects so permanent and so pervasive that we do not notice them at all."[18] The end of the act or of the "action" in the colloquial expression lies in the "deeper root of the Augustinian and Puritanical opposition to the theater." "Some capital texts in the New Testament tell us that God is no respecter of persons— . . . 'not taken by masks'; not captivated, not crazy about them, not taken in, not deceived by them. . . . This God cares not for visible distinctions; or visible achievements, outer works. The faith that saves is internal and invisible." Personality is to end in the dawn of the irrational, the irrational carefully defined by Brown as the opposite of formalisms, rational subjections, false calculations—"defense mechanisms," in other words, the opposite from mechanisms that defend not at all. The "insane" are "closer to the truth," for they consciously conceive their magic and readily make their manipulations visible. To eradicate works, Brown struck for sensing the truth of the magic displayed in some neuroses and psychoses, then called for doing nothing as in a doing of nothing as all:

> The parts are not real: for ye are all one in Christ Jesus; he is not your personal Saviour. In the Last Judgment the apocalyptic fire will burn up the masks, and the theater, leaving not a rack behind. Freud came to give the show away; the outcome of psychoanalysis is not "ego psychology" but the doctrine of "anatta" or no-self. . . . And with the doctrine of no-self goes the doctrine of non-action: action is proper only to an ignorant person, and doing nothing is, if rightly understood, the supreme action.[19]

This is Saint John of the Cross and his dark night of the soul.

Brown's popular imagination is to be understood in the structure of his books in the context of his history, not by using his books to reflect any immediate cultural revolution. He had given to America the revision of itself as Satan's land, and when he spoke of the coming triumph not of work but of play, surely play is to be read as faith. His is the transcendent that Wise had come to bury. But play could be read as play, and for all his textual apparatus, as thorough as any Puritan's, Brown could be taken as a singer, as autoerotic as any child in his own celebration.

This book has not undertaken an etiology or a natural history of the obsessional malaise. It has not offered a diagnosis or a symptomatic expression of what it was, clinically, that the subjects of this book suffered. Diagnosis, for the presumed obsessional patient, is hard enough to attain with that patient living,[20] let alone to attain for the historical figure who has offered himself as an exemplum or type, with his own history further re-created in the writing of psychobiography. History offers enough symptomatic "evidence" of obsession to make the evidence itself a type, a configuration (in historic "actuality" perhaps quite rare, for the obsessional neurosis, clinically referred to, is rare) that appears to run like a Puritan strain through the American character.[21] The weight of the evidence alone should offer some thought that before arguing natural causation—whether "nature" is perceived as an underlying economy, culture, or physiology—one should consider the structure, or the reason for the text having been so often expressed.

Yet a model of economic transition and social disruption is appealing; indeed, in one form or another such a model has dominated the American historical imagination for the last half century. Weber's rationalization, or modernization in the more recent term, Töennies' *Gemeinschaft und Gesellschaft*, and Durkheim's *anomie* are worked together to explain the agonies of both the seventeenth-century Puritan village and the twentieth-century Yankee city. These are histories that offer the prepositions "from" and "to" in their titles and speak as Perry Miller so brilliantly did of the arrival in America of the secular state.

For Miller himself, this rationalization came ironically. Puritan evangelical thought created a peculiar, and for Miller tragic, entrepreneurial reality, and thus the Puritans fashioned their own destruction as their early pietistic ideals were crushed in a New England that was moving from "colony to province," from holy community to modern state. As a model of "declension" Miller's history is predestined; it is capable of explaining the underlying function of the ministers' jeremiads that were but "purgations of soul" preached by those who were furnishing the ethic of this-worldly activity that produced the new capitalism and created the new Yankee the ministers could then only despise. "There is something of a ritualistic incantation about them [the jeremiads]; . . . they do not discourage but actually encourage the community to persist in its heinous conduct." This reading imbues new social and psychohistorical probes of Puritanism, for however much such studies dismiss Miller's methodology, his reliance upon literary documents and ministerial elites, these histories nevertheless follow Miller's sense of evolutionary friction and find in the steps of Puritan declension an engine of explanation. A movement from pietistic community to capitalistic society, it is now argued, damaged psychology and created a tension, one that the Puritans expressed in their own peculiar despair. The "growth" of Puritanism as a social body and a guilt-ridden mind, in other words, creates a crisis of self, though historians differ as to when, exactly, the crisis occurred. Nevertheless, this anthropomorphic image returns Puritan studies to the themes that Weber had originated—to studies of Puritanism as a uniquely ironic temperament creating works before which persons stand estranged.[22]

The art of such history, and in many respects its brilliant form, is that it is not so much American history as America's history. The demonic is uncovered in the New World land, the ghost of the machine is found, along with the waste, inside "the piles of wrecked and rusted cars, heaped like Tartar pyramids of death-cracked, weather-browned, rain-rotted skulls, to signify our passage through the land."[23] It is this reality that the text of pathology is said to reflect, the internal hell of the person and the external state in which he lives. Whether for the social pathologist, the psychohistorian, or even the analyst of American architecture—Henry Glassie, for example, writing of the American transforming the "square" to ward off early American nature[24]—the proof of the tension is held to be a reflection, the text. In America compulsive pathology has been readily expressed—inevitably, since here a compulsion tried to cage nature and make of the self itself a machine, to the end of making a waste. There are few post-Eriksonian psychohistories that refer to anything other than obsessive or compulsive behaviors (though once there was vague mention of a paranoid American character, and there are writings now of a new void of hollow narcissism). Such behaviors, like the prevalence of the model of declension, should make one think that there is perhaps a deeper structure, an innateness not to be rooted in time or to be given momentarily to the crisis of the person transforming himself; that there is perhaps something other than nature reflected; that there exists instead a form, the re-expression of a significant pattern, a way that Americans for over three centuries have had for seeing, for putting together the meaning of their lives, for choosing, in a sense, their neurosis.[25]

Psychohistorians have failed to look beyond the rather general dynamics of character and identity and into the specifics of neurotic symptomatology itself. Usually, of course, the evidence has been sparse, particularly for the so-called compulsive person whose neurosis, if any, is far less visible than his "Protestant character." But here, from Nathanael Mather to Royce and Putnam, the evidence is available, allowing the historian to ask how such symptoms themselves act as "texts"—as speech acts, let us say—holding linguistic meaning within the culture in which they "occur." The evidence for such trauma is there, but the question again is why it is there, why the text appears as it does, why indeed the self is expressed, and *so* expressed.

What one does find in Puritan culture, and particularly within Puritanism as it developed in America, is a certain literary genre and style of self-examination—the idea that to be of the saints is to be mentally beset. Miller, again, opened the discussion: "The grace of God, as most men experienced it, is elusive; . . . the sins of the best of men . . . terribly visible, while the book remains inaccessible to mortals. The creature lives inwardly a life of incessant fluctuation. . . . The science of biography"—and of autobiography—"required clinical skill in narrating these surgings and sinkings, all the time striving to keep the line of the story clear." In America, as Edmund S. Morgan so brilliantly pointed out, this besetment—and its "story"—were a unique requirement for membership in the church and, by extension, for membership within the New England community. Thus, as in Cotton Mather's relation of his brother's history, one finds at least one of the origins of the psychological history in America, the origin of a type of literary exposé of psychic lurkings and hidden distresses that permeates Sacvan Bercovitch's "auto-American-biography," a peculiarly confessional mode of literature that only American Puritans demanded—by law, as it were—prior to entry into the church.[26] Bunyan, it should be remembered, composed his own "brief relation" or autobiography in its earliest form most likely to fulfill a requirement of his Bedford congregation.[27] In England such a requirement was local: it was "separatist" in its inclination and in no manner to be read as a requisite "English" form. Melancholy appeared—indeed, it appeared as "the English Malady," as Boswell commented when approaching the subject in the matter of Johnson. This is the "'morbid melancholy,' which was lurking in his constitution," "this dismal malady." "But let not little men," Boswell warned, "triumph upon knowing that Johnson was an HYPOCHONDRIACK," and there the matter was more or less dropped. Johnson's affair was the affair of the scholar, and melancholy was the learned man's disease.[28] Acedia, the sin of sloth, and ennui, boredom, were figures that had run through Western literature for centuries,[29] but in the diagnostics of melancholy, in the fine presentation of the minutest of obsessional symptoms, the Puritans achieved a sense of new literary realism.[30] They undertook a clinical probe, as Miller said, that demanded an opened expression of self—not writing in apology or putting malady aside, but in organizing the self through such a text, in composing one's life against writings of melancholy by weaving the expression in letters, small confessions, at times in a crisis carefully derived. This writing of conversion could then be repeated: in William James repeating his father's expression; in Henry James repeating what he thought Swedenborg had lived; in Royce identifying with the struggles of Bunyan; in Edwards identifying with the steps of his New England ancestors; in Cotton Mather identifying with the memory of his father and brother. For Winthrop, again, nothing made sense until he read Perkins, for Perkins too provided a writing that could order Winthrop's own expression.

This is to examine how the language of the psychomachia became the language, in Bercovitch's terms, of the American self. It is to ask whether the American intellectual has suffered alienation because he has lacked an occupational structure (a prevailing theme of "status anxiety" that runs from the younger Henry James to modern intellectual historians), or whether vocational crisis is not the American scholar's way of defining himself by giving himself a waste in which to work. Whether as an outcast minister or estranged academic, the American scholar's sense of his self as strange makes of the self a saint, and allows for the making of art. It allows for a unique genre of American art—a *Walden*, a "new journalism," a "documentary expression," a "history as . . . novel, . . . novel as history"—in which there is a particular combining of factual expression—lists, maps, expenses, figures, photographs—with spiritual quest. It allows for addressing the self as an other and for speaking of the self as strange, thereby altering conceptions of author and narrator. It allows for mixing times, times now, times infinite, and for juxtaposing spaces, places fixed, places far removed.[31] It allows, most particularly, for affixing to the self a people, land, or event, for giving to the self, as it were, a geopolitical crisis. Mary McCarthy's Vietnam, for example, is the divided land, as she would have it, that expresses her own identity crisis.[32]

The genre stems from the Puritan spiritual autobiography, from the psychomachia Bercovitch has discussed. In America, where the genre was demanded, however briefly, the alienation could be held as real; Bunyan's dream could be set in time and made to work in the wastes America offered. As Francis Jennings has written, speaking to another issue, "Puritan John Winthrop declared that most land in America was *vacuum domicilium*—i.e., legally 'waste'—because the Indians had not 'subdued' it."[33] America was a vacuum, sealed from the intrusions of other texts, and thus became available for acting the drama out.

Alienation is not the unique expression of a modern society or a secular state, even with the arrival of the large machine (how great, one asks, were the volumes of the pyramids, or the mass of the estrangement contained in their construction?). Alienation is not the product of revolutions in industry, for there were images of mechanization before the machine or before the sight of any particular thing. A crisis of identity is not the creation of Auden's age of anxiety, for Protestantism, admitting to the reification involved, *is* an age of anxiety and has defined its identity as such. Protestantism has given itself a structure by declaring that it has no structure at all; it has provided itself identity by saying that it has no identity at all. Protestantism, as protestation, or as a bearing witness in protest—an antinomian or "mystical" strain that may hardly be of a sect at all, let alone an ism, has demanded a deconstructed universe: the burning of a text (post-structural erasures), the removal from a chamber, the leaving of a cabin—but only after those texts, chambers, and cabins have in themselves been well constructed, built as exercises in useless mechanics. However precisely the measurements are made, whatever the array of statistics displayed, a depth such as Walden is not to be measured. As an age of anxiety, or more properly as Auden's "The Enchafèd Flood,"[34] Protestantism has provided form for studies in the American character. The American spiritual autobiography with its peculiar fusing of technology and story, measurement and myth, creates the means of its destruction. "Cetology," for Ishmael, precedes "The Chase. Third Day."

The building can be formal enough, since ritual is pitted against decay and death in a precision of language: "I got out my check-book and deducted four checks drawn since the first of the month, and discovered I had a balance of $1832.60."[35]

[Says Thoreau:]
I address myself now to those of my readers who have a living to get. And to meet this I have for farm produce sold

	$23 44
Earned by day-labor	13 34
In all	$36 78,

which subtracted from the sum of the outgoes leaves a balance of $25 21 3/4 on the one side. . . .

Edwards measured his time, Thoreau his space; Ishmael arrays the lengths and breadths of whales, dissecting their forms, creating the machine that creates his life. Ahab's ship, the factory Leo Marx uncovers, re-creating for another century the discovery of the demon's mechanics, is broken in the face of its measurements, sundered by the thing unmeasured.

Whatever its origin, neurosis is to remain an expression of division to be celebrated as myth, as in a "myth of madness." Even the psychoses, in particular the schizophrenias, are approached as "mythic" in both the colloquial and scholarly meanings of that word. Even educated circles still speak of the psychoses on the one hand as "nervous breakdowns" caused by overwork or by some particular moment of strain, or on the other hand as magic, as Laingian expressions of alienation possessed by seers who are viewing the truth of the modern world's demonics: the radios and bombs set in their stomachs, the machines encasing their chests, the bits and pieces of electronics encircling their heads. But Moloch arrives when the pained are told their pain is myth or their madness an expression of mythic dimensions. Moloch arrives when these magic people are celebrated and allowed (or asked) to continue to suffer or die in some waste of suicide, thereby killing themselves according to some artist's holy conception. Moloch arrives when the sick are held as the suffering servants and saints of the land, when the mentally ill are brought back to "community" and asked to offer some message from the desert of an institution on the outskirts of a city, brought back from the care of a physician who, it is thought, can provide only the merest physic of cure, to be placed in the cells of the motel rooms that the community offers. Such is the power of mythic words like madness (a word that we both want and want not to use), that we cannot but accept that madness is a terribly special disease. Such is the power myth evokes, the wanting and yet not wanting to see the special being, that we anoint and then push the person away, refashioning the holy ship of fools.[36]

Whatever the cause, neurosis is an expression of self-division no more definable in that sense than the words of Paul. But as a dramatic reenactment, in a recovery and reworking of texts, neurosis becomes a way of organizing and giving meaning to lives. Neurosis—the word that we often hold as strange, either as foreign when applied to ourselves or as suspicious when applied to others—becomes a way of making sense of one's self when a culture demands an estrangement. American Puritanism demanded such an alienation, and demanded that the alienation be expressed. This act is re-created when we write that early American culture was in fact mentally sick, its atavisms explaining the sickness of later American culture. With such an argument, economy is forgotten. In the act of explanation is the act of re-creation, for mental death is to bring salvation from the depths of what Auden phrased the Romantics' "Mechanized Desert."[37] The Puritans demanded the self's revelation within this American desert. They placed the self in a satanic bath and made the traveler go through a waste, like an acidic or an acid trip.

But should we then say the metaphor is to be removed, as though we could speak without the trope? Should we say the art is to be destroyed, the myths sundered, the words made "plain"? Is that not in itself a way of expression, a way again of organizing lives? Should we ask that journeys not be expressed, that ways of making sense be removed? Did the Puritans, in their own mythic creations, make more sense of sickness when such sickness actually arrived? Are the estranged to be truly estranged and told their pains and re-creations make no meaning at all? And is the teller speaking myths? Or telling lies? Are we so to confuse art and life that we sunder the former to make of the latter a truth? Is sense not still to be made?

I saw the best minds of my generation destroyed by madness,
starving hysterical naked, . . .
who cowered in unshaven rooms in underwear, burning their money
in wastebaskets and listening to the Terror through the wall . . .
who ate fire in paint hotels or drank turpentine in Paradise Alley . . .
. . . Third Avenue iron dreams . . .
and who were given instead the concrete void of insulin metrasol
electricity hydrotherapy psychotherapy occupational therapy . . .
returning years later truly bald . . . to the madtowns of the East,
Pilgrim State's Rockland's and Greystone's foetid halls, bickering
with the echoes of the soul, . . .
Moloch the incomprehensible prison! . . . soulless jailhouse and Congress of
sorrows! . . .
Moloch whose mind is pure machinery! . . . Moloch whose breast is a cannibal
dynamo! . . .
. . . Moloch whose factories dream and croak in the fog! . . .
Carl Solomon! I'm with you in Rockland
where you're madder than I am
I'm with you in Rockland
where you must feel very strange . . .
I'm with you in Rockland
where you laugh at this invisible humor . . .
I'm with you in Rockland
where fifty more shocks will never return your soul to its body again from
its pilgrimage to a cross in the void . . .

The Iron of Melancholy

I'm with you in Rockland
  in my dreams you walk dripping from a sea-journey on the highway across
  America in tears to the door of my cottage in the Western night[38]

Work, piety, death, as Cotton Mather constructed his Nathanael, the killing of the self as a satanic machine, remain the categories of life. American nature is *natura*, or becoming, as Emerson said.

Notes

1. Twice-Born and Sick Soul: The Awakening of New England's Conscience

Today the estimate of those actually suffering from an obsessional neurosis is among the lowest given for a psychiatric disorder. Within a psychiatric population alone, the estimates range between 0.1 and 4.6 percent. For a discussion of the incidence and prevalence of obsessional states, and the estimates here provided, see Alan Black, "The Natural History of Obsessional Neurosis," in *Obsessional States*, ed. H. R. Beech (London: Methuen & Co., 1974), pp. 21–22. One might argue that the Puritans' theology created such suffering and that what one is observing is a strong relationship between culture and personality—that an obsessional personality, in other words, was the creation of Puritan child-raising techniques. Philip Greven, for example, in his thorough study, *The Protestant Temperament: Patterns of Child-Rearing, Religious Experience, and the Self in Early America* (New York: Alfred A. Knopf, 1977), has most recently argued the point that such relationships can be found. But theories of culture and personality, as well as culture and abnormality, remain fluid and vague; they are, in any event, open to attack from several points of view. In this regard see Alex Inkeles, "Some Sociological Observations on Culture and Personality Studies," in *Personality in Nature, Society, and Culture*, ed. Clyde Kluckhohn and Henry A. Murray, with the collaboration of David M. Schneider, 2nd ed., rev. and enl. (New York: Alfred A. Knopf, 1962), pp. 577–92; as well as the discussion in David E. Stannard, *Shrinking History: On Freud and the Failure of Psychohistory* (New York: Oxford University Press, 1980), pp. 100–56. Theories of neurotic behavior such as David Shapiro's, contained in his *Neurotic Styles*, The Austin Riggs Center Monograph Series Number 5 (New York: Basic Books, 1965), rely heavily on a "formal" argument (see pp. 176–99) and on very early determinates and instinctual drives—on a certain innateness, in other words, that belies drawing fine distinctions, let us say, between an "Anglican" and a "Puritan" culture. Furthermore, studies of the obsessional disorder as a cultural malaise, few as they are, have yet to produce evidence that the neurosis and/or character type belongs to one culture holistically and not to another. In this latter regard, see Black, "Natural History of Obsessional Neurosis," who calls evidence regarding a social class determinate "limited" (p. 30), and who notes that "the reported proportions of men to women suffering from obsessional disorders range from 8 percent to 73 per cent" (p. 29). But most especially see P. D. Slade, "Psychometric Studies of Obsessional Illness and Obsessional Personality," in Beech, ed., *Obsessional States*, pp. 106–08. Citing from the "one cross-cultural study of psychometric differences in obsessionality" of which he is aware—M. J. Kelleher, "Culture and Obsession: A Comparative Study of Irish and English" (M.D. thesis, University College, Cork, 1970)—Slade does note that "the Irish obtained significantly higher scores than the English on both the symptom and trait items." Religion, however, was not a factor, nor was social class. Three variables were significant: that unmarried Irish males scored higher than married Irish males, that rural Irish females scored higher than urban Irish females, and that Irish women not working outside the home scored higher than Irish women who did work outside the home. These three variables accounted for the Irish as a whole scoring higher than the English, for in regard to all three there was, Slade notes, "a cultural difference." It is at this point that Greven's analysis of Puritan evangelicals becomes significant—not the fact that they were Protestant, but that they were, Greven believes, relatively isolated, particularly the women (see, for example, pp. 25–28 of the *Protestant Temperament*). It is this factor of "isolation" that Slade, using the data of Kelleher, sees as conjoining the three variables of being unmarried, rural, and working only within the home—in this case, presumably, the isolation of Irish Catholics.

There is still, however, little reason for supposing that the incidence of such a neurosis was higher in the seventeenth and eighteenth centuries than today, unless one argues that isolation is indeed important and that it has decreased in a movement, say, from the country to the city. The form, however, of the Puritan evangelical confession remains, obscuring any attempt to derive "evidence" from such confessions. One may thus make a strong argument that when such neurotic behavior did occur, it was strongly supported, perhaps even hysterically imitated (conversation with Howard Shevrin, Department of Psychology, University of Michigan, in November 1977), and certainly expressed, for the behavior was not considered abnormal at all in the sense that it had to be hidden. It is this point that should make the historian wary of reading expressions of trauma literally—as Greven, for example, does—of accepting the Puritan rhetoric of temptation without asking why such a rhetoric is there. Certainly, in the confessions Greven employs, more is required than a circular argument that patterns of child rearing caused the expressions, and the expressions in turn created patterns of child rearing.

Newer histories of American Puritanism seeking the unconscious and interior of life claim not a discourse but a fact of pathology. Robert Middlekauff, in his exquisite study, *The Mathers: Three Generations of Puritan Intellectuals, 1596–1728* (New York: Oxford University Press, 1971), refused the word neurotic in describing the American Puritan temper, choosing instead the phrase "reasoned anxiety." Nor did Darrett B. Rutman's study, *American Puritanism: Faith and Practice,* The Lippincott History Series (Philadelphia: J. B. Lippincott Company, Pilotbooks, 1970), published the preceding year, discuss neurosis. Like John Demos in his *A Little Commonwealth Family Life in Plymouth Colony* (New York: Oxford University Press, 1970), published that same year, Rutman was choosing to write of life course and conversion within the terms set by Erik H. Erikson's model of identity crisis, using Erikson's stages of psychological development like a palimpsest to explain the Puritans' morphology of conversion. But though neither Middlekauff nor Rutman called the American Puritan neurotic, both historians clearly found in Puritan culture what Middlekauff described as an "objective" basis outside the text for strain and anxiety.

But within writings on Puritanism stronger themes exist: psychological "charges" that may be traced to the American Puritans' own community of discourse—to Giles Firmin and his *Real Christian*, for example, charging New England ministers with the creation of anxiety and even terror. Importantly, however, the charge may be traced to the works of the New England writers Firmin considered—to Thomas Shepard's *Sincere Convert* (London, 1648), for example, a text providing spiritual definition for those willing to be called "crazie brains," who would hear the words others said led only to suicide or "madnesse" (pp. 158, 167, 170).

Within twentieth-century scholarship, the work of Erich Fromm in 1932 first coupled the writings of Freud and Weber, specifically Freud's essay on "Character and Anal Eroticism" and Weber's essay on the "Protestant Ethic." By way of textual extension—of the Protestant for Fromm as a mechanical, compulsive character type—Norman O. Brown's *Life Against Death* opens Protestant rationalism and rigidity into a vision, behind a Weberian ethic of work, of sadism and excrement. There is also Erikson's study of Luther, of absolute and yet ignored importance for relating themes of psychopathology to Protestant theology in a movement Erikson traces from compulsive "works" to calling or "work." In the terms of compulsive acts—"obsessive actions," in Freud's phrase—Erikson demonstrates that sixteenth- and seventeenth-century Protestant writers used semeiology to provide psychopathological symptoms with religious significance.

American historians were using life cycle and conversion as objective integrative functions, however, and Middlekauff, Rutman, and Demos were unconcerned with thematic expressions of Protestant psychopathology. Nor were Middlekauff and Rutman concerned with characterology, with the Puritan, in Fromm's terms, as an "authoritarian" or obsessive-compulsive character type. Demos however was, at least as regarded "a tight cluster of anxieties about aggression" and a subsequent overdetermination of "law and order" (pp. 137, 139). But given Erikson's founding of psychohistory as an academic discipline and the availability of the earlier, anthropological concern with "culture and personality," the turn from intellect to piety discussed by Michael McGiffert in "American Puritan Studies" could now end in the recovery of two interrelated themes. First, there was the argument that American Puritanism constituted a particular cultural character formation—an "obsessive style" in the phrase of David Leverenz, or an "authoritarian temperament" in the words of Philip Greven, the last word chosen by Greven to replace Max Weber's "ethic." Specifically this was a compulsive temperament, though Greven used no such word. And second, there was the argument that American Puritanism embedded a deeper neurotic structure—for Greven's evangelical, as opposed to his more integrated, characteralogical "moderate," an obsessive-compulsive neurosis, though again Greven used no such phrasing.

Whether discussing identity formation or social strain, recent historians have argued, usually by implication, that American Puritans suffered from what Freud first formulated as an obsessional or obsessive-compulsive neurosis, or from what T. W. Adorno and others labeled an authoritarian personality. In its most general phrasing, the theme is one of the Protestant ethic as a mental pathology, though beyond studies of witchcraft and hysteria the theme, again, is without a specificity of symptomatological expression.

David Leverenz, however, is diagnostically more precise in his recent book on *The Language of Puritan Feeling: An Exploration in Literature, Psychology, and Social History* (New Brunswick, N.J.: Rutgers University Press, 1980). Leverenz speaks overtly of Freud's "obsessional neurosis," of David Shapiro's "obsessive-compulsive style," and of the long-assumed "relationship between Puritanism, obsession, and anality." He quotes from the scatology—"'dung,' 'excrement,' 'pollution,'"—as do Greven, Bercovitch, Brown, and of course Erikson in his writing of Luther. Leverenz speaks of "obsessional states" as "linked with depression and paranoia," arguing however that "overtly ambivalence is avoided, like ambiguity and often feeling itself, through meticulous precision in work and exasperating repetition compulsions over trivialities. Obsessionals tend to be intolerant, unable to accept bad qualities or imperfections, authoritarian even as they seek authority. They seek in repetitive daily rituals to ward off inward dangers." Leverenz speaks of the obsessive-compulsive style as "comprehensively manag[ing] tensions to enable one to survive in a threatening world," and of the "obsessions" themselves as "satisfy[ing] the self by reducing tension and allaying fears, often at the cost of negating new experience" (pp. 110–21).

The word obsession, however, remains itself vague, and Leverenz fails to offer any specific evidence of either obsessional ideation or compulsive acts in the American Puritan experience—other, that is, than his own close and well-crafted reading of early American literature within the characterological terms of rigidity, dependence, and ambivalence toward authority, the moderation of character type as opposed to neurosis. Philip Greven, on the other hand, within the broader range of his meticulous archival research, uncovers documentation that appears less removed through the artifice of literary distancing. And Greven has provided two pieces of obsessional evidence, though he fails to inquire into the discursive formations entailed, seemingly unaware of the specificity of the expressions he has found. Greven is writing of the anxiety he finds in the evangelical temperament, here reading from the eighteenth-century spiritual relation of Susanna Anthony. Emphasis has been added to the significant phrasing of obsession:

> After listening to Whitefield preach, fourteen-year-old Susanna found that she had gotten "more acquaintance with the work of God in the souls of his people," and she "resolved more diligently to labor after a life of holiness, and inward conformity to God." But immediately she found herself beset by Satan, who "roared after his prey" and tried, she said, "to persuade me my day of grace was over; that all my strivings would not signify any thing; that God had cast me off." Her case seemed hopeless, and she felt "the arrows of God within me. I roared, by reason of the disquietude of my soul; *and was strongly beset to lay violent hands on myself*, verily fearing, if I lived, I should be a most blasphemous wretch; *being strongly and violently urged to utter some shocking imprecations on God, and my own soul, and every thing sacred.*" "O!," she added, "how many hours have I spent bewailing a lost God, and a lost Heaven; crying out, 'I am undone! I am undone! condemned already, and shall be damned!'" Soon she was "on the brink of despair," yet she told no one of her desperate situation. [For William James the writing would be the same in this Biblical injunction to speak to no one in such a state—the "panic fear" or "melancholy" which he refused, he wrote in his *Varieties of Religious Experience*, to mention to his mother.]

Greven continues the relation of Susanna Anthony's own expression of distress: her bodily mortifications, her agony of thought, her sense of sin—common expressions for his evangelical that once again culminate, quite later in Greven's account, in a specificity of symptom: exactly what Freud meant by obsession. Again, emphasis has been added:

> Susanna Anthony almost succumbed to the temptation to kill herself. . . . The "cruel instrument was present to accomplish the hellish design. *This temptation rushed on me with such impetuous force, that I found it would be highly dangerous" to stay in the room.*

Rushing through the house, she happened to see a book of her sister's on "Advice to Sinners Under Conviction, &c. with some Scruples of the Tempted resolved," which spoke directly to her experience and prevented her from commiting "that soul shuddering sin, self-murder." Suddenly, she recalled, "satan felt the force of these commissioned lines, and fled the field." . . . "The darkness and horror disappeared. This was the Lord's doing. . . . There was no human contrivance in it" (pp. 72–73, 82–83).

Susanna Anthony, then, is returned to God, the satanic temptations being restrained, as she wrote, by the commissioned lines of a book. The book to which Anthony refers is a slight work by Samuel Corbyn (Corbin), a seventeenth-century English nonconformist—probably a published sermon, on *Advice to Sinners Under Convictions, to Prevent Their Miscarrying in Conversion. To Which is Added, Some Scruples of the Tempted Resolved*, a reprinted edition of which is listed in Charles Evans's *American Bibliography* (Boston: S. Kneeland & T. Green, 1741). Greven then offers a less full account of temptation, in this case wholly to suicide: that of Nathan Cole, again taken from a mid-eighteenth-century spiritual confession. The words Greven here employs are significant, if only because the historian has extended a past written text; his own words remain within a discourse of Mather's and Edwards's earlier histories, the one treating of witchcraft and the other of religious awakening.

The question remains as to how to construct the meaning—or offer the significance—for such evidence: how is the historian to pursue the course of Susanna Anthony's own lines and ask in her word what it was that her labors and her words did in fact "signify"? For Leverenz and Greven, as for Middlekauff, Rutman, Demos, and the social historian in general—Richard L. Bushman, for example, and his studies of compulsion and identity strains during the period of religious awakening in which Anthony wrote—for all these, such texts are to be understood as symptomatic expressions. They are to be read as the reflections of underlying fractures, mirrors of historic tension and transformation. And in the case of seventeenth- and early eighteenth-century America, the most obvious term of fracture, the underlying transforming material reality, is capitalism—the Puritan temperament as a representation of Weber's Protestant ethic. Beginning with Erich Fromm again, whether in the understanding of character type or neurosis, the obsessional personality and capitalism are to be joined, Freud's and Weber's essays mated, to produce the character of an economy. And given what may be assumed was Perry Miller's own close reading of Weber—his reading of the "iron cage" Weber's ascetic capitalism entailed—Miller offered his own detractors this model: the ironic trope of colony turning to province, *Gemeinschaft* to *Gesellschaft*, creating for the student of Miller the anxiety and guilt of the early American temper.

The accounts by Greven, Leverenz, Bushman, and Elliott of such social, generational, and economic tensions are far more subtle and various than such a simple outline allows. Nevertheless, what is demanded is a reappraisal of this social and psychohistorical method. Given the tradition of examining American Puritanism in terms of declension, the historian should be wary of arguing that a transition from community to society created tension and thence expressions of actual malaise, expressions that prove such a transition occurred. Other than in Miller's monumental *The New England Mind: From Colony to Province*, such an argument is best presented by Richard L. Bushman in *From Puritan to Yankee: Character and the Social Order in Connecticut, 1690–1765* (Cambridge, Mass.: Harvard University Press, 1967). It is precisely for their well-ordered form, however, that Puritan texts should, in the first instance at least, be approached structurally rather than viewed as "reflecting" some actual fact, whether that "fact" be the American frontier or, in this case, a peculiar incidence of mental malaise—trauma considered to have emanated from disruptions within the self or the society.

The Den

1. Quoted and in this way used by Howard Mumford Jones, *O Strange New World: American Culture: The Formative Years* (New York: Viking Press, 1964), p. 10. See Mumford's chapters "The Image of the New World" and "The Anti-Image."

2. John Winthrop, "A Modell of Christian Charity," in Perry Miller and Thomas H. Johnson, eds., *The Puritans* (New York: American Book Company, 1938), p. 199.

3. The citations are from an American edition of *The Pilgrim's Progress*, "a new edition, divided into chapters. To which are added, explanatory and practical notes, by Messrs. Mason, Scott, and Burder" (Philadelphia: William G. Murphey, 1814), p. 37. Unless otherwise noted, reference to *The Pilgrim's Progress* is to John Bunyan, *The Pilgrim's Progress from this World to That Which Is to Come*, ed. James Blanton Wharey, 2nd ed. revised by Roger Sharrock (Oxford: At the Clarendon Press, Oxford University Press, 1960). The first edition of *The Pilgrim's Progress* was published in 1678.

4. Note to Bunyan, *Pilgrim's Progress* (Philadelphia, 1814), p. 38.

The Melancholy Desert

5. Hayden White, "The Forms of Wildness: Archaeology of an Idea" (1972), in his *Tropics of Discourse: Essays in Cultural Criticism* (Baltimore: Johns Hopkins University Press, 1978), p. 181, n. 25, on the etymology of "wild" (*ferus*) and "iron" (*ferrum*).

6. For discussion of Bunyan's character as a man "outside time, . . . like the Freudian Id," see Perry Miller, "John Bunyan's Pilgrim's Progress," in *Classics of Religious Devotion* (Boston: Beacon Press, 1950), p. 78.

7. William Bradford, *Bradford's History "Of Plimoth Plantation,"* Commonwealth edition (Boston: Wright & Potter Printing Co., 1898), pp. 459, 460.

8. Cotton Mather, *The Wonders of the Invisible World: Being an Account of the Tryals of Several Witches, Lately Executed in New-England* . . . (Boston, 1693), in Samuel G. Drake, ed., *The Witchcraft Delusion in New England: Its Rise, Progress, and Termination* . . . , (1866; rpt. New York: Burt Franklin, 1970), 1:3, 15–16.

9. Mather, *Wonders*, p. 13; and William Perkins, *The Combate Betweene Christ and the Deuill Displayed: Or, A Commentarie vpon the Temptations of Christ* . . . , in *The Workes of that Famovs and Worthie Minister of Christ in the Vniuersitie of Cambridge, M. W. Perkins*, Vol. 3 (n.p.: Printed by Cantrell Legge, Printer to the Vniuersitie of Cambridge, 1609), 375, 376. The British Museum lists a second edition, much enlarged by a more perfect copy, of Perkins's *Combate Betweene Christ and the Deuill Displayed*, first published in London in 1606.

10. Mather, *Wonders*, p. 10; and Cotton Mather, *Magnalia Christi Ameri-*

cana: Or, The Ecclesiastical History of New-England . . ., [ed.] Thomas Robbins, Vol. 2 (London, 1702; Hartford: Silas Andrus & Son, 1853), 448, 490, 447, 446–48, 448–71.

11. Mather, *Wonders*, pp. 79, 24, 57, 242, 27, 121–22, 81, 2, 237.

12. "Remains of Mather's Library . . . Purchased by I. Thomas," Mather Family Papers, Box 12, Folder 11, American Antiquarian Society, under the author "Democritus Junior." The book is no longer held by the American Antiquarian Society. Appreciation is extended to Keith Arbour of the American Antiquarian Society for providing this information.

13. [Thomas Hooker], *The Sovles Humiliation* (London: Printed by I.L. for Andrew Crooke, 1637), pp. 117–18; and Tho: [Thomas] Shepard, *The Sound Beleever, Or, A Treatise of Evangelicall Conversion* . . . (London: Printed for R. Dawlman, 1645), pp. 325–26.

The Temptations that the Melancholy Experience

14. Cotton Mather, *The Angel of Bethesda*, ed. Gordon W. Jones (Barre, Mass.: American Antiquarian Society and Barre Publishers, 1972), p. 132. The edition is the first publication of Mather's manuscript on medicine.

15. An expansive study excluding "Elizabethan and Jacobean melancholy" is the classic study by Raymond Klibansky, Erwin Panofsky, and Fritz Saxl, *Saturn and Melancholy: Studies in the History of Natural Philosophy, Religion, and Art* (London: Thomas Nelson & Sons, 1964), a work dating in its conception to 1923. For further studies of ancient and medieval melancholy simply defined as related to spiritual isolation, see Siegfried Wenzel, *The Sin of Sloth: Acedia in Medieval Thought and Literature* (Chapel Hill: University of North Carolina Press, 1960); and Reinhard Kuhn, *The Demon of Noontide: Ennui in Western Literature* (Princeton, N.J.: Princeton University Press, 1976).

16. Klibansky et al., *Saturn and Melancholy*, pp. 359, 360, 372–73.

17. Mather, *Angel of Bethesda*, pp. 135, 134.

18. In his exhaustive study of the literary expressions of melancholy, Lawrence Babb, in *The Elizabethan Malady: A Study of Melancholia in English Literature from 1580 to 1642*, Studies in Language and Literature (East Lansing, Mich.: Michigan State College Press, 1951), pp. vii and 73, traces "the Vogue of Melancholy" beginning in the 1580s. Babb discusses Bright's location on p. 73, n. 2. From the references cited in the sixth volume of the *Oxford English Dictionary*, "melancholy," as opposed to "melancholia," appears to be the proper word, the first citation for the latter word being 1693, with the second, third, and fourth all coming in the nineteenth century. "Melancholia," then, a more "technical" term of disease, appears to be a nineteenth-century expression. The first citation for "melancholiac" in the substantive is 1863; for "melancholic," it is 1586, that is, from Bright's "melancholicke." "Melancholy" in the substantive dates from 1303; in the adjectival, from 1526. And though the *OED* lists the substantive form of "melancholic" as obsolete, the English translation of Freud's essay on "Mourning and Melancholia" (1917), in *The Standard Edition of the Complete Psychological Works of Sigmund Freud*, trans. and ed. James Strachey, Vol. 14 (London: Hogarth Press and The Institute of Psycho-Analysis, 1957), employs the word for one who is so suffering (pp. 245–46).

19. Robert Burton, *The Anatomy of Melancholy*, ed. Floyd Dell and Paul Jordan-Smith (London: George Routledge & Sons, 1931), pp. 917, 900, 866–67, 917,

900, 890, 919, 942, 970, 917, 941; and T. [Timothy] Bright, *A Treatise of Melancholie*, reproduced from the 1586 edition printed by Thomas Vautrollier (New York: Published for The Facsimile Text Society by Columbia University Press, 1940), pp. 198–204. The first edition of Burton's work (1621) is entitled *The Anatomy of Melancholy: What It Is. With All Its Kindes, Causes, Symptoms, Prognosticks, and Seuerall Cures of It. . . . Philosophically, Medicinally, Historically Opened and Cut Vp*, by Democritus Iunior. For a discussion of Burton's "Anti-Puritan Invective," see Thomas L. Canavan, "Robert Burton, Jonathan Swift, and the Tradition of Anti-Puritan Invective," *Journal of the History of Ideas* 34 (April–June 1973), 277–42; and Gail Thain Parker, "Jonathan Edwards and Melancholy," *The New England Quarterly* 41 (June 1968), 193–94. For support of Burton's originality concerning religious melancholy, see Lawrence Babb, *Sanity in Bedlam: A Study of Robert Burton's Anatomy of Melancholy* ([East Lansing, Mich.]: Michigan State University Press, 1959), p. 93.

20. Bright, *Treatise*, p. 121; Burton, *Anatomy*, p. 342. For the history of hysteria, see Ilza Veith, *Hysteria: The History of a Disease* (Chicago: University of Chicago Press, 1965).

21. For seventeenth-century ideas of melancholy, see Babb, *The Elizabethan Malady*; Babb, *Sanity in Bedlam*; Bergen Evans, in consultation with George J. Mohr, *The Psychiatry of Robert Burton* (1944; rpt. New York: Octagon Books, Farrar, Straus and Giroux, 1972); Judith Kegan Gardiner, "Elizabethan Psychology and Burton's Anatomy of Melancholy," *Journal of the History of Ideas* 38 (July–September 1977), 373–88; and Bridget Gellert Lyons, *Voices of Melancholy: Studies in Literary Treatments of Melancholy in Renaissance England* (London: Routledge & Kegan Paul, 1971). For discussion and diagnostic of English Puritanism as a melancholy, see Henry Ashton Crosby Forbes, "A Study of Religious Melancholy and Seventeenth-Century English Puritan Dissent" (Ph.D. diss., Harvard University, 1961).

22. Bright, *Treatise*, pp. 106, 5, 31, 102, 100, 102, 103, 188, 111. For the life of Bright, see William J. Carlton, *Timothe Bright: Doctor of Phisicke: A Memoir of "The Father of Modern Shorthand"* (London: Elliot Stock, 1911).

23. Bright, *Treatise*, p. 132; and Burton, *Anatomy*, pp. 329, 964, 328, 967, 871, 328–30. Themes of fear, sorrow, and solitude are discussed by Babb, *Elizabethan Malady*, pp. 30, 38, 32–33.

24. Bright, *Treatise*, pp. 130, 131, 135, 200; Burton, *Anatomy of Melancholy*, pp. 333, 334, 940, 959, 334, 332–33, 334.

25. Babb, *Sanity in Bedlam*, p. 27; and Burton, *Anatomy*, p. 356.

26. Burton, *Anatomy*, pp. 337–38, 891, 335.

27. Bright, *Treatise*, pp. 220, 193–95, 207–08, 228, 229, 230.

28. Burton, *Anatomy*, pp. 331, 332, 336, 348, 948, 949, 957, 958, 336–37.

29. Bright, *Treatise*, p. 187 and "Dedicatorie," n.p. For a discussion of melancholy and the conscience of sin, see Babb, *Elizabethan Malady*, pp. 51–54.

30. See Babb, *Elizabethan Malady*, pp. 23–24; and Babb, *Sanity in Bedlam*, pp. 93–94.

31. Burton, *Anatomy*, pp. 942, 938; and William Perkins, *The Whole Treatise of the Cases of Conscience, Distingvished into Three Books* (1606 and 1608), in *The Workes of that Famovs and VVorthy Minister of Christ in the Vniuersitie of Cambridge, M. VVilliam Perkins*, Vol. 2 (n.p.: Printed by Iohn Legat, Printer to the Vniuersitie of Cambridge, 1609), 54.

32. Bright, *Treatise*, p. 193; Burton, *Anatomy*, p. 942; and Bright, *Treatise*, p. 190.

33. Bright, *Treatise*, pp. 192, 206; Burton, *Anatomy*, pp. 967, 950, 951–52, 959–60, 970.

Obsessional Temptation and the Movement of Puritan Conversion

34. The idea of visible saints in American Puritan thought, so critical for an understanding of the uniqueness of American Puritanism, is presented by Edmund S. Morgan in his *Visible Saints: The History of a Puritan Idea* ([New York]: New York University Press, 1963). Morgan discusses what he has termed the "morphology of conversion" on pp. 66–73. For an important discussion of Puritan signification that has influenced this essay, see Michael P. Clark, "The Crucified Phrase: Puritan Semiology and Its Development in Colonial America" (Ph.D. diss., University of California, Irvine, 1977). See also Norman Pettit, *The Heart Prepared: Grace and Conversion in Puritan Spiritual Life*, Yale Publications in American Studies 11 (New Haven: Yale University Press, 1966), p. 56.

35. See Darrett B. Rutnam, *American Puritanism: Faith and Practice* (Philadelphia: J. B. Lippincott, Pilotbooks, 1970), pp. 97–107; Perkins, *Whole Treatise of the Cases of Conscience*, p. 15; and Morgan, *Visible Saints*, pp. 68–69. For Perkins's important location within English Puritan thought on the question of preparation, see Pettit, *Heart Prepared*, p. 61. Ronald A. Boscow has appended Perkins's steps of conversion to his edition of Cotton Mather, *Paterna: The Autobiography of Cotton Mather*, ed. Ronald A. Bosco (Delmar, N.Y.: Scholars' Facsimiles & Reprints, 1976), pp. 319–20, taken from William Perkins, *The Whole Treatise of the Cases of Conscience*, in *The Workes of That Famous and Worthy Minister of Christ . . . William Perkins* (London, 1612–13), 2:13.

36. William Ames, *Conscience with the Power and Cases Thereof, Divided into V. Bookes. . . . Translated Out of the Latine into English . . .* (n.p., 1639), 2:8–9.

37. On Hooker and the morphology of conversion, see Pettit, *Heart Prepared*, and most especially Sargent Bush, Jr., *The Writings of Thomas Hooker: Spiritual Adventure in Two Worlds* (Madison: University of Wisconsin Press, 1980). Thomas Shepard, *The Sound Believer: A Treatise of Evangelical Conversion . . .* (1645), in *The Works of Thomas Shepard . . .*, ed. John A. Albro (Boston: Doctrinal Tract and Book Society, 1853), 1:116–17, 267. Other references to the *Sound Believer* will be to this 1645 edition.

38. Perry Miller, *The New England Mind: From Colony to Province* (Cambridge, Mass.: Harvard University Press, 1953), p. 63; Morgan, *Visible Saints*, pp. 64–112; Perry Miller, "'Preparation for Salvation' in Seventeenth-Century New England," *Journal of the History of Ideas* 4 (June 1943), 253–86; and Pettit, *Heart Prepared*, pp. 83–85. It is Morgan who has given emphasis to setting the morphology of conversion into practice in New England. Set against Miller and Morgan and the emphasis given to preparation, arguing instead for a dialectic, is the account by William K. B. Stoever, *"A Faire and Easie Way to Heaven": Covenant Theology and Antinomianism in Early Massachusetts* (Middletown, Conn.: Wesleyan University Press, 1978).

39. Perkins, *Cases*, p. 55.

40. Perkins, *Cases*, pp. 16, 25, 26, 29–30, 31; Burton, *Anatomy*, pp. 970, 472–78.

41. Perkins, *Cases*, pp. 45–46, 46, 47. See also Perkins, *Combate Betweene*

Christ and the Deuill Displayed, pp. 371–409, especially p. 376; William Perkins, *A Discovrse of Conscience . . .*, 2nd ed. (1st ed., 1597), in *Workes*, 515–54, especially p. 536; and William Perkins, *A Graine of Mvsterd-Seed: Or, the Least Measvre of Grace that Is or Can Be Effectual to Saluation* (1597), in Perkins, *Workes* 1:643–44. See also the *Oxford English Dictionary*, s.v. "tentation," "temptation."

42. Perkins, *Cases*, pp. 56, 53–56, 47. For a close discussion of Puritan as opposed to scholastic theories of will, see Norman S. Fiering, "Will and Intellect in the New England Mind," *The William and Mary Quarterly*, 3rd ser., 29 (October 1972), 515–58, though Fiering argues (p. 528) that in attacking intellectualist models of the will, seventeenth-century Puritans used Ovid more than Paul or Augustine.

43. Ames, *Conscience*, 2:8–9, and 1:32–33; Perkins, p. 29; Perkins, *Combate Betweene Christ and the Deuill Displayed*, p. 373; and Thomas Hooker, *The Application of Redemption, By the Effectual Work of the Word, and Spirit of Christ, For the Bringing Home of Lost Sinners to God* (London: Printed by Peter Cole, 1656), p. 264. For Ames's importance in furthering the doctrine of preparation, see Pettit, *Heart Prepared*, p. 79. For a note on Ames's position in the morphology of conversion, see Morgan, *Visible Saints*, p. 66, n. 3.

44. See the opening remarks to these notes.

45. *Westminster Confession of Faith*, chapter XVIII, section IV.

46. Ames, *Conscience*, 2:44–45; Arth. [Arthur] Hildersam, *A Sermon Preached in Ashby-Chapell, Oct. 4. 1629* (London: Printed by George Miller, for Edward Brewster, 1633), p. 7; John Preston, *The Saints Qvalification . . .*, in [*Preston's Works*] (London: Printed by R.B. for Nicolas Bourne, 1633), [IV], pp. 84, 31; Hildersam, *A Sermon Preached*, p. 7; Arth. [Arthur] Hildersam, *The Doctrine of Fasting and Praier, and Hvmiliation for Sinne* (London: Printed by George Miller, for Edward Brewster, 1633), p. 122; Fiering, "Will and Intellect in the New England Mind," p. 539, discussing John Flavel, *Pneumatologia: A Treatise of the Soul of Man . . .* (1685), in *The Whole Works of the Reverend John Flavel* (Edinburgh, 1731), 1:283–84; and Baxter, *The Cure of Melancholy*, pp. 834, 835, 836, 843.

47. Richard Baxter, *The Cure of Melancholy and Overmuch Sorrow by Faith* (1683), with the title addendum "by Faith and Physick . . ."), in *The Practical Works of the Late Reverend and Pious Mr. Richard Baxter* (London: n.p., 1707), 4:832–45.

The Pilgrim's Progress

48. The debate of Bunyan's psychology—his health and/or neurosis—is heated, pitting Roger Sharrock's statement in *John Bunyan* (1954; London: Macmillan, 1968), p. 62, for example, against a host of pathological portraits. For a bibliography of the psychological studies of Bunyan, see Richard L. Greaves, *An Annotated Bibliography of John Bunyan Studies*, Bibliographia Tripotamopolitana: A Series of Bibliographies published occasionally by the Barbour Library, Pittsburgh Theological Seminary, Number V (Pittsburgh: Clifford E. Barbour Library, Pittsburgh Theological Seminary, 1972), section IX, "Psychological Studies," entries no. 381–92. For a more current psychological study emphasizing an Eriksonian point of view, see Monica Furlong, *Puritan's Progress: A Study of John Bunyan* (London: Hodder and Stoughton, 1975). For the essence of scandal

in the Puritan spiritual autobiography, see Sacvan Bercovitch, *The Puritan Origins of the American Self* (New Haven: Yale University Press, 1975), p. 16. For the statement that Bunyan "has his detractors . . . now as when he lived," see Ola Elizabeth Winslow, *John Bunyan* (New York: Macmillan Company, 1961), pp. 155–56.

49. *Pilgrim's Progress*, pp. 178, 9, 27, 84, 91, 34–35.

50. *Pilgrim's Progress*, pp. 15, 20; John Bunyan, *Grace Abounding to the Chief of Sinners*, ed. Roger Sharrock (Oxford: At the Clarendon Press, Oxford University Press, 1962), pp. 13–14. The first edition of *Grace Abounding* was published in 1666. Sharrock, in an end note on p. 315 of Bunyan, *Pilgrim's Progress*, notes the relation of the scene of the hill with the scene from *Grace Abounding*.

51. Bunyan, *Grace Abounding*, p. 13. See the editorial comment by Sharrock relating the scene of the hill with the experience of terror under Mosaic law in Bunyan, *Pilgrim's Progress*, p. 315. Another example, provided by Sharrock in *John Bunyan*, p. 64, of Bunyan's merging theology and psychopathology is Bunyan's belief—held by most Englishmen—that verses from the Bible when taken out of context held meaning, a belief that in Bunyan assumed superstitious dimensions.

52. *Pilgrim's Progress*, pp. 61, 63–64, and for the parallel noted by Sharrock, p. 324n; and Bunyan, *Grace Abounding*, pp. 31, 31–32, 33, 42. Also Karl Joachim Weintraub, *The Value of the Individual: Self and Circumstance in Autobiography* (Chicago: University of Chicago Press, 1978), a broad, thematic study on the rise of personality as self-consciousness, including (pp. 232–42), a Weberian reading of Bunyan; the quotation and comment appear on p. 237.

53. *Pilgrim's Progress*, pp. 114, 115.

The American Spiritual Relation

54. See Bercovitch, *Puritan Origins of the American Self*, pp. 1–34; Northrop Frye, *Anatomy of Criticism: Four Essays* (Princeton: Princeton University Press, 1957), pp. 307–08; Perry Miller and Thomas H. Johnson, eds., *The Puritans* (New York: American Book Company, 1938), p. 461; John N. Morris, *Versions of the Self: Studies in English Autobiography from John Bunyan to John Stuart Mill* (New York: Basic Books, 1966); Roger Sharrock, "Spiritual Autobiography," Ch. 3 of his *John Bunyan*, pp. 52–68; Daniel B. Shea, Jr., *Spiritual Autobiography in Early America* (Princeton: Princeton University Press, 1968); and especially Cecilia Tichi, "Spiritual Biography and the 'Lords Remembrances,'" in *The American Puritan Imagination: Essays in Revaluation*, ed. Sacvan Bercovitch (London: Cambridge University Press, 1974), pp. 56–73. Wayne Shumaker has written of *English Autobiography: Its Emergence, Materials, and Form*, University of California Publications, English Studies 8 (Berkeley: University of California Press, 1954); and more recently Weintraub has presented his *Value of the Individual*. See as well Owen C. Watkins, *The Puritan Experience* (London: Routledge & Kegan Paul, 1972); Paul Delany, *British Autobiography in the Seventeenth Century* (London: Routledge & Kegan Paul, 1969), pp. 167–74; and G. [George] A. Starr, *Defoe & Spiritual Autobiography* (1965; rpt. New York: Gordian Press, 1971). Eighteenth- and nineteenth-century discussions of autobiography would include John O. Lyons, *The Invention of the Self: The Hinge of Consciousness in the Eighteenth Century* (Carbondale, Ill.: Southern Illinois University Press, 1978), his Ch. 5 on "Autobiography," pp.

55–74; and William C. Spengemann and L. R. Lundquist, "Autobiography and the American Myth," *American Quarterly* 17 (Fall 1965), 501–19.

55. For the manner in which Mather composed his spiritual autobiography, see M. [Michael] G. Hall, "The Autobiography of Increase Mather," introduction to *The Autobiography of Increase Mather*, ed. M. G. Hall (1961; rpt. Worcester, Mass.: American Antiquarian Society, 1962), p. 272. On the "public nature" of American Puritan spiritual autobiography, see Shea, *Spiritual Autobiography*, pp. 93–94, 111–13, 118–19. See also "Diary-keeping in seventeenth-century England," the opening chapter to Alan Macfarlane's *The Family Life of Ralph Josselin, A Seventeenth-Century Clergyman: An Essay in Historical Anthropology* (Cambridge: At the University Press, 1970), pp. 3–11. G. Thomas Couser, *American Autobiography: The Prophetic Mode* (Amherst: University of Massachusetts Press, 1979), particularly pp. 1 and 13, gives emphasis to spiritual autobiography as the passage of a model self down through a family.

56. Bercovitch, *Puritan Origins of the American Self*, p. 16. For a discussion of the emergence of Puritan spiritual autobiography in relation to Augustine, see Tichi, "Spiritual Biography and the 'Lords Remembrances,'" p. 60.

57. Bercovitch, *Puritan Origins of the American Self*, p. 23; Emory Elliot, *Power and Pulpit in Puritan New England* (Princeton: Princeton University Press, 1975), p. 41, quoting in part from Norman Pettit; and Philip Greven, *The Protestant Temperament: Patterns of Child-Rearing, Religious Experience, and the Self in Early America* (New York: Alfred A. Knopf, 1977), pp. 79, 82. Greven most dramatically portrays his Puritan evangelicals in the terms as well of "paranoid vision," "rage," "impotency," "latent homosexuality," "intense alienation from their own bodies" (pp. 110, 126, 132, 73).

For a theme of the American Puritan's conversion as reflecting the historical fact, the actual exigency, of Erik Erikson's crisis of identity—a theme that denies Erikson's own historical location—see John Demos, *A Little Commonwealth: Family Life in Plymouth Colony* (New York: Oxford University Press, 1970), pp. 129–44; B. [Barry] R. Burg, *Richard Mather of Dorchester* ([Lexington]: University Press of Kentucky, 1976), pp. 171–72, n. 9; and most especially Darrett B. Rutman, *American Puritanism: Faith and Practice*, The Lippincott History Series (Philadelphia: J. B. Lippincott Company, Pilotbooks, 1970), pp. 114–24. Robert Middlekauff, in his searching exploration, *The Mathers: Three Generations of Puritan Intellectuals, 1596–1728* (New York: Oxford University Press, 1971), finds the Puritans' potential for morbidity displaced in their release of energy within the world, and thus has taken another, more reasoned tact—one closer, indeed, to that which the Puritans themselves claimed: "It [Puritan anxiety] rose from the objective world; it was, paradoxically, reasoned anxiety, and there lay its difference from modern anxiety which is neurotic and which has its sources in the irrational and the abnormal" (pp. 7–8). The only question remaining concerns the fact of such a historical disjunction itself. The most recent psychopathologically informed discussion of American Puritanism is David Leverenz, *The Language of Puritan Feeling: An Exploration in Literature, Psychology, and Social History* (New Brunswick, N.J.: Rutgers University Press, 1980).

58. Psychopathological specificity as regards hysteria is most ably displayed by John Demos in his "Underlying Themes in the Witchcraft of Seventeenth-Century New England," *The American Historical Review* 75 (June 1970), 1311–

26. For the question of obsessional psychopathology in early American studies, see the opening remarks to these notes.

59. See Robert Middlekauff, "Piety and Intellect in Puritanism," *The William and Mary Quarterly*, 3rd ser., 22 (July 1965), 457–70.

60. On the historiographical turn to the emotions and interior life of early America, see Michael McGiffert, "American Puritan Studies in the 1960's," *The William and Mary Quarterly*, 3rd ser., 27 (January 1970), particularly 49, 50, 52, 59, 61.

61. Samuel Hopkins, [ed.], *The Life and Character of Miss Susanna Anthony, Who Died, in Newport, (R.I.) June 23, MDCCXCI, in the Sixty Fifth Year of Her Age. Consisting Chiefly in Extracts from Her Writings, with Some Brief Observations on Them* (Worcester, Mass.: Printed by Leonard Worcester, 1796), p. 127; with acknowledgment to Greven, *Protestant Temperament*, for pointing to the significance of Anthony's writing.

62. Bercovitch discusses the "Auto-Machia," a term he derives from an early seventeenth-century poem by George Goodwin, on pp. 15–25 of his *Puritan Origins of the American Self*. The phrase "auto-American-biography" is used on p. 134.

63. Roger Sharrock, "Introduction" to Bunyan, *Grace Abounding*, pp. xviii, xix; Morgan, *Visible Saints*, pp. 64–112; and Weintraub, *Value of the Individual*, p. 235.

64. It is for this reason that the work of Sacvan Bercovitch, rather ignored by historians, is so important, for Bercovitch has pulled the jeremiad out of time and has offered the spiritual autobiography, the "auto-American-biography," as a genre unique, it would seem, to America, peculiar in its merging of fact and fancy, in its use of the self as social exemplum, in the writing of "History as a Novel, The Novel as History," as Norman Mailer would have it. If one follows the work of Bercovitch closely, most particularly his "Horologicals to Chronometricals: The Rhetoric of the Jeremiad," *Literary Monographs*, Vol. 3, ed. Eric Rothstein (Madison: Published for the Department of English by the University of Wisconsin Press, 1970), pp. 1–124—revised as *The American Jeremiad* (Madison: University of Wisconsin Press, 1978)—and ignores his claim that the Puritans were reflecting the trauma they described, then one finds within the language of the Puritan conversion the beginnings of this peculiar form of literature: Thoreau's *Walden*, Adams's *Education*, Agee's *Let Us Now Praise Famous Men*, Mailer's *Armies of the Night*, and Annie Dillard's *Pilgrim at Tinker Creek*.

65. See Robert G. Pope, *The Half-Way Covenant: Church Membership in Puritan New England* (Princeton: Princeton University Press, 1969). His pages discussing requirements for membership and varying church modifications are listed in his index under "Regenerate membership," including "modifications of," p. 318.

66. On the methodological employment of the past written text, see Sande Cohen, "Structuralism and the Writing of Intellectual History," *History and Theory* 17, no. 2 (1978), especially 208. On the procedure for offering the confession of faith and the examination and questions entailed, see Morgan, *Visible Saints*, pp. 87–93.

For early American spiritual relations recorded for entry into the church, see the relations appended to "The Diary of Michael Wigglesworth," ed. Edmund S.

Morgan, *Publications of the Colonial Society of Massachusetts, Transactions, 1942–1946* 35 (Boston: Colonial Society of Massachusetts, 1951), 426–44; the relations inscribed within *The Notebook of the Reverend John Fiske, 1644–1675*, ed. Robert G. Pope, *Publications of the Colonial Society of Massachusetts, Collections* 47 (Boston: Colonial Society of Massachusetts, 1974); "Relations of Conversion by Various Members of the Church of Dorchester and the Church of Boston," contained in folder 7, box 13, of the Mather Family Papers, Mather Collection, American Antiquarian Society; and "Relations (Confessions of Sins) for Members of the Westborough Church . . . ," contained in folder 2, box 2, of the Parkman Family Papers, American Antiquarian Society. Morgan, in *Visible Saints*, p. 91, n. 44, references fifty narratives recorded by Thomas Shepard, the manuscript held by the New England Historic Genealogical Society. See also Bruce Chapman Woolley, "Reverend Thomas Shepard's Cambridge Church Members, 1636–1649: A Socio-Economic Analysis" (Ph.D. diss., University of Rochester, 1973). An edition of these relations, edited by George Selement and Bruce C. Wooley, has been published by the Colonial Society of Massachusetts. Christopher M. Jedrey, in *The World of John Cleaveland: Family and Community in Eighteenth-Century New England* (New York: W. W. Norton & Company, 1979), pp. 117–19, discusses the structure of fifty-three narratives in the John Cleaveland papers of the Essex Institute in Salem, Massachusetts. Ross W. Beales, Jr., has told the author that he knows of no other such collections of spiritual relations for early America.

For extracts of relations from John Roger's *A Tabernacle for the Sun* (1653), taken in Dublin, see John H. Taylor, "Some Seventeenth-Century Testimonies," *Transactions of the Congregational Historical Society* 26 (1949–51), 64–77.

67. For descriptions of spiritual relations in terms of patterns, see Taylor, "Some Seventeenth-Century Testimonies," p. 66; Geoffrey F. Nuttall, *Visible Saints: The Congregational Way, 1640–1660* (Oxford: Basil Blackwell, 1957), p. 114; and Jedrey, *World of John Cleaveland*, pp. 117–19. The Edwards phrase is from Jonathan Edwards, *A Faithful Narrative of the Surprising Work of God . . .* (1737), in *The Works of President Edwards* (London, 1817; rpt. New York: Burt Franklin, 1968), p. 27.

68. Morgan, *Visible Saints*, p. 89. For discussion of debates in seventeenth-century New England as to whether women should speak their relations publicly, see Mary Maples Dunn, "Saints and Sisters: Congregational and Quaker Women in the Early Colonial Period," *American Quarterly*, 30 (Winter 1978), 588–89, 593.

69. Increase Mather, "Increase Mather's Confutation of Solomon Stoddard's Observations Respecting the Lord's Supper, 1680," eds. Everett Emerson and Mason I. Lowance, *Proceedings of the American Antiquarian Society* 83 (April 18, 1973–October 17, 1973), 41, 55, 63.

70. Jonathan Edwards, *An Humble Inquiry into the Rules of the Word of God, Concerning the Qualifications Requisite to a Complete Standing & Full Communion in the Visible Christian Church* (1765), in *Works* 7:20–21, 194, 121, 41, 59.

71. On the argument that the relation did not serve as a test, see John S. Coolidge, *The Pauline Renaissance in England: Puritanism and the Bible* (Oxford: Clarendon Press, 1970), pp. 65–66 and n. 33. The quotations are from Increase Mather, "Confutation of Solomon Stoddard's Observations," p. 42;

Jonathan Edwards, *Misrepresentations Corrected, and Truth Vindicated, in a Reply to the Rev. Mr. Solomon William's Book . . .*, in *Works* 7:185 (see also p. 141); and Jonathan Edwards, *The Distinguishing Marks of a Work of the Spirit of God . . .* (1741), in *Works* 8:591. An analogy may be drawn between the giving of spiritual testimony and Peter Brown's interpretation of the latitude and communal function of the medieval ordeal: Peter Brown, "Society and the Supernatural: A Medieval Change," *Daedalus* 104 (Spring 1975), 133–51.

72. Increase Mather, "Confutation of Solomon Stoddard's Observations," p. 63.

73. *Notebook of the Reverend John Fiske*, pp. 29–30.

74. "The relation of Mr Collins," in Wigglesworth, "The Diary of Michael Wigglesworth" (1951), p. 426.

75. See "Relations for Members of the Westborough Church" in the Parkman Papers of the American Antiquarian Society. Also Kenneth A. Lockridge, *Literacy in Colonial New England: An Enquiry into the Social Context of Literacy in the Early Modern West* (New York: W. W. Norton & Company, 1974).

76. Shepard, *Sound Beleever*, pp. 79, 49, 60–61, 78–79, 77, 130–31, 134, 133, 132; Hooker, *Sovles Humiliation*, pp. 30, 45; and Shepard, *Sound Beleever*, pp. 134, 135–36, 150.

77. Murray G. Murphey, "The Psychodynamics of Puritan Conversion," *American Quarterly* 31 (Summer 1979), 140.

78. Jack Goody, *The Domestication of the Savage Mind*, Themes in the Social Sciences (1977; Cambridge: Cambridge University Press, 1977, paperback).

79. "The relation of Mr Collins," in Wigglesworth, "The Diary of Michael Wigglesworth" (1951), p. 428.

80. See "Relations for Members of the Westborough Church" in the Parkman Papers of the American Antiquarian Society.

81. Quoted by Terence Hawkes, *Structuralism & Semiotics* (1977; rpt. Berkeley: University of California Press, paperback, 1977), p. 40. The quotation is from Claude Lévi-Strauss, *Structural Anthropology*, trans. Claire Jacobson and Brooke Grundfest Schoepf, [Vol. 1] (New York: Basic Books, 1963), 198, from his essay on "The Effectiveness of Symbols" (1949).

82. Roy Pascal, *Design and Truth in Autobiography* (London: Routledge & Kegan Paul, 1960), pp. 33–34. We would not detract from this fine account, but take exception to the following statement: "But it is Bunyan's mental inarticulateness, his helplessness, that makes these incidents most moving, not his insight; and like many sectarian, pietistic autobiographers he fails to recognise the relevance of many experiences to his spiritual progress." (*ibid.*).

83. Lévi-Strauss, "Effectiveness of Symbols," quoted by Hawkes, *Structuralism*, p. 198.

84. Morgan, *Visible Saints*, p. 71.

Self-Murder

85. Increase Mather, *A Call to the Tempted. A Sermon on the Horrid Crime of Self-Murder . . .* (1724; Boston: Printed by B. Green, 1734), p. 1.

86. "Joseph champney's relation," in Wigglesworth, "The Diary of Michael Wigglesworth" (1951), p. 441.

87. As Greven states in the *Protestant Temperament*, suicide itself actually appears to be rare (p. 83). To the author's knowledge, there is no study of suicide

in seventeenth-century New England to support the contention that it was unusually common. Lyle Koehler, in *A Search for Power: The "Weaker Sex" in Seventeenth-Century New England* (Urbana: University of Illinois Press, 1980), has listed all suicides he has found. In Appendix 3, "Suicides in New England, 1620–1709," pp. 467–70, he lists 56, with 7 attempted. For Rhode Island, he lists 3. In any event, references to texts reflecting upon suicidal impulses offer, if anything, evidence that the authors of such texts themselves held a less than average potential for self-murder—that is, if one accepts the findings summarized by two studies of obsessional thought. In the words of Alan Black, "The Natural History of Obsessional Neurosis," in H. R. Beech, ed., *Obsessional States* (London: Methuen & Co., 1974), "The suicidal attempt rate was unrelated to whether or not suicidal/homicidal ideas formed the content of the obsessions" (p. 48). And in the words of H. R. Beech and Andrée Liddell, "Decision-Making, Mood States and Ritualistic Behavior among Obsessional Patients," in Beech, ed., *Obsessional States*: "The findings of this inquiry suggested that depression is indeed a common complication of obsessional neurosis although, interestingly, other hazards such as alcoholism, drug addiction or suicide appeared to be reduced risks for this group" (p. 145).

88. Increase Mather, *A Call to the Tempted*, p. 8.

89. Samuel Willard, *The Fiery Tryal No Strange Thing* . . . (Boston: Printed for Samuel Sewall, 1682), pp. 6–7; Shepard, *Sound Beleever*, p. 79; Solomon Stoddard, *A Guide to Christ, Or, The Way of Directing Souls that Are Under the Work of Conversion* . . . (1714; Boston: Printed by J. Draper, for D. Henchman, 1735), pp. 33–34. See also Giles Firmin, *The Real Christian, or A Treatise of Effectual Calling* (London, 1670; Boston; Printed by Rogers & Fowle, for J. Edwards . . . and J. Blanchard, 1742), pp. 57–60, 75–76, 311; Thomas Hooker, *The Poor Doubting Christian Drawn to Christ* (Boston: Printed by Green, Bushell, and Allen, for D. Henchman, 1743), p. 52;—a first edition published in London, 1629, as part of *The Saints Cordials* . . . , with subsequent significant changes (see George H. Williams et al., eds., *Thomas Hooker; Writings in England and Holland, 1626–1633*, Harvard Theological Studies, XXVIII [Cambridge, Mass.: Harvard University Press, 1975], pp. 394–96); Cotton Mather, *The Case of a Troubled Mind* . . . (Boston: Printed by B. Green, for S. Garrish, 1717); Tho. [Thomas] Shepard, *The Sincere Convert; Discovering the Small Number of True Believers* . . . , 5th ed. (London: Printed by Richard Cotes for John Sweeting, 1648), pp. 7–8 (1st ed., London, 1640 or 1641); Michael Wigglesworth, "Light in Darkness," particularly Song VII and Song VIII, in *Meat Out of the Eater: Or, Meditations Concerning the Necessity, End, and Usefulness of Afflictions Unto God's Children* . . . , 5th ed., corrected and amended by the author in 1703 (Boston: Printed by J. Allen for N. Boone, 1717, pp. 52–57 (first ed., 1669); and Samuel Willard, *The Christians Exercise by Satans Temptations* . . . (Boston: Printed by B. Green and J. Allen, for Benjamin Eliot, 1701), pp. 26–27.

90. In Wigglesworth, "The Diary of Michael Wigglesworth" (1951), p. 428.

91. "John Dane's Narrative, 1682," *New England Historical and Genealogical Register* 8 (April 1854), pp. 154–55.

92. Increase Mather, *A Call to the Tempted*, pp. 1, 2.

93. Cotton Mather, *Wonders of the Invisible World*, 1:237; and Jonathan Edwards, *A Faithful Narrative of the Surprising Work of God* . . . (London, 1737), in *The Great Awakening* . . . , ed. C. C. Goen, *The Works of Jonathan Edwards*,

John E. Smith, general ed., Vol. 4 (New Haven: Yale University Press, 1972), 206–07.

94. Greven, *Protestant Temperament*, p. 83.

95. "The Spiritual Travels of Nathan Cole," ed. Michael J. Crawford, *The William and Mary Quarterly*, 3rd ser., 33 (January 1976), 100 and n. 23.

96. "Spiritual Travels of Nathan Cole," pp. 101–03.

97. "Spiritual Travels of Nathan Cole," p. 105.

The Self-History and Melancholy

98. Ebenezer Parkman, "Memoirs of Mrs Sarah Pierpont; late amiable Consort of James Pierpont A. M. of New Haven, in New England: who departed this Life" [1754], in the Parkman Family Papers, box 2, folder 4, American Antiquarian Society, Worcester, Mass.

Thomas Cooley, *Educated Lives: The Rise of Modern Autobiography in America* (Columbus: Ohio State University Press, 1976), p. 3, traces the origin of the word "autobiography" to William Taylor, a linguist, dating from 1797.

99. See the opening remarks to these notes.

100. Increase Mather, *Autobiography*, p. 277.

101. For a discussion of anonymity in Cotton Mather's autobiography, and for one of the few discussions of the autobiography itself in early America, see Ronald A. Bosco's excellent "Introduction" to Cotton Mather, *Paterna: The Autobiography of Cotton Mather* (Delmar, N.Y.: Scholars' Facsimiles & Reprints, 1976), pp. xiii–lxi, in particular, pp. xliii, liii–lvi.

102. See "Thoreau and 'I'," pp. 1–11, in Charles R. Anderson, *The Magic Circle of Walden* (New York: Holt, Rinehart and Winston, 1968).

103. As by Leon Edel, in *Henry D. Thoreau*, University of Minnesota Pamphlets on American Writers, no. 90 (Minneapolis: University of Minnesota Press, 1970).

104. For an apology, see Walter Harding in a note to *The Variorum Walden*, annotated by Walter Harding (New York: Twayne Publishers, 1962), p. 289, n. 12: "As Roland Robbins discovered when he began his research on the location of Thoreau's cabin, the passage about the mink ["As I sit at my window this summer afternoon, . . . a mink steals out of the marsh before my door and seizes a frog by the shore," p. 107] was not in Thoreau's original journal entry for August 6, 1845, but was added later when he had left Walden and had forgotten that he could not see the marsh from his cabin door." Wherever the swamp, Thoreau had not forgotten that it lay at his feet and was plainly there for all to see.

Only recently have critics approached *Walden* as Charles R. Anderson has done so well in *The Magic Circle of Walden*, as a "poem." In his chapter "Thoreau and 'I'" (pp. 1–11), Anderson discusses the failure of approaching the work "as nature essays or as social criticism" or "as literal autobiography" (pp. 1, 3). Yet even this designation of poetry fails to account for the genre of *Walden*: Thoreau clearly provides himself as the actor just as the Puritans had, creating confusion as to whom it is one is speaking of.

105. Quentin Anderson, *The Imperial Self: An Essay in American Literary and Cultural History* (New York: Alfred A. Knopf, 1971).

106. Bercovitch, *Puritan Origins of the American Self*, p. 14; and Bunyan, *Pilgrim's Progress*, p. 287.

107. *Walden*, Vol. 2 of *The Writings of Henry David Thoreau*, Walden Edition

(1906; rpt. New York: AMS Press, 1968), p. 72. The work was first published in 1854.

108. Edward Taylor, Meditation 25 (second series), Meditation 26 (second series), Meditation 3 (first series), Meditation 40 (first series), in *The Poems of Edward Taylor*, ed. Donald E. Stanford (New Haven: Yale University Press, 1960), pp. 127, 129, 8, 64, 8. See Bercovitch, *Puritan Origins of the American Self*, pp. 14–15, 16, 20–21; and Bert C. Bach, "Self-Deprecation in Edward Taylor's Sacramental Meditations," *Cithara* 6 (1966), 49–58.

109. Edward Taylor's confessional is published in Donald E. Stanford, "Edward Taylor's 'Spiritual Relation,'" *American Literature* 35 (January 1964), 467–75. Anne Bradstreet's confessional, "To My Dear Children," is contained in *The Works of Anne Bradstreet in Prose and Verse*, ed. John Harvard Ellis (1867; rpt. New York: Peter Smith, 1932), pp. 3–10. The lines quoted are from Anne Bradstreet, "Of the Four Humours in Mans Constitution," in *Works*, pp. 139–41. The poem was first published in London as a part of Bradstreet's collection, *The Tenth Muse lately Sprung up in America . . .* (1650), the collection republished in Boston as *Several Poems Compiled with Great Variety of Wit and Learning . . .* (1678).

110. Cotton Mather, *Diary of Cotton Mather* [ed. Worthington Chauncey Ford], American Classics (1911–12; rpt. New York: Frederick Ungar Publishing Co., [1957], 1:195. See also Shea, *Spiritual Autobiography*, p. 163.

111. Discussed by Frank Shuffelton, *Thomas Hooker: 1586–1647* (Princeton: Princeton University Press, 1977), pp. 28–70, especially pp. 32–35. The quotation is from Jasper Hartwell, *The Firebrand Taken Out of the Fire, Or, the Wonderfull History, Case, and Cure of Mis Drake* (London, 1654), quoted by Shuffelton, p. 35.

112. The case of Mather and Mercy Short is discussed by Richard Slotkin, *Regeneration through Violence: The Mythology of the American Frontier, 1600–1860* (Middletown, Conn.: Wesleyan University Press, 1973), pp. 128–45. See also Mather, *Wonders of the Invisible World*, p. 139.

113. Bunyan, *Grace Abounding*, pp. 31, 22, 42, 57; and Perkins, *Whole Treatise*, p. 3.

114. John Winthrop, "John Winthrop's Christian Experience," (1636–37), in *Winthrop Papers* (Boston: Massachusetts Historical Society, 1929), 1:155, 156, 157, 158, 159. See also Morgan, *Visible Saints*, pp. 71–72; and Shea, *Spiritual Autobiography*, pp. 100–10.

115. "It is not experience that organizes expression, but the other way around—*expression organizes experience*." Thus Marshall Sahlins, *Culture and Practical Reason* (1976; rpt. Chicago: University of Chicago Press, Phoenix Edition, 1978), p. 145, citing from V. N. Vološinov [Mikhail Bakhtin], *Marxism and the Philosophy of Language*, trans. Ladislav Matejka and I. R. Titunik, Studies in Language (Leningrad, 1930; New York: Seminar Press, 1973), p. 85.

116. See William James, *The Varieties of Religious Experience: A Study in Human Nature: Being the Gifford Lectures on Natural Religion Delivered at Edinburgh in 1901–1902* (1902; New York: Random House, Modern Library, n.d.), pp. 196–97; and William James, "Preface" to Edwin Diller Starbuck, *The Psychology of Religion: An Empirical Study of the Growth of Religious Consciousness* (London: Walter Scott, 1899), p. vii. Conversion for Starbuck was "*a*

distinctly adolescent phenomenon," few cases ranging outside the bounds of ten and twenty-five years, a process he correlated with puberty, or what James in *Varieties*, pp. 196–97, spoke of as "growth-crisis." For this, see Starbuck's chapter on "The Age of Conversion," pp. 28–48; the quotation here is from p. 28. Given this model, Erik Erikson has explained late or extended identity crises in terms of moratoriums experienced by his great men. Yet Gerald F. Moran, in "Conditions of Religious Conversion in the First Society of Norwich, Connecticut, 1718–1744," *Journal of Social History* 5 (Spring 1972), 331–43, has shown that for his community, at least, the age of conversion prior to the Great Awakening was, in modern terms, quite high, more in alignment with the adult cases James considered for his Edinburgh lectures. For women, the average age of conversion was 25.6 years, and for men, 30.3 years—"behavior," as Moran writes, that "runs counter to the traditional interpretation of religious conversion as an experience encountered predominantly by adolescents" (pp. 333, 335). Certainly the impression one receives in reading Puritan spiritual autobiographies of the seventeenth century is that conversion was to be considered a mature experience; these were not, as James wrote of Starbuck's cases, "conversions . . . mainly those of very commonplace persons, kept true to a pre-appointed type by instruction, appeal, and example"—that is, by "suggestion" (*Varieties*, p. 196). Moran, pp. 335–36, 342, n. 23, speculates that perhaps the late age of conversion reflects "processes peculiar to a pre-industrial agrarian society," arguing not, as he says, for a theory of "physiological change but for possible variation in the rate of ego development . . . fostered by disparate sets of societal, cultural and behavioral norms." Whether that is indeed the case, Moran's important study does show that so-called delayed conversions—or the adult cases that seemed for James in the *Varieties*, as for Erikson in his studies, peculiar to a few religious geniuses or great men of history—are as much of a type as the adolescent cases. The experience of the wanderer as mature as Bunyan's Christian, reasonably and singularly leaving family and friends, and old enough to loose his way and his ways, could only be adult. A conversion composed as a literary type demanded a maturity of reflection, before a sociology, as it were, came to replace a literature. As Moran has shown for the years of the Great Awakening itself, the age of conversion lessened considerably (pp. 336–38), as one might expect, thereby turning, it would appear, the composition of conversion into a moment of experience, the figure into stereotype.

117. Winthrop, "Christian Experience," and John Winthrop, "John Winthrop's Experiencia, 1616–1618," in *Winthrop Papers* 1:160, 161, 160, 201, 194, 193, 197, 207.

118. "John Winthrop's Experiencia," pp. 196, 198–99, 200.

119. The definitive account of spiritual autobiography in early American is Shea, *Spiritual Autobiography*, who notes the communal function such literature served (pp. 153–54, 182–83).

120. Thomas Shepard, *God's Plot: The Paradoxes of Puritan Piety: Being the Autobiography & Journal of Thomas Shepard*, ed. Michael McGiffert, The Commonwealth Series ([Amherst]: University of Massachusetts Press, 1972), pp. 38, 43, 170, 169, 186, 91, 182, 102.

121. Michael Wigglesworth, *The Diary of Michael Wigglesworth, 1653–1657: The Conscience of a Puritan*, ed. Edmund S. Morgan (1951, 1965; rpt. Glouces-

ter, Mass.: Peter Smith, 1970), pp. 5, 6, 93, 3, 21, 22, 50, 55, 33–34, 50, 81, 82, 84, 53, 69–70, 101, 84. See also Edmund S. Morgan, "Introduction" to Wigglesworth, *Diary*, pp. vi–vii.

122. *Autobiography of Increase Mather*, pp. 291, 292, 293, 294, 295, 296, 298, 303–04, 350. See David Levin, *Cotton Mather: The Young Life of the Lord's Remembrancer, 1663–1703* (Cambridge, Mass.: Harvard University Press, 1978), pp. 18–22, for an excellent discussion of Increase Mather's fright and terror and the effect Levin believes it had on Cotton, though Levin reads the incident rather literally and without psychological apparatus. "Increase Mather's account of these miseries allows us insight," Levin writes, "into young Cotton's anxieties and also into the practical discrepancies between Puritan theology and the methods that individual men actually used to survive the warfare waged between God and Satan inside mortal heads" (p. 20). It is with this statement that one must take exception, if one is to understand the use of psychopathology as text, as signification opposed to "discrepancies" and what "men actually used"—a word and phrase that return the reader to Perry Miller's conception that somehow the Puritan had to work around, or get around, the matter of predestination. The text of Mather's hypochondria is no such instrument, no more than covenant theology was.

123. Increase Mather, *Life and Death of Richard Mather (1670)*, facsimile rpt., Introduction by Benjamin Franklin V. and William K. Bottorff (Athens, Ohio: n.p., 1966), pp. 25, 33.

124. For admirable analyses of Cotton Mather and his works, see Middlekauff, *The Mathers*, Book III; and Levin, *Cotton Mather*.

125. Editorial comment by William R. Manierre II in Cotton Mather, *The Diary of Cotton Mather D.D., F.R.S. for the Year 1712*, ed. William R. Manierre II (Charlottesville, Va.: University Press of Virginia, 1964), p. 91, n. 6.

126. *Paterna*, p. 7; and *Diary for 1712*, p. 124.

127. *Paterna*, pp. 11, 10; and *Diary* 1:61–62.

128. *Diary for 1712*, pp. 35, 66; *Paterna*, pp. 33–34; *Diary* 2:75, 601, 616, 67, 69; and *Diary* 1:80–81, and editorial comment by Ford, p. 6, n. 2. Middlekauff, *The Mathers*, discusses Cotton's asceticism in his chapters on "The Psychology of Abasement" and "The Experimental Religion," pp. 231–46, 305–19.

129. *Paterna*, pp. 9–10; *Diary* 2:533, 534; *Diary* 1:239; *Paterna*, pp. 10–11; and *Diary*, 2:264.

130. *Diary* 1:31, 79–80, 255, 98, 285, 475, 585; *Diary* 2:704, 3; *Diary* 1:585, 109, 377–78, 54; and *Diary for 1712*, p. 111.

131. *Paterna*, p. 264; *Diary* 2:518, 524; and *Paterna*, pp. 97–98.

132. *Diary* 1:475, 2:705. See Clark, "The Crucified Phrase."

The Transit of New England's Conscience: Jonathan Edwards

133. Benjamin Colman, *The Case of Satan's Fiery Darts in Blasphemous Suggestions and Hellish Annoyances* . . . (1711; Boston: Printed by Rogers and Fowle, for J. Edwards, 1744), pp. 59, 35, 15, 52, 25–26, 11, 10, 27, 61. The author is indebted to an article by Gail Thain Parker, "Jonathan Edwards and Melancholy," *New England Quarterly*, 41, pp. 193–212, for reference to this set of sermons by Colman and, as cited earlier, to a sermon by Richard Baxter in relation to the writings of Edwards.

134. Jonathan Edwards, "Benjamin Colman's Abridgment, November 1736,"

in *The Great Awakening* . . . , ed. C. C. Goen, *Works* 4:123; Edwards, *A Faithful Narrative of the Surprizing Work of God* . . . (London, 1737), in *The Great Awakening, Works,* 4:206–07.

135. Jonathan Edwards, *The Life and Diary of the Rev. David Brainerd: With Notes and Reflections,* in *The Works of President Edwards* [ed. Edward Williams and Edward Parsons], Vol. 3 ([London: James Black and Son], 1817; rpt. New York: Burt Franklin, Research and Source Work Series No. 271, 1968), 197; and David Brainerd to John Brainerd, April 30, 1743, in Jonathan Edwards, *Mr. Brainerd's Remains, Consisting of Letters and Other Papers,* in *Works* 3:487. Brainerd's diary was originally published by Jonathan Edwards as *An Account of the Life of the Late Reverend Mr. David Brainerd* . . . *Chiefly Taken from His Own Diary,* and *Other Private Writings* . . . (Boston: Printed for and Sold by D. Henchman, in Cornhill, 1749); the *Account* included Brainerd's letter to his brother John (pp. 261–63).

136. Jonathan Edwards, "Sermon II," in *The Works of Jonathan Edwards, A. M.,* [ed.] Edward Hickman (London: William Ball, 1839), 2:833; and "Sermon III" (September 1737), *ibid.,* 846. Edwards's "demythologizing of the biblical term *wilderness,*" of which "like his contemporary John Wesley he largely interiorized and individualized the meaning," is discussed by George H. Williams in his *Wilderness and Paradise in Christian Thought: The Biblical Experience of the Desert in the History of Christianity & the Paradise Theme in the Theological Idea of the University* (New York: Harper & Brothers, Publishers, 1962), pp. 110–11.

137. "Sermon XII," in *Works of Edwards, A. M.* 2:935; and "The Manner in which the Salvation of the Soul Is to Be Sought" (September 1740), in *Works of Edwards, A. M.* 2:53, 54.

138. Brainerd, *Life and Diary,* pp. 239, 252, 90, 194, 213, 207, 211, 141, 261.

139. *Ibid.,* pp. 96, 177, 183, 182, 95, 166, 102, 220, 239, 144, 173, 215.

140. *Ibid.,* pp. 84, 82, 84, 86, 203.

141. Edwards, *Faithful Narrative,* pp. 191–205; the quotation is from p. 200.

142. Jonathan Edwards, "Preface" to Brainerd, *Life and Diary,* pp. 76, 77, 79, 77, 79.

143. For psychologically informed discussions of Edwards's character, see Richard L. Bushman, "Jonathan Edwards and Puritan Consciousness," *Journal for the Scientific Study of Religion* 5 (Fall 1966), 383–96; and Richard L. Bushman, "Jonathan Edwards as a Great Man: Identity, Conversion, and Leadership in the Great Awakening," *Soundings,* 52 (Spring 1969), 15–46. For a discussion of Edwards and melancholy from a point of view contrasting with this book, see Parker, "Jonathan Edwards and Melancholy."

144. Jonathan Edwards, "His Diary," in S. [Sereno] E. Dwight, *The Life of President Edwards* (New York: G.&C.&H. Carvill, 1830), pp. 76, 81, 76, 81, 77, 78, 77, 78, 82, 77, 78, 80, 88, 91, 84, 90, 82, 80.

145. Samuel Hopkins, *The Life and Character of the Late Reverend Mr. Jonathan Edwards* (1765), republished in David Levin, ed., *Jonathan Edwards: A Profile,* American Profiles (New York: Hill and Wang, 1968), pp. 40, 42, 41, 42. Levin's is the definitive contemporary edition of Hopkins's work.

146. Quoted in Hopkins, *Life and Character of Edwards,* p. 75.

147. Edwards, "His Diary," pp. 88, 93. Edwards's spiritual autobiography ("An Account of his Conversion . . . ," variously published as the "Personal Narra-

tive") was printed by Hopkins in *Life and Character of Edwards*; the quotations are from pp. 25, 27. See also Shea, *Spiritual Autobiography*, p. 192.

148. Jonathan Edwards, *Religious Affections* (originally published as *A Treatise Concerning Religious Affections . . .*, 1746), ed. John E. Smith, *The Works of Jonathan Edwards*, ed. Perry Miller, Vol. 2 (New Haven: Yale University Press, 1959), 151, 446.

149. Edwards, *Religious Affections*, pp. 127, 131, 135, 138, 142, 151, 294, 288, 290, 142; and James Robe to Jonathan Edwards, August 16, 1743, in Dwight, *Life of Edwards*, p. 201.

150. Edwards, *Religious Affections*, pp. 142, 289–90.

151. Edwards, *Faithful Narrative*, p. 162; Edwards, *Religious Affections*, pp. 156–57, 157, n. 6; and *Faithful Narrative*, pp. 162, 206, 206–07.

152. *Faithful Narrative*, p. 162; and *Religious Affections*, p. 426, n. 2.

153. Jonathan Edwards, *Some Thoughts Concerning the Revival* (originally published as *Some Thoughts Concerning the Present Revival of Religion in New-England . . .*, 1742), in Edwards, *Great Awakening*, pp. 334, 336, 334–35, 338, 340, 341.

154. *Religious Affections*, pp. 195, 361–62, 195, 442, 422, 443–44.

155. Perkins, *Whole Treatise of the Cases of Conscience*, p. 15; and Edwards, *Religious Affections*, p. 157, n. 6. Such is the theme of Erik H. Erikson that runs throughout his work, most particularly in the images he draws from "The Meaning of 'Meaning It,'" the title of a chapter from his *Young Man Luther: A Study in Psychoanalysis and History* (New York: W. W. Norton & Company, 1958), pp. 170–222; it is a theme to which this book is indebted throughout. Erikson, however, tends to place the meaning of his own phrase in Luther's distinctions between faith and works on the one hand, and between works and work on the other, and not in this equally important distinction that the Puritans drew between legal fear and sorrow, the latter to be located in the heart, not in impressions falsely wrought. Such dualities drawn by the Puritans are of course a major theme of Perry Miller's work, particularly in his architecture of their mind, *The New England Mind: The Seventeenth Century* (New York: Macmillan Company, 1939); see Miller's discussions, for example, of "historicall faith" (pp. 31–32), "synteresis" (pp. 192–193), and the "mechanical" (pp. 28–29).

156. This theme has been developed in discussions of the Puritans' interaction with American Indians, most creatively by Slotkin, *Regeneration through Violence*, pp. 57–179. Other studies with similar themes are cited by Robert F. Berkhofer, Jr., *The White Man's Indian: Images of the American Indian from Columbus to the Present* (New York: Alfred A. Knopf, 1978), pp. 27 and 83, and pp. 205, n. 61, and 219, n. 31.

157. The correspondence is reproduced in "Related Correspondence," in Edwards, *Religious Affections*, pp. 463–513, with an introductory note and information on Gillespie in the "Introduction" to the letters, pp. 465–69. The correspondence was first published, according to Sereno Dwight and as related by the introduction, in the *Edinburgh Quarterly Magazine* 1 (1798). Thomas Gillespie to Jonathan Edwards, November 24, 1746, pp. 476–77.

158. Edwards to Gillespie, September 4, 1747, in *Religious Affections*, pp. 482, 489, 487; and Gillespie to Edwards, September 19, 1748, *ibid.*, pp. 497, 498, 497.

159. Edwards to Gillespie, April 2, 1750, in *Religious Affections*, pp. 511, 512.

160. Edwards, "Sermon II," p. 830; and Perkins, *Combate Betweene Christ and the Deuill Displayed*, p. 375.

161. Martin Luther, *Lectures on Galatians, 1535*, in *Lectures on Galatians, 1535, Chapters 5–6; Lectures on Galatians, 1519, Chapters 1–6*, ed. Jaroslav Pelikan, trans. Jaroslav Pelikan [for 1535], *Luther's Works*, Vol. 27 (St. Louis: Concordia Publishing House, 1964), 406, 80–81, 406, 405. See in particular Erikson, *Young Man Luther*, pp. 218–20.

162. Bunyan, *Grace Abounding*, pp. 40–41.

163. Max Weber, *The Protestant Ethic and the Spirit of Capitalism*, trans. Talcott Parsons (1904–05, 1930; New York: Charles Scribner's Sons, 1958), pp. 79, 79–92. For the translation of Luther's term, see the translator's note, p. 194, n. 11.

164. Winthrop, "John Winthrop's Experiencia," pp. 209, 206; and Cotton Mather, "Early Piety, Exemplified in the Life and Death of Mr. Nathaniel Mather," in Mather, *Magnalia Christi Americana* 2:157, 158, 170, 164, 158–59, 171, 158, 175–76, 157. Elliot, in his *Power and the Pulpit in Puritan New England*, discusses Nathanael's case, though toward the end of naturalism and reflection rather than form (see p. 85).

165. Edwards to Gillespie, April 2, 1750, in *Religious Affections*, pp. 512–13; Jonathan Edwards, *Original Sin* (originally published as *The Great Christian Doctrine of Original Sin . . .*, 1758), ed. Clyde A. Holbrook, *Works of Jonathan Edwards*, gen. ed. John E. Smith, Vol. 3 (New Haven: Yale University Press, 1970), 424–25; and Shepard, *The Sincere Convert*, pp. 149–50, 158, 167, 170–99.

166. Edwards, *Some Thoughts Concerning the Revival*, p. 356.

167. Ralph Waldo Emerson, "Works and Days," in *Society and Solitude: Twelve Chapters*, Vol. 7 of *The Complete Works of Ralph Waldo Emerson with a Biographical Introduction and Notes*, Centenary Edition (Boston: Houghton Mifflin Company, Riverside Press, Cambridge, 1912), 157, 158, 159, 158, 171, 165, 164, 166. First presented as a lecture in 1857, "Works and Days" was published in the first edition of *Society and Solitude* (1870). The author is indebted to Daniel T. Rodgers, *The Work Ethic in Industrial America, 1850–1920* (Chicago: University of Chicago Press, 1978), pp. 1, 233, for drawing attention to "Works and Days," and particularly to the passage on edge tools, though Rodgers uses Emerson for a different end in his own finely crafted work.

168. Emerson, "Works and Days," pp. 181, 163–64.

169. Joseph Riddel, "Decentering the Image: The 'Project' of an 'American' Poetics?," in Josué V. Harari, ed., *Textual Strategies: Perspectives in Post-Structural Criticism* (Ithaca, N.Y.: Cornell University Press, paperback, 1979), pp. 340, 357.

2. Conscience to Moral Psychology: The Elder Henry James

Inheritance

1. [Henry James,] *Immortal Life: Illustrated in a Brief Autobiographic Sketch of the Late Stephen Dewhurst*, edited, with an Introduction, by Henry James, in Henry James, *The Literary Remains of Henry James*, ed. William James (1884; rpt. Upper Saddle River, N.J.: Literature House/Gregg Press, 1970), pp. 145–46.

2. Henry James, *Substance and Shadow: Or Morality and Religion in Their Relation to Life: An Essay Upon the Physics of Creation* (Boston: Ticknor and

Fields, 1863), pp. 23–24. See also Paul K. Conkin, *Puritans and Pragmatists: Eight Eminent American Thinkers* (New York: Dodd, Mead & Company, 1968), p. 268.

3. H. James, *Substance and Shadow*, p. 75; and William James, "Introduction" to H. James, *Literary Remains*, p. 49.

4. H. James, *Substance and Shadow*, pp. 75, 74; and W. James, "Introduction," p. 50.

5. Henry James, *The Secret of Swedenborg: Being an Elucidation of His Doctrine of the Divine Natural Humanity* (Boston: Fields, Osgood, & Company, 1869), pp. 161, 162, 161; and W. James, "Introduction," pp. 50–51.

6. Ralph Waldo Emerson, *Nature* (1836), in *Nature, Addresses and Lectures* (Vol. 1 of *The Complete Works of Ralph Waldo Emerson: With A Biographical Introduction and Notes*, Centenary Edition) (Boston: Houghton Mifflin Company, Riverside Press, Cambridge, 1903), p. 72; and Jonathan Edwards, diary entry for January 12, 1723, in Samuel Hopkins, *The Life and Character of the Late Reverend Mr. Jonathan Edwards* (1765), republished in David Levin, ed., *Jonathan Edwards: A Profile*, American Profiles (New York: Hill and Wang, 1968), pp. 12–13.

7. Quoted in C. [Clinton] Hartley Grattan, *The Three Jameses: A Family of Minds: Henry James, Sr., William James, Henry James* (1932; [New York]: New York University Press, 1962), p. 18. See also Leon Edel, *Henry James: The Untried Years 1843–1870* (Vol. 1 of *The Life of Henry James*) (London: Rupert Hart-Davis, 1953), pp. 27–28. The most thorough analysis of William James of Albany and his relation with his son is presented by Howard Marvin Feinstein, "Fathers and Sons: Work and the Inner World of William James: An Intergenerational Inquiry" (Ph.D. diss., Cornell University, 1977). Feinstein mentions William of Albany as a salt manufacturer (pp. 8–9), and offers the most careful consideration to date of the litigation of the father's will (see in particular pp. 60–61). See also H. James, *Secret of Swedenborg*, p. 172.

8. Quoted from a letter of May 11, 1843, in Austin Warren, *The Elder Henry James* (New York: Macmillan Company, 1934), p. 50.

9. W. James, "Introduction," pp. 10–11.

10. In *The New England Conscience* (Ann Arbor: University of Michigan Press, 1966), p. 3, Austin Warren states that he was unable to find the phrase occurring before Henry James. As Warren notes, it appears first in a notebook entry of October 31, 1895: *The Notebooks of Henry James*, ed. F. O. Matthiessen and Kenneth B. Murdock (New York: George Braziller, 1955), p. 227; and then in an entry of five years later (p. 375), this time in quotation marks and thus constituting for Warren a phrase that "was presumably . . . already current." In reply to Warren, Raymond Thorberg, "Henry James and the 'New England Conscience,'" *Notes and Queries*, n.s. 16 (June 1969), 222–23, finds the phrase in the novel *Confidence*, serialized in *Scribner's Monthly* in 1879–80, without, Thorberg feels, "indication of any sort that it was to be regarded as of special interest" (p. 223).

Vastation

11. H. James, *Immortal Life*, pp. 153, 185. The author is indebted to Feinstein, "Fathers and Sons," pp. 24–25, who makes reference to the phrase "a red-hot iron" and joins the phrase with the father's injury.

12. See Henry James [Jr.], *Notes of a Son and Brother* (New York: Charles Scribner's Sons, 1914), p. 105; Henry James, *Society the Redeemed Form of Man, and the Earnest of God's Omnipotence in Human Nature: Affirmed in Letters to a Friend* (Boston: Houghton, Osgood and Company, 1879), p. 158.

13. H. James, *Society the Redeemed Form of Man*, pp. 43–52; the passage is partially quoted in W. James, "Introduction," pp. 57–67.

14. H. James, *Society the Redeemed Form of Man*, pp. 44–45.

15. William James, *The Varieties of Religious Experience: A Study in Human Nature: Being the Gifford Lectures on Natural Religion Delivered at Edinburgh in 1901–1902* (1902; New York: Random House, The Modern Library, n.d.), pp. 157 and n. 1.

16. H. James, *Society the Redeemed Form of Man*, p. 159; W. James, *Varieties*, p. 157; and H. James, *Society the Redeemed Form of Man*, p. 45.

17. W. James, *Varieties*, p. 158; and H. James, *Society the Redeemed Form of Man*, p. 46.

18. *Society the Redeemed Form of Man*, pp. 46, 49–51, 46, 51–52. The volumes purchased were Emanuel Swedenborg, *On the Divine Love and the Divine Wisdom*, selections from the *Apocalypse Explained* (London, 1840; Boston: Otis Clapp, 1841); and Emanuel Swedenborg, *Angelic Wisdom Concerning the Divine Providence*, 2nd American ed., a new trans. (Boston: Published for the New Church Printing Society by Otis Clapp, 1840), a work originally published in Latin at Amsterdam in 1764. Neither work gives consideration to the vastation, which indeed seems not a centerpiece of Swedenborg's theology at all, at least not in the sense of the devastation (de-vastation) that James wanted, the being "*re*-born," the "*unlearning*," the "natural demolition or undoing" (this in a letter to Mrs. Tappan of 1860 printed in H. James, Jr., *Notes of a Son and Brother*, pp. 218–19). For references to Swedenborg's discussions of vastation as contained in his *Arcana Coelestia*, see his own note to his *Heaven and its Wonders and Hell: From Things Heard and Seen*, trans. J. C. Ager (New York: American Swedenborg Printing and Publishing Society, 1909), a work first published in Latin in London in 1758, note 1 to n. 513, pp. 327–28 (n. 513 being the section, to which by convention references to Swedenborg are usually made).

It is in *Heaven and its Wonders* that vastation "is simply being let into one's internals," a state after death into which one "unconsciously glides" (n. 551, pp. 355–56; n. 502, p. 319). In the *Arcana Coelestia: The Heavenly Arcana . . .*, Vol. 1 (New York: American Swedenborg Printing and Publishing Company, 1873)—a work first published in Latin in 1749, and in English in London in 1783—vastations occur for the ignorant yet outwardly good "*in the lower earth*" (n. 1106, pp. 455–56). The forms of vastation (or devastation, for those who are evil prior to their emergence into hell) are several and the lengths of time various, as Swedenborg observed when permitted to descend into the inferior earth, there to see such forms of instruction as fear and senseless, mechanical work. In this regard see *Arcana Coelestia*, Vol. 5 (1873), n. 4942, p. 454; and Vol. 1, nn. 1106–13, pp. 455–57, and nn. 698–700, pp. 244–45. For a discussion of devastation, see *Arcana Coelestia*, Vol. 7 (1875), n. 7502, pp. 427–28. For a brief discussion of Swedenborg on vastation, "a specifically Swedenborgian expression," see Signe Toksvig, *Emanuel Swedenborg: Scientist and Mystic* (New Haven: Yale University Press, 1948), p. 240. For bibliographic information on Swedenborg—enormously complex—see James Hyde, *A Bibliography of the Works of Eman-*

uel Swedenborg: Original and Translated (London: Swedenborg Society, 1906).

19. Ralph Waldo Emerson, "The American Scholar: An Oration Delivered before the Phi Beta Kappa Society, at Cambridge, August 31, 1837," in Emerson, *Nature: Addresses and Lectures,* pp. 111, 112, 112–13. The imputation of strangeness to Swedenborg flows throughout Emerson's later lecture, "Swedenborg; Or, the Mystic," in *Representative Men: Seven Lectures,* Vol. 4 of *The Complete Works of Ralph Waldo Emerson,* Centenary Edition (Boston: Houghton Mifflin Company, Riverside Press, Cambridge, 1903); the words quoted are from pp. 135–36. The lecture was part of the series presented in 1845–46, with *Representative Men* published in 1850. For bibliographic information, see the finest of the Emerson anthologies: *Selections from Ralph Waldo Emerson: An Organic Anthology,* ed. Stephen E. Wicher (Riverside Press, Cambridge, paperback, 1960).

20. Ralph Waldo Emerson, "The Poet," in *Essays: Second Series* (1844), *Complete Works of Emerson,* 3:35–36.

21. *Society the Redeemed Form of Man,* pp. 71, 44. For a description of Swedenborg's garden, see Cyriel Odhner Sigstedt, *The Swedenborg Epic: The Life and Works of Emanuel Swedenborg* (New York: Bookman Associates, 1952), pp. 348–49, 241–42.

22. Emerson, "Swedenborg," p. 133.

23. W. James, *Varieties,* p. 157.

24. Swedenborg, *Angelic Wisdom Concerning Divine Providence,* nn. 48, 49, pp. 50–51; n. 321, p. 344.

25. W. James, *Varieties,* p. 157.

26. In quoting and referring to relations from Swedenborg's *Spiritual Diary* (publication in English began in 1846) Toksvig, *Emanuel Swedenborg,* pp. 247 and 245, notes that it was the distance Swedenborg placed between himself and his own compelling thoughts that accounted for the mystic's sense of sanity, for his sense that insanities were being acted without him as opposed to within him: his sense "it was granted me to know that it proceeded from spirits and not from me," that "'it is wonderful,' he comes right out and says, 'that I have been obsessed, and yet nothing has ever injured me—further, I could enjoy my rational mind, just as if they were not present.'" Such were seemingly compelling forces attempting to make Swedenborg "eat greedily," to take up delicacies "with his hands and shove them into his mouth, or to make him buy or steal something they [the spirits] covet." They were forces that came in the form of worries and petty fears, "inconvenient, troublesome and evil suggestions," as Swedenborg called them, worries when abroad about his garden, of who was in charge, "of my being called home, of money matters, of the state of mind of those who were known to me, of the state or character of those in my house, of the things that I was to write and the probability that they would not be understood, of new garments that were to be obtained, and various other things of this kind." "He also warned," Toksvig writes, "(as we should say) against getting a compulsion neurosis. He said it was bad to make up one's mind that something had come to pass in a certain way, if it were only a trivial matter, because spirits might seize on the idea and add to it and induce the thought that it absolutely must be so, blowing it up into undue importance, and in that way man lost his liberty. This, he said, he also knew from experience." (The *Spiritual Diary* citations are from nn. 2772, 192, 2659, 3858, 3624, 2176.)

And it is in *The Spiritual Diary . . .* , trans. W. H. Acton and A. W. Acton (London: Swedenborg Society, 1962), Vol. 1, that Swedenborg wrote of evil spirits and devils attempting to destroy a man: "Evil spirits continually wanted to cast me into danger, even when I was not at all aware of it, for example, wishing to cast me under carriages. It became very manifest to me that they as it were [again there is metaphor] wanted to compel me, but in vain. Likewise, when I was walking beside the water, a similar endeavor [to do me harm—translator's note] continually persisted, but it was restrained by the Lord. It was the same in many other cases" (n. 1043, p. 282). Yet such thoughts—most particularly one of compelling evil—served their purpose, as they had for the Puritan autobiographers, allowing, as Toksvig also notes (p. 276), a man to see the evil within himself, to watch it being brought to the surface, dredged up where it could then be confronted and seen in the dawn of the light of the Lord: "The Lord will cause the man not only to see the evil but not to will it and finally to detest it" (the source for this quotation is unnoted). (Toksvig uses the word "obsession" to designate such thoughts, though she is not particularly interested in psychiatric classifications or diagnoses, which in any event remain various, as they have since the *Spiritual Diary* and Swedenborg's *Journal of Dreams* were published.) Swedenborg disassociated such thoughts from deeds, from the acting out of the evil fancy. Toksvig (pp. 276–77) provides a quotation from *Heaven and its Wonders and Hell* of thinking and willing "without doing" as an enclosed flame extinguished or "seed cast upon the sand." In extending the quotation she uses: "Every one can know that willing and not doing, when there is opportunity, is not willing" (n. 475, pp. 297–98), not willing, that is, with the whole man, for "it must be understood that in deeds or works the whole man is exhibited, and that his will and thought . . . are not complete until they exist in deeds or works, which are his exteriors, for these are the outmosts in which the will and thought terminate, and without such terminations they are interminate, and have as yet no existence, that is, are not as yet in the man" (n. 475, p. 297).

For this reason, as Toksvig further relates (pp. 276–77), Swedenborg saw man as needing to act, for in the act was the self and self-definition, and in the act was the test and experimental faith—the experiential movement not away from but into the world, the deed to be considered in some other form than ascetic retreat. (Toksvig's quotation from Swedenborg is in this instance misplaced; see *Heaven and its Wonders and Hell*, n. 528, p. 338, and also the sections to which Toksvig does refer: nn. 475, 478, 524, 534.) Concomitantly, deeds and works for Swedenborg implied an interior volition to be ascribed to the self as a product of will and thought, and of faith, "otherwise it would be nothing but a movement like that of an automaton or image"—"not deeds and works, but only inanimate movements" (*Heaven and its Wonders and Hell*, n. 472, pp. 295, 296). A comparison may be drawn to Edwards (as to Erik Erikson's Luther), who in arguing against a freedom of the will and an efficacy of works nevertheless argued, and quite consistently, for work, for the act or deed as a test or sign. Edwards argued that to give up, to give in, to lie slothful and indolent and refuse the "trouble," when faced with the doctrine of a determined will, was in itself a contradictory inference. For in such a choice *was* determination. The universe, one says, is fixed, thus I will not move, neither add to nor subtract from my happiness or misery—to "save myself the trouble of labor" when the saving itself is such a move (Edwards, *Freedom of the Will*, pp. 369–70; see note 47 following for reference).

27. Inge Jonsson, *Emanuel Swedenborg*, trans. Catherine Djurklou, Twayne's World Authors Series, TWAS 127 (New York: Twayne Publishers, 1971), p. 120. The citation is from Rudolph L. Tafel, ed., *Documents Concerning the Life and Character of Emanuel Swedenborg*, collected, translated, and annotated by R. L. Tafel, 2 vols. (two parts) (London: Swedenborg Society, 1875–77), 2:149 [?], though Jonsson also cites from an edition of the *Documents* published in London in 1890, to which he may be referring. For further reference to Swedenborg's mechanical imagery, see Wilson Van Dusen, *The Presence of Other Worlds: The Psychological/Spiritual Findings of Emanuel Swedenborg* (New York: Harper & Row, Publishers, 1974), p. 129.

28. Quoted by Toksvig, *Emanuel Swedenborg*, p. 206, from Emanuel Swedenborg, *The Word [of the Old Testament] Explained*, ed. and trans. by Alfred Acton (Bryn Athyn, Penn: Academy of the New Church, [1928–48], n. 1150; see also her chapters on "Automatic Writing" and "Psychical Research," pp. 201–16, 168–79.

29. From Toksvig, *Emanuel Swedenborg*, pp. 142–43 (without the quotation from Paul); and Jonsson, *Emanuel Swedenborg*, pp. 120–21. Toksvig is citing from *Swedenborgs Drömar* [1744; *Jemte Andra Hans Anteckningar*] (Stockholm: J. and A. Riis, 1860), pp. 10ff., also referred to as *The Journal of Dreams*, the manuscript discovered in 1858 and first published the following year; see George Trobridge, *Emanuel Swedenborg: His Life, Teachings and Influence*, 1st American ed. (New York: New-Church Press, [1918?]), pp. 72–73. *The Journal of Dreams*, translated and published as well by Tafel, in *Documents Concerning the Life and Character of Emanuel Swedenborg* (London, 1877), Vol. 2, is central for recording this point of conversion in Swedenborg's life. For other accounts of the episodes, variant only in minor matters, see Jonsson, *Emanuel Swedenborg*, his chapter "The Religious Crisis," pp. 119–36; Trobridge, *Life of Swedenborg*, "Between Two Worlds," pp. 70–84; and Sigstedt, *Swedenborg Epic*, "The Turning Point," pp. 182–93.

The earliest English translation of the *Drömar*, apparently, was made by J. [James] J. G. [Garth] Wilkinson, *Swedenborg's Dreams, 1744; With Some Other of His Pieces*, edited from the original manuscripts by G. E. Klemming, n.d., a manuscript in the library of the Swedenborg Society, presumably of London (see Hyde, *Bibliography of the Works of Swedenborg*, entry 431, p. 98). And whatever James's comments on the good woman he met, the Mrs. Chichester who informed him of Swedenborg and the vastation, it was Wilkinson who more than anyone was responsible for turning Henry James to Swedenborg. In *The Thought and Character of William James: As Revealed in Unpublished Correspondence and Notes, Together with His Published Writings* (Boston: Little, Brown and Company, An Atlantic Monthly Press Book, 1935), 1:20–22, Ralph Barton Perry described the influence that developed into a lifelong friendship and "intimacy" (James would name his third son, born the year following that spring of 1844, Garth Wilkinson; see Warren, *Elder Henry James*, p. 59). This influence appears to have begun with an article Wilkinson annotated on Swedenborg in 1841, and was "confirmed," Perry believed, by the experience at Windsor: the "crisis of doubt and depression, associated with physical exhaustion" (pp. 21, 20). Concerning the vastation, see the following: Quentin Anderson, *The American Henry James* (London: John Calder, 1958), pp. 83–98; Edel, *Henry James: The Untried Years*, pp. 31–42; Grattan, *Three Jameses*, pp.

40–54; Giles Gunn, "An Introduction" to *Henry James, Senior: A Selection of His Writings*, ed. Giles Gunn (Chicago: American Library Association, 1974), pp. 19–21; Warren, *Elder Henry James*, pp. 55–60; and Frederic Harold Young, *The Philosophy of Henry James, Sr.* (New York: Bookman Associates, 1951), pp. 6–7. And yet for Perry as for commentators following his lead the experience remains as James presented it: not as a re-enactment of Protestant psychomachy but as a natural experience, a relief, in other words, from it: "When James finally enjoyed a profound and lasting sense of salvation," Perry wrote, "it was salvation *from* Calvinism. . . . In other words, Calvinism meant painful if not pathological anxiety over one's eternal fortunes, which unfortunately are not within one's control" (p. 21). The manner of describing the experience of fright, however, remained very much within James's control, leading James's reader not to the sense that it never occurred (something, quite simply, did), but rather to the understanding that James so carefully constructed his narrative that no actual "symptom" may be easily inferred. James's text, in other words, cannot be read as a reflection of trauma *per se*, cannot be read as an expressive text available for an analysis of *him*, but is to be read only as a text reflective of other texts, most particularly the text of Swedenborg. (Feinstein, in "Fathers and Sons," has, as William James did in *The Varieties of Religious Experience*, pointed to parallels between the elder James's and Bunyan's accounts of trauma, most interestingly turning not to the *Grace Abounding*, which is unreferenced, but to *The Pilgrim's Progress*. Most important, through an examination of Henry James's correspondence he has further determined what Perry said: that James was well aware of Swedenborg prior to the experience at Windsor. In this respect, see Feinstein's account of the crisis, pp. 74–91, though the mention of Swedenborg is brief and the reference is simply to *The Apocalypse Revealed*.) No matter whether James had available the *Journal of Dreams*, he most assuredly had Wilkinson's biography: James John Garth Wilkinson, *Emanuel Swedenborg: A Biography* (London: William Newbery, 1849), written indeed with only the *Spiritual Diary* available. Yet even here, with the Wilkinson biography the only Swedenborg text, the parallels between the new mystic's crisis and Henry James's vastation are clear: James's account strongly identifies with the master, or rather with the context of Swedenborg's fright—identifies with words chosen and incidents mentioned and locations considered, including perhaps even the time, season, and date of year. One example of these parallels may be followed in an account Wilkinson provided of one of the series of experiences Swedenborg claimed for his crisis-filled years of 1743, 1744, and 1745: in London in April of 1743, or 1745 as Wilkinson surmises (James would choose the middle year), when he was dining late in his room, laboring then on a natural philosophical study of which, in all its massive complications, his revelations would relieve him, just as James would say that his vastation released him from a massive work he was laboring incessantly upon. "Towards the end of the meal I remarked that a kind of mist spread before my eyes, and I saw the floor of my room covered with hideous reptiles. . . . I was astonished, having all my wits about me, and being perfectly conscious. . . . I now saw a man sitting in a corner of the chamber. . . . I was greatly frightened when he said to me, 'Eat not so much!'" (James, alone in his English room in the spring of 1844, sitting before a dimming fire following a meal, spoke of his digestion and then of things putrid, though it was not the Christ who was coming to him, at least not yet and never as a vision, but as that "fetid" thing akin to "a literal nest of hell within my own entrails," as related in *Society the Redeemed Form of Man*, pp. 45, 74.) "The unexpected alarm hastened my return home. I did not suffer my landlord to perceive that anything had happened. . . . From that day forth I gave up all worldly learning, and labored only in spiritual things" (pp. 75, 77, 74, 75–76). And it was from the *Diary* that Wilkinson accounted at least one of the lessons, open of course to Freudian significance, though holding still to the melancholic image, "that all the vermin . . . generated by unseemly appetite, were thus cast out of my body, and burnt up, and that I was now cleansed from them. . . . Smile not, reader, at this plain representation of what lies under thy sumptuous table" (pp. 76–77).

The event, an episode that remains central to Swedenborgian mythology, is discussed by Sigstedt, *Swedenborg Epic*, pp. 197–99, with extended quotations. See as well Toksvig, *Emanuel Swedenborg*, pp. 151–53, who also discusses parallel Freudian imagery, Swedenborg's fear of being "avaricious, a vice he particularly detested, and in some of his dreams he noted that he wanted to hold on to his money" (p. 144).

30. Quoted by Jonsson, *Emanuel Swedenborg*, p. 121, in his discussion of Swedenborg's self-division at this time between science and his scientific ambitions—represented then by the "Anatomy," his *Regnum animale*—and faith, "*Pura fides*, the pure faith in which the child has unquestioning confidence" (see pp. 119–25). The quotation is from Tafel, *Documents Concerning the Life and Character of Swedenborg* 2:154–61, presumably from the *Journal of Dreams*.

31. H. James, *Society the Redeemed Form of Man*, pp. 43, 44. The digestion which James mentions may seem out of place, but when considered in relation to the "diet" Swedenborg held so terribly important for himself—at least as reported by Wilkinson (see *Emanuel Swedenborg*, pp. 236–39)—it seems less so, and particularly when Swedenborg pulled away only somewhat from the psychosomatic thesis of melancholy of the seventeenth century and discussed melancholy and conscience in terms of "pangs to the stomach": it was "there" that spirits talked and related their "undigested and foul" affection, "sadness and melancholy anxiety." When turned away, the anxieties ceased, and "from this it has been made clear to me why some who do not know what conscience is, because they have no conscience, ascribe its pangs to the stomach." Thereby Swedenborg could speak of "true conscience, spurious conscience, and false conscience," true conscience being more than "natural," and yet involved with bodily evil (*Heaven and its Wonders and Hell*, n. 299, pp. 176–77, and note 1 to n. 299, p. 177).

Composition of the Crisis

32. An approach to this theme is considered by Roy Pascal, *Design and Truth in Autobiography* (London: Routledge & Kegan Paul, 1960), particularly his chapter "The Structure of Truth in Autobiography," pp. 179–95.

33. In this regard the words of Raymond Williams, writing in *Marxism and Literature*, Marxist Introductions (1977; rpt. Oxford: Oxford University Press, paperback, 1977), p. 166, should be considered. For a discussion of "literariness," see Terence Hawkes, *Structuralism & Semiotics* (1977; rpt. Berkeley: University of California Press, paperback, 1977), pp. 61, 71.

34. W. James, *Varieties*, p. 158 and n. 1.

35. See the discussions in Jonsson, *Emanuel Swedenborg*, pp. 125–28, 138–43; Sigstedt, *Swedenborg Epic*, pp. 438–39, and 481–82, n. 769; and Toksvig, *Emanuel Swedenborg*, pp. 156–67, especially 159–60.

36. John Stuart Mill, *Autobiography* (New York: Henry Holt and Company, 1873), pp. 133, 138, 155, 139. For considerations of Mill's "crisis in my mental history" as portrayed in the *Autobiography*—perhaps the most considered of its kind for the nineteenth century, and published, it should be noted, prior to Henry James's account in *Society the Redeemed Form of Man* (1879)—see John N. Morris, *Versions of the Self: Studies in English Autobiography from John Bunyan to John Stuart Mill* (New York: Basic Books, 1966), pp. 3–35; Morris draws notice in this introduction to William James. See also most particularly Bruce Mazlish, *James and John Stuart Mill: Father and Son in the Nineteenth Century* (New York: Basic Books, 1975).

Mazlish approaches the crisis (discussed directly on pp. 205–30) and the Mills from a psychohistorical view, weaving themes of Oedipal complex and generation conflict for a nineteenth century in social, political, industrial, and demographic upheaval. Feinstein, in "Fathers and Sons," for whom a vogue of neurasthenia in late Victorian America was real, offers a similar thesis of "vocational uncertainties" accounting for the sweep of neurasthenia—a word, however, that is left undefined (see pp. 305–07). For Mazlish, in an earlier and more complex analysis, it is a theme of *Gemeinschaft* and *Gesellschaft* (pp. 15–43, 138), one of the most powerful and often used models of historical explanation. Mazlish weaves themes of work, mechanization, and production, as well, in some of his most interesting discussions (see particularly pp. 358–62)—themes he grounds historically in time and in the psychology of the subjects he treats.

In the *Autobiography*, and recounting "the dry heavy dejection of the melancholy winter of 1826–7," the crisis having begun in "the autumn" of 1826, Mill speaks of his own work inhibitions, of proceeding "mechanically" in his occupations, and of having been considered a manufactured man, a phrase referring to the impress of his father and to other, more universal themes of alienation as well (pp. 139, 133, 139, 155). The crisis, as Mill wrote, was to be a passage through a "stage" in a movement "onward." Reflections of Bunyan may be found in Mill's description of the mechanics of his mind—an obsession, as it were, that occurs as Mill pulls himself out of depression: "And it is very characteristic both of my then state, and of the general tone of my mind ["my general mental character"] at this period of my life, that I was seriously tormented by the thought of the exhaustibility of musical combinations. The octave consists only of five tones and two semitones, which can be put together in only a limited number of ways, of which but a small proportion are beautiful: most of these, it seemed to me, must have been already discovered, and there could not be room for a long succession of Mozarts and Webers, to strike out, as these had done, entirely new and surpassingly rich veins of musical beauty. This source of anxiety may, perhaps, be thought to resemble ["may appear perhaps (as ridiculous as)"] that of the philosophers of Laputa, who feared lest the sun should be burnt out" (p. 145). The bracketed quotations appear in *The Early Draft of John Stuart Mill's Autobiography*, ed. Jack Stillinger (Urbana: University of Illinois Press, 1961), p. 124, the parenthetical phrase (p. 124, n. 355) from an earlier deleted reading. Such had appeared "ridiculous" to Bunyan as well, his "tormenting cogitations," but Mill's recounting of his compelling fear is now without Bunyan's theological texture. Indeed it seems even more inconsequential, without any apparent meaning at all (open as it is, however, and opened by Mill himself, to a reading of a young man afraid that he will be unable to surpass, to lay claim to, or to strike out at his father). The fear is more secular and therefore seemingly more "real," more symptomatic, one should think, of everyday matters. Yet a structure of ridiculous thoughts serving their point has in this case remained a fear that the universe is closing, becoming mechanically sealed by some imagined bars of (musical) restraint.

37. For a discussion of the relationship between depression and obsessional activity, see Leon Salzman, *The Obsessive Personality: Origins, Dynamics and Therapy*, rev. ed. (New York: Jason Aronson, 1973), pp. 107–26. For a discussion of depression, obsessional character, and aggression, see Myer Mendelson, *Psychoanalytic Concepts of Depression*, 2nd ed. (Flushing, N.Y.: SP Books Division of Spectrum Publications, 1974), pp. 185–95. Qualifications to the thesis, psychoanalytic in origin, of depression as aggression are discussed in Aaron T. Beck, *Depression: Clinical, Experimental, and Theoretical Aspects* (New York: Harper & Row, Publishers, Hoeber Medical Division, 1967), pp. 245–49. Freud put the idea most poetically in his essay on "Mourning and Melancholia" (1917), in *The Standard Edition of the Complete Psychological Works of Sigmund Freud*, trans. and ed. James Strachey, Vol. 14 (London: Hogarth Press and The Institute of Psycho-Analysis, 1957), when he wrote that melancholics' "behavior still proceeds from a mental constellation of revolt, which has then, by a certain process, passed over into the crushed state of melancholia" (p. 248). "In mourning it is the world which has become poor and empty; in melancholia it is the ego itself. The patient represents his ego to us as worthless, incapable of any achievement and morally despicable; he reproaches himself, vilifies himself and expects to be cast out and punished" (p. 246).

38. Henry James, *Spiritual Creation: and the Necessary Implication of Nature in It. An Essay Towards Ascertaining the Rôle of Evil in Divine Housekeeping*, in H. James, *Literary Remains*, p. 216; quoted in W. James, "Introduction," p. 25.

39. *Secret of Swedenborg*, p. 172.

40. *Society the Redeemed Form of Man*, p. 71.

41. W. James, *Varieties*, pp. 155, 216, 155–57.

The Nature of Swedenborg's Temptations

42. Quoted by George H. Williams, *Wilderness and Paradise in Christian Thought: The Biblical Experience of the Desert in the History of Christianity & the Paradise Theme in the Theological Idea of the University* (New York: Harper & Brothers, Publishers, 1962), p. 93. Williams discusses Swedenborg's Biblical themes of wilderness and desert on pp. 93–94. The quotation is from Emanuel Swedenborg, *The Apocalypse Explained According to the Spiritual Sense . . .*, Vol. 4 (New York: American Swedenborg Printing and Publishing Society, 1899), n. 730, p. 2036. Williams treats as well the idea of the desert as a place of temptations, the location for purgation prior to birth (see pp. 5, 12–15, 17–19), and it is to this theme that Swedenborg seems constantly to refer, as for example in *Apocalypse Explained*, Vol. 4, n. 730, p. 2040, and n. 650, pp. 1700–01.

43. Swedenborg, *Arcana Coelestia*, Vol. 8, n. 8403, p. 170; n. 8405, p. 171;

n. 8406, p. 171; and Emanuel Swedenborg, *The True Christian Religion Containing the Universal Theology of the New Church . . .*, trans. John C. Ager, Library Edition (New York: American Swedenborg Printing and Publishing Society, 1906), Vol. 1, n. 126, p. 189—a work first published in Latin in Amsterdam in 1771, and in English in London in 1781. See also the selections from *A Compendium of the Theological Writings of Emanuel Swedenborg*, ed. Samuel M. Warren (1875; rpt. New York: Swedenborg Foundation, 1974), pp. 51–58.

44. Swedenborg, *Compendium of Theological Writings*, pp. 301–02, 301, and selections from *Arcana Coelestia*, n. 5036, n. 1820.

45. Swedenborg, *Angelic Wisdom Concerning Divine Providence*, n. 141, p. 130. According to Toksvig, writing in *Emanuel Swedenborg*: "In his book *The Fibre* [a work left in manuscript, 1741, and published in Philadelphia, 1918, he [Swedenborg] wrote at length about the causes of melancholy [of which he had suffered] . . . , the 'supreme cause' . . . due to an 'evil conscience,' otherwise 'temptations'" (pp. 135, 134–35). See Sigstedt, *Swedenborg Epic*, p. 457, n. 238, and p. 500.

46. Swedenborg, *Angelic Wisdom Concerning Divine Providence*, n. 312, p. 333; n. 290, pp. 302–03; n. 294, pp. 306, 307.

47. *Ibid.*, n. 294, p. 306. The idea was worthy of Edwards, for Edwards too had destroyed the idea of a freedom of the will, so as to maintain the consistency of moral necessity with praise and blame. "He that in acting," Edwards had written, "proceeds with the fullest inclination, does what he does with the greatest freedom, according to common sense." The greater the rootedness, the stronger the habit or evil principle, the more violent the propensity—the less, that is, the indifference or "freedom"—then the more the detestation and blame. "And if good inclination or motive has but little influence in determining the agent, they don't think his act so much the more virtuous, but the less. And so concerning evil acts, which are determined by evil motives or inclinations." Here "our wills are in them; not so much because they are from some *property* of ours, as because they are our *properties*." So wrote Jonathan Edwards in *Freedom of the Will*, ed. Paul Ramsey, Vol. 1 of *The Works of Jonathan Edwards* (New Haven: Yale University Press, 1957)—a work first published in 1754 as *A Careful and Strict Enquiry into . . . Freedom of the Will*—pp. 359, 360, 361, 428. See also Paul Ramsey's "Editor's Introduction," pp. 21, 20–23.

As Ramsey discusses, Edwards drew an important "distinction between moral and natural necessity . . . between 'determinism' and 'compulsion.' . . . Free acts are uncompelled acts, not uncaused or undetermined acts. Edwards associates himself with this distinction—in fact he was among the first to formulate fully and adequately this distinction—between determinism and compulsion" (pp. 37–38; see also p. 12). Ramsey quotes as well (p. 42) from Martin Luther, *The Bondage of the Will* (1525), trans. Henry Cole (Grand Rapids, Mich.: Wm. B. Eerdmans Publishing Co., 1931), sec. XXV: "For compulsion is (so to speak) *unwillingness*." And for Edwards, in his words, "compulsion . . . is a person's being necessitated to do a thing *contrary* to his will"; it therefore followed that "that which has no will, can't be the subject of these things"—that is, can't be subject to "force, compulsion, and coaction." Compulsion was predicated not of a weak will or lack of will but of a force of will: a volition and determinacy within the self—an idea that a nineteenth-century utilitarian psychology would attempt to refute, just as a psychoanalytic psychology would attempt to refute Edwards's complementary contention that, in Edwards's words, "'tis absurd, to suppose the same individual will to oppose itself, in its present act; or the present choice to be opposite to, and resisting present choice: as absurd as it is to talk of two contrary motions, in the same moving body, at the same time" (pp. 164, 159). It was in this manner that Edwards could refute charges made against a determinacy of the will, that man, if such were the case, was "a mere machine" acting "from mere compulsion" (pp. 370–71, 430, 280). It was indeed the notion of free will that left man empty, floating in whimsy, lower even than in a state of mechanics: "Whereas machines are guided by an understanding cause, by the skillful hand of the workman or owner; the will of man is left to the guidance of nothing, but absolute blind contingence" (p. 371).

48. Swedenborg, *Angelic Wisdom Concerning Divine Providence*, p. 5; nn. 129–53, pp. 115–39; n. 145, p. 133.

James's Confession of Temptations and Compulsion

49. *Secret of Swedenborg*, pp. 126, 127.

50. *Immortal Life*, pp. 178–79. See pp. 156–57 of this autobiography for a discussion of his youthful sexual desires that may be compared to a passage of his *Spiritual Creation*, pp. 384–84, which insists that such was never "*life*": "No, it was always death."

51. *Immortal Life*, pp. 160–61, 160, 185–86.

52. Henry James, "A Very Long Letter," in Henry James, *Lectures and Miscellanies* (Clinton Hall, New York: Redfield, 1852), p. 378; *Immortal Life*, pp. 183, 181, 172–73, 165–69, 171. See also Ola Elizabeth Winslow, *John Bunyan* (New York: Macmillan Company, 1961), p. 22.

53. H. James, "Very Long Letter," pp. 377, 378, 400; and H. James, *Secret of Swedenborg*, p. 172.

54. H. James, *Substance and Shadow*, pp. 122–23; *Spiritual Creation*, pp. 295–96; and *Substance and Shadow*, pp. 21–22. On Emerson, see *Spiritual Creation*, pp. 266–67, 293–94.

55. H. James, "Very Long Letter," pp. 376–77.

56. Henry James, "Spiritual Rappings," in *Lectures and Miscellanies*, pp. 407–18. See also Henry James, *Christianity the Logic of Creation* (New York: D. Appleton & Co., 1857), pp. 137–38 n, where he also warns of a then popular spiritualist movement. Spirits indeed speak, but not as the voice of the Lord or angels, and indeed not as a voice but rather as a communication through the medium of one's thoughts, the morbidity of one's mind attracting morbid spirits who have often, as James said, tried to seduce the victim involved. Like Swedenborg, James found life beginning with death, that death being the conscience unique to man—the "spiritual nausea" at the moment of gestation (*Christianity the Logic of Creation*, pp. 144–47). And that nausea, as James wrote in *The Nature of Evil: Considered in a Letter to the Rev. Edward Beecher . . .* (New York: D. Appleton and Company, 1855), pp. 188–89, was a matter of "*spiritual possessions*," "utter disorganization and destruction." In a letter to Julia Kellogg of 1869, quoted in Matthiessen, *James Family* (see note 107 following for reference), p. 10, James described his own incessant battle to be rid of such spirits, of what he called in this instance his anxiety: "My besetting sin is anxiety; and no sooner does any occasion for it arise, *ab extra*, than the whole 'clanging rookery' of hell comes darkening the air, and settling down in my devoted bosom as if it

were their undisputed nest. But they find themselves mistaken, *laus deo*! . . . I do not in the least mistake their dusky visages and croaking voices for my own. I loath and hate them."

It is worth quoting from James rather at length to understand his close identification with Swedenborg—with the mystic's own self-described fight with ghostly visitations. James would suffer his vastation as Swedenborg, and he would manifest as well some form of speech impediment; at least, in a letter to Emerson of November 17, 1843, Thomas Carlyle remarked that there was something "shy and skittish in the man," and something as well that "makes his stammer" (quoted in Grattan, *Three Jameses*, pp. 45–46). And Wilkinson, in his *Emanuel Swedenborg*, reported the same for the mentor (pp. 239–40). And now James used Swedenborg to explain the suffering that remained, a turn as he took it upon his orthodox faith that was hardly a turn at all: "When I speak of the influence of ghostly communications upon 'weak-minded persons,' I mean persons who, like myself, have been educated in sheerly erroneous views of individual responsibility. After my religious life dawned, my day was turned into hideous and unrelieved night by tacit ghostly visitations. I not merely repented myself, as one of my theological teachers deemed it incumbent upon me, of Adam's transgression, but every dubious transaction I had engaged in from my youth up, no matter how insignificant soever, crept forth from its oblivious slime to paralyze my soul with threats of God's judgment." It was through "ritual," he continued, that he "managed indeed to stave off actual despair," the committing, that is, of the unpardonable sin, for the form had remained. "But I had no satisfactory glimpse of the source of all the infernal jugglery I had undergone till I learned from Swedenborg." "I of course did not deny an external or instrumental connection with them; I did not deny that my *hand* had incurred defilement, but with my total heart and mind I resisted any closer affiliation. . . . Hence I had little doubt that the fact might be as Swedenborg alleged, and that I had been all along nourishing, by means of certain falsities in my intellect, a brood of ghostly loafers" ("Spiritual Rappings," pp. 411–13). Thus, like Swedenborg, James attained a sense of his sanity by setting as an object such thoughts as these, placing distance between himself and what he could only determine were (metaphorically) ghosts—alien spirits attempting to appear internal and thus a part of his being. The voices of hell, he could thereby understand, were not the voices of himself. In this way James preserved the Calvinist psychomachy, though it seemed to require a new psychology—and Swedenborg—to re-establish this faith.

This was a deeper understanding than spiritualism alone, for what James was saying was embedded in his Puritan faith and quite at odds, as he said, with any psychomancy—with any conjuring of the dead or, in a similar vein, with any of the mesmerism then sweeping the land: what James simply called "salvation through electricity" ("Spiritual Rappings," p. 419).

57. Henry James, "Intemperance," in *Lectures and Miscellanies*, pp. 429, 426–27, 427–28.

The Conscience of Sin and the Conscience of Crime

58. H. James, *Substance and Shadow*, p. 123, 122–23, 123, 126.

59. H. James, *Substance and Shadow*, pp. 128, 131–32. See as well James's attack on the "natural" and the "moral" law in his *Moralism and Christianity:*

Or Man's Experience and Destiny. In Three Lectures, 2nd ed. (New York: J. S. Redfield, 1850), p. 17. Therein he speaks of nature's "lurking miasms and pestilences" awaiting the person attempting to fulfull perfectly some law of nature—to achieve health, for example, through some enslavement to bodily function. And so also, he continued, with the moral law that "sting[s] me into despair and madness. The letter of the law appears brief and easy, but the moment I indulge the fatal anxiety, have I fulfilled it? I begin to apprehend its infinite spirit . . . , I am worried and fretted into my grave, . . . and the law . . . turns out a minister of utter death." In his *Nature of Evil*, pp. 190–91, 125, and his *The Church of Christ Not an Ecclesiasticism: A Letter of Remonstrance to a Member of the Soi-Disant New Church*, 2nd ed. (London: W. White, 1856), pp. 118–121, 131, James speaks of the madness of such law as well.

60. H. James, *Substance and Shadow*, pp. 138, 155, 174, 175–76, 177, 179, 175, 130.

61. *Ibid.*, pp. 174, 179, 180, 181, 179–80.

62. *Ibid.*, pp. 180, 181, 182, 183, 184.

63. H. James, "Very Long Letter," p. 376; Ralph Waldo Emerson, "The Transcendentalist: A Lecture Read at the Masonic Temple, Boston, January, 1842," in Emerson, *Nature: Addresses and Lectures*, p. 339; and H. James, "Very Long Letter," p. 379.

Moral Works

64. Henry James to Joseph Henry, July 9, 1843, and Joseph Henry to Henry James, August 22, 1843, in Perry, *Thought of William James* 1:16–17, 18.

65. H. James to Ralph Waldo Emerson (1842?), in Perry, *Thought of William James* 1:42–43. The letter is also found in H. James, Jr., *Notes of a Son and Brother*, pp. 170–71, and there is dated 1842 (p. 169).

66. See H. James, *Secret of Swedenborg*, pp. 172–73. The problem of vocation is Erik Erikson's theme, informing the body of his work, including Erikson's understanding of William James, and a theme to which this essay and its earlier form as a dissertation are deeply indebted. The subsequent availability of Howard Feinstein's "Fathers and Sons" furthers the theme of the problem of vocation in the lives of the elder James and his son, though by accounting the problem as the cause, historically defined, of the elder James's and William's sickness—"By using Freud's method, the crisis of 1844 becomes firmly linked to his vocational battle with William of Albany and the breaking of his will" (p. 90)—Feinstein offers too literal a rendition, removing the crisis from any broader context of what—and how—the Jameses were speaking. Familial rebellion is, of course, a Christian figure, and the character of Bunyan's Christian, for the ways of the fathers are to be left, while the texts of the fathers are to be preserved. The problem of vocation or "work" is an American figuration for recounting the struggles of the New World artist and "intellectual," alienation that informs the younger Henry James's portrait not only of his father but of Hawthorne as well, alienation that informs Emerson's often misread words over the grave of Thoreau, alienation that informs Henry Adams's portrayal of himself. It is a problem, simply, of justification, and work, job, or business—busyness in the simplest of terms—is, as sanctification, never cause to justify anyone.

67. See *Henry James: The Untried Years*, p. 29.

68. H. James to Ralph Waldo Emerson (1842?), in Perry, *Thought of William James* 1:42.

69. H. James to J. J. Garth Wilkinson, September 6, 1852, *ibid.*, 23.

70. *Society the Redeemed Form of Man*, p. 48. Feinstein's "Fathers and Sons" is to be credited for calling Henry James's account of his crisis "a parable," though Biblical allusion and a use of *The Pilgrim's Progress* are seen as disguise for what Feinstein himself has artfully constructed, thereby separating reality and text, James's own rhetoric serving no particular point: "Mr. James could not remove all of the clues that unconsciously tied it [the account of breakdown] to the fight over his father's will" (p. 86a). To say the "crisis tale proceeds" simply from *The Pilgrim's Progress*—"reading the bible [*sic*], being cast into despair, keeping the matter from his family as long as possible, and then communicating the awful truth" (p. 81)—does not make of James's story a "myth" but a way rather of constructing sense using meaningful historical texts.

> I was dumb with silence, I held my peace, *even* from good; and my sorrow was stirred.
> My heart was hot within me, while I was musing the fire burned: *then* spake I with my tongue,
> Lord, make me to know mine end. (Psalms 39:2–4).

It is for the historian reworking James's myth—remaining, that is, within his text—to say that "the author [James] would have us believe" and then to uncover as "historical actuality" the real thing that was the matter, and which is to be uncovered in other texts, in "another version" that seems "more compelling" (pp. 75, 87): "inheritance," "property," "his vocational battle," "a very revealing allusion to the parable of the prodigal son" (pp. 90, 86a)—as if those words and phrases were less symbolically fraught, or less likely to be used by James and his sons as ways of saying what had gone wrong. As Freud well enough said, no patient would simply have us believe, or for that matter take anything "right out" of another.

71. A part of the actuality, most interestingly, that Feinstein uncovers in his "Fathers and Sons" is that the manuscripts James claimed to have been working on prior to his collapse are not to be found, and probably never existed (pp. 85–86). But this does not make James's account a lie, unconscious or otherwise: "it is essential to separate spiritual myth-making from historical actuality if we are to establish the connection between that awesome event and the will of William James" (pp. 74–75)—the nonexistence of such Biblical labors points to the necessity for James to make of his experience an appropriate text, demonstrating for his reader his ineffectual compelling labors, works that serve to shatter the self and his ego's endeavors.

72. *Society the Redeemed Form of Man*, pp. 93, 70–71.

73. H. James, *Substance and Shadow*, pp. 209–10, 516–17; see as well *Society the Redeemed Form of Man*, pp. 439–40, 440–41n.

74. Henry James, "Christianity," in *Lectures and Miscellanies*, pp. 440–41.

75. *Substance and Shadow*, pp. 211–12.

76. Swedenborg, *Divine Love and Divine Wisdom*, pp. 22–23, 81, 80, also 16–17, 82: See as well H. James, "Spiritual Rappings," pp. 409–11.

77. *Substance and Shadow*, pp. 212 and 213, n. 1. See as well H. James, *Church of Christ Not an Ecclesiasticism*, pp. 150–51, and Appendix B, pp. 154–156.

78. H. James, *Christianity the Logic of Creation*, pp. 102, 164, 151–52, 102.

79. H. James, *Moralism and Christianity*, p. 16; and H. James, *Christianity the Logic of Creation*, p. 151.

80. *Moralism and Christianity*, p. 47; and *Society the Redeemed Form of Man*, p. 218.

81. *Moralism and Christianity*, pp. 32, 164.

82. *Moralism and Christianity*, pp. 10, 5–13 (republished as "The Perfect Man" in *Henry James: Selection of His Writings*, pp. 124–33), 9, 6; see also p. 38 of *Moralism and Christianity*. For a discussion of James's artist in relation to Emerson's poet and that poet as Thoreau (and of "an aesthetic so devoted to the *activity* of creation that it denies finality to the results of that activity," and of a contemporary art as "an action" as opposed to "a product of action"), see Richard Poirier, *A World Elsewhere: The Place of Style in American Literature* (New York: Oxford University Press, 1966), pp. 21–26 (the quotations are from p. 21); for a relation of James to Hawthorne, see pp. 111–13.

83. Discussions of James's interest in Fourier may be found in Warren, *Elder James*, pp. 87–126; Perry, *Thought of William James* 1:28–38; and Young, *Philosophy of Henry James*, pp. 70–87.

84. H. James, *Substance and Shadow*, pp. 214–15; and Henry James, "The Principle of Universality in Art," in H. James, *Lectures and Miscellanies*, pp. 111, 118, 119, 120–21.

85. Henry James, "Old and New Theology," and "The Old and New Theology. Part Second," *Lectures and Miscellanies*, pp. 154, 238.

86. Emerson, "The Transcendentalist," p. 347.

87. Emerson, *Nature*, pp. 72, 35; and "Works and Days" in *Society and Solitude: Twelve Chapters* (1870), Vol. 7 of *Complete Works of Emerson* (1912), p. 172.

James's Otherworldly Endeavor

88. H. James, *Secret of Swedenborg*, pp. 172–73; Henry James, "The Scientific Accord of Natural and Revealed Religion," in *Lectures and Miscellanies*, p. 313; and H. James, Jr., *Notes of a Son and Brother*, pp. 167–68.

89. Comment by E. L. Godkin in *Life and Letters of Edwin Lawrence Godkin*, ed. Rollo Ogden (Macmillan Co., 1907), 2:117–18, and quoted in Perry, *Thought of William James*, 1:105.

90. Quoted by Charles Eliot Norton in *Letters of Charles Eliot Norton* (Boston: Houghton Mifflin Company, The Riverside Press, Cambridge, 1913), 2:379, and quoted in Perry, *Thought of William James* 1:129–30.

91. W. James, "Introduction," p. 9. The monotony of the father became a figure ritually intoned, his working in those "fifty stout octavos," as Emerson had said of his "Swedenborg" (p. 110), buried in "the vast, even though incomplete, array of Swedenborg's works, . . . anciently red," and anciently read, ". . . forming even for short journeys the base of our father's travelling library and . . . the accepted strain on our mother's patience." "No more admirable case of . . . solitary singleness of production unperturbed, can I well conceive," said his son Henry, who thought it better spoken "in the thin wilderness" of America "than in the thick" of Europe (*Notes of a Son and Brother*, pp. 148, 58).

92. H. James, Jr., *Notes of a Son and Brother*, p. 155.

93. Henry James, [Jr.], *A Small Boy and Others* (New York: Charles Scribner's Sons, 1913), p. 190.

94. Henry James to Ralph Waldo Emerson [March 3, 1842?], in Perry, *Thought of William James* 1:41.

95. *Notes of a Son and Brother*, p. 68.

96. H. James, Jr., *A Small Boy and Others*, pp. 48–49. These quotations from Henry James, Jr., are also contained in Warren, *Elder Henry James*, pp. 128–29. See also Austin Warren's chapter, "'Father's Ideas': The Elder Henry James," in his *New England Saints* (Ann Arbor: University of Michigan Press, 1956), pp. 74–105.

97. *Notes of a Son and Brother*, p. 69. Henry Jr.'s phrase "the New England conscience" (see Warren, *New England Conscience*, p. 3) appears in the *Notebooks* in portraits for a project that would become *The Ambassadors*, first as the sketch of an elderly man and then as Lambert Strether; James's earliest problem was to provide his character with a vocation. As a friend this character is "fatigued, overworked, threatened with nervous prostration." He is "on the verge of an experience," a man of "perception, humour, melancholy" (pp. 226, 375, 376, 377). For a discussion of *The Ambassadors* in relation to the thought of the elder James, see Anderson, *American Henry James*, pp. 207–231.

98. W. James, "Introduction," p. 16.

99. J. J. Garth Wilkinson to Henry James, 1850, in Perry, *Thought of William James* 1:115, n. 26.

100. William James to Henry James, September 26, 1867, in Perry, *Thought of William James* 2:706–07; and William James to Henry James, October 28, 1867, *ibid.*, 711.

101. William James to Henry James, Jr., 1868, in Perry, *Thought of William James* 1:151; and see *ibid.*, pp. 146–66.

102. H. James, *Secret of Swedenborg*, p. 171.

103. Quoted in W. James, "Introduction," p. 55, unreferenced.

104. *Secret of Swedenborg*, pp. 90, 91–92.

105. H. James, *Substance and Shadow*, pp. 56, 57, 58, 59.

106. *Substance and Shadow*, pp. 59, vi–viii, 80, 52: For the theme of "The Fortunate Fall" in the thought of the elder James, see R. [Richard] W. B. Lewis, *The American Adam: Innocence, Tragedy and Tradition in the Nineteenth Century* (Chicago: University of Chicago Press, 1955), pp. 54–73.

107. *Substance and Shadow*, p. 38; *Society the Redeemed Form of Man*, pp. 485, 410; *Spiritual Creation*, p. 364; and *Christianity the Logic of Creation*, pp. 138, 140. In *Christianity the Logic of Creation*, see also pp. 20, 68–69, 107n, 233–34 and n, and 235n for James's discussions of the physical law of excrement for growth and regeneration, of the need to defecate one's person of selfhood, of an analogy drawn to manure—the good of which should be recognized as the good of evil in the world—and of morality as a menstrual flux, "a vastation of the native grossness of the body" prior to conception and birth. And from James's essay, "Some Personal Recollections of Carlyle" (1881), in H. James, *Literary Remains*, pp. 462–67, see his discussion of the irony of the need—as demonstrated, he felt, by Henry Carey—of "the abject waste and offscouring of the planet, which we ourselves are too fastidious even to name," the redeeming virtue for economic salvation, that is, of the as yet to be used "noisome excrement" of sewage (the scatology, if not ecology, a derivative of Swedenborg).

Swedenborg's own scatology did not go unobserved in the nineteenth century; indeed it led Emerson, in his essay "Swedenborg," to observe that this man of "astronomic punctuality"—the mystic who had begun his career "in the smelting-pot," writing of "mines and metals"—had turned to a science of "excrementitious hells." "Except for Rabelais and Dean Swift nobody ever had such science of filth and corruption" (see pp. 103, 101–02, 131–32). Emerson warned of a caution needed to use such books of filth and revenge, books of a man who had explored "the atom of magnetic iron," books that bothered Emerson for their incredibly "coherent and elaborate . . . system," the universe set in "magnetic sleep," the hell beneath (pp. 106, 135, 133). But there was, as Emerson said, a certain "stereotyped language" involved. And "these pictures are to be held as mystical, that is, as a quite arbitrary and accidental picture of the truth,—not as the truth. Any other symbol would be as good; then this is safely seen" (p. 132). It was as though Emerson were searching for a semeiotics for an understanding of what Swedenborg had seen.

What Swedenborg had seen may be found, for example, in the *Arcana Coelestia*, Vol. 1, nn. 938–46, pp. 363–67: the "excrementitious hells" and other sights to which Emerson was probably making reference, an excremental vision—as well as an emphasis given to smell—that appears to suffuse much of Swedenborg's writings, including the books that James first read (see *On the Divine Love*, p. 55, and *Angelic Wisdom Concerning Divine Providence*, n. 38, p. 44; n. 296, pp. 312–13; n. 304, pp. 321–22; and pp. 386–87). It is an obvious metaphor, these anatomical descriptions that Swedenborg provides for purification, the material base underlying spiritual transformation. For further references to Swedenborg's "sexual and excremental fantasies" as contained in the spiritual diaries, see Jonsson, *Emanuel Swedenborg*, p. 127 and n. 21, p. 205. For a description of Swedenborg's use of "odors," see Toksvig, *Emanuel Swedenborg*, pp. 267–69. And for a brief description of Henry James's scatology in relation to Swedenborg, see Young, *Philosophy of Henry James*, pp. 59–60.

James's language is open of course to a Freudian probe, as indeed is Thoreau's, but such must be preceded if not superseded by a contextual examination—a simple referral of James to Swedenborg and thence to a whole understanding of the themes and perceptions of melancholy. Freud then becomes not the discoverer but the continuation of the text, as does any psychoanalytic history of such life against death. Another approach, verging on tautology, is to submit such language anonymously to a variety of separate psychoanalytic readings, thereby achieving an aura of objectivity—the patient placed, as it were, before a board of examiners. For a submission of Thoreau's language to such an examination (the imagery of the thawing sandbank—the railroad cut—from *Walden*'s chapter on "Spring" before two Rorschach analysts), see the discussion of a seminal dissertation on Thoreau by Raymond Dante Gozzi, "Tropes and Figures: A Psychological Study of David Henry Thoreau" (Ph.D. diss., New York University, 1957), in Michael West's "Scatology and Eschatology: The Heroic Dimensions of Thoreau's Wordplay," *PMLA* 89 (October 1974), 1062–63, n. 25. Gozzi's work has remained influential, informing, for example, Carl Bode's essay, "The Hidden Thoreau," in his *The Half-World of American Culture: A Miscellany* (Carbondale: Southern Illinois University Press, 1965), pp. 3–15, and Richard Lebeaux's *Young Man Thoreau* (Amherst: University of Massachusetts Press, 1977). A similar approach to Thoreau, more subtle in its themes and formal in its approach—focusing, it would seem, only on images, particularly on a controlling metaphor of the water lily, the mud through its roots leading to white—is Stephen Railton, "Thoreau's 'Resurrection of Virtue!'" in *American Quarterly* 24 (May 1972), 210–27.

For James the philosophy of waste—in his son Henry's words, in *A Small Boy and Others*—was the "converting to its uses things vain and unintended, to the great discomposure of their prepared opposites," meaning by that "the inveterate process of conversion," "the particular precious metal our chemistry was to have in view," not success or morality or moralism, not, that is, "the *conscious* conscience," but something else: his and William's "Virtue." "We were to convert and convert, . . . were to form our soluable stuff; with only ourselves to thank should we remain unaware . . . of the substance finally projected and most desirable" (pp. 214, 215, 216, 215). This was the son's "own variant," as F. O. Matthiessen phrased it, in *The James Family: Including Selections from the Writings of Henry James, Senior, William, Henry, & Alice James* (New York: Alfred A. Knopf, 1961), "of the doctrine of the conversion of waste" (p. 77). For Matthiessen, the waste was the education of the sons, or at least the appearance "of their unconventional rearing" (p. 77), which remains in this case too literal a reading of the younger Henry James's words.

108. H. James, *Christianity the Logic of Creation*, pp. 86–87.

109. Emerson, *Nature*, pp. 48–49, 38–39, 13, 11.

110. William James to Henry James, September 5, 1867, in Perry, *Thought of William James* 2:705–06; or William James, *The Letters of William James*, ed. Henry James [III], two volumes in one (Boston: Little, Brown and Company, 1926), 1:47.

The Moral Desertion of Henry James's Father

111. H. James, *Immortal Life*, pp. 188, 170, 169–70.

112. *Immortal Life*, pp. 169–70, 170–71, 152: See also Anderson, *American Henry James*, pp. 94–95.

113. *Immortal Life*, pp. 146–47, 188.

114. *Immortal Life*, pp. 159–60, 148.

115. *Immortal Life*, pp. 147–49; H. James, *Society the Redeemed Form of Man*, p. 330; H. James, Jr., *Small Boy and Others*, p. 220; W. James, "Introduction," pp. 76, 75: See Edel, *Henry James: The Untried Years*, pp. 24–25, for a description of some of these aspects of the elder James's family life.

116. *Immortal Life*, pp. 151–52; H. James, "Property as a Symbol," in *Lectures and Miscellanies*, pp. 88–89, 91; and H. James, "The Old and New Theology," *ibid.*, pp. 187–88.

117. H. James, *Substance and Shadow*, pp. 21, 538–39.

118. This theme is central to, and derived from, Andras Angyal's discussion of "The Pattern of Noncommitment," a chapter from his *Neurosis and Treatment: A Holistic Theory*, ed. E. Hanfmann and R. M. Jones (New York: John Wiley & Sons, 1965), pp. 156–89. "In the childhood of people who develop this pattern ["the obsessive-compulsive pattern"] one traumatic factor always stands out: the *inconsistent behavior* of a significant adult or adults that made it impossible for the child to discover even moderately reliable ways of gaining acceptance" (see pp. 156, 157–58). Such for Angyal creates a wilderness scene, the "conception of the world as a jungle, of life as a fight of all against all," an image "held con-

sciously by many of these patients" (pp. 160–61). James gave his own "shame" over to God by asking that it be compared to "a whole menagerie of fierce robust animals, or of alert poisonous reptiles, . . . asking him or his attorney to explain why this crowd of futile things . . . are practically so immoral as never to have felt a blush of shame" (*Spiritual Creation*, p. 222).

119. H. James, *Nature of Evil*, pp. 305, 306, 307.

120. W. James, "Introduction," pp. 75–76: See Perry, *Thought of William James* 1:119–20.

121. J. J. Garth Wilkinson to Henry James, May 20, 1879, in Perry, *Thought of William James* 1:26.

122. *Thought of William James* 1:133.

123. Henry James to Ralph Waldo Emerson, October 30 [1851], in Perry, *Thought of William James* 1:71–72; and Ralph Waldo Emerson to Henry James, February 25, 1850, *ibid.*, 62.

124. Henry James to Henry James, Jr., December 21 [1873], in Perry, *Thought of William James* 1:3–4.

125. Edmund S. Morgan in his seminal study, *The Puritan Family: Religion & Domestic Relations in Seventeenth-Century New England*, new ed., rev. and enl. (1st ed., 1944; New York: Harper & Row, Publishers, Harper Torchbooks, The Academy Library, 1966) spoke of putting children out beyond the home (pp. 75–79), his theory being "that Puritan parents did not trust themselves with their own children, that they were afraid of spoiling them by too great affection" (p. 77). And in *A Little Commonwealth: Family Life in Plymouth Colony* (New York: Oxford University Press, 1970), John Demos has discussed the practice as well, providing more of a functional, vocational explanation, yet on the whole supporting Morgan's point of view (pp. 71–75). A further step was taken by David E. Stannard, "Death and the Puritan Child," in *Death in America*, ed. David E. Stannard ([Philadelphia]: University of Pennsylvania Press, 1975), pp. 9–29—an article that first appeared in 1974—with the argument that the emotional distance the Puritans presumably maintained was a function of their knowledge of their children's high rates of mortality (see especially pp. 19–21). For broader discussion, see David E. Stannard, *The Puritan Way of Death: A Study in Religion, Culture, and Social Change* (New York: Oxford University Press, 1977).

126. James's ambivalence, if that indeed is the proper word, comes out best in the *Nature of Evil*, pp. 99–101, where in discussing his role as a parent he speaks of surrounding the child with freedom and yet providing "strict discipline." ". . . and if accordingly he misuses my gift . . . I am led by the very interests of his freedom to punish him."

127. H. James, *Immortal Life*, p. 178; and H. James, Jr., *Notes of a Son and Brother*, pp. 50–51. The whole of the son's autobiography, constituting three volumes—*A Small Boy and Others, Notes of a Son and Brother*, and *The Middle Years* (1917)—has been published as *Henry James: Autobiography*, ed. Frederick W. Dupee (New York: Criterion Books, 1956).

The Moral Wilderness of Henry James's Sons

128. Erik H. Erikson, in *Identity: Youth and Crisis* (New York: W. W. Norton & Company, 1968), p. 151, has perhaps put this thesis (derived ultimately from Perry, *Thought of William James*) best, stating that William James's father "by a combination of infirmity, inclination, and affluence was permitted to spend his

days at home, making his family life a tyranny of liberalism." See also Gay Wilson Allen, *William James: A Biography* (1967; rpt. New York: Viking Press, Viking Compass Edition, 1969), pp. 64–87, a chapter entitled "The Paternal Grip." And see Perry, *Thought of William James* 1:171.

129. H. James, Jr., *Notes of a Son and Brother*, p. 156; and H. James, *Substance and Shadow*, pp. 21, 538–39.

130. H. James, *Nature of Evil*, p. 121; and *Substance and Shadow*, pp. 121–22.

131. H. James, *Spiritual Creation*, p. 172.

132. *Notes of a Son and Brother*, pp. 66, 160. The quotation on the glass is contained in Warren, *Elder Henry James*, p. 169.

133. *Notes of a Son and Brother*, pp. 145–46, 151, 146, 66: See also Warren, *Elder Henry James*, pp. 168–70, which contains some of these quotations on the work of the father. The study, often used as opening the problem of vocation for the American artist, is Henry James, *Hawthorne*, with introduction and notes by Tony Tanner (1879; London: Macmillan; New York: St. Martin's Press, 1967); the book first appeared in the "English Men of Letters" series.

134. H. James, Jr., *Small Boy and Others*, pp. 233–34, 226.

135. *Ibid.*, pp. 30, 86–87, 216, 411.

136. H. James, *Christianity the Logic of Creation*, pp. 120–22.

137. H. James, *Church of Christ Not an Ecclesiasticism*, p. 67; and *Society the Redeemed Form of Man*, p. 172.

138. *Notes of a Son and Brother*, pp. 277–78, 276.

139. Edel's five-volume study, *The Life of Henry James*, remains the outstanding psychological study, approaching in the first volume, *The Untried Years*, several of the themes here discussed, though rather from a different, psychoanalytically informed point of view. See in particular p. 24 for a discussion of the "parental disregard" the elder James found. In the elder James's own house, Edel feels (pp. 40–47), it was the strength of the mother, Mary James, that conflicted with the passivity of the father; Edel quotes from a letter of Mary James to William describing herself as "strong in the back, strong in the nerves" (p. 46), the points of physiology in which William considered himself so lacking. But Edel also mentions that Mary James was herself inconstant, "inconsistent in firmness; and this firmness itself was in contradiction to her husband's theory that children should be 'free and uncommitted.' A parental tug-and-pull upon the emotions of their offspring that was alike irrational and anxiety-provoking gives a deep significance to Henry James's remark," that as children they breathed inconsistency (p. 49; see p. 52 as well). Edel also speaks of Henry James's conception of themselves as hotel children, his concern indeed for having presented to his reader "our poor father's impulsive journeyings," as well of his admitted suppression of at least one of the trips as making perhaps too plain, in *Notes of a Son and Brother*, an "absence of plan and continuity" (pp. 46, 141, 142). Edel therefore concludes: "He had a terrible need for order, for design, for apprehending—and later communicating—the world around him in an elaborately organized fashion. It stemmed undoubtedly from the disordered fashion in which, as a boy, he was asked to cope with it." It is only with the further conclusion that one might disagree: "In a sense the circle came full round: William of Albany sought to impose discipline and order on the senior Henry; the elder Henry carefully refused to impose such order upon his novelist son, who in the end imposed it, as a consequence of inner needs, upon himself" (pp. 119–20). The

pattern, to the contrary, was rather consistent, and it was indeed a pattern and consciously conceived as such by both the elder James and the younger. For the novelist's perceptions of work, his sense of his work as indeed his salvation, see pp. 213–14 of Edel's study; for his visits to monasteries, pp. 305, 311–312; and for his bodily ailments, including digestive disorders, pp. 311–12. For Henry Jr.'s own trauma—that twenty-minute period of presumed terror so variously interpreted by scholars, as Edel well shows—see pp. 176–86. Edel ingeniously pulls together the threads of the story, finding a repetition for the son of the father's experience, and discovering a hurt only to the back that counters the myths some scholars had contrived; see in particular p. 184.

Henry Jr.'s autobiographical volumes are treated intensively by Robert F. Sayre in his *The Examined Self: Benjamin Franklin, Henry Adams, Henry James* (Princeton: Princeton University Press, 1964). The interlacing of the thought of the younger Henry James with that of his father—an important consideration—is the theme of Anderson, *American Henry James,* who employs several of the quotations from *Notes of a Son and Brother* that this essay uses earlier, though Anderson's position is Freudian. Anderson speaks of orality, the stammer of the younger James as that of the father related to those "whose emotional lives center about their mouths" (p. 96 and n. 27). He speaks of anality, as in the father's vastation and the younger Henry's dream of the Galerie d'Apollon, "the image of a man as a pipe, liable to obstructions" (pp. 173–74 and 174, n. 19). He speaks of "the teasing, evasive quality of neurotic compulsion" in the father's books (p. 97), and of the utter "fantastically presumptuous" role in his coming to terms with himself and anxiety, "a terrible arrogance completely disguised by a maternal care for the whole world. The disguise served to conceal from him his own masculinity, which he deeply feared, and it entailed an incessant compulsive activity" (p. 93). Anderson's emphasis on form, however—the experience of the son in coming to understand form as a container of experience (see, for example, pp. 80–81)—is worthy of consideration; the book as a whole shows important interconnections, a maintenance, as it were, of an American style.

140. H. James, Jr., *Small Boy and Others,* pp. 348–49: See Edel, *Henry James: The Untried Years,* pp. 75–80, for an analysis of the dream and its surrounding events: See also Anderson, *American Henry James,* his chapter "The House of Life," pp. 161–82, and p. 166, n. 4, for other critics' accounts; and F. [Frederick] W. Dupee, *Henry James,* The American Men of Letters Series (n.p.: William Sloane Associates, 1951), his chapter "The Dream of the Louvre," pp. 3–35.

141. Henry James has lent himself well to structural approaches, as evidenced by the work of Tzvetan Todorov, "The Structural Analysis of Literature: The Tales of Henry James," in David Robey, ed., *Structuralism: An Introduction,* Wolfson College Lectures, 1972 (Oxford: Clarendon Press, Oxford University Press, 1973), pp. 73–103. See also Hawkes, *Structuralism & Semiotics,* p. 150. The image of the younger Henry James as a designer, once again, is taken from Edel, *Henry James: The Untried Years,* pp. 119–20.

Hawthorne

142. Nathaniel Hawthorne, "Wakefield" (1835), in *Twice-Told Tales* (1837), Vol. 9 of *The Centenary Edition of the Works of Nathaniel Hawthorne* ([Columbus]: Ohio State University Press, 1974), pp. 136–37. See also Henry G. Fair-

banks, "Sin, Free Will, and 'Pessimism' in Hawthorne," *PMLA* 71 (December 1956), 975–89, especially 976.

143. Henry James to Ralph Waldo Emerson [1861] in Perry, *Thought of William James* 1:88, 89–90. The letter was printed by Henry James, Jr., in his *Notes of a Son and Brother*, pp. 194–96—"No better example," as the younger James said, "of my father's remarkable and constant belief, proof against all confusion, in the imminence of a transformation-scene," reflecting an ability, that is, "to see his own period and environment as . . . a great historic hour" (p. 196), a preservation, certainly, of the Puritans' and Edwards's sense.

144. H. James, Jr., *Hawthorne*, pp. 78–80, quoting from the first volume of the *American Note-Books*. In his "Introduction" to James's book, Tony Tanner points to a seeming overuse of the adjective "dusky"; it is indeed as though James were trying to drive home a point a bit too forcefully as to the nature of Hawthorne's conscience (pp. 13–14). Swedenborg's involvement with ores, iron furnaces, and salt—including "a little treatise called *New Ways of Detecting Mineral Veins*, in which he makes the suggestion that since each mineral 'exhales' a vapor . . . , we ought to be able to tell where treasures lie hidden by 'smelling them out'"—is described by Sigstedt, *Swedenborg Epic*, pp. 42, 52–54, 92–101; the quotation from p. 53.

145. Nathaniel Hawthorne, "Fancy's Show Box: A Morality" (1837), in *Twice-Told Tales*, pp. 223, 220, 224, 225, 221, 224, 223.

146. Hawthorne, "Fancy's Show Box," pp. 225, 226. As J. Donald Crowley has noted in his superb "Historical Commentary" to the Centenary Edition of the *Twice-Told Tales*, pp. 510–13, of "the contemporary response to Hawthorne's work: all focused primarily on the spiritual character of the man, his sensibilities and singular mode of consciousness, and then on the tales as indications of the spiritual and psychological qualities of the writer"—"as personal spiritual autobiography," in other words, and one that Crowley seems a bit suspicious of, noting that one reviewer thought "Hawthorne" probably a fictitious name (pp. 511, 512–13). In *The Power of Blackness: Hawthorne, Poe Melville* (New York: Alfred A. Knopf, 1958), p. 44, Harry Levin employs the connection Julian Hawthorne established between "Fancy's Show Box" and an incident in the elder Hawthorne's life involving the death of a friend in a duel, a death the father was said to have felt responsibility for, though Levin feels the incident is closer to "Alice Doane's Appeal." In this regard, see Julian Hawthorne, *Nathaniel Hawthorne and His Wife: A Biography*, 4th ed. (Boston: James R. Osgood and Company, 1885) 1:170–75, and the son's concluding remarks to the incident: "Those who wish to obtain more than a superficial glimpse into Hawthorne's heart cannot do better than to ponder every part of this little story"—that is, "Fancy's Show Box" (p. 175). Yet as early as 1909 William Dallam Armes, writing in *The Nation* 88 (1909), 356–57, on "Hawthorne, Cilley, and 'Fancy's Show-Box,'" pointed out that the death of Cilley had occurred after the appearance of the tale, obviating any immediate biographical reference, any act precipitating the writing of such memory and fear. Ironically enough, that is the point and the form of the tale—a spiritual autobiography, but as that autobiography had always been written and was meant to be read, as a construction rather than a reflection, expression, or symptom of any actual fact. Nevertheless, as Crowley says (p. 513), Hawthorne's reviewers "succeeded in establishing a cult of personality" with the appearance of the tales.

147. On *The Blithedale Romance* remaining "the least admired of Hawthorne's longer narratives," see Frederick C. Crews, *The Sins of the Fathers: Hawthorne's Psychological Themes* (New York: Oxford University Press, 1966), p. 194.

148. "That abominable gold-mine! . . . It is my opinion that a man's soul may be buried and perish under a dung-heap, or in a furrow of the field, just as well as under a pile of money." The comment, in a letter to Sophia Peabody of June 1, 1841, and first published in *Passages from the American Note-Books of Nathaniel Hawthorne* (1883; Boston: Houghton, Mifflin and Company, Riverside Press, Cambridge, 1900), p. 235—an edition of which Sophia first published in 1868—is perhaps the most remembered of Hawthorne's relations of his Brook Farm experience, and a comment that has obviously been carefully construed.

149. Nathaniel Hawthorne, *The Blithedale Romance* (1852), in *The Blithedale Romance and Fanshawe*, Vol. 3 of *Centenary Edition of Hawthorne* (1964), p. 17. Henry James's remarks are in a letter to Edmund Tweedy, September 5, 1852, in Perry, *Thought of William James* 1:36.

150. *Blithedale Romance*, pp. 37–38, 46, 38.

151. *Blithedale Romance*, pp. 46–47, 233, 234, 236, 38, 37. The finest of the psychological, psychoanalytically informed studies of Hawthorne's works remains Crews's *Sins of the Fathers*, a book that considers *The Blithedale Romance* in the chapter "Turning the Affair into a Ballad" (pp. 194–212). This study is indebted to Crews on a number of points: Coverdale's "prying concern" (p. 196), the figures of the romance acting as the narrator's "characters" (pp. 197–98), the midnight scene of "sadistic fantasy" (p. 209). Crews, however, can only deny Hawthorne's conscious production, offering a theme that "Hawthornian art is necessarily an art of ideality, of flight from unacceptable truth," that "obsession . . . in *The Blithedale Romance* . . . remains cryptically hidden in the narrator's attitude toward the story he is telling" (pp. 211, 267).

Crews's study and often brilliant readings are built upon such themes as "obsession" and "compulsion"—words, however, that he fails to define, using them loosely, almost placing them within a nineteenth-century definition of monomania, though Crews is quite aware of Freudian ideas of obsessional neurosis. The problem, of course, that plagues any psychoanalytic reading of a writer such as Hawthorne—and quite visibly plagues a comparable reading of any post-Freudian writer—is that the subject is here aware, though in another sense, of such themes as well, aware of the meanings he employs, so that one may not assume what Crews demands: "that the obsession of *The Blithedale Romance* is jointly owned by the hero and the author." Having accepted this, says Crews, "we must infer that Hawthorne as well as Coverdale is at the mercy of unconscious logic" (p. 205). Perhaps Crews's most intriguing reading is that of "Roger Malvin's Burial," first and most thoroughly related in "The Logic of Compulsion in 'Roger Malvin's Burial,'" *PMLA* 79 (September 1964), 457–65. Here Crews uses such unconscious logic to argue against a reading of "Christian moralism" into Hawthorne—a new critical approach, as opposed to his own symptomatic reading, and as such a typical division—as though a religious reading were at odds with what Crews will find, "a deeper level than the ethical— . . . how a man may become the victim of unconscious hypocrisies over which he has no ethical control at all. Indeed, the working-out of this plot is strictly dependent, not on a religious attitude of Hawthorne's, but on an amazingly rigid logic of unconscious compulsion in the protagonist" (pp. 457, 458). Ruben is "in the grip of a destructive obsession," "directing the self-accused 'killer' to perform an expiation that is not simply plausible, but absolutely necessary and inevitable" (pp. 462, 464, 465). Such is almost too literal a reading of Freud's *Totem and Taboo*, where the killing of the father takes place in a mythical, "literary" past where Freud, with his own genius for weaving fancy and fact, locates crimes quite out of time, somewhere between the mythical and actual.

Compulsion is not a fatal necessity, but compulsion is so presented by Hawthorne and then by Crews, in a further extension of the text, to provide a battleground—Ruben's forest—for the struggle, the "moralism," to work itself out. And Hawthorne was not unaware of the text involved. If, for example, as Crews and others have noted (Crews, *Sins of the Fathers*, pp. 160–61), *Fanshawe* is in some sense autobiographical, then the identification is conscious between the author, the protagonist (lost as he is on "deserted" paths, anxious and "bewildered"), and "Nathanael Mather," most assuredly Cotton Mather's Nathanael, the hard student Fanshawe emulates as he grinds himself to death. The quotations are from *Fanshawe* in Hawthorne, *The Blithedale Romance and Fanshawe*, pp. 449, 460. The noting of the use of Nathanael Mather, though to a different end, is in Levin, *Power of Blackness*, p. 72.

Bequest

152. H. James, *Spiritual Creation*, p. 216; *Society the Redeemed Form of Man*, p. 432; and *Secret of Swedenborg*, pp. 199, 192.

153. Henry James, Jr., to William James, December 26, 1882, in Henry James, [Jr.], *The Letters of Henry James*, ed. Percy Lubbock (New York: Charles Scribner's Sons, 1920), 1:97–98; and William James to Henry James, [Jr.], 1883, in Perry, *Thought of William James* 1:165. A fuller version of Henry James's letter to his brother, written the day after Christmas, is contained in Matthiessen, *James Family*, pp. 131–32, saying again that his father "*wished* to die," "prayed and longed to die," that "Aunt Kate repeats again and again, that he *yearned* unspeakably to die." There is a letter as well from Alice James to her brother Henry of December 20, 1882, saying that "I am sure you will feel as thankful as I do that the weary burden of life is over for him" (p. 130). See also H. James, Jr., *Notes of a Son and Brother*, pp. 166–67, on "his loss of interest." The father had died the week before Christmas, as Matthiessen notes. The full version of Henry James's letter is contained in *Henry James: Letters, 1875–1883*, ed. Leon Edel (Cambridge, Mass.: Belknap Press of Harvard University Press, 1975), 2:393–96.

154. H. James, Jr., *Notes of a Son and Brother*, p. 162; comments by William James in a notebook, n.d. [a few years after 1868], quoted in Perry, *Thought of William James* 1:161; and Henry James, "Some Personal Recollections of Carlyle," in H. James, *Literary Remains*, p. 433.

155. *Society the Redeemed Form of Man*, pp. 402–03.

156. W. James, "Introduction," p. 118; and *Varieties*, pp. 254, 355–56, 359–60, 359.

3. Conscience to Neurosis: William James

Nature

1. Paul K. Conkin, *Puritans and Pragmatists: Eight Eminent American Thinkers* (New York: Dodd, Mead & Company, 1968), pp. 274–75.

2. William James, *The Varieties of Religious Experience: A Study in Human Nature: Being the Gifford Lectures on Natural Religion Delivered at Edinburgh in 1901–1902* (1902; New York: Random House, The Modern Library, n.d.), pp. 53–76, 155. (Cited hereafter as *Varieties.*)

3. William James to his sister [Alice James], September 13, 1863, in *The Letters of William James*, ed. Henry James [III] (Boston: Atlantic Monthly Press, 1920), 1:50. (Cited hereafter as *Letters.*)

4. William James to his mother [Mary R. Walsh James], c. September 1863; and William James to Mrs. Katharine James (Mrs. William H.) Prince, September 12, 1863; in James, *Letters* 1:46, 44, 46. See also Ralph Barton Perry, *The Thought and Character of William James, As Revealed in Unpublished Correspondence and Notes, Together with His Published Writings* (Boston: Little, Brown and Company, An Atlantic Monthly Press Book, 1935), 1:215, n. 19.

5. Conkin, in *Puritans and Pragmatists*, p. 414, notes a similarity of Santayana's later writings with the spiritualism of the elder James, and notes as well (pp. 253, 259) a certain use of the elder James by Charles Sanders Peirce.

6. See D. H. Meyer, "American Intellectuals and the Victorian Crisis of Faith," *American Quarterly* 27 (December 1975), 585–603, an article that incorporates James.

7. *Varieties*, pp. 269–73, 269, 21. On Peirce, see John J. Fitzgerald, *Peirce's Theory of Signs as Foundation for Pragmatism* (The Hague: Mouton & Co., 1966), p. 104.

8. "The effect of the American environment . . . was to break down commonsense distinctions between art and life. . . . Instead of writing about it—or *merely* writing about it—he [Thoreau] tries it." This from Leo Marx, *The Machine in the Garden: Technology and the Pastoral Ideal in America* (New York: Oxford University Press, 1964), pp. 246–47. The only objection, other than the innocence with which Marx offers the pastoral figure, is that such an impulse cannot be ascribed to America's nature, the physical setting of its landscape, but to the Puritan tropes re-enacted by Thoreau of art as the enactment of nature seen, Thoreau transposing nature and mechanics from the Puritans' emphasis on the body and bodily humors to a naturalism that is now externally there, as it is for Marx himself as he rends his own garden into his "Epilogue: The Garden of Ashes," an industrial waste.

9. I have discussed this theme in James, posing it against the many psychological studies of James, in a paper entitled "On the Effectual Work of the Word: William James and the Practice of Puritan Confession." The paper is to be published in *Texas Studies in Literature and Language* in the spring of 1983.

10. To sustain this argument would require more than this essay can achieve. See the discussion of the imperfection of spiritual luxury by Saint John of the Cross, in the fourth chapter of the first book of the *Dark Night of the Soul*, in Vol. 1 of *The Complete Works of Saint John of the Cross, Doctor of the Church*, translated from the critical edition of P. Silverio de Santa Teresa, C.D., and

edited by E. Allison Peers (Westminster, Md.: Newman Bookshop, 1945), pp. 358–63. Within the chapter, Saint John of the Cross discusses the "most foul and impure" of images that Satan brings through the medium of melancholy—a phase, perhaps, but clearly one without terrible significance. In this respect, see the editorial comment on p. 362, n. 1, concerning Saint Teresa writing to her brother that "I am convinced that they are of no account, and that it is best not to notice them"—this from the *Letters of S. Teresa*, trans. Benedictines of Stanbrook (London: n.p., 1921), 2:241–42. See as well Evelyn Underhill's comment on Saint Teresa in her *Mysticism: A Study in the Nature and Development of Man's Spiritual Consciousness*, new [3rd] ed. [1911; New York: E. P. Dutton and Company, [1912]), p. 469, where, though Underhill is focusing on psychological themes in the manner of James—on "automatism," that is—she writes that Saint Teresa failed to recognize such "absurdities" as "an episode in her normal development." Reference, too, may be made to the discussion "[Concerning Scruples]" by Saint Ignatius, *The Spiritual Exercises of Saint Ignatius of Loyola*, trans. W. H. Longridge, 3rd ed., new and rev. (London: A. R. Mowbray & Co., 1930), pp. 195–97.

11. *Varieties*, pp. 502, 229, 81, 24, 502, 229, 48, 131.

12. James offered so much writing about his psychological traumas that, even before his death in 1910, he became, more than any other intellectual in Victorian America, personally identified with his own writing. Consequently, he has invited more psychological interpretations than any other American scholar. Within the last two decades in particular, James's biographers have combed through his often striking confessions—especially the case of "melancholy" or "panic fear" that James spoke of in his Gifford Lectures, *The Varieties of Religious Experience*—utilizing psychologies from classical psychoanalysis to behavioral learning theory to explain his mental struggle.

The recent psychological investigations run from a "psychographic profile" by A. [Abraham] A. Roback, in *William James: His Marginalia, Personality and Contribution* (Cambridge, Mass.: Sci-Art Publishers, 1942), pp. 214–38, to informed Eriksonian writings. See Howard M. Feinstein, "William James on the Emotions," *Journal of the History of Ideas* 31 (January–March 1970), 133–42; Howard Marvin Feinstein, "Fathers and Sons: Work and the Inner World of William James: An Intergenerational Inquiry" (Ph.D. diss., Cornell University, 1977), an application of classical psychoanalysis; Cushing Strout, "William James and the Twice-Born Sick Soul," *Daedalus* 97 (Summer 1968), 1062–82; Cushing Strout, "The Pluralistic Identity of William James: A Psycho-historical Reading of *The Varieties of Religious Experience*," *American Quarterly* 23 (May 1971), 135–52, an application of ego psychology; S. P. Fullinwider, "William James's 'Spiritual Crisis,'" *The Historian* 38 (November 1975), 39–57, an application of humanistic psychology; and Marian C. Madden and Edward H. Madden, "The Psychosomatic Illness of William James, *Thought* 54 (December 1979), 376–92, an application of behavioral learning theory. See as well Gary T. Alexander, "William James, the Sick Soul, and the Negative Dimensions of Consciousness: A Partial Critique of Transpersonal Psychology," *Journal of the American Academy of Religion* 48, no. 2, 191–205; Howard M. Feinstein, "The 'Crisis' of William James: A Revisionist View," *The Psychohistory Review* 10 (Winter 1981), 71–90; and *The Psychohistory Review*, Vol. 8 (Summer–Fall 1979), an issue devoted to James.

Psychological motifs in James are discussed by Cordell Strug, "Seraph, Snake, and Saint: The Subconscious Mind In James' *Varieties*," *Journal of the Academy of Religion* 42 (September 1974), 505–15; and Don Browning, "William James's Philosophy of the Person: The Concept of the Strenuous Life," *Zygon* 10 (June 1975), 162–74.

James's psychological interpreter necessarily reads through his confessions as if those confessions stood as verbal façades. Given James's choice to write about himself, however—a choice that he made along with many Victorian intellectuals—his psychological biographer should look first not for unarticulated meanings hidden behind his words, but for the practices of writing that encouraged James to compose the confessional documents that he did. Brilliantly construed as many of these interpretations are, they can only assume that James should have provided the words that allow the psychological analysis to proceed. Not all cultures encourage men and women to speak of mental anguish, and not all literate societies reward writings that permit self-revelation. The psychological interpretation necessarily invokes writing as a mirror of disruptive personal, social, or economic forces that a confession of self-alienation often is said to reflect. Prior to such interpretation, however, whether arguing that James's narrative of panic fear resulted from his Victorian dread of masturbation or from his fear of bodily harm (and by implication castration), intellectual historians have the "right," as Sande Cohen has written, to consider first the force of the text. (See Feinstein, "William James on the Emotions"; Strout, "William James and the Twice-Born Sick Soul"; and Sande Cohen, "Structuralism and the Writing of Intellectual History," *History and Theory* 17, no. 2, 206.)

13. *Varieties*, p. 23.

14. See the quotation from Dickinson S. Miller, "Beloved Psychologist," reprinted in *Great Teachers*, ed. Houston Peterson (1946; rpt. Vintage Books, n.d.), p. 226, in Gay Wilson Allen, *William James: A Biography* (New York: Viking Press, 1967), pp. 302–03.

15. *Varieties*, pp. 209–10, 23.

16. William James, "The Will to Believe" (1896), in his *The Will to Believe and Other Essays in Popular Philosophy* (New York: Longmans Green and Co., 1897), p. 31; *Varieties*, pp. 230–31; and James, "Will to Believe," p. 31.

17. *Varieties*, p. 237. On Luther and Calvin, see Baird Tipson, "The Routinized Piety of Thomas Shepard's Diary," *Early American Literature* 13 (Spring 1978), 70.

Brazil and the Lost Garden

18. William James to his father [Henry James, Sr.], September 12–15, 1865, in *Letters* 1:65; to his brother [Henry James, Jr.], July 15 [1865], in Ralph Barton Perry, *The Thought and Character of William James: As Revealed in Unpublished Correspondence and Notes, Together with His Published Writings* (Boston: Little, Brown and Company, An Atlantic Monthly Press Book, 1935) 1:220 (cited hereafter as Perry); and to his mother [Mary R. Walsh James], December 9, 1865, in Perry, 1:225.

19. William James to his parents, April 21, 1865, in *Letters* 1:58.

20. William James to his brother [Henry James, Jr.], July 15 [1865], in Perry 1:220–21.

21. William James to his parents, May 3–10, 1865 and to Henry James, Jr., July 23, 1865 1:221, 219.

22. William James to his father, June 3, 1865, in *Letters* 1:61. See also the editorial comment by Henry James [III] to the *Letters* 1:63, n. 1.

23. William James to his parents, May 3–10, 1865, quoted by Perry 1:220; to his mother, August 23–25 [1865]; and to his parents, October 21–22, 1865—all in Perry 1:222, 223.

24. Samuel Hopkins, *The Life and Character of the Late Reverend Mr. Jonathan Edwards* (1765), in David Levin, ed., *Jonathan Edwards: A Profile*, American Profiles, ed. Aïda DiPace Donald (New York: Hill and Wang, 1969), pp. 11, 14; William James to his mother, December 9, 1865, in Perry 1:225; to his father, June 3, 1865, in *Letters* 1:63, 61, 62–63; and to his mother, December 9, 1865, in Perry 1:225. Hank Greenspan, in a talk presented to the Michigan Society of Fellows at the University of Michigan in the winter of 1980, has offered a thematic of "William James's Eyes," independently derived. His paper now appears in the issue of the *Psychohistory Review* (10, Winter 1981) that is devoted to James.

25. See George M. Fredrickson, *The Inner Civil War: Northern Intellectuals and the Crisis of the Union* (New York: Harper & Row, 1965), pp. 156–61, 229–38.

26. William James to his father, June 3, 1865, in *Letters* 1:62; to his mother, August 23–25 [1865], in Perry 1:222; and to his father, June 3, 1865, in *Letters* 1:62.

27. Henry James [III], editorial comment, in *Letters* 1:54; and William James to Charles W. Eliot, August 13, 1902, in Perry 2:337–38. Pragmatism as semeiotics is discussed by Charles Morris, *The Pragmatic Movement in American Philosophy* (New York: George Braziller, 1970), in his chapter "Pragmatic Semeiotic," pp. 16–47, though a distinction between Peirce and James is drawn—and mitigated in comparison with earlier accounts (see p. 30).

28. William James, *The Principles of Psychology* (1890; rpt. New York: Dover Publications, 1950), 1:649, 2:442–85; William James, "The Will to Believe" (1896), in *The Will to Believe and Other Essays in Popular Philosophy* (1897), *The Works of William James*, ed. Frederick H. Burkhardt (Cambridge, Mass.: Harvard University Press, 1979), pp. 13–33; *Varieties*, p. 371; and *Principles of Psychology* 1:373–74.

29. William James to his mother, December 9, 1865, in Perry 1:225; and to his father, June 3, 1865, in *Letters* 1:62.

30. William James to his mother, December 9, 1865, in Perry 1:225; and Henry David Thoreau, *Walden* (1854), Vol. 2 of *The Writings of Henry David Thoreau*, Walden Edition (1906; rpt. New York: AMS Press, 1968), 351. See Marx, *Machine in the Garden*, pp. 264–65, for the sense of an ending, in Frank Kermode's phrase, in Thoreau.

31. *Walden*, p. 367.

32. *Varieties*, p. 23; and *Walden*, pp. 7, 100–01, 100, 12–13.

33. William James to his parents, October 21, 1865, in *Letters* 1:67; to his mother, December 9, 1865, in Perry 1:225; and to his father, June 3, 1865, in *Letters* 1:61–62.

34. William James to his parents, October 21 and 22, 1865, and to his father, June 3, 1865, in *Letters* 1:68, 69, 63, 67.

35. The problem of vocation for the nineteenth-century American intellectual, considered by writers such as Henry James and Van Wyck Brooks, was opened in a seminal essay by Henry Nash Smith, "Emerson's Problem of Vocation: A Note on the American Scholar," first published in *The New England Quarterly* 12 (1939), 52–67, and republished in Brian M. Barbour, ed., *American Transcendentalism: An Anthology of Criticism* (Notre Dame: University of Notre Dame Press, 1973), pp. 225–37. The theme is brilliantly discussed in relation to transcendentalism as a whole by R. [Raymond] Jackson Wilson in the opening chapter, "The Plight of the Transcendent Individual," to his *In Quest of Community: Social Philosophy in the United States, 1860–1920*, American Cultural History Series (New York: John Wiley and Sons, 1968), pp. 1–31. The problem for late nineteenth-century intellectuals is perhaps best considered by Christopher Lasch in his *The New Radicalism in America [1889–1963]: The Intellectual as a Social Type* (New York: Alfred A. Knopf, 1965). The "particularly prolonged identity crisis which drove William from art school to a 'scientific school' to medical school, and from Cambridge (Mass.) to the Amazon to Europe and back to Cambridge," is the theme of Erik H. Erikson, *Identity: Youth and Crisis* (New York: W. W. Norton & Company, 1968), pp. 19–20, 150–55, 204–07; the quotation is from p. 151. Considerations of the "vocational problem" of James from a post-Freudian psychoanalytic point of view are provided by Strout, "William James and the Twice-Born Sick Soul," and most particularly by Feinstein, "Fathers and Sons." See as well Millicent Bell, "Jamesian Being," *The Virginia Qvarterly Review* 52 (Winter 1976), 115–32, especially 125–27. And for discussion of "William James and the Crisis of Work" and "Pragmatism and the Work Ethic," see James B. Gilbert, *Work Without Salvation: America's Intellectuals and Industrial Alienation, 1880–1910* (Baltimore: Johns Hopkins University Press, 1977), pp. 180–96, 197–211.

36. Perry, 2:685–86.

37. *Varieties*, p. 479.

James's Fear of His Father's Ascetic

38. *Varieties*, p. 19.

39. *Varieties*, pp. 354, 50, 20, 216, 296.

40. *Varieties*, pp. 255–56.

41. Henry James, *Substance and Shadow: Or Morality and Religion in Their Relation to Life: An Essay upon the Physics of Creation* (Boston: Ticknor and Fields, 1863), p. 75; and William James, "Introduction" to Henry James, *The Literary Remains of the Late Henry James*, ed. William James (Boston: James R. Osgood and Company, 1885), p. 49. The confluence of these phrases has been noted as well by Strout, "Pluralistic Identity of William James," p. 145.

42. William James's son, Henry James III, quite readily revealed the source of the "anonymous 'French correspondent'" in editorial comment to *Letters* 1: 145–47, having observed the confessional tone of the lectures themselves. He surmised that the date of the experience was the winter of 1869–70.

43. *Varieties*, pp. 80, 157–58, 167, 291–92.

44. William James to Theodore Flournoy, September 28, 1909, in William James, *The Letters of William James*, ed. Henry James [III], two volumes in one (1920; rpt. Boston: Little, Brown, and Company, 1926), 2:328. Cited hereafter as *Letters* (1926).

45. "Degeneration and Genius" (1895), in William James, *Collected Essays and Reviews*, ed. Ralph Barton Perry (New York: Longmans, Greene and Co., 1920), pp. 402, 404, 405; and *Varieties*, pp. 8, 184, 472.

46. In particular see "The Explosive Will" in William James, *The Principles of Psychology* (1890; rpt. New York: Dover Publications, 1950), 2:537–45; and *Varieties*, pp. 24, 25.

47. *Varieties*, pp. 167–68.

48. Perry 2:323; and William James to Alice H. Gibbens James, 1882, in *ibid.*, 323.

49. James, "Introduction," p. 73.

50. *Ibid.*

51. *Principles of Psychology* 1:318, n.; and *Varieties*, pp. 357, 359, 356–57.

52. *Varieties*, pp. 290, 341–42, 347; see also pp. 362, 333, 290–91, 268.

53. James, "Introduction," pp. 117–18.

Panic Fear

54. See the comment by Henry James in James, *Letters* (1926), 1:147–48; Perry, 1:322; and Allen, *William James*, pp. 165–67.

55. William James to O. W. Holmes, Jr., September 17, 1867, in *Letters* (1926) 1:100; and *Varieties*, p. 158.

56. *Varieties*, p. 158; and James, *Principles of Psychology* 2:421–22.

57. William James to Henry James, Sr., September 5, 1867, in *Letters* (1926), 1:96; and Mary Robertson Walsh James, 1874, quoted in Perry 2:673.

58. See for example Sigmund Freud, "An Autobiographical Study" (1925), in Sigmund Freud, *The Standard Edition of the Complete Psychological Works of Sigmund Freud*, trans. and ed. James Strachey, (London: Hogarth Press and the Institute of Psycho-Analysis, 1959), 20:52.

59. Comment by Henry James [III] in *Letters*, vol. 1, p. 84; William James to Thomas W. Ward, September [12], 1867, in Perry 1:244; William James to Alice James, June 4, 1868, quoted in Allen, *William James*, p. 145; Allen, *William James*, pp. 89–90; William James to Theodore Flournoy, June 14, 1904, in *The Letters of William James and Theodore Flournoy*, ed. Robert C. LeClair (Madison: University of Wisconsin Press, 1966), p. 157; and William James to Theodore Flournoy, June 15, 1906, in *Letters of James and Flournoy*, pp. 176–77. See also comment by Henry James [III] in *Letters* 1:141.

60. William James, diary entry of 1869, quoted in Allen, *William James*, p. 163; William James to G. H. Howison, July 17, 1895, in *Letters* (1926), 2:23; to O. W. Holmes, Jr., September 17, 1867, *ibid.*, 1:99–100; and to Mrs. Henry Whitman, October 15, 1890, *ibid.*, 303.

61. William James to Thomas W. Ward, June 8, 1866, in *Letters* (1926), 1:77; and to Thomas W. Ward, January 1868, *ibid.*, 128–29.

62. William James to Theodore Flournoy, May 29, 1910, in *Letters of James and Flournoy*, p. 233; Henry James [III], comment in *Letters* (1926), 1:84–85; William James, diary entry of January 1, 1870, quoted in Allen, *William James*, pp. 163–64; William James to Mrs. E. P. Gibbens, August 22, 1899, in *Letters* (1926), 2:96; and William James to Theodore Flournoy, January 3, 1908, in *Letters of James and Flournoy*, pp. 200–01. See Thomas Shepard, *God's Plot: The Paradoxes of Puritan Piety: Being the Autobiography & Journal of Thomas Shepard*, ed. Michael McGiffert, The Commonwealth Series ([Amherst]: University of Massachusetts Press, 1972); and Cotton Mather, *Paterna: The Auto-*

biography of Cotton Mather, ed. Ronald A. Bosco (Delmar, N.Y.: Scholars' Facsimiles & Reprints, 1976), pp. 31, 9–10.

63. William James to Thomas W. Ward, September [12], 1867, in Perry 1:244; to Henry James, Sr., September 5, 1867, in *Letters* (1926), 1:98; to Henry P. Bowditch, December 12, 1867, *ibid.*, 123; and to Thomas W. Ward, September [12], 1867, in Perry 1:244.

64. William James to Henry James, Sr., June 3, 1865, in *Letters* (1926), 1: 62–63.

65. Allen, *William James*, p. 45.

66. Perry 1:169–70; Allen, *William James*, p. 64; F. [Francis] O. Matthiessen, *The James Family: Including Selections from the Writings of Henry James, Senior, William, Henry, & Alice James* (New York: Alfred A. Knopf, 1961), p. 73; Henry James, Sr., to Samuel Ward, September 18, 1859, in Allen, *William James*, p. 55; and Leon Edel, *Henry James: The Untried Years, 1843–1870* (London: Rupert Hart-Davis, 1953), p. 49.

67. William James to Henry James, Sr., [August 19, 1860], in Perry 1:197; William James to his parents, July 9, 1868, *ibid.*, 283; "Philosophical Correspondence Between William James and His Father," Appendix I, *ibid.*, 2:705–16; William James to Henry James, Sr., October 28, 1867, *ibid.*, 2:715; and William James to Henry James, Sr., September 5, 1867, in *Letters* (1926), 1:95–96.

The Context of the Crisis

68. William James to Charles Renouvier, July 29, 1876, in *Letters* (1926), 1:188; to Thomas W. Ward, March 27, 1866, *ibid.*, 75; to Thomas W. Ward, January 1868, *ibid.*, 129; and to Thomas W. Ward, March 27, 1866, *ibid.*, 75.

69. William James to O.W. Holmes, Jr., September 17, 1867, in *Letters* (1926), 1:99; to Thomas W. Ward, c. November 1867?, *ibid.*, 119; to Robertson James, January 27, 1868, in Perry 1:259; and to Thomas W. Ward, November 7, 1867, in *Letters* (1926), 1:119.

70. William James to Henry P. Bowditch, December 12, 1867, in *Letters* (1926), 1:121; and to Thomas W. Ward, January 1868, *ibid.*, 128, 129–30, 133.

71. William James to Thomas W. Ward, June 8, 1866, in *Letters* (1926), 1:78; and to Thomas W. Ward, January 1868, *ibid.*, 130–31.

72. William James to Thomas W. Ward, June 8, 1866, in *Letters* (1926), 1:78, 79; to Mrs. Katharine James (Mrs. William H.) Prince, September 12, 1863, in *ibid.*, 43; and James, *Principles of Psychology* 1:293, 310.

73. The theme and phrase of vocation and doubt are central, of course, to the work of Erik Erikson. For his discussion of James, see *Identity: Youth and Crisis*, pp. 19–25, 150–55, 204–07. See as well Strout, "William James and the Twice-Born Sick Soul," and Feinstein, "Fathers and Sons."

74. See Erikson, *Identity: Youth and Crisis*, p. 19; and William James to Mrs. James (wife), c. December 1878, in *Letters* (1926), 1:199. See also James to Mrs. Whitman, October 5, 1899, quoted in Allen, *William James*, p. 403; to Theodore Flournoy, December 31, 1893, in *Letters of James and Flournoy*, p. 30; and to Thomas Davidson, March 30, 1884, in *Letters* (1926), 1:235.

75. James in his diary, February 1, 1870, quoted in Allen, *William James*, p. 165.

76. William James in a notebook, April 30, 1870, in *Letters* 1:147–48.

77. William James, notebook entry of April 30, 1870, in *Letters* 1:148; and the

diary entry of May 27, 1868, in Perry 2:271, the quotation completed with different excerpts from Allen, *William James*, p. 149.

78. Editorial comment to Sigmund Freud, "Obsessive Actions and Religious Practices" (1907), in Vol. 9 of Freud, *Standard Edition* (1959), p. 117, n. 1.

79. William James, notebook entry of April 30, 1870, in *Letters* 1:148.

80. William James to Henry James, Jr., in *Letters* 1:158; and notebook entry of April 30, 1870, *ibid.*, 148.

81. This essay is indebted to William A. Clebsch, *American Religious Thought: A History*, Chicago History of American Religion (Chicago: University of Chicago Press, 1973), p. 145, who, though to a different end, has pointed to the conjunction in these two writings of the phrase in question.

82. James, *Principles of Psychology* 2:284 and 284–85n.

83. Henry James, Sr., to Henry James, Jr., March 18, 1873, in Allen, *William James*, pp. 179–80; Henry James [Sr.], "Man," in his *Lectures and Miscellanies* (Clinton Hall, N.Y.: Redfield, 1852), pp. 353–54; Henry James, Sr., to Henry James, Jr., January 14, 1873, in Allen; *William James*, p. 179; and Henry James, Sr., to Henry James, Jr., March 18, 1873, *ibid.*, p. 180.

84. A reading list, containing in part physiology and mental pathology, from William James's diary, January 1, 1870, is provided by Allen, *William James*, p. 531n.

Renouvier, Bain, and Obsessive Ideation

85. For brief discussions of ideomotor activity in relation to pragmatism and James, see Philip P. Wiener, *Evolution and the Founders of Pragmatism* (Cambridge, Mass.: Harvard University Press, 1949), pp. 68, 109–10, 266, n. 17, 274–75, n. 52; John Wild, *The Radical Empiricism of William James* (Garden City, N.Y.: Doubleday, 1969), pp. 254–56; and Craig R. Eisendrath, *The Unifying Moment: The Psychological Philosophy of William James and Alfred North Whitehead* (Cambridge, Mass.: Harvard University Press, 1971), pp. 114–15.

86. William James, "What the Will Effects," *Scribner's Magazine* 3 (February 1888), 242.

87. See Perry 2:88.

88. William James to Charles Renouvier, March 29, 1888, in Perry 1:702; William James, "Bain and Renouvier" (1876), in William James, *Collected Essays and Reviews*, ed. Ralph Barton Perry (London: Longmans, Green and Co., 1920), pp. 30–31; James, "What the Will Effects," p. 244; James, *Principles of Psychology* 2:307–11; and James, "What the Will Effects," p. 244.

89. "What the Will Effects," p. 245, 246, 247, 248, 246.

90. Ch. [Charles] Renouvier, *Essai de critique générale, Deuxième Essai: Traité de Psychologie rationelle d'aprés les Principles du criticisme* (1859; Paris; Librairie Armand Colin, 1912), 1:277–79. The author wishes to thank Jane Schmidt for a translation of this portion of Renouvier's work.

91. James, *Principles of Psychology* 2:309; and James, diary entry, spring 1873, in *Letters* (1926), 1:170–71.

92. A meticulous consideration of Bain's influence on American pragmatism is presented by Max H. Fisch, "Alexander Bain and the Genealogy of Pragmatism," *Journal of the History of Ideas* 15 (June 1954), 413–44.

93. *Principles of Psychology* 2:554.

94. Alexander Bain, *The Emotions and the Will*, 4th ed. (London: Longmans,

Green, and Co., 1899), pp. 14, 390. This edition is in effect a reprint of the third edition (New York: D. Appleton & Company, 1876). Alexander Bain, *The Senses and the Intellect*, 3rd ed. (New York: D. Appleton & Company, 1874), p. 342 (1st ed., 1855).

95. *Principles of Psychology* 2:553–54, 558–59.

96. Norman S. Fiering, in his "Will and Intellect in the New England Mind," *The William and Mary Quarterly*, 3rd ser., 29 (October 1972), 515–58, finely considers this debate in relation to seventeenth- and eighteenth-century American thought.

97. Alexander Bain, *The Emotions and the Will* (London: John W. Parker and Son, 1859), p. 500; William James, *Talks to Teachers on Psychology: and to Students on Some of Life's Ideals* (1899; New York: W. W. Norton & Company, The Norton Library, 1958), pp. 59–60; and Bain, *Emotions and Will* (1859), pp. 504, 505, 502, 506, 508, 511, 508.

98. Bain, *Emotions and Will* (1859), pp. 433–38, 417–18. See also Bain, *Emotions and Will* (1899), pp. 379–82; *Emotions and Will* (1859), pp. 72–93; *Emotions and Will* (1899), pp. 158, 154, 164; and *Emotions and Will* (1859), p. 515. As in Puritan thought, where a rather minor psychological point of a seemingly obsessive temptation repugnant to the conscience could assume enormous pastoral considerations, the fixed idea could assume considerable importance in nineteenth-century associationist or analytic psychology—in the work, as seen, of Bain. The problem of the fixed idea may be followed as well in Bain's and John Stuart Mill's editorial emendations to James Mill's chapter on the will in the second volume of his *Analysis of the Phenomena of the Human Mind*, with notes illustrative and critical by Alexander Bain, Andrew Findlater, and George Grote, edited with additional notes by John Stuart Mill, 2nd ed. (London: Longmans, Green, Reader, and Dyer, 1878), pp. 327–95, a work first published in 1829. See in particular pp. 340 and 340, n. 61; 379–82, n. 67; and 382–84, n. 68. In his *Autobiography* (New York: Henry Holt and Company, 1873), John Stuart Mill resolved his depression and crisis not with an advocacy of the freedom of the will but rather like Edwards, drawing distinction, as he wrote, between "the doctrine of circumstance, and Fatalism; discarding altogether the misleading word Necessity" (see pp. 169–70). For a discussion, see Th. [Théodule] Ribot, *English Psychology*, translated from the French (New York: D. Appleton and Company, 1874), pp. 108–13.

Work

99. William James to Margaret Mary James, May 26, 1900, in *Letters* (1926), 2:132.

100. *Varieties*, pp. 196–97; and William James, "Preface" to Edwin Diller Starbuck, *The Psychology of Religion: An Empirical Study of the Growth of Religious Consciousness* (London: Walter Scott, 1899), p. vii. Conversion for Starbuck was "*a distinctly adolescent phenomenon*," few cases ranging outside the bounds of ten and twenty-five years, a process he correlated with puberty or what James, in *Varieties*, pp. 196–97, spoke of as "growth-crisis." For this, see Starbuck's chapter on literature. As Moran has shown for the years of the Great Awakening itself, the age of conversion lessened considerably (pp. 336–38), as one might expect, thereby turning, it would appear, the composition now into a moment of experience, the figure itself into imitation and stereotype.

101. *Varieties*, pp. 197, 239; Thoreau, *Walden*, pp. 4–5; and *Varieties*, p. 240.

102. William James to Henry James, Jr., August 24, 1872, in Perry 1:328; to Henry James, Jr., November 24, 1872, *ibid.*, 332; diary entry for April 10, 1873, *ibid.*, 343.

103. William James to Alice James, November 23, 1873, in *Letters* (1926), 1:176; to Henry James, Jr., May 25, 1873, in Perry 1:347; to John Jay Chapman, May 18, 1906, in *Letters* (1926), 2:257; to Charles Renouvier, August 4, 1896, *ibid.*, 44; to Theodore Flournoy, August 30, 1896, *ibid.*, 47; and to Miss Rosina H. Emmet, September 9, 1898, *ibid.*, 84.

104. Allen, *William James*, p. 193; William James to Henry James, Jr., June 11, 1896, in *Letters* (1926), 2:37; Ernest Earnest, *S. Weir Mitchell: Novelist and Physician* (Philadelphia: University of Pennsylvania Press, 1950), p. 155; William James, "Laura Bridgman" (1904), in James, *Collected Essays and Reviews*, p. 453; William James to Mrs. Alice Howe Gibbens James, July 9, 1898, in *Letters* (1926), 2:75–78; and James, *Principles of Psychology* 2:543. See as well, on the "anaesthetic revelation" of Benjamin Paul Blood, William James, "The Sentiment of Rationality" (1879), in James, *Collected Essays and Reviews*, pp. 134–35, n. 1; William James, "On Some Hegelisms" (1882), in James, *Will to Believe*, pp. 294–98n; William James, "A Pluralistic Mystic" (1910), in his *Memories and Studies*, ed. Henry James, III, his son (1911; London: Longmans, Green, and Co., 1917), pp. 369–411; and Perry's chapter on "Blood and Boutroux," 2:553–69.

105. *Principles of Psychology* 2:537.

106. *Principles of Psychology* 2:543 (see note). Here James referenced works on "impulsive insanity": Henry Maudsley, *Responsibility in Mental Disease*, The International Scientific Series (New York: D. Appleton and Company, 1874), pp. 133–70; and "Forbes Winslow's Obscure Diseases of the Mind and Brain, chapters VI, VII, VIII," this latter reference to Forbes Winslow, *On Obscure Diseases of the Brain, and Disorders of the Mind . . .* (Philadelphia: Blanchard & Lea, 1860), 2nd American ed. entitled *Obscure Diseases of the Brain and Mind* (Philadelphia: Henry C. Lea, 1866).

107. Alice James, *The Diary of Alice James*, ed. Leon Edel (New York: Dodd, Mead & Company, 1964), p. 149. For a discussion of hysteria in terms of role conflict, a conflict that Alice James expresses elsewhere in this passage from her diary, see Carroll Smith-Rosenberg, "The Hysterical Woman: Sex Roles and Role Conflict in 19th-Century America," *Social Research* 39 (Winter 1972), 652–78.

108. Alice James to Mrs. William James, February 5, 1890, in Matthiessen, *James Family*, p. 271, n. 1.

109. In particular see Maudsley, *Responsibility in Mental Disease*, pp. 133, 139–40, 143–45, 148–49, where the author speaks of "impulsive insanity," as well as William James's review of Maudsley's book in the *Atlantic Monthly* 34 (September 1874), 364–65. For Maudsley, in these pages, the impulsively insane is in the grip of a "despotic possession": "like the demoniac of old . . . , he is possessed by a power which forces him to a deed of which he has the utmost dread and horror; and his appeal sometimes to the physician whom he consults in his sore agony, when overwhelmed with a despair of continuing to wrestle successfully with his horrible temptation, is beyond measure sad and pathetic" —a sentence that, when carefully read, shows the confusion involved, for the deed here is both acted and not acted out. Maudsley was unable to resolve a con-

tradiction he observed though barely considered, that exhaustion of nervous and physiological energy loosed the imperative conception, the loss of defenses setting the stage for the impulsive acting out; and yet, in a case observed, a man so possessed appeared otherwise than exhausted. Whether the imperative idea itself was not a means of control—a way of excluding, as this man did, and of offering good reason for remaining apart from others close to him—Maudsley of course could not consider. "The fact that he does successfully resist the insane impulse by calling up ideas to counteract it, or by getting out of the way of temptation, is assuredly not, as many persons think, and some argue, a proof that he might continue to do so on all occasions." The disease could ebb and flow, organic functions remaining in fluctuation, a linearity of argument that for Maudsley made sense, given the idea that only counterforces held the idea in check. When counterforce failed, the "*idea*" became "a violent *impulse*," swallowing will and ending in "convulsive action." For a not dissimilar discussion, see Winslow's *Obscure Diseases of the Brain and Mind* (1866), his chapter (cited by James) on "The Stage of Consciousness," pp. 146–65, where the imagery is stronger and where the steps of Bunyan's conversion have been horribly reversed, such thoughts leading not to light but to death and suicide. Bunyan's understanding of the function of blasphemous suggestions, his frame of reference for the signification such thoughts had, appears constructive in the face of a case Winslow provided (pp. 146–47, 149): "A gentleman of great accomplishments, high order of intellect, known literary reputation, and of admitted personal worth, had his mind for years tortured by morbid suggestions to utter obscene and blasphemous words. He eventually destroyed himself, and in a letter which he wrote to me . . . said his life was embittered and made wretched by these terrible thoughts; but he thanked God he had never once yielded to them, and that, although he was a Christian in belief and conduct, he felt he was not sinning against God by committing self-destruction, if by so doing he could effectually destroy all chance of giving utterance to expression that might contaminate the minds and morals of others!" The case and the manner of its presentation should argue against the notion—indeed, the assumption—that for obsessive behavior, at least, psychiatry by the mid-nineteenth century had emerged from the darkness and demonology of its past, evolving as a science or objective art so as to be rational in its treatment. In its pragmatics Bunyan's psychology was a better explanation of experience, more life-saving certainly, in that it provided a quite rational explanation for saving the victim's life, thereby offering meaning and in that sense preserving sanity.

110. In his *Evolution and the Founders of Pragmatism*, Wiener discusses briefly, among other works, the importance of William B. Carpenter's *Principles of Mental Physiology, with Their Applications to the Training and Discipline of the Mind, and the Study of Its Morbid Conditions* (New York: D. Appleton & Company, 1875), and Isaac Ray's *A Treatise on the Medical Jurisprudence of Insanity*, 2nd ed., with additions (1st ed., 1838; Boston: William D. Ticknor and Co., 1844), for James's writings on ideomotor activity (pp. 109–10, 266, n. 17). Ray's book was reviewed by Nicolas St. John Green, a lawyer and friend of several American pragmatists, including James (See Wiener, *Evolution*, p. 161).

111. Ray, *Treatise on Medical Jurisprudence*, pp. 196–97, 198, 199, 200. Ray's confusion of terminology and types, or at least his misconception of obsessive behavior, is continued in the "Editor's Introduction" to a modern edition of his

book, *A Treatise on the Medical Jurisprudence of Insanity*, ed. Winfred Overholser (Cambridge, Mass.: Belknap Press of Harvard University Press, 1962), p. xiv, in a discussion of the nineteenth-century conception of "moral insanity."

112. Ray, *Treatise on Medical Jurisprudence* (1844), pp. 202–03, 224. The clear alliance of melancholy with the presence or susceptibility to fixed ideas, however vaguely that phrase is defined, is seen as well in another work, one cited in *Varieties*, pp. 143, 493, n. 2: Th. [Théodule] Ribot *The Psychology of the Emotions*, The Contemporary Science Series (London: Walter Scott, 1897). See pp. 70–71 for the melancholiac as "shut up in his grief"—what James, in *Varieties*, p. 133, would call the "prison-house" of consciousness. Ribot considered depressive forms of the religious sentiment, as would James, in terms of fear (pp. 324–25), fear growing "on the soil of melancholia," "fear in all its varieties, ranging from the simple scruple to panic terror; and the intellectual criterion [or analogy], the possession by a fixed idea. Religious madness follows a course depending on character, education, environment, epoch, and form of belief. So those who believe in predestination are tortured by the idea of having committed the unpardonable sin. This obsession, frequent among Protestants, is rare among Catholics, who admit the possibility of absolution." Following this sociological theme, and citing from Hack Tuke that only one such case of this religious madness was found by him among Catholics, Ribot continued: "One form, which we might call subjective, consists in religious melancholy pure and simple, in which the patient believes himself continually guilty, rejected, damned. In its anxious form it is characterised by scruples about everything, lamentations over imaginary crimes or faults." In the second form, the objective, "demoniac melancholia," the person feels the powers without, as in voices, visions, and smells—clearly a psychotic form (to use a later term), not related to what James felt. There is no evidence, of course, and indeed no reason, to attribute any of this subjective melancholia, and the asceticism Ribot offered as one of its functions, to James. But Ribot's words are important, not only because James used his work, but also because the words help indicate what James assumed when he spoke to his audience of melancholy as panic fear. Ribot's words and, to a lesser extent, the case of the peasant lad seem a better or at least a more accessible place from which to begin an inquiry into the case of the anonymous Frenchman, less fraught with assumptions, than Strout's attributing of the case, in "William James and the Twice-Born Sick Soul," pp. 1066–67, to William Acton's *Functions and Disorders of the Reproductive Organs* and its condemnations of masturbation and introspection. Strout does so because of Acton's phrase describing such asylum patients—"The pale complexion, the emaciated form, the slouching gait, the clammy palm, the glassy or leaden eye, and the averted gaze," in Strout's quotation, and not all that close to James's less stereotypical description; Strout links the fear to James's "sexual frustration" and "vocational problem" of then being a physician, as opposed to his philosopher father. Such may well be true, though it is an assumption that can be made only after the ground for James's words has itself been considered—just what he meant in the first place when he spoke of "the worst kind of melancholy . . . panic fear." And it is an assumption that must be considered in the light of James's use of historical terms, his case as composed hardly specific to him, unique in the sense of reflecting only his nature. James's experience, once again, was not simply "there," "actual," "real," or "specific"; it was remembered and

constructed, using available forms as much as that of any fictional character, which does not in any sense make of James's experience a fiction.

113. *Principles of Psychology* 2:542.

114. *Ibid.*, 542–43, 543–45.

115. *Ibid.*, 545.

116. *Ibid.*, 548. Elsewhere in the *Psychology* James applauded habits as a mechanism "to fund and capitalize our acquisitions," seeing not habit but morbid "indecision" as tyranny (1:122).

117. *Ibid.*, 2:549, 563, 566.

118. James, interview with the *Boston Journal*, July 29, 1903, in Perry 2:317; and William James, "What Is an Emotion?" (1884), in *Collected Essays and Reviews*, p. 261.

119. William James, "The Physical Basis of Emotion" (1894), in *Collected Essays and Reviews*, p. 361.

120. *Principles of Psychology* 2:436, 421, 420, 423–26, 430–36, 435n.

121. *Ibid.*, 409–10, 437–38. Along with John Stuart Mill and James, Darwin remains a famous case of nineteenth-century neurasthenia and work inhibition. For a discussion of his sensibility, see Donald Fleming, "Charles Darwin, the Anaesthetic Man," reprinted from *Victorian Studies* 4 (1961), 219–36, in Philip Appleman, ed., *Darwin*, A Norton Critical Edition (New York: W. W. Norton & Company, paperback, 1970), pp. 573–89.

122. *Principles of Psychology* 2:548, 549, 534.

Compulsion and Doubt

123. James, *Talks to Teachers*, pp. 122–23, 121–22.

124. For a nicely presented discussion of ideas and movements of relaxation in late nineteenth-century America, see Daniel T. Rodgers, *The Work Ethic in Industrial America, 1850–1920* (Chicago: University of Chicago Press, 1978), "Play, Repose, and Plenty," pp. 94–124.

125. James, *Talks to Teachers*, pp. 62, 122; and William James, "The Gospel of Relaxation," first published in its revised form in his *Talks to Teachers on Psychology: And to Students on Some of Life's Ideals* (New York: Henry Holt and Company, 1899), pp. 197–228, and republished in William James, *Essays on Faith and Morals*, [ed.] Ralph Barton Perry (New York: Longmans, Green and Co., 1943), the edition here used, the quotations from pp. 248, 249, 254, 252, 240–41. For bibliographic information, see the "Annotated Bibliography of the Writings of William James" appended to *The Writings of William James*, ed. John J. McDermott (New York: Random House, The Modern Library, 1968), pp. 811–58.

126. See Marx, *Machine in the Garden*, Ch. 2, "Shakespeare's American Fable."

127. Ralph Waldo Emerson, "The American Scholar: An Oration Delivered Before the Phi Beta Kappa Society, at Cambridge, August 31, 1837," in *Nature, Addresses and Lectures*, Vol. 1 of *The Complete Works of Ralph Waldo Emerson*, Centenary Edition (Boston: Houghton Mifflin Company, The Riverside Press, Cambridge, 1903), p. 83; Ralph Waldo Emerson, journal entry for October 1837, in *Selections from Ralph Waldo Emerson: An Organic Anthology*, ed. Stephen E. Whicher, Riverside Editions (Boston: Houghton Mifflin Company, The

Riverside Press, Cambridge, paperback, 1957), p. 81; and Emerson, "American Scholar," p. 96.

128. James, "Gospel of Relaxation" (1943), pp. 243, 252, 247, 252; and Emerson, journal entry for October 1837, in *Selections from Emerson*, ed. Whicher, p. 81.

129. Emerson, "American Scholar," p. 81; and James, "Gospel of Relaxation" (1899), p. 221, the quotation in the text from the headnote.

130. The following citations are from *Letters* (1926): James to Henry James, Jr., [c. 1890], 1:225; to Charles Renouvier, August 5, 1883, 1:230; to Henry James, Jr., April 12, 1887, 1:269; to Mrs. Henry Whitman, July 24, 1890, 1:297; to Mrs. Henry Whitman, October 15, 1890, 1:303.

131. William James to Margaret James, April 2, 1908, in *Letters* (1926), 2:302; and to Henry James, Jr., April 15, 1908, *ibid.*, 302. It was Arthur O. Lovejoy, in "William James as Philosopher," an essay first published in the *International Journal of Ethics* 21 (1911), and republished in *The Thirteen Pragmatisms and Other Essays* (Baltimore: Johns Hopkins Press, 1963), pp. 79–112, who first observed in critical form not only the austerity and pessimism in James but also, as Lovejoy took it, the laboriousness. Feinstein, in his "Fathers and Sons," has provided a unique analysis of James's drawings, many for the first time published, sketches that show, as Feinstein well argues, the terrible anger and fears involved.

132. James, "Gospel of Relaxation" (1943), pp. 256–58.

133. William James to Mrs. Henry Whitman, June 16, 1895, in *Letters* (1926), 2:22; to Henry James, Jr., June 11, 1896, *ibid.*, 36; and to Dickinson S. Miller, August 18, 1903, *ibid.*, 198.

134. William James to Francis R. Morse, September 24, 1903, in *Letters* (1926), 2:200. See William James to Theodore Flournoy, October 4, 1908, *ibid.*, 313–14; and to Henri Bergson, July 28, 1908, *ibid.*, 308.

135. See William James to John Jay Chapman, May 18, 1906, in *Letters* (1926), 2:256, for his opinion of Mrs. Whitman's unsimple life; to Henri Bergson, October 4, 1908, *ibid.*, 315; to Theodore Flournoy, June 2, 1902, in *Letters of James and Flournoy*, p. 122; to John Jay Chapman, May 18, 1906, in *Letters* (1926), 2:257; to Charles Renouvier, August 4, 1896, *ibid.*, 44; to Theodore Flournoy, August 1901, in *Letters of James and Flournoy*, p. 112; and to Theodore Flournoy, December 26, 1901, *ibid.*, p. 115.

136. The following citations are from *Letters* (1926): James to Clifford W. Beers, April 21, 1907, 2:274; to Henry James, Jr., June 11, 1896, 2:36; to Henry James, Sr., September 12–15, 1865, 1:66; to Alice James, September 13, 1863, 1:50; comment by Henry James [III], 1:233; James to Mrs. E. P. Gibbens, August 22, 1899, 2:98–99; to Theodore Flournoy, August 13, 1895, 2:24; to Henry James, Jr., September 22, 1893, 1:347; to H. G. Wells, September 11, 1906, 2:260; to Alice James, December 17, 1873, 1:178; to T. S. Perry, January 29, 1909, 2:319; to Henry James, Jr., and William James, Jr., February 14, 1907, 2:265; and to Mrs. Frances R. Morse, December 26, 1878, 1:198.

137. A theme best treated by Perry Miller, *The New England Mind: From Colony to Province* (Cambridge, Mass.: Harvard University Press, 1953), in his chapter on "Do-Good," pp. 395–416, especially pp. 400ff.

138. William James, "The Energies of Men," *The Philosophical Review* 16 (January 1907), 1–20. Subsequent references to this essay are to the article as it

appeared in *The Philosophical Review.* The article appeared in an altered form as "The Powers of Men" in the *American Magazine* for October 1907. For James's comment on misunderstanding, see William James, "Introductory," to William James, *The Energies of Men*, new ed. (New York: Moffat, Yard and Company, 1917).

139. Historians have yet to consider neurasthenia as other than a vague Victorian malaise incident to the industrialism to which Beard thought it was symptomatically related—which is not surprising, given the enormous contemporary literature on the subject from a variety of sources, as any perusal of the *Index Medicus* will indicate. For discussions, see Philip P. Wiener, "G. M. Beard and Freud on 'American Nervousness,'" *Journal of the History of Ideas* 17 (April 1956), 269–74, an article of bibliographic importance for Beard; Donald Meyer, *The Positive Thinkers: A Study of the American Quest for Health, Wealth and Personal Power from Mary Baker Eddy to Norman Vincent Peale* (Garden City, N.Y.: Doubleday & Company, 1965), "The Discovery of the 'Nervous American,'" pp. 21–31; Francis G. Gosling III, "American Nervousness: A Study in Medicine and Social Values in the Gilded Age, 1870–1900" (Ph.D. diss., University of Oklahoma, 1976); and Gilbert, *Work without Salvation*, "Neurasthenia: The Mental Illness of Industrialism," pp. 31–43. Of related interest, see Barbara Sicherman, "The Paradox of Prudence: Mental Health in the Gilded Age," *The Journal of American History* 62 (March 1976), 890–912.

140. In particular see George L. Walton, "The Classification of Psycho-Neurotics and the Obsessional Element in Their Symptoms," *The Journal of Nervous and Mental Disease* 34 (August 1907), 489–96.

141. William James, comment on J. J. Putnam, "Psychical Treatment of Neurasthenia," *Boston Medical and Surgical Journal* 132 (May 23, 1895), 516–17. James Jackson Putnam's paper appeared as "Remarks on the Psychical Treatment of Neurasthenia," *ibid.*, 132 (May 16, 1895), 505–11.

142. Pierre Janet, "On the Pathogenesis of Some Impulsions," *The Journal of Abnormal Psychology* 1 (April 1906), 1–17.

143. Janet, "On the Pathogenesis of Some Impulsions," pp. 1, 1–2, 2, 7–8, 13–14, 16.

144. James, "Energies of Men," pp. 2, 8.

145. *Ibid.*, pp. 9–12.

146. William James to W. [Wincenty] Lutoslawski, May 6, 1906, in *Letters* (1926), 2:252–55.

147. William James to Theodore Flournoy, January 3, 1908, in *Letters of James and Flournoy*, pp. 193–94, 195.

148. James, *Principles of Psychology* 1:126.

149. *Varieties*, pp. 230–31, 235, 236, 240, 259, 261, 267, 268, 341–42, 347.

150. *Varieties*, pp. 309, 313, 312, 356–57.

151. *Varieties*, pp. 362, 363, 368–69.

152. *Principles of Psychology* 2:9n; Thomas Shepard, *The Sound Believer: A Treatise of Evangelical Conversion . . .* (1645), in *The Works of Thomas Shepard . . .*, ed. John A. Albro (Boston: Doctrinal Tract and Book Society, 1853), 1:117; and Jonathan Edwards, *A Faithful Narrative of the Surprising Work of God . . .* (1737), in *The Works of President Edwards* (London, 1817; rpt. New York: Burt Franklin, 1968), p. 23.

The steps in the *Varieties* are clear enough, perhaps, though this construction of the *Varieties* was seen only when pointed out by Elizabeth Ann Huetteman, a student of the author in an undergraduate colloquium. Cushing Strout, in "The Pluralistic Identity of William James," has also commented on the "lack of variety" in the *Varieties*, though by that he means the emphasis James gives to the sick soul as opposed to the healthy-minded (pp. 136–37). Strout has provided a well-informed Eriksonian reading—stressing in James's life a "working through," though his reading is literal and evolutionary—of James as working toward Erikson and ego psychology, balancing two worlds: "Certainly his own conversion was connected with 'deeper forces,' deriving from an over-identification with a disturbed father. Such a son, with less suffering today, might 'work through' a similar problem with the sustained and expensive help of a psychoanalyst or psychiatrist. But James lived between the two cultural worlds of religious conversion and psychoanalytic therapy" (p. 148). "Pluralism would be James's contribution to metaphysics, and in psychological terms pluralism of identity was the mark of his character. His fundamental sympathies were divided between the healer and the patient, the agnostic and the believer, the strenuous will and the mood of 'letting go,' the 'healthy-minded' moralist and 'the twice-born sick soul,' the scientist and the metaphysician" (pp. 149–50). Such is rather a traditional view of James, stemming indeed from Ralph Barton Perry who in *Thought and Character of William James* entitled his last two chapters "Character and Thought: Morbid Traits" and "Character and Thought: Benign Traits." But process rather than pluralism (or Perry's dualism) defines James's texts, including (as the psychobiographer desires), the text of his life, removing the need to hold James's self in "tension," to see his life divided, when division itself is the figuration, the structuring of self holistic and complete. Health, sickness, mechanism, and faith remain in their order, the text James wrote as he moved through the (vocational) process of conversion, never allowing the end to be anything other than his sighting, and citing from, the so-called mystics' texts, rather as Bunyan held the Celestial City within the distance of Christian's eye.

Scholars have neglected Edwards's presence in James's thought. Instead, they read the *Varieties* exclusively within the radical shifts of nineteenth-century thought, most obviously the shifts that occur with the advent of Darwin and Freud. They also approach the book as an expression of James's freely moving pluralism, viewing the lectures as individual essays rather than in terms of the lectures' order and process. See most particularly Henry Samuel Levinson, *The Religious Investigations of William James* (Chapel Hill: University of North Carolina Press, 1981).

153. *Varieties*, pp. 183, 242, 236; and Shepard, *Sound Believer*, p. 267.

154. *Varieties*, pp. 370, 379, 375, n. 1.

155. *Varieties*, pp. 383–84, n. 1.

Radical Empiricism

156. William James, diary entries for December 21, 1869, and January 1, 1870, quoted in Allen, *William James*, pp. 163, 163–64, Allen providing the reading list William recorded on p. 531n.

157. Henry Maudsley, *The Physiology and Pathology of the Mind* (1867; New York: D. Appleton & Company, 1871), pp. 330–31.

158. William James, *A Pluralistic Universe: Hibbert Lectures at Manchester*

College on the Present Situation in Philosophy (London: Longmans, Green, and Co., 1909), pp. 309, 305–06, 320–21, 258–59, 263–64.

159. William James to Margaret Mary James, May 26, 1900, in *Letters* 2:131, 132.

160. James, *Pluralistic Universe*, pp. 313, 303, 304–05, 330.

161. William James to Thomas W. Ward, January 1868, in *Letters* 1:132.

4. Conversion through Ethical Salvation: Josiah Royce

1. See R. [Raymond] Jackson Wilson, *In Quest of Community: Social Philosophy in the United States, 1860–1920*, American Cultural History Series (New York: John Wiley and Sons, 1968), pp. 148–49.

2. For the legend of Thoreau's box, equated by Perry Miller with death, see Miller's "Introduction" to *Consciousness in Concord: The Text of Thoreau's Hitherto "Lost Journal" (1840–1841), Together with Notes and a Commentary* (Boston: Houghton Mifflin Company, Riverside Press Cambridge, 1958), pp. 3–7.

3. Josiah Royce, "Diary," March 10, 1879, quoted in J. [Jacob] Loewenberg, "Editor's Introduction" to Josiah Royce, *Fugitive Essays by Josiah Royce*, [ed.] J. [Jacob] Loewenberg (Cambridge, Mass.: Harvard University Press, 1920), p. 34.

Imitation

4. Royce to Mary Gray Ward Dorr, October 31, 1889; to William James, September 12, 1900; to Horace Elisha Scudder, May 21, 1888; and to George Bucknam Dorr, August 12, 1887. The letters are found in Josiah Royce, *The Letters of Josiah Royce*, ed. John Clendenning (Chicago: University of Chicago Press, 1970), pp. 241, 407, 214, 210 (hereafter cited as *Letters*). For Royce's brief autobiographical sketch in which he discusses personal estrangement, see Josiah Royce, "Words of Professor Royce at the Walton Hotel at Philadelphia, December 29, 1915," in Royce, *The Hope of the Great Community* (New York: Macmillan Company, 1916), pp. 122–36. For firsthand accounts of Royce's personality, see Richard C. Cabot, "Josiah Royce as a Teacher," *The Philosophical Review*, 25 (May 1916), 466–72; John Jay Chapman, "Portrait of Josiah Royce, the Philosopher," *The Outlook* 122 (July 2, 1919), 372 and 377; Harry T. Costello, "Recollections of Royce's Seminar on Comparative Methodology," in *Josiah Royce's Seminar, 1913–1914: As Recorded in the Notebooks of Harry T. Costello*, ed. Grover Smith (New Brunswick, N.J.: Rutgers University Press, 1963), pp. 189–95; J. [Jacob] Loewenberg, *Royce's Synoptic Vision* ([Baltimore]: Department of Philosophy of the Johns Hopkins University, 1950); George Herbert Palmer, "In Dedication: Josiah Royce," in *Contemporary Idealism in America*, ed. Clifford Barrett (New York: Macmillan Co., 1932), pp. 1–9; Ralph Barton Perry, "Two American Philosophers: William James and Josiah Royce," in Perry, *In the Spirit of William James* (New Haven: Yale University Press, 1938), pp. 1–43; and George Santayana, "Josiah Royce," in *Character and Opinion in the United States* (1920; New York: George Braziller, 1955), pp. 57–59.

5. Royce to William James, May 21, 1888, in *Letters*, p. 215; and James Harry Cotton, *Royce on the Human Self* (Cambridge, Mass.: Harvard University Press, 1954), p. 6.

6. Royce to William James, January 12, 1908, in *Letters*, pp. 518–19.

7. Chapman, "Portrait of Josiah Royce," p. 377; comment by John J. McDermott, in Josiah Royce, *The Basic Writings of Josiah Royce*, ed. John J. McDermott (Chicago: University of Chicago Press, 1969), 2:829, n. 1; Loewenberg, *Royce's Synoptic Vision*, p. 5; and Cotton, *Royce on the Human Self*, pp. 6–7.

8. Royce's lecture is described by Peter Fuss in *The Moral Philosophy of Josiah Royce* (Cambridge, Mass.: Harvard University Press, 1965), p. 64. Fuss mentions Royce's "personal confession" in n. 12 on that page, accepting the incident in the manner Royce presented it. For his citation, Fuss references Josiah Royce, "Topics in Psychology of Interest to Teachers," Harvard University Archives, folio 64, lecture 5, pp. 42–76, giving the date of the lecture on p. 61.

9. In a footnote (pp. 31–32) to "The Case of John Bunyan" (1894), in Josiah Royce, *Studies of Good and Evil: A Series of Essays Upon Problems of Philosophy and of Life* (New York: D. Appleton and Company, 1898), Royce referenced an article by Edward Cowles on "Insistent and Fixed Ideas" which appeared in *The American Journal of Psychology* 1 (February 1888), pp. 222–270, and compared Bunyan (p. 43) to the case study of obsession Cowles had discussed at length. In his article Cowles cited as part of the case history of a Miss M. her morbid fear of doing harm to a friend. "On one occasion," Cowles wrote, "in a public library, she read in one of Dickens' stories a graphic account of a murder by cutting the throat. This affected her very painfully, as if it described a crime of her own. She had no peace till she went again to the library, and from the same book had secretly torn the leaves upon which the murder was described and rended them into shreds" (p. 248). This fear of committing a criminal act, as well as the attempt to remove the object which had aroused the fear, is similar to Royce's own experience, as he must have realized by this following year, described in his earlier essay on imitation.

10. Richard Slotkin, *Regeneration Through Violence: The Mythology of the American Frontier, 1600–1860* (Middletown, Conn.: Wesleyan University Press, 1973), Chs. 4 and 5, pp. 94–145.

11. Royce's essays on imitation include "The Imitative Functions, and Their Place in Human Nature," *The Century Magazine* 48 (May 1894), 137–45; "The External World and the Social Consciousness," *The Philosophical Review* 3 (September 1894), 513–45; and "Preliminary Report on Imitation," *The Psychological Review* 2 (May 1895), 217–35. It is in the last of these articles that Royce describes his experiments, speaks of the aspect of mocking (p. 224), and writes that "imitation is, psychologically speaking, the one source of our whole series of conscious distinctions" (p. 230). For an extended discussion of Royce on imitation, see Fuss, *The Moral Philosophy of Josiah Royce*, "Imitation," pp. 59–75.

12. Josiah Royce, "The Problem of Job" (1898), in Royce, *Studies of Good and Evil*, pp. 22, 21.

13. *Ibid.*, p. 21.

14. Josiah Royce, *The Spirit of Modern Philosophy: An Essay in the Form of Lectures* (1892; rpt. New York: W. W. Norton & Company, The Norton Library, 1967), p. 212 (cited hereafter as *Spirit*); Royce, "Problem of Job," pp. 22, 23; and Royce, *Spirit*, p. 211.

15. See Josiah Royce, *The World and the Individual*, Gifford Lectures Delivered before the University of Aberdeen, Vol. 2 (New York: Macmillan Company, 1901), 348; and Royce, *Spirit*, pp. 213, 210, and for the quotation, p. 211.

16. George Santayana, *Character & Opinion in the United States, with Remi-*

niscences of William James and Josiah Royce and Academic Life in America (New York: Charles Scribner's Sons, 1920), p. 100; and Josiah Royce, "Meditation before the Gate," an unpublished meditation dated February 12, 1879, published in Loewenberg, "Editor's Introduction," p. 7.

17. John Clendenning, "Introduction" to *The Letters of Josiah Royce*, p. 11.

18. Josiah Royce, "Words of Professor Royce at the Walton Hotel at Philadelphia, December 29, 1915," in *Papers in Honor of Josiah Royce on His Sixtieth Birthday*, a volume that originally appeared as Vol. 25 of *The Philosophical Review* (May 1916), pp. 279–80; and Cotton, *Royce on the Human Self*, p. 8.

19. From a conversation with Paul K. Conkin; and Santayana, *Character & Opinion* (1920), pp. 119–20.

20. George Santayana, "A General Confession," assembled from separate writings published in 1930 and 1936, in *The Philosophy of George Santayana*, ed. Paul Arthur Schilpp, *The Library of Living Philosophy*, 2nd ed. (New York: Tudor Publishing Company, 1951), p. 11.

21. Josiah Royce, "The Possibility of Error," Ch. 11 of his *The Religious Aspect of Philosophy: A Critique of the Bases of Conduct and of Faith* (1885; rpt. Gloucester, Mass.: Peter Smith, 1965), pp. 384–435. For discussions, see Bruce Kuklick, *Josiah Royce: An Intellectual Biography* (Indianapolis: Bobbs-Merrill Company, 1972), pp. 32–39; and Bruce Kuklick, *The Rise of American Philosophy: Cambridge, Massachusetts, 1860–1930* (New Haven: Yale University Press, 1977), pp. 150–57; as well John E. Smith, *Royce's Social Infinite: The Community of Interpretation* (New York: Liberal Arts Press, 1950), pp. 11–16; and Cotton, *Royce on the Human Self*, pp. 117–21.

22. Royce, *Spirit*, p. 261; and Josiah Royce, *The Philosophy of Loyalty* (New York: Macmillan Company, 1908), p. 241. For a discussion of themes of social alienation in late-nineteenth-century American intellectuals, including Royce, see Jean B. Quandt, *From the Small Town to the Great Community: The Social Thought of Progressive Intellectuals* (New Brunswick, N.J.: Rutgers University Press, 1970).

23. Royce, "Diary," March 10, 1879, in Loewenberg, "Editor's Introduction," p. 35; and Royce, *Religious Aspect of Philosophy*, p. 125. For the influence of Goethe's *Faust* on Royce, see Vincent Buranelli, *Josiah Royce*, Twayne's United States Authors Series, TUSAS 49 (New York: Twayne Publishers, 1964), pp. 29–30.

24. Royce, *Spirit*, pp. 33–34, 192, 206, 207–08; and Royce, "Problem of Job," p. 23. On estrangement as "making strange," see Raymond Williams, *Marxism and Literature*, Marxist Introductions (1977; rpt. Oxford: Oxford University Press, paperback, 1977), p. 191; and Terence Hawkes, *Structuralism & Semiotics* (Berkeley: University of California Press, 1977), pp. 63–64.

25. Royce, "Problem of Job," p. 23.

California and Royce's Childhood

26. Royce, "Words of Professor Royce," in Royce, *Hope of the Great Community*, pp. 124, 125, 126–27, 130–31.

27. Royce to Henry Lebbeus, July 29, 1886; to George Buchanan Coale, September 23, 1880; and to George Buchanan Coale, December 5, 1881 (Royce, *Letters*, pp. 196, 92, 104). [See Santayana, "Josiah Royce," in Santayana, *Character and Opinion* (1955), p. 60.] For themes of doubt and order in late Victorian

America, see Robert H. Wiebe, *The Search for Order: 1877–1920*, The Making of America series (1967; New York: Hill and Wang, American Century Series, 1968); Walter E. Houghton, *The Victorian Frame of Mind: 1830–1870* (1957; rpt. New Haven: Yale University Press, published for Wellesley College, paperback, 1957), especially Houghton's chapters on "Anxiety," "Dogmatism," and "Rigidity"; and D. H. Meyer, "American Intellectuals and the Victorian Crisis of Faith," *American Quarterly* 27 (December 1975), 585–603, especially 587–91.

28. Royce to Daniel Coit Gilman, September 16, 1878; and to William James, August 10, 1888 (Royce, *Letters*, pp. 61, 219). See Andras Angyal, "The Pattern of Noncommitment," Ch. 11 of his *Neurosis and Treatment: A Holistic Theory*, eds. Eugenia Hanfmann and Richard M. Jones (New York: Viking Press, 1965).

29. Clendenning, "Introduction" to Royce, *Letters*, pp. 11–13.

30. Josiah Royce, "Doubting and Working" (1881), in Royce, *Fugitive Essays*, p. 344.

31. Clendenning, "Introduction," pp. 12–13; Royce, "Words of Professor Royce," in Royce, *Hope of the Great Community*, p. 123; and Perry, "Two American Philosophers," pp. 6–7. See also Clendenning, "Introduction," p. 13.

32. Sarah Royce, *A Frontier Lady: Recollections of the Gold Rush and Early California*, ed. Ralph Henry Gabriel (New Haven: Yale University Press, 1932), pp. 11, 17, 67, 125–26, 114, 118, 119, 117, 126, 104, 114. Royce, "Words of Professor Royce," in Royce, *Hope of the Great Community*, p. 124; and Clendenning, "Introduction," pp. 12–13.

33. For Peirce, signification, and pragmatism, see John J. Fitzgerald, *Peirce's Theory of Signs as Foundation for Pragmatism* (The Hague: Mouton & Co., 1966), and Douglas Greenlee, *Peirce's Concept of Sign*, Approaches to Semiotics Paperback Series, ed. Thomas A. Sebeok (The Hague: Mouton, 1973), on both of which these present statements on Peirce rely. The central discussion of the sign without its pragmatic relation is contained in Charles Sanders Peirce, *Collected Papers of Charles Sanders Peirce*, ed. Charles Hartshorne and Paul Weiss, Vol. 2 (Cambridge, Mass.: Harvard University Press, 1932), 134–73, sections 2.227–2.308.

34. Greenlee, *Peirce's Concept of Sign*, pp. 120–31; Greenlee speaks as well of "convention." See also Fitzgerald, *Peirce's Theory of Signs*, pp. 154–59. On the "social character of the knowing process" for Royce, see Mary Briody Mahowald, *An Idealistic Pragmatism: The Development of the Pragmatic Element in the Philosophy of Josiah Royce* (The Hague: Martinus Nijhoff, 1972), pp. 78–85.

35. Josiah Royce, *The Feud of Oakfield Creek: A Novel of California Life* (Boston: Houghton, Mifflin and Company, 1887), pp. 12, 10–11, 12, 21–22.

36. *Ibid.*, pp. 14, 13, 14–15.

37. Harry Stack Sullivan, *Clinical Lectures in Psychiatry*, ed. Helen Swick Perry, Mary Ladd Gawel, and Martha Gibbon (New York: W. W. Norton & Company, 1956), pp. 266, 267–68; and Royce, *Feud of Oakfield Creek*, pp. 482–83.

James and Harvard

38. Royce to Alfred Deakin, April 18, 1908, in Royce, *Letters*, p. 522; Loewenberg, *Royce's Synoptic Vision*, p. 15. On the theme of Royce's own pragmatism, see the important discussion by Kuklick, *Josiah Royce*, as well as Mahowald, *An Idealistic Pragmatism*.

39. Quoted in Cotton, *Royce on the Human Self*, pp. 4–5, from *Harvard*

Graduates' Magazine 18 (June 1910), 631. On California, see Royce to William James, July 16, 1878; to William James, January 14, 1879; to George Buchanan Coale, December 5, 1881; to William James, June 7, 1880; to George Buchanan Coale, September 23, 1880; to Daniel Coit Gilman, September 16, 1878; and to William James, October 31, 1882 (*Letters*, pp. 59, 66, 103, 83, 93, 60, 121).

40. Perry, "Two American Philosophers," in Perry's *In the Spirit of William James*, pp. 24–27.

41. For the discussion of what is taken as "the Roycean myth" of an imported philosophy, begun by Santayana and extended by Perry, see Daniel Sommer Robinson, "Josiah Royce—California's Gift to Philosophy" (1950), in Robinson, *Royce and Hocking: American Idealists, an Introduction to Their Philosophy, with Selected Letters* (Boston: Christopher Publishing House, 1968), pp. 17–32. For the finest discussion of Harvard philosophy, see Kuklick, *The Rise of American Philosophy*.

42. William James to Royce, September 26, 1900, in Ralph Barton Perry, *The Thought and Character of William James: As Revealed in Unpublished Correspondence and Notes, Together with His Published Writings* (Boston: Little, Brown and Company, An Atlantic Monthly Press Book, 1935), 1:817.

43. Josiah Royce, *The Sources of Religious Insight: Lectures Delivered before Lake Forest College on the Foundation of the Late William Bross*, The Bross Library, Vol. 6 (New York: Charles Scribner's Sons, 1912), 178.

44. William James, *Pragmatism, The Works of William James* (Cambridge, Mass.: Harvard University Press, 1975), pp. 62, 31–32, 34, 40, 44, 119, 141, 142, 124. (First published as *Pragmatism: A New Name for Some Old Ways of Thinking*, 1907.) And see Josiah Royce, "Schiller's Ethical Studies" (1878), in Royce, *Fugitive Studies*, p. 59. Royce's discussion of Peirce and the interpretation of signs is contained in Josiah Royce, *The Problem of Christianity: Lectures Delivered at the Lowell Institute in Boston, and at Manchester College, Oxford* (New York: Macmillan Company, 1913), Vol. 2, lectures XI–XIV.

45. James, *Pragmatism*, p. 111.

46. Royce to Charles Rockwell Lanman, August 14, 1882, in *Letters*, p. 115.

47. Royce, "Problem of Job," pp. 20–23, 19, 20–21, 21–22. The earliest citation of "ambivalence" in *A Supplement to the Oxford English Dictionary* (1972) is 1912, from the *Lancet*. For a comment by Freud—"the very apt term introduced by Bleuler—'ambivalence'"—see Sigmund Freud, "Instincts and Their Vicissitudes" (1915), in Vol. 14 of *The Standard Edition of the Complete Psychological Works of Sigmund Freud*, trans. and ed. James Strachey (London: Hogarth Press and The Institute of Psycho-Analysis, 1957), 131, as well as the editorial comment in n. 2, p. 131, on Bleuler's use of the term in 1910 and 1911. In his *Autobiography* (New York: Henry Holt and Company, 1873), p. 136, John Stuart Mill wrote that an understanding such as Royce's of associational psychology was so taught.

48. Quoted in Sheldon M. Stern, "William James and the New Psychology," in Paul Buck, ed., *Social Sciences at Harvard, 1860–1920: From Inculcation to the Open Mind* (Cambridge, Mass.: Harvard University Press, 1965), pp. 213–14; Santayana, "Josiah Royce," in Santayana, *Character and Opinion* (1955), p. 58. And see Chapman, "Portrait of Josiah Royce," p. 377, and comment by Dickinson Miller, quoted in Ralph Barton Perry, *Thought of William James* 1:819, n. 1.

49. Chapman, "Portrait of Josiah Royce," pp. 377, 372; Costello, "Recollec-

tions of Royce's Seminar on Comparative Methodology," p. 189; and Chapman, "Portrait of Josiah Royce," pp. 372, 377, 372. And see Perry, "Two American Philosophers," pp. 37–38, 40; Chapman, "Portrait of Josiah Royce," p. 377; John Jay Chapman, "Mrs. Whitman," in John Jay Chapman, *Memories and Milestones* (New York: Moffat, Yard and Company, 1915), p. 106; Santayana, "Josiah Royce," in Santayana, *Character and Opinion* (1955), pp. 59, 69. [See Perry, *Thought of William James*, 1:819, for James's marginal notation in his copy of *World and the Individual*; and for Royce's reply to charges of abstraction, see Royce, "Words of Professor Royce," in Royce, *Hope of the Great Community*, p. 131.]

50. Quoted in Kuklick, *Josiah Royce*, p. 201, from a book inscription, c. 1901.

51. Josiah Royce, "Dr. Abbot's 'Way Out of Agnosticism,'" *International Journal of Ethics* 1 (October 1890), republished in *The American Hegelians: An Intellectual Episode in the History of Western America*, ed. William H. Goetzman (New York: Alfred A. Knopf, 1973), p. 247. See Kuklick, *The Rise of American Philosophy*, note on p. 250.

52. Royce to William James, September 12, 1900, in *Letters*, p. 407; William James to Josiah Royce, September 8, 1900, and June 18, 1901, both letters in Perry, *Thought of William James* 1:814, 818.

Breakdown

53. Clendenning, "Introduction," p. 20.

54. Quoted in Perry, *Thought of William James* 1:800, apparently from a letter from Royce to William James.

55. Royce to William James, May 21, 1888, in *Letters*, p. 215. For Royce's description of his breakdown, see Royce to Daniel Coit Gilman, February 9, 1888; to Francis Ellingwood Abbot, February 9, 1888; to Charles Rockwell Lanman, May 21, 1888; to Horace Elisha Scudder, May 21, 1888; and particularly to William James, May 21, 1888—all published in *Letters*, pp. 211–18. Royce, though no more public about his crisis than James, was nevertheless open in his troubles, beginning an article on "Hallucination of Memory and 'Telepathy,'" for example—in *Mind: A Quarterly Review of Psychology and Philosophy* 13 (April 1888), 244–48—with the remark that "my health obliges me to suspend all work for some time, and I must leave this, like other matters, in other hands" (p. 244).

56. Ralph Henry Gabriel, "Concerning the Manuscript of Sarah Royce," introduction to Sarah Royce, *Frontier Lady*, p. xi; Sarah Royce, *Frontier Lady*, pp. 5, 49, 17, 49–50, 44; Gabriel, "Concerning the Manuscript of Sarah Royce," p. x; and Clendenning, "Introduction," p. 12.

57. Royce to William James, May 21, 1888, in *Letters*, p. 216; Sarah Royce, *Frontier Lady*, pp. 66–67; Royce to William James, May 21, 1888, in *Letters*, p. 215; and Royce to Daniel Coit Gilman, February 9, 1888, in *Letters*, p. 211. Royce's travel to Australia has been recently placed in a psychological setting by Frank M. Oppenheim, *Royce's Voyage Down Under: A Journey of the Mind* (Lexington: The University Press of Kentucky, 1980).

58. Sarah Royce, *Frontier Lady*, p. 5. Royce to Daniel Coit Gilman, February 9, 1888; to William James, May 21, 1888; to Horace Elisha Scudder, May 21, 1888; to William James, May 21, 1888 (in *Letters*, pp. 211, 216, 214, 215, 217–18, 215).

59. Royce to William James, May 21, 1888, in *Letters*, pp. 215–16.

60. *Ibid.*, p. 216.

61. Royce to Horace Elisha Scudder, May 21, 1888, in *Letters*, p. 214; Royce to Daniel Coit Gilman, February 9, 1888, in *Letters*, p. 211; and Cotton Mather, *The Wonders of the Invisible World* . . . (1693), in *The Witchcraft Delusion in New England: Its Rise, Progress, and Termination* . . . , ed. Samuel G. Drake (1866; rpt. New York: Burt Franklin, 1970), 1 : 132.

62. Royce to Daniel Coit Gilman, February 9, 1888, in *Letters*, p. 211.

63. Josiah Royce, *Outlines of Psychology: An Elementary Treatise with Some Practical Applications*, Teacher's Professional Library, ed. Nicholas Murray Butler (New York: Macmillan Company, 1903), p. 362.

64. Royce to Horace Elisha Scudder, September 25, 1886, and to Henry Lebbeus Oak, September 1, 1886, in *Letters*, pp. 202, 201–02; and Josiah Royce, *California: From the Conquest in 1846 to the Second Vigilance Committee in San Francisco: A Study of American Character* (Boston: Houghton, Mifflin and Company, 1886), p. 148. See Buranelli, *Josiah Royce*, pp. 37–39, for a discussion of Royce on Frémont.

65. Royce to George Buchanan Coale, January 14, 1884; to Henry Lebbeus Oak, November 12, 1885; to George Buchanan Coale, December 30, 1885; and to Henry Lebbeus Oak, August 29, 1885 (in *Letters*, pp. 129, 181, 176–77).

66. Royce, *Outlines of Psychology*, p. 363; and Royce to Daniel Coit Gilman, February 9, 1888, in *Letters*, p. 211.

67. Royce to Charles Rockwell Lanman, May 21, 1888, and to William James May 21, 1888, in *Letters*, pp. 213, 216.

68. Royce to Thomas Davidson, May 13, 1899, in *Letters*, p. 389.

The Reconsideration of the Crisis

69. This is an impression gathered from the number of citations to neurasthenia in the *Index Medicus: A Monthly Classified Record of the Current Medical Literature of the World*.

70. Josiah Royce, "Introduction" to Royce, *Studies of Good and Evil*, p. vii; Royce, "Case of John Bunyan," pp. 31–32n and p. 29; and Royce, "Introduction" to *Studies of Good and Evil*, p. vii.

71. Royce to William James, May 21 and August 10, 1888, in *Letters*, pp. 215, 219.

72. Royce, "Introduction" to *Studies of Good and Evil*, pp. vii–viii; Royce, "Case of John Bunyan," p. 74; Royce, "Introduction" to *Studies of Good and Evil*, p. vii; and Royce, "Case of John Bunyan," pp. 30–31.

73. Royce, *Problem of Christianity*, Vol. 2, in particular 49–53.

74. Royce, "Case of John Bunyan," p. 29.

75. Joseph H. Crooker, "Jonathan Edwards: A Psychological Study," *The New England Magazine*, new series, 2 (April 1890), 162, 165, 164, 163. This essay is indebted to a discussion of Crooker by Gail Thain Parker, "Jonathan Edwards and Melancholy," *The New England Quarterly* 41 (June 1968), 193.

Modern Psychiatric Literature

76. Neurologists began giving attention to Samuel Johnson's compulsive acts at the turn of the century. See, for example, Bertram M. H. Rogers, "Medical Aspect of Boswell's 'Life of Johnson,' with Some Account of the Medical Men Mentioned in that Book," *The Alienist and Neurologist* 32 (May 1911), 277–96; and

D. Hack Tuke, "Imperative Ideas," *Brain* 17, part II (1894), 183. A convenient reference to Johnson's "peculiarities" is contained in the index to *Boswell's Life of Johnson: Together with Boswell's Journal of a Tour to the Hebrides and Johnson's Diary of a Journey into North Wales*, ed. George Birkbeck Hill, rev. and enl. ed. by L. F. Powell, 2nd ed. (Oxford: At the Clarendon Press, 1964), 6:210. Walter Jackson Bate has provided in his brilliance the psychologically measured discussions of Johnson: *The Achievement of Samuel Johnson* (New York: Oxford University Press, 1955), and *Samuel Johnson* (New York: Harcourt Brace Jovanovich, 1977). For a consideration of Boswell in the tradition of English autobiography, and his melancholy, see John N. Morris, *Versions of the Self: Studies in English Autobiography from John Bunyan to John Stuart Mill* (New York: Basic Books, 1966), pp. 169–210.

77. See David Shapiro, *Neurotic Styles*, the Austen Riggs Center Monograph Series, No. 5 (New York: Basic Books, 1965).

78. See Ilza Veith, *Hysteria: The History of a Disease* (Chicago: University of Chicago Press, 1965).

79. For a discussion of Freud's views on this matter and a thesis that phobias are in fact a part of the obsessional syndrome, see Leon Salzman, *The Obsessive Personality: Origins, Dynamics and Therapy* (New York: Science House, 1968), pp. 127–47.

80. An example of this "use" of an obsessive thought, reinforced in a peculiar interaction between alienist and patient, was provided by a leader of the American neurological profession, William A. Hammond, in *A Treatise on Insanity in Its Medical Relations* (New York: D. Appleton and Company, 1883). In a section on "Intellectual Objective Morbid Impulses" (pp. 389–400), contained within a chapter on the "Intellectual Insanities," Hammond provided a case example, having first offered a definition: "An intellectual objective morbid impulse consists of an idea occurring in the mind of an individual contrary to his sense of what is right and proper, and urging him to the perpetration of an act repugnant to his conscience and wishes. . . . If yielded to, . . . the circumstance is often of such a character as to demand the serious consideration of society, for it is generally the case that the impulse tends to the committal of a deed of crime or violence. As in the previously described form of morbid impulse, there is no delusion and no necessary emotional disturbance, except such as would naturally result in the average man from the existence in him of an irresistible impulse to commit crime." "He is perfectly aware of the nature of the act he is prompted to commit," Hammond continued, "and perpetuates it only because he is impelled thereto by a force which he feels himself powerless to resist." And yet, having said that, Hammond allowed himself to be drawn into the purpose of the thought itself, to become partner, as it were, to the drama involved: "It frequently happens that the subject of an intellectual objective morbid impulse struggles successfully against the force which actuates him even when on the very point of yielding, or when he takes such means as experience has shown him are sufficient to direct him." The words had hardly changed from the seventeenth century; the psychotherapeutics, however, had a different tone. Hammond cited the example of a man who wrote to him, saying that when his child came into his garden—appropriate, it seemed, as a garden of temptation—he was seized with the impulse to kill her with his spade. "Now, I love this child better than I do the apple of my eye, and why I was seized with that impulse I

can't say." Hammond's advice, in letter correspondence, was that the man had this impulse "under control; that he was able to reason calmly and intelligently in regard to it; that he had applied to me for advice, and that I urged him without delay to place himself under the restraint of an asylum. I further told him that, if he disregarded this advice, and finally yielded to this impulse, he would be fully as guilty of murder as though he had killed his child through deliberate malice, and that he ought to be just as surely executed as any other murderer" (pp. 389–92)—which was, ironically, the point of the thought in the first place: to allow the victim to set himself aside.

81. For brief discussion of the development of terms and diagnostic entanglement, see John Owen King, "Labors of the Estranged Personality: Josiah Royce on 'The Case of John Bunyan,'" *Proceedings of the American Philosophical Society* 120 (January 1976), 48–49, n. 17.

82. C. L. Dana, "Folie du Doute and Mysophobia," *The Alienist and Neurologist* 5 (July 1884), 514–15.

83. See the quotations from Borrow's *Lavengro* in W. Julius Mickle, "Mental Besetments," *The Journal of Mental Science* 42 (October 1896), 733, 735, 743.

84. A. Kampmeier [ed.], "Confessions of a Psychasthenic," *Journal of Abnormal Psychology* 2 (August–September 1907), 113, 115.

85. *Ibid.*, pp. 121, 117, *passim.*

86. Edward Cowles, "Insistent and Fixed Ideas," *The American Journal of Psychology* 1 (February 1888), 230, 239, 239–40, 241.

87. *Ibid.*, pp. 243, 244–45, 245, 247, 246, 248.

88. *Ibid.*, pp. 256, 258–59.

89. *Ibid.*, pp. 262–63, 268, 265–66.

Kant and the Constructive Imagination

90. Josiah Royce, Joseph LeConte, G. H. Howison, and Sidney Edward Mezes, *The Conception of God: A Philosophic Discussion Concerning the Nature of the Divine Idea as Demonstrable Reality* (New York: Macmillan Company, 1898), p. 277; Josiah Royce, *The World and the Individual*, Gifford Lectures Delivered before the University of Aberdeen, Vol. 2 (New York: Macmillan Company, 1901), 258, 258–59, 253–54, 253; Royce, *Conception of God*, pp. 276–77; Royce, *World and the Individual* 2:265, 259; and Cowles, "Insistent and Fixed Ideas," p. 243.

91. Josiah Royce, *The Spirit of Modern Philosophy: An Essay in the Form of Lectures* (1892; rpt. New York: W. W. Norton & Company, The Norton Library, 1967), pp. 106, 106–107, 120, 108, 120–121.

92. Royce, *Spirit of Modern Philosophy*, p. 120; and extracts from Royce's "Diary," August 9 and 20, 1880, quoted in J. [Jacob] Loewenberg, "Editor's Introduction" to Josiah Royce, *Fugitive Essays by Josiah Royce* (Cambridge, Mass.: Harvard University Press, 1920), pp. 35–36.

93. Royce, *Spirit of Modern Philosophy*, pp. 108–109, 128, 132, 125, 124, 128, 127, 126, 130, 128, 128–129.

Bunyan and the Mocking of the Tempter

94. Josiah Royce, *Lectures on Modern Idealism* (1919; rpt. New Haven: Yale University Press, paperback, n.d.), p. 228.

95. Josiah Royce to Henry Rutgers Marshall, July 17, 1890, and Royce to Mar-

shall, July 12, 1890, in *Letters*, pp. 247–48, 246. In his review of James's *Psychology*—Josiah Royce, "A New Study of Psychology," *International Journal of Ethics* 1 (January 1891), 143–69—Royce focused as a last and emphatic point on James's discussion of insistent ideation, of the ironic meaning that this bit of naturalistic psychology had for pleasure and pain as motivation. "I confess," Royce opened a brilliant review, synthesizing the two volumes and placing the work within the history of two hundred years of psychology, "there is something very sad about the crudity and *naiveté* of many ethical writers who nowadays still treat the question of pleasure and pain as motives, without the least sense of the entirely novel light in which modern biological research, and, yet more, modern pathological psychology, have put all the problems involved in this question." For this, see pp. 166–68.

96. Royce to Henry Rutgers Marshall, July 17, 1890, in Royce, *Letters*, p. 248.

97. Royce read his essay on "The Case of John Bunyan" before the second annual meeting of the American Psychological Association on December 27–28, 1893. The association published the article in the *Psychological Review* 1 (1894), 22–23, 134–51, 230–40. The essay is reprinted in Royce's *Studies of Good and Evil: A Series of Essays Upon Problems of Philosophy and of Life* (New York: D. Appleton and Company, 1898), pp. 29–75. This bibliographic information is taken from Ignas K. Skrupskelis, "Annotated Bibliography of the Published Works of Josiah Royce," in Josiah Royce, *The Basic Writings of Josiah Royce*, ed. John J. McDermott (Chicago: University of Chicago Press, 1969), 2:1194. All subsequent references to "The Case of John Bunyan" are from *Studies of Good and Evil*. For a more complete discussion of Royce on Bunyan, see King, "Labors of the Estranged Personality."

98. "Case of John Bunyan," pp. 62, 65, 64, 66, 67, 66, 66–67, 68, 64, 68–69.

99. Royce, "Case of John Bunyan," pp. 69, 70, 30–31.

Work as Self-Creation

100. Royce, *Spirit of Modern Philosophy*, pp. 157–58; and see Josiah Royce, "Loyalty and Insight" (1910), in Josiah Royce, *William James and Other Essays on the Philosophy of Life* (New York: Macmillan Company, 1911), p. 64; and Royce, *Spirit of Modern Philosophy*, p. 165.

101. Royce, *Conception of God*, p. 209; Royce, *Spirit of Modern Philosophy*, pp. 127, 128; and Royce, *Lectures on Modern Idealism*, pp. 55, 133.

102. Josiah Royce, *The Philosophy of Loyalty* (New York: Macmillan Co., 1908), pp. 167–68; and Royce, *Spirit of Modern Philosophy*, pp. 165, 157–58.

103. Royce, *Lectures on Modern Idealism*, pp. 178, 133, 99, 228.

104. Royce, *Lectures on Modern Idealism*, pp. 208, 209; and Josiah Royce, "The Problem of Job" (1898), in Royce, *Studies of Good and Evil*, pp. 26–27.

105. Josiah Royce, *The Sources of Religious Insight: Lectures Delivered before Lake Forest College on the Foundation of the Late William Bross*, The Bross Library, Vol. 6 (New York: Charles Scribner's Sons, 1912), 190–95; and Royce, *Lectures on Modern Idealism*, p. 186.

106. Royce, *Spirit of Modern Philosophy*, a portion of the title of the third lecture.

107. See for example Erik H. Erikson, *Young Man Luther: A Study in Psychoanalysis and History*, Austen Riggs Monograph, No. 4 (New York: W. W. Norton & Company, 1958), pp. 220, 219, 8, 220.

108. Hannah Arendt, *The Human Condition*, Charles R. Walgreen Foundation Lectures (Chicago: University of Chicago Press, 1958), p. 80 and p. 80, n. 3.

109. Josiah Royce to George Buchanan Coale, December 5, 1881, in Royce, *Letters*, p. 105; John Clendenning, "Appendix A: Biographical Notes on Addressees," *ibid.*, p. 655; and Royce to George Buchanan Coale, December 5, 1881, *ibid.*, p. 106.

110. *The Feud of Oakfield Creek*, pp. 64–65.

The Contrite Consciousness

111. *Feud of Oakfield Creek*, pp. 61–64, 49. For these characterizations of Royce's living, see George Herbert Palmer, "In Dedication: Josiah Royce," in *Contemporary Idealism in America*, ed. Clifford Barrett (New York: Macmillan Co., 1932), p. 7; James Harry Cotton, *Royce on the Human Self* (Cambridge, Mass.: Harvard University Press, 1954), p. 6; and Royce to George Bucknam Dorr, August 12, 1887, in Royce, *Letters*, p. 210. Royce's essay on physical training, "Some Relations of Physical Training to the Present Problems of Moral Education in America," is contained in his collection, *Race Questions, Provincialism and Other American Problems* (New York: Macmillan Company, 1908), pp. 229–87.

112. For discussion, see John Owen King III, "The Ascetic Self: Mental Pathology and the Protestant Ethic in America, 1870–1914" (Ph.D. diss., University of Wisconsin, Madison, 1976); the chapter on Royce, "The Varieties of Alien Experience," traces Royce's later concerns with the obsessional neurosis.

113. Josiah Royce, *Lectures on Modern Idealism*, ed. J. [Jacob] Loewenberg (1919; rpt. New Haven: Yale University Press, paperback, n.d.), p. 138.

114. Josiah Royce, trans., "Phenomenology of the Spirit: The Contrite Consciousness," by Georg Wilhelm Friedrich Hegel, in Benjamin Rand, ed., *Modern Classical Philosophers: Selections Illustrating Modern Philosophy from Bruno to Spencer* (Boston: Houghton, Mifflin and Company, The Riverside Press, Cambridge, 1908), pp. 614–28; and Benjamin Rand, "Preface," to *Modern Classical Philosophers*, p. vii.

115. Royce, "Contrite Consciousness," p. 614n. See G. [Georg] W. F. Hegel, *The Phenomenology of Mind*, trans. J. B. Baillie, 2nd ed., rev. and corrected (London: George Allen & Unwin, 1931), p. 264, and Royce, "Contrite Consciousness," p. 626, for the variety of the translations of the petty acts.

116. Royce, *Lectures on Modern Idealism*, pp. 180–89, *passim*.

117. *Ibid.*, p. 184.

118. Royce, "Contrite Consciousness," pp. 627, 625, 615, 625, 626, 620, 621, 615, 623.

119. Royce, *Lectures on Modern Idealism*, p. 185; and Royce, "Contrite Consciousness," p. 628.

120. Josiah Royce, *The Problem of Christianity: Lectures Delivered at the Lowell Institute in Boston, and at Manchester College, Oxford*, 2 vols. (New York: Macmillan Company, 1913).

Modern Alienation

121. Josiah Royce, "Some Observations on the Anomalies of Self-Consciousness," in Royce, *Studies of Good and Evil*, p. 176. Royce read this paper before the Medico-Psychological Association of Boston on March 21, 1894. For a discussion

of the essay from a philosophical point of view, see James Harry Cotton, *Royce on the Human Self* (Cambridge, Mass.: Harvard University Press, 1954), pp. 44–51. F. [Fred] H. Matthews, in "The Americanization of Sigmund Freud: Adaptations of Psychoanalysis before 1917," *Journal of American Studies* 1 (April 1967), 39–62, argues that the later (and peculiarly American) post-Freudian emphasis on ego, social integration, and interpersonal dynamics was well embedded in the American interpretation of Freud prior to 1917. For a discussion of this argument in relation to Royce, see John Owen King, "Labors of the Estranged Personality: Josiah Royce on 'The Case of John Bunyan,'" appendix 2, 57–58.

122. See King, "The Ascetic Self," pp. 182–237.

123. See Jean B. Quandt, *From the Small Town to the Great Community: The Social Thought of Progressive Intellectuals* (New Brunswick, N.J.: Rutgers University Press, 1970), pp. 155–57, 130, 132, and *passim*; Kevin Starr, *Americans and the California Dream, 1850–1915* (New York: Oxford University Press, 1973), pp. 142–71; R. [Raymond] Jackson Wilson, "Josiah Royce: The Moral Community," in his *In Quest of Community: Social Philosophy in the United States, 1860–1920* (London: Oxford University Press, 1968), pp. 144–70; and Morton and Lucia White, "Provincialism and Alienation: An Aside on Josiah Royce and George Santayana," in Morton and Lucia White, *The Intellectual Versus the City: From Thomas Jefferson to Frank Lloyd Wright* (Cambridge, Mass.: Harvard University Press, 1962), pp. 179–88. And see Josiah Royce, "Words of Professor Royce at the Walton Hotel at Philadelphia, December 29, 1915," in Royce, *The Hope of the Great Community* (New York: Macmillan Co., 1916), pp. 129–30; Josiah Royce, "Provincialism," in Royce, *Race Questions*, p. 55–108; and Josiah Royce, "Provincialism: Based Upon a Study of Early Conditions in California," *Putnam's Magazine* 7 (November 1909), 232–40.

124. Royce, *California: From the Conquest in 1846 to the Second Vigilance Committee in San Francisco: A Study of American Character* (Boston: Houghton, Mifflin and Company, 1886), pp. 287, 285–313; Royce, *The Religious Aspect of Philosophy: A Critique of the Bases of Conduct and Faith* (1885; rpt. Gloucester, Mass.: Peter Smith, 1965), pp. 212–13; and Royce, *Sources of Religious Insight*, 274–75.

125. See Royce, *War and Insurance: An Address Delivered before the Philosophical Union of the University of California at its Twenty-Fifth Anniversary at Berkeley, California, August 27, 1914* (New York: Macmillan Company, 1914), for Royce's utopian construction.

126. See Royce, *Outlines of Psychology: An Elementary Treatise with Some Practical Applications*, Teachers' Professional Library (New York: Macmillan Company, 1903), pp. 74–80. Royce described an obsessional character in the following manner: "Whether he rushes about or lies still in pretended rest, whether his mood is this or that, he is all the while incited to act, and is busy holding himself back from effective action. His endless question, 'What shall I do?' his motor restlessness, his petty and useless little deeds [note the similarity of this phrase with Hegel's unhappy consciousness], all express his inability to choose between the numerous tendencies to movement which his situation arouses. Countless motor habits are awakened, and then at once suppressed. In his despair he tries to inhibit all acts until the plan—the saving plan—shall appear. And so, accomplishing nothing, he may do far more motor work than an acrobat" (p. 79).

127. See Royce, *The Philosophy of Loyalty* (New York: Macmillan Company, 1908), pp. 239, 238. For a discussion of the use of Hegel's term by Royce, and of alienation less specified in the work of several turn-of-the-century American intellectuals, see Quandt, *From the Small Town to the Great Community*, pp. 213–14, n. 22. Of the nine "progressives" she surveys, only Royce uses *Entfremdung*, Hegel's term for estrangement or alienation. For additional comment on Hegel's concept of alienation, see Daniel Bell, "The Debate on Alienation," in *Revisionism: Essays on the History of Marxist Ideas*, ed. Leopold Labedz, Library of International Studies, Vol. 1 (London: George Allen and Unwin, 1962), 195–211, the source that Quandt uses as the basis for her brief discussion of the word. For a history of the concept of alienation, see Richard Schacht, *Alienation* (Garden City, N.Y.: Doubleday & Company, 1970). For alienation in Marx, see István Mészáros, *Marx's Theory of Alienation* (London: Merlin Press, 1970); and Bertell Ollman, *Alienation: Marx's Conception of Man in Capitalist Society*, Cambridge Studies in the History of Politics (Cambridge: At the University Press, 1971).

128. Quandt, *From the Small Town*, p. 132. See Cotton, *Royce on the Human Self*, pp. 257–59, for a consideration of Royce's discussion of alienation. Royce, *Loyalty*, pp. 219, 239.

129. Royce, *Loyalty*, pp. 223, 241, 89, 241–42, 222, 240, 241, 240, 219, 240, 240–41, 212, 222, 10, 6, xi, 28.

130. Quandt, *From the Small Town*, pp. 213–14, n. 22; and Royce, *Loyalty*, p. 240. The word "self-alienation" is taken from Royce, *Lectures on Modern Idealism*, p. 228.

131. Royce, *Loyalty*, p. 245.

132. Josiah Royce, *The Problem of Christianity* (1913; Chicago: University of Chicago Press, 1968), pp. 262, 112, 106–19, 112; cited hereafter as *Problem*. Royce uses the phrase "mechanically cooperative social life" to describe high civilization (p. 262). See Cotton, *Royce on the Human Self*, for an analysis of Royce's theory of self-consciousness.

133. *Problem*, pp. 115, 112–13, 116, 112, 116, 113, 128, 106–07, 104, 73, 117, 115–16.

134. *Ibid.*, pp. 115–16, 115, 127, 116.

135. *Ibid.*, pp. 110–12, 110, 114, 128–29, 129.

136. *Ibid.*, pp. 128, 118, 148, 194.

137. *Lectures on Modern Idealism*, pp. 201–03.

138. *Problem*, p. 131.

139. *Ibid.*, pp. 166, 169, 145, 169, 144, 145. And see John E. Smith, "Introduction" to *Problem*, p. 15; and *Problem*, pp. 151–52.

140. *Problem*, pp. 148, 163, 161, 162.

141. *Ibid.*, pp. 198, 204, 207, 156, 152, 155, 180–81, 181, 182.

142. *Ibid.*, pp. 184, 185, 186, 215–17.

143. See Royce, *Loyalty*, pp. 239, 238.

144. Josiah Royce, *The Problem of Christianity: Lectures Delivered at the Lowell Institute in Boston, and at Manchester College, Oxford* (New York: Macmillan Company, 1913), 1:229, 236–37, 388–89, 218, 229.

145. The theme is expressed in Royce's *Philosophy of Loyalty*.

Death

146. John Clendenning, "Introduction" to Royce, *Letters*, p. 39; and Horace M. Kallen, "Remarks on Royce's Philosophy," *The Journal of Philosophy* 53 (February 2, 1956), 132–33.

147. Royce to Edward Bagnall Poulton, July 6, 1915, and to Lawrence Pearsall Jacks [June 1915?], the letter printed in the *Hibbert Journal* 14 (1915), 37–42 (in Royce, *Letters*, pp. 632, 629).

148. Kallen, "Remarks on Royce's Philosophy," p. 137.

5. Conversion through Psychoanalysis: James Jackson Putnam

Working Through

1. H. [Henry] Stuart Hughes, *Consciousness and Society: The Reorientation of European Social Thought, 1890–1930* (New York, 1958; London: Macgibbon & Kee, 1959), p. 321.

2. Josiah Royce, *The Spirit of Modern Philosophy: An Essay in the Form of Lectures* (1892; rpt. New York: W. W. Norton & Company, The Norton Library, 1967), p. 214.

3. See Sigmund Freud, "Psychical (or Mental) Treatment" (1905), in *The Standard Edition of the Complete Psychological Works of Sigmund Freud*, ed. James Strachey, Vol. 7 (London: Hogarth Press and The Institute of Psycho-Analysis, 1953), 289–90. Unless otherwise noted, subsequent references to the works of Freud are from the Strachey edition. The theme of psychoanalysis recapitulating aspects of Puritan thought is interestingly discussed by Howard M. Feinstein, "The Prepared Heart: A Comparative Study of Puritan Theology and Psychoanalysis," *American Quarterly* 22 (Summer 1970), 166–76, though Feinstein's approach is rather different from the current discussion. The "Americanization of Sigmund Freud: Adaptations of Psychoanalysis before 1917," is presented by F. [Fred] H. Matthews in the *Journal of American Studies* 1 (April 1967), 39–62, an article stressing well the "ethic of service" (p. 60) in early American thought. The monumental discussion of Freud in America is Nathan G. Hale, Jr., *Freud and the Americans: The Beginnings of Psychoanalysis in the United States, 1876–1917* (New York: Oxford University Press, 1971), the first of a planned two-volume study. This essay is indebted to all three of the above studies, as well as to John Chynoweth Burnham, *Psychoanalysis and American Medicine, 1894–1918: Medicine, Science, and Culture*, monograph 20 of *Psychological Issues*, Vol. 4, no. 4 (New York: International Universities Press, 1967). Slightly older studies include C. P. Oberndorf, *A History of Psychoanalysis in America* (New York: Grune & Stratton, 1953); and Hendrik M. Ruitenbeek, *Freud and America* (New York: Macmillan Company, 1966). The standard biography of Freud is Ernest Jones, *The Life and Work of Sigmund Freud*, 3 vols. (New York: Basic Books, 1953–57).

4. Sigmund Freud, "Lines of Advance in Psycho-Analytic Therapy" (1919), in *Standard Edition*, Vol. 17 (1955), 162, 164.

5. Sigmund Freud, "Five Lectures on Psycho-Analysis" (1910), in *Standard Edition*, Vol. 11 (1957), 52, 53.

6. Quoted in Adelbert Albrecht, "Prof. Sigmund Freud: The Eminent Vienna

Psycho-Therapeutist Now in America," interview with Freud in the *Boston Evening Transcript*, September 11, 1909, part three, p. 3.

7. Sigmund Freud, "Remembering, Repeating and Working-Through (Further Recommendations on the Technique of Psycho-Analysis II)" (1914), in *Standard Edition*, Vol. 12 (1958), 156–57.

8. James Jackson Putnam to Ernest Jones, July 21, 1915, in James Jackson Putnam, *James Jackson Putnam and Psychoanalysis: Letters Between Putnam and Sigmund Freud, Ernest Jones, William James, Sandor Ferenczi, and Morton Prince, 1877–1917*, ed. Nathan G. Hale, Jr., trans. of German texts Judith Bernays Heller, A Commonwealth Fund Book (Cambridge, Mass.: Harvard University Press, 1971), pp. 290–91. Cited hereafter as *Letters*.

9. E. [Edward] W. Taylor, "James Jackson Putnam: His Contributions to American Neurology," *Archives of Neurology and Psychiatry* 3 (March 1920), 307.

10. James Jackson Putnam, *A Memoir of Dr. James Jackson; With Sketches of His Father, Hon. Jonathan Jackson, and His Brothers Robert, Henry, Charles, and Patrick Tracy Jackson; and Some Account of Their Ancestry* (Boston: Houghton, Mifflin and Company, 1905). Cited hereafter as *Memoir*.

11. That Putnam was a descendent of John Putnam who emigrated to Salem before 1641 is mentioned by H. R. V., "Putnam, James Jackson," in the *Dictionary of American Biography*, ed. Dumas Malone, Vol. 15 (New York: Charles Scribner's Sons, 1935), 282. For genealogies and documents of the Putnam family's involvement in the witchcraft trials, see *Salem-Village Witchcraft: A Documentary Record of Local Conflict in Colonial New England*, eds. Paul Boyer and Stephen Nissenbaum, The American History Research Series (Belmont, Calif.: Wadsworth Publishing Company, 1972), pp. 202–25, and *passim*. For a particularly wrenching confession of recantation by Anne Putnam, Jr., see Chadwick Hansen, *Witchcraft at Salem* (New York: George Braziller, 1969), p. 215.

Putnam's Character

12. Quoted in Taylor, "James Jackson Putnam" (1920), p. 314.

13. Frederic A. Washburn, *The Massachusetts General Hospital: Its Development, 1900–1935* (Boston: Houghton Mifflin Company, 1939), pp. 175, 314, 318.

14. Anonymous [Edward W. Taylor], "James Jackson Putnam," *The Boston Medical and Surgical Journal* 179 (December 26, 1918), 810.

15. Marian C. Putnam, "Foreword" to Putnam, *Letters*, p. xii; Anonymous, "Charles G. Putnam, M.D.," *The Boston Medical and Surgical Journal* 92 (February 11, 1875), 163, 164–65, 164; and Putnam, *Memoir*, p. 350.

16. Nathan G. Hale, Jr., "Introduction: Putnam's Role in the Psychoanalytic Movement," Putnam, *Letters*, p. 65; and Aunt Anna [Cabot Lowell] to James Jackson Putnam, October 21, 1867, quoted by Hale, *ibid.*, p. 5.

17. Hale, "Introduction," p. 5; also Elizabeth Cabot Putnam to James Jackson Putnam, Sunday noon [1864], and Elizabeth Cabot Putnam to Putnam, unsigned, undated, in the handwriting of Elizabeth Cabot Putnam, both letters quoted by Hale, *ibid.*

18. For an extended discussion of the relation between inconsistent parental behavior and compulsive mechanisms, see Andras Angyal, "The Pattern of Noncommittment," chapter 11 of his *Neurosis and Treatment: A Holistic Theory*, eds. E. [Eugenia] Hanfmann and R. [Richard] M. Jones (New York: John Wiley & Sons, 1965), pp. 156–89. The idea of the double bind runs as a motif in the work

of Gregory Bateson and R. D. Laing. See Bateson's essays, "Toward a Theory of Schizophrenia" (1956) and "Double Bind, 1969" in his *Steps to an Ecology of Mind: Collected Essays in Anthropology, Psychiatry, Evolution, and Epistemology* (San Francisco: Chandler Publishing Company, 1972), pp. 201–27, 271–78; and R. [Ronald] D. Laing, *Self and Others*, 2nd ed. (New York: Random House, Pantheon Books, 1969), pp. 125–31.

19. Quoted and interpreted, though to a different end, by Hale, "Introduction," pp. 5, 6. As documentation, Hale cites two unpublished essays by Putnam in the Putnam Papers, the Francis A. Countway Library of Medicine, Boston: "St. Francis," June 15, [no.] 20, and "On Education," Forensic I, October 6, 1865, pp. 5, n. 12, and 6, n. 17, respectively.

20. Taylor, "James Jackson" (1918), p. 810; and Marian C. Putnam, "Foreword," pp. xi–xii. As to Putnam's inability to relax, Edward W. Taylor provides a similar observation in "James Jackson Putnam" (1920), p. 313.

21. James Jackson Putnam to Marian C. Putnam, [Summer–Fall] 1911, in Marian C. Putnam, "Foreword," p. xiii.

22. Taylor, "James Jackson Putnam" (1920), p. 308.

23. The photograph appears in Putnam, *Letters*, p. ii.

24. Taylor, "James Jackson Putnam" (1920), pp. 308, 309, 311, 312. See also H. Addington Bruce, "A Tribute to the Late Dr. Putnam," reprint of "Lives that Illumine" from the Associated Newspapers, *The Boston Medical and Surgical Journal* 18 (February 27, 1919), 262.

25. Taylor, "James Jackson Putnam" (1920), pp. 312, 313–14, 313, 314; Taylor, "James Jackson Putnam" (1918), p. 811; and James Jackson Putnam to Sigmund Freud, February 15, 1910, in Putnam, *Letters*, p. 95.

26. James Jackson Putnam to Marian C. Putnam, 1911, in Marian C. Putnam, "Foreword," p. xiv; and see Taylor, "James Jackson Putnam" (1920), p. 313.

27. Taylor, "James Jackson Putnam" (1920), p. 314.

28. Marian C. Putnam, "Foreword," p. xii; Putnam, *Memoir*, p. 243; and Taylor, "James Jackson Putnam" (1920), pp. 312–13.

Family and Neurasthenia

29. Putnam, *Memoir*, pp. 159–60.

30. James Jackson Putnam, "A Study in Heredity," and Philip Coombs Knapp, "Heredity in Disease of the Nervous System," together with a discussion, *Transactions of the American Neurological Association* (May 1907), pp. 92, 93, 92. The papers and discussion are reprinted in *The Journal of Nervous and Mental Disease* 34 (December 1907), 769–76.

31. Putnam, "A Study in Heredity," from the discussion, pp. 97, 98, with comments by Putnam's assistant, G. L. Walton. James Jackson Putnam's papers on neurasthenia include: "Neurasthenia," in *A Reference Handbook of the Medical Sciences . . . ,*" ed. Albert H. Buck (New York: William Wood & Company, 1887), 5:160–65; "Remarks on the Psychical Treatment of Neurasthenia," *The Boston Medical and Surgical Journal* 132 (May 16, 1895), 505–11; "Neurasthenia," in *A System of Practical Medicine by American Authors*, ed. Alfred Lee Loomis and William Gilman Thompson (New York: Lea Brothers & Co., 1898), pp. 549–95; and with George A. Waterman, "Neurasthenia," in *A Reference Handbook of the Medical Sciences . . .* , new ed., revised and rewritten, ed. Albert H. Buck (New York: William Wood and Company, 1903), 6:249–54.

George M. Beard's conception of neurasthenia may be traced in the following articles and books. Though Beard introduced his first article on neurasthenia in 1868, publishing it the following year, he did not return to the subject until 1879, at which time morbid fears were introduced as an important component of the disease: "Neurasthenia, or Nervous Exhaustion," *The Boston Medical and Surgical Journal* 3 (April 29, 1869), 217–21; "The Influence of Mind in the Causation and Cure of Disease—the Potency of Definite Expectation," *The Journal of Nervous and Mental Disease* 3 (July 1876), 429–34 (James Jackson Putnam was in attendance at the presentation of this paper); "The Nature and Diagnosis of Neurasthenia (Nervous Exhaustion)," *New York Medical Journal* 29 (March 1879), 224–51; abstract of "The Differential Diagnosis of Neurasthenia," *The Journal of Nervous and Mental Disease* 6 (April 1879), 367–69; "Other Symptoms of Neurasthenia (Nervous Exhaustion)," *The Journal of Nervous and Mental Disease* 6 (April 1879), 246–21; "Morbid Fear as a Symptom of Nervous Disease," *The Hospital Gazette* 6 (July 19, 1879), 305–08 (on p. 307 of this article Beard wrote, "These morbid fears [including mysophobia], rarely exist alone. They almost always appear in connection with other symptoms of neurasthenia. . . . Like all these symptoms of neurasthenia morbid fears very often occur in those of great, even enormous muscular strength and endurance"); "Morbid Fear as a Symptom of Nervous Disease," *The Journal of Nervous and Mental Disease* 4 (October 1879), 693–97 (this abstract contains the recorded discussion of Beard's paper presented before the annual meeting of the American Neurological Association in June 1879. James Jackson Putnam participated in the discussion. Again, this time in the discussion, Beard said, "These morbid fears were symptomatic of cerebrasthenia [brain exhaustion]"); *A Practical Treatise on Nervous Exhaustion (Neurasthenia): Its Symptoms, Nature, Sequences, Treatment* (New York: William Wood & Company, 1880), particularly pp. 22–41; *American Nervousness: Its Causes and Consequences* (New York: G. P. Putnam's Sons, 1881); *Sexual Neurasthenia (Nervous Exhaustion): Its Hygiene, Causes, Symptoms, and Treatment, With a Chapter on Diet for the Nervous*, ed. A. D. Rockwell (New York: E. B. Treat, 1884); *A Practical Treatise on Nervous Exhaustion (Neurasthenia): Its Symptoms, Nature, Sequences, Treatment*, edited with notes and additions by A. D. Rockwell (New York: E. B. Treat, 1888).

Helpful secondary discussions of Beard, none of which, however, probe his diagnostic classifications, include the following: Charles L. Dana, "Dr. George M. Beard: A Sketch of His Life and Character, with Some Personal Reminiscences," *Archives of Neurology and Psychiatry* 10 (October 1923), 427–35; Philip P. Wiener, "G. M. Beard and Freud on 'American Nervousness,'" *Journal of the History of Ideas* 17 (April 1956), 269–74; Charles E. Rosenberg, "The Place of George M. Beard in Nineteenth-Century Psychiatry," *Bulletin of the History of Medicine* 36 (May–June 1962), 245–59; and the first chapter, "The Discovery of the 'Nervous American,'" of Donald Meyer's *The Positive Thinkers: A Study of the American Quest for Health, Wealth and Personal Power from Mary Baker Eddy to Norman Vincent Peale* (Garden City, N.Y.: Doubleday & Company, 1965), pp. 21–31. Where Meyer cautiously stresses the new sociological theme of Beard, Rosenberg cautions against such an approach, emphasizing that for Beard and for other nineteenth-century alienists, a functional disease was still a material disease. For an incomplete history of neurasthenia, see Henry Alden Bunker, "From Beard to Freud: A Brief History of the Concept of Neurasthenia,"

Medical Review of Reviews 36 (March 1930), 108–14. For a more recent discussion, see Francis G. Gosling III, "American Nervousness: A Study in Medicine and Social Values in the Gilded Age, 1870–1900" (Ph.D. diss., University of Oklahoma, 1976).

Neurasthenia still appears in psychiatric texts, usually in conjunction with hypochondria, though it is generally considered an outmoded classification. One may look at a 1930 article, Paul Schilder, "Neurasthenia and Hypochondria: Introduction to the Study of the Neurasthenic-Hypochondriac Character," *Medical Review of Reviews* 36 (March 1930), 164–76, or a more contemporary discussion: Gerard Chrzanowski, "Neurasthenia and Hypochondriasis," in *Comprehensive Textbook of Psychiatry*, eds. Alfred M. Freedman and Harold I. Kaplan (Baltimore: Williams & Wilkins Company, 1967), pp. 1163–68.

The relegation of neurasthenia to a general malaise of misplaced Americans, particularly American intellectuals, is best displayed by Christopher Lasch, *The New Radicalism in America [1889–1963]: The Intellectual as Social Type* (New York: Alfred A. Knopf, 1965). No one has yet explored an understanding of neurasthenia and its vogue in Victorian America, in relation to the ongoing presentation of the American self as psychically beset—in relation, indeed, to the obsessional malaise that had long been seen as besetting the land. For all the complications Beard presented, morbid fear and obsessional ideation centered his discussion, and centered as well his understanding of why within a mechanical land—a new industrial land of waste—such fears had come to possess a people. Beard hardly discovered the sociological cause of nervousness, whatever the new machines introduced or the new sense of "hurry," nor was that idea incompatible with the physiological orientation given for such a functional disease, since the psychosomatics of Bright and Burton, Perkins and Ames still remained—the displayed mechanics of the devil's bath.

32. Putnam, "A Study in Heredity," from the discussion, pp. 97, 98.

33. Putnam, "Neurasthenia" (1903), p. 249; Putnam, "Remarks on the Psychical Treatment of Neurasthenia," pp. 505, 507; and Putnam, "Neurasthenia" (1898), p. 551.

34. "Neurasthenia" (1898), pp. 562, 558, 559, 566, 584, 587, 581–82.

35. "Neurasthenia" (1903), pp. 251, 249, 253; and "Neurasthenia" (1898), p. 588.

36. "Neurasthenia" (1898), p. 588; and "Neurasthenia" (1903), pp. 252, 253, 254.

37. "Neurasthenia" (1903), pp. 253, 254; and "Remarks on the Psychical Treatment of Neurasthenia," pp. 505, 507, 508, 505, 506, 507.

38. "Neurasthenia" (1903), pp. 254, 253; and "Remarks on the Psychical Treatment of Neurasthenia," pp. 508, 505.

39. "Neurasthenia" (1898), pp. 574, 559, 565, 583, 584, 587, 595.

40. Putnam, *Memoir*, pp. 436–37. See also James Jackson Putnam, "Physical Exercise for the Sick," *The Boston Medical and Surgical Journal* 95 (September 28, 1876), 371–77; James Jackson Putnam, "Neuralgia," in *A System of Practical Medicine by American Authors*, ed. William Pepper (Philadelphia: Lea Brothers & Co., 1886), 5:1211–40; James Jackson Putnam, "Neuralgia," in *Reference Handbook of the Medical Sciences* (1887), 5:153–60; and James Jackson Putnam, "The Relation between Neuralgias and Migraine," *The Journal of Nervous and Mental Disease* 27 (March 1900), 129–34.

41. *Memoir*, pp. 259, 258–62.

42. Gregory Zilboorg, in collaboration with George W. Henry, *A History of Medical Psychology* (New York: W. W. Norton & Company, 1941), p. 286.

43. *Memoir*, pp. 428, 258.

44. For example, see James Jackson Putnam, "Certain Aspects of Treatment of the Nervous Breakdown," *Transactions of the Association of American Physicians* 22 (1907), 433; and James Jackson Putnam, "The Treatment of Psychasthenia from the Standpoint of the Social Consciousness," *The American Journal of the Medical Sciences* 135 (January 1908), 91. Putnam planned a study of Bunyan which he never carried out. See Putnam to Ernest Jones, July 17, 1914, in *Letters*, p. 281, and the editorial comment on p. 218, n. 2.

The Memoir of James Jackson

45. *Memoir*, pp. 299–303. Writing to his children in November of 1817, James Jackson described the anxieties of his wife (*Memoir*, pp. 300, 302–03).

46. Putnam, "Neurasthenia" (1903), pp. 250, 251.

47. *Memoir*, pp. 71, 29, 13, 27, 54, 61, 56, 57–58.

48. *Memoir*, pp. 141, 154, 131, 132, 130–31, 138, 143, 135, 131, 137, 155.

49. *Memoir*, pp. 418, 282–83, 395, 357–58, 365, 184–85, 416, 419, 184, 171, 376, 333, 384–85, 332, 387.

50. *Memoir*, pp. 160, 239, 233, 383, 414.

51. *Memoir*, p. 360.

52. *Memoir*, p. 310.

53. *Memoir*, pp. 166–67.

54. *Memoir*, pp. 167–68.

55. *Memoir*, pp. 169, 168.

56. *Memoir*, pp. 168–69, 175.

Freud and the Analerotik

57. Marian C. Putnam, "Foreword," p. xii.

58. Sigmund Freud to Karl Abraham, December 18, 1910, in Sigmund Freud and Karl Abraham, *A Psycho-Analytic Dialogue: The Letters of Sigmund Freud and Karl Abraham, 1907–1926*, ed. Hilda C. Abraham and Ernst L. Freud, trans. Bernard Marsh and Hilda C. Abraham (London: Hogarth Press and The Institute of Psycho-Analysis, 1965), p. 98; and Sigmund Freud to Carl Jung, October 1, 1910, in Sigmund Freud and Carl Gustav Jung, *The Freud/Jung Letters: The Correspondence Between Sigmund Freud and C. G. Jung*, ed. William McGuire, trans. Ralph Manheim and R. F. C. Hull, Bollingen Series XCIV (Princeton, N.J.: Princeton University Press, 1974), p. 357.

59. Jung to Freud, February 14, 1911, *Freud/Jung Letters*, p. 392; and Jung to Freud, January 18, 1911, *Freud/Jung Letters*, p. 385.

60. See Freud to Jung, April 2, 1911, *Freud/Jung Letters*, p. 413; Freud to Jung, January 13, 1910, *Freud/Jung Letters*, pp. 286–87; and Jung to Freud, February 14, 1911, *Freud/Jung Letters*, p. 391.

61. Freud to Putnam, November 5, 1911, in Putnam, *Letters*, pp. 132–33.

62. See Putnam to Freud, December 3, 1909, and early 1915 in *Letters*, pp. 88–89, 179.

63. James Jackson Putnam, "On Freud's Psycho-Analytic Method and Its Evolution" (January 25, 1912), in James Jackson Putnam, *Addresses on Psycho-*

Analysis, International Psycho-Analytical Library, no. 1 (London: International Psycho-Analytical Press, 1921), p. 121; and James Jackson Putnam, "Recent Experiences in the Study and Treatment of Hysteria at the Massachusetts General Hospital; with Remarks on Freud's Method of Treatment by 'Psycho-Analysis,'" *The Journal of Abnormal Psychology* 1 (April 1906), 41. And as taken from Ralph Barton Perry, "Annotated Bibliography of the Writings of William James," in *The Writings of William James: A Comprehensive Edition*, ed. John J. McDermott (1967; New York: The Modern Library, 1968), p. 832: William James, Notice of J. Breuer's and S. Freud's *Ueber den Psychischen Mechanismus Hysterischer Phänomene*, in the *Psychological Review* 1 (1894), 199.

64. Putnam to Freud, September 11, 1912, in *Letters*, p. 147. See Putnam to Freud, November 17, 1909, in *Letters*, p. 86; and James Jackson Putnam, "The Present Status of Psychoanalysis" (June 11, 1914), in Putnam, *Addresses*, p. 254.

65. Ernest Jones, *Free Associations: Memories of a Psychoanalyst* (New York: Basic Books, 1959), p. 189; and Putnam to Freud, December 3, 1909, in *Letters*, pp. 88–89.

66. Putnam to Freud, November 17, 1909, in *Letters*, pp. 86–87.

67. James Jackson Putnam, "The Relation of Character Formation to Psychotherapy," in *Psychotherapeutics: A Symposium*, ed. Morton Prince *et al.* (Boston: Richard G. Badger, 1910), pp. 185–204. The symposium was held on May 6, 1909, with all papers except Putnam's originally published in *The Journal of Abnormal Psychology* 4 (June–July 1909), 69ff.

68. For a bibliography of Freud's studies of the nature of character and a notation of their paucity, see the editorial note 2 to p. 175 of Sigmund Freud, "Character and Anal Eroticism" (1908), in *Standard Edition*, Vol. 9 (1959).

69. Freud to Putnam, December 5, 1909, in *Letters*, p. 90.

70. See Philip Rieff's comments in *Freud: The Mind of the Moralist* (New York: Viking Press, 1959), pp. 53–54.

71. Putnam to Fanny Bowditch, December 10, 1913, quoted to a different end by Hale, "Introduction: Putnam's Role in the Psychoanalytic Movement," p. 40; and Hale, "Introduction," p. 60.

72. Hale remarks in *Freud and the Americans*, p. 5, that Freud made one of his few mentions of sublimation before the First World War in his lectures at Clark University.

73. Sigmund Freud, "The Disposition to Obsessional Neurosis: A Contribution to the Problem of Choice of Neurosis" (1913), in *Standard Edition*, Vol. 12 (1958), 317–26.

74. Freud, "The Disposition to Obsessional Neurosis," pp. 317–26. See also the editor's note to Freud, "Character and Anal Eroticism," p. 168.

75. Sigmund Freud, "Obsessive Actions and Religious Practices" (1907), in *Standard Edition*, Vol. 9 (1959), 117–27, 119.

76. Freud, "Obsessive Actions and Religious Practices," p. 118.

77. *Ibid.*, p. 119.

78. *Ibid.*, p. 123.

79. See, for example, Freud's comments in "Lines of Advance in Psycho-Analytic Therapy" (1919), in *Standard Edition*, Vol. 17 (1955), 166, and the editorial comment in note 1 to this page.

80. Silas Weir Mitchell was perhaps the most influential neurologist in America during the nineteenth century. The work of Mitchell and the rest cure may be

traced in the following books: *Wear and Tear, or Hints for the Overworked* (Philadelphia: J. B. Lippincott & Co., 1871); *Fat and Blood: And How to Make Them* (Philadelphia: J. B. Lippincott & Co., 1877), 4th ed., rev. with additions, entitled *Fat and Blood: An Essay on the Treatment of Certain Forms of Neurasthenia and Hysteria* (1885); and *Lectures on Diseases of the Nervous System, Especially in Women*, 2nd ed., rev. and enl. (Philadelphia: Lea Brothers & Co., 1885). It is in the last of these books that a typical comment is provided, Mitchell speaking here of one of his patients: "I saw clearly that I had to do not with a clever woman who may be won over, . . . but with a child who, to be made well, had to be calmly and firmly ruled, and held day by day to rigid account. She was at once shut up, with a good nurse, and kept at rest in bed, not being allowed to use her hands even to feed herself. As she had been able to knit and sew, and be read to, and to receive many visits, the sense of the irksomeness of the treatment soon made her eager to do anything I wished" (pp. 32–33). It is, indeed, one of his more calmly considered remarks. See as well: "Rest in Nervous Disease: Its Use and Abuse," *A Series of American Clinical Lectures*, ed. E. [Edward] G. Seguin, no. 4 (April 1875), 83–102 (in which Mitchell writes on p. 84: "As to women, for some reason they take more kindly to rest than do men, and will stay in bed, when once there, as long as you wish, and longer sometimes"); "Clinical Lecture on Nervousness in the Male," *The Medical News and Library* 35 (December 1877), 177–184; *Nurse and Patient, and Camp Cure* (Philadelphia: J. B. Lippincott & Co., 1877); "Neurasthenia, Hysteria, and Their Treatment," *Chicago Medical Gazette* 1 (April 5, 1880), 155–56; *Doctor and Patient* (Philadelphia: J. B. Lippincott & Company, 1895); "The Evolution of the Rest Treatment," *The Journal of Nervous and Mental Disease* 31 (June 1904), 368–73 (in which, on p. 372, Mitchell described his success with one patient: "She has remained, save for time's ravage, what I made her"); "The Treatment by Rest, Seclusion, etc., in Relation to Psychotherapy," *The Journal of the American Medical Association* 50 (June 20, 1908), 2033–37; and discussion of "Rest Treatment in Relation to Psychotherapy," *The Journal of Nervous and Mental Disease* 35 (December 1908), 781–85.

Mitchell himself was an inordinate worker and considerable writer, a poet, novelist, and physician whose output of work in terms of sheer words probably surpassed that of any American Victorian intellectual. He liked a neat and ordered world of work and schedule with set times and prescriptions, having that habit of mind "which excludes nothing" and sees things "minutely." "This is the Sunday calm of my office," he once wrote to his son. "The day outside is gray and threatens change, and I have on me my Sunday mood, which is grim enough, and has been so for years—yet why I can hardly tell, since on the whole life ought to satisfy me, but does not. Indeed I have had great luck to have had work always, for otherwise. . . . But enough of self." For these remarks, see Silas Weir Mitchell to John K. Mitchell, November 16 and 29, 1873, in Anna Robeson Burr, *Weir Mitchell: His Life and Letters* (New York: Duffield & Company, 1929), pp. 165, 166.

Mitchell's long infatuation with rattlesnakes and his belief that the evil in the Garden was that not of the serpent but of Eve, that she was the tempter—indeed, Mitchell's whole view of the woman as potential vampire—speaks to the physician who for decades dominated the American neurological profession, and yet whose work has yet to be thoroughly evaluated. Mitchell himself suffered from periods of severe depression that he called neurasthenic breakdowns. And there is some evidence buried within his not-quite-anonymous case histories that he suffered as well, or presented himself as suffering, from compulsive mannerisms. The evidence may be traced in the following articles by Mitchell: "Reversals of Habitual Motions, Backward Pronunciation of Words, Lip Whispering of the Insane, Sudden Failures of Volition, Repetition Impulses," *The Journal of Nervous and Mental Disease* 30 (April 1903), 193–203; "The Treatment by Rest, Seclusion, etc., in Relation to Psychotherapy"; and "Some Disorders of Sleep," *The American Journal of the Medical Sciences*, new series, 100 (August 1890), 109–27.

W. W. Keen, in "Silas Weir Mitchell (1829–1914)," *Proceedings of the American Academy of Arts and Sciences* 59 (January 1925), 647, 649, records Weir Mitchell's demand for hard work while serving with him during the Civil War. Mitchell, right down to his death in 1914, was exceedingly materialistic and somatic in his approach to mental disease, and thus what was a compulsive movement, a small ritual performed seemingly without the express volition of the person, was for Mitchell analogous to a form of "habit chorea" or a "mental tic." Such confusions (from a less somatic view) and corrections by other alienists may be followed in the discussion of the paper by Smith Baker, "Christian Pseudo-Science and Psychiatry," *The Journal of Nervous and Mental Disease* 27 (August 1900), 438–43; and the discussion of the paper by Wharton Sinkler, "Habit Chorea," *Transactions of the Association of American Physicians* 11 (1896), 149–60; as well as the paper and following discussion by Mitchell, "Motor Ataxy from Emotion," *The Journal of Nervous and Mental Disease* 36 (May 1909), 257–60; and *The Journal of Nervous and Mental Disease* (July 1909), 413–14. It was as though Mitchell and his materialization were threatening to remove any symbolic or emblematic significance—any signification—from the compulsion or "habit" of which Henry James, Sr., had spoken, to remove the psychomythology of a Bunyan pushing his arms and elbows, relegating these habits and small works to the meaning they held for a Boswell's Johnson. Such, indeed, was the potential held within the new field of neurology itself, from the mechanics of which Freud emerged to re-establish the symbol.

And yet there is evidence—a "text," however assembled in retrospect—that Mitchell suffered from a compulsive or obsessional syndrome; more appropriately, that he so presented himself, though he refused an understanding of the neurosis in Putnam's terms. The evidence is partially contained in the one article in which Mitchell discussed obsessional and compulsive dynamisms; "Reversals of Habitual Motions, Backward Pronunciation of Words, Lip Whispering of the Insane, Sudden Failures of Volition, Repetition Impulses," where his confusing juxtapositions are clear enough from the title and readily apparent, particularly since clearer taxonomies had emerged in the field by the time the article appeared in 1903. To quote from pp. 198–99 and 201:

> The line between habit and obsessions is very narrow, and disliking the term obsessions I prefer to describe that [*sic*] I now deal with as despotic habits. . . . They may be today mere controllable habits, and at another time despotically beyond volitional rule. . . .
>
> Perhaps no case more curious can be found than that of Samuel Johnson. . . .
>
> He was a prodigious worker, had some irregular movements which were analogous to habit chorea, and was subject to attacks of profound melancholy. . . .
>
> The obsessions of childhood appear so far to have escaped study. In my own home one

brother, in later days an army officer of distinction, had, as a child, a great dread of feathers, and of all fluffy objects. A bunch of cotton, or a feather, laid on the lintel of an open door kept him an easy captive. He could not pass over it or by it. Another brother, who also served in the Civil War as Colonel, would not, when young, go out of doors without an umbrella. This lasted for some years from the age of ten. How it ended I do not recall.

In this paper on reversals of habitual motions, with the childhood of his brothers though not of himself discussed, Mitchell cites another case (pp. 193–94), that may be juxtaposed to another text, an autobiographical account that appeared in his article, "The Treatment by Rest, Seclusion, Etc.," p. 2035:

I am a little in doubt how to label the symptom. I must content myself with calling the phenomena Reversals.

The patient, a man in mid life, was an officer of the navy. . . . Mentally he was very competent, but was what I should call anxious-minded, a man who put a needless amount of work into all he did. He first suffered after a time of unusual strain during the war of the rebellion. No warnings preceded the primary symptoms. He described himself as at this time exhausted in mind and body. When on the landing of a staircase intending to go up the next flight of stairs, instead of doing so, he found himself going down the flight he had just ascended, and going down backward. After descending a few steps he had the sense of mental shock, which all wholesome-minded men would experience under such conditions, and went up the stairs as usual although with some incomprehensible difficulty. Thereafter, at long intervals, and when overworked, this reversal happened. In the street if the action of walking suddenly ceased to be automatic, and he recalled the fact that he was walking, he would sometimes walk backward a few steps, and finally recovering himself, would go on as before. After a while he had great difficulty in ascending the stairs in the usual way, and was practically unable without effort to go up stairs foremost. When he was alone he was apt to go up backward, and generally, if not watched, descended the stairs in the same way. By and by this peculiarity began to be troublesome. He would go to a door to unlock it and would find himself making an effort to lock it. I had at one time notes of this interesting case, and have mislaid them. I do not think the peculiarity went much farther and I believe he continued to be a man of mental value in all the ordinary affairs of life. I may add that during the years of this peculiarity he served in the war with distinction.

And from the article on rest:

As I read, and I have read patiently, the wearisome detail of psychopathic analysis and treatment, I find a gathering belief that neurasthenia is always a malady of the mind alone—a psychogenesis. I know that it often has a background or a foreground of hysteria or hypochondria, but I also know that there is a goodly proportion of neurasthenia which has no more psychic origin or symptoms than has a colic. There are purely bodily neurasthenias. . . . [He then offered an example of soldiers during the Civil War.]

My second experience was too personal for full record. In 1872 I had an attack of neurasthenia with grave insomnia. It was rapid in its march, and so complete that I could not ascend three flights of stairs without sitting down on the way to rest. I had no depression that was abnormal or unreasonable. My surprise at my condition was great, but I felt that I had thoroughly earned disaster. My psychic treatment should have come beforehand.

For Mitchell the pilgrimage—Thoreau's "walking"—seemed to have become a matter of physics, and the odd movement on three stairs a matter of simple fatigue, things the matter with such marching itself. In his paper on "Some Disorders of Sleep," Mitchell wrote of mental aberrations immediately preceding sleep, pseudo-visions of which he said, "I first knew of it in my own case, during an attack of neurasthenia, many years ago, and soon learned that it was immediately due to my cigar" (p. 122). Mitchell included here a number of case studies, including (p. 116) another of a man who could not walk up three flights of stairs without resting. "In this case the spmptoms [*sic*] were neurasthenic, and absolutely no other cause could be assigned for it. Recovery was complete." But Mitchell also included the case of a professional man beset with a foolish fear (pp. 112–13), and then a second case described (pp. 113–14) as follows:

I will let a sufferer tell his story as he wrote it for me.

He was fifty years old, of nervous, restless intelligence, anxious always, successful past the common, free from disease, endowed with a perfect stomach, and habitually insomnic. . . . He says:

"This trouble haunts the time close to sleep. I lie down; am easy, and assured of sleep. Suddenly, I think, Is the gas turned off properly? I get up and look; return to bed; get up again, and so on. At last, I become anxious as to my son, aged six. Is he safe in bed? will he fall out? My wife goes to see, reassures me, and then I go myself, and go a dozen times. Next, it is the furnace, or the locks, or fear of fire, until, worn out, I am surprised by sleep. It seems as if this thing waits for me at the gates of sleep, and I can understand that just then one's fancies may run wild. But once awake, the thing goes on until I am ashamed of the demands made upon my wife, and, too, of my own folly. I know of others who have the same trouble, but never in the day season."

The assemblage of these cases and brief confessions forms as a whole a text, hardly a spiritual autobiography but still, in the openings and juxtapositions that Mitchell allowed, a composite that becomes a portrait. And Mitchell, as recorded in Burr, *Weir Mitchell* (pp. 41, 155), wrote that "I have always been a nervous, excitable person, needing to have a sudden grip on myself in danger or in wrath," and though his health was consistently good he suffered from headaches and intermittent insomnia. The aberrations of those moments preceding sleep did concern Mitchell, as he described in "Remarks on the Effects of Anhelonium Lewinii (The Mescal Button)," *The British Medical Journal* 2 (December 5, 1896), 1625–29, an essay based on his experience with the mescal he introduced to William James. There he cautioned against excessive dosages which might, he feared, match "a painful experience of some years ago," the nature of which he did not elaborate. But Mitchell did say: "From childhood I, like some others, can at night, before sleep arrives, summon visions. These are not always just what I desire. Once present I cannot alter them; they shift, change, and disappear under influences not within my capacity to control or analyze" (*ibid.*, pp. 1628, 1627).

For a bibliography and discussion of Mitchell's medical career, see Richard D. Walter, *S. Weir Mitchell, M.D.—Neurologist: A Medical Biography* (Springfield, Ill.: Charles C Thomas, 1970).

William A. Hammond's paper on "Mysophobia," the most common of compulsions discussed, and which Beard prominently added to his syndrome of neurasthenia, first appeared in *Neurological Contributions*, no. 1 (April 1879) and was reprinted in *The [Independent] Practitioner* 1 (March 1880), 115–25. Hammond, a prominent American physician and Surgeon General of the United States, was a friend of Mitchell.

For a discussion of the relation between the ideas of John Brown (1735–88) and Beard's conception of neurasthenia, see Zilboorg, *A History of Medical Psychology*, p. 286. For Sigmund Freud's early approach to both Mitchell and Beard, see Freud, "Review of Weir Mitchell's *Die Behandlung Gewisser Formen von Neurasthenie und Hysterie*," in Freud, *Standard Edition*, Vol. 1 (1966), 36, a review which first appeared in 1887; and Freud, "On the Grounds for Detaching a Particular Syndrome from Neurasthenia Under the Description 'Anxiety Neurosis,'" *Standard Edition*, Vol. 3 (1962), 90–115, a paper first published in 1895.

The reaction of the Neurological Department of the Massachusetts General Hospital under the direction of James Jackson Putnam to neurasthenia may best be followed in the important article by George L. Walton, assistant to Putnam, entitled "The Classification of Psycho-Neurotics and the Obsessional Element in Their Symptoms," *The Journal of Nervous and Mental Disease* 34 (August 1907), 489–96, and the discussion following the paper—a paper (p. 491) in which the ironies of so-called neurasthenic behavior are clearly delineated, and in which the malaise is given to "the ideo-obsessive," Walton returning the malaise to the seventeenth-century text of melancholy. Walton concluded: "In the Neurological Department . . . the tendency has increased to class such cases under the psychoneuroses, at the expense particularly of neurasthenia. During the year 1906 the diagnosis psychoneurosis was made 91 times; the diagnosis neurasthenia was made only three times, whereas it was made during the same time in the medical department 127 times" (p. 494). And though neurasthenia was to remain, a revolution—in the strict meaning of the word—had occurred, a question not of how much but of the manner in which work was done, the significations involved when one spoke of the sickness of one's labors.

81. Sigmund Freud, "Five Lectures on Psycho-Analysis," p. 50; and Sigmund Freud, "Sexuality in the Aetiology of the Neuroses" (1898), in *Standard Edition*, Vol. 3 (1962), 272.

Moral Regeneration

82. Putnam to Freud, late March 1911, in *Letters*, pp. 117–18.

83. Putnam to Freud, late March 1911; to Freud, February 15, 1910; and to Freud, November 17, 1909—all in *Letters*, pp. 117–18, 96, 87.

84. For a discussion of "The Themes of Work and Play in the Structure of Freud's Thought," see David Riesman in *Individualism Reconsidered and Other Essays* (Glencoe, Ill.: Free Press, 1954), pp. 310–33. Reisman probes such themes in Freud as dream work, though he does not touch upon the aspect of work involved in the psychoanalytic therapy itself.

85. Freud to Putnam, December 5, 1909, in *Letters*, p. 90.

86. Freud to Putnam, May 14, 1911, in *Letters*, pp. 121–22.

87. Rieff, *Freud*, pp. 20–23, 23n, 115–18.

88. Freud to Putnam, August 20, 1912, and Putnam to Freud, December 25, 1913, in *Letters*, pp. 146, 167, 169.

89. Putnam to Freud, May 19, 1915, and December 25, 1913, in *Letters*, pp. 186, 168.

90. Putnam, "Recent Experiences in the Study and Treatment of Hysteria," pp. 27, 30.

91. Putnam to Freud, October 20, 1911, and Freud to Putnam, November 5, 1911, in *Letters*, pp. 132, 133.

92. Ernest Jones to Putnam, October 29, 1911, in *Letters*, pp. 270–71. Putnam's letter to Jones describing the dreams is missing.

93. Putnam to Freud, June 19, 1912, in *Letters*, p. 141.

94. Putnam to Freud, September 30, 1911; Freud to Putnam, October 5, 1911; and Putnam to Freud, September 20, 1911—all in *Letters*, pp. 125, 129, 126–27.

95. Putnam to Freud, September 20, 1911, in *Letters*, pp. 127–28.
96. Putnam to Freud, September 20, 1911, in *Letters*, p. 128.
97. Freud to Putnam, October 5, 1911, in *Letters*, pp. 129, 130.
98. Freud to Putnam, October 5, 1911, in *Letters*, p. 130; and Putnam, "Relation of Character Formation to Psychotherapy," pp. 198, 194.
99. Putnam to Freud, September 30, 1911, in *Letters*, p. 128; and a relation by Marian C. Putnam, September 22, 1966, to Paul Roazen, in Paul Roazen, *Freud and His Followers* (New York: Alfred A. Knopf, 1975), p. 377.

Analysis

100. Noted by Hale, *Freud and the Americans*, p. 183.
101. Delivered in October and November of 1906, Pierre Janet's lectures were published as *The Major Symptoms of Hysteria: Fifteen Lectures Given in the Medical School of Harvard University*, 2nd ed., with new matter (1st ed., 1907; New York: Macmillan Company, 1929).
102. Sigmund Freud, "Preface" (1921) to Putnam, *Addresses*, p. iii.
103. James Jackson Putnam, "Personal Impressions of Sigmund Freud and His Work: With Special Reference to His Recent Lectures at Clark University" (December 1909), in Putnam, *Addresses*, p. 28, n. 1, and p. 28.
104. James Jackson Putnam, "On the Etiology and Treatment of the Psychoneuroses" (July 21, 1910), in Putnam, *Addresses*, pp. 66, 69, 58, 57–58, 62–63, 78, 70, 67, 77.
105. For Putnam's views on rest treatments, see James Jackson Putnam, "Recent Views Respecting the Diagnosis and Treatment of Lithaemia," *The Boston Medical and Surgical Journal* 109 (December 13, 1883), 560; and James Jackson Putnam, "In Memory of Silas Weir Mitchell, M.D., LL.D.," *The Boston Medical and Surgical Journal* 170 (May 28, 1914), 821–25. For hypnotism, see James Jackson Putnam, "Some of the Important Aspects of the Therapeutics of the Nervous System," *Transactions of the New York Neurological Society* 1 (November 1894), 42–45. Putnam made several contributions to the psychotherapeutic movement in Boston which appeared in various issues of *Psychotherapy: A Course of Reading in Sound Psychology, Sound Medicine, and Sound Religion*, ed. W. B. Parker, all published in 1909. These include "Psychology of Health—I," 1 (no. 2), 24–32; "Psychology of Health—II," 1 (no. 3), 5–13; "Psychology of Health—III," 1 (no. 4), 37–49; "Psychology of Health—IV," 2 (no. 1), 35–44; "Philosophy of Psychotherapy," 3 (no. 3), 13–24; "Philosophy of Psychotherapy—II," 3 (no. 4), 28–38; and "The Nervous Breakdown," 3 (no. 2), 5–15. For Putnam's relation to the Emmanuel Movement, see James Jackson Putnam, "The Service to Nervous Invalids of the Physician and of the Minister," *Harvard Theological Review* 2 (April 1909), 235–50.
106. James Jackson Putnam, "Remarks on the Desirability of a More Careful Study and Extended Use of Hydrotherapeutics," *The Boston Medical and Surgical Journal* 140 (March 9, 1899), 225–28; and James Jackson Putnam, "Practical Experience with Hydrotherapy," *The Boston Medical and Surgical Journal* 146 (March 13, 1902), 284–87.
107. James Jackson Putnam, "On the Remote Results of the Removal of the Ovaries and Tubes," with "Discussion," *Transactions of the Association of American Physicians* 6 (1891), 112, 106.
108. See Putnam, "Neurasthenia" (1903), p. 254; and James Jackson Putnam,

"Not the Disease Only, But Also the Man: The Shattuck Lecture," *The Boston Medical and Surgical Journal* 141 (July 20 and 27, 1899), 80. This lecture, delivered on June 13, 1899, is also printed in *Medical Communications of the Massachusetts Medical Society* 18, no. 1 (1899), 47–79. For Richard C. Cabot's writings on work and rest, see the following articles from *Psychotherapy: A Course of Reading*, ed. W. B. Parker: "The Use and Abuse of Rest in the Treatment of Disease," 2, no. 2 (1909), 23–38, including editorial commentary; "Work Cure—I," 3, no. 1 (1909), 24–31, including editorial commentary; and "Work Cure—II," 3, no. 2 (1909), 20–29, including editorial commentary.

109. Putnam, "On Freud's Psycho-Analytic Method and Its Evolution," p. 120. For a qualification of the significance of heredity, however, see Putnam, "On the Etiology and Treatment of the Psychoneuroses," p. 58.

110. See James Jackson Putnam, "On the Etiology and Pathogenesis of the Post-Traumatic Psychoses and Neuroses," *The Journal of Nervous and Mental Disease* 25 (November 1898), 789, and the "Discussion," *The Journal of Nervous and Mental Disease* 25 (June 1898), 485–88.

111. Putnam, "Treatment of Psychasthenia from the Standpoint of the Social Consciousness," p. 79. See also James Jackson Putnam, "The Bearing of Philosophy on Psychiatry, with Special Reference to the Treatment of Psychasthenia," *The British Medical Journal* 50 (October 20, 1906), 1201–23.

112. James Jackson Putnam, "A Consideration of Mental Therapeutics as Employed by Special Students of the Subject," *The Boston Medical and Surgical Journal* 151 (August 18, 1904), 180.

113. James Jackson Putnam, "Typical Hysterical Symptoms in Man Due to Injury, and Their Medico-Legal Significance," *The Journal of Nervous and Mental Disease* 11 (July 1884), 498; James Jackson Putnam, "The Medico-Legal Significance of Typical Hysterical Symptoms Occurring in Men after Railway and Other Injuries," *The Boston Medical and Surgical Journal* 111 (July 3, 1884), 8–9; and Putnam, "Typical Hysterical Symptoms in Man Due to Injury," pp. 496–501.

114. "Not the Disease Only, But Also the Man," p. 79.

115. "Certain Aspects of Treatment of the Nervous Breakdown," p. 442.

116. *Ibid.*, pp. 447, 431; and see Putnam, "Neurasthenia" (1903), p. 249.

117. "Certain Aspects of Treatment of the Nervous Breakdown," p. 432; and "Treatment of Psychasthenia from the Standpoint of the Social Consciousness," p. 85.

118. "The Relation of Character Formation to Psychotherapy," pp. 195, 197, 203, 204.

119. "Recent Experiences in the Study and Treatment of Hysteria," pp. 30, 36, 38, 39; and "Not the Disease Only, But Also the Man," pp. 77, 57, 77, 79.

120. For example, see "Not the Disease Only, But Also the Man," pp. 77–78; and "Treatment of Psychasthenia from the Standpoint of the Social Consciousness," p. 92.

121. James Jackson Putnam, *Human Motives*, Mind and Health Series (Boston: Little, Brown, and Company, 1915), pp. 117, 108, 160, 162, 168, 168–69, 173, 146–47.

122. For Putnam's use of Royce's triadic community, see James Jackson Putnam, "The Interpretation of Certain Symbolisms" (April 1918), in Putnam, *Addresses*, pp. 434–35.

123. James Jackson Putnam, "Dream Interpretation and the Theory of Psychoanalysis" (April 1914), in Putnam, *Addresses*, p. 250. And see James Jackson Putnam, "Services to Be Expected from the Psycho-Analytic Movement in the Prevention of Insanity" (November 28, 1914), *ibid.*, pp. 274–96.

124. "Dream Interpretation and the Theory of Psychoanalysis," p. 251; James Jackson Putnam, "On Some of the Broader Issues of the Psychoanalytic Movement" (March 1914), in Putnam, *Addresses*, pp. 212, 221; "Services to Be Expected from the Psychoanalytic Movement," p. 279; and "On Some of the Broader Issues of the Psychoanalytic Movement," pp. 210–11, 221–22.

125. "On Freud's Psycho-Analytic Method and Its Evolution," p. 100; and "On Some of the Broader Issues of the Psychoanalytic Movement," p. 196.

126. "On Freud's Psycho-Analytic Method and Its Evolution," pp. 109, 107; and James Jackson Putnam, "Comments on Sex Issues from the Freudian Standpoint" (June 15 and 22, 1912), in Putnam, *Addresses*, p. 134. And see "The Present Status of Psychoanalysis" (June 11, 1914), in Putnam, *Addresses*, p. 272; "On Freud's Psycho-Analytic Method and Its Evolution," pp. 118–19; "On Some of the Broader Issues of the Psychoanalytic Movement," p. 217; and "The Present Status of Psychoanalysis," pp. 264–65.

127. "On Some of the Broader Issues of the Psychoanalytic Movement," p. 222.

Putnam's Ethical Bias

128. James Jackson Putnam, "On the Utilization of Psychoanalytic Principles in the Study of the Neuroses" (August 1916), in Putnam, *Addresses*, p. 343; and Putnam, *Human Motives*, pp. 39–40.

129. James Jackson Putnam, "Sketch for a Study of New England Character" (June 1917), in Putnam, *Addresses*, pp. 375, 373, 374–75, 377, 396, 366.

130. See James J. Putnam, "Memorial of Miss Katharine Burrage," *The Boston Medical and Surgical Journal* 174 (February 3, 1916), 151–53; and Washburn, *Massachusetts General Hospital*, pp. 475–77. And see Putnam, "Treatment of Psychasthenia from the Standpoint of the Social Consciousness," pp. 89–91.

131. For the possible effect of Putnam on Freud's ideas of sublimation, see Hale, "Introduction: Putnam's Role in the Psychoanalytic Movement," p. 62.

132. Sigmund Freud, "James J. Putnam" (1919), in *Standard Edition*, Vol. 17 (1955), 271; and Sigmund Freud, "An Autobiographical Study" (1925), in *Standard Edition*, Vol. 20 (1959), 51.

133. Sigmund Freud, "Five Lectures on Psycho-Analysis," pp. 54–55, 50.

134. Sigmund Freud, "A Seventeenth-Century Demonological Neurosis" (1923), in *Standard Edition*, Vol. 19 (1961). See in particular pp. 82, 87, 91–92, 100–01, 104.

135. Sigmund Freud, *Civilization and Its Discontents* (1930), in *Standard Edition*, Vol. 21 (1961), 77–78, 93, 96–97, 93.

136. James Jackson Putnam, "On the Utilization of Psychoanalytic Principles in the Study of the Neuroses" (August 1916), in Putnam, *Addresses*, p. 343; and James Jackson Putnam, "Certain Features of the Work of the Late J. Hughlings Jackson of London," *The Boston Medical and Surgical Journal* 169 (July 17, 1913), 76.

137. Max Weber, *The Religion of China: Confucianism and Taoism*, trans. and ed. Hans H. Gerth (Glencoe, Ill.: Free Press, 1951), pp. 232, 235. The essay has been translated from the first volume of Weber's *Gesammelte Aufsätze zur*

Religionssoziologie (Tübingen: J. C. B. Mohr, 1920–21), 276–536; see Reinhard Bendix, *Max Weber: An Intellectual Portrait* (Garden City, N.Y.: Doubleday & Company, 1960), his "Bibliographical Note on the Writings of Max Weber," pp. 9–12.

Freud's Mechanics

138. The quotations—from Sigmund Freud, *The Interpretation of Dreams* (1900), *Standard Edition*, Vol. 5 (1953), 456–57—are presented by Alexander Grinstein, *On Sigmund Freud's Dreams* (Detroit: Wayne State University Press, 1968), pp. 338–39. For discussion of Freud's "'phobia' of traveling by train," and of his need to be at the station well ahead of time, see Jones, *Life and Work of Sigmund Freud*, Vol. 1 (1953), 13, 181, 305, and particularly 306–08 for the chronological relation of that anxiety to Freud's working through in the 1890s to the Oedipus complex.

139. Grinstein, *On Sigmund Freud's Dreams*, p. 339. The quotation Grinstein juxtaposes here is from Sigmund Freud, *The Interpretation of Dreams* (First Part) (1900), *Standard Edition*, Vol. 4 (1953), 260.

140. Sigmund Freud, *Extracts from the Fliess Papers* (1892–99), in *Standard Edition*, Vol. 1 (1966), 254, 224–25.

141. *Ibid.*, pp. 250–51, 256, 256–57, 251.

142. *Ibid.*, pp. 257–58, 259.

6. American Apocalypse: Max Weber

Work and Person

1. Michel Foucault, "What Is an Author?," in Josué V. Harari, ed., *Textual Strategies: Perspectives in Post-Structural Criticism* (Ithaca, N.Y.: Cornell University Press, 1979; paperback), pp. 141, 149, 143, 150. The translation is by Harari; an earlier version of the essay appeared in 1969 (see p. 13 of *Textual Strategies*). See as well Foucault's comments in Michel Foucault, "The Discourse on Language," an appendix to his *The Archaeology of Knowledge*, trans. A. M. Sheridan Smith (New York: Harper & Row Publishers, Harper Colophon Books, 1976), pp. 221–22; the essay first appeared in French in 1971.

2. Roland Barthes, "From Work to Text," in Harari, ed., *Textual Strategies*, p. 78. The essay, first appearing in 1971, is translated by Harari.

3. Max Weber writing to Karl Rothenbücher, excerpts from a letter quoted in Marianne Weber, *Max Weber: A Biography*, trans. and ed. Harry Zohn (New York: John Wiley & Sons, A Wiley-Interscience Publication, 1975), pp. 664–65, 665–66. Zohn's translation is based upon the first edition of Marianne Weber's biography (Tübingen: J. C. B. Mohr [Paul Siebeck], 1926), along with the corrections and emendations contained in the abridged second edition (Heidelberg: Lambert Schneider, 1950).

4. Quoted by Marianne Weber, in Marianne Weber, *Max Weber* (1975), pp. 689–90.

5. Erich Fromm, "Psychoanalytic Characterology and Its Relevance for Social Psychology" (1932), in Erich Fromm, *The Crisis of Psychoanalysis* (New York: Holt, Rinehart, Winston, 1970), pp. 135–58; and Norman O. Brown, *Life Against Death: The Psychoanalytic Meaning of History* (Middletown, Conn.: Wesleyan University Press, 1959), p. 203. Adumbrations of the argument appear in Sandor

Ferenczi, "The Ontogenesis of Interest in Money" (1914), in *First Contributions to Psycho-Analysis*, The International Psycho-Analytical Library, No. 45 (London: Hogarth Press and The Institute of Psycho-Analysis, 1952), pp. 319–31; and Isador H. Coriat, "A Note on the Anal Character Traits of the Capitalistic Instinct," *The Psychoanalytic Review* 11 (October 1924), 435–37.

6. Joseph Riddel, "Decentering the Image: The 'Project' of an 'American' Poetics?," in Harari, ed., *Textual Strategies*, p. 324; and see Sande Cohen, "Structuralism and the Writing of Intellectual History," *History and Theory*, 17, no. 2 (1978), 175–206.

Work and Text

7. Michel Foucault, "What Is an Author?" in Michel Foucault, .*Language, Counter-Memory, Practice: Selected Essays and Interviews*, ed. Donald F. Bouchard, trans. Donald F. Bouchard and Sherry Simon (Ithaca, N.Y.: Cornell University Press, 1977), p. 137. The essay was first published in the *Bulletin de la Société française de Philosophie* in 1969; and Michel Foucault, "What Is an Author?," in Josué V. Harari, ed., *Textual Strategies*, pp. 141, 149, 144, 143, 150, Harari's translation being of the earlier version of the essay that appeared in 1969 (see p. 13 of *Textual Strategies*). And see as well Foucault's comments in Michel Foucault, "The Discourse on Language," an appendix to his *The Archaeology of Knowledge*, trans. A. M. Sheridan Smith (New York: Harper & Row, Publishers, Harper Colophon Books, 1976), pp. 221–22, the essay having first appeared in French in 1971.

8. Barthes, "From Work to Text," p. 76.

9. Riddel, "Decentering the Image," pp. 347–48.

10. Max Weber to Marianne Weber, spring 1920, quoted in Marianne Weber, *Max Weber* (1975), p. 691.

11. *Ibid.*, pp. 697–98, 234, 698.

12. *Ibid.*, pp. 234–35.

13. Max Weber, *The Protestant Ethic and the Spirit of Capitalism*, trans. Talcott Parsons, new ed. (New York: Charles Scribner's Sons, Student's Edition, 1958), pp. 181, 182, 181–82. The edition here used is a reprint of the first English translation (New York: Charles Scribner's Sons, 1930). The essay, *"Die protestantische Ethik und der 'Geist' des Kapitalismus,"* was first published in *Archiv für Sozialwissenschaft und Sozialpolitik* 20 (1904) 1–54, and 21 (1905), 1–110. For the correspondence of Weber's writings with English translations, see Reinhard Bendix, "Bibliographical Note on the Writings of Max Weber," in his *Max Weber: An Intellectual Portrait* (Garden City, N.Y.: Doubleday & Company, 1960), pp. 9–12, supplemented with, but not replaced by, a similar note to the new edition of Bendix's work (Berkeley: University of California Press, 1977), pp. xxxviii–xliii. The Marianne Weber quotation is from her *Max Weber* (1975), pp. 237–38.

14. H. [Henry] Stuart Hughes, *Consciousness and Society: The Reorientation of European Social Thought, 1890–1930* (New York, 1958; rpt. London: Macgibbon & Kee, 1959).

15. Stanley E. Fish, *Self-Consuming Artifacts: The Experience of Seventeenth-Century Literature* (Berkeley: University of California Press, 1972), in particular his chapter on Bunyan, "Progress in *The Pilgrim's Progress*."

16. H. [Hans] H. Gerth and C. [Charles] Wright Mills, "Introduction: The Man

and His Work," Max Weber, *From Max Weber: Essays in Sociology*, trans. and ed. H. H. Gerth and C. Wright Mills (1st ed., 1946; rpt. New York: Oxford University Press, A Galaxy Book, 1958), p. 27; and Max Weber, *Ancient Judaism*, trans. and ed. Hans H. Gerth and Don Martindale (1952; rpt. New York: Free Press, paperback, 1967), pp. 287, 306, 284, 298, 303, 294, 295.

Weber's Collapse

17. Max Weber, "Science as a Vocation" (1919), in Weber, *From Max Weber*, p. 149; Marianne Weber, *Max Weber* (1975), p. 286; and Weber, *Protestant Ethic*, pp. 232–33, n. 66. For indications of the amount of Weber's research in America, see *Protestant Ethic*, pp. 250–51, n. 154, and pp. 252–53, n. 169; Max Weber, "The Protestant Sects and the Spirit of Capitalism" (1922–23), in Weber, *From Max Weber*, p. 308; Gerth and Mills, "Introduction," p. 16, 18; and Marianne Weber, *Max Weber* (1975), pp. 279–304. Weber mentions speaking to William James in his essay on the "Protestant Sects," p. 308. In this respect, see Hughes, *Consciousness and Society*, pp. 321–23.

18. William James, *The Varieties of Religious Experience: A Study in Human Nature: Being the Gifford Lectures on Natural Religion Delivered at Edinburgh in 1901–1902* (1902; New York: Random House, The Modern Library, n.d.), pp. 11, 481.

19. *Protestant Ethic*, p. 63.

20. Arthur Mitzman, *The Iron Cage: An Historical Interpretation of Max Weber* (1969, 1970; rpt. New York: Grosset & Dunlap, The Universal Library, 1971), p. 155. The author is indebted to Mitzman's psychological probe of Weber, more than the end notes indicate. Though the emphasis here is on Weber's use of asceticism as a nonauthoritarian mode of life, indeed as antiauthoritarian, and on his abiding mistrust of eros and mysticism, it is Mitzman who garnered the quotations and put together the portrait of Weber as, in effect, an ascetic self, one that Mitzman believes Weber came to deny, beginning by 1904, as an expression of the authority and autocracy of his father.

21. Marianne Weber, *Max Weber, ein Lebensbild* (Heidelberg, 1950), p. 276, translated by and quoted in Mitzman, *Iron Cage*, pp. 155, 156.

22. Marianne Weber, *Max Weber* (1975), p. 235.

23. Mitzman, *Iron Cage*, p. 155; and Gerth and Mills, "Introduction," p. 26.

24. Marianne Weber, *Max Weber* (1950), pp. 191, 274, translated by and quoted in Mitzman, *Iron Cage*, pp. 85, 152; and Gerth and Mills, "Introduction," p. 28.

25. Gerth and Mills, "Introduction," pp. 12–14.

26. On a structural approach to neurosis, see David Shapiro, *Neurotic Styles*, The Austen Riggs Center Monograph Series, No. 5 (New York: Basic Books, 1965).

27. The Oedipal theme is that of Mitzman, *Iron Cage*; the generational, that of Guenther Roth, "Max Weber's Generational Rebellion and Maturation," *The Sociological Quarterly* 12 (Autumn 1971), 441–61.

28. Gerth and Mills, "Introduction," p. 29. See also Hughes, *Consciousness and Society*, p. 297, as well as Mitzman, *Iron Cage*.

29. Most particularly, see Mitzman, *Iron Cage*; and Roth, "Max Weber's Generational Rebellion and Maturation."

30. From Eduard Baumgarten, ed., *Max Weber: Werk und Person* (Tübingen:

Mohr, 1964), p. 629, translated by and quoted in Roth, "Weber's Generational Rebellion," p. 444.

31. Gerth and Mills, "Introduction," p. 11.

32. Max Weber, October 21, 1887, in Max Weber, *Jugendbriefe* (Tübingen, 1936), p. 276, translated by and quoted in Mitzman, *Iron Cage*, pp. 58–59.

33. Andras Angyal, *Neurosis and Treatment: A Holistic Theory*, ed. Eugenia Hanfmann and Richard M. Jones (1965; New York: Viking Press, Viking Compass edition, 1973), his chapter, "The Pattern of Noncommitment."

34. Marianne Weber, *Max Weber* (1950), p. 207, translated by and quoted in Mitzman, *Iron Cage*, p. 90; and *Protestant Ethic*, pp. 130–31.

35. Michel Foucault, *The Birth of the Clinic: An Archaeology of Medical Perception*, trans. A. M. Sheridan Smith (New York: Random House, Vintage Books, 1975), pp. xvi–xvii, xix. *Naissance de la clinique* was first published in France in 1963.

36. Hughes, *Consciousness and Society*, p. 299.

37. Gerth and Mills, "Introduction," pp. 10–11, the quotation translated by and quoted in Gerth and Mills, "Introduction" (from Marianne Weber's biography of her husband, though no citation is provided; see Marianne Weber, *Max Weber*, p. 202); and Marianne Weber, *Max Weber* (1950), pp. 122, 226, translated by and quoted in Mitzman, *Iron Cage*, pp. 48, 49–50. Mitzman has addressed the issue of Weber's "compulsive need to work": following his depression, as Weber wrote and Mitzman quotes, "An icy hand has let me go"—a quotation that appears as well in Gerth and Mills, "Introduction," p. 12. "For my sickly disposition expressed itself in past years in a desperate clinging to scholarly work as to a talisman, . . . [now] extinguished" (Mitzman, *Iron Cage*, pp. 49–50). Gerth and Mills had extended the quotation from Marianne's biography (see *Max Weber*, 1975, p. 236) to include the following sentence: "I do not believe that I shall achieve less than formerly in my inner treadmill, of course, always in proportion to my condition" ("Introduction," p. 12). This provides some modification of Mitzman's arguing that here for Weber was a turn against such asceticism, though Mitzman's point remains. Mitzman considers the *Protestant Ethic*—"it is hardly accidental that his study of Puritanism and the capitalist spirit followed shortly after the worst phase of that misfortune" (p. 50)—to have been written against the demonic of work and capitalism, such an economy of asceticism being for Mitzman a singular, historically unmodified text without Weber's distinctions of types of capitalism: the "ascetic" as opposed to the "high." And still, Weber was embedding himself in the trope of a narrative of conversion, the law that, as for Bunyan, had to fall, and the compulsive works that needed to be acknowledged; Weber, then, was released from the icy hand not of work, but of work as "talisman," of labor, that is, as magic and charm.

Weber's Obsessive Actions

38. See Mitzman, *Iron Cage*, the most thorough and considered of psychological studies.

39. Mitzman, *Iron Cage*, p. 276. One must consult as well Martin Green, *The von Richthofen Sisters: The Triumphant and the Tragic Modes of Love: Else and Frieda von Richthofen, Otto Gross, Max Weber, and D. H. Lawrence, in the Years 1870–1970* (New York: Basic Books, 1974), particularly pp. 118, 129–30,

366–83, tempered with Marianne's words in *Max Weber* (1975), pp. 373–84.

40. Mitzman, *Iron Cage*, p. 277.

41. Gerth and Mills, "Introduction," p. 27; and Marianne Weber, *Max Weber: ein Lebensbild* (Tübingen: Verlag Von J. C. B. Mohr [Paul Siebeck], 1926), pp. 605–06. The author wishes to thank Barbara Cline for this translation from Marianne Weber's biography.

42. Weber, *Ancient Judaism*, pp. 107, 167, 288–89, 286, 287; the work was first published as essays in the *Archiv für Sozialwissenschaft und Sozialforschung* (1917–19). See also Weber, "Social Psychology of the World's Religions," pp. 290–91, 293, 290, 281, 291.

43. Weber, *Ancient Judaism*, pp. 273, 286–87, 288–89, 286–87.

44. *Ibid.*, pp. 303, 288, 293.

45. *Ibid.*, pp. 290–91.

46. *Ibid.*, pp. 290, 297, 400, 294, 306.

The Worldly Ascetic Ethic

47. Erik H. Erikson, *Young Man Luther: A Study in Psychoanalysis and History* (New York: W. W. Norton & Company, 1958); Weber, *Sociology of Religion*, p. 188; Marianne Weber, *Max Weber* (1926), p. 317; the author is indebted to Barbara Cline for translations from the 1926 edition.

48. On the translation of the phrase, see Talcott Parsons's note to *Protestant Ethic*, pp. 193–94, n. 1.

49. Weber, "Science as a Vocation," pp. 139, 152; and *Protestant Ethic*, p. 105.

50. Ephraim Fischoff, "Translator's Preface" to Max Weber, *The Sociology of Religion*, trans. Ephraim Fischoff (1963; rpt. Boston: Beacon Press, paperback, 1964), p. x. The translation is from the 4th ed., rev., of Weber's *Religionsoziologie*, published in Germany in 1956 (1st ed., 1922).

51. *Protestant Ethic*, p. 31.

52. Marianne Weber, *Max Weber* (1975), p. 326.

53. See Edward W. Said's discussion of Foucault's *Folie et déraison* in his *Beginnings: Intention and Method* (Baltimore: Johns Hopkins University Press, 1975; paperback, 1978), pp. 300–01. The figure from Adams appears in Henry Adams, *The Education of Henry Adams: An Autobiography* (Boston: Houghton Mifflin Company, The Riverside Press, Cambridge, Sentry Edition, 1961), p. 380. The edition here used is a reprint of the *Education*, first published privately in 1906, as published by Houghton Mifflin Company (1935?).

54. *Protestant Ethic*, p. 154. On the economic rationalization of monasticism, see Max Weber, *Economy and Society: An Outline of Interpretive Sociology*, ed. Guenther Roth and Claus Wittich, trans. Ephraim Fischoff *et al.* (New York: Bedminister Press, 1968), 2:538–39, 555, 586; and 3:1168–70, 1172–73, 1184. (This translation is based upon the fourth edition of Weber's *Wirtschaft und Gesellschaft*, first published in Germany in 1956, with a revision of 1964, and with appendices from Weber's *Gesammelte Aufsätze zur Wissenschaftslehre* and *Gesammelte politische Schriften*.) See also Max Weber, "Religious Rejections of the World and Their Directions" (November 1915), in Weber, *From Max Weber*, p. 332. See as well Talcott Parsons, *The Structure of Social Action: A Study in Social Theory with Special Reference to a Group of Recent European Writers*, 2nd ed. (1st ed., 1937; Glencoe, Ill.: Free Press, 1959), p. 518—a study to

which this book is indebted throughout for Parsons's analysis of Weber's ascetic capitalism.

55. Mitzman, *Iron Cage*, p. 277. In his *Iron Cage*, Mitzman translates the phrase as "housing hard as steel," thereby changing Parsons's "iron cage" "to its literal meaning in the German, which has a significance beyond the phrase 'iron cage' used by Parsons" (p. 172 and p. 172n). Weber of course was well read in Bunyan, so whether Parsons's text is that of Weber or Weber requires more literal translation is, perhaps, immaterial—that is, if one demands a continuation of such a "text" through to and including Parsons, the son of a former Congregational minister (see Talcott Parsons, "On Building Social System Theory: A Personal History," *Daedalus*, 99 [Fall 1970], 877, n. 23), who so closely identified with Weber's design of vocation and ascetic capitalism.

56. *Protestant Ethic*, pp. 244, n. 113; 167; 247, n. 131. As Weber wrote in the essay following his American visit, Protestant asceticism was "always hostile to authority," a "part of the historical background of that lack of respect of the American which is, as the case may be, so irritating or so refreshing" (*Protestant Ethic*, pp. 255–56, n. 178). The third type of capitalism for Weber was the adventuristic and profiteering, a type that Weber located throughout history in the form of the timeless buccaneer.

57. *Protestant Ethic*, p. 17; and Max Weber, *The Religion of China: Confucianism and Taoism*, trans. and ed. Hans H. Gerth (Glencoe, Ill.: Free Press, 1951), p. 245. The latter work comprises a portion of the first volume of Weber's *Gesammelte Aufsätze zur Religionssoziologie* published in Germany in 1920–21. Weber did present a compassionless and hoarding entrepreneur: his third type of capitalist, the speculator, moneylender, and "irrational" booty hunter, an archetypal figure appearing throughout history (*Protestant Ethic*, pp. 20, 81, 119). Weber's ascetic indeed conquered petty, compulsive acquisition as if Weber realized how terribly irrational such activity could be. Writing later of the Confucian, Weber stressed how consuming "acquisitiveness" was when it became a business of magic and ritual, of work "magically and ceremonially" construed:

> The Puritan was taught to suppress the petty acquisitiveness which destroys all rational, methodical enterprise—an acquisitiveness which distinguishes the conduct of the Chinese shopkeeper. . . . That is to say, the Confucian way of life was rational but was determined, unlike Puritanism, from without rather than from within (*Religion of China*, pp. 243–44, 247).

The most that could be said for equating Freud's portrait—Sigmund Freud, "Character and Anal Eroticism" (1908), in *The Standard Edition of the Complete Psychological Works of Sigmund Freud*, trans. and ed. James Strachey, Vol. 9 (London: Hogarth Press and The Institute of Psycho-Analysis, 1959), 169–75—with Weber's Puritan entrepreneur, was that beneath Weber's apparently clear theme that Protestantism generated unique economic behavior there could appear ambiguities. Weber vacillated, leaving himself open to a variety of interpretations, leaving his text open indeed to its own destruction—the interpretive cutting that Freudian scholars could perform in revealing what Weber's ascetic capitalism now stood for or meant. Thus Fromm's reading in his "Psychoanalytic Characterology," or Brown's reading in his *Life Against Death*, or even Erikson's reading in his study of Luther, of the hoarding and aggressive anality destroyed the meaning of Weber's work, undercutting his character. In that manner the whole of a text was preserved: as the Puritans' mask of morality was uncovered through the excrementitious humor of their melancholy, so Weber's ascetic character was torn apart.

58. See for example Thomas L. Canavan, "Robert Burton, Jonathan Swift, and the Tradition of Anti-Puritan Invective," *Journal of the History of Ideas* 34 (April–June 1973), 227–42.

59. These excremental manifestations are evident from the first English work on melancholy in the vernacular: again, T. [Timothy] Bright, *A Treatise of Melancholie*, reproduced from the 1586 edition printed by Thomas Vautrollier (New York: Published for The Facsimilie Text Society by Columbia University Press, 1940).

60. Again, the estimate of those actually suffering from an obsessional neurosis is low. See Alan Black, "The Natural History of Obsessional Neurosis," in *Obsessional States*, ed. H. R. Beech (London: Methuen & Co., 1974), pp. 21–22.

61. *Protestant Ethic*, p. 175.

62. Quoted in Mitzman, *Iron Cage*, p. 48, from Marianne Weber, *Max Weber* (1950), p. 122.

63. Weber, *Sociology of Religion*, p. 183.

64. *Protestant Ethic*, pp. 118–19; Max Weber, "The Social Psychology of the World Religions" (1922–23), in Weber, *From Max Weber*, p. 271; *Sociology of Religion*, pp. 27, 152. See also Talcott Parsons, "Introduction" to Weber, *Sociology of Religion*, p. lvi.

65. *Sociology of Religion*, pp. 260, 114, 184, 12, 25, 26, 27, 38, 44, 41.

66. Max Weber, *General Economic History*, trans. Frank H. Knight (1927; rpt. Glencoe, Ill.: Free Press, 1950), p. 117. (The lectures constituting the work were first published in Germany in 1923.) Weber did, however, join the early specialization of work skills to magic and magical occupations. See Felix Krueger, "Magical Factors in the First Development of Human Labor," *The American Journal of Psychology* 24 (April 1913), 256–61, writing of the discipline of magical ceremony as an origin of disciplined labor (particularly pp. 257–58).

67. Weber, *Religion of China*, pp. 238, 232, 235.

68. *Protestant Ethic*, pp. 105, 114; *Religion of China*, p. 240; and *General Economic History*, pp. 361, 362.

69. *Protestant Ethic*, pp. 97, 149, 117.

70. See *Protestant Ethic*, p. 244, n. 114; Max Weber, *The Theory of Social and Economic Organization*, trans. A. M. Henderson and Talcott Parsons, ed. Talcott Parsons (1947; rpt. New York: Free Press, paperback, 1964), pp. 108–09; and *Protestant Ethic*, p. 128. The *Theory of Social and Economic Organization* is a translation of part 1 of volume 1 of Weber's *Wirtschaft und Gesellschaft*, a second edition published in Germany in 1925.

71. *Protestant Ethic*, pp. 107–09, 111–12, 232, 118–19, 148, 153, 159, 158–59.

72. *Protestant Ethic*, pp. 117–18, 105.

73. For this theme within Puritan writing, see Michael Clark, "'The Crucified Phrase': Sign and Desire in Puritan Semiology," *Early American Literature* 13 (Winter 1978–79), 278–93.

74. *Protestant Ethic*, pp. 111–12, 119.

75. Weber, *Sociology of Religion*, p. 188; and William James, *The Varieties of Religious Experience: A Study in Human Nature: Being the Gifford Lectures on*

Natural Religion Delivered at Edinburgh in 1901–1902 (1902; New York: Random House, The Modern Library, n.d.), p. 469; James cited from W. Sanday, *The Oracles of God* (London, 1892), pp. 49–56. Typology and topology, to a different end, are juxtaposed briefly by Sacvan Bercovitch, *The Puritan Origins of the American Self* (New Haven: Yale University Press, 1975), p. 138, seemingly contrasting two orders of history.

76. See Marianne Weber, *Max Weber* (1926), p. 249, translated by and quoted in Gerth and Mills, "Introduction," p. 12.

77. Gerth and Mills, "Introduction," p. 4; and *Protestant Ethic*, p. 220, n. 5.

78. Gerth and Mills, "Introduction," p. 26; and Ephraim Fischoff, "Translator's Preface" to Weber, *Sociology of Religion*, p. xv.

79. Hughes, *Consciousness and Society*, p. 290; and Bendix, *Max Weber*, p. xxi.

80. Weber, "Social Psychology of the World Religions," p. 296.

81. *Sociology of Religion*, p. 238; and *Protestant Ethic*, pp. 244, n. 113; 167; 247, n. 131.

82. Weber, "Religious Rejections of the World," pp. 328–29.

The End of the Worldly Ascetic Ideal

83. The major portions of Weber's American letters appearing in Marianne Weber's *Max Weber* have been translated and edited by Henry Walter Brann, "Max Weber in the United States," *The Southwestern Social Science Quarterly* 25 (June 1944), 18–30; this quotation referring to Oklahoma appears on pp. 24–25. And see Marianne Weber, *Max Weber* (1975), the portion of her chapter on "The New Phase," pp. 279–304.

84. Max Weber, "Capitalism and Rural Society in Germany" (1906), in Weber, *From Max Weber*, p. 366.

85. Quoted in Brann, "Max Weber in the United States," p. 25.

86. Weber, *Theory of Social and Economic Organization*, pp. 205, 26; and see a writing of 1906, published in the *Archiv für Socialwissenschaft und Sozialpolitik* 12 (no. 1), 347ff., quoted in Gerth and Mills, "Introduction," p. 71.

87. *Protestant Ethic*, pp. 181, 182; and Marianne Weber, *Max Weber* (1975), pp. 341–42. On the translation of the phrase, see note 55.

88. John Bunyan, *The Pilgrim's Progress from This World to That Which Is to Come*, ed. James Blanton Wharey, 2nd ed. revised by Roger Sharrock (1678; Oxford: At the Clarendon Press, 1960), pp. 34–35.

89. Weber, *Religion of China*, p. 238.

90. *Sociology of Religion*, pp. 205–06; see also pp. 172–73. See as well Weber, *General Economic History*, pp. 368–69.

91. *Protestant Ethic*, pp. 180–82.

92. *Protestant Ethic*, p. 182.

93. From a letter by Weber of 1904, quoted in Marianne Weber, *Max Weber* (1975), p. 286; and *ibid.*, pp. 287, 304.

Work and Death

94. Barthes, "From Work to Text," p. 75.

95. Josué V. Harari in his "Preface" to *Textual Strategies*, p. 10, quoting from Roland Barthes in *Tel Quel* 47 (1971), 9–10.

96. Remarks made by Weber in a debate at the convention of the *Verein für*

Sozialpolitik in 1909, translated by J. P. Mayer in *Max Weber and German Politics* (London: Faber & Faber, 1943), pp. 127–28, and quoted in Bendix, *Max Weber* (1962), pp. 455–56.

97. Barthes, "From Work to Text," p. 75.

98. Said, *Beginnings*, pp. 320, 324–25.

99. Weber never met Freud; indeed, he disliked what he had read of psychoanalysis. Such therapy, he thought, was but another form of the Catholic confession—a momentary relief, perhaps, but also an excuse (Gerth and Mills, "Introduction," p. 20). For Weber's reading Freud about 1907 and his initial disgust, see Marianne Weber, *Max Weber* (1975), pp. 373–84, a discussion which includes (pp. 375–80) Weber's reply concerning an article submitted for publication by Otto Gross. See as well Hughes, *Consciousness and Society*, pp. 297–98; and Green, *The von Richthofen Sisters*, p. 55.

Freud's belief that repression could produce, among other neuroses, a "*Zwangsneurose*," Weber found absurd. Repression, he countered, was obviously necessary for the health of the nerves (Marianne Weber, *Max Weber*, 1926, p. 380). But in August 1907 Weber referred to a recent essay by Freud in the same journal in which Freud's article on "Obsessive Actions and Religious Practices" had appeared the preceding April (Marianne Weber, *Max Weber*, 1926, p. 379). (For the publishing history of Freud's essay, see the editorial preface to Sigmund Freud, "Obsessive Actions and Religious Practices" [1907], in *Standard Edition*, Vol. 9 [1959], 116.) Thus Weber may have known, through direct reading, of Freud's own reading of religious ceremony as neuroticism. And if Weber later read *Totem and Taboo*, then he may have written intentionally to Freud's thesis of all religion as an obsessive grid repressing primal violence. Weber may have wished to show, in other words, a historically efficacious time of accepting rigidity to release the self from magical encumbrance—tension, as opposed to a neurotically obsessional life. This last sign of work and rationality is followed by the acceptance of faith.

100. Riddel, "Decentering the Image," p. 332.

101. Shapiro, *Neurotic Styles*.

102. Barthes, "From Work to Text," pp. 76–77.

103. James, *Varieties of Religious Experience*, pp. 208, 481–82. The "Deep Cut" of Thoreau is displayed by Leo Marx, *The Machine in the Garden: Technology and the Pastoral Ideal in America* (New York: Oxford University Press, 1964), pp. 260–62; the pointing to the seven miles of beans is on p. 255.

104. See Hayden White, "The Forms of Wildness: Archaeology of an Idea" (1972), in his *Tropics of Discourse: Essays in Cultural Criticism* (Baltimore: Johns Hopkins University Press, 1978), p. 181, n. 25, on the etymology of "wild" (*ferus*) and "iron" (*ferrum*).

Conclusion

1. Wilhelm Reich, *Character Analysis*, 3rd ed., enl., trans. Vincent R. Carfagno (New York: Farrar, Straus and Giroux, 1972), p. 215. Again, for the phrase of the subtitle of the chapter, "making strange," see the account in Terence Hawkes, *Structuralism & Semiotics* (1977; rpt. Berkeley: University of California Press, paperback, 1977), pp. 62–63, where Hawkes discusses Viktor Shklovsky and "*ostranenie*."

2. W. Julius Mickle, "Mental Besetments," *The Journal of Mental Science* 42 (October 1896), 721.

3. C. [Carl] G. Jung, *Psychological Types or the Psychology of Individuation*, trans. H. Godwin Baynes (London: Routledge & Kegan Paul, 1923), p. 480. See also Erich Fromm, *Escape from Freedom* (New York: Holt, Rinehart and Winston, 1941); Harry Stack Sullivan, *Clinical Studies in Psychiatry*, ed. Helen Swick Perry, Mary Ladd Gawel, and Martha Gibbon (New York: W. W. Norton & Company, 1956); and C. [Charles] Wright Mills, *White Collar: The American Middle Classes* (New York: Oxford University Press, 1951).

4. Henry David Thoreau, *The Journal of Henry D. Thoreau*, eds. Bradford Torrey and Francis H. Allen (1906; Boston: Houghton Mifflin Company, The Riverside Press, Cambridge, 1949), 9:45, with acknowledgment to Roderick Nash, *Wilderness and the American Mind* (New Haven: Yale University Press, 1967), p. 87, for pointing in the direction of, though not to, this quotation; Edwin T. Layton, Jr., *The Revolt of the Engineers: Social Responsibility and the American Engineering Profession* (Cleveland: Press of Case Western Reserve University, 1971), pp. 193–94, speaking of Herbert Hoover's call for the Federated American Engineering Societies to undertake such a study, and the beginning for Hoover of an efficiency campaign; and Herman Melville, *Moby-Dick [or, The Whale]: An Authoritative Text, Reviews and Letters by Melville, Analogues and Sources, Criticism*, eds. Harrison Hayford and Hershel Parker, a Norton Critical Edition (1967; rpt. New York: W. W. Norton & Company, paperback, 1967), from Ch. 113, "The Forge," pp. 404–05, a "constructed text" following the first American edition (New York, 1851).

5. 2 Sam. 23:7; Deut. 3:11; and Melville, *Moby-Dick*, pp. 468–69.

6. David W. Marcell, *Progress and Pragmatism: James, Dewey, Beard, and the American Idea of Progress*, Contributions in American Studies, No. 9 (Westport, Conn.: Greenwood Press, 1974), pp. 162–63, and quoting from William James, *The Principles of Psychology* (New York: Henry Holt, 1890), 1:288–89.

7. William James, *The Principles of Psychology* (1890; rpt. New York: Dover Publications, 1950), 2:688.

8. Frank Kermode, *The Sense of an Ending: Studies in the Theory of Fiction*, The Mary Flexner Lectures (1966; London: Oxford University Press, paperback, 1968); to be placed beside Edward W. Said, *Beginnings: Intention and Method* (Baltimore: Johns Hopkins University Press, 1975).

9. Stanley E. Fish, *Self-Consuming Artifacts: The Experience of Seventeenth-Century Literature* (1972; Berkeley: University of California Press, paperback, 1974).

10. Melville, *Moby-Dick*, p. 160. Hennig Cohen and James Cahalan have provided a needed reference: *A Concordance to Melville's "Moby-Dick"* (n.p.: Melville Society, 1978); available through Imprint Series, Monograph Publishing on demand; produced and distributed by University Microfilms International, Ann Arbor, Michigan.

11. Dan. 2:1, 2, 5, 31, 33, 40, 44.

12. Dan. 2:5, 35; and Melville, *Moby-Dick*, pp. 454–55.

13. Melville, *Moby-Dick*, p. 459; and Dan. 2:35.

14. Norman O. Brown, *Life Against Death: The Psychoanalytic Meaning of History* (Middletown, Conn.: Wesleyan University Press, 1959), his chapter "The Excremental Vision," pp. 179–201, and pp. 222–23. The motif, obses-

sional sickness as Protestant curse, and salvation, is less artistically expressed by Arthur Guirdham as though approaching something analytically new, in his *Obsession: Psychic Forces and Evil in the Causation of Disease* (London: Neville Spearman, 1972), particularly in his opening pages.

15. Brown, *Life Against Death*, p. 1, from the headnote, speaking of his entry into Freud.

16. The motif of Mather and the Franklins is Perry Miller's, presented in his *The New England Mind: From Colony to Province* (Cambridge, Mass.: Harvard University Press, 1953), in his chapter "A Secular State," pp. 367–84; for particular references to Mather and Benjamin Franklin, see pp. 292, 300–01, 360, 419, 442, 484. For Miller, who had read Weber thoroughly, the declension and its irony were historically real. The quotation from John Wise appears on p. 292 and is given in reference not only to Mather but also to James and Benjamin Franklin. For Miller's own brief account of his experience, a spiritual autobiography of five sentences, see the "Preface" to his *Errand into the Wilderness* (Cambridge, Mass.: Belknap Press of Harvard University Press, 1956), p. vii: "The adventures that Africa afforded were tawdry enough, but it became the setting for a sudden epiphany (if the word be not too strong) of the pressing necessity for expounding my America to the twentieth century." The very form of his history, and his choice of titles, speaks to the issue Miller claimed, that "the literature of self-condemnation must be read for meanings far below the surface, for meanings of which, we may be so rash as to surmise, the authors were not fully conscious, but by which they were troubled and goaded. They looked in vain to history for an explanation of themselves" ("Errand into the Wilderness," in the aforementioned volume, p. 15). Surely history offered the form, as Miller himself so clearly said, that the Puritan "had to tell everything," "the slightest event," that "a life story had to be an example—an *exemplum*—whether for good or evil; it had to be organized into a drama, in which the ultimate meaning would emerge out of a welter of fact." This is from an introduction to one of the pieces of his abridged collection, *The American Puritans: Their Prose and Poetry* (Garden City, N.Y.: Doubleday & Company, Anchor Books, 1956), p. 225. A clear example of Miller's point, that everything was to be exposed, was provided by Samuel Sewall, and in a manner that might readily be passed by. The following is from the first volume of *The Diary of Samuel Sewall, 1674–1729*, newly edited by M. Halsey Thomas (New York: Farrar, Straus and Giroux, 1973), p. 543: "*March 27th* [1706] I walk in the Meetinghouse. Set out homeward, lodg'd at Cushing's. *Note.* I pray'd not with my Servant, being weary. Seeing no Chamber-pot call's for one; A little before day I us'd it in the Bed, and the bottom came out, and all the water run upon me. I was amaz'd, not knowing the bottom was out till I felt it in the Bed. The Trouble and Disgrace of it did afflict me. As soon as it was Light, I calld up my man and he made a fire and warm'd me a clean Shirt and I put it on, and was comfortable. How unexpectedly a man may be expos'd! There's no security but in God, who is to be sought by Prayer." And there the entry for the day ends. Certainly the small incident is real and, with the exception of the last two sentences, matter-of-factly presented, but the construction is careful: Sewall's failure to pray with his (suffering) servant, to humble himself with the servant Christ; his weariness; his trouble—the bottom falling out; the dawning light.

17. Norman O. Brown, *Love's Body* (1966; rpt. New York: Vintage Books, A Division of Random House, 1966), p. 80, with appreciation to Sharon C. King for pointing to the poems of Wallace Stevens.

18. Brown, *Love's Body*, pp. 90, 103, 90, 91, 93, 94, 95, 96, 98, 100, 102, 103, 96, 102.

19. Brown, *Love's Body*, pp. 104, 108, 105.

20. For perhaps the best and most current discussion of the diagnostic problems involved with the obsessional neurosis—of obsessional symptoms, that is, acting as a "façade" for other disorders—and for a recent discussion of this century's literature and the complications that literature involves, see Humberto Nagera, *Obsessional Neuroses: Developmental Psychopathology* (New York: Jason Aronson, 1976), Ch. 3, "Obsessional Neuroses as a Façade" (pp. 125–36): "Rarely indeed do I see a systematic approach to diagnosis, with our metapsychological tools used to penetrate behind the descriptive façade and to examine in minute detail the basic fabric and actual structure of the building behind the façade, before we affix to the patient the labels *obsessional or hysteric*" (p. 129). See also Ch. 2, "Contributions by Other Analysts" (pp. 71–124). Nagera, a psychoanalyst, notes the paucity of literature on the obsessional disorder (p. 73), an irony, he feels, in the face of Freud's words in *Inhibitions, Symptoms and Anxiety* (p. 13): "Obsessional Neurosis is unquestionably the most interesting and repaying subject of analytic research. But as a problem it has not yet been mastered"—irony even further removed from that which Nagera feels.

21. See n. 38 of Ch. 1 of this essay, to be softened, perhaps, by Nagera's comment in *Obsessional Neuroses*, p. 211, "that obsessional characters and obsessional neuroses are very rare entities indeed"—for children and adolescents, that is, "yet clinical experience with adults contradicts this paucity," the "discrepancy . . . partly accounted for by a developmental tendency to keep conflicts fluid and flexible for as long as possible during childhood." For discussion of "Familial and Social Roots of Obsession" and summaries of literature on the subject, see Paul L. Adams, *Obsessive Children* (1973; New York: Penguin Books, paperback, 1975), pp. 21–65.

22. Perry Miller, "Errand into the Wilderness," in his collection of essays by the same title, pp. 8–9. For "Implicit Irony in Perry Miller's New England Mind," though without reference to Weber, see Gene Wise, *Journal of the History of Ideas* 29 (October–December 1968), 579–600. And for a presentation of the tensions in Miller's thought, including "a tension between 'the Conscious' and 'the Mechanical,'" see David A. Hollinger, "Perry Miller and Philosophical History," *History and Theory* 7, no. 2 (1968), 189–202. The finest of the early American histories that display the thesis of tension and exoneration include, as mentioned in our Ch. 1, Richard L. Bushman, *From Puritan to Yankee: Character and the Social Order in Connecticut, 1690–1765*, a Publication of the Center for the Study of the History of Liberty in America, Harvard University (Cambridge, Mass.: Harvard University Press, 1967); as well as Paul Boyer and Stephen Nissenbaum, *Salem Possessed: The Social Origins of Witchcraft* (Cambridge, Mass.: Harvard University Press, 1974). The theme of identity and crisis in American Puritanism was introduced, and well argued, by Darrett B. Rutman, *American Puritanism: Faith and Practice*, The Lippincott History Series (Philadelphia: J. P. Lippincott Company, Pilotbooks, 1970). A return to Weber's themes,

meticulously presented and well constructed in arguing (though no such words are used) obsessive and compulsive aspects in evangelical presentations of self, is, again, Philip Greven, *The Protestant Temperament: Patterns of Child-Rearing, Religious Experience, and the Self in Early America* (New York: Alfred A. Knopf, 1977). The model for study of the New England town moving from community to society is the engrossing study by Kenneth A. Lockridge, *A New England Town: The First Hundred Years: Dedham, Massachusetts, 1636–1736,* The Norton Essays in American History (New York: W. W. Norton & Company, 1970). The image of immediate, Turnerian change offered in the pioneering work of Sumner Chilton Powell, *Puritan Village: The Formation of a New England Town* (first published in 1963 but completed earlier), was to be modified by the new social histories such as Lockridge's work and an equally important study by Philip J. Greven, Jr., *Four Generations: Population, Land, and Family in Colonial Andover, Massachusetts* (Ithaca: Cornell University Press, 1970). Greven, for example, placed "declension" within its place and attacked Parsons's ideas that the "nuclear" family had only recently emerged (see p. 284, including the appended note). And yet for both Lockridge and Greven, establishing early stability in the New England town allowed their texts to create alienation—allowed their communities, that is, to break and scatter—fine craftsmanship turning their work into the art it is.

Richard D. Brown has offered a model of "Modernization and the Modern Personality in Early America, 1600–1865: A Sketch of a Synthesis," *The Journal of Interdisciplinary History* 2 (Winter 1972), 201–28, arguing a case for the emergence of an achieving personality; see also his *Modernization: The Transformation of American Life, 1600–1865,* American Century Series (New York: Hill and Wang, 1976). Michael Zuckerman, "The Fabrication of Identity in Early America," *The William and Mary Quarterly,* 3rd ser., 34 (April 1977), 183–214, has offered the emergence of an identity incorporating both "the communal and the individualistic elements of American life," a model, most important, that stresses the Protestant emphasis upon "the dichotomous ordering of experience that emerged after the Reformation" (pp. 185, 186). A close look at the historian's use of modernization theory—in this case, the labor historian—is offered by Daniel T. Rodgers, "Tradition, Modernity, and the American Industrial Worker: Reflections and Critique," *The Journal of Interdisciplinary History* 7 (Spring 1977), 655–81. For a consideration of social theory in relation to the problem of community in American historiography, see Thomas Bender, *Community and Social Change in America,* Clarke A. Sanford-Armand G. Erpf Lecture Series on Local Government and Community Life (New Brunswick, N.J.: Rutgers University Press, 1978). The subject of "Toennies in America," including Tönnies own talk at the St. Louis Congress of Arts and Science, is treated by Werner J. Cahnman in *History and Theory* 16, no. 2 (1977), 147–67.

23. Richard Slotkin, *Regeneration Through Violence: The Mythology of the American Frontier, 1600–1860* (Middletown, Conn.: Wesleyan University Press, 1973), the last sentence of his work, p. 565.

24. Henry Glassie, *Folk Housing in Middle Virginia: A Structural Analysis of Historic Artifacts* (Knoxville: University of Tennessee Press, 1975).

25. The "choice of neurosis" is a Freudian theme, references to which may be found in the index to the *Standard Edition*—"General Subject Index," Vol. 24 (1974), 331—under the heading "Neurosis, choice of . . ."

26. Miller, *The American Puritans,* introductory remarks to the "Personal Narrative," p. 225. The references, again, are to Edmund S. Morgan, *Visible Saints: The History of a Puritan Idea* ([New York]: New York University Press, 1963); and Sacvan Bercovitch, *The Puritan Origins of the American Self* (New Haven: Yale University Press, 1975).

27. Roger Sharrock, "Introduction" to John Bunyan, *Grace Abounding to the Chief of Sinners,* ed. Roger Sharrock (Oxford: At the Clarendon Press, 1962), pp. xviii–xix.

28. *Boswell's Life of Johnson . . . ,* ed. George Birkbeck Hill, rev. and enl. edition by L. F. Powell (1934; rpt. Oxford: At the Clarendon Press, 1971), 1:63–65, with references to melancholy in the indexes, 2nd ed. (1964), 6:208. Discussion of melancholy as a disease of scholars in seventeenth-century English thought is to be found in Lawrence Babb, *The Elizabethan Malady: A Study of Melancholia in English Literature from 1580 to 1642,* Studies in Language and Literature (East Lansing, Mich.: Michigan State College Press, 1951), with references in the index under "Melancholy types, scholar or man of letters" and "Melancholy, intellectual." For a recent formal analysis of Burton's *Anatomy of Melancholy* laying stress on the self-creative aspects of the book in the making of itself, giving industry and thereby order to itself (and providing an ironic meaning to melancholy as the scholar's disease), see Ruth A. Fox, *The Tangled Chain: The Structure of Disorder in the "Anatomy of Melancholy"* (Berkeley: University of California Press, 1976).

29. Siegfried Wenzel, *The Sin of Sloth: Acedia in Medieval Thought and Literature* (Chapel Hill: University of North Carolina Press, 1960); and Reinhard Kuhn, *The Demon of Noontide: Ennui in Western Literature* (Princeton, N.J.: Princeton University Press, 1976), with appreciation to George McClure for calling attention to these works.

30. In arguing against "the persisting belief that Mather's biographies are an exercise in filiopietism," Bercovitch, in *Puritan Origins of the American Self,* offers "the sheer bulk and diversity of information," for example, Mather's medical information, as well as Mather's "comments on Winthrop's shortcomings . . . his descriptions," again as example, "of what might be called clerical melancholia—William Thompson's psychosomatic distempers, Nathanial Mather's suicidal depressions, Ezekial Rogers's morbid sense of isolation." This is what Bercovitch, in arguing for "Mather's historicism," sees in the biographies: not "pious *exempla,*" not hagiography, but a beginning realism—"a transitional mode between hagiography and modern biography. Though it insists on details, it forces them into the framework of the ideal. Its aim is to teach by use of examples. It rebels against medieval allegorization without really allowing for realism, in our empirical sense of the term." "Significantly, he [Mather] was the first American to use the term 'biography,' associated from its appearance in the late Renaissance with the revolt against panegyric. With his contemporaries, he advocated a direct, detailed investigation of personality and events" (pp. 2, 3, 4, 3). There is for Bercovitch, in other words, a new Protestant empiricism—if not a realism then an exemplary observation of nature; Bercovitch, indeed, was infatuated with "the haunting arguments of Max Weber" (p. 20). His is essentially an evolutionary trope, the moving of the Puritan from eulogy to detail; that detail—the empiric unassembled, presumably real; the morbidity Mather discussed, as in Winthrop; as well as the "tumors, circulatory ailments, hypochondria" (p. 2)—is

not, for Bercovitch, the stuff of filiopietism. Structurally, however, it is medicine as available for metaphor—as Susan Sontag, in her *Illness as Metaphor* (New York: Farrar, Straus and Giroux, 1978), has well shown, though she would have the metaphor removed—just as psychopathology is itself exemplum, quite available for the praise of the fathers. For the contrasting approach to the idea of an evolving realism, see Roland Barthes, *S/Z*, trans. Richard Miller (New York: Hill and Wang, 1974).

31. The idea of placements of time and space is taken from the writings of Bercovitch, most particularly Bercovitch's latest discussion of Melville's "Chronometricals and Horologicals" in *Pierre; or, The Ambiguities*. See Sacvan Bercovitch, *The American Jeremiad* (Madison, Wis.: University of Wisconsin Press, 1978), pp. 28–30. "Documentary expression" is a phrase from a title by William Stott: *Documentary Expression and Thirties America* (New York: Oxford University Press, 1973); see Ch. 1, "What is Documentary?," pp. 5–17. Bercovitch refers to Mailer's "diary-essay-tract-sermon," *The Armies of the Night*, in a note to p. 204 of *The American Jeremiad*.

Of the problem of the American intellectual not being able to stand outside of the text (or of the culture), to assume that Weberian position of prophet beyond the walls, see the work of Christopher Lasch. His discussion of the American intellectuals' confusion of culture and politics is best displayed in *The New Radicalism in America [1889–1963]: The Intellectual as a Social Type* (New York: Alfred A. Knopf, 1965). It is a problem that focuses the work of Bercovitch and the irony he displays toward the American jeremiad, because "in every case, the defiant act that might have posed fundamental social alternatives became instead a fundamental force against social change"; because "in this country, the *unmediated* relation between social structure and social ideal has made the very exposure of social flaws part of a ritual of socialization—a sort of liminal interior dialogue that in effect reinforces the mainstream culture" (*The American Jeremiad*, pp. 204 and 204–05n). See as well R. [Raymond] Jackson Wilson, "The Plight of the Transcendent Individual," Ch. 1 of his *In Quest of Community: Social Philosophy in the United States, 1860–1920*, American Culture History Series (New York: John Wiley and Sons, 1968), pp. 1–31.

32. Mary McCarthy, *The Seventeenth Degree: How It Went, Vietnam, Hanoi, Medina, Sons of the Morning* (1974; rpt. New York: Harcourt Brace Jovanovich, 1974, paperback).

33. Francis Jennings, "Virgin Land and Savage People," *American Quarterly* 23 (October 1971), 521–22, citing from John Winthrop, "General Considerations for the plantation in New England, with an answer to several objections," ed. Allyn B. Forbes, *Winthrop Papers* (Boston: Massachusetts Historical Society, 1929–47), 2:118. Of Milton, Bercovitch has written: "He acknowledged his failure—which is to say, the failure for him of the metaphor of national election—by singing the paradise within and, in his *History of Britain*, by moralizing over the futility of providential affairs. 'One's country,' he wrote to a European correspondent in 1666, 'is wherever it is well with one'" (*Puritan Origins of the American Self*, p. 83). And again, see Morgan, *Visible Saints*, for evidence of the American practice.

34. W. [Wystan] H. Auden, *The Enchafèd Flood: Or the Romantic Iconography of the Sea* (New York: Random House, 1950).

35. Ernest Hemingway, *The Sun Also Rises* (1926), in *The Hemingway Reader*, ed. Charles Poore (New York: Charles Scribner's Sons, 1953), p. 110. For an analysis of the cash value as a thematic tie in the novel, see Claire Sprague, "*The Sun Also Rises*: Its 'Clear Financial Basis,'" *American Quarterly* 21 (Summer 1969), 259–66. And on a measure of Thoreau's, see Albert F. McLean, Jr., "Thoreau's True Meridian: Natural Fact and Metaphor," *American Quarterly* 20 (Fall 1968), 567–79.

36. The metaphors of schizophrenia, of anatomical wastes and bodily mechanics, of "implosion," "petrification," "depersonalization," are derived from R. D. Laing, *The Divided Self: An Existential Study in Sanity and Madness* (London: Tavistock Publications, 1960). Laing's beautiful art becomes enacted in life, wrenchingly so in David Reed's account, *Anna* (New York: Basic Books, 1976). The work of Thomas S. Szasz is to be mentioned: *The Myth of Mental Illness: Foundations of a Theory of Personal Conduct* (New York: A Hoeber-Harper Book, 1961); and *The Manufacture of Madness: A Comparative Study of the Inquisition and the Mental Health Movement* (New York: Harper & Row, Publishers, 1970); along with a collection of essays, *Ideology and Insanity: Essays on the Psychiatric Dehumanization of Man* (Garden City, N.Y.: Doubleday & Company, Anchor Books, 1970). For a perspective on Laing and Szasz in a book considering the earliest models of mental illness, see "The Development of Models of Mental Illness," Ch. 2 of Bennett Simon, *Mind and Madness in Ancient Greece: The Classical Roots of Modern Psychiatry* (Ithaca, N.Y.: Cornell University Press, 1978). A debate on the efficacy, again, of the nineteenth-century American asylum places the work of Gerald N. Grob—*The State and the Mentally Ill: A History of Worcester State Hospital in Massachusetts, 1830–1920* (Chapel Hill: University of North Carolina Press, 1966); and *Institutions in America: Social Policy to 1875* (New York: Free Press, 1973)—against that of David J. Rothman: *The Discovery of the Asylum: Social Order and Disorder in the New Republic* (Boston: Little, Brown and Company, paperback, 1971). The materialization of the ship of fools—"Madness will no longer proceed from a point within the world to a point beyond, on its strange voyage; it will never again be that fugitive and absolute limit. Behold it moored now, made fast among things and men. Retained and maintained. No longer a ship but a hospital"—is contained in Ch. 1, "'*Stultifera Navis*,'" of Michael Foucault, *Madness and Civilization: A History of Insanity in the Age of Reason*, trans. Richard Howard (1965; New York: Random House, Vintage Books, 1973), published in France as *Histoire de la folie* in 1961. In his *Mental Illness and Psychology*, trans. Alan Sheridan (New York: Harper & Row, Publishers, Harper Colophon Books, 1976), published in France in 1954 as *Maladie mentale et psychologie*, Foucault writes: "The contemporary world makes schizophrenia possible, not because its events render it inhuman and abstract, but because our culture reads the world in such a way that man himself cannot recognize himself . . . in it" (p. 84). A relatively recent discussion of the problem of coming to any causal psychodynamic theory of schizophrenia—including the effect of the double bind and the magnitude of different familial pathologies, all of which makes control of a singular variable almost an impossibility—is contained in Manfred Bleuler, *The Schizophrenic Disorders*, trans. Siegfried M. Clemens (New Haven: Yale University Press, 1978), first published in West Germany in 1972, his section entitled "The Role of Psychotraumatic Experiences," pp. 474–80.

37. Auden, *The Enchafèd Flood*, pp. 29–39.

38. Allen Ginsberg, "Howl," in his *Howl and Other Poems* (1956; San Francisco: City Lights Books, 1959, paperback), pp. 9, 13, 15, 17, 19, 20, the quotations including the first and the last lines of the poem.

Index

Abbot, Francis, 215–216
Abraham, Karl, 269
Acton, William, 395*n*
Adams, Henry, 120, 142, 209, 310, 321, 324
Agassiz, Louis, 148, 150, 152, 153
Agee, James, 324
agoraphobia, 160, 182
Agrippa of Nettesheim, 22
alcoholism, 109, 177, 287
Alcott, Bronson, 86, 127
Alfieri, Vittorio, 181
alienation:
  American sense of, 2, 84, 116, 185, 199, 205, 206, 240, 244–251, 291, 332
  artistic, 117, 130, 134, 136, 151, 153–154, 285, 333, 372*n*
  doubt and, 205, 207
  Edwards on, 73–77
  estrangement vs., 199, 235, 246
  from God, 15, 35, 122–123, 138, 258
  guilt and, 246–249, 300
  of modern man, 242, 247, 251, 334–335
  physical origin of, 172
  Royce on, 199, 205, 206, 209, 221, 232, 234, 236–251
  self-, 226, 232, 234, 246
  self-possession vs., 234, 237–239
  sin and, 104, 111, 113, 121, 249
  Weber on, 11, 240, 245, 291, 300, 306, 312–313, 315, 322
  of work, 117–118, 134, 165, 206, 240, 246
alienists, *see* psychiatrists, psychology
Alline, Henry, 102
Ambassadors, The (Henry James), 375*n*
ambivalence, concept of, 214, 404*n*
America, *see* United States
American character:
  frontier and, 17
  origins of, 2, 17, 81
  Protestant ethic and, 8, 10–11, 184
  psychopathological nature of, 6–8, 186, 188, 240, 244–251, 257, 280, 285, 291, 323, 327, 329–331, 332
  studies of, 1, 8, 17–18
"American Scholar, The" (Emerson), 96, 118
Ames, William, 30, 34–36, 38, 40, 48, 51, 68, 71, 112, 192
amnesia, 189, 224
anal eroticism, 3, 270–274, 311
Anatomy of Melancholy, The (Burton), 21, 23–29, 311
Ancient Judaism (Weber), 297, 304
anger:
  guilt and, 211
  in obsessional neurosis, 5, 64–65
Angyal, Andras, 207, 300, 377*n*–378*n*
Anschauungen, 168
Anthony, Susanna, 42, 340*n*–341*n*
antinomianism, 29, 31, 148, 333
Apocalypse Explained, The (Swedenborg), 103, 145
Arbella, 18
Arendt, Hannah, 240
Armies of the Night (Mailer), 82
Arminianism, 31, 84, 168, 175
asceticism, 205, 324
  of elder Henry James, 87–88, 90, 107–110, 115, 138–140, 154–159
  of transcendentalists, 87–88
  as "twice-born philosophy," 154–155
  Weber on, 6, 11, 57, 78, 115, 191, 255, 265, 286, 290, 295–296, 300, 303, 308–319, 433*n*–434*n*
  of William James, 154–159, 174, 184, 190–191
Auden, W. H., 333, 335
Augustine, Saint, 41, 59
autobiographical writing:
  "autobiographies" vs., 40, 54, 147, 294, 304
  diaries vs., 54–55
  narrator in, 55–56
  see also confession, confessional literature; *individual authors*
automatic writing, 99, 100

Index

Babb, Lawrence, 343*n*
Bain, Alexander, 166, 172–175, 178, 180, 190, 202
Barthes, Roland, 319–321
Bartlet, Phebe, 68, 128
Baxter, Richard, 35–36, 76, 290
Beard, George, 188, 257, 264, 282, 416*n*–417*n*
Bercovitch, Sacvan, 1, 41, 42, 56, 81, 331, 332, 349*n*, 441*n*–442*n*
Bergson, Henri, 187, 197
Bible:
  Jeremiah in, 296, 304–308, 316
  Job in, 203–205
  as literary model, 46, 49–50, 67, 102, 108, 217, 250, 326
  quoted, 11–12, 13, 41, 50, 76–77, 99, 113, 161, 214, 317
  wilderness in, 11, 76, 199
Binnenleben, 184
Bleuler, Eugene, 214
Blithedale Romance, The (Hawthorne), 136–138, 381*n*
Borrow, George, 227
Boswell, James, 222, 331
Bradford, William, 20
Bradstreet, Anne, 57
Brainerd, David, 66–69, 79, 147
Breuer, Josef, 283
Bright, Timothy, 23–28, 31–32, 36
Brown, Norman O., 8, 327–328
"Brunonian system," 264
Bunyan, John, 7, 59, 74, 77–78, 101, 108, 109, 123, 154–157, 169, 227, 346*n*–347*n*, 351*n*, 394*n*
  autobiographical writing of, 6, 19, 36, 39, 40, 42, 48–49, 53, 58, 92–93, 102, 110, 112, 200, 221, 237, 296, 331
  Pilgrim's Progress written by, 11, 17–19, 36–40, 56, 58, 64, 93, 145, 147, 155, 318, 321, 365*n*
  Royce and, 198, 204, 207, 217, 220–222, 232, 234–237, 240, 242, 244, 251, 264, 283, 332
Burton, Robert, 5, 21, 23–29, 31–32, 36, 42, 58, 311

Cabot, Richard, 280
Calvin, John, 147, 320
Calvinism, 6, 45, 86, 205, 227, 296, 314–315
  commercial, 106–107, 110–111, 117, 124, 129
  decline of, 198, 220, 222
  rejected by elder Henry James, 10, 82, 84–86, 91, 106, 129, 209, 365*n*
  see also Puritans, Puritanism
capitalism, Protestantism and, *see* Protestant ethic
Carlyle, Thomas, 371*n*
"Case of John Bunyan, The" (Royce), 235
Case of Satan's Fiery Darts in Blasphemous Suggestions and Hellish Annoyances, The (Colman), 65
Cases of Conscience (Perkins), 31–32
Catholicism:
  confession in, 279, 313
  Protestantism vs., 115, 313, 395*n*
Channing, William Ellery, 259, 266–267
Chapman, John Jay, 215
"Character and Anal Eroticism" (Freud), 3
child development, 259, 281, 283
  Bain's theory of, 174, 202
  Royce's theory of, 200, 202, 203, 207–212, 247, 248
Clendenning, John, 208, 252
Clinical Lectures on Mental Disease (Clouston), 169
Clouston, T. S., 169
Coale, George Buchanan, 241
Cohen, Sande, 43
Cole, Nathan, 52–54
Coleridge, Samuel Taylor, 216
Colman, Benjamin, 65–66
compulsive behavior, 102, 109, 178, 181, 184, 189, 222–231, 235, 300
  Freud on, 271–273, 302–304, 307, 313 313
  habit vs., 272
  obsessive neurosis vs., 4, 303
  of Puritans, 3, 60, 240
  Weber on, 243, 297, 302–308, 319
  see also obsessional neurosis
confession, confessional literature, 40–65, 162, 203, 349*n*
  in Catholicism, 279, 313
  as church membership requirement, 42–49, 331
  disappearance of, 83–84
  Edwards on, 44, 100
  interpretation of, 8–9, 47–49, 50, 53, 55–56, 67–68, 100–101, 105, 147, 209–210, 297, 301, 386*n*
  melancholy in, 54–65
  narrator in, 55–56

Index

origins of, 2–3, 9, 16, 41, 315
psychoanalysis as, 279
psychomachy in, 41, 94–95, 112, 240
tradition of, 6–10, 81–82, 85, 86, 92, 94–95, 112, 121, 147–148, 192, 200, 216–217, 240, 311
see also individual authors
Confessions (Augustine), 41, 59
"Confessions of a Psychasthenic," 227–228
conscience:
consciousness of, 204
contrite, 112
"distempered," 32
melancholy and, 27–28, 31–33
"New England," 89, 183, 222–223, 227–228, 255–257, 262, 268
Puritanical, 2, 6, 16, 27–28, 105–108, 184
"socially trained," 247
see also guilt
Conscience with the Power and Cases Thereof (Ames), 34
conversion, *see* spiritual conversion
Cooper, James Fenimore, 17
Cotton, James Harry, 201
Cotton Mather (Levin), 356*n*
Cowles, Edward, 220, 228–232, 285, 401*n*
crime, *see* sin
Critique of Pure Reason (Kant), 232
Crooker, Joseph H., 222
Culture of Narcissism, The (Lasch), 1

Dane, John, 52
Darwin, Charles, 123, 127, 153, 192, 396*n*
Day of Doom, The (Wigglesworth), 51
defensive mechanisms, 102
"Degeneration and Genius" (William James), 156
delusion, obsession vs., 229
depression, *see* melancholy
Descartes, René, 234
desert, *see* wilderness
despair:
in *Pilgrim's Progress*, 37, 39, 155
as sin, 14
devil, *see* Satan
dipsomania, 177, 287
"Disposition to Obsessional Neurosis, The" (Freud), 271
"distraction," 24, 26
"double-bind," 208, 259
doubt:
alienation and, 205, 207
in obsessional neurosis, 168–169
dream interpretation, 276–278, 284, 286–287
Dürer, Albrecht, 22
Durkheim, Émile, 329

Edel, Leon, 132, 379*n*–380*n*
Education of Henry Adams, The (Adams), 120
Edwards, Jonathan, 43, 52–53, 65–82, 104, 105, 106, 112, 143, 199, 222, 255, 263, 332, 334, 357*n*, 369*n*–370*n*
on alienation, 73–77
on confession, 44, 100
diary of, 69, 70, 149, 201
elder Henry James vs., 85, 86, 88, 89, 91, 103, 110, 118, 128
life of, 16–17, 66–76, 83–84
on melancholy, 10, 16, 67–76, 80, 184
Royce compared to, 142, 204, 252
William James compared to, 146, 147, 149, 168, 192, 195, 325
Edwards, Sarah, 73, 75
"Effectual Work of the Word" (Hooker), 34
election, *see* spiritual conversion
Elizabethan Malady, The (Babb), 343*n*
Emanuel Swedenborg (Toksvig), 362*n*–363*n*
Emerson, Ralph Waldo, 67, 80–81, 92, 136, 149, 151, 153, 157, 167, 185–186, 311, 322, 336
elder Henry James and, 85, 86, 91, 95–96, 107–108, 113, 114, 118, 123, 128
on Swedenborg, 91, 96, 185, 376*n*
as transcendentalist, 87–88, 142
Emotions and the Will, The (Bain), 172
Enchafèd Flood, The (Auden), 333
"Energies of Men, The" (William James), 187–188
epilepsy, 180
Erikson, Erik H., 8, 59, 299, 308, 327, 338*n*–339*n*, 372*n*
on Luther, 5–6, 77, 240, 358*n*
Experiencia (Winthrop), 78

Faithful Narrative of the Surprising Work of God, A (Edwards), 52
"fall line," 17
"Fancy's Showbox" (Hawthorne), 83, 135–136, 381*n*

Index

fathers, father figures:
  in American society, 209, 245
  society as, 248–251
  in Victorian era, 209
  "Fathers and Sons" (Feinstein), 360*n*, 367*n*, 372*n*, 373*n*, 397*n*
fear:
  of filth, *see* mysophobia
  of idleness, 63, 78
  legal, 30–31, 38, 74, 107, 111, 175
  in melancholy, 25–27, 65
  obsessional, 202, 222
  panic, *see* James, William; spiritual conversion
  "systematizing" of, 154, 157, 182
  of touching, 224
  see also phobias
Fechner, G. T., 197
Feinstein, Howard Marvin, 360*n*, 367*n*, 372*n*, 373*n*, 397*n*
Ferenczi, Sandor, 270
Feud of Oakfield Creek, The (Royce), 210–212, 241–242
Fichte, Johann Gottlieb, 237, 238
Fiering, Norman, 35
Fish, Stanley E., 296
Fiske, John, 45
fixed ideas, 4, 96, 102, 146, 147, 155, 171, 173–174, 189, 228–229, 272, 297, 307, 308
  see also obsessional neurosis
Flavel, John, 35
Fliess, Wilhelm, 288
Flournoy, Theodore, 187
Foucault, Michel, 9, 291, 293–294, 301, 310
Fourierism, 117, 136
Franklin, Benjamin, 67, 168, 187, 325, 327
Frémont, John C., 219
Freud, Sigmund, 18, 184, 214, 290, 291, 318, 320, 321, 325, 383*n*, 436*n*
  on anal eroticism, 270–274, 311
  on compulsive behavior, 271–273, 302–304, 307, 313
  on melancholy, 368*n*
  on "New England conscience," 256
  on obsessional neurosis, 3–5, 155, 188, 224, 225, 257, 260, 271–273, 286–288, 303, 315
  on psychoanalysis, 254, 256, 273, 279
  Putnam and, 10, 206, 251–252, 254–258, 267–286
Fromm, Erich, 3, 8, 311, 323
fugue state, 189, 224

Gandhi, Mohandas K., 240
General Economic History (Weber), 289
genius:
  obsession vs., 156
  passivity of, 192
Germany, philosophy and psychology in, 199, 206, 239
Gerth, Hans, 297
ghosts, 108, 370*n*–371*n*
Gifford, Adam, Lord, 143
Gillespie, Thomas, 75–76, 79–80, 204
Ginsberg, Allen, 335–336
Glassie, Henry, 330
glorification, Puritan concept of, 29, 31, 192–193
"Gospel of Relaxation, The" (William James), 184–186
Grace Abounding to the Chief of Sinners (Bunyan), 36, 39, 40, 48–49, 53, 200, 311, 347*n*
Great Awakening, 65–68, 70–72, 83–84, 86, 355*n*, 392*n*
Great Christian Doctrine of Original Sin Defended, The (Edwards), 252
Greenlee, Douglas, 210
Greven, Philip, 1, 337*n*–341*n*, 440*n*
Grinstein, Alexander, 287
guilt, 83, 106, 107, 273, 313, 319
  alienation and, 246–249, 300
  anger and, 211
  origins of, 163, 211, 225, 227
  see also conscience

Hale, Nathan G., 271
Hammond, William A., 407*n*–408*n*, 423*n*
handwashing ritual, 4, 181, 183, 223, 226–227, 272
  see also mysophobia
Hawley, Joseph, 72–73
Hawthorne, Nathaniel, 83, 130, 133–136
  fiction of, 85, 135–138, 143, 199, 381*n*, 382*n*–383*n*
Hegel, Georg Wilhelm Friedrich, 203, 204–206, 234, 237, 238, 240, 242–245, 249
Heine, Heinrich, 233
Henry, Joseph, 114
Hildersam, Arthur, 35, 49
holiness, *see* sainthood, saintliness

Index

Hooker, Thomas, 22, 30, 34, 46, 53, 58, 70, 78, 144, 148
Hopkins, Samuel, 69–70, 106, 143
Howells, William Dean, 119
Hughes, H. Stuart, 296
Huizinga, Thomas, 18
humoral psychology, 16, 22, 24, 28, 32, 84, 103, 203
Hutchinson, Abigail, 68
hypochondria, 169, 171–172, 177, 194, 299, 331, 417*n*
hysteria, 41, 178, 281–282, 283, 288, 300
  anxiety, 224
  concept of, 3
  melancholy vs., 24, 26–27, 35, 67, 71
  neurasthenia and psychasthenia vs., 189, 203
  obsessional neurosis vs., 223, 224, 227, 303–304
  religious, 83, 86

ideas:
  actions vs., 33, 51, 112, 133–136, 138, 144, 156, 170–172, 178–180, 189, 214–215, 225, 369*n*–370*n*, 407*n*–408*n*
  fixed (*idées fixes*), *see* fixed ideas
identity crises, 166, 333, 355*n*, 388*n*
imitative behavior, 185, 200, 202–207, 214, 221, 247, 401*n*
individualism, collectivism vs., 247–248
"Insistent and Fixed Ideas" (Cowles), 228–231
"iron," metaphoric uses of, 3, 11, 18, 19, 21, 29, 37, 40, 93, 102, 154, 155, 224, 290, 296, 305, 307, 311, 318, 320, 322, 324, 326
"iron of melancholy," 3, 102, 154

Jackson, Henry, 265
Jackson, James, 258, 259, 261, 264–269, 278
Jackson, Jonathan, 265
Jackson, Patrick, 265
James, Alice, 128, 145, 178–179, 383*n*
James, Henry, 89, 128–135, 138–139, 187, 209, 257, 360*n*, 372*n*, 374*n*, 375*n*, 379*n*–380*n*
  father criticized by, 87, 88, 118–120
James, Henry, Sr. (the elder), 83–178, 184–185
  asceticism of, 87–88, 90, 107–110, 115, 138–140, 154–159
  autobiographical writing of, 10, 84–86, 88–89, 106, 107–109, 120–121, 123, 142, 159
  Calvinism rejected by, 10, 82, 84–86, 91, 106, 129, 209, 365*n*
  death of, 90, 138–139, 214, 383*n*
  Edwards vs., 85, 86, 88, 89, 91, 103, 110, 118, 128
  Emerson and, 85, 86, 91, 95–96, 107–108, 113, 114, 118, 123, 128
  as father, 110, 118–120, 128–133, 163–164, 169–170
  life of, 85, 88, 91, 106–107, 114, 124–126
  mother of, 125
  Royce compared to, 199, 201–202, 205–206, 218, 240, 244
  son Henry's criticism of, 87, 88, 118–120
  son William compared to, 85, 86, 97, 98, 100, 101, 142–143, 145, 148, 160, 182, 186
  son William's ambivalence towards, 139–140, 142, 153, 154–159, 176, 191, 214
  son William's criticism of, 87–90, 113, 119, 120–121, 123, 148, 213
  Swedenborg and, 91, 95–99, 101, 108, 116–117, 119, 122–123, 128, 131, 136, 140, 151, 175, 176, 205–206, 213, 332, 364*n*–366*n*, 370*n*–371*n*
  transcendentalists and, 85–88, 113–114, 118, 142
  vastation of, 59, 89, 90–102, 108, 114–115, 144, 159, 160, 174, 197, 216, 218, 365*n*–366*n*
  work as viewed by, 87–90, 97, 116–118, 134
James, Henry, III, 143, 159, 166, 167, 187
James, Margaret, 196
James, William, 10, 11, 85–94, 100–102, 106, 127, 128, 130–133, 141–197, 224–225, 255, 256, 262, 264, 269, 279, 283, 298, 302, 316, 321, 324–326, 332, 399*n*
  ambivalence toward father, 139–140, 142, 153, 154–159, 176, 191, 214
  as artist, 151
  on asceticism, 154–159, 174, 184, 190–191
  asylum visited by, 11, 98, 151, 166, 167, 175, 180, 206, 243
  autobiographical writing of, 8, 92,

James, William (*continued*)
142–143, 147, 149–151, 166–167, 192, 209, 385*n*–386*n*
in Brazil, 148–153, 163, 165, 167, 218
career choices of, 146, 153, 163, 164–165, 208, 388*n*
drug experiments of, 177
Edwards compared to, 146, 147, 149, 168, 192, 195, 325
emotion theory of, 150, 182
empiricism of, 147, 176, 194–197
father compared to, 85, 86, 97, 98, 100, 101, 142–143, 145, 148, 160, 182, 186
father criticized by, 87–90, 113, 119, 120–121, 123, 148, 213
in Germany, 164–165, 170
Gifford Lectures of, 87, 92, 143, 154–157, 166, 190, 192, 196
on melancholy, 3, 92, 143, 155, 157, 175–176, 181, 183–184, 185, 194, 214
mother of, 160, 379*n*
as naturalist, 148–153
on neurasthenia, 188–189
on obsessional neurosis, 155–156, 168–175, 190–191
panic fear of, 59, 92–94, 100, 101, 105, 153, 155, 159–164, 174, 216, 386*n*
physical weakness of, 148–149, 160–164, 176, 212
poor eyesight of, 149, 160–161, 164, 166, 176–177
pragmatism of, 146, 168, 191, 212, 213
on relaxation, 184–186
Royce and, 10, 185, 196–197, 199–202, 203, 205, 208, 212–216, 218, 235, 237, 240, 251–252
on saintliness, 158, 184, 190, 193
as scholar, 144–146, 164
Swedenborg and, 98, 101, 145, 213
volition theory of, 170–171, 181
on writing, 9, 93–94, 100, 150–151, 163, 186
James, William (grandfather), 86, 88, 106–107, 114, 119, 120, 123–129, 134, 139–140, 163, 360*n*
"James-Lange" theory, 182
Janet, Pierre, 188–190, 225, 279, 282
Jennings, Francis, 322–333
Jeremiah, 297, 304–308, 316
Jesus Christ:
crucifixion of, 59
imitation of, 15, 20–21, 29, 33, 49–51, 56, 65
Puritan view of, 20–21
Job, 203–205
John Bunyan (Sharrock), 346*n*–347*n*
"John Dane's Narrative, 1682" (Dane), 52
John of the Cross, Saint, 384*n*–385*n*
Johnson, Samuel, 222–223, 331, 406*n*–407*n*
Jones, Ernest, 270, 276
Journal of Abnormal Psychology, The, 189
Jung, Carl, 269, 270, 323–324

Kallen, Horace, 252
Kant, Immanuel, 88, 199, 220, 221, 231–234, 237
Klibansky, Raymond, 22
Krafft-Ebing, Richard von, 167
Kuklick, Bruce, 142

Lasch, Christopher, 1
Levin, David, 356*n*
Lévi-Strauss, Claude, 49
Life Against Death (Brown), 327
literature:
American, 17, 54–65, 67, 81–82, 85, 142, 151, 199–200, 204, 300
confessional, *see* confession, confessional literature
English, 5, 24
neurotic nature of, 151
Puritan, 2, 6–10, 40–49, 54–65, 81, 86, 94, 112
seventeenth century, 40–49, 54–65, 81, 86, 162, 315
eighteenth century, 67
nineteenth century, 17, 24, 67, 85, 142, 151, 199–200, 204, 216
see also individual authors and titles
Locke, John, 234
Lockridge, Kenneth A., 440*n*
Lowell, A. Lawrence, 258
Lowell, Anna Cabot, 259, 266
Luther, Martin, 24, 77–78, 147, 176, 196, 316, 320
Erikson on, 5–6, 77, 240, 358*n*
Lutoslawski, Wincenty, 190

McCarthy, Mary, 332
Magnalia Christi Americana (Cotton Mather), 78–79
Mailer, Norman, 82

Index

Marcell, David W., 324
Marcuse, Herbert, 8
Martineau, James, 192
Marx, Leo, 321–322, 334
Marx, Karl, 205–206, 240, 243, 289, 318, 384*n*
Massachusetts General Hospital, 188, 258, 266, 285
Mather, Cotton, 52–53, 66, 69, 98, 123, 142, 168, 182, 187, 199, 218, 253, 263, 324, 327, 332, 356*n*
  autobiography of, 55, 57–58, 60, 62–65, 162, 201
  brother's biography written by, 78–79, 81, 106, 221, 331, 336, 441*n*
  on melancholy, 16, 20–23
  on Satan, 20–21
Mather, Increase, 41, 43–44, 50, 51–52, 94, 100, 170, 333, 356*n*
  autobiography of, 55, 60, 61–62
Mather, Nathanael, 78–79, 81, 106, 221, 331, 332, 336, 441*n*
Mather, Richard, 60, 62
Maudsley, Henry, 178, 194, 393*n*–394*n*
Max Weber (Marianne Weber), 304
melancholy:
  Bright on, 23–28, 31–32
  Burton on, 23–29, 31–32
  in confessional literature, 54–65
  conscience and, 27–28, 31–33
  Cotton Mather on, 16, 20–23
  definitions of, 3, 5, 15, 19, 20, 22–23, 343*n*
  "distraction" vs., 24, 26
  Edwards on, 10, 16, 67–76, 80, 184
  fear in, 25–27, 65
  Freud on, 368*n*
  in humors theory, 16, 22, 24, 28, 32, 84, 103
  hysteria vs., 24, 26–27, 35, 67, 71
  "iron" of, 3, 102, 154
  monomania vs., 35
  as obsessional neurosis, 25–27, 32–33, 36, 74, 105, 222, 224, 288, 331–332
  as obsolete term, 224
  Perkins on, 28, 32–35, 58, 61, 71, 73
  in *Pilgrim's Progress*, 36–39
  and Protestantism, 22, 227–228, 395*n*
  psychiatrists on, 3, 33
  psychosis vs., 24, 26
  among Puritans, 5, 6, 9–10, 14–15, 20–29, 35–36
  religious, 5–6, 23–29, 102, 156, 397*n*
  symptoms of, summarized, 9, 24–27
  temptation as symptom of, 32–36, 43, 64, 157, 221
  William James on, 3, 92, 143, 155, 157, 175–176, 181, 183–184, 185, 194, 214
Melencolia I (Dürer), 22
Melville, Herman, 17, 199, 204, 324–326, 333–334
Memoir of Dr. James Jackson, A (Putnam), 257, 261–262, 264–269, 278
Mill, John Stuart, 101, 209, 367*n*–368*n*, 392*n*
Miller, Perry, 31, 81, 329–332
Mills, C. Wright, 8, 297, 323–324
Mitchell, Silas Weir, 189, 280, 419*n*–423*n*, 438*n*
Mitzman, Arthur, 311, 430*n*, 431*n*, 433*n*
monomania, 4, 35, 156, 172, 174, 178, 179, 222, 272
  love as, 181
  melancholy vs., 35
  obsessional neurosis vs., 225, 229
"moral insanity," 4, 10, 33, 54, 86, 112, 133, 144, 179
Moran, Gerald F., 357*n*
Morgan, Edmund S., 29, 42–43, 48, 331, 378*n*
Munsterberg, Hugo, 278
mysophobia, 4, 183, 224, 262, 272
  see also handwashing ritual
mysticism, concept of, 193
myths:
  American, 1, 17–18, 333
  of the garden, 1–2, 17–18
  of madness, 334
  see also wilderness

narcissism, as modern neurosis, 8
Nature (Emerson), 67, 85, 92, 118, 151, 153, 157, 311
Nature of Evil, The (Henry James), 148
neurasthenia, 144, 161, 177, 178, 203, 220, 223, 224, 257, 280, 281–283, 285, 323, 416*n*–417*n*, 422*n*–424*n*
  hysteria vs., 189, 203
  psychasthenia vs., 189, 282–283
  in Putnam family, 262–265
  symptoms of, 262–263
  William James on, 188–189
  see also obsessional neurosis
neurology, 221
  function of, 223, 231, 282
  see also psychiatrists, psychology

Index

neuroses:
 classifications of, 224
 concept of, 3, 144, 146, 223–224, 284, 334
 work and, 188, 274
 see also specific neuroses
New England:
 settlement of, 2, 7, 13–14, 30
 suicide in, 51
 theocracy in, 41–45, 329, 331
 as wilderness, 14, 16, 19–22, 31, 80–81, 333
 see also Puritans, Puritanism
"New England conscience," 89, 183, 222–223, 227–228, 255–257, 262, 268, 360*n*, 375*n*
New England Town, A (Lockridge), 440*n*

Obscure Diseases of the Brain and Mind (Winslow), 178, 394*n*
obsessional neurosis, 3–10, 178–183, 222–231
 anger in, 5, 64–65
 compulsive behavior vs., 4, 303
 connotations of, 225–226
 as cultural malaise, 285, 329–331
 delusions vs., 228
 doubt in, 168–169
 fear in, 202, 222
 Freud on, 3–5, 155, 188, 224, 225, 257, 260, 271–273, 286–288, 303, 315
 hysteria vs., 223, 224, 227, 303–304
 Janet on, 189–190
 monomania vs., 225, 229
 neurasthenia and psychasthenia vs., 188–189, 220, 223, 224, 280, 281–283, 285
 orderliness in, 267–268, 286
 prevalence of, 337*n*–338*n*, 439*n*
 of Puritans, 3, 4, 8, 25–27, 60–61, 239–240, 249
 as religious ritual, 4–6, 226, 240, 271–273, 280
 Royce on, 4, 240, 242, 411*n*
 as spiritual conversion, 144, 191, 312
 symptoms of, 4, 146, 155, 182–183, 189–190, 194–195, 226, 267–268, 286, 323, 340*n*, 393*n*–394*n*, 411*n*, 439*n*
 temptation in, 4, 103–105, 312
 William James on, 155–156, 168–175, 190–191
 see also melancholy
"Obsessive Acts and Religious Practices" (Freud), 271–273
Oedipal struggle, 299–301
"On the Pathogenesis of Some Impulsions" (Janet), 189–190

panic fear, *see* James, William; spiritual conversion
Panofsky, Erwin, 22
paralysis:
 hysterical, 224, 281, 288
 metaphoric uses of, 98, 115, 169, 174, 175, 183, 189, 324
Parsons, Talcott, 290
Paterna (Cotton Mather), 55, 162
Paul, Saint, 22, 29, 34, 49–50, 52, 99, 157, 196, 214, 240, 247, 249, 250, 251
Peirce, Charles Sanders, 146, 209–210, 213, 237, 241
Perkins, William, 28–36, 38, 39, 40, 59, 68, 76, 332
 Christ as viewed by, 20
 on melancholy, 28, 32–35, 58, 61, 71, 73
 spiritual conversion outlined by, 29–32, 35, 48, 49, 74, 77, 192
 on thought vs. behavior, 33, 51, 112, 225
Perry, Ralph Barton, 127, 139, 143, 157
Pettit, Norman, 29
Phänomenologie des Geistes (Hegel), 242
Philosophy of Loyalty, The (Royce), 198
phobias, 189
 agora-, 160, 182
 myso-, 4, 183, 224, 262
 see also fear
"Physical [or Mental] Treatment" (Freud), 254
Physiology and Pathology of the Mind, The (Maudsley), 194
Pierpont, Sarah, 54–55
pilgrims, 13–14, 20, 23
 see also Puritans; Puritanism
Pilgrim's Progress, The (Bunyan), 11, 17–19, 36–40, 56, 58, 64, 93, 145, 147, 155, 296, 318, 321, 365*n*
 despair in, 11, 37, 39, 93, 155, 318
 Iron Cage in, 11, 37, 40, 93, 155, 296, 318
 melancholy in, 36–39
 wilderness in, 38

Index

pleasure vs. pain, psychological theory of, 172–173, 235
Plymouth Colony, 20
pragmatism, 146, 168, 179, 191, 212, 213
"Pragmatism and Religion" (William James), 141
precisians, 3, 13, 23–24, 80, 106
  saints vs., 42
  see also Puritans, Puritanism
predestination, implications of, 45, 48, 289–290, 314, 318, 395*n*
Preston, John, 35
Prince, Morton, 276, 279
Principles of Psychology (William James), 93, 158, 168, 172, 174, 178, 183, 194, 196, 222, 235, 325
Problem of Christianity, The (Royce), 244, 251
Protestant ethic, 88, 227–228, 320
  American character and, 8, 10–11, 184
  virtues of, 57
  Weber on, 2, 3, 10–11, 57, 115, 255, 265, 286, 290–292, 294–295, 303, 309–314
Protestant Ethic and the Spirit of Capitalism, The (Weber), 3, 191, 290, 295, 298–299, 309–314
Protestantism:
  Catholicism vs., 115, 313, 395*n*
  melancholy and, 22, 227–228, 395*n*
  see also Puritans, Puritanism
Protestant Temperament, The (Greven), 1, 337*n*–341*n*, 440*n*
Psalms, 11–12, 41, 77, 161
psychasthenia, 144, 161, 189–190, 224, 227–228
  hysteria vs., 189, 203
  neurasthenia vs., 189, 282–283
  see also obsessional neurosis
psychiatrists, psychology:
  Freudian, 279–284
  humoral, 16, 22, 24, 28, 32, 84, 103, 203
  imperfection of, 279
  on melancholy, 3, 33
  Victorian, 2–4, 27, 33, 133, 144, 156, 160, 178–180, 188–190, 220–232
psychoanalysis:
  as confession, 279
  Freud on, 254, 256, 273, 279
  popularity of, in U.S., 275, 279–284
  Putnam on, 10, 275–283
  as spiritual conversion, 10, 254–256, 280
psychogenesis, concept of, 325, 422
psychohistory:
  development of, 1, 240
  function of, 81, 330–331
Psychology of the Emotions, The (Ribot), 395*n*
psychomachy, 291, 321, 332
  in confessional literature, 41, 94–95, 112, 240
  origin of, 41
  as psychobiography, 221–222, 240
  Puritan concept of, 76, 81, 112, 235, 240
psychopathology, 33, 47, 154–155, 168, 222, 225, 250, 267
  social, 244, 285
  see also specific types
psychosomatic diseases, theory of, 28, 32
Puritan Origins of the American Self, The (Bercovitch), 1
Puritans, Puritanism:
  American vs. English, 16, 31
  compulsive behavior of, 3, 60, 240
  conscience of, 2, 6, 16, 27–28, 105–108, 184
  decline of, 198, 220, 222
  definitions of, 13–16
  excremental language of, 37, 42, 46–47, 56
  glorification stage of, 29, 31, 192–193
  Jesus as viewed by, 20–21
  literature of, 2, 6–10, 40–49, 54–65, 81, 86, 94, 112
  melancholy of, 5, 6, 9–10, 14–15, 20–29, 35–36
  Miller on, 31, 81, 329–332, 438*n*
  obsessional neurosis of, 3, 4, 8, 25–27, 60–61, 239–240, 249
  as precisians, 3, 13, 23–24, 80
  psychomachy among, 76, 81, 112, 235, 240
  sainthood in, 2, 14–15, 24, 29, 35, 42–44, 77, 84, 86, 112, 147, 203
  salvation as viewed by, 9, 14, 24, 26, 29–34, 314–315
  sin as viewed by, 6, 14, 23, 30, 46
  temptation as viewed by, 6, 9, 14, 15–16, 20–21, 27, 104, 199, 315
  Weber on, 45, 48, 289–291, 297, 309, 311–312, 314–315, 322

wilderness sought by, 13, 15, 18, 25, 66–67, 68, 84, 251, 335
see also Calvinism
Putnam, Ann, 257
Putnam, Charles (father), 258
Putnam, Charles (son), 258
Putnam, Elizabeth Cabot Jackson, 258–259
Putnam, James Jackson, 142, 188, 221–222, 254–288
character of, 258–261, 271, 277–278
death of, 269, 286
dreams of, 276–278
family of, 257–262, 264–269, 278
Freud and, 10, 206, 251–252, 254–258, 267–286
genealogical writing of, 257, 261–262, 264–269, 278
on moral regeneration, 274–279
on psychoanalysis, 10, 275–283
Royce and, 251–252, 255, 258, 260, 274, 279, 281, 283, 284
Putnam, John, 257
Putnam, Marian Cabot, 261, 267–268, 277

Ramsey, Paul, 368*n*
rationality, concept of, 310, 313
rationalization, concept of, 122, 329
Ray, Isaac, 178–179, 394*n*–395*n*
reaction formation, 267, 271
Reich, Wilhelm, 323
"Relation of Mr. Collins, The" (Wigglesworth), 51–52
relaxation, importance of, 184–186, 220
Religionssoziologie, 309
Religious Affections (Edwards), 192
Renouvier, Charles, 166, 170–172, 175, 179, 180, 190
repression, 256, 285, 302–303, 436*n*
Ribot, Théodule, 395*n*
Riddel, Joseph, 82, 320
Riesman, David, 8
Royce, Christopher, 201
Royce, Josiah, 142, 198–253, 275
on alienation, 199, 205, 206, 209, 221, 232, 234, 236–251
autobiographical writing of, 200–202, 205–207, 210, 216, 233, 248
breakdown of, 216–221
Bunyan and, 198, 204, 207, 217, 220–222, 232, 234–237, 240, 242, 244, 251, 264, 283, 332
on child development, 200, 202, 203, 207–212, 247, 248
childhood of, 205, 207–212, 248
on contrite consciousness, 242–244
death of, 202, 252
Edwards compared to, 142, 204, 252
elder Henry James compared to, 199, 201–202, 205–206, 218, 240, 244
on evil, 203, 206
experiments of, 203, 401*n*
as father, 201–202
on imitative behavior, 185, 200, 202–207, 214, 221, 247, 401*n*
Kant and, 199, 220, 221, 231–234, 237
as lecturer, 215
as novelist, 210–212, 218–219, 241–242
on obsessional neurosis, 4, 240, 242, 411*n*
Putnam and, 251–252, 255, 258, 260, 274, 279, 281, 283, 284
on saintliness, 204–205
on self-creation, 220, 231–234, 237–243
on temptation, 204–205
William James and, 10, 185, 196–197, 199–202, 203, 205, 208, 212–216, 218, 235, 237, 240, 251–252
on work, 201, 206, 209–210, 220, 231–232, 237–243, 283–284
Royce, Sarah, 207–212, 217
Royce, Stephen, 201
Rutman, Darrett B., 29

sadism, "ethical bias" and, 285
Sahlins, Marshall, 7
Said, Edward, 320
sainthood, saintliness:
precisians' aspiration to, 42
Puritan concept of, 2, 14–15, 24, 29, 35, 42–44, 77, 84, 86, 112, 147, 203
Royce on, 204–205
William James on, 158, 184, 190, 193
Salem village, witchcraft trials in, 21, 257
salvation, *see* spiritual conversion
Santayana, George, 146, 205, 207, 213, 215
Satan:
Cotton Mather on, 20–21
as source of evil thoughts, 33, 38, 50–53, 71, 103–104, 236–237, 315
Saussure, Ferdinand de, 82
Saxl, Fritz, 22

Schelling, Friedrich Wilhelm Joseph von, 237
Secret of Swedenborg, The (Henry James), 119
self-alienation, 226, 232, 234, 246
see also alienation
self-creation, 220, 231–234, 237–243
self-possession, 234, 237–239
self-punishment, 107, 189–190, 226, 231
Senses and the Intellect, The (Bain), 173
sexual drives:
control of, 263, 277
in infancy, 279
Shakespeare, William, 185
Shapiro, David, 320, 337*n*
Sharrock, Roger, 346*n*–347*n*
Shepard, Thomas, 22, 30–31, 46, 60–61, 66, 70–71, 80, 148, 162, 192, 325
Short, Mercy, 58
sin:
in action vs. thought, 33, 51, 112, 133–136, 138, 144, 156, 178–180
alienation and, 104, 111, 113, 121, 249
consciousness of, 204
despair as, 14
Puritan view of, 6, 14, 23, 30, 46
"Sketch for a Study of New England Character" (Putnam), 285
Social Psychology of the World Religions, The (Weber), 304–305
Society the Redeemed Form of Man (Henry James, Sr.), 97
Soul's Preparation for Christ, The (Hooker), 46
Sound Believer, The (Shepard), 30–31, 192
Spencerianism, 113
Spira, Francisco, 227
Spirit of Modern Philosophy, The (Royce), 231
spiritual conversion:
age for, 59, 159, 175, 216, 299, 355*n*
concept of, 7, 14–16, 147–148, 213–214, 235, 325
expression of, *see* confession, confessional literature
as identity crisis, 166
journey as metaphor of, 14–15, 147–148
as obsessional neurosis, 144, 191, 312
Perkins on, 29–32, 35, 48, 49, 74, 77, 192
psychoanalysis as, 10, 254–256, 280
in revivalism, 83–84, 86
season for, 159
steps to, 29–34, 73–74, 105, 147–148, 192–193, 239–240, 296
spiritualistic movement, 108–109, 370*n*
"Spiritual Rappings" (Henry James, Sr.), 108–109, 370*n*–371*n*
"split" personality, 226
Starbuck, Edwin, 175, 354n–355*n*
Stoddard, Solomon, 79, 83
Strout, Cushing, 395*n*, 399*n*
"Study in Heredity, A" (Putnam), 261–262
sublimation, 271, 284, 285–286
suicidal thoughts, 15, 21, 23, 27, 39, 41, 43, 60–61, 80, 162, 164, 168, 178, 228, 351*n*–352*n*, 394*n*
acting out of, 51, 72, 138
as convention, 49–54
suicidal act vs., 229
Sullivan, Harry Stack, 211, 323
superstition, 25, 64, 106, 109, 240, 308, 309
Swedenborg, Emanuel, 117, 134, 159, 361*n*, 362*n*–363*n*
elder Henry James and, 91, 95–99, 101, 108, 116–117, 119, 122–123, 128, 131, 136, 140, 151, 175, 176, 205–206, 213, 332, 364*n*–366*n*, 370*n*–371*n*
Emerson on, 91, 96, 185, 376*n*
philosophy of, 91, 96–99, 101
on temptation, 99, 103–105, 112
William James and, 98, 101, 145, 213
Swedenborg's Dreams (Wilkinson), 364*n*–366*n*

Talks to Teachers on Psychology (William James), 183
Taylor, Edward, 57
temptation:
in obsessional neurosis, 4, 103–105, 312
Puritan view of, 6, 9, 14, 15–16, 20–21, 27, 104, 199, 315
Royce on, 204–205
Swedenborg on, 99, 103–105, 112
as symptom of melancholy, 32–36, 43, 64, 157, 221
"tentation" vs., 33
see also sin; suicidal thoughts
Tennyson, Alfred, Lord, 193
Teresa, Saint, 385*n*
Thoreau, Henry David, 85, 88, 118, 151–153, 176, 200, 204, 321, 324,

Thoreau, Henry David (*continued*)
325, 326, 327, 333–334, 384*n*
Walden written by, 17, 56–57, 67, 79, 85, 114, 353*n*
Töennies, Ferdinand, 296, 329
Toksvig, Signe, 362*n*–363*n*
Tolstoi, Leo, 216
Totem and Taboo (Freud), 18, 307, 318, 320, 383*n*, 436*n*
transcendentalists, 85–88, 113–114, 118, 142
Treatise of Melancholie, A (Bright), 23, 27–28
Treatise on Insanity in Its Medical Relations, A (Hammond), 407*n*–408*n*
Treatise on the Medical Jurisprudence of Insanity, A (Ray), 179–180, 394*n*–395*n*
Turner, Frederick Jackson, 17

Unitarianism, 222, 256, 259, 260
United States:
alienation in, 2, 84, 116, 185, 199, 205, 206, 240, 244–251, 291, 332
fatherhood in, 209, 245
liberalization of, 220
literature of, 17, 54–65, 67, 81–82, 85, 142, 151, 199–200, 204, 300
myth of, 1, 17–18, 333
prevalence of psychoanalysis in, 275, 279–284
Weber on culture of, 317–319, 321–322
see also American character; New England

Varieties of Religious Experience, The (William James), 3, 10, 11, 92, 143, 151, 155, 157, 158, 163, 167, 175, 184, 191–193, 196, 222, 298, 316, 399*n*
Vastation, 91, 95, 361*n*
see also James, Henry, Sr.; spiritual conversion
"Very Long Letter, A" (Henry James, Sr.), 108
Victorian era:
fatherhood in, 209
psychological concepts of, 2–4, 27, 33, 133, 144, 156, 160, 178–180, 188–190, 220–232
Vološinov, V. N., *see* Bakhtin, Mikhail

Walden (Thoreau), 56, 67, 79, 85, 146, 151, 176, 214, 300, 353*n*
Ward, Thomas, 162, 165
Warren, Austin, 259, 360*n*
Way Out of Agnosticism, The (Abbot), 215–216
Weber, Marianne, 294–297, 299, 302, 304, 306, 310, 312, 313, 319, 322
Weber, Max, 39, 122, 289–322, 324, 329, 330, 436*n*
on alienation, 11, 240, 245, 291, 300, 306, 312–313, 315, 322
on American culture, 317–319, 321–322
on asceticism, 6, 11, 57, 78, 115, 191, 255, 265, 286, 290, 295–296, 300, 303, 308–319, 433*n*–434*n*
autobiographical writing of, 291–298, 301–308
collapse of, 287, 295, 298–303, 306, 313, 315
on compulsive behavior, 243, 297, 302–308, 319
death of, 295
father of, 298, 300, 311, 316
mother of, 299–300
on Protestant ethic, 2, 3, 10–11, 57, 115, 255, 265, 286, 290–292, 294–295, 303, 309–314
on Puritans, 45, 48, 289–291, 297, 309, 311–312, 314–315, 322
Weintraub, Karl Joachim, 39
Weltanschauung, 296
Wesley, John, 312
Westminster Confession of Faith, 35, 48
"What the Will Effects" (William James), 170
White, Hayden, 322
Wigglesworth, Michael, 51–52, 60, 61, 64
wilderness:
in Bible, 11, 76, 199
garden myth vs., 1–2, 17–18, 127
in myth and metaphor, 1–2, 15, 17–18, 66–67, 68, 80–81, 86, 103, 121, 135, 217, 234, 253, 257, 298, 319, 321–322, 357*n*
New England as, 14, 16, 19–22, 31, 80–81, 333
in *Pilgrim's Progress*, 38
Puritan concept of, 13, 15, 18, 25, 66–67, 68, 84, 251, 335
Wilderness and Paradise in Christian Thought (Williams), 368*n*
Wilkinson, J. J. G., 364*n*–366*n*, 371*n*
Williams, George H., 368*n*
Winslow, Forbes, 178, 394*n*

Winthrop, John, 18, 58–61, 78, 332, 333
Wise, John, 327
witchcraft trials, 21, 58, 257
Wonders of the Invisible World (Cotton Mather), 52
work:
  alienation of, 117–118, 134, 165, 206, 240, 246
  elder Henry James on, 87–90, 97, 116–118, 134
  neuroses and, 188, 274
  over-, 188, 273–274, 280, 282, 299, 301
  Royce on, 201, 206, 209–210, 220, 231–232, 237–243, 283–284
  see also Protestant ethic
Wyman, Jeffries, 145

yoga, 190

Zwangsneurose, 3, 224, 257, 311, 436*n*
  see also obsessional neurosis
Zwangsvorstellung, 167

About the Author

John O. King, III, was born in Houston, Texas, and was graduated from Princeton (B.A., 1965) and from the University of Wisconsin (Ph.D., 1976). He served for three years as an infantry officer in the U.S. Marine Corps, including one year in Vietnam. He is now assistant professor of history at the University of Michigan. His home is in Ann Arbor, where he lives with his two children.

About the Book

The text and display type are Trump Medieval. Composition and typesetting were done by G & S Typesetters of Austin, Texas. The book was printed on 50 and 60 lb Warren's Old Style Wove paper and bound in Holliston Roxite by Kingsport Press, Kingsport, Tennessee.

Design and production were by Joyce Kachergis Book Design & Production, Bynum, North Carolina.